FRAGMENTS

FRAGMENTS

Portraits from the Inside

Andre de Toth

Foreword by Martin Scorsese

faber and faber
LONDON · BOSTON

First published in 1994
by Faber and Faber Limited
3 Queen Square London WC1N 3AU

Photoset by Parker Typesetting Service, Leicester
Printed in England by Clays Ltd, St Ives plc

The Foreword by Martin Scorsese first appeared
in *Double Exposure Take Three* by Roddy McDowall
(William Morrow and Company, Inc.)

A CIP record for this book is available from
the British Library

ISBN 0–571–17222–9

10 9 8 7 6 5 4 3 2 1

Contents

List of Illustrations

Foreword

Andre de Toth is a 'director's director', a special category that speaks for itself.

He is not a 'popular' director – audiences may recognize the titles of his films rather than his name. Like other genre directors, de Toth is an unsung hero, mainly appreciated over the years by those who make movies.

I've always been fascinated by Andre de Toth's movies. Their under-lying anger and determination often make them very disturbing. Take *Play Dirty*, for instance. The characters have no redeeming social value; they don't think, they just act. They have a job to do, and they're going to do it. The nihilism, the pragmatism – it's at least unsettling. Disguise becomes a way to survive that brings doom at the end: soldiers killed by their own countrymen fooled by the uniforms. Take *House of Wax*: it's the best 3-D movie ever made – and de Toth has one eye! Throughout the first third of the film, the camera keeps tracking around Vincent Price, and around the wax figures – which look very much like real people. And every time somebody comes into a frame, you don't know whether it's a wax or a real person. When the wax museum burns, the eyes start to fall out of the dummies' eye sockets, and it's tremendously effective. (And I like that it takes place in Mulberry Street – my old neighborhood.)

My favorite de Toth picture is perhaps *Ramrod*, a grim, cynical Western which remains so surprisingly fresh. But I also like the gothic quality of *Dark Waters*, the way the psychology of the characters is reflected through the environment of the Louisiana bayous. Other de Toth titles that are favorites of mine include *Pitfall*, *Slattery's Hurricane*, *Springfield Rifle*, *Riding Shotgun*, *The Indian Fighter*, *Two-headed Spy* and *Day of the Outlaw*. There is a tension in de Toth's visual style that seems to reflect this continuous struggle between people and their surroundings. Be it in his 'film noir', or in his 'Westerns', de Toth's characters always move in a treacherous world where deception and cynicism are aimed at one goal: survival. In de Toth's movies there are no happy endings, only ambiguous ones.

MARTIN SCORSESE

Preface

First of all, I owe some marvellous childhood memories to Andre de Toth, when my love of movies still surpassed my love for the cinema: amazement at the magnificently colored images of horsemen in the snow, or backlit against the desert sky (*The Last of the Comanches*); the unforgettable emotions caused by some dramatic twist in the plot. I shall always remember the scene in *Springfield Rifle* (I remember even the framing of the shot and Max Steiner's music) where Gary Cooper is dismissed from the army for cowardice. Even more, I still feel the same shock when a broad yellow line is painted on his back – the ultimate shame – which ruins his white shirt. I was twelve years old. I was appalled, and yet at the same time I knew that this could not be 'true', even in fiction, and that Gary Cooper (my idol then, as now) could not have behaved like this. In spite of it all, I had to keep believing in him and remain loyal.

There were also all those daydreams in front of film posters and the bizarre French film titles: *The Stranger Wore a Gun* became *Les Massacreurs du Kansas* (*The Killers of Kansas*); *Man in the Saddle* was *Le Cavalier de la mort* (*The Rider of Death*). *The Indian Fighter* was poetically transformed – an admirable rendering for once – into *La Rivière de nos amours* (*The River of our Loves*). The tag line for *Les Conquérants de Carson City* (*Carson City*) promised 'a film with 99 fistfights'. I didn't see that film until twelve years later, on American TV at three o'clock in the morning. But this was nothing compared to the thirty-five years I had to wait before finally managing to see *Slattery's Hurricane* at the Museum of Modern Art. It was an often powerful and personal film noir, and I knew the trailer by heart, having seen it three times (once after *Thieves Highway*, twice after *The Black Swan*) at the Studio Obligado, an obscure local cinema between the Etoile and Porte Maillot where I was a student. I can still remember not only all the cinemas where I saw Andre de Toth's films and the trailers for them, but also the people I saw them with and even the conversations we had on leaving the cinema.

Then came the film buff era, and the Nickel Odeon – a film club which I founded with some friends in the early 1960s which aimed to explore and re-examine the history of cinema. We showed films which we found interesting but which had disappeared from the cinemas. There were, of course, many de Toth films among them, and one of the very first screenings was *Man in the Saddle*.

It was then that we began to notice certain peculiarities about de Toth, apart from the fact that he was the fourth one-eyed man in Hollywood (the fifth really, but we did not know that Tex Avery was one too). He had a taste of stylized visual effects, such as 360° panning shots. Sometimes these were fast and combined with abrupt camera movements, which were used to connect various fragments of a scene (as seen in *Springfield Rifle*). Sometimes he played with the length of the shots in a more internal way – for example, the dance in *The Indian Fighter* and, above all, in *Day of the Outlaw*, a most impressive sequence where, without cutting away, the camera follows several women who are passed from the arms of one outlaw to another, as they are forced to dance. These long, circular panning shots accentuate the feeling of chaos, imposing a sudden eruption of physical and mental imbalance, and thus creating a tension, an atmosphere of extremely powerful violence.

We also discussed at length his dazzling aesthetic ambitions, which would suddenly invade a more or less conventional narrative (the wide shots of a gunfight in a pitch-black saloon lit only by the flash of gunfire – *Man in the Saddle*); and the way he handled violence with a dry, implacable style, a no-frills harshness quite opposite to the mannerisms, the running gags so dear to Ford and Tay Garnett. At the end of *Man in the Saddle*, Randolph Scott wounds Alexander Knox again and again before finishing him off – a moment of rare sadism in Scott's filmography. (De Toth, by some strange coincidence, has just telephoned me and confirms that he had to battle with his star in order to film these shots.) In *Day of the Outlaw*, during a memorable fistfight in the snow, he accentuates the scene's harshness by passing abruptly from a very long camera shot to a huge close-up, echoing the painful impact of some blows, while others send up a rain of shattered ice or melted snow – a wonderful stroke of inspiration.

It was also at this time that, while accompanying Jean Pierre Melville on one of his visits to the cinema, I discovered the remarkable *Crime Wave*

– 'one of the swan songs of film noir', as I wrote in *Trente ans de cinema Américain* (*Thirty Years of American Cinema*) back in 1968. Melville, moreover, loved this work enough to 'borrow' a few scenes – the ending of *Le Deuxième souffle* (*Second Breath*) – and a few props – in *Le Doulos* (*The Finger Man*), the toothpick chewed by Jean Desailly came straight out of the mouth of Sterling Hayden.

In short, at the time de Toth seemed to us to be a picturesque filmmaker, strong in his use of colour, often interesting, indeed inspired, even if this only happened occasionally in the course of a single scene (Raymond Massey offering champagne in *Carson City* to the people he robbed, the death of a traitor or the subliminal black images after a gunshot in *Thunder Over the Plains*). More inspired, at any rate, in *Day of the Outlaw* and *Crime Wave* than in *The Indian Fighter* – his greatest critical success in France and, for some (Patrick Bureau in *Le Western*), even 'one of the most beautiful pantheistic poems that the western has given us'. This is something of an exaggeration, despite the undoubted eroticism (accentuated by excellent use of CinemaScope) of the love scenes between Kirk Douglas and Elsa Martinelli in the river, which provided the wonderful French title of the film.

I found him sufficiently interesting to want to interview him, during a visit to London, for the *Cahiers du cinema* (no 197, December 1967–January 1968). I believe this was the first, and for many years the only, interview published in a film magazine. I still have vivid memories of that encounter: his old-pirate air, of course, at the same time casual and elegant; that mischievous look; and his replies, elliptical and precise, where the silences outweighed the frivolity. In contrast to what one might expect, he told few anecdotes and avoided talking about certain films, preferring to expound on the subject of *The Gunfighter*, which he had written with the very talented William Bowers, and taking me completely by surprise when he declared that his favorite film-maker was Satyajit Ray.

This surprise was compounded over the next few years as I discovered several of his major successes: *Riding Shotgun*, the best of the Randolph Scott movies; his last film, *Play Dirty*; and, above all, those extremely personal and unknown masterpieces, *None Shall Escape* and *Pitfall*, which illuminate the rest of his work. By bringing out the contradictions and the strengths of his work, they reflect his true stature as an artist.

The originality, ambition and force of *None Shall Escape* are so evident that one cannot understand why it received little recognition. Ahead of its time, this film was shot in 1943 and released in February 1944. It follows the trial of war criminals by an international tribunal, more than two years before Nuremberg. It is also an extremely intelligent analysis of the rise of Nazism and the ideological devastation that went with it, avoiding most of the clichés which weigh down nearly all the contemporary propaganda films. Refusing all anti-German racism, it doesn't hesitate to underline the responsibility of the Allied governments, a theme mentioned again in several chapters of *Fragments*. Within a Hollywood context, the script – perhaps the best with which Lester Cole (one of the Hollywood Ten) was associated – takes a surprisingly radical stance on anti-semitism and the Holocaust. But it is de Toth's extraordinarily inventive and vibrant direction, with its great crane shots, its unusual, very European visual composition (the scene in the fields where Marsha Hunt tries to help one of her students, a young girl who will kill herself later) which lends life and weight to this denunciation. The film traces the way in which the Nazis created false news footage (an autobiographical memory, which he relates in the terrifying chapter devoted to the invasion of Poland); the rebellion of the Jews who refuse to board the death train, and the massacre which follows. Here he tosses us this tremendous (autobiographical?) dialogue between the Nazi leader (Alexander Knox) and the teacher (Marsha Hunt):

> 'I am trying to find a glimmer of pity.'
> 'In which eye?'
> 'The left.'
> 'That's the glass one.'
> There is a pause, then Marsha Hunt says, very calmly: 'I know.'

The tone, very Fullerian, is, however, also very personal. The black humour, the corrosive or exultant conciseness, the economy of narrative punctuated by snatched incisive judgements and the absence of sentimentality are all found in many films (*Slattery's Hurricane*, *Pitfall*, *Play Dirty*, *Day of the Outlaw*) and throughout his autobiography.

If he dwells at length in his book, justifiably, on *None Shall Escape*, de Toth is not forthcoming enough about *Pitfall*, one of the best film noirs and one of the most incisive (the dialogue by Bowers and de Toth is a constant delight), but, above all, one of the most original. This film clearly distances itself from all the most embarrassing conventions of the genre, starting with misogyny. The two female characters, written in a very modern way, are the main movers of the action and, at the same time, the principal victims of this action. They are devoid of all duplicity and selfishness (here Lisbeth Scott, perfectly cast, plays a part in stark contrast to the majority of her roles, the image associated with her). One is far removed from the evil temptress; the other not at all the symbol of domestic virtue. We are touched by their painful fragility, in no way synonymous with submission, but quite the opposite.

There is no puritanism or hypocrisy in de Toth's view of his two heroines. The conventions of married family life are depicted, beneath the light relief, with an unyielding ferocity, anticipating work in the 1960s such as *Loving* by Kershner. As Philippe Garnier quite rightly observed in his excellent essay on de Toth (*Bon Pied, Bon Oeil*, Institut Lumière Actes Sud):

> It is on Jane Wyatt's haggard face that one's attention finally rests . . . This pretty little face, usually so strong and witty, is suddenly broken by pain, humiliation and incomprehension. And this is the same face found in the last scene, eyes fixed on the car windscreen in order not to look at her husband while, in a feeble voice, she announces the sort of pardon which has nothing to do with a happy ending . . . One of the most chilling endings in the history of cinema. And also one of the most realistic.

In this film, by the way, de Toth gives Raymond Burr one of his most spectacular roles. His briefest appearance makes your blood run cold; he exudes a formidable air of menace and inevitable catastrophe, all with a minimum of violence, which is particularly striking in the scenes with Lisbeth Scott.

It is evident that de Toth really knew how to give a real colour to his 'heavies', endowing them with real personality. He had a very sharp sense of casting (he proved this with, among others, *Slattery's Hurricane*, *Crime Wave*, *Dark Waters* and *Day of the Outlaw*). This is a laudable quality, although shared with many action or film noir specialists: Boetticher, Phil Karlson, Henry Hathaway.

What was much more original was his handling of women, his way of getting the best out of his female characters, giving them a consistency and a very rare force. *None Shall Escape* and *Pitfall* are two clear examples of this. And long before *Johnny Guitar*, *Ramrod* made women the real heroines of the story. Faced with ultra-conventional subjects, he managed to give his actresses real presence. Look how he inspired Barbara Hale with energy and rapidity of movement in *Last of the Comanches* in order to mask the absence of a role. He drew from Tina Louise, the perfect example of a non-actress, the only good acting of her career (*Day of the Outlaw*); he removed all insipidness and sentimentality from Diane Foster (*Monkey on my Back*); and he showed himself to be particularly inspired by the delightful Phyllis Kirk, a modest and underrated actress who he rewarded for rescuing many inadequately written characters (*Thunder over the Plains*) by giving her at last a role worthy of her in *Crime Wave*, where she is splendidly dignified and straightforward.

At his best, de Toth is not simply an illustrator of genres – sometimes brilliant, inventive. On the contrary, his successes, whether they are entire films or sequences within a film (such as the extraordinary battle scene – so harsh, so true – in *Monkey on my Back*), reject the rules and principles of those genres, taking the exact opposite course, both in form and ideology. In de Toth's films there is no exaltation of 'positive values'. There is no plea for individualism, no feeling of attachment to roots, to a country. The Nature that in so many American films is a redeeming factor, a lost paradise, a garden of Eden where the sins of civilization can be forgotten, is given a threatening, lethal presense, and can be deadly. What strikes you is the sharp, cutting way de Toth looks at his characters, mixing affection and scepticism, doubt and irony.

More often than not, he refuses to follow typically American dramatic outlines – for example, one which Anthony Mann defines as 'a man decides to do something and must do it'. De Toth's heroes generally do the opposite of what they intend to do: Sterling Hayden frees Gene Nelson and Phyllis Kirk and lights up a crushed cigarette (*Crime Wave*); Ryan gives up his plans for vengeance (*Day of the Outlaw*); and Michael Caine is killed by mistake in a particularly brutal and realistic ending. One could list numerous other examples. This taste for 'open endings' explains, on the other hand, the impression of lack of care that one feels about certain 'happy endings' which seem to have been tacked on: the end of *Slattery's Hurricane*, where Widmark rejoins the navy, jars with the rest of the film.

In fact, together with other European emigré film-makers – Tourneur, Lang, Preminger – de Toth shares a distrust of affirmative cinema, positive at all costs. He goes out of his way to cloud the issue, to shift the focus of interest, to deal with subjects by refraction. Paralysed by certain routine and pedestrian western scripts, he comes to life when he confronts chaotic sets (the ruins in *Last of the Comanches*) or closed places (*Riding Shotgun*), and he proves to be inspired by the claustrophobic atmosphere and stifling ascetism, lit by some dazzling lyrical flashes, in *Day of the Outlaw* – a western as original and ahead of its time as *Johnny Guitar*.

Like Tourneur, he is one of those whose films, underrated for far too long, are appreciated more and more each time one sees them. As the years go by, they have become indispensable companions which stimulate me and restore my confidence.

Rereading what I have written, I only hope that this preface does not appear to make excuses for the book. It was not written with that intent and *Fragments* does not need it. It stands up very well by itself. I am not about to forget the delight and surprise I felt reading it, right from the first typical de Toth phrases. In Lyon, when I asked him who had really written *Day of the Outlaw*, he replied, 'You've read my book, you've heard the dialogue . . . Judge for yourself.' I also like the fact that it contains no bitterness or denigration of contemporary cinema in favour of a mythical Golden Age. De Toth is above all that. Just like Michael Powell, whose verve, invention and keen sense of description *Fragments* recalls. It is fascinating to compare the two great portraits of Korda and Selznick drawn by Powell and de Toth. The two men also share a genuine curiosity about other art forms and a very personal enthusiasm for certain films. It is astonishing to see an American director cite Mattarazo's *Treno Popolare* and Renoir's *La Vie est à nous* (*The People of France*).

In writing this preface my only wish is to prevent de Toth being reduced to the definition 'the one-eyed man who made the first 3-D movie'. Or that people simply praise an excellent book written by 'a colourful B-movie director'.

I simply wanted to say that this is an excellent book, written by an excellent film-maker. And a man I respect.

BERTRAND TAVERNIER

Dedications

This book is dedicated to: Loránt Basch, Ferenc Molnár, Steven 'Hapshi' Eiben, and two other wonderful people, my mother and my father; they shouldn't have been cursed with a son like I was.

To my mother's oldest brother, a real son-of-a-bitch. He gave me an example of what not to be. For this I am grateful to him.

To Eddie Cline, my first Range Boss, who took the polo mallet out of my hand and put me on a western saddle to chase fifteen hundred head of ugly, smelly Herefords, opened up the wide open spaces for me, busted my ass on the broncs, and Bishop my Pinto, and made me fall more in love with this beautiful country. To Lloyd McMurry, my roping partner, for my twisted fingers. To Tap Canutt and George Ross for keeping the wagon wheels rolling in the dust of the westerns. To Elisha Cook, my fishing buddy. And in memoriam of Macko, my great Komondor, whom one of my lovely wives ordered to be shot, because she said I loved him more than I loved her – which wasn't difficult.

To Captain Carl Streed, a true friend, in the cockpit or on the ground, and a 'general' of the mothballed fleet, in Kingman, Arizona. To H. R. 'Fish' Salmon, a test-pilot with whom it was just as much fun to test the upper limits of the 'wild blue yonder' as the lower limits of nirvana on a bar-stool.

To Tony Costello, only a Major-General in the Forces under Patton, but a seven-star General above me on the golf courses of Olgiata and Aqua Santa in Rome.

To my Squadron Leader, Captain Sewell Griggers, whose usual after-midnight sport was shooting from ten paces cigars out of my mouth, the only non-smoker in his Squad. I still hear your voice, Sewell, as you were about to pull the trigger, 'We all have to take equal chances.' Sewell, you've wasted an awful lot of lead, I am still a non-smoker.

To my nineteen children, and their mothers, wherever they are, including Elaine and Michael, and to those who stuck around – Diana and Claire, Michelle, Patrick, Charly and Chuck, Schuyler Marie, Tierney Dawn and Nicholas and Holly Ann (without an 'e'!), and to my seventh wife Ann (without an 'e'!), to whom I owe special thanks for making up for what the others never had to offer. For her integrity, her love, devotion and patience, specially while helping to prepare this book, no thanks are sufficient.

My undying thanks to the Flurys for their mistake in not letting me kick the bucket. My appreciation goes to Bob Gitt and Tony Slide for their friendship and encouragement. To Todd 'cowpoke' McCarthy for his vitriolic and unjust criticism while on the grind. To Thierry Fremaux for being what he is. And to the 'always busy' but ready to be on the spot Richard Schickel for his thoughtfulness and boost. To Larry Cohen of Larco, for sinking another de Toth into the sometimes snakepit but always fun picture business. Thanks Kevin, David, Vicki-the-Dynamo, for not completely screwing up every page of this book, to Allan Dye, for gluing together the fragments on cover of *Fragments*. And above all thanks to Walter Donohue for his invaluable editorial help in preparing this book.

To Elliot Midwood, his Gremlins and Joe at American Fine Arts for putting up with me in the studio and still pouring my bronzes. To 'half-cup-four-eleven-111-Mal', for one-one-one. No special thanks to the slave-driving wizards Bob Koster of StarComp, Kameron and Hovik of PatioComp for robbing me of my excuse to loaf by fixing up my often screwed-up computer always so promptly, and absolutely no thanks to Tammy, for her torture she calls physiotherapy with the excuse of keeping me in shape.

My affection and thanks go to the Kordas, especially to Zoltán and Vincent, the artistic pillars of the Korda empire. To Harry Cohn of Columbia Pictures for giving me my first American feature in the USA and not firing me after going over seven days on a seven days schedule. To Jack Warner of Warner Bros, who had the wisdom, foresight and the guts to trust me with a 3-D picture with one eye.

This book is also dedicated to some of the wise doctors in Los Angeles and Lausanne, Switzerland who went sailing, hunting, fishing, played golf or tennis instead of wasting their valuable time with me, and to the memory of Dr Erdös in Vienna.

Thanks to Jack and Jill and Bill, whom I never met. Thanks for their bones from the bone bank to fuse my third-fourth-fifth-sixth and seventh cervical vertebrae when I broke my neck the third time.

And my special thanks to Martin Scorsese and Bertrand Tavernier for their faith in me which I value more than all the money I have made and unwisely spent.

This book is neither a self-eulogy nor an apology, nor was it intended to be an entrée in a name-dropping contest, nor an historical document, although the happenings are true, the geographies are correct.

I want this book to be your guide through an era gone by. Fragments, images, portraits in a shattered mirror under a magnifying glass. I wanted to present the real people hiding behind the fronts, not publicity-created phantoms. Stepping-stones from my path.

I hope you will enjoy reading it as much as I did living it.
Don't be careful, have fun!

1 Breakfast in the Café New York

The rain falls everywhere except in Budapest. In Budapest the rain doesn't fall, it hangs in the air, invisible. You only feel it. It crawls up inside your pants legs, up your crotch, cold. Your brain feels wet, soggy.

It all started on a night like that on Teréz Körút. I stood in a doorway opposite the theater. It was ridiculous to stand in a doorway, in Budapest the doorways offer no protection from the rain. It was only a rumor spread by foreigners to confuse us Hungarians. And I was confused. At eighteen it isn't very difficult to be confused.

The light sparkled through the wet air, the black letters stood out harsh on the painfully white marquee of the theater across the Körút, like mourners at a funeral. My funeral. The muted drumbeat came from the direction of Andrássy Ut. The hooves of a fiacre's tired horse clippety-clonking on the soaked wooden blocks of the wet pavement. Clonk, clap, clippety-clonk, clap. 'Clap – Jesus! I hope she didn't give me the dose too! That's all I needed now!'

I hated her. I was sure because of her they were now taking off my name from the marquee. Not even a first night after the dress rehearsal. She must have told him I fucked her, the bitch. Hold it! Maybe the wardrobe lady saw us and spread the news. But how could the wardrobe lady know it was her who led me on to start with. I hated her. But what about that poor son-of-a-bitch on the top of a stepladder in the rain taking off those thick black letters from the marquee; he should hate her too, poor slob, and he is innocent.

Here goes the first letter of my name. He has difficulty with it. Good. 'Shit, is this the end? No!'

I started to laugh but the raindrops off my hose and cheeks dribbled into my mouth. They tasted foul. That the rain is pure is a myth. It tasted like hell that night anyway. I stopped laughing and stopped hating. Hate. What a waste of energy and emotion. I have never hated anybody or anything ever since.

I kept on repeating, 'They can't do this to me,' as I watched them doing it. That's funny. My name was half off. 'Who cares? Nobody, if I won't. What matters is that I enjoyed what I was doing, writing that play. That's more than the poor man now taking the letters off, in the rain, can say.'

Credits since then have meant little or nothing to me. Some say I'm wrong. Could be, but I feel sorry for credit hogs, they are clinging to their past. Only care about the next thing, whatever that is, and enjoy it.

'What are you looking at?' came a voice from the damp night.

I ignored it, I was watching the stagehand trying to reach for a letter almost out of his reach. He was too lazy to move the ladder over. I was hoping he would fall. It's not a nice thought, but that's what I was thinking.

'Are you connected with the theater?' continued the voice.

The man across the street tottered on the ladder, grabbed the next letter of my name off the marquee, slipped to the ground to shuffle the ladder further.

'I'd like to buy you a cup of coffee,' went on the voice.

Without turning toward the voice I moved away to the next doorway. I didn't want to leave. I had watched my name being put up there, I would watch it being taken off. 'I won't be defeated, I won't run away. Face facts.'

A gentle scent of Yardley's drifted through the mixed stench of peeling, sodden wooden doors and naked mortar patches of the old baroque walls. Then the voice, 'If you are who I think . . .'

I cut him off without turning, 'I am not. Now, get lost.' This was no deterrent. 'Are you by any . . .'

I faced him. A man in a grey flannel double-breasted suit, silver-blue marcel wavy hair, a monocle dangling from his lapel as shiny as his sparkling shoes. Calm, smiling. Confident. Elegant. Be polite, flashed through my mind.

'Look don't waste your time, I am not that way. Now, fuck off!'

This didn't faze him either. He had an aura about him that even the rain respected. He didn't have a drop of water even on his monocle. He nodded. His smile irked me as he was now looking across the street, while he spoke unhurried, 'Yes . . . That's what I thought. You are the author of the play they took off.'

The man across the street removed the last letter of my name from the marquee. The white harsh emptiness glared at me and now the credits of the two other plays looked more impressive.

'My play is better,' I spat out loud in my defiance.

He said flatly, 'No, it is the worst play I have ever seen, but it has promise . . . I wanted to meet you.' Before I could strike out he continued to shut me off. 'My name is Ferenc Molnár.[1] I know how you must feel. Don't lose heart, you'll be able to write. Patience and some audacity, which you have, so patience. Now, let me buy you that cup of coffee.'

Yes, he was *the* Ferenc Molnár, but why was he doing it? He was a known womanizer. It could not be a homosexual pick-up.

Like a well-trained docile dog a locomotive-size Austro-Daimler was following us, hugging the curb, splashing through the water in the potholes.

Three gibbering girls in flopping black oilskins, like birds fleeing from a storm, whipped around the corner, stretching newspapers over their heads to protect their hair-dos. Silver, blue, gold and white sequins sparkled through the slits of their makeshift raingear. Their white teeth flashed as they said hello to us on the run. Show girls from the Moulin Rouge, out to grab a late bite between performances.

I knew only one, Gina, but Molnár obviously knew all three of them. Without turning he spoke to the Austro-Daimler, not to the driver, 'take 'em back,' the car halted, the girls piled in with giggling thanks. Molnár never changed his pace, never looked back. I did.

Before shutting the car door, Gina gestured me a 'what's up?' I shrugged. Then, picking up my pace, I caught up with Molnár just as he rounded the corner.

'Which one do you know?' he asked.

'Gina,' I answered. He was obviously aware of my contact with one of them. He nodded almost imperceptibly, and we kept on walking in silence, in the rain. The road seemed to be stretching farther and farther as we walked. What the hell does he want from me, I mused.

The car caught up with us with purring engine and tires slushing on

---

1 Ference Molnár (1878–1952) enjoyed international fame with such plays as *The Swan*, *The Guardsman*, and *Liliom*, which became the basis for the Broadway success, *Carousel*. He was one of the greatest playwrights of his day.

the wet pavement, and fell into pace again. He ignored it. I spoke out loud, too loud, louder than was necessary just to break the silence. 'Gina is a very nice girl.'

'I hope you never reach the point or the age when you think that all girls aren't nice,' he retorted.

'Oh well . . . well, I mean . . .' I stuttered, 'I mean just . . .'

He looked at me and smiled. 'Relax. Never speak just to break the silence. Speak only when you have something to say. Do you have something to say?'

'Well . . . I . . .' I stuttered again.

'Well?' He looked at me sideways. 'You want to ask me why I am doing this.'

'Well . . .'

'You use the word "well" too often. Watch it. I am doing this because a friend of mine asked me to help you.'

'Who?' I asked eagerly. He ignored me. No answer, not a word, but it seemed he enjoyed the situation, or was it a smirk instead of a smile on his lips. Shall I be grateful for it? Or shall I break some necks? I was puzzled, confused, furious but decided not to press on with any more questions.

I followed Molnár like his Austro-Daimler. The only difference between the car and me was that the car couldn't get annoyed. I didn't know anything about its driver but I got more and more perturbed, fuming, pissed off with every step we took; I felt I was shrinking smaller and smaller. I had to speak, I was not a dumb machine. I wanted to be sarcastic. 'And where are we going?'

He took several steps, ignoring me, and started some breathing exercises. After a while he acknowledged my existence, 'I like to walk in the rain, it's so refreshing.' Before I busted wide open he continued, 'To the Japán Kávéház (Café Japan).' He turned toward me. 'It's all right with you.' But it wasn't a question.

In Hungary, as in all other countries in that part of the world, the coffee houses were important focal points of everyday life. Your intellectual, social, political status could be pegged by knowing which coffee house you called home away from home. For some they were more than a home away from home, some men spent most of their time there.

Every artist, foreign or Hungarian, when in Budapest just had to be seen in the Fészek (Nest) Club where usually the élite of the time gone by congregated with tears in their eyes, treading the sentimental molasses of yesteryears, flavored with their never-dying imagination and humor. Only the Hungarian was created to cry, smile, be happy, all at the same time.

The service in the Club was excellent. Before their shifts, the waiters were taken out of mothballs, wound up like mechanical toys; they didn't walk, they glided, surely, slowly, very slowly. If you were an habitué, you didn't have to order, they knew what you wanted. It was there as you sat down. And exactly as you wanted it: boiling hot, tepid, cold. Exactly right. But God couldn't save you from a disaster if you changed your mind. Because then somehow your order ended up with you, on your shoulder, on your sleeve, on your trousers, on your shoes. I could never figure out how they decided what was the key to the magnitude or geography of the accident. They never apologized but looked at you with rheumy eyes – most of them had blue eyes, as I remember – they creaked as they shrugged and disappeared. Then a busboy, a kid of sixty-five or seventy, turned up and spread the mess around. You had to tip the busboy.

The New York Kávéház (Café New York) was a marble and mahogany, crystal-chandeliered, burgundy and gilt depository. It was a public place, provided you were one of the chosen few who were selected by the Fö-úr (Maître d') to attend this cathedral of coffee houses. The food was excellent, the service depended on how you tipped. The tip always had to be folding money, of course, which disappeared like magic into the headwaiter's accordian-like wallet.

The place was always full, but never crowded. After a late show or at dawn after living it up in one of the locáls (nightclubs, of which Budapest had almost as many per capita then as Las Vegas has now), or returning from one of the tiny restaurants in Buda full of barack pálinka (apricot brandy) and gypsy music – to have breakfast in the Café New York was a must. They spoiled you there, with the morning papers on their cane frames with handles so the news print never smudged your fingers, the crisp, white linen napkins the waiters draped on your knees, the always fresh hot coffee. They sent you off to face the day not thinking, but knowing you are the king. It all depended, of course, on how well you tipped.

The coffee house in the Royal Hotel was a pre-dinner, pre-show hang out. Mirrors, mirrors and mirrors in ornate gold-gilded frames. Red plush carpets, Louis Quatorze imitation chairs, pink, embroidered napkins and table cloth.

The twenty-four-hours-a-day Café Japan with its black, grey and white décor and naked marble tables was more austere and ear-splittingly more noisy. If the one-hundred-and-fifty-year-old Turkish occupation had left any heritage in Hungary, it was the bazaar-like atmosphere in the Café Japan, and that is where we were heading for now.

As we walked in, Moses's legendary miracle of parting the Red Sea was a secondary feat to me compared to Molnár's path through the throng of arguing, reading, billiard-, pool-, card- or chess-playing crowd plus the darting zig-zagging waiters, balancing enormous trays, loaded with glasses, cups of all sizes and shapes, filled to the brim with various liquids, some steaming hot. The waiters, like charging kamikazes, changed their minds at the last minute, always veering off from what looked like an inevitable disaster.

This scene reminded me, many years later, of that tragic Grand Prix in Monte Carlo when the brilliant young British racing driver Peter Collins was killed, with several others; among those who littered the track with wreckage but survived was Stirling Moss, a fantastic, unique, brilliant British driver who probably set more lap records on courses all over the world than any one else, who said he had to 'climb the wall to avoid ploughing through the carnage'. Juan Manuel Fangio, holder of more world championships than anybody else, said later very simply, 'What carnage? I saw only a path.'

Molnár followed the magic path of the super champions. For him the way was clear. If I had not been stepping on his heels, one, two, three, waiters zipping between us, tilted legs of chairs and outstretched limbs of human beings, my path would have been a hurdle-dotted labyrinth to eternity. Still I had to mumble 'pardon mes' and 'excuse mes' to which nobody paid any attention. Before Molnár sat down, like magic there was on the table in front of him an obviously hot cup of coffee, a bottle of brandy and a large brandy snifter askew on a delicate, gleaming copper stand with a small blue flame dancing under its bulbous belly. I stopped short, causing a traffic jam and, by another miracle, or by the miraculous dexterity and reflexes of the waiters following me, there was no major accident.

Molnár joined two people. Only two people at a table where this time of the night normally there would be six or eight stuck together like cordwood in front of a mountain cabin before winter's onslaught. The two smiled as I reached the table and sat down, defiantly, without much ado, next to Mihály Babitch, one of the great Hungarian poets.

Naturally I had never had the chance to meet him before. Molnár sat next to Dr Loránt Basch, the attorney, art connoisseur and collector, with piercing blue eyes, if you could see them through the dirty funny glasses he wore. When I met Alex Korda later (not Sir yet), I found his glasses were almost as funny but crystal clear, while Vincent Korda's[2] glasses, on occasions when he wore them, were always smudgy. It is strange: the two people I had the great privilege of meeting who both were art connoisseurs and lived almost exclusively for art's sake, were looking at the world and the world of art through the dirtiest glasses; and even stranger, they not only lived for art but they could judge it too. However, they were different, in that Vincent looked at life through pastel-diffused colors and seldom acknowledged it, while Dr Basch evaluated it as if looking through an electronic microscope. He was now twirling his half-full bottle of Vichy water. For him to consume that much, they must have been sitting at that table at least two and a half hours.

Babitch nodded at me, then turned his limpid brown eyes toward the remains of a glass of wine which looked to be more like red ink with dirt in it than wine. One could judge how many swallows he had taken by the lip marks on the rim of his glass. To hide his widening smile he lifted his glass and drained it.

Nobody said a word. A waiter came with a bottle of Törley champagne in a cooler. I turned to him, 'I would like to – ' Molnár cut me off, 'You're having it,' indicating the champagne, 'We'll celebrate.'

Another waiter appeared and carefully rotated Molnár's brandy snifter over the flames. Molnár patiently waited till the waiter finished the manoeuvre, then told him to take it away, off the table, he did not want his usual tonight. The other waiter poured champagne, elegantly, but only for three of us; Dr Basch wasn't offered any, he stayed with his Vichy water; obviously the waiter knew his habits.

There was still silence around the table. The hubbub in the café around us, the whole situation became overbearing and I started to fight the world.

2 Vincent Korda (1897–1979) was a gifted painter and later award-winning art director, the youngest and the most talented of the Korda brothers.

'I enjoyed writing it and I don't give a damn what anybody thinks.'

'Yes, you do,' said Dr Basch turning towards me. I guessed he looked at me but I couldn't see his eyes through the dirty glasses. 'Otherwise you wouldn't be so belligerent.' He indicated Molnár, 'He must have liked it, some of it, because if he didn't he wouldn't have talked to you. We agreed on that.'

Molnár touched glasses with Babitch, I followed suit, and when we clinked our glasses together Molnár stated flatly he didn't like my play at all. However, he was amused by my courage, innocence and audacity. Nobody without those assets would touch such a worn, bedraggled situation I had tackled in my blissful inexperience; which in spite of my refreshing new approach was doomed. He spoke in dulcet, quiet tones and elegantly dissected my still-born baby. Then he summarized: 'When you touch shit, it remains shit, and the more gold you pour on it, the more it shows up the shit.'

This broke the tension. We all laughed and talked and talked, and I listened and I listened, and we drank and drank. Even Dr Basch finished his first bottle of Vichy water. And dawn came through the large windows of the coffee house. A swarm of window-cleaners with squeegees on their long poles attacked the tall windows. A skeleton of a horse with the hide still on it was dragging a milk wagon which must have been white on its maiden voyage, eons ago. Its snail's pace and bumpy progress didn't seem to bother the driver dozing blissfully on the hard seat. A baker's apprentice with snow-white apron and a white chef's hat whizzed by on his bicycle, its baskets heaped with all sizes and shapes of bread and croissants. Save a periscope, no possible way could he see over the top load in the front basket; still, wildly, surely, he was careening around the potholes, oblivious of or dismissing the possibility of a disaster. And I learned from him: don't think of disasters; then they are less likely to happen.

The Fö-úr came to the table to announce that fresh croissants had just arrived, and I had one of the most memorable breakfasts in the Café New York that morning. There was another breakfast some years later I remember so well, my first breakfast on the range as a working cowpoke. But this breakfast with Dr Basch, Ferenc Molnár, Mihály Babitch was a turning point in my life. I was put on a track, on a straightforward track. Until then my path had been a zigzag which could have led me to tumble into the bottomless pit of the millions of living dead.

From a very early age I had nothing but trouble, but soon learned to be generous and give trouble. Don't have headache or ulcers, just give them. Foolishly, I believed this would work; later on I had ulcers.

In Hungary, as in most parts of Europe, parents stuck their little darlings between the ages of four and six in a preparatory school or kindergarten, if they couldn't afford to have a governess (a German fräulein, French mademoiselle or occasionally an English nanny) to chase after you, to watch out for your table manners and teach you the language the parents thought would be the best for your future. But teach you only one language, maybe two, nothing more, since the old wives' tale had it, to learn too much too soon could have a bad effect on your nervous system later on.

As I remember, we always had one of those ladies. All of them smoked secretly, some of them rolled in the hay with the stable boys. I could not understand why they were doing it when they continuously protested, 'Oh no-no-no!' and called God's name more often than I heard it in church. I got along well with all of them. They didn't bother me and I didn't bother them. Now I can blame them that I can murder only five languages.

When you reached the ripe old age of six, off you went to what was called the elementary or grade school. After four years of attendance and passing grades, you were sent to what was called a föiskola or gymnasium, for eight, usually miserable, years of your life.

Miraculously I survived the first four years in one grade school, attending it from home. But I was bored, I didn't believe the lore about the necessity of education. Furthermore, I was quite well versed in subjects they wanted to instil in us sometimes through the wrong end, since caning was still very much the fashion. Even then I did not understand why they were so stupid as to think that the most effective way to reach the brain was through a red welt-covered ass.

To bide my time I painted with water colors, I painted on whatever was to hand and became more and more convinced that my teachers' art appreciation was as low as their intelligence.

My next eight years in the föiskola could not be called dull or monotonous. During those eight years I was asked to depart from five of them. Except for one, the rest were all for trivial reasons.

I have never been a surly child, I never carried grudges, but I suppose my sense of humor was different from others and I still think it was funny when the twenty-some sparrows fluttered out of the desk drawer of our history teacher. I didn't have a crystal ball to tell me he would throw himself against the edge of the blackboard and gash his head and knock himself out.

In the next school, with the Latin professor it was a pure accident. He thought I was a useless good-for-nothing, and one cold winter day he ordered me to be of some use and hold his chair above the big red-hot pot-bellied iron stove during the recess, to keep it warm, to soothe his rheumatism when he sat down behind his desk. He didn't understand that I needed the recess to do my homework, so I just hooked the chair, legs up, on the top of the stove and finished my homework.

This was a real advanced school, co-educational. We had five girls in our class but they could not enter the classroom before the professors arrived. So I arranged with one of the lovely little buttercups to knock on the door when they saw the professor coming down the corridor. This they did and the signal gave me time to unhook the chair, so when the professor marched in I was holding the chair as he instructed me, high above the stove. My parents were sticklers for etiquette, so I followed the professor up to the podium and politely shoved the chair under his fat posterior. He sat down and wrapped his knees in a blanket. Suddenly his eyes bulged, he opened his mouth but no sound came out, then frantically he started to untangle his feet from the wrap. His voice returned in a high-pitched hysterical scream as he was running toward the door, with the chair sticking to the seat of his pants. I thought it was funny. The whole class thought it was funny. But the school principal had a different sense of humor, he did not agree at all it was funny.

My next involuntary departure was caused by a difference of opinion. We had a very nice professor of history and Greek mythology. I wanted to prove to him how much he impressed me with his theory that the heart, the soul, the spirit were more important and more beautiful than their encasement, that those magnificent Greek statues were so beautiful, as he expounded to us, because you could feel the spirit of their creator in the cold marble.

While preaching this, he had on a toupee like a soiled mop from a public toilet, woven into a steel helmet. This toupee was independent, not only of the professor's spirit but of his body too. It seemed to stand still when he moved, as if it were independently suspended above wherever he was. He always wore a hat, which he carefully took off when he entered the classroom and never put on during the recess if he had two consecutive hours in class. So one day I took this opportunity to put glue on his hatband.

Actually our class missed the resulting climax. But we had the joy of the anticipatory suspense of events impending when the professor put on his hat carefully, as usual, and marched out toward the next classroom, to spread the wisdom.

This report is from unreliable sources: fellow students, and some enraged professors.

The glue I used turned out to be so effective that it stuck the hatband not only to his toupee but to his forehead too. To remove the hat from his head he needed medical assistance. His toupee could never be restored, transformed as it was into a steel helmet, wrinkled by a tank. To add to the disaster, the poor professor was not able to put on a hat, since his scalp needed constant medical attention, because a large part of the skin from his forehead was still on the hatband. But after a few weeks he got used to the breezes, and never wore another toupee again.

I thought I had done him a favor. I helped him, no matter how inadvertently, giving him a chance to prove he believed what he was advocating, the real value, the essence of life he was so fervently selling to us, the inner beauty. I was not thanked. I was not expelled. I was thrown out of this backward establishment.

During the beginning of my seventh grade in the föiskola I was provoked again into a quick change of geography. It all happened so fast on a lovely September afternoon. The term had barely started. The sun had the full bite of July, the water was warm, the swimming pool was crowded, a perfect afternoon of an Indian summer. One of the professors, actually a member of the Order of Pius, was accompanying a group of students who were living in the school's boarding facility, run in conjunction with the school.

Even now there is no question in my mind, the professor was a man of good taste and I shared his feeling, that around the pool there were more uplifting sights than watching a bunch of rumbunctious, cavorting boys trying to drown each other; unfortunately unsuccessfully.

The professor was squiring a lovely lady. To prove to him that we were on the same wavelength, I made a remark to which he took offense and slapped me. A rash, wrong move. The next moment, less four teeth, he was on the ground. Then, flailing on his back, he kicked me. I kicked him, but my aim was better.

My mother's comment on the incident: 'Oh my God!' My father said, 'You were wrong to knock his teeth out! If he slapped you, you should have knocked his head off!'

The professor was transferred to a monastery to regain his composure and his dignity. To evoke a miracle to grow back his four front teeth was a futile attempt, but the other injured part of his body was ignored, since according to his vows he wasn't supposed to use that anyway.

Subsequently the lady in question engulfed me with her throbbing charm. And I am eternally grateful to the professor, not for the lady's sudden, surprising rush of attention but for his slapping me. Without that slap I probably wouldn't be having this breakfast in the Café New York.

I was expelled from the school, effective immediately, and, disaster of all disasters, I had to take a few weeks of enforced vacation. But she kept up my education. The lady taught me things they were not teaching in schools then. As a matter of fact they wouldn't be teaching them now, especially with demonstrations.

Through friends, relations, donations and various other persuasions, another school finally accepted me. I liked this school. I stayed there for almost two years, finishing my time in the föiskola. I lived in the governor's mansion, boarding with the lieutenant-governor's family. As I walked through the gate, the guards always saluted me smartly. I appreciated it so much, for the first few days I kept walking back and forth through the gate, fifteen, twenty times a day. I asked my classmates to observe this obnoxious ritual; this school was also co-educational, and both sexes of the student body were duly impressed. However, the guards had a different opinion of me and would happily have wrung my neck. Well, we all have our own crosses to bear.

In this school, like all other schools in that part of the world, there were class principals who were concerned, beyond their own speciality, with general and particular class activities: academic, social, or sporting. My class principal was a short man, high cheekbones, and a Taras Bulyba[3] moustache; he had a small hump on his right shoulder blade and

3 Taras Bulyba: famed for his cruelty, a chieftain of the Tartar Mongolian tribes, with Ghengis Khan's horde, which overran Europe.

it seemed his slightly bowed legs started at his Adam's apple. He taught French, Italian and Literature. He was the editor and part-owner of the *Nógrády Hirlap* (*Nógrád News*).

His first words, when he interviewed me before being admitted to the school, were: 'Did you do it? Did you really do it?'

Well, I thought here we go again, we'll have to look for another school. I nodded.

He nodded, and mumbled a 'good'.

I was relieved, or did I hear it right?

He was watching me as he opened the cover of my fat file in front of him on the desk; he studied it, then mumbled again, louder this time, 'I don't believe in corporal punishment no matter what you did.' He was slowly turning the pages of the file. In the silence the buzzing of an autumn fly desperately trying to get through the window sounded unnaturally loud, I watched its losing battle. I had nothing better to do.

'It's not very clear what really happened in your last little . . . oh . . .' he sighed and slammed close the cover of the file. I had the feeling he was nailing me to the wall with his jet-black eyes. Yet another school, here I come, I resigned myself to it. He tapped the file.

'Quite a history you have here. Quite an achievement. However, in spite of your not very illustrious record the consensus of opinion is, you have one redeeming feature. You show some talent in writing. Stick with it. No painting. No sculpting. Writing.' He picked up a slip of paper and handed it to me. 'My cub reporter, let's say, quit. Now, after school you will go to this address. My partner, the publisher of the *Nogrády Hirlap*, will teach you what you should know about typesetting. It's easy but messy.'

Messy it was, and I became a typesetter, a delivery-boy-and-cub-reporter on the paper, gaining more and more muscle. I was filling four pages out of eight of this bi-weekly newspaper, the most important paper in the county. In truth, the only paper in the county.

The building was the size of a twin privy in the 1880s on the Kansan plains, but in one corner of it was a special desk. My desk. I put a sign above it: 'City Room', and slowly I began to realize the power of the press. And occasionally misused it, of course, as any seventeen-year-old with sense would do. Any time I wanted to cut a class, I just had to go to the City Room, but strangely enough I had better grades in this school than any previous establishment I had attended and been kicked out of. I began to be known in town, only to discover that sometimes fame can be a double-edged weapon.

My father came to visit me. He was a happy carefree man. He didn't live for the day, he lived for the hour. He always said, 'Who knows what the twenty-fourth hour will bring?' He and my mother made a happy couple. There was never once a hard word, a dirty look between them. In their thinking they were way ahead of the time and place they lived in.

My earliest memory of my father is gypsy music in the night. He used to go out quite often to raise hell, then came back with a gypsy band to serenade Mother. Mama would put a lit candle in the window, a sign of welcome, a signal they were invited in. Four, five, six of his friends piled in for breakfast. I looked forward to seeing him, he was a good friend.

He was surprised by the fine reports from the school and impressed with the City Room. He said during our first luncheon, 'It seems you're growing up. Don't do it too fast'. He came to watch me compete in discus, javelin and four hundred meters against the regional schools. I got lucky that day, I was happy, so was he. During dinner he looked at the medals and said, 'Well, now we have a reason to celebrate.' Would I have been the last, not the first, it would have been just as good a reason for him to celebrate. He just loved to celebrate.

He suggested after dinner we should take a walk, and checked his watch, something he seldom did. He slowly sipped his brandy. After a while he checked his watch again, then off we went. We didn't head for the park or the river. Strange. But he knew this town, I followed him. He kept on talking, wondering about the duck, the pheasant, the deer seasons, was concerned about the diminishing wildlife. He was an excellent shot, an avid hunter and a dedicated conservationist. His den was full of trophies, antlers, stuffed birds and animals of all kinds. It's a way to conserve too.

Our back yard was full of various breeds of gundogs, specialists in their different fields. But the king of the roost was Sam, the giant grey crane Father saved from extinction in the swamp when he found him with broken wings, starving. He turned out to be a better watchdog than our watchdogs, our fearless and worldwide-feared Komondors. With his long, snake-like neck stretched out horizontally, his broken wings flopping, long legs goose-stepping, beak opening and shutting, emitting terrifying screeches, Sam was a frightening sight.

Sam was one of my best friends, especially during the years while I was under the dictatorial thumb of one of my fräuleins. When I was locked in my room with the remains of a meal I hadn't finished at the table, all I had to do was open the window and Sam came running to my rescue. His long neck, like a giant snake, slid through the window and he ate what I was supposed to. Sam ate everything, I swear with a smile, Sam had no taste at all, he was no gourmet.

I would sooner have been without my tongue than ask my father where we were heading. Away from the plush section of villas and shopping district toward the 'other side' of town. He kept on talking, as parents do. They dream their dreams for you. He didn't mind now my playing around with writing. 'After all, there are some people who are writers and are very respectable; novelists, playwrights, top playwrights of course. But the future is with the military. Naturally, the Huszárs. That's the future.' He had already talked to his first cousin, General Szirmay, the commander of the Ludovica Academia, the Hungarian equivalent of West Point or Sandhurst. 'As far as writing goes, historians, specially military historians, they have their place in society. But can they enjoy life; I mean, can they afford to do what they want?'

'Maybe writers want self-satisfaction more than anything material?' I interjected. He shrugged, looked at his watch again as we passed the last street lamp on our way to the dark section of town.

Dogs were barking in the distance, strains of gypsy music and singing drifted from the direction of the kis kocsmák, the small restaurants fringing the dignified silence of the dull side of town. White picket fences embraced the adobe houses with thatched roofs and geraniums in their windows. I had never been in one of those kocsmákba where the food, usually a selection of one, was the rule, and it was supposed to be superb. The wine and the barack pálinka (apricot brandy) flowed freely. And the gypsies, if they didn't shred at least half the strands of the horse hair on the bows of their violins or cellos, they didn't do so well. And if the mulatók, the celebrants, didn't smash every glass in the place the evening was a dismal failure. These were the places where the men went. Could he be taking me to one of those places, I wondered. But would they let me in?

We kept on walking, then we turned right towards the house. It was a big baroque building surrounded by ancient trees and a once beautiful garden. Kids were told it was a haunted house. Haunted by the ghost of the count whose family once owned the house. He blew his brains out because he couldn't pay his card debts in twenty-four hours as was required by the 'code'.

The fields that once surrounded it had been sold in parcels. The house now looked like a beached whale.

No, we aren't going there.

But yes, we were. And with every step my father took I lagged two behind. He turned with a mischievous grin on his face and motioned me to catch up.

From some of the large downstairs windows of the house, slits of light cut into the night. Faint strains of music filtered through the still imposing, but once magnificent front door. As it opened, light, music and laughter poured out. And Madame Frieda, silver hair shining, black lamé dress shimmering, stood there, elegant, dignified. The rumor-spiced legend had it, unverified of course, that she was once married in Paris to a Russian prince. She held out her hand like a princess.

'Oh – so good to see you, Mr . . .' She stopped, looked at me, behind my father. Then both arms outstretched she passed him, beaming, 'Oh, Bandi [my nickname at that time], I didn't expect to see you today,' and embraced me.

My father froze. She was fast, 'Oh you two are together?'

My father, wooden-faced, turned as he spoke, 'We were,' and backed into the night. I shrugged and went in, feeling the burden of fame a newspaper man had to carry sometimes.

It had a stigma, but I don't think Maison Frieda was an out-and-out whorehouse. It could have been an out-and-out confessional for misunderstood, misjudged men, feeling sorry for themselves. I have often seen some of them with cover charge refunded, no charge for what they've consumed, and, no sex allowed, sent back to their wives; absolved of their self pity. Madame Frieda made all of them feel like kings. The burgundy rugs on the marble stairway were not threadbare but somewhat worn from the traffic, while the mahogany on top of the railing, once gold, now white, shone from the sliding hands of Madam Frieda's hostesses, because they all caressed it as they descended. That was one of Madam Frieda's rules: they had to descend with one hand on the railing, shoulders forward 45 degrees to the line of the stairs. They looked more regal this way.

There were no meals served in the house but the best of hors d'oeuvres and titbits, from beluga caviar to grandma's cookies. The coffee was the best this side of Italy, the connoisseurs said. So were the drinks, plentiful and expensive, although the prices varied. I have often wondered since what ESP guided Madame Frieda's pencil to guess the extremities of the freight. The cover charge was the same for everybody, for which you could have a cup of coffee and if any of the hostesses was bored and felt like talking to you, she did. No extra charge.

There were newspapers, magazines, fresh and ancient, domestic and foreign, from Paris, Vienna, Berlin. I even found editions of the *Corriere della Sera*. Our editor, a.k.a. my class principal, subscribed to it too. I used to read it in the City Room. Being a fine investigative reporter, I marked a few copies of *Corriere della Sera*, which I found together with our *Nogrády Hirlap* there. This address was not on my delivery list. My hunch was right. An enlightening discovery.

Yes, Maison Frieda was a haven for all from the daily miseries. How much you spent made no difference, all were treated equal, in a quiet, dignified, simple way. It was a place where personal, emotional, economic, political problems could be settled.

Similar and still so vastly different from the lobby of the Willard Hotel in Washington, D.C. where according to the bronze plaque above the Round Robin Bar: 'President Ulysses Grant used to escape the pressure of the presidency with a brandy and a cigar in the Willard lobby. Many would-be power brokers approached him on individual causes and he called these people "lobbyists". And the word "lobbying" sired by Ulysses Grant was born.' The Willard is now rejuvenated to its old glory, its lobby is still full of PR dust-clouds of political prostitution, past and present. I often think establishments like Madame Frieda, with their simplicity, would do a hell of a business, and an awful lot of good, with less dust. And less diseases spread.

The next morning, I was supposed to meet my father for breakfast at the hotel where he was staying. I had rewritten and rehearsed and re-rehearsed my attitude toward him several times.

He was already in the breakfast-room, seated at the best table of course, in the corner, the only table with a view overlooking the little park and the pond which they laughingly called the lake. On it floated the only crooked-necked swan I have ever seen. My father was reading the *Nógrády Hirlap* neatly stretched out on a cane frame. He smiled at me as usual, put the paper aside and, indicating it, said, 'After breakfast show me the articles you have written.'

I had barely put the napkin on my lap when the waiter arrived to serve him and me. He said apologetically, 'I took the liberty to order your favorite breakfast too.'

My favorite breakfast was: paprikás salona (specially prepared Hungarian bacon, smoked and covered with red Szegedi paprika), various sausages, head-cheese, fresh baked bread, warm from the baking oven, not reheated (I can smell it even now), various cheeses, a pitcher of milk.

My father downed a schnapps and the waiter promptly poured a second. A conversation, interrupted by large swallows, about which team is going to win the football championship. Then he changed his mind, and said it would be more sporting if he guessed which articles I had written in this edition of the paper. 'You said you wrote more than one, right?' I nodded with my mouth full. And he picked out two out of four of my pieces, after the third schnapps.

The breakfast was great fun. The crooked-necked swan flapped its wings, emitted some horrible noises like a cracked trombone. The hotel yardman appeared with a basket to give the swan the breakfast it was clamoring for. I became more and more relaxed. Finally, father's second cousin arrived to take him to the station, we hugged each other and we parted. Not a word, not one word was spoken about the previous night.

It is strange. The first and only time it came up was many years later, on Spaulding Drive in Beverly Hills, when my mother mentioned it with a big broad smile.

I always guessed she was fully aware of my father's philandering. She was a great woman. Very strong and very proud. They had the most idyllic marriage I have ever known and she was very sure of herself and sure of his real love for her. She knew that he belonged to her.

Bringing up the Maison Frieda incident, I believe, was more of a hint to one of the very lovely but misfortunate ladies who was foolish enough to ask me to marry her. My mother had noticed this lady kicking me in the shin under the table even if I only said a nice thank you to a waitress; it did not matter how the waitress looked, or how old she was.

Time went fast and I was enjoying every minute of my last two terms in the föiskola, and to my surprise harvesting very good grades. But slowly I started to feel a pressure. Gentle but continuous pressure like the sides of a canoe would feel, if it could feel at all, when left in the water in sub-zero temperature. It was building up and up and up.

My mother maintained, 'It's his life, let him choose.'

My father gently objected, 'But he hasn't got the experience to make the wise choice.'

I watched Mother's reaction, there was none. 'How do you know, haven't you ever been surprised in your life?'

My father nodded hastily. 'Yes . . . oh yes, eh but . . .' But he kept up the pressure on me about my future as he saw it. I kept on writing. One advantage that had, surely, said Father, it was less messy than my painting and sculpting.

The day of the decision had to come. My father made it for me. I was to leave for Budapest for a week's stay to rest up and then meet his famous cousin General Szirmay. And off I went, loaded to the gills with presents, food, clothing, as if I were to embark on an expedition to circle the globe through the North and South Poles.

On the train I assessed my nutritional supplies and the presents for the multitude of relatives, and decided to check into a small room in a small hotel instead of staying with the 'loving you to death' cousins, aunts and uncles and answering, or trying to answer, their millions of ever-probing questions, questions and questions, which I either didn't want to answer or didn't have the answer to. It all made sense to me, but I caused a larger commotion than I anticipated.

I reported in at the Ludovica exactly on time of course, and even the guards showed some consternation. Hurried quiet phone calls, surprised glances, a second identification was required, then I was ushered up the wide red marble, very imposing stairway to the General's office. I mean directly into the General's office, without stopping in the outer offices where lesser mortals, wearing identical uniform to the General's but with less gold braid and medals, were sitting.

I had never met General Szirmay before and I was immediately impressed by the office, and above all by him. A bronzed silver-haired man in this very spacious wood-panelled office full of portraits of generals; so I quickly guessed that only a general could have the honor of having his picture here, among the large paintings of battle scenes, ancient and new maps.

Above the panelling, a shelf full of silver, gold, bronze statues, mostly Huszárs on horses, jumping, running, flying through the air. In a corner there was the most beautiful globe I have ever seen. The room was elegant, dignified not gaudy. Impressive. Impressive is the word, and I stood to attention, which I had never done before. I did it automatically, the best way I could in front of the General's large desk. Silence.

When he finally spoke, after an eternity, he had a deep, very good voice, commanding but not gruff. 'Where have you been?' I glanced at my wrist watch. But before I could say anything he continued matter-of-factly, 'Of course you're on time. But you disappeared for four days and everybody was very concerned about you, where you were.'

It wasn't a question, but you just knew you had to answer him. 'Oh . . .' My thoughts whirled, then an idea struck me. 'I just didn't want to bother anybody, sir.'

He seemed to like that. There was no change in his expression, but I felt it. There was something, just like electricity around him. You knew it was there but you couldn't peg it. I started to like him.

'Your father told me you would like to be a Huszár, like he was. I'm glad, but understand, that's not enough. That you are a sásvári-farkasfalvi-tóthfalusi-Tóth, that's not enough. That we are related that's-not-enough. All this is just good enough to open the door for you.' For the first time he moved, leaned forward slightly. 'But don't ever forget all this only puts added responsibility on your shoulders. You'll have to pass certain tests, with honours, you understand, because of your responsibilities you must be one of the best!'

'I am the best,' I cut him off.

A silence can be deafening, and what followed was. Then he leaned back, I thought, or I would have liked to think, with an ill-hidden smile.

I really liked him. You had to like him. 'Well,' he grunted, 'we'll see what we can do, then I want to see what you can do.'

The interview was over. I straightened up even more. I wanted to look tall, as tall as I thought he was. 'Thank you sir, but – '

He cut me off, no change in the volume of his voice but still it was a whiplash, 'But what?'

'I want to be a pilot.'

In an endless silence he scrutinized me again. I was sure the hint of the smile, if there ever was one, had gone. I was facing a razor's edge. 'Did you tell this to your father?'

'No, sir.'

'Why not?'

'I thought it was between you and me, sir.'

He mulled this over for a while, then, 'Why?'

'It's my future.'

'I didn't mean that. I meant, why the airforce?'

'The future of war is in the air, sir. I read all I could find about the First World War aces and –'

I believe I rattled him. It may be my conceit, but the way he shot me down: 'Are you giving me a lecture on the future of warfare?'

This question required no answer either. And this was the last question he asked me, because he never spoke to me again. Not one word, ever. He didn't even say leave, finished, out.

He pushed a button on his desk, picked up a telephone perfectly befitting the ambiance of his office but which today you could find only in extravagantly elegant large dressing-rooms or next to toilets in seven-figures-plus mansions. Then I was on the street. 'I am the best!' Ha ha.

On another street, sitting at a table in a sidewalk café, Doney's, in Rome, I saw a beautiful man waltz down the street, the Via Veneto, stopping by tables where he heard American spoken, which was at most tables, and announcing with a bright smile, 'I'm the best! You'll see, I'll get the gold!' And he did. Nineteen sixty, Cassius Clay.

I still didn't get my gold but I am having fun waiting for it. No. Not waiting for it, digging for it.

I never returned to live at home, refused my relatives' invitations. And the hassle started.

I found a small furnished room, paid the rent for two months in advance and subsisted on the food presents I was supposed to deliver to my darling relatives. Now I was independent and started really to write.

My first play. I wrote, I rewrote and rewrote, then I hated what I wrote and rewrote it again. The play never reached the curtain of its first performance. I have never, ever suffered like that before or since in my life. But that made up for all my misdeeds of the past and a payment in full for the future.

Strangely enough, the rougher it became, the more I enjoyed it.

I looked around the hockshop, this mausoleum of failure, the cemetery of broken dreams and fizzled-out plans. The first I have ever been in, and the last. I went there to sell my gold wristwatch, a barely few-weeks-old graduation present. The events I competed in gave only silver medals, small ones for second and larger ones for first, bronze for third, but in this pawnshop they were not interested in bronze. My trophies went too, silver vases, plates and a large silver ashtray. Ridiculous, we were always warned of the dangers of smoking and they were giving ashtrays as trophies in sporting events.

Smelling of mothballs and with a layer of cobwebs on his bald pate, a wizened little man with receding chin, barely higher than the top of the counter he stood behind, was smiling. Yellow teeth, brown lips, a wart on his right nostril. He had on very thick, round, bevelled-edge glasses set in thin dark frames. Why was he smiling? Did he enjoy the misery of others? Or was it a smile of consolation? No, I didn't think so. Maybe he was the reason I disliked Alexander Korda's glasses so much.

Even before he became 'Sir Alex', when he was just plain Laci, his family nickname, he was always so immaculately elegant. But those glasses he wore. Made me wonder if Korda was ever in the same hockshop on Király utca, the aptly named King's Road. Could he have picked up the idea for those hideous glasses there? He was fussy, fastidious about everything, to the smallest detail, except ideas. He took them from anywhere.

As I walked up to the sunshine from the wet stench of the semi-basement on the worn iron steps I wondered if the sweat, the effort, the time, the energy and the dreams were worth only that little. Suddenly I realized they weren't giving out awards for dreams.

No one could have appreciated a large family more than I did while the parcels of food lasted. They all were extremely well off, they didn't need the food, so I had absolutely no guilty conscience about this self-help. It was an even trade, I kept my freedom while they were left alone in peace during their Sunday luncheons. But after I had demolished my stolen independence I had to rely and count on pure family relations and I realized that liberty and freedom are not synonymous and freedom is not necessarily free and sometimes one has to buy it – dishonestly? – with more than money. Of course you are at liberty not to, but as the goodies vanished I suffered, with dismay, through those degrading but lifesaving family luncheons.

I wrote, then rewrote, then revised the rewrite over and over, again. I was never satisfied. I worked only at night or when it was raining or heavily overcast. It's not that I had more inspiration then, but I split my determination between finishing my play to my satisfaction and getting my wings – General Szirmay and his Huszárs or not.

The birthplace and very hub of Hungarian gliding was on the Hármas

Határ Hegy (the Mountain of Three Borders). As far as mountains go it was only a hill, not too far from Budapest. They needed beef up there to supply launching power for the gliders and that I could supply – six feet, 210 pounds of it. I was very strong, even my head was full of muscle, as General Szirmay commented to my father. He couldn't fathom, nor could my father, how anybody could turn down an 'invitation' to become a Huszár Officer. A Hungarian Huszár Officer.

Hungarians are a strange breed, to say the least. Their love for horses goes back thousands and thousands of years. Hungary has no seashore, but Hungary's regent was then an Admiral who rode a magnificent white stallion not only on parades but to the toilet. I can understand General Szirmay better now than I could then.

The gliders were launched, usually unsuccessfully, with bungee cords. The tail of the glider was affixed with a releasable hook to a dead-man not too far from the rim of a deep precipice. The bungee cord was fastened with another gadget, a pelican hook, to the nose of the glider and we, the beef, the launching power, four, six, eight of us, ran, scrambled to the very edge of the precipice to stretch the elastic cord as far as we could. When we were barely able to run even on the spot – just before we were about to be snapped back – came the moment of truth. Success, failure or disaster rested with the pilot's skill, it was all up to him, he had to know to feel that magic split-second to hit the release button to be successfully airborne.

The equipment mortality rate was high. If you could be airborne at least for one whole minute, you were awarded a little blue circular emblem with the silhouette of one white seagull on it. If you were skillful enough to stay airborne for two minutes, you were admired, and were entitled to sport the little emblem with two white seagulls on it. And if you were lucky enough to stay aloft beyond three minutes, you received the ultimate: a certificate of your gliding skill and a little blue emblem with three seagulls on it. You became officially a fully-qualified sailplane-glider pilot.

It sounds ridiculous, but the fact was if one could stay up for three minutes, usually one could stay afloat for hours – provided you could master the art of launching yourself successfully. From there on only experience could teach you where to look for updrafts. You were on your own, alone, really alone.

The sad fact was that we spent more time gluing the kites back together than we spent in the air. This sport was then strictly for the daring idle rich and a few dedicated nuts. We, the beef, we were paid for our power and had a chance to fly when the weather was lousy.

Actually this helped us. With less help from nature we became better pilots. We took our turns on the kites and prayed together for Lady Luck to be with us and not mangle the kites too badly. When it happened, as it did, there were no traumatic upheavals. The love of the sport and the excitement fused us into one and I learned something more, much more important than flying, spreading my wings there. The bungee taught me if you wanted to fly high, to be successful, then stretch it to the limit, to the very very edge of the limit, but know damned well where that limit is.

Sometimes I wish that we could all go back in time and up to the Hármas Határ Hegy to watch that bungee, and watch those on the bottom end of the bungee duck, shrivel, scamper to avoid the deadly whip. Watch those below, the ones who launched us to fly high. The world would be so much nicer and motion pictures maybe even shorter and better, if we would do that.

Under the bungee-influence, instead of writing a three-act play I decided to write only a one-act play to begin with. But about what?

My mother tracked me down and caught up with me bringing a hamper full of food, enough for a picnic for six weeks for a regiment. Almost shyly, she said she would like to ask me a favor. She had never, ever asked me to do anything before and never did after, throughout all the years. She left us when she was only one hundred and three years young, and was never sick for one single day of her short and happy life.

To show her how receptive I was, I jumped, 'Yes, yes, you're right, I really should have – '

She cut me off, 'No.' She smiled, 'I don't want you to visit anybody you don't want to visit. I understand.'

Forty-love, in her language. She played an excellent game of tennis. I don't play tennis. I was treading air, like Donald Duck running off the diving board. Cleverly she kept me there, then she came to the point. Without ever losing her refinement she could come down like a meat axe, hard and direct and sometimes with the blunt end first. As it turned out, this was to be one of those occasions.

She asked me if I had started to paint again, or were there any new sculptures. She looked around the room, not approving nor disapproving, just looking as if understanding that no one, but no one could paint or sculpt, or even live here: if you were a midget you could easily touch any two opposite walls simultaneously.

I told her I was writing a new play now. She thought it was an 'excellent idea' and asked, 'Do you miss your newspaper?' 'Yes, I do.' I couldn't analyze it then, but what I really missed was being important. One grows up, hopefully.

I didn't shock her with my flying exploits. She thought there was a future in it but then the axe came down, blunt end first. She wanted me, note, she didn't ask me, this time she wanted me to enrol and finish, to have a diploma of law and political sciences from the Királyi Magyar Pázmány Péter Tudomány Egyetem of Budapest – in short the University of Budapest. To have something to 'fall back on . . . just . . . just in case'. It was the only time I ever heard her stutter, but she went on. She thought, with that diploma, and my knowledge of languages, and our family connections, a possible position in the diplomatic service could be arranged.

She told me she was aware I didn't believe in the fall-back theory, the 'just in case' policy attitude, and I was right not to go into a battle admitting being half defeated before it all started. A true champion believes only in victory, which is right but . . . but . . . but! Tears welled up in her beautiful dark eyes. She tried to hold them back. She was no actress. If any fault she ever had, she was no actress.

What could I do? I agreed, and I got my diploma in the shortest possible time, in four years, with honors, and I learned a great deal. The most important thing discipline, self-discipline. I gave the framed diploma to my mother with a dozen red roses. She wasn't surprised at all, took it for granted, she said, because she knew I would get the diploma when I promised I would, and I gave her roses often, without there needing to be a special occasion. Above all, she had absolute faith in me.

She had faith in me. Thanks. I was annoyed with her faith that time. As I found out actually before she came up to Budapest to convince me to attend the university, she had already secured a place for me in the Diák Otthonban (a student home) on Ferenciek Terén (Franciscan's Square), the poshest of posh addresses in the Belváros, the Mayfair of Budapest. Only sixty students. Four of us had a ballroom-sized room, the place had a well stocked library, a club-like comfortable study, a community room with billiards, ping-pong and all kinds of other games, but no card games were allowed.

According to the legend, years and years ago a student lost a formid-able sum of money playing Alsos (a special Hungarian card game), and being of good Hungarian gentry he knew he had to blow out his brains if he could not pay his debt of honor within twenty-four hours. So he did. And now his ghost came back occasionally to haunt the Friars at midnight on the very spot of his noble deed. None of us students ever saw his ghost. But of course we were handicapped, we didn't know where to expect his appearance, where the exact spot was where he committed his final grandiose gesture. I added to the guesses and con-fusion of this legend by spreading my theory that it actually happened in the dining-room, and not because of his card debt but because he couldn't take the lousy slop they were serving then, same as they served us now. To add weight to my 'information from reliable sources' – an expression from my 'newspaper days' – I further augmented my theory with watertight proof to anybody who listened: 'You see, we don't have to eat here. We pay for three meals a day but we don't-have-to-eat-here.'

News travels fast, especially if it comes from 'reliable sources'. It reached Father Benedict, a bulbous, purple-nosed Friar, with lilac-colored forehead, snow-white beard, tonsure and silvorium- (Hungarian plum brandy) flavoured breath. He had heard about my theory, based on 'iron-clad-logic', of course.

He put two of his ham-fisted hands on my shoulders and whispered in my ear, engulfing me in silvorium fumes. I needed a quick chaser of cold water after he had left me. 'You are cynical; so young and already cynical, but funny.'

He leaned closer; I'll have heartburn for sure if he has a lot to say, I thought. And he went on inconsiderately. 'Don't spread the . . . well I shall be polite and I will say legend . . . I mean, don't if you want to stay here. Lying is a sin, you know, and you know the confessionals are open daily from six-thirty to seven.'

He was moving away, thank God, as he continued, 'See you at mass tomorrow morning.' And he chuckled as he shuffled away in his open heel-and-toe sandals, exposing his blue and grey naked ankles. Before he turned the corner he waved goodbye.

He had a deep, grumbling voice and a good sense of humor. The longer I stayed the more I liked Father Benedict. He was an avid reader. He had finicky taste, but he liked very much whatever I wrote and encouraged me to keep on writing. Occasionally we snuck a drink together, naturally silvorium and of course for health's sake.

I wanted to stay there, but it always bugged me that it was all arranged before I said 'yes'. It all went through an uncle who happened to be a professor of criminal law at the university of Budapest. The fact that I would yet have to pass an exam was blithely ignored. For them it was a minor detail. They took it for granted I'd pass. I did, but it was an uncomfortable feeling that had I failed, I still would have gotten in, because we had 'protectio' – the word for back-door influence in Hungarian.

Dammit, this was no way to run a railroad. These kinds of 'little' things added up to my decision finally to leave the country. It took some time to realize it, but it all added up. The truth is, at that time I actually enjoyed and was proud of the unfair privileges we, our class, enjoyed.

Mother came up to Budapest to check up on me and bring some home-baked goodies. The semester was well on the way, I was established in the Diák Otthonban. She even came up once to the Hármas Határ Hegyre to watch me soar for a whole one and a half minutes, breaking my personal best to that date, and she also watched my lackluster finale. I not only broke my personal best, but turned the kite into a heap of matchsticks, as I unexpectedly crashed among the trees.

Her observation: 'Was that short minute and a half worth all the fuss and bother? And those poor boys scrambling down that hillside, oh, you could have splintered that thing more efficiently and so much quicker.'

I had no answer. Both of my parents had that terrible habit of asking devastating questions with no answers. And both had terrible relatives. Mother came from a large Catholic family. Thirteen children, seven girls and six boys, Mother being the seventh girl and the thirteenth child of the litter. Her oldest brother was an attorney and created the eighth deadly sin: not attending Sunday lunches on time at his house with their children, all dull, boring puppets, plus an addition of equally boring relatives visiting Budapest, or occasionally some professors from various universities, with their bible-bleached families sitting around like clean, scrubbed wax figures.

Reigning at the head of the football-field-sized table sat this uncle of mine with his sparkling pince-nez wobbling on his nose ready to fall into the pea soup – any soup, anything messy – but disappointingly it never did. I committed the eighth deadly sin my uncle devised more often than any other sins.

I didn't like attending his command performances, and I stayed away very often without even offering an obviously transparent lie for an excuse. That added to the gravity of my offense. But I could not swallow him, even when that big Sunday lunch would have been my only hot meal for the week.

I didn't mind eating there once or twice when the 'grown-up' crowd was so large that the 'kids' ate at a separate table in the small dining room, but usually on those occasions I was excused from attending. They were worried that my subversive power would corrupt their white-fleeced flock. Who in hell would believe at twelve that the storks bring the babies? I concede that to discuss the propagation of human life in detail may not be the most appropriate Sunday lunch conversation, but after all! Well, so I was often excused from attending.

It was during one of those ceremonial luncheons, however, that I met Dr Basch. Despite the fact that the main table was overflowing with 'grown-ups', I was not 'cancelled' because my mother was there. It was an occasion on which I didn't expound my contaminating theories of life in general at our separate table because I was listening to the voices coming through the door connecting the small dining-room with the big one.

I heard my mother's voice – and she never raised her voice – arguing with her brother, defending what her brother called my antics, my irresponsible bohemian attitude. 'Now, a play yet, well, at least he's not messing up your floors and Persian rugs with paint and clay. You hold the reins too loose or not at all. You have nothing but trouble, and you'll have nothing but more trouble. I think you went through enough misery. We have to do something drastic if necessary.'

Another voice was raised, backing my mother on my behalf. Whose, I had no idea. I had my belly full, not only with superb food, which was always identical to what was served at the big table. I decided to serve the grown-ups a surprise extra dessert.

Just before coffee was brought in for them in the salon, I appeared. My uncle snapped his head around toward the door at my unexpected appearance, his pince-nez jiggled violently, but to my great and eternal disappointment it stayed on his nose.

I was ready to let fly, but before I could open my mouth a mid-sized middle-aged silver-grey man, in a rumpled but not shabby silver-grey suit, with the dirtiest glasses on his nose, stood up and came toward me. 'I was so anxious to meet you, Bandi. I would like to read your play and see some of your art work. I am Loránt Basch.' We shook hands.

My sails were deflated for the moment. 'Sit down,' suggested my mother; knowing her eldest brother, and me, she was trying to avoid a showdown. 'I told Dr Basch about your writing a play,' she moved to give me room next to her on a small love seat. Defiantly I sat, no, I didn't sit, I plopped down on the Gobelin upholstered dainty piece of furniture, which was built more to look at than to sit on. Its delicately carved wooden legs remonstrated painfully with a creak which blended with my aunt's sigh.

'Have a little brandy,' said Dr Basch to no one in particular. 'It's all right,' he continued to me, 'I am sure you've had it before.'

'I'd like a drop of Delamain.'

'Good choice,' agreed Dr Basch.

My uncle went purple, his wife turned away to hide a smile, my mother didn't.

The chambermaid, Gabriella, winked at me as she poured; we were friends, very good friends. Her name actually was Gina, but my uncle didn't think it was dignified enough. She had to be called Gabriella. Of course I thanked her extra loud, 'Thank you, Gina.'

Otherwise it was silence in the room, Dr Basch slowly swirled his Vichy water in a crystal clear glass in his hand but the glasses on his nose were all smudged up; they always were soiled, as I discovered, but I never asked him why.

I was sure my mother was sitting on pins-and-needles, fingers crossed for no blow-ups. Basch was enjoying the situation; he repeated, to break the silence, I thought, 'As I just told you, I'd like to read your play. Have you finished it?'

'No.'

'I do hope you still have some of your old paintings and statues left.' He opened a wound, noticed it, then made a joke of the world 'old'.

'No.'

'Any new ones? I would like to see them.'

'No more, I quit. The only thing I have ever quit in my whole life.'

This must have sounded ridiculous and bitter. Dr Basch nodded, 'Hm. Quit? Oh well, when you restart show them to me.'

'No, I am only writing now. I'll be . . . I *am* a writer. Those stupid fucking idiots . . .'

Oops – That was not exactly fitting dialogue in this quaint Biedermayer salon on Sunday, after a family luncheon.

The chambermaid dropped a silver tray of bonbons as she was about to serve them to the ladies. First, the bonbons scattered onto a glass-topped sideboard, from there to the floor.

My mother lifted a hand to defend me, herself or the propriety of her oldest brother's house. I never found out why. I knew I had boobed.

There was no way out. Defiantly I continued, 'Yes, you heard me. I – '

Dr Basch came up again to bridge the gap, 'You must have been very badly, deeply hurt.'

'Yes.'

Until I was barely fourteen I was only content when I could paint, draw, make messes with clay as I was doing my sculptures.

It was interesting to me how both my paintings and my statues achieved so vastly different effects on various people. They still do.

My mother said they were beautiful. My father asked, 'What are they?' But both said, 'Go ahead if you like it.'

I was even then aware, of course, that all great artists had the anatomical knowledge of a neurosurgeon, but who would expect that ripened knowledge from a kid barely past thirteen.

Idiots, the idiots! It never came to their hazelnut-sized, feeble brains that I actually didn't want to depict with meticulous exactness the world around me. What I was trying to do was to recreate the emotional impact on canvas, in clay, the impact I felt living in the world at that particular moment; hoping that you, when you look at my paintings, statues, you will feel the same impact, feel the same emotional involvement I felt at the moment of creating them.

Well, I succeeded, I involved them all right but not the way I dreamed I would.

In school we had an art teacher, tall, dry and sad. He lived with four cats and two dogs and had a moustache like a convoluted mess of barbed wire from which icicles dangled in the winter. His landscape aquarelles were quite decent, but what destroyed my respect for him were his plump, Raphael-ish rosy-assed little angels with chubby cheeks and fat wings crawling on the rims or peering into his terracotta bowls, vases, trays, ornamental dishes. Some of the angels were – ugh – painted to boot. I asked him once how could he tell one angel from another and their faces from their asses, because both parts of their anatomy had identical expressions; what I meant was, no expression. Surprise surprise, he laughed, but the last laugh wasn't his. Time will tell, he said facetiously. However, inadvertently he helped me, God bless him.

We had a maths teacher, a pig of a man, a Pink Pig. He despised me. I enjoyed that. Rather be despised or hated than ignored is one of my commandments. God gave us ten commandments and how many of them are we keeping? I gave myself a lot more commandments, so by the process of elimination I hoped to keep some and survive.

This Pink Pig, by pink I mean the color of his flesh not his political leaning, caught me. During one of his boring lectures instead of struggling with Pythagoras I was enjoying myself studying a book my father had given me on the new wave of German Expressionists, full of illustrations of paintings, statues, carvings, some of the figures with overexaggerated anatomy. My inattention enraged him for two reasons: first, I was not paying any attention to him, and second, I preferred this pornographic trash to Pythagoras. He dragged me down to the Principal's office demanding I should be expelled. Immediately.

Luck and miracles, thank God and Lady Luck, again as so often, they were on my side. My art teacher was present in the Principal's office and without batting an eye, he said the book was his and he had given it to me.

Of course I shouldn't have ignored Pythagoras. However, he thought, since the book was his, my not paying due attention to Pythagoras wasn't sufficient enough reason to expel me. 'I asked him to bring the book back to me today, I needed it.'

With this he reached for the book, snapped it up from the Principal's desk – 'It is my book' – put it under his arm and left the room. I never saw the book again. He kept it. I suppose he didn't want to be a liar.

'Go,' growled the Principal at me, and as I was walking out of his large office he turned to the maths teacher, and raised his voice to be sure I could hear him. 'We should have thrown him out before he exhibited that appalling insult to art.'

'I was all for that, you know it. And you know how I despise vandalism,' chimed in the Pink Pig, 'but I certainly would like to congratulate those vandals who destroyed that decadent trash. They had taste at least. I don't understand, it doesn't make sense for a teacher to be involved with this offensive muck. Even if he is an art teacher, he should know better, and giving a filthy book like that to a student. I just can't understand him. After all, art is not a license for immorality!'

I reached the door, swung it open with what I thought then was grandeur and struck a pose Douglas Fairbank Sr and Errol Flynn, put together, would have envied. I threw my head back à la John Barrymore and, facing them defiantly, exclaimed, 'Ha-haa!' To emphasize my contempt I just stood on the threshold, then whirled dramatically and slammed the door behind me, hard, hoping the glass squares in it would shatter. I failed. They didn't.

Any time I think of this scene, even now I shudder and have to laugh. Had those two stalwart guardians of civilization had any sense of humor they would have had to split their sides laughing at my performance.

I walked down the long corridor. Where the ancient walls met the ceiling the winter storms had left their calling cards and I felt I was carrying the whole weight of the hoary roof. I went in the WC, I wanted to be alone, and nowhere can one be more alone than sitting on the toilet. But it did not work for me that time.

I don't know how long I sat there, a minute, an hour, when two seniors came in to share a cigarette. Before lighting up they checked the cubicles for security, and spotted me. They climbed up on the toilet seat in the next cubicle and looked over the partition.

'You're okay?'

'Yep.'

'Sure?'

'Yep.'

'Y'ave constipation? Then better take your pants off while you sit there, just in case.' And they went off to a corner to enjoy their forbidden smoke. I kept on sitting on the toilet confused, disturbed. The seniors finished their smoke.

'Sure you don't need any help?'

'Nope.' A door slammed and they were gone.

Alone again in the shithouse, riddled with questions I could not answer. The 'whys'. Why this blind hatred of something they cannot understand? Why did my art teacher arrange for me a 'one-man show' and then exhibit his own work next to mine? I exhibited because of pride, he exhibited for charity, neglecting to mention that the charity was for himself, for his cats and for his dogs. The simpletons just 'ooohed' and 'aaahed', loved his stuff, it was a sell-out success. My 'one-man show', the first show I ever had, was a complete fiasco. They made fun of me, laughed at my pieces. I have to give them credit though, they didn't ridicule me behind my back but straight up front, one on one, they-laughed-at-me-smack-in-my-face! First I wanted to strike out, slap-them-hit-them-kick-them; then suddenly I felt sorry for them. I felt they were the losers. But still, I just had to blow.

The very same night I busted the big window, the biggest, of the exhibition hall and slashed every one of my paintings and smashed every one of my statues; wondering, whom did my dreams hurt, why were people so cruel? I didn't realize then how deep the hurt was.

I never felt revenge, I never touched any one of the other 'pieces of art' in the show; the aquarelles of the Puszta, white farmhouses with thatched roofs, white longhorn steers, prancing horses, mallard ducks flying over snow-spotted grounds, blue ponds. Ugly, fat arse-angels crawling all over rims of vessels.

The sound of the opening door, scurrying footsteps suddenly stopping.

'Who-is-smoking-in-here?' The shrill voice of the Pink Pig yanked me out of my reverie. With bloodshot myopic eyes he was peering at me from below the cubicle's door, his pink face slowly getting purple.

I knew I was wasting my breath, but I still spoke up, 'I'm not smoking.'

'Of course not, you just like to sit on the toilet with your pants on, fully dressed, always!'

I was thrown out of yet another school, not for reading a porno-graphic book in class, but for smoking in a toilet, and because of my deplorable behaviour in general. But of course I couldn't be con-gratulated for destroying my own dreams, and being the hero with 'taste' who destroyed the 'decadent trash'. He remained anonymous.

They all listened to my saga, even my uncle. I knew when he paid attention – his pince-nez was not quivering.

My mother put her hand on my knee to comfort me.

After draining his Vichy water, Dr Basch said, 'I think I understand how you must have felt,' and motioned to me to follow his example, which I did: I gulped down my brandy like he gulped down his Vichy water, but with more style. I did it like I have seen in the movies, in cowboy pictures.

As our respective glasses were replenished my uncle asked, 'How do you feel now?' I knew what he meant, but I didn't want to give in. I indicated the snifter in my hand with the second drink in it, 'Fine, sir, just fine.'

He got impatient, 'I mean . . .' I interrupted him, 'Oh thanks for asking, sir, I'm just fine, and strong. That exhibition was the best thing that ever happened to me. I don't feel sorry for myself, I'll never, ever be a loser and nothing can ever hurt me from now on, I'll . . .' Maybe I overplayed my cards.

My uncle motioned at the drink in my hand, 'You don't have to finish it if . . .' I interrupted him again. I knew he didn't like to be interrupted. 'Oh-I-know, but . . . I really enjoy this drink.' I added, 'Sir'. For good measure.

'I want to read your play when you're finished with it,' wedged in Dr Basch, again at the right time.

'You better give it to Dr Basch when it's presentable if he is so kind as to read it.' Then Mother turned to Dr Basch, 'It is very kind of you, Loránt, to do this for him.' Her voice changed as she spoke to me, 'Now, Bandi, put the glass down and off you go with the others.'

I drained my drink, put the glass down slowly, to annoy my uncle. 'You said the glass, Mother,' kissed her on the cheek and marched off. But on the way out I heard my beloved uncle, 'How could you put up with him?' I didn't hear my mother's answer. Whatever it was, I knew I had wonderful understanding parents. I had a beautiful example to follow, but I didn't. I guess I was born to be a single drifter.

I had an additional incentive now. Somebody wanted to read my play. Somebody important. I didn't know who Dr Basch was, but I was sure he must be important. My uncle would not invite anybody who was not influential. He harangued his mentally anemic offsprings incessantly on the importance of this 'cornerstone of life'. A nice man, he was.

I didn't feel the pavement underneath my feet. I was floating on my way to my room. I suppose the two brandies had something to do with it or at least added to my elation.

When I got to my room, the door had barely slammed behind me and I dove into still another rewrite of my play. I was not aware of the dangers of rewriting. I didn't add yet to my dozens of commandments: If it needs a rewrite, throw it away. Sometimes I fell into another trap, I clung to words, to unreal situations, hopelessly fighting the glue of repetition. I was determined, now more than ever, no extracurricular activity, of any kind, nothing, until I finished the play to my satisfaction, so I could show it to Dr Basch.

I was sitting there with obstinate tenacity staring at a stack of blank paper with an equally blank mind, I don't know for how long. I didn't even notice it had turned dark outside. Would I have had an idea I could not have put it on paper; it was now pitch black in the room. Was it the brandy, or had I dug myself into a deep hole with no way out?

There was a knock on the front door, tentative, faint, then again. I opened it. The light barely squeezed through the dust cover on the naked light bulb dangling overhead. The chambermaid from my uncle's house stood there. I stood inside the door, in the dark. She was clutching a small satchel with both hands.

Neither of us moved or said a word, seemingly for hours. Finally she shrugged apologetically, opened the satchel, pulled out a brown paper bag and held it to me. 'The bonbons the Nagyságos úr (the highly honorable sir) wanted me to throw out.'

I didn't connect, stood there puzzled. She smiled, embarrassed. 'I think you should have them, there is nothing wrong with them . . . here, you should have them.' I hesitated, she pressed on. 'I tasted some, the ones that dropped to the floor when you said . . .' she giggled, covered her mouth and blushed. 'It was funny. You really gave it to him.'

She thrust the paper bag at me, I took it from her and we stood there on both sides of the threshold. She spoke up again, 'I never have Sundays off till seven in the evening, you know, the guests and all that long luncheon. I have only Mondays off.'

'You want to come in, Gabriella, for a few minutes?' and she was in the room pronto. On her way in she protested, 'You know I am not really Gabriella, I am Gina, you know it. The Nagyságos úr, your uncle, said it was a too common name, it's for chorus girls, and you know . . . like that, and you know with all the important guests and all that I have to be Gabriella. Silly. You know it.'

'Would you like some coffee or tea?'

'Tea would be fine, just fine with the bonbons.' And we had all the bonbons, and she told me she missed the train today that she usually took home on Sunday nights. Somehow I didn't believe she was telling the truth. Later we had the salami I kept between the two panes of the window facing the courtyard. And much later she asked me if she could trust me not to tell. Something was fishy I thought, if she was really worried that I would tell my uncle about her bringing me the bonbons, she should not have brought me the bonbons. If something else was on her mind she should have asked me sooner, very much sooner if she could trust me at all. 'It's too late to worry about the bonbons now, Gina,' I laughed, 'we have finished them.'

'Ohhh-it's-not-the-bonbons,' she broke down, started to cry, hung on to me tight and explained, sobbing, she had a problem, a big problem, a big secret she could not live with any longer and didn't know what to do. She was afraid.

A searing thought flashed through my mind. All I needed now was a pregnant Gina. It must have been an atavistic male reflex movement to shy away from being tied down. I certainly was not aware of it, but she must have sensed something subconsciously for she moved away, looked at me with tear-striped face.

'No, no, no-no it's not that!'

The dam of her pent-up emotions cracked, she clung to me desperately and poured out her pitiful, sordid story. She had to talk to somebody and there was nobody else she could trust. She saw clearly today how much I disliked my uncle, so she had decided to take a chance and tell everything.

'My mother would commit suicide if she knew. My father would kill me and your uncle if he found out.'

'My uncle?'

Her sobs became uncontrollable, with clenched fists, she rubbed away her tears. 'I hate him, God forgive me but I hate him, I can't take it any longer!'

She was almost unintelligible as she blurted out that he kept on molesting her; he not only took her virginity but asked her, forced her to do 'all kinds of things' knowing she could not do anything about it. She couldn't complain to anybody and 'bring shame' to her own family. After all, her father was 'a first conductor in uniform, on the fast train, the express train, between Budapest and Vienna.' She knew how important my uncle was and that he could put her in jail and have her father fired. When I protested, how could he do that, she kept on repeating she just knew because he was very important and he had her Cseléd Könyv.

I had forgotten about that passport of slavery. Even as late as the thirties, servants couldn't have a job without it. It was issued by the government with photos and fingerprints affixed, controlled by the police.

When leaving an employment, the employer graded the employee's performance and behaviour, ticking off the boxes for trustworthiness, diligence, orderliness, religion, stability, etc., and it could have been the death sentence to future employment if there was in the General Remarks section the code, the code everybody was aware of: 'Parted in good health'. It was a cruel, criminal practise upheld by the law. The law? There was no defense against a vindictive employer's cruel vengeance. There was no appeal.

Gabriella's mysterious disappearance created lots of waves crashing against many shores. The least affected were the police. They were used to this kind of disappearance story, only very few caused concern or had serious consequences. I felt sorry for her family but Gina was adamant about not letting them know her whereabouts. She was more worried about her father getting into deep trouble if he found out what really happened. She wanted to stay away from her family till she 'got settled in and clean'.

The next Sunday I showed up uninvited for lunch. I was curious what, if any, changes Gina's disappearance had caused in my uncle's clockwork house. Oh, I know it was not very nice, wanting to enjoy the situation. My concern for Gina's parents' grief was somehow lessened by the formidable commotion she worked up in my uncle's house. My aunt was sitting on thorns. My uncle was present at the table only in body.

When the new chambermaid, in her fifties, grey and plump, appeared, I innocently asked the children where Gabriella was today. For a while my uncle didn't even hear what we were talking about at the low end of the table, but pretty soon the pasty, wall-flower children of his bloss-omed out and spoke up. They bubbled and freely expressed their pent-up theories from suicide to abduction for white slavery in Turkey. We chatted uncurbed for a while; this had never happened before. They buttoned us up, even if we tried to discuss a banal sports event.

I wanted some action. Taking the proverbial bull by the horns, I asked my uncle point blank if he thought Gabriella could serve as a white slave in Turkey without her Cseléd Könyv. Well, this brought him out of his reverie and he shut us up gruffly. Even my aunt was surprised by his uncivil, unnecessarily rude tone. I couldn't hide my satisfaction. His ice-clad cover cracked, at least for me. From that moment on I watched him quite openly. I only took my eyes off him when he looked at me, but just slow enough to make him aware of my surveillance. For me it was one of the most satisfying meals I ever had there; except one to follow quite a while later, but it was worthwhile waiting for it.

During the remainder of the more than usually discomforting, sour luncheon for my uncle and his brow-beaten family, he performed a mental autopsy on me, he thought, surreptitiously.

I had barely put down my dessert fork and wiped my mouth as required by the code of etiquette after a meal, needed or not, when he dismissed me from the table. From the table? From the apartment. That hypocritical son-of-a-bitch uncle of mine. I really shouldn't say that, after all my mother had the same mother. The genes sure screwed him up, or was it life?

Gina stayed with me for a while. I threw away stacks of paper of re-re-re-rewrites, and, based on my illustrious uncle, I started to write my new play, a one-act satire, *One in the Family*.

Strange that a play, in spite of the fact it never saw its first performance, could have brought me wherever I am.

As I wrote, Gina watched me with silent admiration, she was feeding my ego, my confidence, and my belly with fabulous meals cooked on a single burner hotplate. The first lady who ever stayed with me, she spoiled me for most of the rest that followed.

My landlady was the cigarette concessionaire for two of the biggest night clubs. Her gentleman friend was the Fö-úr in one of them. She and Gina met and a kinship was forged through their similar contamination by society; through their degrading experiences, which were known but never discussed, and were silently accepted by society, despicable as they were.

This is as late as the early thirties, when some of the Földes urak and Nagyságos urak, like my vermin uncle, flagrantly committed outrageous atrocities against all human rights and dignity, as vicious as a medieval lord's right to the 'first night', which was tolerated as a matter of routine. How should we feel about ourselves, about our society, today, stepping into the twenty-first century when only the offenders' titles changed? My landlady set out to emancipate Gina, to liberate her from her odious memories of the past. She tried to rebuild her crushed self-esteem.

The choreographer of one of the nightclubs was a friend of my landlady.

He took Gina on, taught her how to walk; did you ever notice how few people really know how to walk? She was a natural, and in no time she was at ease doing entrechats, plies, arabesques and without the humiliation of a cattlecall she was accepted in the chorus line. In the last row, but she was there. And she never looked back.

Gina's gratitude to me was almost embarrassing. We remained friends. Her career was short-lived; she got married to one of the assistant managers of the biggest department store in Hungary. I was the godfather of their first child.

What bothered me was that my uncle had shed the jitters and was clad again in his ice crust and remained placid in those rarer and rarer occasions when somebody happened to mention Gabriella.

I decided I had to do something about it and I did. To sweeten the dessert which was about to be served, by another very young and very pretty chambermaid, by the name of Elizabeth. I was sure her real name was Böshke, a very common peasant name, but that wouldn't do.

Overriding the polite hubbub of the boring conversation, I mentioned casually, but loud enough to be sure everybody around the table was going to hear it: 'I saw Gabriella in the Moulin Rouge.'

The sudden silence was dotted by the clinking of silver utensils dropping onto the fine Herendi porcelain plates. Now I had everybody's riveted attention and went on merrily. 'Actually her real name is Gina. Did you know that? Oh, and she looked – wow! I mean, she was very, very nice.' I turned to my uncle. 'We talked. We talked a lot.'

My uncle choked, and in hoarse whispers he blamed it on the hazelnuts in the cake. Little did I know that my prank would not end there. My uncle got up from the table with the excuse of clearing his throat. In reality he went to notify the police. Of course, by then the police already knew Gina was alive and well, very well.

My uncle came back to the table. To me he looked like a drenched, beaten dog. I don't know if anybody else was aware of it. He explained in a shaky, emasculated tone that he wasn't sure if we had overheard his conversation from the other room, but it was his duty to notify the police; how relieved he was that Gina had been found. But that wasn't enough for him. Not for that . . . oh, how could my mother have the same mother! He got to Gina's family – as I found out from her – he told them she had gone to the dogs, ruined and degraded on Harlot Street. Shame and dishonor she had brought down on the family.

Neither Gina's family nor anybody else, not even the police, could find Harlot Street on the map, but the police gave them Gina's address and Gina's mother notified her immediately, in panic, that her father was on his way to Budapest to see her.

I was sorry. I mean I was sorry I did not plan what subsequently happened, it was all spontaneous. The awful truth is I was more sorry I did not witness the subsequent payoff.

Her father arrived on the Keleti Pályaudvar, Railway Station East: the terminal for all passenger trains coming from or going toward the West. This is the norm in Hungary. To go to, or arrive from the West the station has to be called Railway Station East. This is very useful information if you travel in Hungary, still a magnificent country. Now you know which railway station you should go to if you want to travel south, you won't have any trouble. Right?

Gina's future husband sent his car, a Steyr XII, to pick up Gina's father. For this occasion he had a driver, no problem if you knew of the many young car enthusiasts who couldn't afford a car and were happy to chauffeur you around for the joy of driving free. There was a valid accepted objection in Hungary: 'You can't talk to me this way, I own a bicycle.' Imagine your status if you owned an automobile. And how the Steyr XII impressed Gina's father. It was a strong solid box of a vehicle for solid citizens, and when Gina introduced her father to her fiancé who was treated like a king in the department store where her father had never dared to enter before, and when he saw the engagement ring on her finger, diamond not zircon, a real diamond, and the lovely large sunny apartment with a view on the Danube, all furnished, waiting for the newlyweds to move in, he was satisfied.

I could never guess if Gina's father's ensuing action was impromptu or carefully planned. When he was asked by his future son-in-law what he would like as a present from the department store – anything – he picked out a thick, heavy, expensive bamboo walking cane. A shillelagh, supreme. It fitted her father, he was six foot two.

The following morning he walked in unannounced to my uncle's office. The reports must be true and accurate since they were overheard and/or witnessed not only by my uncle's large office staff, but also by the people in the adjoining corridors and offices. They all had clearly heard the tête-à-tête. And tête-à-tête became more than just an expression, as in his bull-horn-like voice Gina's father made it extremely clear what was on his mind.

'You don't know what the fucking hell you were talking about. Harlot Street. Where is it? And what's that "shame" crap my daughter brought down on my family? I am proud of her. I like her fiancé, I like the store he manages. I like the real diamond wedding ring he gave her. I like their apartment more than I like your stuffy office here, and I'll be goddamned if I'll be ashamed of the Steyr XII they drive.' (My uncle had the same type of car, and was very proud of it.) 'You're a sick, crazy son-of-a-bitch if you think this is the way she is going to the dogs, to her ruin. If that's the way to go to the dogs, just let her! Hear me, just-let-her-I-am-proud-of-her! Furthermore it's none of your God-damned fucking – forgive-me-God-for-taking-your-name-in-vain – business anyway. You almost gave me a heart attack, you stupid, old, bald son-of-a-bitch!' With that preface, to add more emphasis to his sentiments, he whacked my uncle squarely over the head with the brand new gift from his future son-in-law.

Gina and I had dinner together that night. She quit the Moulin Rouge to celebrate her new future. I could hardly wait for the next Sunday luncheon.

Again I appeared unannounced. I planned to be late. Everything there worked like clockwork. I knew exactly when they were going to sit down at the table and that is when I wanted to make my entrance. The soup was being served. My aunt gave prompt orders to Elizabeth, the new, very pretty chambermaid who I thought had red-rimmed eyes from crying.

My uncle barely greeted me. He turned his head away, lifting his chin to hide a fat long, over-broiled Polish-sausage-like welt adorning the exact center of his semi-bald dome.

He was, like always, polite, but his politeness could cut like a rusty hacksaw. 'Welcome to lunch but don't be late if you want to eat here.' My aunt worried that I might walk out. Under usual circumstances I would have done just that, but this was a special occasion. I would not have missed this, the best luncheon I ever had anywhere for any insult.

A table setting appeared on the table in front of me. My aunt jabbered on, trying to excuse her husband's behaviour, complaining about the constant electrical failures and the many uncalled for accidents they caused. That was true enough. The lights used to go out regularly at the most inconvenient times. But the longer she kept on prattling about how this terrible malheur happened, without actually pointing at her husband's head, the fishier her story sounded and the more her husband squirmed.

I couldn't stand it any longer, I wanted to have my fun. I tried to imitate my uncle's attitude and brisk delivery. I announced my verdict direct, talking to my aunt and impolitely pointing at my uncle's bruised head. 'It looks to me more like somebody whacked him right on the top of his noggin with a shillelagh.'

My uncle whirled around toward me. It was a violent move, his pince-nez finally flew off his nose and landed right in the middle of his tomato soup, freckling him and everybody around him.

I was satisfied. I was repaid for all the unpleasant moments I had spent with him. And as a result, there were not many more moments pleasant or unpleasant I had to spend in his company. I became definitely persona non grata in the household.

It just proves again, good deeds pay for themselves. But this wasn't the final blow, this was only a jab. I delivered the blow, a well set-up right cross when I read out loud after one Sunday lunch the new one-act play I had just finished.

It was the perfect day to do it. I knew it would be a big turnout and Dr Basch would be present. My excuse was to do it for Dr Basch, who must have noticed my uncle's trepidation too. I guess he knew my uncle better than I thought he did, because the moment I finished reading and before anybody had a chance to voice an opinion, he put his on the table.

'You'll see it on the stage.' And right then Dr Basch picked up the phone; in front of everybody he arranged a meeting for me with Alexander Marton, a famous agent and impresario. During the conversation my uncle with ashen face and shivering pince-nez whispered to Dr Basch, 'Are you sure, Loránt?' Dr Basch lifted a hand for him to be quiet and kept on talking.

All this led up to this breakfast now in the Café New York. And as the sun was coming up, three men decided my future. For a while they went about it as if I weren't there, as if I were an object of dubious value they weren't sure where to place. I sat there listening, awestruck – the first time in my life. They were talking about somebody I didn't know.

Dr Basch insisted I had to finish university because I promised. Molnár said, 'Poppycock,' I had some chance to become a writer, a degree in law and political science would not help me to become one. There were no short cuts to writing. I had to write, write and keep on writing. Babitch spoke occasionally and softly, repeating he had no law degree. Basch had the same retort for him every time, 'But you are a poet.'

By then Molnár had had two additional eye-opener brandies and grumbled dissidently, 'He'll never be a writer by attending that university.' He poked a finger toward Basch as if telling him what to do. 'That university is horseshit. Write, write, write. That's the only way to become a writer, and I wouldn't care if he couldn't spell.' 'And he has to read a lot,' interjected Babitch.

'Right, learn to read life.' For the first time Molnár agreed with anything or anybody that night. 'Most important, learn to read life.' Then, agitated, he turned nose-to-nose to Basch. 'What the hell does he need a law degree for? If you don't believe in him, then what the hell is he, what are we doing here?'

There was a momentary silence at the table. The first time I realized how noisy the Café New York was this early in the morning. An ancient waiter brought another brandy for Molnár, then floated away, silent as a ghost.

It seemed to me Molnár didn't believe in the fall-back theory either. Good, I thought; finally I could, I really should get involved in this discussion. I surprised them when I spoke up. They had forgotten that I was present.

'After all, it is my life you are talking about and I –' Molnár had already started on his next brandy and drowned me with it, 'You stay out of this!' Well, what would you have done? I stayed out of it for a while.

At the end Dr Basch had the last word, 'Film is the future. It is a new budding artform. It would suit his talents. Words and Images would suit his temperament. To make motion pictures, successful motion pictures, one has to have audacity.' 'That he has,' acquiesced Molnár. The only point on which all three of them agreed on that occasion, for the next hour or so.

My knowledge of motion pictures was very limited. As they kept on forming my future around me I tried to remember films I saw; I could recall only somebody by the name of Jack Holt, playing a sea captain, strutting up and down on a pier. Invincible and brash. I was duly impressed.

I loved westerns. I couldn't recollect the names of any of the actors, or wouldn't have recognized them if they had walked in and sat at the next table, but I would have recognized their horses.

I was an avid reader. I had read all Karl May's[4] westerns before I finished reading the Bible. I lived with his heroes, Old Shatterhand and that magnificent Indian, Winnetou. They turned my path to the West. Little did I know then, Karl May had never left Germany. He never left the jail cell where he was planted for alleged embezzlement while writing his novels. His imagination sparked my love of the West and opened vistas for me that he, himself, never could ride.

But Hollywood can breed Hungarian cowboys saturated by Louis L'Amour and inspired by an alleged German embezzler.

4 Karl May (1842–1912). His fair-haired German hero Shatterhand even influenced Adolf Hitler, but filmmakers did not pay him any attention until the 1960s, when his westerns were filmed in Yugoslavia and Italy. Long after his books had been published, just before his death, he visited the country he described so vividly.

2   An Eiben Coffee

It was a very long walk from the Café New York to the river. The city was beginning to be peopled by the cog-wheels of life, defiling the purity of the night. The Homo Sapienses, with ugly, loud sniffs and death-row coughs were splattering sputum on the freshly washed pavements. A covey of birds fluttering from tree to tree, relieving themselves in flight, was helping to befoul the morning. I plowed through the uncaring half-asleep crowd. The further I walked, the more irritated I became. The champagne, the too-much talk, washed away my awe of the illustrious group. 'Don't talk if you have nothing to say.' Hell, don't talk too much even if you have something to say, is just as important, maybe even more, it seemed to me. I became rattled, whom were they trying to convince, me or themselves, of what I should be doing with my life.

Mist drifted above the river. I sat on the steps on the shore below the Corso. Across on the top of the Gellért Hegy (Mount Gellért) the Fortress Citadella stood, impressive and vulnerable. A skiff glided over the choppy waves in silence, the man in it was rowing seemingly with no effort. From far away a coxswain's voice echoed between the buildings, an eight came into view, a great contrast to the silent skiff. Even from the distance one could feel the effort, smell the sweat of the crew. Their oars almost lifted the shell out of the water. The coxswain, dissatisfied as they always are, was yelling through the megaphone fastened to his chin, riding like a jockey just before the finish line. I admired them as they passed, they were one, one well-oiled unit. Little did I know how soon I'd be one of that eight.

The waves slapped the stairs, the sun hit the water and painted little rainbows around the small oil patches drifting from the passenger boats and freighters moored along the shore. The Blue Danube was far from being blue. It looked more like clay-yellow mixed with greenish-grey. I don't believe it could have ever been blue. I was blue.

The man in the skiff came back, rowing smoothly against the flow. Suddenly it occurred to me how ridiculous he would feel to have three coxswains with him in the shell. Actually only two and a half, like I had two and a half with me, Babitch being the least assertive. I didn't want to be ungrateful, but. And the 'but' came.

'What in hell do you want me to do with him now?' Molnár attacked Basch. 'A conceited jackass –'

'Now hold it, just a minute . . .' I yelled at him.

'You stay out of it!' Molnár yelled back at me.

Babitch lifted a hand, his other hand held a glass of his eternal red wine. He spoke quietly, Molnár listened, he had respect for him. I hardly could hear what Babitch said in the noisy Café. All I caught was '. . . After all, it's his life.'

'His life, my ass!' Everybody could hear Molnár, even across the street. 'He'll get lost and he could be . . . Oh fuck him!' He got up, carrying his snifter, went to sit with a group of newspapermen. Babitch stretched his smile. Basch was smug and satisfied, as he watched Molnár go, 'He paid you the highest compliment . . .'

'Me? A compliment?'

'Didn't you notice, he was so upset he forgot he should not carry his own glass.'

'He likes you,' said Babitch, who drained his glass, stood up. 'Got to go home, now,' and left.

'I'm sorry for all the trouble I have caused.'

'What trouble, sorry for what? You did exactly what I was hoping you would do. Molnár is with you, but you bug him. He has to realize you're not his toy. It's your life. Any plans?'

'None.'

The classrooms were built like amphitheaters, with places for fifty to one hundred and fifty students. In some of the classrooms the last couple of rows were about two stories up. The roll calls were irregular and read by an assistant to the professor. I found out while this went on the professors dozed, read the morning or afternoon papers mixed in with their notes, or indeed read their notes for the lectures of the day. We had actual close personal contact with them only during the exams.

Before the exams we were thoroughly scrutinized and identified. On those rare days when I actually attended classes, I made a point to seek the professors out with some specific inquiries about their subject of the day, hoping they would remember me on the day of judgement.

I bribed the readers of the roll calls to tick me off 'present' on the list, regardless of my actual presence. It worked. I had a one hundred per cent attendance record, and passed the tests with flying colors, after several weeks of day and night cramming before exams. This approach kept me free to prepare for my real future: Motion Pictures. It was all fine in theory, but where to start?

I read everything I could about films and film-making. There was not very much available, but enough to get me excited. Dr Basch's view on the possibilities of this future art form was right on line.

Words and images. Yes. Motion Pictures. Movement, rhythm, highlights and shadows.

And the word. Yes, the Word, but what is more important, to see or to hear? If you had to lose one of these, sometimes blessings, sometimes curses, which one would you keep? Balance. Balance? There is no balance. Do you want to live half blind and half deaf? No, go for it. The story should dictate on each frame which one, sight, or sound – music – should carry the alpha influence to your brain.

Molnár kept on nodding, I couldn't tell if he was dozing, agreeing or disagreeing or thinking of something else. I turned off my ramblings.

After a sip of brandy Molnár looked at me, and actually smiled. 'Thinking is dangerous, you know.' He had another sip, I shrugged, embarrassed. 'You're really getting ready to set the film world on fire.'

'Yeah . . . but where to start this arson?'

'We'll see.'

There were no courses readily available on campuses anywhere around as there are now. There was only one way to learn, I still think probably the best, on the floor, one-on-one, hands on. But where to put my hands on?

I found out where through Molnár during one of his not too frequent visits to Budapest. He introduced me to Imre Farkas, a fellow author. He called him, like everybody else, by his nickname, Mokucy (Squirrelly). He looked like a squirrel, and acted like one. He was more proud of the fact that he never owned or wore an overcoat, rain or snow, than all of his quite illustrious literary achievements.

As luck – again – would have it, one of his novels was about to be filmed at the Hunnia Studios, right in Budapest. He arranged a pass for me to visit the set while they were shooting.

Lady Luck again. My first day in a studio I found where to put my hands on.

It was a coffee mug on the top of a box which was covered with a black cloth. Under this black cloth was not only that box, but a man's head, of course still attached to the man. He was seated on a bar stool on a baby buggy-like contraption, which was rolled around, back and forth.

My first thought was it was absurd to try to rock the man to sleep in this cacophony of loud voices, hammering, sawing and ringing bells. I was happy to note, my first judgement on a motion picture set was right. The man under the black cloth was not asleep. He reached out from under his cover, groping for the mug on the top of the box. He had difficulty finding it. Being brought up to be polite I risked my safety, dodging swinging two-by-fours, dangling ropes – actually cables for the overhead lights – as I ran to help him. I handed him the mug under the cover. He whipped back the black cloth, and I was bludgeoned by the strongest whiff of rum. He stared at me first then drained the mug and handed it over to me, 'Get me another one,' and disappeared under the cover.

I knew, like everybody else must have known within a mile radius, what was in the mug; my only problem was where to get it. I just stood there, holding the empty but still reeking mug as I watched the seemingly headless, noisy commotion around me.

'Across the street at the Schraettner.' A skinny harassed man clutching a megaphone, the assistant director who arranged my pass, yelled at me on the run, then added, 'Be sure it's hot.'

Schraettner was a restaurant across from the studio. The minute I walked in, before I could open my mouth, the man from the cash register took away the mug and hollered toward what I guessed was the kitchen, 'An Eiben coffee.' I yelled 'Hot!' He looked at me appalled, 'Of course hot,' but repeated it for good measure, 'hot!' When the fresh mug came in, steaming, I snatched a napkin from a table, wrapped the mug in it; not to keep it hot, but to avoid getting drunk on rum fumes.

When I got back to the studio the security guard at the gate stopped me, not too politely. 'Hey, hold it! Where you think you're going?'

'I was in before. I just went across to . . .'

He was sniffing the air as I was speaking, pointed at the wrapped up mug, 'Eiben coffee.'

'Yeah!'

'Don't just stand here, get going, he's waiting, move.'

The big door of the stage was wide open, groups were standing around in front of it, smoking, chatting. A short well-fed man, sporting a dark-blue beret, left one of the groups and headed directly toward me. 'Where have you been?' I had never seen him before in my life. He reached for the wrapped up mug, 'Finally, somebody is thinking . . . who are you?'

I like to be wrong. I feel if I am not wrong I have lost something. Being right you gain nothing, it feels like treading water in a stagnant pool. Being wrong is a step forward, you learn, you have gained. I was wrong to wrap up that mug to keep me sober, I should have done it to keep it warm . . . It makes a big difference. That's life.

The consumer of the Eiben coffee fished out of one of his pockets a crumpled cigarette and I thought we'd be blown up by the fumes when he went to light it. He ignored this possibility, lit his cigarette and we survived. I am still convinced it was due to a major miracle. During all this he nailed me to the wall with scrutiny. 'What are you doing here?' Before I could answer he fired a second question, 'And how did you get in?'

I tried to be short, people were going back inside, I didn't want to miss anything.

'So you're looking for a position.'

'Yes sir!'

'You got one.' He handed back the mug, empty of course. 'Get me another one.'

This was my first job in the motion picture industry, and for twenty-four hours the only job.

It was late. Everybody was gone, I was sitting on the deserted, dark stage in the director's chair, dreaming . . .

'What on earth are you doing here, I was looking for you all over . . .' A double-sized matron with flaming red hair and mezzo-soprano voice shredded my fantasies. Her sledgehammer steps rattled the lights overhead as she marched across the set. 'Come on . . . I have tickets to *Rigoletto*, I don't want to spend all night here with you . . .' and she held the stagedoor open for me.

Now I recognized her, she was the wardrobe lady. I followed her down a narrow long corridor, puzzled, lagging behind. I thought, I don't want to spend all night with her, here or anywhere else, nor with *Rigoletto* at the opera.

'Move . . .' and she charged through the wardrobe department's door, leaving it wide open behind her. As I reached the door, I was hit by a bundle of clothes flying through it and before I could untangle myself I was hit by another batch, which she followed, 'Get in there,' pointing at a dressing-room, 'and put 'em on.'

An actor who was supposed to start his part the following morning had been taken ill and this had caused two big problems. One for the production, to find a replacement for the actor, two, for the wardrobe lady, how to catch *Rigoletto* that night.

The wardrobe lady found the solution for both problems. She was sure of her keen eyes and good judgement and suggested I should replace the actor, because the wardrobe would fit me without a stitch of alteration. It did, and she got her wish and, happily humming *Rigoletto*, off she went to the opera, and I became an actor. Luck?

My father and General Szirmay got a sliver of their wish too: I was wearing a uniform of the Hungarian Huszárs, the uniform of a lieutenant no less. But! I was schlepping Eiben coffee across from Schraettner to Hunnia Studios hour after hour. I must have been some sight, and smell too, carrying gingerly a mug of Eiben coffee, in that glorious semi-dress uniform, while trying to overcome three serious obstacles; one, the mirror-shiny black boots were way, way too small, because I hadn't wanted to rob the wardrobe lady of *Rigoletto*, and had accepted them. Two, the gleaming saber dangling from my waist was too, too long. Three, and worst of all, the mug – always filled to the brim – was slopping over.

I was glad then and I am just as glad now that my father or General Szirmay didn't see me. They would have either shot me or committed suicide, or most likely both. *Requiescat in pace.*

That symbol of manhood, that damned saber was the cause of my first faux pas in the motion picture industry, with many more big and glorious faux pas to follow throughout the ensuing happy years.

My second faux pas in order of discovery was actually connected with the Eiben coffee and the high praises I had received for serving such full mugs always so hot. I achieved both faux pas within my first forty-eight hours on the threshold of a new career.

By now I knew how important the Eiben coffee could be to my career and after a few trips I decided to order two mugs. When I got close to the stage I poured what was left in the two mugs into one mug to make the full portion I was praised for, and what was left in the second mug I emptied over the fence on the grass. Nobody told me that the pet jack rabbit belonging to the executive secretary of the studio lived there.

New words, new expressions filtered through my ears, saturated my brain. It seemed bedlam held the reins to an organized confusion – almost like today, with one very important difference: there was no line of demarcation between the crafts. I felt they were one and all in love with making motion pictures. Whoever was closest to a job to be done did it. Except for a few specialists, like the man under the black cloth, he just stuck his hand out from under the black cloth and pointed at things to be done.

And the clapper-loader, he was a real specialist, a kid of sixty-five–seventy. He had lost his right leg just below his knee in the first war, the war we were told then was to end all wars. He had a strap-on wooden leg, but he used it only when he was 'drinking heavily'; he never owned a pair of crutches, he owned only a gnarled cane, which 'came in handy' during winter months. With all this, I cannot say handicap because he was the fastest clapper-boy I ever worked with any time anywhere, zig-zagging like lightning over the usual clatter on stage floors to end up rock steady in front of the lens. Whacking the stick to the board and out he was even faster than he zig-zagged in.

I could never forget him. I owe him a lot. He was my inspiration when I broke my neck for the first time in Switzerland, skiing, showing off, of course, and I was told by the professors I would never walk again.

I was itching to look through that box, the camera. I hadn't seen anybody looking through it all day except the man with the Eiben coffee. I could hardly wait for the next 'take five' to come, I had decided to take my chances.

My biggest obstacle was that clumsy saber, dangling between my legs. As I was trying to saddle the barstool on top of the baby buggy, I almost overturned the whole contraption. To avoid disaster I unhooked the saber, left it on the prop box, lifted the black cloth, withstood the shock of the mixed odor of rum, coffee and acetone, and for the first time I looked through a movie camera.

Looked through? I couldn't see a thing. Now I understood why the black cloth was needed to cover the box, a Debrie Super Parvo,[1] which had

---

1 The best known of motion picture cameras in Europe was the Debrie, named after its inventor André Debrie (1880–1967). He introduced the 'Parvo' (compact) camera in 1908, and the 'Super Parvo' for shooting sound films in 1932.

a direct through film and lens view. Ideal for the perfect framing of set-ups, but it was a special art to operate. The camera was resting on a gimbal, had no gear head, it had to be panned or tilted with a 'schwenk arm', a fancy name for a pipe screwed to either left or right lower corner of the box. This one had it on the left, of course, the right was reserved for another function. It is a marvel what superior photographic quality was achieved, in every aspect, by some of the masters of the period, without alibiing for the inferior chemical structure of the film. They, at least, stand up with today's masters of black-and-white photography. My respect grows for them every time I see a movie or step behind a camera now.

Luck again that I was to start off with a master like the man under the black cloth, the man with the Eiben coffee: István 'Hapshi' 'Pishta' Eiben.[2]

'What the hell you think you're doing?' and the black cloth was roughly yanked off my head, off the box. 'Who in hell you think you are?' Eiben snapped the black cloth with a sharp crack, 'Get off.' Not much else I could do. I clambered off, half blinded by the sudden light, trying to get my bearings. 'You're fired!'

'You can't fire him, Pishta [one of Eiben's nicknames], he's in a few more scenes yet,' butted in an aghast first assistant, then he ran out.

There was an impasse, I took advantage of it. 'I wasn't even hired yet.' Turning to Eiben directly, 'I didn't know I shouldn't do it, sir. This is my first time on a set and I am trying to learn as much as possible about the camera since the name of the game is making motion pictures. Pictures. Without knowing the camera, how can one make 'em, I thought.'

The stage door burst open, the director rushed in with his assistant, 'What's going on here?' he asked panting, 'I need him.'

'Nothing is going on, we were waiting for you,' said Eiben, then turned to me. 'What the hell are you standing around here, go and get it.' And I ran.

It is not true. I flew. What a relief. Instead of being fired on the spot, I felt I had connected with Eiben. And the following years proved my instinct was correct.

2 István 'Hapshi' 'Pishta' Eiben (1902–58). Cameraman, one of the early pioneers of optics, camera and lighting techniques. Refused to be called Director of Photography. 'There is only one director and I refuse to be a second!' He photographed four out of Andre de Toth's first five films between January 1939 and October 1939.

At first I didn't notice that that useless piece of chrome-plated steel was not dangling between my legs. I was sure I was going to break my round-trip record with the mug. The security guard was yelling at me from across the street as I emerged from Schraettner with the usual two mugs, wrapped in napkins, of course. 'Get moving, boy, they're waiting for you, all set up. Don't slow down because you think you're an actor now, not a busboy.' He laughed at his sarcasm, I speeded up.

Now I really flew. I didn't want to keep them waiting, I was already aware of the number-one nemesis of picture-making, 'schedule'. The Eiben coffee was slushing over the brim of the mugs more than usual because of my speed, dripping off the soaked napkins. 'Watch the wardrobe,' flashed through my mind just as I reached the fence. On an impulse I threw my load over it, all of it so I could speed up.

The small pedestrian door of the stage opened a slit. 'Come on,' yelled the assistant director, and almost cut my heels off as he closed the door quickly behind me. 'Ready,' he yelled.

Before I could take my second deep breath I was ushered on the set, shoved to a chalk mark on the floor. 'Action!' yelled the director, unnecessarily loud. Since then I have had an aversion to calling 'Action'.

The scene was shot. Eiben wanted it 'once more'. The director yelled even louder than when he called 'Action', 'Oh shit, he'll never do it again.' I immediately learned how to give confidence to an actor. The scene was shot; second take, it was printed. Eiben got off the baby buggy. On his way to the next set he thumbed toward the stage entrance, smiled at me, 'Get it, Hapshi.'

Hapshi. A word I had never heard. It could have been an insult, but he smiled when he said it. Well, I'd better 'get it,' and flew.

Every time 'on my way out' I picked up the mugs and napkins I had left on the grass 'on my way in', but they were not there now and nobody brought them back to Schraettner.

'Lost,' concluded Schraettner. 'They are a bunch of thieves over there. Now, don't you dare quote me, over there, you hear.'

The chimes above the entrance door were almost ripped off as the security guard swung it open. 'Stop lally-gagging here, they –'

'– fresh brew is coming up,' Schraettner yelled.

'They want him on stage, didn't you know he is an actor now, ha ha. I'll take the stuff.'

'What happened?'

'Don't blabber, it's some miss-match, go.'

The small stage door was wide open, in front of it the director, the assistant director, the wardrobe lady and the script girl. (That's what they were called then. No man would take that job. I never could figure out why it was stamped as not a man's job.) They were yelling at each other, gesticulating wildly. They looked very undignified. One of the 'don't do's' I learned within my first forty-eight hours was, don't lose your dignity.

The group noticed me and all started to yell at me, all at the same time, but the shrill mezzo-soprano of the wardrobe lady cut through and above their voices, 'Where the fucking hell is your saber?'

The saber? The saber! Where is it? whirled around my brain. Oh!

'I left it on the prop box.' That started another war between them for the time being, but after a while they zeroed in on the silver-haired hatchet-faced script girl, who was at least sixty. Her dried-apple-color face went magenta.

She spat on the wardrobe lady. And while the wardrobe lady was cleaning herself, the script girl collected some more saliva and spat at the assistant director, but she missed him. He was half way through the door, following his boss. She now turned to me, I was flinching. 'You stupid ass!' but no spit, she went inside. (Today she would have called me an asshole, time marches on, courtesies are changing.) The wardrobe lady grabbed the epaulet on my tunic and stiff-armed me through the door. I didn't like it, but I thought it was wiser not to fight her. One, she was a lady, two she was six foot three, with a forty-six cup.

I still didn't know what was going on. 'Don't you dare to take that saber off again till I tell you. You'll eat with it, you'll shit with it, you'll fuck with it and you'll sleep with it on! Got it?' She stopped shoving me, I faced her. Only one thing came to my mind: 'How was *Rigoletto* last night?'

We stood nose to nose, she had garlic breath. God she was sharp, she must have noticed my grimace, 'I had garlic toast for breakfast, I like it –'

'With schnapps?'

She smiled and exhaled through her mouth, 'You're a son-of-a-bitch, but you're OK. It wasn't your fault, don't worry.'

Eiben called out, 'Where is it?'

'Fresh brew, sir, it's coming.'

There was no propman around, he was too busy with new set-ups, the wardrobe lady affixed the saber, the assistant led me back on the set, to the same spot where I was before. Eiben called out from under the black cloth, 'I told you, can't tell if the saber is on him or not.'

A Babylonian gibberish started up again, should they re-shoot the scene or not. The cutter came in. (There were no editors at that time.) He reported the lab wouldn't be able to deliver the rushes for at least forty-eight hours or so. To re-shoot or not re-shoot, that was the question. The problem was, if anybody had an answer, it would have been lost in the noise.

Eiben stayed aloof, cool, and silently supplied the solution. 'Get it, Hapshi, I'll be on the other set.' Off he went one way, I went the other way with that damned saber dangling between my legs again. The wardrobe lady's detailed instruction didn't include keeping it on while carrying the Eiben coffee, but I thought it safer, wiser to have it on. I blamed myself for the slip-up. One down, many more to come.

On the way out I spotted the security guard coming toward me, concentrating on the mug, shuffling gingerly like an LA driver at midnight going through a sobriety test. When he saw me he stopped. 'Look at me, look at me.' The Eiben coffee was dribbling down his knuckles, the sleeves of his uniform, the bottom of his pantaloon, his shoes, everything he had on was polka-dotted with Eiben coffee.

'This is for the birds.' He was concentrating so hard he didn't notice the sparrows following him. 'I'm a security guard – I wasn't hired as a waiter like you. Here, have it.'

When he handed the mug over I slapped the bottom of it, hard. 'You have it,' and whatever was left in the mug splattered all over his face, his shirt, on the front of his uniform.

'Keep the mug, I'll get a fresh one.' Before he recovered, I was gone.

'I wish more coffee had been left in that mug,' commented Schraettner.

'And hotter,' I augmented his feeling.

'Fresh ones are coming up,' he said and I followed him back into the restaurant.

Waiting for fresh hot mugs to be filled, I asked Schraettner what 'hapshi' meant. 'Oh, that's an Eiben word, don't look for it in the dictionary. He makes things up. If he likes somebody he calls them Hapshi, if he likes somebody very much he calls them Hapshikám.'

'He called me Hapshi.'

'Well, now did he? Be proud of it, "lieutenant". He's a no bullshit man.

They were making a picture over there with horses and with a director who came back home from Berlin. You know what he did? He called the director a horse's ass, then turned to the horses and apologized to them for comparing any part of their body with the director and walked off the show. That's Eiben.'

Many years later, I quoted him verbatim to an actor and to some horses, but Charlie Einfeld and David Loew of Enterprise were real producers, not star-gazers with brown noses. They wouldn't let me walk off, and we needed the horses, so they asked the horse's ass to leave the show.

Have you ever seen a drunken jack rabbit? Or have you ever seen a jack rabbit as large as a small Saint Bernard? I never did either, before that very day.

They were on their last shot now, with end of the day tension in the air. Ignoring the red light, the warning 'Do not enter' sign, the security guard stormed through the stage door, yelling, 'Help . . . Heeeelp, first aid, first aaaaid.'

A straw-blond, flat-chested woman about the size of the wardrobe lady was on his heels, squealing like a stuck pig and bleeding profusely from her right hand. 'Attila bit me . . . he bit meee . . . look, look at it . . .' Everything stopped, of course.

The director pushed his chair under the bottom of the bleeding woman, the assistant was running toward the cubbyhole of the first aid, screeching through his megaphone, 'First aaaaaid.' The electricians holding on to the sides of the ladders were sliding down to the floor, the ever present morbidly curious surrounded the woman. Eiben, with the 'schwenk arm' under his armpit, resting comfortably under the black cloth, was the only one on the stage who didn't even move.

Like an ice-breaker, the security guard was parting the throng around the still hysterically 'Attila bit me . . . bit meee,' crying woman. The assistant director, through his megaphone, started to yell in his director's ear, 'We'll be behind . . .' the director knocked the megaphone away, luckily no teeth flew with it. The assistant finished his sentence, now whispering, 'schedule'.

The security guard pointed at me, 'There he is. He did it, I saw him do it.'

I was sitting on a box next to the baby buggy. 'I did what?'

All eyes turned toward me. Eiben still didn't move.

'He got him stoned. Come 'n' see him, he could've killed Attila.' They all swarmed after the guard through the door to see Attila.

The first aid person, he or she, it was impossible to tell from where I was, slipped away to get medical supplies, I supposed. The injured woman, mumbling to herself, mesmerized by her still bleeding hand, was now all alone on the set.

Attila, the small Saint Bernard-size jack rabbit stole all the company from his bleeding mistress. He was, for sure, a sight to behold. In one second he was charging at the fence head on, like rams butt heads during mating season; in the next, he was trying feverishly to dig a hole under the fence. Then again abruptly he turned, picked up the Eiben mug determined to lick out the last remaining drops, then, as if he were disgusted, threw it against the fence; during all this he was intermittently emitting short very high-pitched squeals.

If you think this is abnormal behaviour for a drunken rabbit, Harvey or not, you're wrong. He really went over-the-hill berserk when he picked up the Eiben coffee-soaked napkins. He chewed on them with venom, then shook and shook them wildly. Then, with a running start, he tried to climb the trees with the napkins clamped between his teeth, only to end up on his back, covered by the napkins, his four feet clawing towards the sky faster and faster.

Then, unexpectedly, he went rigid for a minute or so, but he had another surprise coming: Attila urinated on himself, on the napkins. When he finished, suddenly he jumped to his feet and with his powerful hind-legs kicked the napkins away, sending the soggy bundle against the fence, splattering foul-smelling light-brown liquid on the bystanders. After that the whole performance started all over again, in the exact same sequence as before, but faster and faster.

With bandaged hand, Attila's mistress finally joined the dwindling group outside watching Attila and she spoke softly to the drunken rabbit. 'Oh baby, baby what did they do to you? Oh . . . oooh you stink.' She whirled around, her voice now sounded like a mean drill sergeant's: 'Where is that bastard?'

The security guard was right on the ball, 'There he is,' pointing at me. I got scared, I didn't know what I should do if this big hunk of irate female started to lambast me. Hit her back – I too believed in the equality of sexes that Mother was fighting for all her life. After all, I couldn't let my mother down. I was ready for the onslaught. Why not? Is there equality or not?

She was screaming at me from a long distance. Never since have I been called so many names in one language. None of them was flattering. By the time she reached me, she ran out of insults. She stopped two steps away, towering above me, and I was no midget at six feet.

'Why did you do it, why did you want to poison my baby with that shit?' With tears streaming down her cheeks, she was about to haul off.

'Hold it, Maria.' Eiben joined us, 'I have been drinking that shit now for a few years and it didn't harm me, did it?' Eiben's question was sharp. 'Now, did it?'

She was stumped for a moment, and she knew she had run into a dead-end street. Eiben put the screws on, 'I asked him to do it, OK?' She became unglued, started to bawl, unashamed, loud. 'Why? . . . Why?' She ran to Attilla, to her drunken jack rabbit, still on the rampage.

'On the set . . . On the set. Let's go, let's gooo!' yelled the assistant director, through the megaphone grown to his lips, herding the sheep.

Eiben turned to me. 'I am curious, what happened?' He rarely spoke to me beyond 'Get it.' I felt I was still on thin ice, but I had no choice but to explain, hesitantly, what I had done with the two mugs. He laughed, 'I never had a full mug before, I was wondering how it was happening now. Very clever.'

Strange. I had to thank God, my Lady Luck and a drunken jack rabbit for the wonderful friendship with Eiben which started then.

My second faux pas during the first forty-eight hours in the 'business', instead of bringing disaster, brought success. I was relieved of being in charge of the Eiben coffee delivery, at the request of 'Attila's mother', but first I had to teach the second-second assistant what to do so the mug was hot and full, in order of importance, upon arrival at Eiben's right hand. We had to have several rehearsal runs to be sure. Eiben was a tremendous help, he consumed a great deal more than usual during the training period of the second-second. All in all, my first 'directorial assignment' was a success. My pupil performed well.

By the end of the week I was trusted to keep the camera lenses and the filters clean and, most important, keep the 'hair'[3] out of the gate in the

---

3 Occasionally, as the 'pin' or 'claw' pulled the film through behind the lens, dirt accumulated in the little 'window' – the 'gate' – through which the light reached the negative and exposed it. When the positive image was projected, on the edges of the screen this accumulated dirt sometimes looked like a picket fence, sometimes like telephone poles.

Debrie Super Parvo. It was an important assignment with grave responsibilities.

By the end of the week the director started to talk to me, seeing Eiben was not only letting me look through the camera but allowing me occasionally, during rehearsals, to operate it, and this was unheard of before. This director hardly, if ever, looked through the camera, to Eiben's great dismay. He had little or no respect for directors who neglected the image. 'After all,' he told me between sips of his coffee, 'we are supposed to be making motion pictures . . . pictures,' he sighed.

Seeing my sponge-like interest, he talked to me about lenses, filters, the light, the framing; the rhythm of the images, movement. 'Look at it,' and he kicked the baby buggy. 'I invented this so we could move but no, we are anchored.' He kicked the baby buggy again. 'When you direct, don't let them tell you, you can't move. Only a constipated imagination will stop you from moving the camera. But watch it, don't let the movement interfere with the dramatic impact you're after . . . Oh shit.'

Disgusted, he emptied his mug, then looked for the second-second assistant, 'Hey, get it!' The second-second ran, and I felt I had arrived.

Finally the shooting came to an end, two days behind schedule. I was sorry it was over. I told Eiben, watching the last few set-ups, 'If he had taken two more days, the picture would've turned out to be only half as bad.'

I sopped up every move, every word, every minute of the two weeks' shooting. I decided never to compromise. But it took me years to learn the difference between no compromise and being stubborn.

Harry Cohn of Columbia taught me a few little tricks about that. But sometimes I like to think I showed him a few little tricks too. It makes me feel good to think that. Actually we ended up fifty-fifty, he won in the financial court but I got the best of him on the principles. Each of us got what we thought was the most important. It is a great luxury when one can afford to learn from the mistakes of others. Sometimes it is more important to know the don'ts than the dos.

During the wrap-up party Eiben told the director, pointing at me, 'You'll have him with you in the cutting room.' It was not a question, it was not a request, he told him. And for almost two months I lived with acetone fumes, hot-splices, razor blades and silver-nitrate film wrapped around the director's neck, just missing his cigar. Little did I know then how close we sometimes came to being fried to crisp smithereens, obviously he didn't know it either, or blithely ignored it, as he ignored, for me, very important details. He was a typical good-enough man. However, he was called 'a good cutter', because he hardly lost a frame. Based on this, my first experience alone, I do understand why 'editors' object to be called 'cutters'. But I can't fathom why someone should have the credit 'director of the toilet' for keeping the WC clean.

The chicken paprikás with lots of sour cream, surrounded by a wagon-load of Hungarian galushka (dumplings) was savoured with a couple of bottles of Badacsonyi Kéknyelüvel. By the time we were finishing the Dobosh Torta and we were enjoying the Five Puttonosh Tokay Aszu, a pink morning sun was peeking through the Eiben dining-room. The Eibens had no servants, which was very unusual. Mrs Eiben was a shiny, smiling, fiery little butter-ball and a cooking maniac. She tiptoed back in the dining-room, waited till her husband finished his sentence and asked us what we would like to have for breakfast. 'The car will pick you two up at seven,' she reported. I was suprised by the plural. Eiben got up from the table, tenderly hugged his wife, 'I didn't tell him yet.' He laughed from the bottom of his heart, 'You'll start with me today on this new picture.'

It was as simple as that, and I was on my second feature, a big one – foreign money, three weeks' schedule. By the fourth week of the three week schedule I was beginning to grasp the shortcomings of light meters, how to veer off the center-norm to achieve unusual effects. Occasionally I was allowed to operate the camera when shooting inserts. It all accelerated. Now thanks to the second-second, and not to a drunken jack rabbit. Of course, in my thanks God and Lady Luck are always included.

The second-second on this picture was in real life the second cousin of the director. He thought it was beneath his social status to play waiter to Eiben, and with a systematic but cowardly rebellion neglected his most important duty; when Eiben was ready for his mug, the mug just was never there. I pitched in without much ado. Every second time when Eiben reached up from under the black cloth the Eiben coffee was there, in a full mug and hot.

On this occasion, breaking all his rules, Eiben lifted his cover and stared at me, with pupils dilated to their limits so that all one could see was a blur. He grunted a 'hm' and ducked back under the black cover.

The first assistant director, a pompous jackass, who came back from

Germany with the director, specially for this picture, one day called me Eiben's lackey. I kept my cool and thanked him for the compliment, adding that I was very proud to be Eiben's anything. Eiben overheard this exchange, surfaced from under his black cloth, and made it very clear that he assigned the second-second to be in charge of his mug, and I was his first assistant, 'Do you hear, schmuck, he is the first to me just like you are to . . .' he hesitated, nodded toward the director, 'whatever-his-name-is.'

He ducked back under his cover. From that moment on he worked my butt off and really took charge of my indoctrination in the mysteries of photography. Eiben could be a very tough hombre, whether he liked you or disliked you made little difference to him. But he was a pro to the nth degree.

It is amazing how coincidence guided my path, for better or for worse, all through the years, with the big 'what if's' lurking inevitably in the back of my mind.

A new hand was on the tiller of my life, replacing the brilliant triumvirate of Molnár, Babitch and Basch: Eiben. I didn't know anything about his background, his education, but his technical and chemical knowledge of photography was unsurpassed, his dramatic sense was flawless, and his photographic effects never overwhelmed but always enhanced the moment. I started to think maybe Molnár was right: what did I need a law and political sciences degree for. When I mentioned this to Eiben, at first he was surprised and impressed that I was 'attending' the university, then, unexpectedly, he blew his top. He really blew it. He threatened to fire me on the spot, never to speak to me again if I quit my studies. 'I never thought you were stupid, but . . .' He didn't finish his sentence, ducked under his black cloth and kept on mumbling to himself. He didn't speak to me for the rest of the afternoon. But as we were breaking for the day he called to me, 'You'll have dinner with me. See you at Schraettner in twenty minutes.' He didn't wait for any answer, just left.

When I walked into the restaurant they led me to a secluded table way in the back, the worst table in the place. When I questioned the choice, I was told this was the table Mr Eiben wanted.

I sat, ordered nothing and sat and sat. When I was about ready to leave he showed up, around thirty or so minutes late. He sat down. I sat and he sat. Neither of us spoke. We just sat opposite each other at the table, no waiter came to take our order. Eiben was openly watching me with that peculiar squint he usually used to size up a new set before he started lighting it.

All at once two waiters appeared and served an obviously pre-ordered dinner, and we were poured two glasses of water, no alcohol. Strange, I thought. Still no exchange of words. The moment the waiters had departed he spoke. 'I am going to eat this shit because I didn't want my wife to hear what I am going to tell you. And I don't want you to say one fucking word till I am through with you. Got it?' Before I could say yes sir, he barked at me, 'not a word, just listen.'

He took a sip of his water, made a terrible face, then started. 'You'll do what I tell you or you're fired. Right here on the spot, don't come in tomorrow, I don't want to waste my time with you if you don't agree.' As a reflex motion he took a sip of his water again only to spit it back into the glass, wrinkled his nose and went on. 'It seems you could finish your studies and work here at the same time, right?'

'Right,' I said automatically.

'Shut up! Then you have no excuse. You'll finish whatever you have started in the university. During your summer vacations you'll go to Vienna, or Berlin. Better yet, you will have to go to London sooner or later. English is important, you have to speak English.' He twirled his glass, watched the vortex in it with a mile-away stare – he was here in body only. He spoke at first like he was only speaking to himself. 'All who spoke languages are gone, some of them were good, I miss those.' His thoughts rejoined his body.

'If you want to succeed, be on the top of the world, you have to go, the stupid world won't come to you. There are only two places to hit, Germany, specially UFA in Berlin, or America. Yes, Hollywood, the most important. Paris is important too, it is a different style of film-making, it is wonderful, but it can be very tough for a foreigner. London, with Laci Korda there now, may wake up or they may put him in jail.' He took again a sip of water and to my surprise he swallowed it. It must have been a big shock to his system, he pushed the glass too far to be within easy reach, then went on, 'In the meantime I'll teach you, whatever . . . Take your time, then, I'll tell you when, get out of here, find a job, any job in pictures in Berlin or London. Then, after a couple of years, please, promise you'll come back. You know we like imports here. The Ferenc Jóshka (the Hungarian nickname for Franz Joseph of Hapsburg, Emperor of Austria, King of Hungary) instilled insecurity still lives on.' He indicated the director sitting with his entourage at a table, noisy, boisterous. 'Look at him, he doesn't know his asshole from his mouth. I wouldn't take him for a second-second. He was hanging around here for a while, got nowhere, then went to Berlin. He was an occasional extra there, that's all. Then he came back after a couple of years, full of hot air, saying he was a director. Now this is his second picture. The pompous ass. Imagine, when he got off the train people were waiting for him, flowers and all that stuff, and you know what his first words were, speaking only in German, never guess it, "Please help me, I forget what's the Hungarian name for Mother." And his dear mother was standing right next to him with flowers. The shithead.'

He turned abruptly and called a waiter, made a large sweeping gesture, 'Take this crap away and bring us some food.' He ordered broiled Hungarian sausages, Egri Bikavér (bull's blood, a heavy Hungarian red wine) and lángosh (pancake-like, pan-fried fresh bread dough); it was definitely not a diet meal. After a long discussion with the waiter about how all this should be prepared, interspersed with the waiter's deep sighs – 'We're doing this for you all the time, Mr Eiben, the cook knows,' 'And fucks it up all the time . . . OK, get it,' – he turned back to me: 'Your answer is yes.' He didn't wait for my answer, he got up and went to the toilet.

We had a hell of a meal. The dessert was the best, plans for the future, washed down with schnapps. It was strange, not too many years later, for sentimental reasons, to sit at the same lousy table, eating an identical, suicidal meal to reminisce. The occasion was the first night of the first day of shooting of my first full-length feature. You would never guess, it was being photographed by Hapshi Eiben.

It was unfortunate he could not photograph all of my five Hungarian films shot in 1939 between January and October because of previous commitments. I missed him, always remembering my odyssey started with him. All in all a happy trip.

As the summer vacation loomed around the corner, I was prepared. I bought a used 125 cc belt-driven Excelsior motorcycle. It sounded like a sewing-machine, but it moved, especially downhill. Uphill was another story; I had to walk it up, but the bike was a bargain.

Through some connections, as usual, and the extra help of Father Benedict of the student home where I was living in Budapest, I got into another student home, in Vienna. It wasn't as luxurious as the one I took for granted in Budapest, but it served the purpose. I'll be working all day anyway, I thought.

When finally the day came, to eliminate the immediate sentimental upheavals usually attached to departures of this magnitude, I decided, instead of leaving from home, to leave direct from Budapest. Loaded with suitcases tied to the back-seat of the bike, plus a packed-to-bursting-point rucksack strapped on me, I took off to conquer the picture industry of the world.

Before reaching the outskirts of the city, my rear tire blew, downhill. By the time, with luck, I brought the dancing machine under control and stopped, the carcass of the tire was a shredded, entangled mess of spokes, cords and ribbons with the twisted rim of the wheel and drive-belt.

I thought I had been smart to leave before the crack of dawn to avoid the milk carts and the slow traffic of the tradesmen. That's what I thought. Now I had four hours in hand to think, sitting on the curb in front of a garage, before it opened. The bike was a sad sight.

Finally the garage opened, they helped me to drag in the bike, but that didn't minimize the damage. The garage master picked up a paper and, hanging on to a pencil as if hanging on for dear life dangling off a cliff, licked his lips as he started to write up what had to be done. Even before he finished I knew I had no other choice but to sell the bike. I was offered less than half of what I paid for the bike, plus a free trip to Vienna the following morning on one of their trucks delivering produce to Austria. I just had no choice. I didn't want anybody to know what happened, so I spent the longest day and night hanging around the garage, watching the mechanics cannibalize my ex-bike and other vehicles.

I had time on my hands to think and proposed to myself yet another commandment. Don't get anything second-hand. I married only two divorced ladies in a momentary lapsus memoriam of this commandment and the disasters that followed are best forgotten. For me there have never been second-hand bargains.

3 Mausoleum of Yesterday

That I survived at all in Vienna was sheer luck, but otherwise it was not a city of bargains for me. I always felt under the transparent 'Gemüt-lichkeit' was a cold, decaying, sad city.

It never bothered me that there was no blue or otherwise Danube actually in Vienna, like the dirty Seine of Paris, or the muddy Thames of London, or the grey-yellow Danube of Budapest. The people as a whole bothered me, desperately clinging to the scattered straw of memories floating in the sewers of history, to the forever vanished yesteryears' glory of which the only intact reminders were the Lipizzaner horses and the Spanish Riding School. The horses retained their class and pride. They were the least affected by the crumbling of the Austro-Hungarian Empire.

Bella gerent alia, felix Austria nubet/others wage war, lucky Austria weds, noted the contemporary historians. Unfortunately, when the divorce came, the judge turned out to be the bloodthirsty and revenge-hungry Clemenceau, and Austria had to give back not only the trous-seaux but part of her own flesh. This is a polite way of saying Austria was being raped, then left alone with toothpick legs, no backbone, muscle nor body to support the giant head: Vienna. More than three-quarters of Austria's population live in Vienna, in a self-pity-spiced dream world of a long past glory and splendor. It's a great place to live in if you enjoy phony laughs through genuine tears.

Their tears were well justified, mourning the decaying skeleton of the once fortress city founded by the Romans. During the Middle Ages, Vienna exerted increasing political, intellectual, artistic and economic influence in Europe and it became the capital of the Holy Roman Empire of German denomination until 1806, when Napoleon conquered the city. Ironically the Corsican's fate was decided in 1815 at the Congress of Vienna. And now I was on my way to conquer the city.

After repairing five flat tires, replacing a shredded fan-belt and driving twenty-eight hours in one stretch, finally we found the address in Vienna. The truck came to a painful stop. The driver and I sat in the cab for a little longer before kicking open the squeaking doors, then sat for a bit longer before getting out with cramp-bent legs. Neither of us spoke. We dumped my luggage, the driver climbed back into the cab and rattled down the cobblestone street in a self-created camouflage-cloud of dust. We said no goodbyes.

My teeth felt like each one was wearing its own fur jacket. I spat out some mud before yanking on a bronze ball attached to an iron rod, which in turn was connected to a thick wire, which in turn went through a hole rimmed with a bronze ring embedded in the wood of the ancient, large, one-time carriage gate. I waited. Nothing happened. Waited and tried again. After the fourth try I stepped back to size up the building. I was interrupted: a small door in the big gate was opened a crack by a rumpled, disheveled old man; he held it firm and was not about to let me in. I couldn't blame him, for I must have been a sight – covered with dust, unshaven, no bath, no sleep for forty-eight hours.

I faced an impasse. The man behind the gate refused not only to read but even to touch my ID papers, saying he had no glasses, and ignored my plea to show them to somebody else inside. He asked me if I knew what time it was, but before I could tell him, he assured me he knew it very well, he remembered what time I woke him up and, with finality, he shut the little door.

It was after six in the morning, not a soul in sight on the narrow street. Settling down on the pavement, next to the wheel-guard of the gate-jam, I suddenly realized I was starving. I did the only sensible thing I could, opened my 'goodie-bag' and had my breakfast alfresco. A very inauspicious beginning for my conquest of the international film world. I didn't doze off, I went to sleep, deeply. And it took some time to gather the senses God has sparingly given me to realize where I was. The big gate was already half open, a young man stood above me. My first sudden impression was, he must be a very good athlete.

'What the hell are you doing here?'

'I was having my . . .' I broke off, realizing he was speaking Hungarian to me. 'How did you know I was Hungarian?'

'Who else would be having breakfast with embroidered napkins laid out on the sidewalk?'

He reached down and matter-of-factly picked up a large stick of kol-bász (Hungarian sausage) and spoke with his mouth still full as I was putting away the remnants of my breakfast-snack. He approved it. 'Yeah. You better hide it, they'll lynch you for this kolbász.' He stepped back and assessed my luggage. 'Moving in?'

'I thought so but . . .' and I explained what happened.

'He is a shit. He is the janitor, gardner, handyman of the building, he has nothing to do with our set-up at all, only his wife has. Some of the fellows are banging her and he knows it. The only vengeance the slob has is to hate us collectively and singularly, instead of kicking her ass out. She is quite a dish, I am told . . . Let's go.' He picked up the two largest pieces of luggage, I took the small one and followed him.

The courtyard must have been impressive once. The fountains were still working, but sadists had let the plants kill each other throughout the years. We reached the 'lift', a glued-on-to-the-building affair, con-ceived in Brussels lace, executed in wrought iron. I thought its door would squeak as he opened it. It didn't. 'If you're not a suicidal maniac don't ride in it.' He deposited the two pieces he was carrying in the quaint little cage, took the small piece from me and carefully put it in the lift too, then slammed its door very hard. The little cage started to move immediately.

'Don't push the buttons, they seldom work. This way it goes auto-matically to the third floor,' and taking the wide stairs two and three at a time, off he went. So did I, lagging way behind.

On the third floor landing he was waiting for me. When I joined him, the elevator was not there yet. 'You're having one of the best rooms, only two in a four-bed room, it's Gróf (Count) Eszterházi's during terms.'

'Oh well,' that was about all I could say and he went on, 'you must have some pull to get in here, and in that room. My name is Erdös Pál – Pali – you were expected yesterday.'

I told him what had happened, the elevator arrived, he again picked up the two large pieces, I followed him with the small one. We passed an office, still closed; finally we came to a door. He unceremoniously kicked it open.

The room was in darkness, save the little light coming from the open door behind us. I had a short glimpse of a naked young man throwing himself on the top of one of the beds, stiffening up, trying to pretend he was asleep. Pali ignored him and led me to the fourth bed, quite separate from the other three. 'This is yours for the summer.' He didn't lower his voice, 'I'll show you where the showers are.'

On the way out he leaned to look under the occupied bed. 'Good morning,' he sing-songed in German. When he closed the door behind us he explained, 'He had a girl under the bed. Of course this place is strictly celibate,' he laughed. 'When you want a shower, have it very early or very late.'

'No hot water?'

'No water!'

Before I even realized it, two weeks slid by. I cannot say smoothly. I had a letter to a Herr Vidor, the factotum of Tobis Sascha Studios. Naturally, the day after my arrival, at eight a.m. I was at the gate on Siebenstern Gasse, 32 – I think. At eight p.m. I was still there, hoping to give Herr Vidor the letter of introduction personally, but neither of the two seedy men in their shabby uniforms at the gate were willing to take me in or take the letter to him.

This went on for the next two days. Of course it was an asinine effort on my part, since I had no idea whom I was looking for, what Herr Vidor looked like. On the chance I might be able to slip through the gate with the people going in and out I hung around, but the security was too tight. I couldn't get through to Herr Vidor even on the telephone.

Finally, Luck came to help me again. A motherly lady on a museum-piece bike rode through the gate every day, unmolested, in at nine, out at twelve, in at two, out at six. On the third day, on her two p.m. in-trip, she stopped in front of me. 'What on earth are you hanging around here for, can't you find something useful to do, young man?'

I pulled out of my pocket the by-now wrinkled envelope. The words caused a traffic jam in my throat because of my eager anxiety to explain the predicament I was in. Finally I could talk to somebody who at least seemed to listen. She took the envelope from me, got back on her bike and pedalled through the gate with it.

Waiting for the lady's six p.m. out-bound trip was the longest four hours I ever spent. Finally the lady came. She never stopped, but pedalling through the gate she turned back over her shoulder to say, 'Tomorrow morning at eleven.' And off she went.

At about ten-thirty the following morning I sauntered up to the studio gate. I felt legitimate now, and inquired if there was any word for me.

Their immediate 'Yes' surprised me, and the rest of the dialogue surprised me even more: 'If you don't stop loitering here we'll call the police.'

I defied their threat, hoping the police wouldn't be there before the lady's twelve o'clock out-bound trip. I stayed put, but further down the ugly street.

Twelve o'clock, on the nose, she was rolling through the gate again. I stepped in front of her. She let go of both ends of the handlebars, twisted her white-gloved hands palms skyward, shrugged, 'Patience,' swung around me without touching the handlebars and pedalled away merrily. I joined her, jogging next to the bike, explaining my problem with the two straw dummies at the gate. 'I'll handle them.' She speeded up, I stopped, out of breath and close to being out of patience.

On her in-trip at two, she completely ignored my presence. She didn't turn her head away – that would've been a negative acknowledgment – she just sailed by. But to my surprise and relief she stopped at the gate and talked to the two blockheads. That made my vigil easier.

Finally, at five o'clock, on the nose, here she came, riding her bike toward the gate. She stopped when she caught my attention. White gloves on her hands, still on, or on again, she waved to me to come. A millstone off my neck. She did not wait for me to reach her, made a U-turn and started off on her damned bike. The closer I got to her the faster she pedalled. The bitch. No! I should not think of her that way, after all she got me in.

What do I expect to get out of this place? The thought hit me. There was nothing around me but dilapidated crumbling old sets, the putrid smell of decay. What am I doing here in this dump? Suddenly I understood why the lady wore white gloves. No wonder. We had disorder in the studio in Budapest, but it was an artistic disorder, it had heart, it was mysterious, never seedy, it never smelled of decay.

The lady pulled up in front of a once-olive-green door, leaned her bike against the wall of the building, which was in urgent need of repair. She motioned me to follow her, I did, down a corridor dotted with gaping doors of empty offices and doom hanging in every nook. Maybe Herr Vidor did not want me to see this, hence the reluctance. I couldn't blame him. I almost bumped into her. She was waiting for me at a door around the corner. I couldn't tell if the glass in the wide door was frosted or just years and years of collected dirt and dust made it opaque.

The outer office of Herr Vidor was a perfect match to what I'd seen so far. Of the four tired desks one was obviously unoccupied. On the one closest to the door to Herr Vidor's inner sanctum towered a skyscraper-like, ancient Underwood typewriter. Behind the other two desks sat two ladies between the ages of long-ago retirement and mummification. One was busy knitting an indeterminable garment, the other, determinedly chewing a pencil, was studying a racing form. An indelible image of efficiency.

Herr Vidor's office was large. It was very large. Every inch of the walls were covered with faded or fading photographs. Every piece of the enormous furniture was heavily carved. Dominating it all was a city-block-long, gaudily ornate, messy desk. Behind it, from a distastefully upholstered heavy throne, Herr Vidor got up – wrong, not got up, got down from the throne. He almost hit his chin on the edge of the desk, he was so short. He came around the desk to greet me. How civilized, I thought.

I was wrong again, he went to a sideboard, picked up a box of cigars and retreated with it behind his bastions. Not a word, he did not even give me a grunt, a cursory glance. For him, I was not there. He was busy preparing his cigar, gingerly pulling off its ring, then carefully slipping it on his bird-claw-like little finger. He was a sparrow with an eagle beak, an ashen, pock-marked face, hard-lined, pink-purple, very thin lips and glued-on, no-color hair.

I kept on shifting my weight from one foot to the other, he was carefully preparing his cigar, cracking it, licking it with his grey tongue, warming it over a match, finally lighting it. I thought I was considerate enough not to break his ritual, but it was now time to break the silence. I thanked him, in Hungarian, for seeing me in spite of his busy schedule. No reaction, not a flicker in his bloodshot beady eyes. I kept on going, telling him about my plans, dreams. Finally I ran out of steam, and patience, and I was more than a bit confused. He was Hungarian, I told him I was told he spoke Hungarian, and asked him point blank what was wrong with him or with me. 'Speak, say something!'

Finally he spoke. He spoke German with a very heavy Hungarian accent, informing me, in case I didn't know, we were in Vienna, and people spoke German here.

From behind me the lady of the bike, now without her white gloves on, standing next to the open door, called Herr Vidor's attention to the possibility that I might not speak any German at all.

He ignored her interruption. More and more riled, he was not only telling me but the whole world how fed up he was with Hungarians who thought, because they were Hungarians, they had no taboos. Flailing his cigar like a rapier, he started to yell at me at the top of his voice, demanding who I thought I was.

To avoid any misunderstanding I answered him in German, that I didn't know who I was, but I knew he was a no-good shit-head-son-of-a-bitch, with that I swept everything off his desk, stomped on his cigar box, turned over, correction, tried to turn over every piece of furniture I could lift – some I couldn't, they were way too heavy. I still laugh about it, I must've looked absolutely ridiculous.

I did not want to overstay my welcome, I walked out of the office. For a moment I wanted to run, get out fast, but then I thought my father and General Szirmay would not have approved of my retreat, even if I had declined to be a Hungarian Huszár officer, so I forced myself to walk slowly down the long corridor, followed by Herr Vidor's hysterical screams repeating over and over 'You're fired! You're fired!' I presumed it was directed at the poor lady with the white gloves and bike as a reward for arranging my interview.

I was concerned when I reached the gate. Not only did nothing happen, the two straw dummies saluted me on my way out. I waved to them. I guessed Herr Vidor and Co. were still in too deep shock to do anything about my interior decorating talent – for the time being anyway.

I thought this was the end of the Herr Vidor affair and maybe my career in the film industry, in Vienna anyway. I was wrong again on both assumptions.

Three days later two uniformed policemen came to the student home, looking for me. They were very polite, and inquired if I knew a Herr Vidor, and if so, what did I know about him. Was there any altercation between us, ever. It wasn't done in private, and the audience in the community room grew, listening. I told the police exactly what had happened from the first minute of my initial arrival at the gate, to the minute of my departure. I held back nothing. I added for good measure, I thought the studio was a dump, a blemish on the Austrian film industry, it should be burned down. They said, 'Hm,' and immediately asked for my passport, took note of it, and requested me not to leave town without telling them first; then they handed back my papers, to my great relief, and left. I became an instant hero of the student home.

I didn't know that the night after my meeting with Herr Vidor there was a fire in the studio. My Lady Luck must have been asleep not to tell me that, or to remind me of one of my most important commandments: 'If you can say something with five words, say it with four, if you can say it with four, say it with three, if you can say it with three, say it with two, if you can say it with two, say it with one. And if you can say it with one it is not worthwhile opening your mouth. So keep it shut.'

A few days later in the papers it was briefly mentioned that no incendiary devices were the cause of the studio fire, but the police were looking for the arsonist. My aura wasn't tarnished, I remained on the hero's list. But the restriction that I couldn't leave town without police permission bothered me.

I was sure Herr Vidor directly or indirectly was responsible for the fire, then sic'ed the police on me as a repayment for moving his furniture around. And if he didn't light that fire, I was just as sure he thought it was my doing. Of course both conjectures turned out to be wrong. The police tracked down an arsonist who, thank God, confessed. I felt free, free again to leave this hell-hole of civilization without police sanction, if I wanted to.

I never wanted to be tied down and refused to sign 'long-term deals', years and years later in Hollywood, even when it was stupid not to. A special tribute to you, Bert Allenberg.[1] Probably very few people remember you, Bert, but I do remember.

I was never in love with this mausoleum of yesterday, Vienna, but loved and still love its music-makers' heritage. I always loved Viennese pastry, but not when it is made of white marble forming an arch over the head of Johann Strauss the Younger, who, frozen in bronze, can't run away from this monument of distaste decorated with reliefs of obese semi-naked bodies, crawling around on it. Were he alive, I am sure he would rather have the birds unload on his head, than have this thing stand around and above him, in the Stadtpark.

A covey of schoolgirls in their dark-blue, immaculately pressed,

---

1 Bert Allenberg (1899–1958) was a very prominent Hollywood agent, who entered show business in 1930, and in 1932 established the Berg-Allenberg Agency in partnership with Phil Berg. When the latter retired in 1949, Allenberg and the agency became part of the William Morris Agency, with which Allenberg remained associated until his death.

pleated skirts and swinging, blinding-white shirts circled the monument. They were having a great time, snickering as they surreptitiously imitated the poses of the women on the piece. Some of them were bold enough to touch them. The chaperoning, hawk-eyed nuns stopped the fun and herded them on the steps under the statue to line up for a group photograph. A lovely, young and smiling nun surfaced from nowhere carrying a shoe-box-size camera fixed to a tripod strong enough to support a railroad bridge. The girls came to life again, chattered, giggled, squirmed around. Two of the nuns, contradicting each other constantly, kept on asking them to change places, two other nuns tried to quiet them down. Pandemonium.

'I am ready,' yelled the nun with the camera. Everything stopped, somber faces turned toward the shoe-box on the tripod. New instructions filled the air, 'Smile,' 'Don't smile,' 'Look over here,' 'No, no, nooo, look over there.'

'I am readeeee,' announced the photographer again.

On an impulse I yelled out, 'Hold it, hold everything.' That froze them. I walked up to the nun at the camera and asked her if she too would like to be in the picture. She blushed, smiled, and shot a questioning glance behind me. I turned. A very stern-faced nun left the group, giving me the once-over as she walked up to the camera. 'Now, what gave you this idea, young man?'

'Well, I . . . I apologize, I just thought . . . maybe the sister would like it if . . . if she could be in the picture too. I am sorry, I didn't want to be presumptuous, or brash or something like that, please forgive me, I am sorry.'

She spoke in a very clipped manner, 'Don't be sorry, it was a very noble thought, young man. Now, Elizabeth, join the group.'

'Thank you, Mother Superior.'

And Mother Superior actually smiled at me when she spoke to Sister Elizabeth, 'Thank this nice young man.'

That she did, the students broke into an applause, which broke off as suddenly as it had started when Mother Superior stopped Elizabeth, 'Come back, please. Don't you think it would be a good idea if you showed this kind young man how to use this camera.'

Blushing again, Sister Elizabeth turned around. The students, being too far away to realize what was happening, started booing, as the flustered Sister was returning to the camera.

'Mother Superior,' I interjected, 'I know how to use this camera.'

Sister Elizabeth stopped and watched me fish the lightmeter out of her large camera bag. After I took several readings she nodded her approval to Mother Superior and even smiled at me when I finished loading the camera with the large glass negative. As both Sisters were returning to the group the applause started again. Mother Superior, satisfied, majestically seated herself in first row center, nodded to me and I took three very nice group shots of them.

I was helping Elizabeth to pack up the camera. In the distance the Kursalon's orchestra started to warm up and its various instruments' C-D-E-F-G-A-B's served as an undulating background music for the chattering, giggling girls milling around us and asking silly questions, funny only for themselves. I felt a tug on the back of my jacket, then again, and again. I reached back. A hand slipped in my palm a piece of paper, rolled up into a little ball. I turned around and faced a very pretty strawberry-blond standing as close to me as it was possible without touching. She spoke Hungarian, 'All the girls appreciated very much what you did. We like Sister Elizabeth very much.'

'How did you know I speak Hungarian?'

'Only a Hungarian would have the guts to do something like that and we – '

'Zsuzsi,' Mother Superior was standing beside us, 'please don't bother – '

'Oh I am not bothering anybody, Mother Superior, I was just saying – ' and she repeated verbatim in German what she had said in Hungarian to me.

'It was nice of you to say that, Zsuzsi, but please don't be chauvinistic, it is – '

'Oh I am not, Mother Superior, I was only saying what's true.'

'Now, Zsuzsi, say goodbye and join your group.'

'Yes-Mother-Superior-goodbye,' she said it all together, with one breath, turned and, swinging her pleated skirt, she was off to join her group. I put the little paper ball in my pocket.

I was sure it was two-twenty, I was certain I was in the Kunsthistorisches Museum (Museum of Art History). Where else would I be surrounded in Vienna by van der Weydens, van Cleeves, van Eycks. I was sure I was in the room of fifteenth- and sixteenth-century Dutch masters, and I had been there sitting on a hard settee since two o'clock, on the nose. I smoothed out the little paper ball and read the crumpled note for the umpteenth time. According to it, I was on time and this was the place. At three o'clock I got up ready to leave. Behind me, on a more comfortable looking settee, was Zsuzsi, sitting smug and smiling. When I reached her she pulled me down next to her.

'Good, I was testing you. You're patient, it's very good. It's important. A friend of mine wants to meet you, my very, very best friend. She is shy, but she is wonderful. Imagine,' she slapped my knee, with a hard, resounding slap.

Some of the disturbed art connoisseurs turned around with dagger glances, she faced them with a smile and shrugged, then pulled my ear very close to her mouth and whispered, it tickled. 'She is a . . . a . . . a-virgin-imagine, a-virgin. Here they come.' She jumped up and dragged me through a side door I didn't even notice existed. Her schoolmates were herded into the adjoining room.

She blithely ignored an 'Employees only' sign on a small door, led me through a not-too-well-kept narrow corridor, a short cut to a shiny, main, wide corridor.

'You certainly know this place.'

'Oh yes. I love art . . . it's so easy to get lost in here, and they believe you really got lost, so no problems. I always meet my boyfriends here.' She stopped. 'So I thought it's a good place for you to meet Lillian –'

'Lillian?'

'Lillian, my very-very best friend, I just told you about her, who thought you were wonderful, and she never said that about any boy, ever, but still, she didn't know if she wanted to meet you or not, well, so I thought you two should meet, so we are here.'

'You said, with the same breath, not even a second ago, she didn't want to meet me.'

'Now she does. She wasn't sure, I said, I have a very good memory. She is just very timid, that's all I said. Finally she agreed. But remember, you're my responsibility, be very nice to her, please.'

Her brashness evaporated, I was facing a new girl, she spoke quietly. 'She is very lonely, so are we all. We call ourselves the parked generation. Our parents can't face us, because they can't face themselves. So they park us for the vacations here, for the school year somewhere else. If you're sick, which is very inconsiderate of you, they pack you into a sanitarium. Oh, it'll be a good one. I haven't been – it would be ridiculous for me to say home – I haven't been where they live now for four years. I am from Budapest. Some of us here are from Germany, some from Italy. Italy for us means Milano, Genoa. None I know of came from Rome, Florence, Naples. None from the South. The same applies to Spain. It's strange. Now, Lillian is one of the few who is actually from Vienna, but she stays with us only for the vacations, to learn French and English. And it is much more difficult for her. We don't know each others' parents. A visit to a "parked-one" means a maximum of an hour, an hour and a half lunch in a hotel or in an expensive restaurant, one or two useless, but very expensive presents. Presents they think are enough payment for the non-existent love, sufficient penance for their negligence.'

She turned abruptly, moved away. I discovered we were standing in front of a 'Ladies Room'. The 'other side' of Zsuzsi surfaced again. 'Shit. What the hell am I jabbering for? What's the matter with you? I have never done that.'

'I am glad you've spat it out. You'll feel better, if not now, tomorrow for sure.'

'She is waiting for me in there, so let's get to the point, she is a beautiful human being, I warn you, be nice to her. Better, be very nice to her or I'll cut your balls off. Get it? I promise, and I always keep my promise. Now wait here.'

She had barely closed the door behind her when two uniformed museum guards came by, inquiring if I had seen three young ladies in a school uniform, and they described the uniform. Three? Three was a puzzle for me, my 'no' answer was honest, but I kept my fingers crossed they should not come out before the guards were out of sight. Keeping my fingers crossed was absolutely unnecessary. It took quite a while before the 'Ladies Room' door opened.

At first I did not recognize Zsuzsi. She had shed her school uniform. She was holding the door open, nodding encouragement to someone to come on out. Finally, in similarly elegant street clothes, Lillian (I presumed) appeared, carrying a very large, identical handbag to Zsuzsi's. She hesitated on the threshold. Zsuzsi put an arm around her waist, 'They may want privacy in there,' and gently closed the door behind her.

'This is Lillian, and . . .' Her laughter bubbled, 'What's your name?'

I don't know, but I would not put it beyond her that she planned it this way. Planned it this way or not, it certainly broke the tension all around. I wanted to live up to the froth of the moment, wanted to be glib and nonchalant: 'I have been called so many names before, just call me Bandi. As long as you call me.' I shiver to think now how it must have sounded.

Zsuzsi turned out to be the self-appointed tour guide. I still believe even Lillian knew nothing about what she was planning. When I wanted to pay for the streetcar fares for all of us, she blasted me, 'None of that Hungarian Huszár bullshit, we all pay our own.' She turned to Lillian, as the streetcar rattled on, shaking like a sieve at the crossroads. 'I told you, you have to watch those Hungarians.' Speaking as if she was not Hungarian herself. 'This young Huszár officer –' she slapped my knee again, turned away from Lillian, who had not said a word yet. 'Did you ever think of being a Huszár? It would suit you.'

Without waiting for a possible answer she turned back to Lillian. 'Now, this Huszár officer met this lovely, young, as the French say, "fille de joie". They spend a hell of a night together, I mean,' she turned, back to me, 'you know.' Lillian squirmed. Zsuzsi didn't slap, only touched her knee. 'It's all right, honey,' then she patted her knee reassuringly. 'It's a true story. So, morning came, as it comes sometimes too soon, but being a Huszár officer, and a gentleman of course, he got dressed very quietly, not wanting to disturb the lady and tiptoed to the door. As he reached it the lady called out, softly, inviting, "Darling, didn't you forget something?"

'The Huszár officer looked at his watch, sadly shook his head. "No, oh no I didn't, but you slept so sweetly, I didn't want to disturb you," he indicated his watch. "It's late, too bad I have to be back in the barracks in an hour."

'The lady stopped him again from opening the door. "Darling, daaarliiing, come here." She reached under the bed, came up with an elaborately carved box and pulled out of it a fistful of money and waved it toward the Huszár, "Didn't you forget this?"

'The young Huszár officer clicked his heels, saluted smartly, "Thank you, madam, but a Hungarian Huszár officer never takes money from ladies," and left.'

I caught Lillian's glance toward me, I shrugged, she didn't try to hide a whiff of a smile.

This was our first contact.

Zsuzsi clearly enjoyed her own story, smugly watched her own image and the reflection of us in the streetcar window. Abruptly she jumped up. 'Jesus, I almost screwed it up,' and started to burrow her way through the crowded aisles of the streetcar to get off. We followed her as close as we could. The streetcar was beginning to move. She reached up and yanked a couple of times on a rope running through loops along the ceiling.

With intermittent screeches the streetcar was coming to a jerking halt. The standing passengers were hanging on for dear life to anything within reach, to each other. That included us. I was steadying Lillian, holding her by her shoulders.

This was our second contact.

We scrambled off the still-moving streetcar, not with the best wishes of the fellow passengers or the streetcar personnel.

'What's your hurry . . . You want to kill us?' Zsuzsi yelled at them, before they had a chance to express their own sentiment about us. She grabbed one of Lillian's hands. 'Help her,' she commanded me. I held on to Lillian's other hand.

This was our third contact.

'We have to change here for Grinzing.'

With absolutely no consideration for anybody, herself included, she jumped off the platform, dragging us with her, scrambling over several naked tram lines and some more platforms. Self-satisfied, she let Lillian's hand go and plopped down on a wooden bench under a sign – 'Line 38' or something like that. Zsuzsi tapped the bench, indicating to me to sit there, next to her.

Simultaneously Lillian and I realized we were still holding hands, we let go. With a sweeping, grand gesture Zsuzsi indicated again where we should sit but Lillian sat next to Zsuzsi not next to me. Zsuzsi got up and sat on my other side, as if it was the most natural thing to do, leaving Lillian on the very edge of the bench alone. And from there on, she ignored her as if she were an unwanted stranger. 'Do you know what a Heurige[2] is?'

'Sure, it's a restaurant where –'

'Tourist,' she cut me off, disgusted. 'The word has two meanings –'

---

2 'Heurige' has two meanings: the new wine grown and made in Grinzing, and/or the place where the wine is drunk. A genuine Heurige serves only their own wine, and they are open only from three weeks to a maximum of six months a year, depending on the crop and the thirst of the patronage. The 'Nobel Heurige' are pseudo Heurige, defiling the tradition on record since the year 1114. Grinzing, a proud community, survived the 1529 Turkish destruction, the Great Fires of 1604 and 1638, the French occupation in 1809 and is now capitulating to the onslaught of tourists and money-grabbing developers.

I tried to get an eye contact with Lillian, Zsuzsi slapped my knee, 'Now listen, I am talking.'

It bothered me Lillian being excommunicated, and I paid little attention to Zsuzsi, but before I could say anything she whacked me again, and if any time thereafter I only glanced toward Lillian, Zsuzsi whacked me. Harder and harder. I learned the history of Grinzing the hard way.

We were being watched; embarrassed, Lillian scooted over, 'I don't want your knee-cap shattered,' and put her hand on it.

Zsuzsi mumbled her approval, 'That's more like it, isn't it,' and rattled on with the history of Grinzing, but no more slaps. 'And now, we're going to one of those real places. It is closed. They had a good year, Hans's father owns it.'

I could finally put a word in edgeways, 'Hans, who is Hans?'

Zsuzsi answered promptly and was very annoyed, 'Who else do you think he is? My boyfriend!' She checked her wrist watch, 'Where the hell is he?' She waited for no answer, unexpectedly she served Lillian a question on a silver platter: 'Does it hurt?'

Lillian smiled, shook her head slightly, a silent 'No.' Zsuzsi acknowledged with a laugh drowned in an 'I told you, dummy.' Lillian's smile broke up as abruptly as it started.

'Where the hell have you been? You're late!'

'I know,' yelled back the approaching figure, following the same illegal path, crossing the tracks and platforms as we had done about half an hour before. Hans arrived, dropped the bulging rucksack he was carrying, threw himself on the bench next to Zsuzsi, kissed her twice. First lightly, then deep. He was tall with extremely wide shoulders and wavy blond hair. He could have done more than justice to any ski resort poster.

I watched Lillian. She had glued her eyes to the floor to let the lovers have their privacy. She was not with us until Hans spoke to me, 'Hi hot-shot-hunky, I heard about you,' and pushed forward a shovel-size hand. It turned out to be a hard handshake. One of those silly whose-grip-is-stronger, jungle grips.

Lillian got to her feet, she and Hans greeted each other – evidently it was a ritual, left cheek against left cheek, right cheek against right cheek, loud kissing noises in the air. They created the silhouette of an inverted 'V' like a steep-roofed Swiss chalet in the high Alps. Cheeks together, feet miles apart.

A streetcar arrived, filled to bursting point. Using the rucksack as a battering-ram, Hans forced his way through the non-yielding crowd, with added help from Zsuzsi, who was pushing him from the rear; they represented a formidable force. The warning whistles and yells of the conductors did not stop the doors from closing and they almost guillotined Lillian and me apart. Once inside the car with luck, and engulfed by discourteous strangers, Lillian was hanging on to me with snow-white knuckles.

Vineyards behind the houses on both sides of the narrow, cobble-stoned streets. Red-white-red Austrian flags in the late afternoon breeze. Fir branches above some entrances. Shredded chords of accordion from 'tourist-infested Nobel Heurige' as Zsuzsi – not Hans – called them. Grinzing.

His large load didn't hinder Hans, with a hand around Zsuzsi's wasp-waist they were leading the way up and down the murder-on-the-feet cobblestone street. Lillian was holding on to my elbow from a foot away, as we walked in silence stealing what we thought were sub rosa glances at each other. Zsuzsi and Hans were prattling merrily, oblivious of the occasional strangled chords of music.

To our great surprise the 'closed' Heurige of Hans's family was packed full with a merry crowd of our age group. Hans appeared to be one of the leaders of this exuberant congregation. He received thunderous applause when he held up his rucksack, other rucksacks surfaced from under the tables, the jubilation grew loud enough to rustle the leaves on the trees overhead. After shouted greetings, frantic waving to a multitude of friends, spotted all over the place, Zsuzsi remembered we existed, 'Oh, I forgot to tell you, we're going to demonstrate today.' As she melted in the potpourri of youth, she yelled back glibly, 'Just stick with the group.'

'Stick with the group? We are swallowed by it,' Lillian smiled. 'It is so ridiculous, it's funny.'

The charged atmosphere was contagious. It swept us with it, we didn't know what we were celebrating but we joined the celebration. Zsuzsi whirled by, 'I told you it was going to be fun,' and she was swallowed in the crowd again.

The singing died away, small groups were forming around what seemed to be their leaders. Tension nibbled at the ebullience. Most of the boys were saddling themselves with rucksacks, the girls were sorting handbills. We paid little attention to the transformation. Lillian and I were getting acquainted. Hans popped up, 'Whatever happens, you two stay with us,' and darted away.

Zsuzsi flew in from another direction, 'Did Hans tell you, you just stay with us whatever happens.'

'What do you mean whatever happens?'

'Never mind. Nothing happens. Come on.'

Befuddled, we followed her to a group of about ten, 'That's our group.' She turned to them, 'This is their first time out, take care of them.' And she was off again. We shook hands all around, wishing each other luck.

'Luck for what?' I asked Lillian, 'do you know what this is all about?'

'No. I trust Zsuzsi. It's going to be fun, that's all she told me.'

Hans joined us and, addressing the gathering, warned them not to call attention to themselves until they all were at the target.

'Target?' I asked Zsuzsi. 'What the hell did he mean?' Zsuzsi shushed me, putting a finger on my lips.

The assemblage broke up into small groups, using various ways of transport so they could unobtrusively reach their 'target'. Hans gave everybody their tickets, but he did not let the group walk out together. Lillian studied the ticket after I asked her if she knew what our destination was. She had no idea and she did not care. She was all thrilled with this excursion. She gave the impression she had been hermetically locked up all her life before today and she was having a great time. I did not want to spoil her fun and talk about my qualms.

She was extremely interested in my home life, what I thought of my parents. I asked her how long they were allowed to stay out tonight. She clouded up. She didn't answer for a long time, staring ahead at the back of Zsuzsi and Hans, way up in front. I felt bad about inadvertently spoiling what had seemed to be a great beginning. I was perplexed. I did not have an inkling about what I had said or done that brought down the curtain so abruptly. I could tell, I felt the wheels were going around her head. It was a hard decision for her. Finally she spoke.

'We don't have to be back in the convent till eight-thirty tomorrow morning.'

'How come?' I was so surprised it slipped out. It was too late to swallow my tongue. I felt I was losing down the line. 'Forgive me, I didn't mean to pry, it is rather unusual that in a convent –'

'I understand, yes, it is very unusual.' Her laughter burst out, it startled me. As she went on I became more than startled. 'You see Zsuzsi and I are having private piano lessons tonight.'

I was baffled, she stopped speaking, then another wave of laughter erupted. It must have cut through the din in the streetcar, Zsuzsi turned around, clasped her two hands above her head, blew a kiss for us. Lillian waved back, lowered her hand on to my knee.

'I didn't slap it.' She kept her hand on my knee, impassive. 'You see, Zsuzsi already called Madame Baklanova, she is her favorite pupil. Madame Baklanova is a music teacher who plays the organ free of charge in the chapel at school. She is very strict, but very considerate of the children's welfare and academic progress. She does not want them to take time off from their studies. So, she arranged for a few, only very few, the most musically inclined students to come to her studio, after they have finished their homework and all that. She was just as concerned about the children's safety as the Sisters were, you know, sometimes going back to the convent late and all that. So, you see, Madame Baklanova made arrangements for the children to have their dinner and stay in her studio overnight. And it was her responsibility that the children were delivered washed and clean, having had their breakfast, to school on time in the morning. Madame Baklanova was very, very proud of the fact that never, ever once were any of her star music pupils late getting back to class. You see, Zsuzsi thinks of everything.'

It all sounded 'Zingo' to me, but all I said was 'Hm.' Then, as an afterthought, I asked Lillian what kind of instrument she was playing.

'Oh I don't play anything at all, so to speak. I fool around with the piano, sometimes. This is my first time with Madame Baklanova. Oh, I know her from choir practice but . . . what I meant this is the first time I'll be staying with Madame Baklanova overnight.'

My 'Oh, I see,' was absolutely superfluous.

'No, you don't.' She laughed, it was a dry nervous laughter. 'Zsuzsi is good in everything she does, but not because of her musical talent, but because she is Madame Baklanova's best customer she has a pull with her and arranged this special lesson for me tonight. You see, Madame Baklanova is very careful, she doesn't take more than four, five at the most, "star potential" music pupils. She doesn't want to lose her extra –' She giggled, it was not like her at all. Her nerves got tighter and tighter as she continued. I felt she wanted to unload. '– her extra large added income. She charges a small fortune to the gullible parents for the special music lessons, the dinners, the breakfasts, none of which of course is taken advantage of by her customers. She will be grossly surprised when I show up tonight and I . . .'

She stopped and looked down, astounded to find her hand was still on my knee. She pulled it away, rubbed her hands for a moment as if they were freezing, then I believe she even stopped breathing. She turned to me. She turned away to stare at her lap. She was working up to a big decision. She faced me. Started to speak. Stopped. Finally she made up her mind, spoke almost inaudibly, 'I . . . I am . . . I . . . I-am-a-virgin.' She dropped her head, neither of us spoke. I could not say I knew it. After a while completely composed she turned back to me, 'I don't want to waste your time.'

'I understand.'

'Now, do you?'

I made up my mind quickly. 'I knew it. And I respect you.'

'Zsuzsi?'

'Yes, and I am here.'

I felt she had dropped a millstone off her neck. The screeching brakes of the streetcar coming to a stop could not drown her laughter. 'Thanks. Leave it to Zsuzsi, she is wonderful.'

On the way to getting off the streetcar she hugged Zsuzsi. Freely, she hooked an arm around my elbow, and we followed Zsuzsi and Hans, not knowing where. After a very short walk we began to meet up with some members of the group from the Heurige. I thought it was strange, so did Lillian, that there were no greetings exchanged in the descending night. I asked Lillian if she knew where we were. She did not, nor did she care, it was all so exciting and she was having a wonderful time . . . she said. Other groups were joining us, emerging from the side streets. Torches and gasoline cans appeared from the rucksacks. The girls unfurled their slogan-ridden placards. In the distance angers swelled. The torches were lit and their smoke and angry shouts were beginning to fill the cooling air.

'It's a pity the torchlight is wasted. I wish they were singing the songs from the Heurige, it would be such a nice picture.'

'I think so too.' Lillian slowed down, 'We've lost Zsuzsi and Hans.' Then she pulled me toward a large doorway. 'Let's watch from there . . . I hope . . . well, I will feel better.' We stopped in the cover of the large doorway.

We stood there, close together. 'I understand you . . . But . . . you think in this mêlée we'll have a chance to meet up with them? . . . They'll be all right.'

We watched the surging crowd. We felt the swells of hatred and anger sweeping the street. She held on to my arm without moving closer. 'Shall we go?'

'Do you know where we are?'

'No, but we'll find a way . . . Firecrackers?'

I knew better. 'Let's get out of here!'

She hung on to me and we ran as one, away from the sounds of the 'firecrackers'.

Torches, placards, rucksacks were flying through the smoke-filled air. Fleeing feet trampled on the dying torches and the street got darker and darker. Lillian slowed down, then halted, 'We should wait for them.'

'No way!' and I dragged her along.

A stampeding crowd was beginning to overtake us. No more protests left, fear was the new king on the street. Suddenly bursts of gunfire came from straight ahead of us. We stopped. Like ocean waves hitting a beached boat, the crowd hit us from behind. Lillian faltered on the pockmarked pavement.

Luck was with me again. There was a side street within the realm of reaching its safety. We forced our way across the torrent of human bodies. The echoes in the narrow street made it impossible to judge from which direction the shots were coming, except they were getting closer. Lillian stumbled, held onto me, got up, and slipped off her shoes. The side street was short, it led to a main artery, well lit, tranquil from the distance. The frenzy of the crowd somewhat subsided. Lillian put her shoes back on, shook her head, 'I only wish I knew what we were demonstrating for or against.'

'So do I.'

The 'firecrackers' sounded very, very close. We started to run again . . . Empty silence . . . Nothing.

4 A Ball 'This Big'

The 'empty silence' now filled my head with the buzz of a swarming beehive. The 'nothing' turned into dark. No. Not dark, it turned into lifeless black. It was cold. Bone-freezing cold.

Pain, deep, dull, heavy pain . . . I was on my back . . . Fear of the unknown drove me to get up . . . I hit my head on the ceiling . . . I fell back . . . The back of my head hit the heartless stone floor . . . Void.

Noises, the opening of a creaking door. Voices in the distance. Every part of me hurt. I had to get up, only to hit my head on the ceiling again. As I was falling back from the sky I thought of Lillian, yelled out for her.

'Lillian . . . Lilliaaaan.'

Voices now filtered through dim yellow light.

'I heard it too.'

'Yeah, but where in the hell did it come from?'

'From there!'

'No! Not from there – from that corner.'

I did not try to get up any more, in the feeble light I saw the ceiling. It was not two feet above me. I was desperate, 'I am here.'

Hard hands grabbed my ankles, they pulled me toward the light; it blurred my vision. Two washed-out phantoms pulled me further out from wherever I was.

'I can see it now.'

'Can you read the tab?'

'Yeah . . . let's get rid o' him.'

They dropped me on the floor. Tore the corpse's ID tab off one of my toes. I cannot recall if it was the left or the right.

They grabbed me under my armpits and dragged me through miles and miles of damp cement corridors, panting, cursing under their foul-smelling breaths. 'We got to get rid o' him.'

'Yeah, he is only half dead.'

'We're lucky. A dead foreigner can cause lots of trouble.' They dragged me on.

One held me against a wall, the other fought a stubborn lock on a rusty iron door. When it opened I was shoved through it into another room.

The peeling walls must have been pukey green once. The cement floor was covered with clothing and shoes. No furniture. One held me upright. The other threw pieces of clothing at me, helter-skelter, picked from the large dirty pile – trousers, a jacket, a pair of shoes – and called to me, 'Hey, put 'm on.'

I tried to pick up the trousers, I stumbled, they cursed me and straightened me up against a corner.

I was naked. My left side was covered with caked blood. I could not move my left arm, when they shoved it through the sleeve of the jacket a searing pain drilled through my body. They had difficulty putting on the shoes. Curses did not prove to be effective shoehorns.

'Leave 'em off, he ain' gonna catch cold.' They laughed and laughed. For them it was a hilarious joke. I could not laugh, I must have lost my sense of humor somewhere. 'Tempora mutantur et nos mutamur in illis.'

I could not walk. They dragged me through endless corridors again, up and down stairs. Both of my feet were trailing behind us like the train of a bride's wedding gown. They stood me up in front of a door, opened it and kicked me down three . . . four steep stairs.

On the street again; 'I am the best', went through my mind as I passed out.

The shower felt wonderful, warm, soothing. I lifted my head, it was raining. Little rivulets crossed the street between the cobble stones. I had no idea of time, where I was, or how long I had been there.

I kept on repeating, 'Get up, get up.' 'I am the best!' Am I? . . . Move. 'I am the best.' Get up then. Finally, finally I did.

The rain washed off some of the blood. My blood I shed for whom, for what?

The rain had added some gloss to the wretched, narrow, back street, but it still looked miserable, like an outdoor jail corridor. Jail? Hell, the morgue.

The realization, belated as it came, hit me that much harder. Get out of here. To the left or to the right. It doesn't matter, move. Fast. Get out of here before they call you back. I moved.

I was staggering from alleys to streets, from streets to alleys. I did not have the faintest idea where I was or, for that matter, what day it was. All I knew I was aching all over, and it was night, and judging by the empty, lonely streets it was late.

When I stumbled onto a main thoroughfare, I got concerned. I did not want the police to pick me up, specially in this less than presentable attire, sporting a threadbare, three- to four-sizes-too-small jacket, its sleeves barely covering my elbows, a torn, full-of-ventilation-holes, baggy pair of pants on a blood-stained, bruised, naked body, bare feet, taking a leisurely stroll at night in the rain. No papers. I would have to do an awful lot of explaining, which I was not well equipped to do.

Suddenly I did not care, I did not look for shelter from the drizzle, I just laid down where I happened to be standing. I did not care.

Instinct, or luck again, one or the other woke me. A fiacre was wobbling down the street. Both the horse and the coachman were sound asleep. Mustering all that was left in me I managed to topple in front of them.

Awakened with a start, the coachman first pulled up, then thought the better of it, started to go around me. With despair-given force, I got to my feet but all I could blurt out was a feeble 'Please . . .' The word 'help' got stuck. All spent, I folded up. The coach halted, then backed up.

'You're in a hell of a mess.'

My chin dropped to my chest, not to indicate my acquiescence, but because I could not hold my head up any longer.

'Please, take me home, but I have no money.'

'No kidding, what happened to you?' I had no strength to answer. 'Were you demonstrating?' I joined the wet pavement. He stood over me. 'You were, weren't you . . . Those bastards, the dirty bastards. I hate 'm too. Where do you live? Get in . . . Get in!'

I could not move. The horse, impatient, started to paw the ground, splashed water on me from the puddles. That helped. 'They jus' let you out-a jail, huh?'

'No, the morgue.'

'The morgue, no shit, the morgue, huh.' And he picked me up like I was a feather and gently laid me down on the back seat of the fiacre.

'Hey, hey, hey!' Somebody was calling from miles. I opened my eyes, their lids were made of lead. 'That's where you live?'

We were in front of the still locked big gate.

'Yes, thanks,' and I fell off the fiacre as I was trying to get out. The coachman caught me.

'What's your hurry, don't ya break your neck now.' He nodded toward the gate, 'It's locked, can't get in.'

I showed him where to ring the bell. He pulled the bell-rod. He yanked it, he jerked it. He kicked the gate and cursed. Finally his curses were answered, muffled, but they were answered from inside the gate. I told him about the caretaker, and he was ready for him, shoved the little door with great force when it was barely cracked open and barked at the startled caretaker before he could have said more than' What the . . .'

'Out-a-the-way,' and we were inside.

At the little elevator the coachman asked me, 'Can you make it from here?' When I asked him to wait till I could get some money to pay him, he was curt, 'No way. I was glad to . . . I mean I was not glad for what happened to you, but I hate them bastards too.' And slamming the elevator door as I asked him to do, the little cage moved immediately. In the courtyard below me the caretaker and the coachman exchanged some compliments.

There was still light in the community room. Under the light in a corner sat Erdös Pali, in front of two pushed-together tables, covered with charts and heavy books. When I stumbled in he looked up. I was hanging on to the door-knob. He stared at me then burst out laughing. 'Where have you been – at a costume ball?'

Through the steam the faces were blurred. Faces of a crowd of hundreds. They were holding me up, they washed and scrubbed me. The water must have been scalding hot. I was numb with pain. I did not feel it.

I was poured into a cement slab, I could not move. The morgue. I screamed, 'I am here, get-me-out . . . get-meeee-ooouuuut.'

'Give him some more.' Hands pried my mouth open and poured fire in it. I wanted to spit it out. Hands clamped my mouth shut, pinched my nose tight. I had to swallow the fire.

I opened my eyes. Light above me, a white ceiling. A circle of faces stared down at me. I was in a pit, not the morgue.

'Give him some more.' Whatever it was, I drank it, eagerly. It was good to feel the warmth sliding down, filling my toes.

'What happened to Lillian . . . What happened?'

'Give him some more. We're about finished. You were very lucky. Two more inches to the right and you would not have given me this head-ache. I took a big chance here with you . . . Give him some more.'

I drank again. It did not taste any more as if I were drinking red-hot nail files. 'Some more, please.'

'No. Not a drop more. I don't want you to throw up.'

'It's dark in here, turn back on the lights.'

'Open your eyes, open them.'

I did, and I could see, not too clearly, but I could distinguish Erdös Pali among the faces above me, he was the one who spoke. We were in the community room. I was tied to two table tops. 'If you promise you're not going to jump around we'll untie you. I've had enough trouble with you already, don't give me any more. Now, give me your word.'

Before the two last letters of 'word' left his lips, I gave him my 'word'. I would have given my word to anything. They untied me and I fell into a bottomless whirlpool.

The three gentle taps did not hurt my cheek, they hurt my throbbing left shoulder. It was not a sharp pain, it was a throbbing, deep pain.

'Wake up, you have to eat something.'

Erdös Pali, Baron Kurt von Walberg, my room-mate, and Otto Schönberg from the next room were standing around my bed. Like a minor catering outfit, they were holding steaming cups, a loaf of bread, some cold cuts. 'Open,' ordered Erdös, touching my lips with a small white piece of paper in the shape of a 'V'. 'Aspirin, stick your tongue out.' I did and he sprinkled the awful-tasting powder on my tongue.

'Swallow!' Kurt touched the steaming cup to my mouth. 'Drink, chicken broth.'

I did, it washed down the taste of the aspirin. I wanted to change position, but a ton of pain in my left shoulder flattened me.

They sat around and helped me with my meal. 'Now, let's hear what really happened. You were pretty delirious, we couldn't get it quite clear. But based on what we got out of you we had decided not to take you to a hospital with a bullet in your armpit. When bullets are involved the police are usually curious, and they would have asked you a couple of questions you maybe did not want to answer.'

My mind moved slow. Bullet. 'Bullet?'

Erdös reached in his pocket, he came up with a bullet. He gently pried my right palm open and dropped the bullet in it. 'Here, have it as a good luck charm. If something goes wrong with you, I may need it more than you do.'

I was looking at the bullet, dazed.

'It came from a Manlicher, I know, because I have taken out a few of those from cadavers in classes.'

'I didn't know you were a doctor.'

'I am not. Not yet . . . practice will make you perfect, didn't you know that.' The room started to spin.

For the next week the three friends watched me like hawks. The days went by. Not knowing what had happened to Lillian bothered me more than the rapidly healing bullet wound. There was nothing in the papers about the incident.

'It happens all the time,' grumbled Otto. 'They run the free press.'

Erdös was annoyed, 'They, they, who are they?'

'They are the ones who run the show. Your life, my life. Our lives. They always were and they always will be "They", the bastards. "They" are all alike, once they grab power. They are all alike. It's the same all over the world, all through history. No matter what their slogan is, or what color their flag is. If you look at –'

'Fuck history, double-fuck politics, and you two.' Erdös cut Otto off. 'Burn your pulpit. It's people like you, the sheep, who follow each other's wet ass. You don't care whom you follow, just follow. You're not even cowards, just duds. That's why governments get away with shitting in your morning coffee.

'Talking of meals, I think our friend here has had enough cold cuts for a lifetime, which will be short if he keeps on demonstrating. Before it gets too late let's take him out to an early dinner. He is fit enough.'

Since my continuous presence zilched Kurt's love life, he was delighted with our plan to go out for dinner. He put down the book he was reading, wished us bon appétit and waltzed through the door into the light of the setting sun seeping through it, advising us to 'have fun'.

My investigative reporter's training with the *Nogrády Hirlap* was not needed to find out the address of Immaculate Heart in the telephone book, but Erdös and Otto dissuaded me from going in and inquiring about Lillian or Zsuzsi, when I did not even know their family names. But it became an obsession with me and the next three days I spent watching the entrance of the convent. Nothing. I did not even spot Sister Elizabeth, whom I would have somehow trusted to ask.

On the fourth day Lady Luck found me again. A fiacre pulled up and waited in front of the convent. After a while Zsuzsi pranced out of the building, crisp and bright as ever. I ran across the street, she saw me and promptly fainted. I dissuaded the panicky coachman from running for help. We revived Zsuzsi and the fiacre took us to Madame Baklanova's address.

Leave it to Zsuzsi, she arranged 'special lessons' for herself and Lillian for the next few weeks. And without consulting Lillian set up a rendez-vous right then.

I was waiting for them at the statue of Strauss, in the Stadtpark. Zsuzsi thought it would be very romantic because that is where we had met. Schmaltzy waltzes floated through the nice evening air, courtesy of the Kursalon's orchestra. Bird-lovers arrived, ignoring the outstretched, pleading hands of the few hungry beggars; they were shaking brown paper bags skywards, offerings to their gods or to the pigeons overhead?

All three of them, Lillian, Zsuzsi and Hans were approaching. Lillian broke away from the two and ran, ran to me and embraced me tight, then tighter. Her cheek was hot against mine. In a tear-strangled whisper she kept on repeating, 'I am sorry, I am sorry.'

'What for?' She pressed her cheek still harder against mine. I kissed her earlobe, gently. She kissed my neck behind my ear, once, twice, three times, 'I thought I'd die when I saw you were hit.'

'Welcome back, Lazarus.' A heavy hand grabbed my shoulder, the left of course, and Hans swung me around. 'How was your trip on the meat wagon? There aren't too many who have a return ticket on those babies.' He smiled, so wide I was concerned his ears would be falling into his mouth. He slapped my shoulders simultaneously. 'Good to have you back. You've got to tell us how it was.' He pointed, 'Up there' pointed again, 'or down there?' It was a great joke, he laughed.

He laughed alone. Zsuzsi embraced me tenderly, kissed me on both cheeks, then gave me a peck on my mouth. 'We are going to celebrate, we're going to have dinner in the Kursalon, then we are going to have a nice long walk in the park.' No questions, Zsuzsi set it.

It was the most miserable, full-of-good-intentions dinner. Hans ordered a typical, expensive tourist slop-deluxe. He was totally out of his sphere. But wines he knew. He ordered two bottles of Badacsonyi Kéknyelüt, not one bottle to begin with, but two. Obviously to please me. Their 'mea culpas' were drowning out the otherwise pleasant orchestra. I had the feeling they wanted to pay me for 'what I went through' as they referred to that memorable evening, over and over again.

Hans asked questions and questions and immediately answered them. That most of the time Lillian's hand was resting on my hand did not ease my revulsion. I wanted to bolt; she felt it, I was sure, so I stayed. But without the British upper lip. I asked our host to order another bottle of wine. 'I knew you would like it, did you ever have it before?' I couldn't answer him fast enough. He informed us around the table, 'It's Hungarian you know.' I had to stop him from ordering two more bottles.

Zsuzsi ended the ordeal. 'Let's go for a nice walk.' Hans paid and left the bill on the table for a long time, so everybody could see it. It was an expensive meal. Irrepressible as ever, Zsuzsi bubbled, 'I want to show you our private bench.'

I told my wife, Ann, about that bench, and some fifty years later, on our first trip to Vienna, we went to look, not for the bench of course, but where it used to be, between the Kursalon and the canal they misleadingly called the Wien Fluss – river Wien.

The river was still there, except more sewage was floating on it. The trees had become more majestic, the bushes around them had grown more impenetrable than I remembered. I tried to wiggle my way through their branches, asked Ann to follow. 'Why, I can see it from here. It is nice, I can imagine how romantic it must have been.'

I was determined, wanted to reach the very same spot where the bench was. 'Ann, please, fight your way, come on.'

'You are achieving the impossible, getting more stubborn every day.' And she squirmed her way through the Viennese jungle.

We stood side by side, silent for a long time. This was the place where Stephen was conceived.

Isn't it strange, as human lives last longer and longer their love dies quicker and quicker. I wondered why. But there is some hope. I hope there is, for some at least.

It was not the same bench, but there was a bench.

It was his third birthday. The third birthday of Stephen. Stephen, my son. My first offspring. He wanted a ball 'this big'. He stretched his arms as far as he could, his hands were trembling from the effort. Red, yellow, and green and blue, and 'this big', he emphasized.

The ball wasn't 'this big'. I couldn't afford a ball 'this big', and there weren't any 'this big' balls anyway. But it was red and yellow and green and, yes, and blue. It was a big ball.

I was on the way to meet him and his mother. Not my wife. Lillian. Lillian von Zweck. The 'von' was very important. She was the daughter of Hofrat[1] von Zweck. He hated me. I had no feeling about him. He was not worth hating.

Stephen, arms stretched to its limits again, hands trembling, announced: 'It is not "this big". Not "this big"!'

I was more disappointed than he was. Lillian came to the rescue. 'Stephen, try to embrace it.' Of course he couldn't. 'You see, it is "this big".'

Stephen studied the ball for a second, grunted an 'oh', then poked the colors with his little pointing finger; it is red, and green and yellow, and blue . . . Yeah.' He approved it, and happily bounced away after the ball. After all, the ball was 'this big' and had all the colors he wanted.

I loved him and I loved Lillian. She went through hell for me. In a convent school, seventeen and pregnant. And above all, the worst, being Hofrat von Zweck's daughter. Pregnant!

We had decided to share our secret with her mother. A secret that was impossible to be kept any longer. She received the news in silence, a silence which seemed to last forever. Lillian and I were just standing there. I watched her, I had never met her before. Slowly, very slowly, tears swelled up in her eyes. Her eyes were beautiful, and that was the only similarity between her and Lillian. She just kept on staring at me. She still didn't utter a word and her tears started to roll down on her fat, red cheeks, dropping down on her water-melon-sized breast.

Suddenly she grabbed her forehead with both hands, speaking in a hoarse whisper: 'Oh-my-God-my-migraine . . . my migraine . . . oh,' as she snatched up her Gobelin purse from her lap, turned away from us as far as she could, trying to hide that she was frantically rummaging in her purse. She came up with a small silver flask and uncorked it with nervous fingers. She almost knocked her front teeth out as she jerked the flask up to take a large swallow. She closed her eyes, cleared her throat, took a second helping, and whispered, 'My migraine medicine.' The medicine smelled even from across the room very much like schnapps.

She cleared her throat again and for the first time she looked straight at

1 Hofrat: Undersecretary of State.

me. Still hoarse, she announced: 'He will kill you . . . and you, Lillian . . . and me!'

It was evident she was most concerned about herself being killed.

I moved closer to her, I thought I took a heroic stance. 'Don't worry, I will . . . I would-like-to marry Lillian.'

Lillian came close to me, reached for my hand. Her mother, without trying to hide it, took another swallow of her medicine, cleared her throat a couple of times before yelling at me, 'You . . . Youuu,' she paused, obviously trying to find a suitable insult. Finally she found it, raised her voice to a shrill pitch. 'You Hungarian, you want to marry Hofrat Leopold von Zweck's daughter . . . get out of here . . . get out while you're alive, get out of this town, get out of this country-get-out, get out! Get out!'

She became hysterical as Lillian led me out of the room. 'You stay, Lillian . . . Lillian, you stay right here. Didn't you hear me, Lillian – Lilliaaaannn!'

Her voice echoed in the marble foyer. As we crossed it one of the servants was scurrying away not wanting to be caught eavesdropping. Lillian called after her: 'Margaret . . . go help Mother, her migraine . . .'

'Yes, Miss Lillian . . .' and with a knowing smirk she changed her course. It was obvious she had overheard everything.

Outside the gate we openly, defiantly kissed. Lillian was clinging to me, desperately holding on, tighter and tighter. I felt something. I backed slightly away, she relaxed her hold, wiped away a tear. 'She started to kick.'

'Is that what I just felt?'

'Yes. She started to kick yesterday.'

'My God, *he* is kicking and I felt it. God, it's wonderful.'

She hung on to me. We kissed gently. I reached in my pocket and came up with a small box, in it a ring. A small ring, not a big zircon. It was a small, perfectly cut blue-white diamond. Erdös Pali loaned me some money, charging a bottle of Cordon Rouge per week interest until it was fully repaid.

Lillian threw her arms around me, kissed my neck just below my ear and answered my yet unasked question, whispering, 'Yes . . . yes of course.'

'Tomorrow . . .'

'Yes . . . yes tomorrow.'

'The same place.'

'The same place, the same time,' and the door closed behind her. I walked home. It was a long walk but I needed it.

It was early dawn but the light was still on in the far corner of the community room. As usual, Erdös Pali was hunched over anatomical charts and impressively well-thumbed books. When I was about halfway through the room he looked up, 'How did it go?'

'Lillian is going to have a baby.'

'If you want an abortion? I –'

'Hell no! We are going to be married, tomorrow.'

'Tomorrow, well, congratulations. Good. The interest on the loan just went up to two bottles of champagne per week, till it is fully paid. With the baby coming I'll be kept in champagne for the rest of my life. Let's celebrate'. And 'celebrate' we did.

Either we had celebrated too loud, or the liquid we used to fuel our celebration had too penetrating a smell. In all justice you couldn't call it aroma. But whatever it was, it woke up some inmates and they all were more than eager to help us to celebrate. Sooner than in due course we saturated even our shoes with the lethal variety of zwetchke-schnapps-barack-silvorium-unicum and lesser known poisons that were all stashed away strictly for medical emergencies.

Well fortified, we had decided the baby's name. It would be Stephen. 'Maybe Lillian will have some other ideas,' interjected Erdös Pali. Slurred as he was, he could not defend his position. He was voted down, unanimously. We all knew it would be a boy, and his name would be Stephen. That was final.

And the wedding was fabulous. And Lillian looked more beautiful than ever in her Brussels lace wedding gown, with a long white train trailing behind her, held up by Stephen in the full dress uniform of the Hungarian Huszárs. Even Lohengrin's wedding march didn't sound too corny, played by a military band, with lots of brass and heavy drums. Her mother was pickled in schnapps in a glass barrel which was rolled down the aisle by Hofrat Leopold von Zweck, dressed in a leotard. I was running down the aisle toward Lillian. Lillian was running toward me. We both were running faster and faster desperately wanting to be together but never getting closer to each other.

The dream was over; it was not as easy to get married as Lillian and I had imagined. I realized the 'tomorrow' could stretch to next week, or longer. We needed parental permissions. We needed more than that. We had to find parents to give us the needed permissions. But what we needed most urgently was to get rid of our king-size katzenjammers (hangovers).

I was naïve, I thought one got married only once in a lifetime. I was sure Lillian would understand our celebration was justified.

Yesterday's 'tomorrow' turned into today, and I was waiting for Lillian. I was on the spot and on time. I was on time an hour ago, on the spot, in front of Madame Baklanova's studio. No Lillian. I was so intent on Lillian that I saw her in anybody coming from the direction I was expecting her to arrive.

Easy, she thinks we're going to be married today. She doesn't know the hurdles we had to surmount yet. She had a thing or two to do. The question of where to live only then hit me. Hit me like a ton of bricks.

A voice from close behind calling my name scattered my worries. As I turned I spread my arms to hug Lillian. Zsuzsi was there. The Zsuzsi who even when she was a mess looked crisp and neat. She looked like a scraggy vision of disaster. Her face was wet from tears. Before I took a breath she threw her arms around my neck, cried out.

'They took her away . . .'

'Who . . .'

'Her father. I don't know . . . I don't know. Something is very-very wrong. She was so happy-she-told-me-what-happened-yesterday – congratulations . . . Then this . . . I am not going to have my lesson today with Madame Baklanova.'

I had no words. I felt I had stepped into an elevator shaft and there was no elevator.

The three of us, Zsuzsi, Hans and myself were sitting across a table in Hans's father's Heurige. We were on our second bottle of wine. Most of the first was consumed by Zsuzsi. She was devastated, and felt totally responsible for what had happened and whatever the future would bring. Hans acted like, or actually was a nice, warm human being. His inferiority-fired bravado was not with him. Zsuzsi told us over and over what happened. Hofrat von Zweck, himself, appeared in the late evening, told Mother Superior, because of grave family problems out of town, Lillian had to leave immediately. He cancelled Lillian's tuition, and he was not sure if Lillian would be able to continue next year or not. It all depended on a medical condition and how soon it could be cleared up.

'Depended on a medical condition and how soon it could be cleared up.' Those were the words that concerned me.

It was late, I was sitting across the table from Erdös Pali, behind his barricade of books. 'No way. Of course if they knock her out without her consent . . . that's a different story.'

'How?'

'It's easy.'

'Thanks. You're a great consolation.'

'Any time . . . don't mention it.'

Erdös didn't hear my 'and funny too'. He did not see me across the table from him. He was far, far away. Cell-mates, as we called each other, came and went. The always polite Erdös Pali did not return their greetings. Abruptly he looked at me. I knew, now I was in focus. I was facing the other side of the coin. Erdös Pali was a hard man.

'What did you say Lillian's father's name was?' he asked unexpectedly.

I told him . . . 'Why?'

'Never you mind.' He got up from the table, walked around the room. It was the walk of the caged tiger. He stopped, came to a decision, it must have been a hard one. He sat across the table, looked straight at me, I felt he was evaluating me. He hesitated then spoke. 'I trust you.'

I was taken aback, I did not expect this opening. What was going to be the next surprise? It came.

'From tomorrow noon on be at this phone.' He pointed at the community phone, which occasionally worked. 'Don't move from it till you hear from me.'

'Yeah?'

Nothing, he ignored me, started to pack up his books. It was unusually early for him to quit his studies. I sat and watched him.

'Good night,' and off he went. I sat there for a long while, dumbfounded. It was a day of surprises. None good.

The next day brought another big surprise. I had to wait for it, but it was worth it. Some things, many things are wrong with me, but one is for certain. Any time, any place, anywhere if I have to wait for somebody, something, anything, I am convinced that is the longest wait I had been subjected to, ever.

The longest wait ever ended; Erdös called, I was to meet him in the Café Fenstergucker. I had never heard about that café, but then there were many other things in life I had never heard about either. I swallowed my questions, because Erdös was rather curt on the phone. I was on my way, on the double.

The Fenstergucker was a large place. It was glossy, but in good taste, far from being garish. It was elegant, with its white wrought iron curlicue legged tables, chairs and settees. The colors for their upholstery were borrowed from Gauguin's palette. The place smelled clean, and it was as busy as a beehive. Waiters glided around with loaded trays floating high above their heads as they negotiated the passages between the tables. I stood in the entrance, surveying a sea of faces. Erdös surfaced, motioned to me, and I joined him at his table.

'The Napoleon is divine here,' and ordered one for me, one for himself, without waiting for my reaction.

'Divine,' nothing wrong with it, but it didn't somehow sound like Erdös, and it was not the same face – confident, reassuring – I remembered seeing through my alcohol-anesthetized half-consciousness. Something was amiss. He ordered himself a double schnapps. Ask? he didn't even look at me to see if I would like one too.

The place was bursting with laughter, yet we sat in silence. The waiter came and delivered the double schnapps. Still not a word. He picked up his drink, swirled it around, sniffed it a couple of times, then slowly replaced it on the table, right in front of him. He looked around, surveyed the café, finally looked at me, straight.

'Exercising self-control?' I was getting to be annoyed with his charade.

'Yeah, congratulations. I am glad you didn't ask how I liked the Napoleon.'

'How was it?'

'What the hell are we doing here, playing a game?'

He nodded, 'Yes –', he wanted to say something more but cut himself off. He picked up his drink, sniffed it, then put it down without touching it.

A couple of people passed the table and the old, friendly Erdös returned their greetings, only to hide anew behind his own, private storm clouds. I didn't know what to expect. Occasionally he looked at the clock in the white wrought iron curlicue frame on the far wall, checked the time against his own watch, then scanned the café. Was he waiting for someone, or was he uncomfortable?

'Let's have another Napoleon.'

'Sure thing.' Somehow, I don't know why, I started to feel sorry for him. He must have felt like I did years later when in an under-powered and over-loaded aeroplane I was trying to take off from a short, rutted, bumpy dirt field, bouncing, bouncing and bouncing but not able to get airborne.

The Napoleon came, no question the best I ever had, before or since. Forgive, Mother. Erdös wiped his mouth, put two elbows on the table, 'Do you know where you are?'

'Sure, the Fensterguck . . .'

'You are in a homosexual meatmarket, deluxe.'

I didn't say anything, I had nothing to say, as a matter of fact I didn't have a thought. I was empty. I was not shocked, or surprised, I was just empty. He was cool, leaned closer, his voice didn't change volume or pitch, he spoke level. 'I wanted you to know I am a male whore.'

It took me some time to absorb this information. Neither of us spoke. He watched me for a reaction. I had none. I felt I had to say something. But what?

'I thought you were a medical student.'

'Right. That is why I am a male whore. I need the money. If I took a regular job I wouldn't have enough time left for studies.' He spoke with monotonous simplicity.

Like what an electric shock does to a heart to restart it, is what and how Erdös, opening himself up, did to me. I was in gear, I was moving. I reached over and put a hand on his forearm. 'Let's go, you're quitting now. I will call my father and things will be done, and you'll be a doctor. That's it, let's go.'

I raised my hand to signal a waiter, he pushed my arm down. 'No, not yet, we still have something to take care of.'

'What?'

He ignored my question. Smiled. The old Erdös rejoined himself. Unburdened, he was at ease. He must have felt like I did years later when under-powered, over-loaded, I cleared the trees on the end of the rutted, bumpy, short dirt field. I thought of Erdös Pali then.

The waiter came with the bill, Erdös ordered two more Napoleons and chatted to while away the time till whatever we were waiting for happened. He picked up his schnapps again but now he did not sniff it, he poured it into the coffee cup. 'You see my father died at the age of forty-one, chased into his grave by delirium tremens, the poor slob. My mother was a drug addict, she sold one of my sisters for a fix. She was twelve. I was ten when one of the priests in school defiled me when we were preparing the vestments for Sunday mass. I was not the only one, nor was my sister. Kids around the blocks were dropping dead or worse, were maimed for life. No help was available. I'll be a surgeon, and a children's specialist.'

He did not have to say he'd be the best – I felt, I knew he would be. To my great surprise he laughed, actually from his heart. 'It all sounds like a corny old Shakespearean plot, I discovered that just now as I heard it. It whirled within me, pent up, but it never left my lips before.'

He checked his watch, looked around, turned back, a satisfied man. 'Let's finish our Napoleon, then we are going to have our real dessert.'

'This is getting kind of ridiculous. Look, Pali, what the hell is . . .'

'This Napoleon is –'

'Look, stop this –'

'OK, follow me.' He got to his feet, he didn't even attempt to pay, when I tried, he waved me off, 'It'll be taken care of later.'

Sure-footed, he weaved his way through a happy crowd, a greeting here, another there. I was on his heels. We stopped at a table occupied by two people in deep, deep conversation, completely unaware of us. One, a very elegant, elderly man with a white handlebar moustache, was wearing a dark suit, pearl-grey waistcoat and a large pearl tie-pin. The other, a sleekly elegant, snow-blond, very handsome young man was the first to realize our presence. He jumped to his feet, he greeted Erdös like a long-lost brother. 'Felix, you look just marvelous!'

Felix? I thought, what in the hell is going on here, while they greeted each other with profuse compliments. The elderly gentleman was visibly annoyed by our interruption, and so far was completely ignored by everybody. Unbefittingly, he squirmed.

Finally 'Felix' and Helmut ran out of compliments for each other. Turning, Helmut gently moved 'Felix' closer to the elderly gentleman, 'Herr Hofrat, may I present my friend, Felix von Grünewald.'

Herr Hofrat? von Grünewald? Shit! This was beginning to be too much for me. They shook hands, 'von Grünewald' clicked his heels, dropped his chin against his chest, whipped it back with a quick jerk. I was standing there like a bump on the log, my jaw dropped in slow motion. 'Felix' reached back and, without anybody's permission, dragged a chair over and sat down. I was not there, I did not exist. They settled comfortably.

'Herr Hofrat,' gushed Helmut, 'this is "Felix" who was so, so anxious to meet you. Thank you, Herr Hofrat, for letting me arrange for my very-verry-verrry bestest friend the privilege of meeting you.' Herr Hofrat obviously enjoyed being flattered. They all were in icky-land flattering each other – unfortunately not – to death.

'Felix' finally acknowledged that I existed, 'Please come closer.' He turned from me to Herr Hofrat, dropped his head now with slow humility, 'Herr Hofrat, I took the liberty of bringing my very best friend with me, who also was extremely eager to meet you, and if you kindly allow him, Herr Hofrat, to ask a few questions from you, Herr Hofrat von Zweck.' Herr Hofrat smiled, condescendingly nodded.

Herr Hofrat Leopold von Zweck! I almost dropped dead, but when he heard my name I thought for a minute he did drop dead.

We left 'Felix von Grünewald' in the Fenstergucker. Erdös Pali and I walked homeward in silence. It was all arranged. Lillian would be brought back to town immediately, she could return to school if she chose to. With Herr Hofrat's blessing, Lillian and I would get married at the earliest 'convenient' (his phrase – not 'possible') time. He saw it as 'natural' that Lillian and I should see each other. It was all arranged. Strange as life is, it was done through Felix von Grünewald.

'Let's have a coffee.'

'Great.'

We walked into the first Café House we came to. Neither of us looked up to see the name of it. The hour before early dinner, it was almost empty. Erdös gazed into his full cup of capuccino as if he wanted to read his fortune before he drained the cup as the pros do. My 'thanks' yanked him off it.

'For what?'

'First, for trusting me, I appreciate that, second, for arranging what you arranged, thanks, OK?'

He was the old Erdös Pali. I was so glad to see him back. He laughed, 'You know, nobody else knows that son-of-a-bitch "Felix" outside the Fenstergucker, but you, you alone.' He stirred his cappuccino, slow and thoughtful, 'I know you'll bury him there.'

'I can't.'

He looked up, sharp, hurt, then smiled again, 'I understand.'

'No. You don't. How in hell can I bury the son-of-a-bitch if I never saw him. I don't know him.'

He ordered again what we had before and two barack pálinkát. 'You see, everybody thinks I am a rich Hungarian Jew, that's why I am so close-mouthed about where my money is coming from. It's not only fine with me, but I am leading them on to think they are right. You know, in some circles it is better to be known as a Jew than a faggot, and that turned the key in Herr Hofrat's mind.'

The orders came, he lifted his glass, I knocked my drink back, lifted my empty glass eye-to-eye as a greeting, noticing he did not touch his drink. He looked around – nobody paid any attention to us or anybody else – and swiftly poured his drink under the table. 'You see, any time I really want one – not to enjoy it, but because I need it badly – I order one, or pour one, then I pour it out. Training. I grew up watching what "I need this one only" can do. Not for me, man.' He looked as if he were hypnotizing his cup of cappuccino. He talked to it, 'Homosexual, bisexual, I don't know what the hell I am . . . All I know is I am a whore now . . . for a while yet. But I pay 'em with more than what the shits give me. Money, shit oh-shit. I am buying with that money what I want to be. And, by God, I know what I am going to be.'

It was almost weird, he smiled when he looked up. 'Thanks for being a friend, I need one, sometimes badly. Let's get out of here, I have a lot to catch up with.'

'From now on I'll believe in miracles!' These were the first words Lillian spoke when I met her. 'How is it possible for someone to acquire something that was totally lacking, the most difficult thing to acquire, and within forty-eight hours: Understanding. You know what he said, he dared to say to me, he, that hypocritical pig, he understands me. Un-der-stands-me! He gave his blessing to our marriage, I can go back to school if and when I want to. Well, to begin with I am not going back to school again, now or ever. I am moving out, away. I didn't tell him yet, but that is what I am going to do tomorrow. I can't look at my drunken mother having migraines twenty-four hours a day now. God! When he said he would be a good grandfather, I wanted to throw up. I am finished. I am grown up in an hour, and thank you.' She kissed me.

When I told Erdös that Herr Hofrat Leopold von Zweck had kept his word, all he said was, 'He had no choice.' When I told him Lillian's decisions to leave school, home, quit everything, he answered only with two words, 'Good choices.' And when I told him how grateful I was for all he had done for us, he looked up from his book and after a long, thoughtful pause he said, heavy-hearted, 'Wait with the thanks. It's not over yet. I don't know,' he shrugged and, with a 'who knows', sunk back into his studies.

Lillian moved into the Heurige with Hans's parents and worked as a waitress for her keep. She absolutely refused to get married or accept any kind of help. 'My daughter and I are just fine, and we shall always be. You did not run up a bill. There is nothing for you to pay for.' She became adamant and hurt every time I brought up the subject of my responsibility. 'If you don't want to see me again, just bring up once, only once more, that you think we are your responsibilities and that's it.'

The first night Lillian moved out of her parents' house we celebrated our engagement in Hans's Heurige. I put the ring on her finger, Zsuzsi screamed for joy, Hans, of course, came up with a lovely, thank God short toast, where he accepted the not-offered honor to be godfather to our baby. We all, except Lillian, drained our glasses; Erdős gave her a lovely antique brooch, which she put on immediately.

Then to our surprise she slipped off the ring, pulled out of her purse a narrow pink ribbon, all prepared, slipped it through the ring and put it around her neck as a pendant, 'Now we are married,' and kissed me on my cheek. The last time we kissed. She stubbornly but elegantly avoided even the possibility of us, just the two of us, being intimately together again. Overnight Lillian became a hard lady. But a lady she remained.

Erdős finally found his way out of the shell he withdrew into after our Fenstergucker meeting. He realized his confidence was not defiled. His happy-go-lucky self reigned once again over his books, charts and the community room in general.

I was on a picture in Budapest, I had absolutely no way to get to Vienna to be with Lillian for the big day. She understood perfectly, actually I had the feeling she was glad. Sooner than anticipated, I received a telegram from Zsuzsi: 'You won, it's a boy, what a boy.' I never liked a picture to come to the end, I always had the feeling it took a big piece of me away. This was the only time when I could hardly wait for the end.

He was not beautiful, he was not ugly. He was a baby. But he was my first boy, it was only natural I thought he was the most beautiful baby. I brought Lillian a simple gold chain for her pendant. She thought it was a great idea and replaced the pink ribbon immediately. 'How do you like him?'

'How do I like him? I like him, actually I couldn't get a good look at him yet, but let's keep him anyway.'

'You didn't ask what his name is.'

'His name, his name, well it doesn't really matter, he is my – our son, that's all.'

'You won twice, you got a son and he is Stephen as you ordered it, you stubborn Hungarian. Your King Saint Stephen must have meddled in up there, thank him and better thank Dr Erdös, he stayed with me for twenty-eight hours in the Heurige.'

'Heurige?'

'Sure, what's the big surprise, you know that's where I live.'

A short weekend, Zsuzsi was still taking lessons from Madame Baklanova, Hans was still full of hot air and plans to buy out every Heurige in Grinzing, and Dr Erdös was now spending every minute of his days and nights in the children's clinic. A lovely, warm reunion. I believe the idea to make a film, to pay a tribute to Dr Semmelweis, the Saviour of Mothers, took root in me then. I should have dedicated on the screen, my fifth Hungarian film, *Semmelweis*, to Lillian, Stephen and Dr Erdös, of course.

It was the first and only time I enjoyed Vienna. Dr Erdös took me to the train, picked up my luggage again and put it on the rack. 'You know,' he said, 'it's funny, I haven't been in the Fenstergucker since we were there together. Thanks.' And my train pulled out.

I could not come back to Vienna for a long time. I missed Stephen's first and second birthdays. Lillian was still working at the Heurige. Hans's parents adopted her, so to speak. Dr Erdös assured me she and Stephen were doing fine.

I finally made Stephen's third birthday. Lillian was content, she didn't change. Unfortunately more ways than one. She still refused to marry me. She firmly, almost rudely, refused a bracelet I bought for her. 'You must have spent a fortune on this, why?'

'I wanted you to have it.'

'You wanted me to have it, or you wanted to buy out your own guilty conscience again. Stop suffering. I keep telling you, you didn't do anything wrong, no need. And I won, I have Stephen, he is with me, he is mine. I am well paid for whatever you still think you owe me. This bracelet, this expensive showy bracelet on the wrist of a waitress in the Heurige? Think, do you want me to put my jewelry on at night and wear it to bed when everybody else takes it off. Please.' She put her hand on my knee, 'But I am glad you got that "this big" ball for your son.'

This was 'Stephen's Park', they came here often. It was an ordinary small outskirts park, sad, worn like the streetcars unloading their habitués, like the old men now playing chess, reading yesterday's newspapers. Faded old ladies with colorful yarns in their laps gossiped with false teeth and bone knitting needles chattering away happily. Even the pigeons looked second-hand. But Stephen loved his park, and that was important, he was showing off his 'this big' ball even to the not very appreciative pigeons.

Lillian and I were sitting on a bench, her hand resting on my knee. Unexpectedly, she put her head on my shoulder. She closed her eyes, I shut mine, excluding each other from our dreams.

The screeching brakes of a streetcar cut through our dreams. 'Too bad,' she said. Suddenly she jumped up, looked around, 'Stephen . . . Stephen.'

There was a noisy crowd around the front of the streetcar. The ambulance came. They had difficulty pulling Lillian out from half way under the front of the streetcar. She grabbed me, her fingernails dug deep into the back of my head. She didn't see the box, as big as a shoe box. She didn't see the Red and the Yellow and Green and yes, the Blue fused eternally with what was left of Stephen. My first son.

5 No Angels Fly Barefoot

'The war to end all wars' officially ended on 4 June 1920. The peace treaty of Trianon was signed. Good old naïve USA pulled the hot potato out of the fire, won the war for Clemenceau[1] and lost the peace. A glorious habit we kept on indulging in. To add insult to injury they dubbed the Versailles-Trianon treaty 'la paix Wilson'[2] after Wilson's brilliant fourteen-point proposal was mostly ignored.

The venom-fed damage sired by Clemenceau, 'Le Père de la Victoire', was irreparable. The Versailles-Trianon peace treaty ultimately cost more lives and hurt the world more than Hiroshima and Nagasaki. And it is doubtful whether 7 December 1941 would ever have occurred without Trianon. Clemenceau's fear and blind hatred of Germany and the Austro-Hungarian Empire made him deaf to Lord Rothermere's plea and prophetic warning, 'The world's conscience not to be allowed rest in view of the injustice done at Trianon, and the consequent danger it represents to the world peace in a foreseeable future.' Heil Clemenceau, father or mother of Herr Hitler.

Clemenceau's Trianon blasted Central Europe to pieces. It destroyed a possible counter-balance for the German might he feared so much. Out of 325,411 square kilometers Trianon misappropriated 232,448 square kilometers, more than sixty per cent of land the Crown of Saint Stephen, Hungary, had held without dispute since the eleventh century in the Danube basin, surrounded by the Carpathian mountain range, a natural

---

1 Georges Clemenceau (1841–1929), the French premier who opposed President Wilson at the Peace Conference.
2 Woodrow Wilson (1856–1926) was the 27th President of the United States from 1913–1921. He viewed the First World War as a necessary evil in making the world 'safe for Democracy'. At the Paris Peace Conference he outlined a fourteen-point imperative for a peace settlement and a new world society, resulting in the establishing of the League of Nations, the basis of today's United Nations.

border. According to Monsieur Clemenceau Hungary was to keep only 92,963 square kilometers. That was not all. Out of Hungary's pre-Trianon population of 20.90 million the chopped-up country was left with 7.62 million people. A loss of close to 70 per cent. Out of the lost 13.28 million population only 10.4 per cent did not claim Hungarian, Magyar, as their mother tongue. Trianon could not happen today, France would be one of the first countries to protest against this genocide.

Trianon, the collapse in mid-June 1931 of the Hungarian Banks, minor details, could not break the Hungarian sense of humor; the spirit of survival flowed freely. In the 600-odd coffee houses in Budapest business thrived better than ever. In patisseries paradise – Gerbeaud, Lukács, Ruszwurm – the portions grew larger.

Jean Renoir[3] based his statement, 'The foundation of all great civilizations is loitering,' on Budapest. He neglected to say loitering in luxury was the trademark of Budapest. And loiterers deluxe, like Kodály, Bartók, Solti, Molnár, and Vértes, who subsequently introduced me in Paris on the terrace of Café Coupole to a fellow artist, 'a brilliant painter, a lazy genius', Vincent. That's all, Vincent.

He could have been twenty-five or thirty-five, he was ageless and obviously penniless. He had a slouched, grey something on his head – some time ago it was probably a hat – a cord instead of a belt holding up his baggy pair of pants, a well-worn tweed jacket of indeterminable color, a surprisingly clean white-white shirt with a bright multicolored scarf and a two-inch-long stack of drooping cigarette ash glued to his lips. He had an aura about him, you had to like him. Soon I learned his surname in Denham, England.[4] Korda. Vincent Korda.

His oldest brother – Kellner Sándor by birth, Lászlo' according to his mother's wish a week after his birth, Korda Sándor according to his own wish, aka Korda László, aka Laci Korda, aka Alex Korda, aka Alexander Korda, aka Sir Alexander Korda – had left Budapest by then. Various reasons were given for his departure. I believe the least political and most dramatic, coming from a 'reliable eye witness account'.

3 Jean Renoir (1894–1979), the son of Impressionist painter Auguste Renoir, considered to have been one of the greatest film directors. His best known works: *Une Partie de Campagne/A Day in the Country* (1936); *La Grand Illusion/The Grand Illusion* (1937); and *La Regle du Jeu/The Rules of the Game* (1939).
4 Denham is a small village north of London, where Alexander Korda created the studios of that name which housed his London Films. The studios closed in 1952 and are now utilized by Rank Xerox (the British division of Xerox Corporation of America).

In those days film-speed was extremely slow, and an enormous amount of light was required to obtain the correct exposure. The Klieg lights used were powerful enough to inflict serious sunburn. Their heat converted the stages into hell-like sauna baths. But they had no substitutes.

The director, Korda, then Laci, wanted the Angel, gussied up in a white, flowing, lace robe, with a pair of large, shiny, silver wings strapped to her back, to descend from the twenty-some-feet-high studio ceiling, converted for this grand occasion into a blue heaven, right down to a big-big close up. The Angel, the star of the film, the star of Korda Laci's life was Maria Corda, aka Maria Korda. A world-renowned star in her own right, she had wanted Laci to direct the film in the first place.

The star nixed Korda's dream shot with one word, 'No!' She refused to be a barefoot Angel, she wanted a silver slipper: 'No Angels fly barefoot.'

And after an hour's discussion nobody could prove her wrong. Maria Korda was a strong-willed, beautiful nut. A dangerous nut.

'Lunch one hour,' and after two hours a pair of silver slippers arrived. They didn't fit. Laci tried to convince the star on his knees that it didn't matter, she didn't have to walk, she would be carried to the harness. When the shot was finished, she would be carried back to her dressing room. 'No! No Angels wear shoes that don't fit.' Nobody could prove her wrong.

'That's all for today, nine in the morning.'

Variations circulating on this story circulated, but all were in accord in that the producer of the epoch got his first heart attack that evening.

And as always the morning came, for some too soon.

The set-up was lit and ready, all go. Finally the Angel descended to the set from her own heights in silver shoes. Her first words shattered everybody. 'I have a great idea!'

After a long silence Laci uttered a 'Yes, dear?'

'Silver is crap for an Angel. Gold is what an Angel should wear!' announced the star of the film and Korda's life.

It was common knowledge that Maria was keeping Laci in a style he would like to be accustomed to, but he shocked everybody with his answer, 'Yes dear, you're right. Absolutely right. Gold, yes gold, is right!'

After this degrading submission in front of everybody he motioned to the wardrobe mistress who brought forward a big satchel and unloaded six pairs of gold shoes with various heights of heels and placed them gently in front of Maria. She assessed them, then declared that she liked the silver shoes more.

Then the hassle started. She refused to put on the harness, she was not sure it was safe. Korda tried his best to convince Maria of the beauty of the shot, her magnificent, big-big close up after the long-long shot, all in one.

No use. She insisted it was not a safe shot.

In the meantime the Klieg lights were heating up the stage, the poor stand-in was going up and down on the wires twenty-thirty times, to convince the star it was safe. Maria watched as she sat majestically on a special chair so as not to wrinkle her wings. Finally, whatever Korda whispered in her ear did the trick. 'Let's go.' She jumped to her silver-shoed feet. You couldn't defeat Korda László.

Every craftsman worked feverishly, and up she went before she could change her mind. Take one brought great applause from the crew. She lived for applause, she loved it, all she said was, 'It's hot up there.' That brought thunderous applause and yells of appreciation of her sacrifice for her art, and up she went, smiling. Take two. And that was it. The wire jumped out of the pulley, the Angel was stuck in heaven at the hotter-than-hell ceiling from where she was flooding the stage with every four-letter word, some in new combinations, in two languages, Hungarian and German.

Her situation got more and more dangerous as she wiggled around. The Klieg lights had to be kept on so the rescue team could see what they were doing, the heat crept up, and up, the wilting and livid Angel was stuck in her hell-like studio heaven. Her anger reached hysterical proportions. Besides her curses and threats she started to throw down everything she could reach dangling up there, her shoes, parts of her wings, all aimed pretty accurately at Korda below.

Korda, seated in his director's chair, stoically smoked his cigar, immobile, watched the silver slippers whizzing by his head, the angel wing feathers floating down and the progress of the crafts building up platforms high enough to save the cursing, kicking, screaming Angel from her hell-hot-heaven. Everybody was fully aware that Maria was crazy enough to carry out her threats once on solid ground.

Korda knew that more than anybody. When the rescuers just about reached Maria, he left the studio and left Budapest.

However, he never could shed Maria. She followed him literally all through his life, right to the proverbial grave in the British mist Sir Alex loved so much. She showed up at his funeral and scattered the handful of mourners; cursing and screaming, she physically attacked Alexa, Sir Alex's reigning wife, whom I never met. It was Zoltán[5] whose cool strength stopped the mayhem. And Sir Alexander Korda was laid to rest at last.

In Paris I drew a blank. My French was atrocious, still is. Later I discovered my French was better than Vincent's, no big discovery. I thoroughly agree with Gabriel Pascal,[6] an ex-Hungarian Huszár officer who rode the rollercoaster of the international film industry, that Vincent spoke every language badly, except Hungarian – that he spoke terribly. But whatever Vincent said in any language it always had a meaning. Little did he know then how much I cherished the hours we bummed through museums and art galleries together.

In his studio he had the best coffee, the most incredible 'artistic disorder', a beautiful young lady-friend, and a lovely screaming baby, who was crawling on masterpieces thrown all over the floor. Some of them were his own paintings, some from other masters which now fetch millions on the auction circuits today. The great majority of Sir Alex's fortune was accumulated through Vincent's knowledge of art and artists, his judgement was impeccable, his instinct was phenomenal.

My time was not wasted in Paris. I met a giant – a warm, beautiful man, bursting with talent, spreading contentment and happiness. When I confessed my 'artistic fiasco' he tried his best to convince me to forget motion pictures – 'Merde.' He shoved me in front of a canvas, 'Paint, God-damn-it, now paint!' I could not touch the brushes. Many, many years later he understood me.

It happened in Hollywood. By then he was Vincent Korda, the

5 Zoltán Korda (1895–1961) was initially a cameraman and editor before becoming a film director in the late 1920s. His films include *Elephant Boy* (1937), *The Four Feathers* (1939), *Jungle Book* (1942), and *Cry, the Beloved Country* (1952). He was adept at handling location filming. He missed being a great director, being tied to his brother, Sir Alexander Korda.

6 Gabriel Pascal (1894–1954) is best remembered for having persuaded George Bernard Shaw to allow him to produce screen versions of four of Shaw's plays: *Pygmalion* (1938), *Major Barbara* (1941), *Caesar and Cleopatra* (1945), and *Androcles and the Lion* (1953).

world-famous, award-winning set designer, art director of motion pictures, a field he was trying to talk me out of in Paris. I never was professionally content in my life, but I was doing fine.

One of the saddest malaises of the picture business is, world-wide, the 'drift apart'. It is contagious. Vincent and I caught it too. Somehow we drifted apart. 'Let's have lunch or dinner,' Vincent came through on the phone, out of nowhere.

'Great, when?'

'Oh, well, now?'

'Sure, now. Lunch and dinner. Why not?' I would have cancelled anything for him, except my own funeral. I felt there was some emergency. There was.

We started lunch late, the Derby[7] on Vine Street was almost empty. I finished my Martini, demolished my rare steak, and a baked potato, and a salad and a cheesecake. Vincent was toying with his food. None of the Kordas ate heartily except Hungarian food.

It wasn't only the silver creeping in his bushy hair, his whole self was un-Vincent like, dull, the wrinkles squeezed the sparkle out of his eyes. We spoke of nothing that explained the long-time-no-see-but ... immediacy of this luncheon.

Between the first and second brandies Vincent shared half of his load with me, emphasizing it with a deep sigh. 'You got to help me, I want to buy a car.'

It still happens to me today when friends want to buy an automobile, my past, limited racing experience catches up with me, they ask my advice then usually don't follow it. With Vincent I knew it would be different, he would follow my suggestion, I was hoping he would.

I was all set to talk him out of buying anything with wheels. He was the world's worst driver. He was the most considerate, courteous human on foot. As a driver I could not decide if he was a suicidal or homicidal maniac. Vincent knew only one speed, twenty miles an hour. He started with that, stopped from that, but immediately. He moseyed along, happily paying little or no attention to minor details like left side or right side

7 The Brown Derby restaurant on Vine Street, immediately south of Hollywood Boulevard, was a favorite dining place for the film community. It opened in 1929 under the guidance of Robert H. Cobb, creator of the restaurant's best known dish, the cobb salad.

of the road. An artist like him, sensitive to colors, ignored red, green, yellow. In the driver's seat colors meant nothing to him. Deep in thought, with an angelic smile on his face, he just kept on driving. He placed a heavy load on my shoulders. He knew it, he felt easier. He unloaded his burden and started to shed his sad-self.

'You don't need a car, Vincent. What in the hell do you want a car for? You like taxis, you like taxi drivers. Why, why do you need a car now?'

'I need it.'

'No, you don't!'

'OK. If you don't want to help me, Bandi, I'll go now and buy one all by myself. Right now. Waiter, the check please.'

'Right now?'

'Right now.'

I was sure Vincent would do it, just for spite. He could be very stubborn. They would probably sell him a Porsche or a Ferrari, why not to a Korda. He knew he'd got me. His furrows disappeared, his foxy smile returned, 'OK' he asked slyly.

'All right, do you know what you want?'

'Yes. I want it to be grey, with this big a trunk . . .' He stretched out his arms.

His voice faded. 'I want it this big and red, and yellow, and green, yes and blue, and this big . . .'

'Hey, come back. Where have you been?'

'I was thinking what to look for. But please, promise me you'll take at least two weeks of driving instructions before you drive it.'

'What are you talking about, I have my license!'

'Yes or no?'

'Uh, yes. Now let's have some good food.'

That happened all the time with the Kordas. In Hollywood good food meant Miki Dóra's 'Little Hungary' on the Sunset Strip. Nadina, Miki's Russian-born mother, did the 'home cooking', Walther Kohner, agent Paul's brother played the piano, it was the Mecca for all expatriates. And, aside from the good food, Dóra gave credit, with uncanny assurance to a chosen few, including Sam Spiegel and Co. If you were one of those who could eat at Miki's place on credit, you could rest easy, you had made it. Six big meals a week in your stomach made it easier to cross your fingers. It was inconsiderate of his mother, but she wanted a day off.

After a few phone calls, the following day Vincent bought his car.

Exactly what he wanted. It was a grey, two-seater Dodge coupe, with the biggest trunk on the market. He picked me up in it and took me for a drive, no way could I have avoided it. The two weeks' instruction turned out to be a complete waste. Vincent was Vincent.

We had breakfast in the Polo Lounge which I loved, he hated; none the less, he ate like he had been starved for a week. He confessed he had asked me to have lunch with him in the Derby because he wanted to tell me how terribly he had failed in life. He said all this with a happy smile. I told him that was plain nonsense, he was at the top of his profession, all the awards he had collected and the money. He cut me off. 'The awards and the money, merde, they are choking me. I am hog-tied. I am not happy. I don't feel free. I was a fool to leave Paris. And painting. You are a fool too not to go back to it. Go back to it. I will. Waiter, check please, now let's go shopping.'

Shopping we went. And I realized why he wanted a big trunk. He bought up an art store, everything a painter ever can dream of he bought; he was as happy as a child turned loose in a candy store. When we were loading his car, he carefully segregated some of the loot.

He took the wheel and pulled out of the parking lot without looking left or right. After the irate honking ceased, he said calmly, 'Now I will show you my secret, and it will be our secret.' The puzzle didn't end. We stopped at a market and Vincent almost bought out the market too, including two cases of very good wine. He spilled no information, I tagged along.

Miracles can happen, he drove without any mishap, his radio was blaring the most unlikely songs for him to listen to, 'Cielito lindo', then 'Amapola'. 'I like them,' were the only words he had spoken since we left the market. He only smiled. Finally on a small street in one of the run-down sections of Hollywood, between Melrose and Beverly, he pulled up in front of those typical early nineteen-hundred bungalows, a triplex.

'Number three, on top. Here are the keys.' He threw a bunch of keys at me, and started to carry up some of the stuff, taking two steps at a time on the not too stable wooden stairs. I had never seen him move so fast, and he kept it up. I had difficulty following him up and down. When I wanted to take out the segregated art supplies he yelled at me from the landing, 'Leave 'em there. They are yours, you're going to paint. Don't drop your jaw, the sidewalk is dirty. Come on up.'

The living-room was spacious, bright, with large windows facing north. A brand new refrigerator that did not fit in the tiny kitchen was pushed against the wall, like every other piece of furniture. In the cleared center of the room two large easels were already set up. 'This is what I wanted, I have a six months' lease to start with. Nobody knows it but you. Now get out, you'll start and I'll start, right now.' I called a cab, gave instructions to the landlady not to disturb Vincent, if something was to be done be sure to call me, and I left the happiest man on Earth.

Vincent's fire sparked me to move. I set up and started to paint. My lady wife arrived from some fashionable charity 'do' and was surprised to find me home so early and doing what I was doing. 'What's that?' Before waiting for an answer she asked the next, for her, important question, 'Do you want a drink?' And before I answered she was walking out with the promise, 'I'll bring it.'

She kept her promise but pronto. Had she kept all her other promises like that we probably still would be wed. Thank God, she didn't.

She hooked both of her long legs over the arm of an easy chair, balancing her drink, naturally on a coaster, on her sharp, boney knee. It was only a question of minutes before one of our dogs would romp in to greet his/her mistress and knock the drink off her knee, as happened at least twice a week. Her only remark about my painting was, 'Oh, that stinks, is that oil or turpentine I smell?' After a generous gulp, she whined on. 'It could give me a headache, you know. If you want a new hobby why don't you find a cleaner one?'

Oblivious of everything beyond the smell of turpentine she sunk into her own world of interests -- who had a new bracelet, a new gown, a new hairdo, a new color lipstick, a new girlfriend, a new boyfriend, a new scandal, a new divorce, a new car, a new . . . 'If you don't listen, how will you know what I would like for Christmas?'

Out of her verbal diarrhea all I remembered was 'divorce'. My answer was obvious, to me at least. 'Divorce.'

She unhooked her legs, the drink was safe for now, 'You're not funny,' she said, as she marched out of my study. Peace at last. No, she stuck her head back through the door. 'Want another, daaahrling?' I hadn't even started my first drink yet.

'No, thanks.'

She came back, irked. 'What is the matter with you today?'

I didn't try to answer her, I knew better, she was not waiting for an answer.

'Better stop playing with that thing there. You know what day it is?' She waited for no answer of course, 'This is Thursday, remember? Dinner with your producer. Eight-thirty-at-your-producer's. A sit-down dinner in our honor.' It was barely eight. 'I love my new dress, daaahrling, you'll just love it.'

'I am not going.'

'You what?' Now she waited.

'I am not going, I am not going to make this picture, I quit the picture business.'

She dropped the glass, it shattered, she stared at me bug-eyed. Aida-Bell materialized, all three hundred pounds of her. Supple as a kitten, she bent down, cleaned up the mess, disappeared. My lady wife stood in the doorway, silent as a window dummy, just as elegant and just as empty. I saw her in a different light now.

'What is this nonsense? Did you rob a bank, or are you planning to rob one or something?'

'I've had enough.'

'You've had enough of what? Making money? What about me? I have commitments. Today, just today I, I had the first fitting of the mink coat, floor-length with a hood, imagine, with a hood. I ordered it six weeks ago as a Christmas surprise for myself, what about that? What-about-that?'

'Ask the minks to find another sucker.'

'You are funny, very funny. Look at me, look at me. I am not laughing.' And gracelessly she flounced out. A door slammed. Fresh breeze. The dogs charged in. It was such a relief. They truly loved me. Me! The bare me, without the trimmings. They loved what I was doing, they loved smelling the turpentine, they loved licking the oil. They were connoisseurs.

I didn't notice it at first, it was almost dark. The phone rang, I didn't pick it up. The lady of the house appeared. She turned on the lights. It was a bit of a theatrical entrance, but a good, effective entrance. The new dress was really stunning. Surprise, surprise, it was subdued. She came to the phone next to me, picked up the receiver and, contrary to the effect she had achieved so far, she did not hand the receiver to me, she shoved it at me. 'Sam's on the line, here he is, Sam.' That was it.

We attended the sit-down dinner. I liked Sam, but his silent partner was anything but silent. I could hardly stand him. The feeling was mutual. I was not very enthused about the script to begin with, I wanted to paint again, my hands felt the yielding of the clay. I could not find a good reason why I should get involved with this half-ass undertaking. I was looking for one desperately, when it was right in front of me all the time. The script.

The script would be my saviour. Not very politely I tore it apart with the appetizer, I tore it apart with the main course, I tore it apart with the dessert, I shredded it with the coffee and brandy. For the first time in his life the silent partner lived up to his title. He remained silent when we were leaving the party, so silent he didn't say goodnight. I wanted to drive the nail securely into my coffin; as Sam, always a gentleman, escorted us to the front door, I summarized my insults. Poor Sam, ashen-faced, shook his head sadly as he whispered, 'Good night.'

On the way to the car, which was parked down the street some distance from Sam's house, I expected a scene. Not a word, not a look. She walked determinedly, but not quite steadily, toward the car. When we had left our house the car was in front, engine running, her sitting behind the wheel to highlight the fact that I had kept her waiting. Now she had the car keys and was heading toward the driver's side of the car. I beat her to it, holding my hand out, 'Please.' Keys in hand, she faced me. For a moment I thought she would throw the keys in my face. No, she sighed and leaned against the car. I stuck my hand out, more positive. 'You drank too much.'

'You talk too much.' She dropped the keys, walked around the car, waited for me to pick up the keys and open the door for her, which I did.

The ride home started like a joy-ride. 'Who in hell do you think you are?' I was sure she did not want my answer to this question. She would answer it herself in due time, which she did. 'You are a selfish bastard . . . all you think about is yourself. Christmas means nothing to you, does it, I mean nothing to you . . . All you care about is you-you-you . . .'

I switched off. She kept on flattering me until she slammed her bathroom door behind her.

The next day, she left for Palm Springs to visit her mother for a couple of weeks. She took one of the dogs with her. I missed the dog. I planned to paint, paint and paint eighteen, twenty hours a day.

It was barely eight in the morning when the phone rang. I got worried on my way to answer it. The morning traffic. She was a reckless driver under normal conditions and she was still very upset at dawn when she informed me of her plan. It was Sam.

I am not easily intimidated or embarrassed, but Sam succeeded on both counts. The longer he talked the more I shrank. I should take a week's vacation, he said. 'On the payroll, of course.' They had already made the arrangements to put the picture back four weeks to comply with all my objections, longer than four weeks, if I thought it was necessary. And he went on. How much everybody admired my integrity. I expressed myself rather strongly, but that was a wonderful sign of my dedication to my profession and to this particular project. End of ice-cold shower.

Roll with the punches. I will have a week of painting, that's a start, a step toward heaven. I thought of Vincent with his unlimited time and I had a vicarious thrill to know he had his fulfilment. He lived a few houses from me down the street on Rexford Drive in Beverly Hills; I kept watching for the grey Dodge coupe. No sign, good sign.

I painted day and night and the week had gone by fast. When I returned to my office, I was handed a stack of messages. Three of them from Vincent's landlady. I called her and she started with, 'You'd better come . . .'

I cut her off, 'Anything wrong?'

'Nooo, and please, don't think I am nosey or something like that but . . . I think you should know . . .'

I cut her off again. Vincent was always very subdued and quiet in mixed company, but by no means was he a celibate monk. I thought he probably had some noisy company. 'I'll be over as soon as I can.'

My first thought was to call Vincent, but I changed my mind. I was sure I would be able to handle the problem without bothering him. He often spoke of how much he liked to paint in Cagnes-sur-Mer because nobody disturbed him there.

The Dodge was there, no dents. It was evenly covered with Southern California's special mix of daytime dust and nighttime dew of slime. It hadn't been moved since Vincent parked it there. I was relieved.

I wanted to be briefed by Vincent before tackling the problem with Mrs Schultz. No luck. She was hovering in wait and intercepted me. I took the bull by the horns, and started off, 'Don't you worry, Mrs Schultz, I'll take care of it. Let's not disturb Vincent, I will see to it that there won't be any more problems, noise or – '

'Noise? He gives me the creeps, he is so quiet up there. I am not nosey or anything like that, but with the other tenants I always knew what was going on . . . I am not curious or anything like that, you know . . .'

'Oh, I understand, Mrs Schultz, of course. You know he is painting away up there and the brushes don't make much noise, but I will tell him maybe put on the radio louder or make some noise.' I thought I was funny, she did not.

'No joke, I am telling you he gives me the creeps. And another thing, both the cards and the leaves, they don't look so good.'

I didn't notice it before, there was a faded, old ornate sign in the window: 'Madame Schultz – Knows your future – Cards and tea-leaves reading – In three languages.'

'And another thing,' she continued, 'you tell me how can he paint in the dark? Tell me that. He hasn't turned on the lights since he moved in,' she checked a little book, 'eight days and nine hours ago. There.'

'He paints only in the daytime, Mrs Schultz.' And I was climbing the stairs three at a time. I knocked on the door several times, no use. I didn't want to call out too loud and create unwanted attention. She was standing at the bottom of the stairs, watching me. 'Do you have a second key or a pass key, Mrs Schultz?'

'I certainly do, but it is illegal.'

I remember I started to talk to her on the way down. 'Mrs Schultz, I want those keys. He is maybe not well and needs help. It will be your responsibility if something terrible happens.'

She straightened up and became several inches taller, shook her head, 'No.'

'Mrs Schultz, maybe the cards and the leaves were right.'

That did the trick. From a big ring hanging from her apron's belt, loaded with keys, she unhooked two and started up the stairs. I physically stopped her, took the keys out of her hand. 'You stay right here, Mrs Schultz. I will call you if I need help . . . Everything is fine, thank you, Mrs Schultz, thank you very much.' I threw the keys down to her and she caught them.

Fine? Vincent was dead.

First impressions are strange phenomenona. They differ from situation to situation, from person to person under identical happenstances.

The stack of cigarette ash always glued to his lower lip was absent. He was always clean-shaven, now he had a heavy, several days' growth of beard. He was slumped askew on the floor with his back propped up against the seat of a large armchair, with unnaturally pigeon-toed feet. Both of his legs were stretched out rigid on the floor.

His eyes, frozen open, stared at nothing.

Every canvas was slashed, and the frames were busted. The two easels were wrecked. Broken brushes littered the floor. The sacks and sacks of groceries were still in their wraps, untouched, so was the half bottle of wine on the table where I had left it.

'I lost it . . .'

He was barely audible as he slowly sat back up in the chair, all spent. I sat down, and we just sat in silence.

After a long while, on his way to the bathroom, he gently pushed the debris out of his way with his foot. 'I am through,' as he closed the door.

How deep was the hurt that drove him – a complaisant, easy-going man – to this violence? I felt it once, but I was hurt by strangers. He was destroyed by his own brother who robbed him and let him live drained and empty. The real tragedy was that Alex loved his brothers. But he didn't love them or anybody else more than he loved himself. I despised Sir Alexander Korda.

For a while I didn't notice Vincent standing in the bathroom door. The Vincent I knew, clean-shaven, 'Don't hate him, Bandi, I love him, he is my brother. He tried to do for me what he thought was the best.'

'For whom?'

'I could've stayed in Cagnes-sur-Mer, he didn't force me to go to Marseilles.'

No, Sir Alex never forced anybody, he was too devious, he worked like a snake trying to swallow a large prey. He surrounded them with saliva and they all slid down easy.

Vincent was smiling. Smiling as he surveyed the room, 'What a mess . . . Let's go, I am hungry.'

Every light in the house was on, lights I didn't know existed. Badly parked cars jammed the driveway. The front door was open. I was about to make a U-turn, the dogs came out running. This was about the time I used to drive around the block six-eight times with the dogs running on the sidewalk, on the soft front lawns, jumping over hedges, left-out baby buggies. How could I disappoint them. I still don't know whether the dogs or I had more fun. So off we went.

'Daaaahhaarling . . . waaaiit . . .' I didn't hear it. I wasn't a nice guy. Worst, I was a coward. The third time around she and her friends blocked the street. I didn't run them down. We all make mistakes.

'Daaaharling ... where-have-you-been-all-day-and-why-didn't-you-call-me-and-tell-me-the-good-news?-Thanks-Betty-Betty.' This was all in one breath, she took another breath and she blew a 'thank you' kiss to Betty-Betty. They literally peeled me out of my car. I was a coward again, I could've slammed the doors and chopped a few hands off, rings and all.

Three sad souls, the two dogs and I were literally herded in the house. 'Of course you didn't tell me on the phone, you wanted to surprise me.' She pinched my face, I shuddered. 'But wait, just wait. Do I have a surprise for you.' I shuddered again, she held up a designer's sketch for everybody to see. They all ooohed and aaahed. 'This is my Christmas present, floor-length with a hood.' She planted a loud kiss on my cheek, 'Thanks for the surprise, darling.'

She noticed I was not looking at her Christmas present, I was looking toward the study, there was no sign left I ever painted there.

'Oh that, aren't you glad I told them to clean up that mess-of-course-you-are!'

I thought I would never see 'that mess' again, and the piece of me that went with it. I was wrong. My wife, Ann, found 'that mess' in dead storage. She was curious what we were paying for for years in Los Angeles when we were living overseas.

'I like these paintings very much. How come your name is on them?' I told her about my first and second painting debacle. All she said was, 'Hm.'

The next day, in one corner of the living room, an art supply store was set up. Dozens of different sizes of canvases, an easel, enough paint and brushes to paint the length of Wilshire Boulevard from downtown to the ocean.

It hit me. I thought of Vincent . . . 'What's that?'

'They told me these are the things you need for painting, please, help me.'

'Help you? Sure, with what, what can I –' I was completely flabbergasted, she cut me off.

'Just follow me.' I followed her to her car, she opened the trunk, 'I can't lift it alone.'

I helped her to carry into the house a wet sack of clay heavy enough to give hernias to two longshoremen. Once inside all she said was, 'Now paint, sculpt and make the biggest mess you want, as long as you don't sing, just paint.'

I didn't agree with her. Maybe I was alone, but I thought I had a very good voice. And, after all those years and Vincent's heart-breaking experience I was reluctant to start to paint and sculpt again. I was sure singing would be less painful, to me anyway. I was wrong again. In a year I was exhibiting and selling my paintings, within a couple of years I had several bronzes on permanent display in museums, including the museum of the Vatican. Well, one cannot be one hundred per cent right all the time. Thanks, Ann.

6 Revolving Doors

This is not only 'from well-informed sources', it is well documented, widely used not only in Hollywood between the early thirties and mid forties but before and since all over the world. I can verify this from personal experience. I benefitted by it as an innocent bystander during 'the years of the dachshund'. The 'dachshund syndrome'.

One day, this dachshund saw a magnificent collie in a park. She was the most beautiful bitch he had ever seen. The lightning of love struck him and he marked every bush and marked every tree and marked every blade of grass in her path week after week, till he ran out of marking fluid. No use. The collie ignored him completely. She was only interested in a big, roadside mutt.

The poor love-sick dachshund couldn't sleep, couldn't eat, he was pining away, ready to expire. With a last desperate effort he confronted the collie and barked, 'Don't you ignore me, I was a Great Dane in Europe!'

And a miracle happened. The collie left the roadside mutt. She followed the dachshund everywhere. And the little dachshund grew and grew and grew and he became the largest ever Great Dane, and they lived happily ever after. Miracles can happen.

Beside going to a movie in Vienna, the closest I came to the motion pictures there was being suspected of arson in connection with a fire in a studio. It was a hot connection while it lasted, but even that connection with the picture business was pretty short. Being a fugitive from the morgue taught me little about picture-making, but a lot about people and prejudices.

I returned to Budapest penniless but richer. Nobody knew I was coming back, only Eiben, he was aware of my Viennese debacle. I called him before I unpacked. Before saying as much as 'hello', he gave me strict instructions, 'If anybody, a-n-y-b-o-d-y asks you anything about Vienna, what you did, or anything, all you say . . .'

Then he acted out on the phone how I had to emphasize the words.

He was a great cameraman but a terrible actor. 'Oh, Vienna! You know Vienna, oh! You know?' He made me repeat it three times to be sure I'd do it right, 'That's all, that-is-all you say.'

'But how can I . . .'

'Did you unpack?'

'No. Not yet.'

'You see, and you are already arguing. By the way, you started work yesterday.'

'I did what?'

'One o'clock lunch at Schraettner tomorrow.' And he hung up, no welcome back, no goodbye. That's all, that was Eiben.

As I walked in the restaurant Schraettner came to greet me. Quite unusual. 'Welcome back, how was Vienna?'

Eiben was already at his table, hawk-eyed, straining his ears to hear my answer. 'Oh, Vienna . . . Oh! You know –'

Schraettner cut me off. 'Do I know Vienna?' Like water out of a burst dam he poured out his knowledge of Vienna.

Eiben was beaming. 'You see, it worked,' he said after I sat down.

It was an amazing experience. Usually before I finished saying what I was supposed to say according to Eiben, people cut in and tried to impress me with their experience in Vienna. Or they simply said, 'Yes, nice city,' or something like that. But nobody, nobody ever tried to pry further.

Eiben was always Eiben, predictably unpredictable, but always to the point. I believe he didn't drive a car because he didn't want to make a turn, he just wanted to go straight. There was another Hungarian genius like him, Kertész Mihály, aka Michael Curtiz.[1] My path crossed with Curtiz's many years later in Hollywood, I will not forget that crossing.

In Hollywood you could tell immediately how important the people were whom you were going to see or how important you were by the allocated parking space. Of course I was curious where my parking space

1 Michael Curtiz (1888–1962), one of the most versatile film-makers, entered the Hungarian film industry in 1912 and became director of many of the most popular American films, including *Yankee Doodle Dandy* (1942), *Casablanca* (1943) and *Mildred Pierce* (1945). His 1933 feature *The Mystery of the Wax Museum* formed the basis for Andre de Toth's 3-D classic *House of Wax*.

was reserved. This was my first assignment with Warner Bros. It would be a clear indication of my status in the company, on the lot.

Right after the war – the second that is – it was very difficult to get new cars. I got lucky, I was driving a brand new Mercury convertible. The top was down, the sun was shining. California. The car was sparkling, driving through the gate of WB on a good assignment, it was living. To hell with where I was going to park. It was a wonderful feeling.

At the gate the security guard explained which stage I was to park next to and how to get there. Easy enough. I couldn't find it.

'It happens all the time,' said the guard after my second inquiry; he drew a map and marked the spot with an 'x'.

I didn't want to argue, I was there, I couldn't find it. I drove off again, looking more carefully. I read the famous names on the wall – Hal Wallis, Henry Blanke, Raoul Walsh, Howard Hawks, Michael Curtiz. Was the guard right? Yes. There was a space between Curtiz and Hawks. I backed up, and there it was. I'll sleep easy tonight, I thought. Pretty good company.

I was wrong. After a glorious day and before a promising evening I was ready to take off, with top down, on Mullholland Drive across the hills, in my pristine new car. New car? The whole side of the car from the passenger's door to the trunk lid was smashed, cut wide open, in one stroke, with a dull can opener.

I didn't move the car. I walked to the front gate and reported it to one of the guards on duty. He was ready to come with me to see the damage. Offhand he asked where was I parked. When I told him, he stopped, yelled back to his colleague, 'We have another complaint.'

The other guard joined us with a stack of forms, 'You will have to fill these out, we'll handle it from there. And may I suggest you ask for another place, sir. Nobody wants to park next to Mr Curtiz's left.'

I felt smaller with every step as we were walking toward my prime parking space. Nobody wants to park there. I wished he had never said that, and the guard droned on.

'This is not a bad week for him, you are only the second. During weeks when he has to go to the back lot often he can "touch" – that's what Mr Curtiz calls it – "touch" as many as seven or eight "things". His "things" mean lamp posts, mailboxes, cars, or whatever "things" are next to the curbs around corners to his right. You see, he doesn't want to turn to the left, he wants to go straight. Mr Curtiz cuts the corners to go straight.'

This was my first day at Warners' and my first 'contact' with Michael Curtiz. He and Eiben were very much alike and spoke the same language, with a grammar of their own.

Eiben was in better form than usual. He was not a frustrated director, he had no ambition to direct. He wanted to be the best in his field. He was for perfection in everything. 'He doesn't know his ass from his elbow. They all just blow in and direct. This one wasn't even on a street where there was a studio in Berlin, let alone try to burn one down. At least you had tried that. You should have directed this picture.'

I cut him off, hard. 'No, thanks. I am not ready yet. Thanks, Hapshikám, no.'

'I'll drink to that, Hapshikám, exactly what I expected.' Eiben never needed an excuse to drink, but if one surfaced he grabbed it.

'This will be the best schooling for you yet. After talking to him, I believe you'll learn things you shouldn't do as a director. You are his first assistant . . .'

'But I . . .'

'You talk too much. Don't interrupt. I think this guy is a lazy pompous ass; we'll be behind schedule, you'll have a chance to shoot some scenes to catch up, now, oops, here he comes. Right over here.' Eiben instructed the director. 'I was talking about you, not very flattering unfortunately. Sit down, please.'

He came, preceded by an onslaught of cologne. A clean, starched Prussian, not an echt, an ersatz, an imitation Prussian. From Magyaróvár through Berlin. He wore a supercilious smile, he was a bit pear-shaped and quite a bit pompous. Eiben cut him to ribbons, the director obviously was not a professional. I felt sorry for him and tried to serve him well.

He was not lazy, he was laid back and let things happen. He had neither talent nor knowledge, nor courage to initiate. He could only criticize if something went awry. He was not a 'director', he was a 'selector'. It was perfect for me. I took the bit and ran with it, right up to delivering the answer print. To my great surprise I received a single card credit on the main title. I thought it was Eiben's doing, but he protested vehemently, too vehemently.

Luck and miracles, overlapping commitments at the time when the 1931 collapse of the Hungarian banking system was still hurting. I could afford to race the latest sports cars, have the best tables. I almost fizzled out in the froth of living, looking for the glitter not the substance. I woke up one morning and luckily remembered miracles didn't last if they were not backed up. I wish I had always remembered it. Hindsight. Some consolation, I had fun.

Dr Basch thought he invented me, which he did in a way. Babitch, when I was mentioned, only smiled and licked the rim of his wine glass as he mumbled, 'Well, well, well.' Molnár was disappointed: 'Shit! I wasted my time, I thought you wanted to be a writer.' When I told him I worked on the screenplays too, he was not flattering, but at least he smiled, 'That prostitute's writing. Don't ever be proud of it.' But he adored Géza Herczeg and Melchior Lengyel,² and a few other 'writers turned prostitutes'.

Much later in Hollywood, when Herczeg reminded him that he was willing to sell some of his material for pictures, he answered, 'Oh, that is different. I am in the highest class of prostitution,' he laughed, 'and I need the money.' Until his dying days he still slighted motion pictures and 'picture people' as a whole, including the 'king of the hustlers', a not-yet-Sir Alexander Korda.

Babitch wiped off the red wine from his handlebars, tapped my arm, 'Don't lose faith,' turned to Molnár, 'Did the shoe hurt you that much?'

I was waiting for an explanation, but Molnár switched the subject to the edge of Bordeaux over other red wines. It took me years and Nemeskürty³ to find out from him that Molnár wrote some of the early Hungarian films, and the title of one was *Pufi cipöt vesz* (*Pufi Buys a Shoe*) in 1914. Molnár was a hypocrite. Babitch was a film buff; for him I was to go-go-go.

My mother was elated, Father was on Molnár's side of the fence; 'But he would have never made a Hungarian Huszár officer,' grumbled General Szirmay, who ignored or had never heard of the two ex-

2 Géza Herczeg (1888–1954) enjoyed an impressive pre-film career; he was a war correspondent from 1912–18, he spent a term with the Royal Hungarian Foreign Office, was a press officer in Hungary and Germany, and a playwright from 1927. As a result he was brought to Hollywood by Warner Bros, who filmed his play *Wonder Bar* in 1934. Films Herczeg co-wrote include the Academy Award-winning screenplay of *The Life of Emile Zola* (1937), *Florian* (1939), *The Shanghai Gesture* (1941) and *Rapture* (1949). During the Second World War, he worked with the Overseas Motion Picture Bureau of the Office of War Information, writing patriotic short subjects. Melchior Lengyel was a prolific writer of essays and plays, his greatest hit was *Ninotchka* with Greta Garbo.
3 Nemeskürty is a Hungarian film historian, and the author of several books.

Hungarian Huszár officers, Géza von Bolváry, and Géza von Cziffra[4] riding tall in the saddle of the world-wide fame of motion pictures.

Eiben remained cool, his only observation was, 'If you don't break your neck in one of those stupid cars you drive, you may make it.' He turned out to be an unreliable oracle. Subsequently I broke my neck three times, but in an automobile only once, shamefully while I was standing still. I have made it so far. Almost anyway, and I still have some time left, I hope.

Eiben went gung-ho when I got an offer to be Géza von Bolváry's assistant on a film to be shot in Hungary, Austria and Germany. He had worked with the man. 'Now you will learn what you should do.' He added, 'Sometimes.' He had to do that, he was Eiben.

My first international assignment was not firmed up yet but we celebrated anyway, and from that celebration lunch I went direct to my interview with Géza von Bolváry.

The Gellért was a lovely old deluxe hotel on the Buda side of Budapest. My appointment was at three. It was quarter to four, I consumed my third espresso in the lobby. I was glad he was late. In the silence before the storm, every head turned toward the entrance as the doors burst open. A bull of a man with dark, shoe-button eyes rode through it. He was swinging his riding crop against a pair of boots with mirror-like polish. He wore tweeds and an incongruous blue beret. Those who weren't running with him were standing at attention. The grand elevator took off with him and half of his entourage, the other half scurried up the stairs.

Reflecting, I believe de Mille's boots and crop were only thrift-store imitations compared to Bolváry's.

The lobby returned to its mid-afternoon slumber. For variety's sake I ordered a capuccino. I had barely taken my first sip when a bell-boy came and asked me to follow him up to Herr von Bolváry's suite. He stopped me from paying my bill. He explained he had strict orders, direct from the 'Master', to take care of everything if I had a bill.

When I walked in, Bolváry said 'thank you' to his retine. They disappeared, melted into the brocade-covered walls. No introductions.

---

4 Géza von Bolváry (1898–1961) was a rebel. He directed light, flossy, big-budget films which had no reference to the political climate of the time. Géza von Cziffra was from the same school as Pascal and Bolváry but their audacity overshadowed him.

'Sit down.' He pulled out a slim, gold cigarette case. I reached for the lighter on his desk. He stopped, suspended animation in mid-air, scrutinized me, then took away the lighter, flipped open the cigarette case again and offered it to me, all in silence.

'No, thank you. I don't smoke.'

'Good, I don't like it.' He snapped the case shut and lit his cigarette. He smoked in silence, turned away to look at the magnificent view of the river, the bridges, the Corso on the Pest side of Budapest.

Abruptly he turned back. 'I understand you have been in Vienna.'

'Yes, sir ... Oh, Vienna ...' I just could not continue the Eiben-prescribed dialogue. A long silence followed. He was watching me.

'Let's get this straight, I don't want anybody to set fire to my sets.'

I stepped into an elevator shaft and there was no elevator there. I was falling down, down, down. How could he, where did he get this information from. I blurted out the first thing that came to mind. 'No sir, I promise I won't.'

'You're fired . . .'

I died, this plume of an opportunity went off in goddamned Herr Vidor's smoke.

He repeated with emphasis, 'You are fired,' then continued, 'if you ever mention the word "schedule" to me. Understand it?'

'Yess-ssir! I never heard that dirty word.'

'Good. Now, did you do it?'

Better be real straight with this man. 'No. I didn't, unfortunately.'

'Too bad. I don't like that son-of-a-bitch either. We'll be shooting in Vienna, we'll have some fun with him.'

The fun started earlier. It started when I met Eiben as agreed at Schraettner. It became clear where Bolváry had got his information about my Viennese fire connection. He was sitting there with Eiben, in an animated conversation with two stunning ladies seated at another table not too far from them.

Bolváry hadn't lost the Hungarian Huszár officer's mandatory approach to life, he loved to play around. In spite of the fact it spelled a very special danger to him. He was married to a very inflammable lady, once a star in her own right, somewhat older then he was. She had little or no inhibition at all about creating mayhem anywhere, any time and always at the most inopportune moments, à la Maria Korda. Here was this bull of a man, who wouldn't hesitate to step in front of a loaded freight train to stop it, and he was petrified of his wife. His dates always had to sit at separate tables. Paparazzi were not an invention of the Via Veneto.

This time, instead of a 125 cc belt-driven Excelsior motor cycle, I drove a 1,500 cc BMW roadster to Vienna, and instead of the student home it was the Hotel Schönbrunn.

Slim Zsuzsi was a fat Viennese hausfrau, running the Heurige, married to Hans, and the mother of a set of twins, awaiting the next arrival, to be delivered by Dr Erdös.

I arrived just in time to be the godfather of Dr and Mrs Erdös's first-born, named after me.

The only blemish of the assignment was Lillian. She had disappeared. She had been working and staying at the Heurige, then one day she just vanished. Erdös checked with the police, with every morgue in the country, no sign, until I stumbled on a clue. In all places, in the cemetery.

I wanted to place a headstone on Stephen's grave – ridiculous as it may sound, a marble ball, 'this big' and Red, and Yellow, Green, and yes, Blue, and 'this big'. The caretaker's office of the cemetery checked the files and advised me there was no such grave as Stephen de Toth listed in the cemetery. That's all, goodbye. They closed the files and the door in my face.

When Eiben and Bolváry found out what had happened in the cemetery, unbeknown to me they went off and hired a private investigator to clear up the mystery. They couldn't solve the mystery, but came up at least with the clarification why the caretaker's office wanted to get rid of me so quickly.

One of the gravediggers admitted he dug up a child's grave illegally because he felt sorry for the lady who had to leave the country and wanted to take the body of her little child with her. The description of the lady fitted Lillian. The gravedigger did not remember the exact date, but it approximately dovetailed with the date Lillian was last seen in the Heurige. Without a trace, Lillian and Stephen had vanished. Dead end.

Vienna surprised me with something bitter again. To eradicate some of the bitterness Bolváry sent me to see Herr Vidor to inquire about his conditions and the prevailing prices. A typical Bolváry gesture, as I left his office he called after me, 'I'll bail you out, don't worry.'

As I was driven through the studio gate in Bolvary's Horche the two guards hopped to an acceptable attention, then dove for the phone. At the office building Herr Vidor was waiting outside and rushed to open the car door, obviously waiting for Bolváry to emerge from his car.

He was watching me over his shoulder as he politely, half a step ahead, led the way down the long corridor; he hadn't put two and two together yet. All the office doors leading off the corridor were shut. The entrance door to his office was now sparkling clean. In the outer office the lady of the bicycle with the white gloves was not present, one of the other ladies sat at her old desk. No knitting needles or racing forms were in sight. When we entered both ladies stood up to greet Herr von Bolváry; surprised, they lowered themselves slowly. So did Herr Vidor, shrinking lower and lower in his throne behind his enormous ugly desk. The furrows on his brow got deeper and deeper, his beady eyes had become two slits as he concentrated on watching me. I could hear his thoughts, where did I meet him before, where did we meet. I wanted to serve an ace for the set, take the play away from him.

'I have to compliment you, Herr Vidor.'

He slightly eased, he was vain as most pompous little people are. He almost smiled as he uttered an anticipatory 'Yeeees?'

'You are absolutely brilliant . . .' Now he smiled knowingly, he knew it, and started to relax . . . 'You know Hungarian is one of the most difficult languages and you didn't speak a word of Hungarian not too long ago, and now you speak it with such perfection. Congratulations, Herr Vidor.'

Like a guppy out of water he kept opening and closing his mouth, the penny had dropped. Let's be generous, pour some salt on the wound, I took my time, looked around.

'It seems to me you didn't like the way I had rearranged your furniture, Herr Vidor, well, obviously we have different tastes.'

Herr Vidor just sat, mummified. I closed his door behind me, stopped in the outer office, asked for and received the address of the lady of the bicycle with the white gloves and walked down the long corridor slowly. It seemed much shorter now. Despicable as it is, revenge can be very sweet.

Bolváry took the address of the lady with the white gloves from me, handed it to his secretary, 'Offer her a job, from tomorrow on.' That was pure Bolváry again.

I am sure Tennessee Williams must have been around and got the title for *Cat On The Hot Tin Roof*, watching Herr Vidor when I met him next time in Bolváry's presence.

Wounds either heal or will be infected with gangrene. The gangrenous part of you sometimes can be amputated and thrown away, you may survive. However a part of you always will be missing. If your wound heals leaving little or no scar, you will forge ahead healthy. On the other hand, if the scar you were left with is ugly and hurts, you may be cursed with self-pity, which is the half-death of impotency.

Lillian and Stephen never completely disappeared in the night of the past. Red, and Yellow, Green, and yes, Blue and 'this big,' haunted me. But after I shed the paralyzing dry rot of the 'if's' – the 'if-I-dids' and 'if-I-did-nots' – they turned into warm memories of a short passage. Thanks to Bolváry and Eiben and luck I forged ahead. And learned a great deal.

Bolváry was a director, as the word goes. With saber drawn, on horseback, he charged through hell and high water. The truth is, sometimes he created both so he could charge through them. Strangely, most of his films were on the light side.

I never worked on a picture I was happy to see end. This one was just about coming to it. I realized there was an additional hand on the tiller of my life, Bolváry's.

'No! No way. Not-Ber-lin!'

I learned long ago if you want information listen. I did. Eiben didn't. He had his own ideas. 'Why not?'

'Because it is dead.'

'But what about . . .'

'But what about what? I grant you from the outside it still glistens. Hatred always had lots of sparks. Germany, Berlin is dead from the inside. It's got to fizzle out like every firework fizzles out in the end. The smart ones have already left. Murnau long ago, Fritz Lang shot Molnár's *Liliom*[5] in France then went off to America. Pabst, Pommer, Dietrich, Stroheim, oh a whole bunch of them went to Hollywood. The next step for him ' – pointing at me – 'is Hollywood. I wish I could speak English.'

'He is not ready, the step is still too big for him. I think London. Korda.'

5 *Liliom* (1909) is the most popular of Molnár's plays. It was first filmed in the United States in 1921 as *A Trip to Paradise*. A 1930 version was directed by Frank Borzage with Charles Farrell in the title role. Fritz Lang directed a French version in Paris in 1934. The play was also the basis for the Broadway musical *Carousel*, filmed in 1956.

'I don't like him.'

Eiben was getting red under the collar. 'Excuse meee! I was not talking about you, I happened to be talking about him.'

A wise old war-horse, Bolváry smiled. 'You're excused. If it's England, why not Gaby Pascal?'

'I like him, but I don't trust him.'

'If I don't trust somebody, I'd rather not trust Gaby Pascal than Korda. Why don't you trust Pascal?'

'He is too up-and-down for me. One minute he is so low he couldn't touch a frog's ass standing on tip-toes on a fireman's ladder, the next he is out of sight above the clouds.'

'All right, but it's straight. Korda's way of putting pictures together reminds me of a photograph I saw once, the tracks of a sidewinder in the sand.'

Two stubborn men, bascially very similar, kept on arguing what would be the best 'next step' for me, Korda or Pascal. Both hustlers, Pascal more audacious, Korda more devious.

There is a historically proven talent of Hungarians of which Alex Korda was the most prominent standard bearer. A Hungarian may let you go through a revolving door first, but he will come out ahead of you on the other side. Pascal's technique was to bust through the wall. Sometimes he succeeded. More often he stood tall with a bloody nose on the side he started from.

Korda's checkerboard career stretched across the Atlantic, from Budapest through Europe, to Hollywood, and to his Mecca: London. His first set of peacock feathers, the Commissarship of the Hungarian film industry, was quickly blown off with the collapse of the Communist government. He scooted from Hungary to escape the wrath of his 'angels', both marital and financial.

Austria was a barren land for the film industry. It was curious: all the plentiful native talent drifted from the necropolis of film-making, Vienna, to frantic, glossy Berlin, or dove into the boiling, happy turmoil of Budapest. Both turned out to be the jumping-off platform for them to Hollywood. Only the dynamo of Michael Curtiz could turn on the lights in Vienna for a very short while. Then he went off to Hollywood. There were no revolving doors in Vienna for Korda.

In the fifth largest city after New York, London, Paris and Tokyo, in Berlin Korda found no greener pastures. It was not his type of city. While

Admiral Horthy, Regent of Hungary, could ride his stallion to the toilet, Korda had great difficulty in fulfilling his old ambition to ride a Rolls Royce to the potty – in the land of Mercedes there were very few Rolls Royces and very few bathrooms. The super deluxe Adlon Hotel with its 400 beds had 250 baths. The posh Bristol Hotel with its 400 beds had only 230 baths. Both were on the impressive Unter den Linden, the 200–250-feet-wide Boulevard, lined with double rows of lime and chestnut trees, with the emblem of Berlin, the Brandenburger Tor, at its west end.

Berlin was a gay city, in more ways than one, a noisy, hustling and brash city without a past. Berlin was hardly noted in history when in Vienna St Stephen's Cathedral, a Gothic masterpiece, was being built and in 1365 the University of Vienna, one of the oldest seats of learning, was founded.

Berlin had something else to offer, what Vienna had lost in its self-pity bogged down in the memory of its glorious past. Behind the functional, sometimes drab façades of the German Bauhauses dwelled a vitality, a great determination to succeed because of or in spite of the disgraceful peace treaty of Versailles–Trianon. Berlin lived, burning the candle at both ends. Restaurants, cafés, wine restaurants, cabarets and theaters were packed. And to the dismay of the British they instituted the afternoon teas à la Berlin.

No tea was served, save the little that went well with and didn't spoil the rum. No cucumber sandwiches but tango, foxtrot, charleston, the Berlin of the afternoon tea. Thé-dansant. In the best hotels, cafés and some restaurants well-nourished hausfraus rubbed belly-buttons with younger ein-tansers or elderly spiessbürgers with schlanke mädels, or with each other, both sexes of all ages looking for business or adventure.

Who cared? There was an almost suicidal abandon in the air. But shame, an indelible shame on all who didn't hear the chords of military marches mixing louder and louder with the tangos, and turned blind eyes on the more and more prevalent glistening boots and sparkling epaulettes of the uniforms on the dance floors competing with the flashy neons above. Heil Hitler snuck up on a nation desperate to regain its former national pride stolen from them by Clemenceau.

The film industry was booming. The production deals were conceived in the high-class restaurants and cafés like Habel, with its historic wine room founded in 1779; the Krantzler and the Könige Victoria, with their tables on the side walk; in the Café Berlin in the Adlon Hotel, and, in the hub of it all, in the Kempinski on Kurfürstendamm.

None of them was as palatial as the Café New York or as the Café Japan in Budapest, but all humming, filled with dreams, plans and hot air. Just like in Budapest. And around at least sixty per cent of the tables Hungarian was the language.

Korda stayed away from these places, his ego could not take the Hungarian flak. To his dismay he was beginning to be known as Maria Korda's director. His angel had forgiven him and descended from the hell-hot heaven of the studio ceiling of Budapest to the Hotel Adlon and became his real angel. It was a noble gesture, so noble that Maria gave herself nobility – to the great dismay of the not-yet-Sir Alex – and started calling herself Maria de Korda. Noblesse oblige, somehow they got connected with an Austrian nobleman, Baron or Count Sascha somebody,[6] who was married to a tobacco heiress of considerable wealth. Sascha's advantages were, he loved to spend the money she had, loved race cars – loved them but could not drive them – loved women regardless of whether he could or could not have them and, most important, he was a film buff.

Maria lost the 'de' and became Corda again to emphasize her own identity. The inevitable had happened and Alex Korda and the Baron or Count Sascha embarked on a film production, *Seine Majestät das Bettelkind*. The film turned out to be a respectable critical and financial success. It had a minor hitch: Alex and his perennial collaborator Lajos Biró had forgotten to obtain the rights to the original from the author, Mark Twain. Alex's excuse, that he thought it was in the public domain, did not stick with the honorable nobleman and it led to the breakdown of their relationship.

With the 'talkies' taking over more and more of the screens, Maria became more and more of a burden. A short and disastrous Hollywood stay almost destroyed Korda. He was no match for the Hollywood biggies. Maria was now a millstone around his neck, so he decided to take advantage of the California divorce laws and unload her legally. Returning to Europe, he ended up in Paris.

The metropolis of art, Paris was a small gossip-filled village when it came to motion pictures and the theater. In spite of an illustrious start

6 Graf Alexander 'Sascha' Kolowrat-Krakowsky was one of the most prominent early Austrian film producers, founding Sascha Film GmbH circa 1910. The company continued in existence under one name or another until 1986.

with Marcel Pagnol's big hit play, *Marius*, with its original cast, Pierre Fresnay and Raimu, the film was a lukewarm hit; Alex was not received with the respect his talent and charm, he thought, should have earned him.

The French may be chauvinistic, but they bow to talent. They bowed to the art of his youngest brother, the half-starving Vincent. They accepted him with his fractured French. They did not succumb to Alex's charm. One could buy great food at Fouquet's or Maxim's, even on credit, but Alex Korda discovered in France one could not buy respect. However, he found the key to his success. He was not aware that with it he had destroyed his brother Vincent's promising future as a world-renowned painter.

Bob Kane, Paramount's head in Paris, was impressed with Korda and with the quality of *Marius* and offered him a job with Paramount, England. He accepted it and Sir Alexander Korda was born.

England was virgin territory. London was full of revolving doors and no Hungarians.

Korda was the greatest chameleon. One week he was directing a propaganda film in Budapest, with impassioned devotion for the Hapsburg Empire. Exactly a week later he was shooting Communist propaganda films for the new Hungarian government, with the same devotion, blazing hurrah and zeal. He had only one firm conviction, do what is best for Alex Korda. By the time he got off the train in London he was more British than the British. And it worked. He was an eccentric strange duck in eccentrics' paradise, England.

Eiben was selling Korda to Bolváry in a strange way. 'You have to admit he was a brilliant entrepreneur. OK, so he bamboozled one of the sharpest, most brilliant statesmen in history, Winston Churchill, to be his "consultant". It's class. Korda was going to make his story, *The Life of Marlborough*. So Korda paid Churchill for his services, that's not a bribe!' The Eiben steamroller went on. 'You have to concede, hats off for his genius.' Then Eiben put his trump card on the table. 'You have to admit he makes pictures, big international pictures, like *Henry VIII* and –'

Bolváry didn't let him finish, 'Yeah, but I liked the original *Henry VIII* he made in Berlin.'

'What are you talking about. He did what?' Eiben snapped back.

'*Seine Majestät das Bettelkind*, with the same writer, Biró, the basic story of Henry VIII, which by the way, they stole from Mark Twain. OK? Now, look at Pascal. He didn't steal the story from G. B. Shaw. No fancy footwork. He paid for it, he bought it with cash!'

Eiben wanted to speak, Bolváry waved him off. 'Don't interrupt. Yeah, it's true he paid only one pound for it, but it was his-last-pound for the rights of *Caesar and Cleopatra*. That's impressive, and that's not all. He told Shaw he had no money left for his return trip to London. Did you know Shaw was so impressed by Gabriel Pascal's honesty he paid for his return fare to London. Now! That-is-what-I-call-guts.'

Eiben, imitating the trumpet call of the Huszárs' saber charge, yelled 'Chaaaaarge!' This caused quite a commotion in the restaurant; we ignored the, to us, flattering remarks from the nearby tables, 'Hungarians.'

Camels are the dirtiest mammals on this earth. They carry all communicable diseases including syphilis. During the filming of G. B. Shaw's *Cleopatra* Pascal wanted one hundred of the beasts lined up in a straight line.

Everybody on the set knew that, if Pascal wanted something, it had to be done. Out of the one hundred camels, ninety-nine knew it and lined up absolutely straight – all except one. This camel was in the straight line all right until Pascal yelled 'Action,' then this one camel always stepped forward. The camel-drivers suggested taking the rebellious camel out of the line. Pascal was adamant. He wanted one hundred, one hundred camels in the shot, and in-a-straight-line. To the camel drivers' plea, 'Please, let us take it out, nobody will know,' Pascal's retort was, 'I would.' End of discussion.

Pascal was not known for his patience and, after a dozen or so takes, he lost it. He yelled 'Action.' True to form the one camel stepped forward. Pascal yelled, 'Keep it rolling.' With that he whacked the camel on its nose with his forever-present riding crop. The camel stepped back in line, the cameras were rolling, the shot was perfect, Pascal yelled 'Print it.'

Pascal was proud of himself, for him the shot was over. Not for the renegade camel. It broke away from the rest of the camels, caught up with Pascal and clamped his head in its large mouth. Camels could be killers, they could crush a human skull easily with their powerful jaws and very large teeth. Luckily Pascal was walking away so the camel didn't get a full bite on his skull, though it was with enough force to tear off his scalp from forehead to nape. Satisfied with its revenge, the camel retreated, leaving Pascal soaked in blood with his scalp dangling round his neck.

Unperturbed, Pascal kept on walking toward the coffee stand, where he was originally headed, followed by a trail of blood and the medics from first aid, deeply concerned about the serious consequences a disease-infected camel's bite could cause. They pleaded with him, 'Mr Pascal, please, let us take care of that wound, camel bites are known to be fatal.' One of the miracles of the desert – camels infected with gonorrhea and syphilis.

Pascal didn't even answer them until he stopped at the coffee stand, tasted the coffee, complained it was not strong enough, it was not hot enough. Only after being satisfied with the coffee, did he face the extremely worried medics. 'Don't you vorry about me. Vorry about the camel. The camel will die.'

The following morning the camel was found dead.

It took some time before the Pascal contra Korda issue resolved itself. By then I had another picture under my belt with Bolváry in Berlin and several with some other directors and so-called directors in Budapest. Both places were full of vibrant activity.

It was frightening looking back how the blissful glitz and glitter had blinded so many. And so many 'new people crawled out from under rocks,' as Eiben put it, 'who knew nothing, who had no right to make pictures.' The tragedy was that their right to make pictures was so shamefully wrong.

'I wish I could go with you.' Eiben dropped the bomb after a short four hours' luncheon at Schraettner.

'Where am I going?'

'To Korda . . . We are trying to plug you in.'

'Who are "we"?'

'I and the mother of that drunken jack rabbit you made an alcoholic out of. And Bolváry agreed too.'

Bolváry agreed it was a good idea this time for me to go to London, but refused to write to Korda. So the circle had closed.

They wanted Molnár to write, he refused. Molnár didn't like Korda.

Again Lóránt Basch oiled the wheels. 'If you don't like Korda,' he told Molnár, 'then write that letter of introduction.' I was with them at the table. Dr Basch pointed at me, 'You thought he was a pain in the ass. So write that letter, give Korda a present.'

Typical Molnár, he wrote the letter. Right then at the table, by hand. It was such a complimentary letter I wanted to hire myself right then and there.

7 It's Not Enough to be Hungarian

Undercurrents and riptides of discontent were cracking the foundations of society from below and the waning emotions of human decency from above. Europe was sitting down to the happy last supper of the doomed.

The café houses beneath their noisy façades degenerated into the hush-hush bourses of the black markets. It was impossible, well, almost impossible to take currency or jewelry in or out of countries. Rare stamps were the easiest to hide and transport. 'Rare stamp factories' sprang up all over. Illegal, shady deals were the norm of the day.

Molnár's letter hit the target and I had to hit the black market for English pounds, or US dollars. Luckily, because of his world-wide royalties, Molnár had more money elsewhere than he had in Budapest and he lived high on the hog, always in need of the Hungarian Pengö. With one hand he did not count the change, with the other he was the stingiest human alive. He demanded and I gave him better exchange rates than the available black market had to offer. With that, plus additional exchanges through the visiting stars' and tourists' 'contribution' to my future, I scrounged enough foreign currency to keep me in London, if I skinned the pennies, for three weeks.

No sky can be more beautiful than a blue British sky, and no sky can be filled more with dirty, continuously unloading pigeons than the sky over London, competing with the stench-saturated skies above Venice.

I was booked into the Cumberland Hotel at Marble Arch. Not a deluxe hotel but a solid first-class establishment, frequented by a better class of British gentry. It was Sunday, a beautiful day. The pigeons behaved. Budding artists hung their hopes on the iron fence around the Park. Hyde Park Corner was in full swing.

It was awesome to experience for the first time the constructive and destructive power of free speech. To see the colorful toy soldiers on their magnificent steeds. After the drab panzers and thundering goosesteps of

Berlin it was an operetta awakening, a beautiful promise of hope for a good tomorrow.

The 'good tomorrow', Monday, had started with a large British breakfast at the hotel. It was followed by an arduous train journey to the promised land of the moment, Denham. Then, an odyssey from the station to the kingdom of not-yet-Sir Alexander Korda.

After the Herr Vidor experience I had no preconceived idea of what to expect. I threw away the Korda coin, in mint condition on one side, blemished on the other. The red carpet was out, I floated above it directly into Korda's elegant office. Before I was able to sit down he asked me in excellent Hungarian how was my trip, what would I 'prefer', tea or coffee?

'Thank you, coffee would be fine, black, no sugar.' The lady who led me in vanished into thin air. And before I leaned back in the chair she reappeared and set up a dainty table within my easy reach, topped with a Royal Doulton cup and saucer and a complete antique silver coffee set befitting any museum. I was embarrassed. I wished I had not mentioned 'black, no sugar'. Korda had an identical set-up on his desk. Before the lady vanished again, Korda asked her not to put any calls through.

I had to be careful not to bump my head on the ceiling, I was floating so high. I was never better received. Never had a more interesting, a more pleasant meeting in my life before or after. How unfair people can be, jealousy I thought. Korda was considerate, genuinely interested in me. Asked about my background, my family. He loved the General Szirmay incident. He was very impressed with Molnár's recommendation. I felt close to him. I stood naked in front of him. I told him about my plans, my dreams for the future.

'By the way,' he asked quite offhand, 'where are you staying?'

'The Cumberland Hotel.'

Somebody turned the lights out. Korda went black, blank and cold. I was facing a black icicle. I was not in the room anymore. He pushed a button on his desk, 'Mrs Fisher,' – I think – 'please put the calls through.' He started to talk on the phone. I was not ignored, I simply did not exist anymore. He didn't say goodbye or good riddance when I excused myself and backed out of the room. I was deflated.

I rattled more than the square-wheeled train on which I was travelling back to London. I was racking my brain, what did I do, where did I go wrong?

'You all right, guv?' asked the man across from me on the second-class bench, with whom I was touching knees out of necessity all through the longest journey of my life. A lady next to him took off her glasses, wiped them thoughtfully with her thumb, put them back on with great care as she stared at me. The rest of the people in the crowded compartment ignored me. I must have spoken out loud in my self-inquisition in search for the 'why'.

I tried to smile at them, uttered a 'Thanks, I'm fine.'

The man shook his head, licked the point of his pencil and went back to his racing form. The lady kept staring at me. I couldn't take it, got up and went to the toilet. Lucky I didn't have to go, there were five people ahead of me. Then it hit me. I found the 'why'. The man from behind tapped me. It was my turn. I left the queue.

I squeezed back into the compartment. The man opposite me nudged the lady next to him with his elbow, exhibited all of his three teeth with a mischievous grin and whispered to her, 'I told you, didn't I?' She bashfully covered her mouth to hide her snicker. He turned to me, 'You had to go, didn't you, laddy,' and went back to his racing form.

Back in the hotel I took a scalding hot, then a cold shower to organize my still whirling thoughts, made my decision and checked out of the hotel.

They looked at me disdainfully at the reception desk in Claridges when I arrived schlepping my own two heavy cowhide suitcases to save money. They had no rooms available at all, until, very offended, I said, 'But Mr Korda was sure you could put me up without any reservation.'

After a few 'hurrrumps', some lengthy whispered conversation behind the desk and stuttered apologies I could hardly understand – they were sooo-British – a hundred-year-old bellboy dragged my luggage off – just like the 'Fészek' in Budapest I thought – and I was escorted to my suite. One of the escorts elegantly opened the door, stepped aside. The other asked me, 'Would that be satisfactory, sir?'

I stood there for a while before answering, not because I was surveying the palatial suite, but to get my breath back, and figured out instead of three weeks in London I had three days, maximum. 'Alia jucta est.'

I nodded, the escorts were visibly relieved, 'We were hoping it would be satisfactory, sir.' On their way out they wished me a 'pleasant stay', and 'If you need something –' I had to sandwich in '– just whistle,' which they couldn't understand. They left and softly closed the ornate door.

I just missed an elevator in the morning. I had to wait for the next one. It finally arrived, the door opened and there he was, Alexander Korda. Lady Luck was with me again. Be on the right spot at the right time, a travesty of justice, but it swings more weight than aptitude or talent.

The lightning of an angry Zeus struck me. Korda was spitting out his words sotto voce, in Hungarian. 'What-are-you-doing-here?' He did not wait for an answer. 'This is my home, we made no appointment, get out!'

He was a hissing snake, striking and striking again. My only hope was that he would stop his tirade before we reached the ground floor where, in the lobby, he would tell them to throw me out. Just as the elevator was coming to a stop Korda had to take a breath and I could interject edgeways, 'I am sorry, sir. I live here.'

The elevator stopped, he stopped spitting fire, the wonderful, benevolent Alexander Korda stepped out of the elevator. Put his hand on my shoulder, 'But I understood you were at the . . .' he screwed up his nose as if he had stepped into dog's excrement on the sidewalk . . . 'Cumberland.'

'Sorry, sir, for the misunderstanding, but my English, you know it is . . .'

He cut me off, 'What are your plans?'

'My first trip to England, I . . .'

'You will love it.'

'. . . I thought I would go to the British Muse . . .'

'Some other time. My brother loves museums, he will take you. We are going now to the studio.'

The seat of the Rolls was more comfortable than the second-class hard seat of the square-wheeled train. He handed me newspapers, he even asked me if the cigar smoke bothered me. I missed my cue, I should have said yes.

A strange, not an ordinary, but a special kind of dignified slime was engulfing me. I did not like it. He talked as if he wanted to impress me. Me? It was ridiculous. What was his reason? And as I listened I realized Alexander Korda was a lonely flagpole sitter. He could not live without adoration. I gave it to him. I felt like a fink.

When we walked through his outer-outer office his freeloading leeches, a rare breed of prideless Hungarians, slapped ingratiating smiles on their faces, got to their feet and kept bowing to him like those drinking birds over the rim of a glass of water. Their high and mighty bread-and-butter-giver failed to notice their accolade.

By the time we sat down in his office the coffee was set up. Before I was able to take my first sip a side door opened, a dishevelled man came through. Unannounced. He did not take off his shapeless hat, his double-breasted grey suit was buttoned up askew, a long stick of ashes was dangling from his lower lip. An obvious intruder in these posh surroundings. The lowest buttonhole on one side was hooked up on to the top button on the opposite. This caused the wide lapel to bulge out. Obviously a gun was hidden there.

With an intercollegiate boxing championship behind me and some experience in judo, this was to be the moment of my glory. Now I would impress Korda, he would have to be grateful. It flashed through my mind.

'Mit akarsz, Lacikám? (What do you want, Lacikám?)' said the intruder in Hungarian. He didn't stand to attention or bow like the flunkies outside, he didn't take the stick of ashes off his lips either as he spoke.

Korda didn't answer him. He told me, 'Wait outside.' No 'please' or at least 'would you'. His imperial impoliteness didn't register until later, I was concentrating on the intruder. I had seen him somewhere. No. He couldn't be the painter from Paris. Here? How could he be? No-no. But the intruder was scrutinizing me too. When I was about half-way through the door he asked Korda, 'Who is he?'

I hesitated, wanting to find out who I was, but I couldn't linger on the threshold and all I heard was, 'Molnár asked me to . . .' before the mirror-shiny mahogany door shut behind me. Damn those thick walls and heavy doors, I couldn't hear a thing, no matter how I strained my ears.

A lady's voice interrupted my concentration, Mrs Fisher, speaking very slowly, as if speaking to a child, 'Please, do not stand there. There is a chair next to you. Sit down.' She was holding a tray with a steaming cup of coffee on it. To impress her that my English was very good, I said 'Thanks,' and gave extra attention to pronounce the 'th' correctly. She noticed, smiled. 'Your English is very good . . . considering you are Hungarian and a recent arrival.' I complimented her on the coffee. She parried the compliment, saying Mr Korda was responsible for the coffee. She had never heard of it before she came to work for Mister Korda, it was from Kenya.

It had to be different if Korda selected it. He would not have ordinary Colombian or Jamaican coffee. It had to come from the elysium on earth. It is too bad tourists now outnumber wildlife, but in spite of that the coffee from Kenya is still good.

She must have read my thoughts. She gave me a second cup of coffee, in a fresh cup, but of course! She said with a smile, 'Yeeees, Mr Korda is a perfectibilian.' I liked her. It was too bad I saw her so very infrequently. Zoltán and Vincent kept me away from their brother. I still haven't figured out why. To save him from me or save me from him? We didn't like each other very much. 'You puzzle him,' said Zoli one day. 'You didn't fit the niche where he wanted to put you.'

The rumpled man with his whimsical, crooked smile came out of the office, hands outstretched, the stick of ashes still glued to his lip. 'This is a surprise!'

'You can say that again.'

'Alex wants to see you now, after that we'll go to have lunch. Too bad Zoli is tied up, but we'll see him for dinner.'

In the office I faced a different Korda. He didn't ask me to sit down. I had the feeling he didn't even notice I had come into his mausoleum-cum-museum office. I stood in silence in his impersonal, antiseptic void. I was not important. His cigar was. With great care and concentration he rolled it between his bony fingers, licked it, and through the blue-grey smoke came the voice, 'You didn't know in Paris that Vincent was my brother?'

'No.'

'He didn't tell you I was his brother?'

'No, why would he, all I knew was what everybody else knew, he was a great artist who in time would be in the circle of immortal painters.' There was smoke-filled silence in the room. I added as an afterthought, 'Isn't that enough to know about somebody whom you liked anyway?'

'Hmmm,' was his immediate retort. After two puffs he continued, 'I understand you paint.'

'I did.' After his 'Hmmm,' I added, 'I gave it up.'

His face became visible through the cigar smoke. I thought I was facing Dr Caligari. Actually he was not a bad-looking man, but with those stupid round glasses he looked like Dr Caligari to me and I didn't like him. He was looking at me with two drill-like eyes as he asked, 'Why?'

'Because people didn't like it.' For him I vanished again, I felt. He was interested only in his cigar. No. He was playing cat and mouse. 'Do you care what people think about you?'

To hell with him. I must have made a mistake again somewhere but I didn't know where, or what. Might as well fizzle out as a hero. I moved over to one of the comfortable chairs opposite him and sat down defiantly as I blurted out, 'Don't you?'

Was it a small smile that had crossed his face or was it my hopeful imagination? Then he looked at me with a glint. A glint that later on I learned to know as the Korda glint. All three brothers had that glint. Vincent's was more mischievous, Zoli's was more noticeable, but Zoli overdid everything.

I sat, sat opposite him as if I had a thousand pounds of lead in my ass. But at least he was looking at me now. It made me feel better. No more shadow-boxing, I was not looking at a phantom through cigar smoke and it became clear that sadistic-son-of-a-bitch sitting across the desk, hanging onto his big cigar, wanted me to squirm. No way! I thought.

Then came his next shot. Bullseye. 'I understand you wrote a play.'

He got me off balance. Defensively defiant, I spoke louder than necessary. Bad poker playing, I showed him my cards. 'It was only a one-act play and it didn't even have one performance. The idiots took it off after the dress rehearsal and I didn't give a shit, and I don't give a shit because I know I will do better. OK?'

Instead of covering, I childishly uncovered my hurt. And of course Korda knew it. He leaned back in his obviously supremely comfortable throne. I followed his glance up towards a magnificent ceiling which was in the process of being defiled by the cigar smoke. Silence. Then, 'Do you have something else?' I didn't, so I said I was working on a couple of things. 'Hmmm, things,' he said, then leaned forward and looked at me straight, really looked at me for the first time and asked, 'What can I do for you?'

It was a big mouthful of a question. He dumped big buckets of icecubes on me while I was sitting naked on the top of North Pole. He himself was moulded of ice, accentuating every syllable of his next question. 'What do you want from me?'

'Well,' I started, but stopped. Turmoil whirled through my head, scrambled my brain. Really, what did I want? I would not tell him how much I wanted to meet him, an idol of so many. How much I was hoping he could perform a miracle, how much I would have liked a job

– and suddenly it hit me, what kind of a job? No, I had had enough. I shrugged.

He was a good fencer, he saw the opening and he thrust again. 'What do you want me to do for you, now?' I didn't answer, he drilled on. 'Do you need any money?' I didn't even stutter an answer. He continued, 'How much do you want? . . . How much do you have?'

I got up. 'I don't want money, I don't want your money. I don't want alms. I was hoping to meet someone who would open the door for me. I want to learn this business and I will learn it, and I will be successful. Thank you for your time, sir, if you ever noticed I was in this room with you.'

I was walking toward the door when he stopped me. 'Hold it.' I turned.

Korda got up and walked around his desk, when he reached me he put a hand on my shoulder as he said, 'It's not enough to be Hungarian, you have to have talent.'

'I saw the sign on your desk, sir. How do you know if I have . . .'

'Ssssh. Talent alone is not enough, you must have luck. Luck and talent, in this order. But that's still not enough if you have no patience. You will find out patience plays a more important role in success than talent.'

It was ludicrous for Korda to talk about patience. He was known to be most impatient. But in all fairness he was impatient with himself too. And this impatience certainly hindered whatever talent he had for directing.

I reached for the doorknob, 'Thank you, sir, for your time.'

He stopped me again. 'Patience, that will be your downfall. Now, I don't want you in Claridges – maybe the Dorchester, yes, the Dorchester would do – or – or – the Savoy. No! The Connaught! Yes! that's it. It is a lovely little hotel, small suites but excellent food, a very good address. That's where you have to move.'

'Don't listen to Alex. If you like Claridges you just stay there.'

'Stay there?' I told Vincent my move from the Cumberland to Claridges, exactly as it happened.

Vincent dropped his fork, hit the table and his whimsical smile widened. 'Zoli will love that. And you will love Zoli. Alex thought you two will get along very well or will kill each other. Hopefully the latter, he wished.'

During luncheon one of Vincent's assistants suggested I should move in to the Mount Royal. He explained it was not far from the Cumberland, behind Oxford Street, and it was on his way to the studio and he could give me a lift both ways. Vincent immediately approved the idea, explaining he would not be able to give me a car allowance as a special effects assistant from the special effects budget.

I was startled, 'I don't know a thing about special effects, at home we –'

Vincent cut me off, which was unheard of. Vincent never cut off anybody. 'You were telling me you wanted to learn, so learn.'

And that I did, I was working with the crème de la crème of film sorcerers of the period. Until Zoli drafted me into the cutting room with him.

The more time I spent with Zoli – and I enjoyed every hectic minute of it all through the years – the more I became convinced that he was unable to, or did not want to learn how to pull a punch. Like Michael Curtiz only knew how to drive a car straight, Zoltán Korda only knew how to live on the straight line. The first time I laid an eye on him, he busted straight through my qualms about Alex.

'He doesn't like you, he doesn't dislike you. He doesn't know where to put you. You were the first "drift-in" Hungarian who refused to take money from him. That bugged him. He likes to buy people to exercise his power over them. You refused him that chance. He was aware of your switch to Claridges, that impressed him. It was something he would have done himself. That disturbed him. He thought you were conceited and obnoxious. Do you want to hear any more of his compliments about you?'

I had heard enough compliments, I asked Zoli to stop or he would make me more conceited. But he made me understand why he and Vincent kept me in jobs out of Alex's sphere. Besides far-away second units, the safest place in town to keep me out of harm's way was the cutting room. Alex hated the slow tedious evolution that editing involved, he was totally benighted about the 'lowbrow efforts' involved in post-production. Except music. He was all there. He was extremely well-read and, in spite of his deep-rooted prejudices, a sharp critic. I never saw him once, save publicity set-ups, in a cutting room.

One fault, one, Alex never possessed. He was no dope. He was extremely sensitive and frighteningly intuitive. He adored his two brothers, Zoltán and his younger brother, Vincent. The tragedy was he loved himself more.

When Korda spoke to people he didn't see them. He saw himself next to them in a mirror. He created an image of himself, which sometimes crystallized, the crystals cracked and he re-glued them. If you watched carefully you could notice the cracks. I did. And that created the chasm between us.

He was always alone, engulfed in the bravado of fear. He hid from you and he hid from himself. Except once, many years later, and only for one fleeting moment he exposed himself to me. One, only one other man I know of had the same insight of Alex Korda – Tom Pryor, the film critic of the *New York Times*. Both our experiences involved Merle Oberon.

Korda was loyal, without any discrimination, as long as you sang the same tune he did. Otherwise he was unforgiving. He was the greatest puppeteer, and he could manipulate people brilliantly. This was probably his only true joy in life. He was a snakecharmer with as much affection for the charmed as a snakecharmer has for his snakes. He was an entrepreneur supreme, a gracious host. A brilliant conversationalist. But if he didn't like you or you were in his way, on the pavement writhing with your guts hanging out, he could step on your guts as easy as walk around you, then accuse you of dirtying his shoes. He was only human. I never accused Alex of being a saint. I was too religious for that blasphemy.

Alex Korda was a Sphinx.

Vincent was a stoic, with the patience of Job.

Zoltán was an open book. An open book with very large print on its pages, all in black and white. For him the black was black, the white was whiter than white. There was a fathomless void in between, which you could have been easily pushed into if you didn't pick one or the other. It sounds almost like a contradiction, but he was open-minded; he was open-minded, despite his prejudices. He didn't care if you were on the other side. He loved to disagree. He demanded you took a side. A positive stand, so he could face the challenge of convincing you that you were wrong. The method of his conviction was short, to the point, batting your head against the wall.

He was a devout hypochrondriac, but his hypochondria was based on bad and real 'lived through' experiences – from tuberculosis to venereal disease in the service, he had had everything. I knew when he felt good because he complained loudly. When he didn't, I was concerned. He always carried in his pockets his bugyli bicskát, short stubs of pencils, pieces of paper, his tobacco, his pipes, his vitamin pills, and other various knapsacks full of surprises.

He was a broad-shouldered, very handsome man, with a good head of steel-grey hair, an impressive forehead. He had burning eyes. They were burning either from fever or from his fanaticism.

He was a much more talented picture-maker than he was given credit for in this industry, where fame is bought through publicity, which he shied away from.

Zoltán Korda had a great inferiority complex, which is easy to understand of one who was living in the shadow of Alexander Korda. Zoli hid it with his outspoken roughness, his unwavering, uncompromising, often stubborn attitude toward everything. He nurtured a lot of enemies, one of the worst was himself. He had a big, soft heart. He loved and was dedicated to his family. I wonder if they ever really knew how much he loved them, how much they meant to him. He was a friend you had to be careful of, because he would needlessly kill himself for you. Others too. How many friends have you had in your lifetime like Zoltán Korda?

Vincent was the youngest of the three, the stoic. He was aware Alex had set him on the wrong track, but he never complained, he blamed himself and suffered in silence. A martyr with a wry sense of humor. A Jewish saint; hands down, the world's most careless dresser. But if you knew him, if you talked to him, after a few minutes you discovered the real values the rumpled clothes couldn't hide.

He wore no braces, no belt. His trousers were always slipping down and when the fringes on the bottom of his pants grew longer than a quarter-inch to a half-inch, he carefully cut them off, but ultimately he was forced to buy a pair of new trousers.

On this particular occasion we were looking for locations and, clambering over barbed wire, he tore the seat of his pants. He felt the slit, which was about a foot and a half to two feet long, and said 'It's not bad, wardrobe will fix it.' While traipsing around the countryside, it took me most of the day to convince him, with the help of some bramble bushes, that it would be better, maybe, if he bought a new pair of trousers. After all, summer was yet far away and he didn't need air-conditioning there anyway.

Grumbling, squinting and smiling, on our way back to the studio we went to a shop on Hollywood Boulevard. Vincent asked for grey flannel trousers and bought the first he put on. The salesman, holding up Vincent's old trousers gingerly with two fingers, asked if he should dispose of them. Offended, Vincent grumbled, 'Oh, no, I will put them on', which he did. He wouldn't let them wrap the new pair of pants, he gathered them up and slung them under his arm.

On our way out of the store I said offhand he should have bought a sweater, since he had been complaining all day how cold it was out in the countryside and we'd be leaving very early in the morning, which he hated. He stopped, thought for a while, squinted again, then grinned, nodded.

He picked out a very nice, grey, crew-neck sweater, took off his jacket, then came the problem. He had forgotten to take off his ever-present hat, which finally he did. He had a good head of hair, auburn red with some strands of silver in it. To everybody's horror he started to put on the lovely sweater he had picked, ignoring the cigarette ashes stuck to his lower lip. The salesman screwed his eyes shut, I crossed my fingers. Vincent, oblivious of the consternation he had caused, emerged on the other side of the crew-neck with the stick of ashes stuck to his lower lip as intact as it was before he started the manoeuvre.

The only time I saw Vincent without the cigarette butt or the ashes glued to his lip was when he was eating. Vincent, without any sign of inconvenience, could enjoy a cup of coffee without ever removing it. This French imprint left him later in his life when, on rare occasions, he sported a pipe.

The afternoon sun was warm and bright. Vincent refused to take the sweater off. 'It was a good idea,' he told me, and proceeded to put on his double-breasted grey jacket, buttoning it, of course, in the wrong way. All through this expedition he did not glance once in a mirror.

We must have been a sight, even on Hollywood Boulevard, marching out of the store with Vincent carrying the rumpled-up pair of new pants, with one pants leg dangling loose under his arm, with the slit on the seat of his pants revealing his colorful underwear – it was grey too, but with big red ants painted all over.

All this was not an act. That was Vincent Korda and everybody loved Vincent.

All three Kordas were alike only in their striving for perfection. But they attacked it from totally different angles. Vincent was searching for it from his sensitive depth. Zoltán from the solid base of his sincere, deep convictions and ideology. Sir Alexander from the peaks of his entrepreneurial nebulae, interspersing facts and fiction as it suited the gloss of his intellectual spasms. He was a perfect chameleon, so much so that occasionally he himself was not sure which suit of armor he was wearing. Alex Korda was a different person for everybody who knew him, and different on every occasion. His confusion and loneliness arose from the fact that he himself was not sure any more who he was and what he really stood for. His only sure aim was to impress. Sometimes at all cost.

Another privilege I had was working with David O. Selznick. If an alchemist with a magic potion could mix all the three Kordas together with their assets and shortcomings, the product would be a Selznick. Their approach to picture-making was poles apart, but both were trying to achieve the same goal, quality. Korda with a razor-sharp rapier, Selznick with a bulldozer. But Selznick could carve an ivory miniature with it. Alex did not have a swagger stick, David O. had an extra large caveman's shillelagh. Korda skirted around, wriggled through problems, difficulties. Selznick blasted through them. Both were quality hounds, both of them had good taste, both thought big. Selznick was strong, Korda was audacious. The big difference was, Korda was devious, but collapsed inside under stress. Selznick was bold, thriving on stress. He never showed it and he was well aware of his shortcomings. In distress Korda had a neurotic fit, Selznick turned into a raging bull.

He was a legend. He liked my foreign films and loved *None Shall Escape*, a film I made for Harry Cohn. I succumbed to the legend, and he lured me away from Columbia. It was against the better judgement of my agent, the dean of all agents of the period, a rare gentleman, Bert Allenberg. 'He was changing directors like mothers change the diapers of their babies. You will get lost. If you go with him we are through. I am representing you, not Selznick.'

He picked up the phone and I was sure Selznick heard him in Culver City from Beverly Drive and Wilshire Boulevard without the help of Alexander Graham Bell. 'David, don't do this to the man, you are ruining his career . . . I don't care how much you pay . . . yes, I do represent him . . . but not any more if he goes with you . . . send the checks directly to him . . . Why, because I am not handling dead clients, that's why . . . You are going to kill him, David, don't do it . . . Yes he is here . . . I'll tell him.

'Bye.' He hung up. We sat in silence for a while. 'Tomorrow at eleven, he wants to meet you.'

I liked and respected Bert Allenberg very much. I had never met Selznick, his offer came through Allenberg's office. I would have never known about it if Allenberg hadn't told me. 'Why did you tell me about Selznick's offer if you didn't want me to – '

He interrupted me, got up and walked me to the door. 'I guess you don't know me well enough otherwise you would have spared me that question.' We stopped at the door, 'I advise my clients, I hope they follow it . . . At eleven tomorrow, it is your decision. It will take you years, if ever, to find out if you made the right or wrong decision. Good luck.'

Allenberg was right. I know it now. But then a Selznick mania was surging through the world and I was caught in its swirl. That evening we celebrated in the, by then, Little Gypsy, because the war was on full blast with Hungary on the wrong side and Miki Dora got worried he might end up in Manzanar with the Japanese, so he changed the name from 'Hungary' to 'Gypsy', saving the expense of repainting 'Little' on the marquee. Very frugal he was indeed and that is one of the reasons he is a fully fledged millionaire today. Couldn't have happened to a nicer ex-Huszár officer.

To illustrate the importance, the 'rightness' of my decision to go with Selznick, Miki 'donated' the dinner. Miki often fed the 'HHs', the Hungry Hungarians, free, in the morning, with last night's leftovers. They were wonderful meals, desserts included. I enjoyed a few 'din-fasts' myself during my very first stay in Hollywood. Yesterday's 'töltött káposzta' (stuffed cabbage) is always better than today's. And quite a few Academy Award ideas were born during those memorable years and meals.

Dora was never cheap, he was frugal but always had class. This he wanted to be a special dinner. Nadina, his mother, who I adored, a music teacher by profession, a fabulous cook on the side, outdid herself for the occasion. Miki invited a large group, some of the people I didn't like, and he knew it. I asked him why. 'Because they don't like you either and I wanted their envy to agonize the bastards.'

No other two groups of people, who are geographically and historically so far apart, are spiritually almost identical as the New Orleanians – Blacks, Whites, Cajuns and Creoles – and the millenniums' old mixture of the Tatárs, Huns and Magyars – the Hungarians – when they think of celebration and the enjoyments of life: food, music, sex, hunting, fishing, and fish stories. Celebration is a contagious disease and Hungarians are certainly contaminated. In Hungary you precelebrated your wake. You wanted to be sure when the time came your friends knew real well how you wanted it done.

And as the curtain came down on the festivities Zoltán Korda slowly and carefully folded his razor-sharp, forever present, special Hungarian bugyli bicskát and pronounced his dictum, 'Don't do it, he is a bloody tyrant, worse than Alex.'

Zoltán was one of, if not the most overlooked directors. He was subjugated professionally by his brother, Alex. I loved and respected Zolki across the board. I listened to him, usually. This time I didn't.

At eleven I walked into Selznick's outer-outer office in Culver City. It was like a beehive, humming with suffocating urgency. Before I could announce myself to one of the secretaries a rather large, impressively elegant, middle-aged lady materialized from the inner-outer office. If I remember correctly, her name was Mary. 'We were expecting you, please follow me.'

I did. Red carpet treatment, it was just like the first time in Denham with Korda. I was looking forward with great anticipation to meeting David O. Selznick. It was strange, we left the office, I followed her. Not a word. She led me to a simple little restaurant on the lot, not too far away.

'The usual table?' asked a waiter as we entered.

Mary said, 'Yes,' then turned to me. 'Mr Selznick regrets he was detained and will be a little late. Please, make yourself comfortable.' She made a gesture, the restaurant was mine. 'Whatever you would like.' And she left. The door was not quite closed behind her when the waiter placed a steaming cup of black coffee in front of me, which nobody ordered. 'Cream 'n' sugar?'

'No thanks, black is fine.'

'New in town?'

'Eh . . . well . . . yes.'

'Actor?'

'No.'

'Ah, writer!'

'. . . No.'

His voice slipped up an octave, 'Oh deeerector, hm.' And he left me.

The coffee was excellent. The second cup was very good, the third was good, the fourth tasted like slop. It was quarter to twelve, when finally Mary came back. I got up before she was halfway across the place, ready to meet Selznick. She held up her hand to stop me, traffic cop fashion. 'No, not yet. He is really sorry, he is still tied up, but he will join you for luncheon here shortly.'

She ushered me back to the same table, it was now set up for lunch for two. She motioned to the waiter and told me confidentially if I wished to order a martini or anything else it was perfectly all right. She repeated 'All right,' to the waiter and left me again.

The first martini was perfect, the second not so perfect, the third was absolutely the best. It was two o'clock. People came, devoured their luncheons and left. Some openly, some surreptitiously were watching me. I felt I was an exhibit. I mentioned this to the waiter between the second and third martinis. 'Oh well,' he said, with a slow shrug. 'This table is called,' he laughed, 'Mr Selznick's outpost for newcomers; that one,' he pointed, 'over there is Mr Selznick's waiting-room for the old hands. They are writers, they had an appointment at four o'clock.'

I checked my watch, it was two-ten. 'They are early.'

He shook his head, 'No, no, no-no. Their appointment was for four o'clock yesterday afternoon.' He must have read my thought, 'No, they came back at nine this morning.'

'This is really terrible,' said Mary as she sat down at the table. I was still naïve, I thought she was talking about how Selznick kept me waiting. No. 'You haven't had your lunch yet, please order something, he is really held up.' She sighed, deeply. It was real, or an Academy Award quality performance, 'And I really don't know for how long.'

The waiter put another martini in front of me, which I did not order, and as I pushed it aside most of it slopped over, as I wished it would.

Mary noticed it. Had she missed it she could not have been Selznick's Number One. The waiter must have had a crystal ball, or others had done it before me. He placed another martini in front of me. I didn't touch it this time. I had to laugh, Mary laughed with me as I said, 'Quite a service.'

'Mr Selznick likes good service . . . I have an idea, why don't you go home and – '

I got up, 'With pleasure. Glad to have – '

'Please, don't jump to conclusions. He is just not aware of time.'

'If you don't tell it to anybody and nobody notices it, I promise I'll keep it as a secret. I would be ashamed of it.'

'Temper-temper, the famous Hungarian temper. I understand. He will like you and you will like him.' She ever so discreetly indicated the martini on the table, 'I have a car here to take you home and pick you up. I shall call you at three-fifteen and let you know.'

The phone woke me up at three-fifteen on the dot. Before I had stretched out, I decided I would not answer the phone. Half asleep, automatically I picked up the receiver, a strange voice, crisp and impersonally polite was on the line. 'The car will be picking you up in forty minutes, sir.'

I was caught off guard, 'I'll be a son of a bitch.'

'I beg your pardon?' queried the voice from the other end.

'Sorry, you just woke me up.'

The voice came back so very clipped, it was almost British. 'The car will be there in forty minutes!' Bang, she hung up. No 'sir' this time either.

There was no sign of the gas rationing. The afternoon traffic was bad even in those days. I had time to get organized. I had decided I was not going to wait for Selznick now, nor for anybody else unreasonably long without a 'force majeure', ever again.

As I walked into the inner-outer office, large, spartan and impeccably orderly, Mary got up from her desk. 'Would you believe it, that meeting which started at eight o'clock this morning is still going on . . .'

'Yes. I would believe it, thanks for the ride.' I turned and started to walk out. She laughed out loud, with a laugh corpulent people usually have, a clear ringing, bubbling laugh. It was so unexpected, so out of place it stopped me. She was enjoying herself.

'Mr Selznick instructed me to break in the meeting when you arrived.' She picked up a file from her desk, motioned to me to follow her. She tapped the file, 'Read your deal memo, you'll be with us for a while.'

I was still ruffled and very inexperienced, 'Don't be so sure.'

She laughed again, it bothered me. 'Nobody leaves Mr Selznick.' And she opened 'the door'.

It was a very large room. It was a very stuffy room. It had several very large windows, all with their shades drawn. As I found out, Selznick was a twenty-eight-hour-a-day man; by keeping the room dark he was never aware of time.

From an ornate ceiling a ballroom-size, beautiful and out-of-place crystal chandelier was hanging above a very, very large desk with a zig-zag edge, topped with thick glass that perfectly matched the complicated zig-zags. Mary put the file on the desk, next to loose, multi-colored script pages, unfinished sandwiches, hamburgers on paper plates and paper cups. No Royal Doulton in sight, no antique silver coffee service on a side table.

Matching the massive pieces of furniture in the room, a pair of extra-large shoes, one of them upside-down, laid next to the desk. A burly man, in stocking feet, shirt unbuttoned, tie undone, swinging a caveman's shillelagh, was strutting up and down the smoke-filled room.

Three men, in various poses of sagging, filled three very large, comfortable-looking armchairs. Like young birds at the rim of their nest opening and closing their beaks expecting their mother to feed them, so did the three men keep opening and closing their mouths in silence, hopelessly trying to override the tirade and the whooshing sound of the caveman's swinging shillelagh.

With a final flourish the caveman concluded 'the discussion' and for emphasis took a full swing at the top of the desk. 'So don't argue with me!' Crash!, and tomahawk-size glass pieces showered the room. The three men ducked. The caveman stood tall and triumphant above the debris. I stood dumbfounded.

On the back wall a hidden door opened, four men in coveralls came in. Two of them carried a new glass top, placed it on the desk. It matched the desktop's intricate zig-zag pattern perfectly. The other two men cleaned up the mess with great expertise. They marched out. All in silence. The three men clambered back into their armchairs. I was still ignored.

The man of this one-sided victory threw a pill in his mouth, finished a bottle of sodapop, acknowledged my presence. 'Mary will give you two scripts. I'll see you tomorrow morning at eight and we'll talk about them.' He turned his attention back to the three unfortunate men, now slouched again in their armchairs. 'Now, let's get on with it.' Mary led me out of the room.

The first time I met David O. Selznick.

The night went by fast. Too fast. I read both scripts. Twice. Neither had a title page. I wasted too much time trying to figure out why.

When at ten-to-eight I was ushered into the inner-outer office, two recipients of yesterday's glass shower were already there having coffee out of mugs. I hit Mary, straight on, 'I was up half the night reading the two scripts, the other half trying to figure out why the title pages on the scripts were missing. I did not believe for a minute you had made a mistake. So why? What is the reason?'

'Well, well, well, thanks for your compliment,' and she laughed. I liked her laugh, it came from her heart. 'I cannot answer your why and what is the reason, you had better ask Mr Selznick about that. He never told me and I never asked.'

'Nor did I,' came a voice from the background.

'Oh,' gestured Mary, 'this is Mr Herman Mankiewicz,'[1] she gestured again, 'and Mr Ben Hecht.'[2]

Sorry, Bert Allenberg and Zoltán Korda, so far so good. Mankiewicz was the founder of the Mankiewicz dynasty. Ben Hecht was Ben Hecht. I found out later he was responsible for me being there. He had liked a film I had made and called Selznick's attention to it. This was the day that started our long association which I was always proud of.

'Better go in now,' suggested Mary. It was eight on the dot, I took a deep breath and followed them.

There was a traffic jam in the doorway, a tall, slim, very elegant man

1 Herman Mankiewicz (1897–1953) was a graduate of Columbia University and the University of Berlin where his career started as the correspondent for the *Chicago Tribune*. Returning to the US, he became prominent in New York's cultural life as the drama editor of the *New York Times* and *The New Yorker*. In Hollywood from 1926. He was largely responsible for the Academy Award-winning screenplay of *Citizen Kane*. He wrote and collaborated on numerous screenplays without credit. A bad habit de Toth picked up from him; their slogan was: 'I know I wrote it. Who cares?' His son Don Mankiewicz (b. 1922) is a novelist and screenwriter, his brother Joe (b. 1909) is a director-writer-producer and won two Oscars in 1949, one as director and one as writer for *A Letter to Three Wives*, also nominated in the same year for best picture. The following year, 1950, he received three Academy Awards; first for directing, second for best screenplay and the third for best picture, *All About Eve*. Quite a dynasty.
2 Ben Hecht (1893–1964) was at the age of 10 a promising concert violinist, at 12 a circus acrobat, and at 16 began his career as a reporter. During WWI he was a daring front line war-correspondent, columnist, short-story writer and novelist. In 1923, he published the *Chicago Literary Times*, which brought him prestige and bankruptcy. In 1925, as usual, he was broke, this time in New York. Herman Mankiewicz, an old friend, brought him to Hollywood. In 1927, he won the first Academy Award given for Best Original story for *Underworld*. In 1935, he received another Oscar for *The Scoundrel*. A most prolific and the highest paid writer, receiving – at that time a fortune – between $50,000 and $150,000 per script, which he delivered within two to six weeks. He wrote and collaborated on countless stories and screenplays and others received credit. 'I know I wrote it. Who cares? The horses are running.' He disliked Hollywood, the horses didn't like him and he was always in desperate financial trouble.

was on his way out. They all knew each other of course. He greeted me with a firm handshake. 'Welcome on board, I am Ray Clune.' I liked him instantly. He was a gentleman. During the short time I was with Selznick I learned a great deal about practical film production values. I got contaminated by the forms of Bill Pereira[3] and the avant-garde dreams of Salvador Dali.

The shades were drawn on the windows. Selznick contributed to the war effort in various other ways but not by saving electricity. There were 'dime-store' thermos bottles and paper cups around. Those cups were not like today's thick, insulated cups. You had to stack three or four together, like the leaning Tower of Pisa. Less stable, but it was the only way to pick up a cup of hot coffee, and when full they tipped over from a hard look.

Selznick was behind his desk. After a smiling 'Good morning,' he went back to his papers, with Mary next to him, feeding additional files with lightning speed to keep up with Selznick as he disposed of them. Nobody spoke. Hecht motioned to me to follow his example, which I did and poured some hot coffee into my paper cup tower.

When Selznick finished, he looked up with a smile. You felt power, he was hypnotic. He took a sip of his coffee. As he put down his cup tower he was about to say something, I beat him to it. I felt had I been closer to Hecht he would have kicked me to shut up.

'Mr Selznick.'

He looked at me, 'David,' he said, then ever so slightly his smile was fading. His 'yes' was tentative.

'David, I was up half the night reading the two scripts you – '

'That-is-exactly what I expected you to do!' A different Selznick cut me off.

I knew immediately I had goofed, but I might as well go down in flames, instead of just fizzling out. 'Sure, that was clear enough, it was fine. What bothered me and kept me awake – '

'I am sorry I contributed to your sleepless night. What bothered you?'

3 William L. Pereira (1909–1986) was the leading Los Angeles architect for some fifty years; among his creations are the CBS Television City, the Los Angeles County Museum of Art, the Disneyland Hotel, the City of Irvine, Pepperdine University, Los Angeles International Airport, and San Francisco's Transamerica Tower. Additionally he won an Academy Award for the Special Effects on *Reap the Wild Wind* (1942) and also produced a couple of films.

His razor had cut my throat, I didn't dare to move my head, I was sure it would fall off. 'You contributed to my sleepless night, sir . . .' He didn't correct it now, David. His eyes kept on narrowing to slits behind his thick glasses, I kept on digging my grave. '. . . because I did not find an answer why, why on earth there weren't any titles on the scripts and it bugged me that I drew a complete blank when I tried to come up with the reason for it. I hated feeling so inept. It just bugged me.' My sails collapsed.

There was silence in the room. Selznick was watching me as he reached for his coffee and almost knocked over his tower of cups. Luck was with me, Mary with amazing quickness averted the disaster. I often thought had she not, what mood would Selznick have been in subsequently. How weird, sometimes little, insignificant incidents could affect one's future. He was not aware of the close mishap, sipped the fresh coffee Mary handed to him. 'Mary, how long have we been handing out scripts without titles or credits on them?'

'Not always. Sometimes for the last ten, twelve years.'

'Have you been asked before the same question he asked?'

'Yes.'

'Yes? When – who – why didn't you tell me?'

'Once. I had no opportunity to tell you. He asked me before we came in. And I told him I didn't know, he should ask you.'

Selznick was blank for a short moment, then laughed out loud. He pointed a heavy finger at me.

'Don't you forget that curiosity killed the cat.'

'I don't know what's better, die wiser or live dumb, happily ever after? Sir.'

He didn't pick it up. He growled at me. 'David, I told you before.'

'Yes-sir, I mean David, but I'd rather die and know the whys and the reasons than live on dumb and happy.' I repeated.

He leaned back, relaxed. He stuffed and lit his pipe. It was a command performance, I presumed, we watched in silence. Loaded with papers, Mary dissolved through the door. David picked up his shillelagh, with his other hand he held on to the corner of his desk, kicked off his shoes and in stocking feet started to walk around the room in silence. His pipe's smoke in his wake left vapour trails in the already stuffy room. All in silence, except for an occasional swoosh from the swinging shillelagh. He stopped, wriggled his well developed behind on the top of his desk.

Maybe he had an itch, I thought, otherwise why would he wriggle on those torturous zig-zag edges. After all he was human, even if he didn't think so. He held his shillelagh between two fingers and made a pendulum out of it and watched it with great concentration for a very long time.

The silence of the warm stuffy room made me doze off. All I remember now is that he was standing in front of his desk and was talking with great enthusiasm. I listened, Hecht and Mankiewicz were listening too, I guessed, because they looked like they were and they were not talking. Only Selznick was talking. I listened so hard it was hurting me but I did not understand what he was talking about, until I stopped trying to connect it with either of the two scripts he gave me to read. And after a while I not only understood what he was driving at, I was swept away by his performance. He visualized what he was talking about, he was dramatic, brilliant. Powerful. Imagine a deluge of words instead of water in Niagara Falls. I was involved with every nuance. When I missed a point, without thinking, I interrupted him. Hecht kicked me.

'It's all right, Ben.' Selznick laughed, then wagged a thick finger at me, 'Don't forget the cat.' He clarified the point and continued as if nothing had happened.

This, my first 'story conference' with David O. Selznick, started at eight in the morning, finished around three-thirty in the afternoon, no food, not even stale coffee. No interruption. He was telling us a story none of us had ever heard before. Recited a film from its first shot to the last, with complete character and visual style analysis. I was spellbound by him. No pun intended. I was ready to comply with most anything he asked me to do. I was walking on air, but the air was in an inflated balloon and the balloon had a slow leak. Slowly, very slowly and with great resentment I was beginning to realize what Allenberg and Zoltán Korda were talking about. Finally after one of those 'story meetings', one late afternoon in the Garden of Allah, Ben Hecht punctured the balloon and I hit the ground. It hurt. He poured salt on my wound and twisted his dagger.

'We are prostitutes,' he gulped down the last few drops of his third martini and was stabbing the lone olive in the bottom of the empty glass with a toothpick. 'Prostitutes, we are god-damned-whores, and don't kid yourself. As long as you know you are making shit you won't drown in it. But you are hypnotized, David gave you shit and you ate it for Sacher torte. Wake up and vomit before it is too late. Quit before you disappear, swallowed, gone. He is a selfish bastard. He needed a good second-unit director for a couple of pictures, a couple of scenes. Nobody with your qualities would take it, so you are it, as long as he needs you, after that he will flush you down the toilet. He would never give you a picture to direct, and even if he did, how long do you think you would last? Cukor, Fleming – a good director and a very tough cookie – Sam Wood – dead wood I call him, but a name – and another few lesser luminaries out-out-out on *Gone With The Wind*, one after the other, out, not even "please". On this one now, the third poor bastard is sweating blood. He goes through directors like a dose of salts or, worse, moulds them in his own mould, they lose their own identity. Do you want to be a has-been before you ever started? I got you into this shit, I'll fish you out of it. You are quitting tomorrow.'

And that was it. Selznick was a gentleman, he agreed with Ben, we shook hands. Less than a year later Selznick didn't remember me at a party.

And I was out of a job. I didn't have to cover the telephone with pillows any more, no agent invited me to have lunch. Invited me to lunch? They didn't return my phone calls. It reminded me of the square-one-days of my visit to Hollywood.

My first assault on Hollywood was to be a curiosity-driven short excursion. But the timing of it came about by accident. An accident in more ways than one.

Racing in Italy I wrecked an Alfa Romeo I was allowed to drive. I thought courage could replace experience. I have loved Italians ever since. Of all nationalities, Italians are the ones who understand that approach to life in general and to any kind of racing in particular.

I was lucky, only my ego was bruised. In memoriam of the demised Alfa my friends arranged a Sicilian wake. I must have been really distraught, because when I woke up in a strange hotel room it was moving and rolling. It took me several hours to discover I was on board the Conte di Savoia, on route to New York. New York? I had a bon voyage note in my pocket with added best wishes and 'bona fortuna' for my planned jaunt to Hollywood, and a number to contact in Detroit, Michigan, at Buick, 'as we discussed'. I felt more of a wreck than the Alfa.

It was a miserable trip. My wardrobe was suitable for a south Italian racing circuit, no tuxedo, which was mandatory in the first-class dining-room for dinner. I ate dinner in my cabin. Two days out I turned blue on deck within fifteen minutes in my light Brioni togs.

As the days passed I was less and less convinced that I would like America. But as it was too far to swim back, I made up my mind to go through with it. I wanted to see Hollywood anyway. Little did I know this decision would become the turning point of my life. 'Hollywood, here I come,' I yelled into the freezing cold mid-Atlantic mist. The few health-nuts on deck walking around dressed like members of Captain Byrd's expedition to the Pole gave me a wide berth.

To arrive in New York not knowing a soul was not the best introduction to America. It felt and smelled like a cold sauna in Finland. Everybody was running from somewhere to somewhere. I didn't blame them. I wanted to run too. And that I did. From the pier to Grand Central, and on to the first train to Detroit, Michigan.

I drove crazy the very polite black train personnel. Every next station I wanted to get off, it had to be Detroit. I had had an idea America was big, but I never imagined it was that spread out.

From Detroit on, my odyssey became if not a joy-ride, at least less eventful. My Italian racing aficionados plugged me in the right circuits; the distance from Detroit to Flint, Michigan, was humanly European. But in Flint the wind was howling, it was snowing, it was freezing. All at the same time. It would have been miserable, but by then I was numb. There were no free taxis to be found, but one driver was kind enough or wanted to kill me, and pointed out the way to the Buick factory, 'about five miles that-a-way.'

I checked in my luggage at the station, and, turning into a snowman with every step, I was on my way to pick up my car at 'factory price', as my Italian friends stressed.

I was the only moving thing around. I must have seemed dubious because a police car pulled up next to me. 'Your car broke down?'

'I have no car, yet. I am on my way to pick one up at the Buick factory.'

That must have sounded weird or suspicious because one of the policemen, braving the weather, got out and gave me a thorough once over. I explained my predicament, he checked my papers, which were not waterproof and have never looked the same since. He had a confab with his partner, who wisely stayed in the car, then asked me to 'get in'.

I got in the back seat of the patrol car and felt at home like a penguin would in a zoo, being separated from the kind officers by a strong steel mesh. But I was grateful and ignored their mumbled observations, 'He is crazy . . .' 'He is just plain nuts.' My first two compliments in the US.

Finally, I picked up my first American car at the factory, a silver-grey Buick roadster. It had red leather upholstery, a rumble seat, spare wheels sunk in the front fenders, a radio that worked. I turned it on and to my biggest surprise Hungarian music blasted through the storm.

I did not know there was a Hungarian station in Detroit, I had no idea that Cleveland, Detroit, Newark, at that time and in that order, were the third, fourth and fifth largest 'Hungarian' cities in the world. Hungary included? Nor did I know whom to thank for tuning in that station. Happily I drove off into the blizzard, without a map and without a driver's license, to discover America.

Rounding the first corner, driving way too fast, I spun out. The car waltzed in slow-motion from curb to curb on the icy road and finally it gently nestled against a big pile of snow next to a driveway. I thought I was hallucinating.

'Hey, Hunky, why don't you learn how to drive!' In Hungarian, in Flint, Michigan, in a blinding, freezing snow storm. Did I hear something? And in Hungarian?

The street was deserted save three children, ten-to-twelve years old, building a snowman and having a ball laughing at me. I yelled at them. 'Did you kids say something?'

No. They couldn't have. The kids who ran to the car were black. 'Better watch out, mister, you're going to kill somebody,' said one in perfect Hungarian. 'And yourself,' said the second. 'Watch that nice new car, mister,' warned the third.

'How did you know that I – '

'The radio, Hunky.'

Luck again. Because I happened to be Hungarian they volunteered to guide me through a short cut to the Department of Motor Vehicles. They would not have done this for anybody else in this 'shitty' weather except for a Hunky. They swore not even for money.

They never thought, of course, that the short cut just happened to pass their favorite, 'the best in Detroit . . . in the world', something I 'had to see', 'real Hungarian cooking', 'maybe taste it?' café.

And while a lovely black lady, who didn't speak a word of Hungarian, served each a double-burger with double fries and ketchup with a large coke, a banana-split, a moron's delight and two sticks of bubble gum, I found out two of them were brothers with a Hungarian mother and a black father, both on lay-off. The third, who loved cars, had a black mother and a Hungarian father who had a job at the Buick factory. I thought they were a wonderful mixture. Hungary was taking over the world.

At the Department of Motor Vehicles a bundled-up middle-aged officer was shivering behind the counter. His first question was, 'Is it cold outside?'

I told him the truth, 'It is freezing.'

'Hmmm,' he grunted. His second question was: 'Can you drive?'

'Yes.' I bragged a little, I was proud of it then, 'I used to race cars in Europe.'

'Hmmm!' He sized me up, 'It's one way to kill yourself.' Then he thoughtfully sized up the ice-flowers-covered windows of the office, listened to the wind serenading him as it whistled through the crack under the door, then came to a decision. He adjusted the blanket on his lap, then pulled out two forms from a drawer, signed one and handed the other to me, pointing, 'Sign there.' Then he stabbed the second form, 'Here too, legibly.'

I signed both and handed them back. He nodded. Put one in a file and dropped the other on the counter, turned back to the paper he was reading when I came in.

I waited patiently. He looked up. 'What are you waiting for? Is your room colder than this damned office?'

'No, I mean . . . my – '

'It's right there in front of you. Drive safely.' As I reached the door he warned me to 'shut it tight!'

He ignored me but I was disliked when I paid for the car and a one year insurance premium with about nine-hundred dollars in cash, in single, ten and twenty dollar bills. The cashiers looked at me strangely as they counted the bills, twice.

Some of the bills were scrutinized with a magnifying glass. It took them forever, and, licking their arthritic purple-blue freezing fingers as they counted the money, they suggested I open a checking account to make it safer and easier for me. What they probably meant was easier for other unfortunate cashiers doing business with me in the future.

I was off to explore the United States of America with over ten thousand dollars in cash, singles, fives, tens and twenties in my pockets and suitcases. Without a map. But with a valid Michigan driver's license. And without the slightest notion of its vastness.

To start with, among the sights I wanted to see, the closest to Detroit was Niagara Falls. Simple, I headed for Buffalo. I drove and I drove. The weather was worse than miserable, snow, sleet. I was beginning to enjoy the challenge of driving in thirty to forty knots cross-winds and temperatures way below zero. It was an exciting new experience. I was beginning to get the hang of it and didn't spin out more than two or three times an hour. It was fun, and if paradise is cold it was Niagara Falls when I first saw it with its icicle wonderland.

I skipped New York. Washington, DC, was the next target. Its extra-large proportions matched its history, the snow-laden trees matched the tranquil beauty of cherry blossom time. But it was cold too. Not like the Buffalo cold, straight, hard. No, the Washington cold cajoled you, it snuck up on you, it was almost like the rain in Budapest, but this cold air was contaminated by politics.

It was extraordinary, in all my close to ten thousand miles of meandering throughout the US at that time, Washington, DC was the only place I did not hear a sincere laugh or run across anybody I would have trusted. I had a feeling it was a city of mistrust and loneliness. The conglomerate, crude, hard city of New York was America. Washington, DC, the capital was foreign land to me.

I loved to ski, the Alps, the snow. Cold never bothered me much, but somehow I had had enough of this cold and its cold people. I asked the concierge what was the shortest way to the sun. 'My target is Hollywood.'

'That is easy,' he said and took great pains to write down a long list of route numbers I was to follow. I did.

The weather was getting better, the people were more gracious the further south I drove, through the yesteryears splendor of the Carolinas. I lingered on, I was bowled over by their history, their cooking and the southern hospitality. Southern Comfort is not only a name of a drink.

Everything was absolutely fine until I passed a sign I thought I had misread. I backed up to check it. I had read it right the first time, 'Welcome to Florida.'

My geographical knowledge of the US was shamefully inadequate, but I knew enough to realize I was in the wrong state, I didn't know there was a Hollywood in Florida. I could not fault the concierge, he did what I had asked him to do, send me the shortest way from Washington, DC to the sunshine and to Hollywood.

I enjoyed Florida, but Texas was something else. It had 'Buda' without 'Pest', it had 'Paris' without the Eiffel Tower, but it made up for it with the wide open spaces. Our Hungarian 'Puszta' was like a suburban back yard compared to it. I liked Texans, their all-engulfing bullshit sounded like the gospel truth and seeded doubts in my mind about some 'historical truths'. The longer I stayed there the more I believed Texas had never joined the Union, the Union joined Texas. I liked the who-gives-a-damn rebellious spirit that filled the red dust in the air.

I made some true friends there, they all stuck with me throughout the years. They introduced me to the western saddle and gave me an inkling about the art of roping. Texas made me feel at home. I could stretch out.

But my imagination did not stretch far enough. It snapped. I was beginning to doubt my sanity. Buying an automobile, a convertible at that. As it turned out it wasn't convertible enough. I could not convert it into a motor boat.

It never rains in sunny California I was told and it was true. It was not raining. It was not pouring. You were just in water. Water above you, water below you, the damned water was on both sides of you. You were in need of a periscope to see which way you were heading if you dared to cross the flash floods-created, ad hoc Amazons that obliterated what once was called the highway. Some years later, shooting the rapids on the Colorado river was child's play in a bathtub compared to negotiating Sunset Boulevard on the day of my arrival in Hollywood.

The town was filled with suicidal maniacs, or the world's worst drivers. Miniature 'Old Faithfuls' added to the thrills as the overladen sewers burped up their burden and that was not only water. Ugh!

Luck. I cannot emphasize enough its impact. I had no connections in Hollywood. The town was deluged. I was running out of gas. The rag-top of my car had succumbed to the weather and started to leak seriously. The wipers were useless. I was starving. To hell with the picture business, I was seriously wishing I was back in Hollywood, Florida.

What always amazed me was the service when you pulled into a filling station. Some of my pit crews weren't much better. I had barely shut off my engine, the hood was open, the dipstick was out and the oil was checked – in spite of the fact we were half-submerged – the water in the radiator was checked and so were the tires. Defying the elements, they cleaned the windows. All that by the time I got out of the car to stretch. And as I did that I looked down the street . . . No . . . It could not be true. The sign was a mirage.

I had left the car at the gas station, swum across the street. Sopping wet, I walked to the door of 'Little Hungary'. Not a mirage.

It was mid-afternoon. The restaurant was closed, the door was locked, but peeking through the streaks cut by beads of water rolling down the befogged window-panes I could see people inside. I knocked. Almost immediately the door opened, as if someone was expected. It was evident someone *was* expected, because, when the man who opened the door saw me, he disappointedly tried to shut it in my face, saying 'Veee open at six,' with a heavy Hungarian accent. 'Pleeaze, move your feet,' grandly indicating my left foot stuck in the door.

I spoke to him in Hungarian, he dropped his chin and cocked his head sideways, his eyes shrunk to two narrow slits as he listened, a perfect image of mistrust.

'Who recommended to you the Little Hungary?'

'Nobody, this is my first visit, actually my first few minutes in town. Driving down the street I spotted the sign and – '

'Vere is your car?' he asked, peering over my shoulder, looking for it. There were no cars parked in sight. 'Vere is it?' he repeated.

'Over there, in the gas station, I was hoping to get a bite to eat while they serviced the car.'

Holding firmly on to the door he opened it just wide enough to stick his head through to be able to check the gas station up the street. There was only one car there, overswarmed with service station attendants. 'Hmmm,' he said and pulled the door tight against my foot again.

The canopy that stretched above the sidewalk from door to curb could not save me from the wind-driven rain. I had had enough. Somebody else inside had had enough too and yelled, in Hungarian, 'Close the damned door, Miki!'

'Thanks a lot for your Hungarian hospitality.'

'Miki' eased the pressure on my foot, I pulled it back and was itching to kick Miki's balls into the gurgling gutter when he said, 'Come in.'

A long wooden bar faced the entrance, its back-bar reached the ceiling, dividing the place into two sections. In the front around the walls the high-sided wooden booths with bench seats looked comfortable, offered privacy. A gate on each side of the bar served as the entrance to the back-room, the actual dining-room, where busboys were snapping snow-white tablecloths before letting them float on the tabletops.

Miki herded me as far as possible from the card-playing groups surrounding most of the tables in the front section of the place. 'Ahhaa!' I thought, this was no restaurant, this was one of those illegal California gambling joints I was warned in Florida to stay away from. I was pretty smart, and quick to put two and two together; that was the reason Miki at the door was so hesitant to let me in. He pointed at a table, 'Sit down,' and yelled out, 'Erick, two coffees, make 'em hot.'

Hard, whistling 'Ssshh-sshhs' came from the concentrating card-players. Their silence was only occasionally broken when a player disgustedly slapped his losing cards on the table, accompanying it with German or fancy Hungarian cuss words. Miki didn't walk. He was like a hard rubber ball, he bounced. He was not a tall man, but he looked tall. He had no hair, he had a wavy lion's mane on his head. Before joining me at the table he surveyed the card-players like a general surveys battlefields from hill-tops afar, before ordering the charge. By the time Miki bounced back to the table to join me I had my passport out and handed it to him to put him at ease. 'Please don't worry, I am not an undercover cop.'

He took the passport, his eyes disappeared again behind the slits of his eyelids, equating me with the photograph in the passport. Erick brought the coffee, Miki took two great gulps. 'Good,' he told Erick, who was waiting for his boss's approval, before shuffling off.

As I was soaked to my skin nothing could have been more appreciated than a cup of hot coffee. Hot coffee? It was liquid hell. A spasm hit my throat. I could not spit it out. I had to swallow it and as the magma slid down, I could have sworn the steam rose from my wet clothes. Miki took another gulp.

Mafia gambling joint or not, it was a raw joke he played. Before he put down his cup I took it out of his hand, ready to slush it across his face. I was wrong again. I almost dropped his cup. It was hotter than mine, he played no raw joke, obviously that was the way he drank his coffee. 'Vat iz wrong?' he asked.

'Nothing. Are you a fire eater in a circus in your spare time, or something? I was hoping yours would be cooler.'

'Some likes it hot,' he said.

Billy Wilder was not within earshot. Actually he was playing gin-rummy in the far corner.

Miki widened the slits as he smiled and almost looked human. He read out loud my name from the passport. Slowly. Twice. It seemed like a penny had dropped. 'It could be,' he said to himself, then asked me, where did I go to school? I started to list the schools, then I stopped. 'What the hell's going on? Are you immigration?'

'I think I owe you a thanks. Thanks.' He curled up his lips to show his teeth. 'Don't you dare to knock *my* front teeth out, I like them.'

'Thanks? Thanks for what?' I thought he was an absolute nut. I got up. 'I thank you for the coffee, and all the damned blisters in my mouth.'

'Wait a minute. Pleeaze, it's still raining. When I saw the name in your passport I had a feeling you might be "it", that's why I asked you where you went to school. Luckily the last school you mentioned before you stopped was the school I was looking for. I knew I guessed right, so thanks, I mean it.'

'OK, so you thanked me, and I thanked you for the coffee, OK? 'Bye.' I wanted to get out, he stopped me.

'Pleeaze, wait. Don't you remember the father from the Order of Pius whose front teeth you knocked out at the swimming pool? They had no more places for boarders, but when you were thrown out, there was an opening and I got in. Get it? I got in, in your place and I didn't lose a year. So-that's-why-thanks-OK? You know you became a legend? Mentioning your name in school was good enough reason to be expelled. Glad to meet you.'

He got up from the table, stood almost to attention as he reached out for my hand, and introduced himself; 'I am Miklós Dóra, of the First Ferencz József Jászkún Honvéd Huszár Ezred, Second-Lieutenant, retired. Now, I own this place.' He had a firm grip. 'We'll have dinner, it's about time we celebrated our – '

There was a knock on the entrance door, he didn't finish his sentence, 'Excuse me,' and bounced away to open the door. Obviously this was the knock he was expecting when I came in. Was one more Huszár added to my life?

A small, small barrel of a man came in and, shaking the water-beads off his thick round glasses and his hat, complained in a potpourri of Hungarian, German and English about the miserable weather.

The scalding coffee must have burned my skull empty. What would Peter Lorre be doing here?

In the restaurant section harsh, blue-white cleaners' lights were turned on, the busboys shed their professional trade mark of lethargy. Dining tables were shoved aside. From nowhere two sides of a ping-pong table appeared and were set up in the center of the dining-room. The newcomer was greeted with great reverence. 'Good evening, Mr Lorre, good evening, Mr Lorre,' went the chant.

The cardplayers slowly drifted into the dining-room to watch the ping-pong match between Peter Lorre and Miki Dóra. It was a twice a week afternoon ritual. They played for five dollars per point. The handicaps changed after each game and the side-bets were marshalled by Jenö, the Fö-úr. According to the handicap, the first time around Miki Dóra had to give two points to Peter Lorre. Miki was a world-class player, strong, very fast, he was on the end and on both sides of the table at the same time, his forehand shots dug furrows on the far side of the table. I didn't believe Peter Lorre ever saw Dóra's bullet-like balls. I was convinced he possessed those miracle genes the bats had, or he inherited them from his ancestors, the dolphins or some other creatures from below the waves. Sonar. He didn't look, he trained one ear toward the table. Peter Lorre played ping-pong by ear.

At five-to-five Jenö tapped his wrist watch. The busboys had a vicarious thrill yanking the table apart while a ball was, so to speak, still in the air above it. That was the house rule. The show was over at five sharp. Miki lost.

Peter didn't win. He just kept plopping back Miki's lightning-fast attacks but his returns were cut and the balls bounced any-which-way, barely over the net on Miki's side of the table. Frustrated, Miki beat himself. According to the rules the losers, bettors included, had to buy the drinks. No limit. This rule was typically Hungarian, 'It's all or nothing.' Bystanders were not included in the post-mortem celebration.

In sprawled-out Hollywood my only possible contact with the people with whom within a few hours after my arrival I was under the same roof could have been nothing more than to follow the map to movie stars' homes then drive by, slowly.

It was luck again. Non-believers would have called it coincidence, but the 'ifs', the big 'ifs', were still there. Had I done what I was supposed to, drive into town through Santa Monica Boulevard – I missed a sign in the confounded rain, thank God – I would have never ended up in the 'Little Hungary' at the time. And if I hadn't knocked the poor horny padre's front teeth out, would I have missed a good friend for life?

Have you ever been accosted by a restaurateur the first time you walked into his place, with 'Where did you go to school, sir?' Even if it was raining outside, it's unlikely it ever happens. Here everything dovetailed, the rain, the misunderstanding through which a new path opened up for me in Hollywood. I called it luck, although there were moments down the road when I doubted it was good luck.

'Where are you going?' asked Miki as I was trying to get out. 'I called them already,' he continued, 'they'll put your car in the back, next to mine, the key will be under the doormat, you'll pay them in the morning. OK? Let's have a drink, OK? Come on.' He led me to a booth, 'I have a new flotsam,' he told the two men. 'Look what the rain washed ashore.' And he went on telling them how I saved a year of his life by knocking out the poor padre's teeth.

Both men became instrumental in my future. One was Paul Lukas[1] – Lukács Pál in Hungarian – the other Géza Herczeg. Both were devout ladies' men. Paul had an advantage, he was better-looking, but one great disadvantage, he was happily married. Married to a lovely Hungarian lady, Daisy, who, like most Hungarian ladies, was extremely possessive, and jealous. Some Jewish men could look very Italian. I mean this as a compliment for both races. Géza looked like an Italian Buddha, but with a little more hair. His sparkling eyes matched his sparkling sense of humor; he was more than unattached, he was looser than loose. Daisy enjoyed Géza's company, his humor, but didn't trust the two of them together. She was a smart and very suspicious wife.

The losers' party was over. Sharp at six Jenö opened the door. The 'Little Hungary' was open for business. At 6.05 the entrance door opened and the first guest, a yellow oilskin-covered figure, blew in, probably directly from a North Atlantic trawler. Water splattered all around as Jenó helped to peel off the rain-gear of a very comely blond lady. She had her bearings pre-set and headed directly to our table, kissed Géza on the top of his head, hugged Miki, then paused to charge up enough energy to greet Paul. When finally they had terminated their unrestrained greeting Paul introduced me to Inga, from Denmark.

She had barely enough time to settle next to Paul when the entrance opened again and the second guest came in. This one entered with slow, chic dignity. Miki whispered, 'Paul,' and got to his feet, Paul whipped his head around and followed Miki immediately to greet the new arrival, and as Paul moved he shoved Inga on the bench seat next to me in the place Miki had vacated. Géza picked up Inga's hand and whispered, 'Mrs

---

1 Paul Lukas (1894–1971), born in Hungary, was a suave leading man in films in Europe and Hollywood. Often cast as a Nazi, it was an anti-Nazi role that brought him the two biggest successes of his life: on the stage in Lillian Helman's Broadway hit *Watch On The Rhine* and in the film of the same title which brought him the coveted Oscar in 1943.

Lukas,' as he kissed it. Inga's big, azure-blue eyes bulged while Géza placed her hands on the top of my hand and as if he were giving us his blessing, patted it.

Miki excused himself to go to check the kitchen, Paul and Mrs Lukas were walking back to the table. Before reaching it, Paul pointed at me, 'Look at him, he got to town two days ago and –' He didn't finish his sentence, pointed at Inga, smiled at her, hugged his wife, 'And this is his first trip to Hollywood.' He nodded to me, 'Congratulations.'

'When are they going to get married?' asked Mrs Lukas.

Her husband ignored the acid remark as if it were never said, smiled at her, 'Daisy, meet Andre de Toth, Bandi, right? And –' he hesitated as if he were groping for the name. I cut in.

'Inga, from Denmark.'

'Thanks,' said Paul. The two ladies nodded to each other like two icicles, hanging on the eave of a Swiss chalet high in the Alps. Paul smiled, slapped my knee as he sat down between his wife and Inga. He was aloof and high above all. No wonder he got an Oscar for acting, he was well versed. He and Daisy were happily married for years.

As Daisy sat down and shook her head, her auburn hair cascaded down from a knot. She reached over the table to pat Géza's hand, 'Wipe the lipstick off your dome, Géza.' She handed another napkin to Paul, who took it, wiped his lips. 'Thanks,' he said as he smiled at his wife.

I was Daisy's next target. With another napkin in her hand she gave me the once-over, 'It seems you were left out of this show, Bandi!' She emphasized my name as she dropped the napkin.

'I don't play for show. I play for keeps.'

'You're a sharp son of a bitch, aren't you?'

Miki appeared to recite the daily specials. He had been in the business long enough to know when to vanish and when to reappear. He would have given his last drop of blood needlessly for a friend on one hand, on the other he was the biggest coward. Daisy was known to have shed blood and Miki was no fool. Nor was Daisy.

After a good dinner and a few drinks, in the WC Paul called me his lightning rod. A moniker that stuck for a while, but as it turned out was not foolproof all the time.

Paul was a matinee idol and he maintained his reputation. Every Wednesday afternoon he met this lovely lady in a motel in the San Fernando Valley, then out of town. They were very steady customers during the lull hours of the day. To help make them feel 'at home' for the two hours and to enable them to keep their incognito, for an extra charge the clever manager let each of them have a key to the room if they promised never to use it any other day or time than agreed. This was a usual arrangement for quite a few devoted husbands, and wives, at the time.

Paul was always punctual and both were eager. When Paul arrived the lady was already in bed waiting for him in the dark room with a sexy 'Hmmmm.' And everything went as usual. As usual until the lights came on. Daisy never looked better naked in bed, but Paul didn't look so good for a few days with a pair of purple-black eyes.

The gold bracelet from Cartier that Daisy exchanged for the motel room key was worth the fun, especially when Paul had to buy Daisy two. Was it tit for tat? 'Daseeeelukas', as we called her, had a marvelous sense of humor.

The lightning rod fizzled, but did not short-circuit our friendship, it lasted through the years. It was Paul Lukas who, several years later, signed the required affidavit which enabled me to become an American citizen, the greatest gift anybody could have given me. It was he who had given me a lady's name in Tijuana, Baja California. 'Look her up, just in case you need some advice, she knows that town better than anybody. You'll find her in the "Molino Rojo", tell her I sent you. Since you don't accept any money, you proud fool, accept this suggestion. I will call her. Good luck, you'll need it.' If ever, I most certainly needed it then.

The Japanese Samurai was cutting a wide swathe in the Far East, Hitler was gobbling up Europe. Hollywood was beginning to overflow with refugees. Most of these were more patriotic deep down inside than the mesmerized mob following the brass bands singing the 'Fahnen Hoch' in the beer halls and on the boulevards. They loved their pre-Hitler homeland. For centuries they had shed their blood and sweat for it and enriched it with intelligence, art and dogged diligence.

The competition became rougher and rougher. It was for survival not for glory. The long knives were out in Hollywood. There was no red carpet out for me.

Knives or no I fell in love with this country. I was determined to sink my roots deep, as deep as the redwoods I loved, and stay as long as they had been here. I never felt I was betraying Hungary, my motherland. I just didn't want to marry my mother.

After a fashion I could drive a race car, fly a plane. I had started to play polo. None of these, nor my limited film experience in Europe, would qualify me to get a job in Hollywood. Nor did I expect it, this was to be only a 'look-around-trip'.

The more I looked around the longer I wanted to stay. I was running out of money. I put the Buick on jacks, to keep it in good shape to drive it back to New York. I stashed enough money in the Security First on the corner of Sunset and Stanley to cover the expenses of the drive back east. I figured I would sell the car in New York, it was all paid for. What I would get for it would more than cover the trip from Southampton to Budapest. My first-class return ticket was in Miki Dóra's safe.

My father always said, 'If you want to add an enemy to your life just borrow from, or loan to somebody money or anything else.' I didn't need any help, I had a great talent for collecting enemies without it. I was proud of that.

To make ends meet, to enable me to stay on, since nobody offered me a plane to fly, or a racing car to drive, I did the next best thing: I drove an old truck from Pomona to the market in Los Angeles, loaded with oranges.

On one of these early dawn pleasure trips, pointing a thumb to the sky, with a pair of legs that made the letter 'O' look like a letter 'I', a cowboy carrying his saddle hitched a ride on his way 'up north to hook a job'. 'It's round-up time, they need hands up there.'

As usual: I delivered the oranges, Jimmy-One-Ear helped me to unload. As unusual: I called and told them where they could pick up their truck. As most unusual and unexpected: now two of us, Jimmy-One-Ear and I, were thumbing rides 'up north'.

'You got a job. Eddie'll fix you up with saddle 'n' all that.' When the force of the tobacco juice he spat out hit the branch of a roadside tree it broke off a few twigs. 'Am tellin' you, don' worry if you can ride. Now if you can't ride don' worry, you'll break your neck and they'll bury you up there. They're decent folk. So don' worry.'

This was the way I met Jimmy-One-Ear. Lloyd McMurry told me later he was on the round-up when Jimmy lost his ear. He was hired as Cookie and he was the lousiest cook. One of the hungry cowpokes, Freddy-Buck-Teeth, got so fed up and angry with him that he bit his ear off and ate it for breakfast. Some said it was on a bet. Jimmy-One-Ear said a jealous woman did it. Whichever way it was, I would not suggest arguing with Jimmy-One-Ear. He was the meanest, dirtiest barroom fighter this side of hell. With him and Lloyd we could clear out any bar in fifteen minutes, guaranteeing nothing left unbroken.

It never has ceased to amaze me how the 'if's' and 'if-nots', coincidences and luck converge. I would never have gotten my immigration quota number, or at least not that easily, without picking up Jimmy-One-Ear on the road. And for sure I would never have directed *Ramrod*. It all hinged on a matter of minutes. On the right spot at the right time. Luck.

The rain was coming down at least as hard as it did when I first arrived in Hollywood. The 'Little Hungary' was almost deserted. It was very unusual. Rain, hell or high water never stopped the crowd before. Miki got curious, called some of the professional gossip-mongers, tried to find out what could have happened.

He came back from his office. 'I'll drive you down to Tijuana after closing,' and handed me all my papers from his safe. He was tense. Before I could ask a question he unloaded. 'The Hungarian immigration quota numbers from Mexico will be assigned in the Tijuana US consulate from nine in the morning. It is a very small quota, I couldn't find out how many numbers will be available. The bastards. They all slipped down this morning without saying a word. Somehow we missed the announcement. Shit!' he said and he seldom used a four-letter word; he hated them, w-o-r-k was one of them.

Paul Lukas came in, in a hurry, followed by a little man with fogged-up glasses; somebody we didn't know. He stopped by the entrance, shaking his umbrella. Paul didn't take his coat off, sat down. 'Did you hear – '

'Yes, we did.'

He looked around and smiled, 'It seems everybody else did too. Now, I have phoned Carmelita in Tijuana, it took me more than an hour to get through. She said the town was chock-a-block full. There was no standing room available, not even in a doorway. You will have . . . I assumed you are going of course.'

We nodded. He said, 'Good,' as he took out a gold fountain pen from his pocket, motioned to the little man at the entrance to join us, 'Would you, Irving, please,' then asked Miki, 'Give me his papers.' Irving joined us at the table with his paraphernalia, 'I appreciate the favor, Irving,' and Paul signed my affidavit with a flourish, guaranteeing he was responsible for me and I would not become a burden on the state. Miki and Jenö were the witnesses, Irving, happy to shed a favor, notarized it and left in a hurry to face the storm. Paul fished out of his pocket two one-hundred dollar bills, put them on the table, 'Sorry I cannot stay, we have a dinner engagement.' On his way out he yelled back, 'The Molino Rojo.' A car was waiting for him outside. Paul Lukas gave me the key to my American Dream. It all happened within two minutes.

I left the bills with Miki, he returned them to Paul the following day, of course. Even if it had not been against my principles, it still would have been useless to accept the money. I needed something else.

I had no contacts and no idea how to go about getting a quota number. Deluxe attorneys were charging between two and four thousand dollars to help you get, or to arrange for you to get a quota number. We knew within a day all the numbers would be gone. What I needed was luck.

Miki's mother, my 'ersatz' mother, Nadina, loaded us up with her home-baked cookies and off we drove into another rain-soaked night. Miki had a grey Chevy convertible identical to my red one. He didn't need to drive it. The car knew the road up to San Onofre by itself. We used to go surfing there with the long hard-boards sometimes three, four times a week, after Miki closed shop. We slept on the beach at San Onofre, where I spent more time eating fresh-caught, steamed fish wrapped in seaweed with the Japanese fishermen when they came back at dawn than on the surf board. Miki was a good surfer. Surfing, ping-pong and chasing girls were his main sports. He excelled in the first two. Oh, he ran fast enough to catch his quarry all right, but didn't know what to do about it later.

The rain left us or we left it behind around Oceanside. By the time we reached Tijuana, after midnight, the stars were out, the town was wide awake. All the street lights, maybe two dozen, were on; anemic neons hissed and flickered above some of the cantinas and hotel entrances.

We cruised around. Expensive cars were parked on the dirt in front of the cantinas. Miki recognized some of his customers' cars. I had great difficulty getting him to give me his word not to piss in their soup as he threatened to do when he spotted them. Disgusted with humanity, he decided to head back to town before he got into trouble with some aspiring citizen and maybe miss the seven a.m. trade deliveries to the restaurant.

He dropped me in front of the 'Molino Rojo', waved me goodbye with crossed fingers. The tires from his jack rabbit start showered gravel and dirt on some of his customers' shiny new cars and off he went. It started to drizzle.

The place was not as crowded as I had expected, possibly because some of the applicants came with their spouses. I stopped at the nearest end of the bar to get oriented. It didn't take long to discover that I had guessed right, the 'Molino Rojo' was a whorehouse. 'Maison Frieda' in Tijuana.

Almost. What was missing was the style, the quiet elegance of 'Maison Frieda' and the ladies of Madame Frieda. The 'Molino Rojo' was trying to make up for that with a noisy abundance of very young, barely dressed, giggling girls, fresh from the farms, loud and happy music with lots of off-key singing. 'Maison Frieda' was subdued, 'Molino Rojo' was bursting. As a whorehouse expert, please take my word for it.

Nobody paid attention to me. I walked around curious to see if there was anybody I knew. And of course there were. It was sadly funny how they all tried to avoid seeing me – their feeble attempts to disappear from my sight, like smelling the food on their plate and picking up imaginary objects from under the table.

Except one, whom Miki fed for over a year free. He was the one, if anybody, who should have told Miki. No. We found out later he sold the information to people who were willing to pay his expenses to get down here for the quota number. That son of a bitch had the gall to look straight at me and ask, 'What are you doing here?'

'I'm soliciting business.'

That kind of puzzled him. 'What business?'

'Cleaning, dry cleaning. I hope I'll get your business.'

He didn't know what to make of that and I didn't give him too much time to figure it out. I picked up his plate and shoved the re-fried beans and eggs in his face, poured the Marguerita over his head – and my feet were off the ground, propelled by expert guides toward the back of the establishment. I knew better than to resist.

The right time at the right place, luck. As the bouncers hustled me through a narrow passageway at the far end, a door was opened by a very well built, very large, very handsome lady of indeterminate age, dressed in a very ornate going-to-church outfit.

I didn't understand a word of the machine-gun-like, rattled Spanish between the two bruisers and the lady – except the name 'Carmelita'. I jumped on that, 'Paul Lukas asked me to give you his greetings,' as I was propelled by the back exit.

Another quick burst of machine-gun-like Spanish, the brutes let me go. I told Carmelita what had happened and how right the bouncers were and complimented the bouncers on how good they were. Carmelita laughed, the bruisers laughed, they shook my hand and kept on smoothing out my jacket, saying 'hombre . . . hombre' and we shook hands again and they left us looking for another prey.

Carmelita's office was very small. To say it was overdone would be an understatement. Two pieces overwhelmed her nest: a large mirror with more light bulbs around it than all the light bulbs together on the streets of Tijuana, and an enormously large, puffy, fluffy, drowned-in-lace bed. As we came in she pointed at the bed with pride. 'It is from France. When I was young that was my office.' Then she laughed. She laughed from her belly, but it was not a bellylaugh, it was a full, sincere, warm laugh. When she laughed you wanted to laugh with her, to hug her. She was a genuine, nice person. We became and stayed friends throughout the years and I took a white orchid, her favorite flower of course, to her funeral.

Carmelita had 'business' to attend to. I moseyed up to the bar, at the back end this time. The bartender could not get to me for a while, serving the loud training-to-be-ugly American emigrés, soaking up Margueritas, Bertas, Tequila Sunrises and, for the braver ones, Swiss-itches. Finally, he managed to reach me. He was surprised when I asked for a shot of Jack Daniel's with a soda chaser.

Now came the Mexican Waltz. 'Sure?'

'Sure.'

Then he went away. Served a few people at the other end of the bar, then he came back. I did not see him look for my order. 'No, no, got it.'

'What do you got?'

'Scotch, booorbon?'

'Bourbon.'

'OK.' Then he went away again but this time he examined the back bar, looked under the counter and came back, 'Foroses.'

'Is that all you got?'

'No. Imperial.'

'Fine, please, bring me a double shot of that and – '

He smiled, happy to get rid of me, cut me off proudly, 'And soda chaser.'

The voice from behind made me think I was back in Texas. 'Ah don't know which is worse, but Ah think Four Roses would'a been not half as bad as the Imperial.' He shrugged, 'Ah think.'

Where the bar joined the back wall, with his back against it, sat a US Marine, I thought, in civvies. Lean, tall, with bull neck and close-cropped hair. I had not noticed him before. I told him I ordered the Imperial for sentimental reasons. And we started a conversation. The conversation consisted mostly of him asking questions.

After the second double shot of Imperial he told me he thought if I could drink that slop for a sentimental reason, it had to be quite a reason. I told him about Jimmy-One-Eye, my first encounter with Imperial.

I spent my wedding night during my first trip in the High Sierras above Lee Vining, on the ground in an oilskin bedroll in sub-zero weather. Instead of an organist the wind played the wedding-march whistling through the pines.

Eddie Cline, my range boss, jarred me out of my wedding night slumber with a hard kick in my ass. The thin sheet of ice crackled and crumbled off the oilskin cover as I sat up. A fire was burning next to the chuck wagon, the Cookie with white-wurst-size fingers was playing his accordion. He stopped his morning serenade only long enough to turn the deersteaks over the fire. Eddie kicked Jimmy-One-Ear next to me on the ground twice in his ass and as he sat up threw him a brown bottle. Jimmy-One-Ear caught it with great dexterity and took a large gulp while the bottle was still flying, it seemed. He slushed the mouthwash around in his mouth and threw the bottle of antiseptic to me.

I thought how civilized it was to start the morning with a mouthwash in this wilderness. I imitated Jimmy-One-Ear and took a big gulp to rinse my mouth like he did. It was the foulest tasting liquid ever. Anti-septic or not I spat it out, dropped back on my bed-roll, gasping.

'What the hell you want, Hunky, Jack Daniel's?' He kicked me again, 'Imperial ain't good enough for you? Cookie, you got olives? Maybe this gentleman wants a martini.'

'Hey, drink it!' barked Jimmy-One-Ear.

He was responsible for me being here. I drank it and – the biggest surprise of my life – I survived. Imitating Eddie and my sponsor, I threw the bottle to Shorty next to me, he was six-foot-seven.

I have never had a better breakfast before or since. Onion and deer liver and spuds and four eggs and deer steak and sheepherder bread and two more swallows of Imperial bourbon. I never felt more at home anywhere. No orchestra ever sounded better than Cookie's accordion, no fire ever smelled better. It was so beautiful even the five ugly faces around it couldn't spoil it.

'Chico!'

The bartender was in front of him before the letter 'o' had left his lips. 'Yes, sir.' Yes, I was sure he was a Marine from the base across the border. The Mexican waltz started again, but it had a different ending. 'Two Jack Daniel's.'

'No. No got it,' said Chico, after giving me a meaningful side glance.

'Two doubles, now!' He didn't have to raise his voice, he knew how to command. 'Yes-sir,' said Chico, and we were drinking Jack Daniel's till dawn.

'My name is Bart, yours?'

'Andre.'

'It's a hell of a name for a Texan. You said you had adopted Texas, right?'

'Right.'

'Then why are you hanging around here for a quota number?'

''Cause I want to adopt the whole goddamn big beautiful country. OK?'

'It's OK with me, but . . . as I heard it, it's going to be tough. Who is your lawyer?'

'Nobody, couldn't afford one. As I learned to say in San Antonio, I ain't got a pot to piss in.'

He laughed, I laughed. 'Ah aaam from Texas,' he said, 'I'd never have guessed it,' and we had a special drink to Texas. And we became closer and closer friends as only two Texans can be as the hours went by.

Unexpectedly he changed the subject. 'Take my advice, never look for a job as a waiter. You'd make a lousy one you know, it's no way to serve re-fried beans an' eggs the way you did it. What happened?' I told him. 'It's sure a dog-eats-dog game. Now, ah tell you, better be at the consulate real early, 'cause ah heard it's first come, first served. And there are a couple of drivers parking in front now!' He checked his wrist watch, got to his feet, steady as a rock. 'Ah-got-to-go-now, it's all taken care o', see-you-'round.' And left.

I felt empty. Chico picked up Bart's glass, knocked back what was left in it, shook his head, shrugged twice and smiled at me.

'Who was he?'

'Ooooh don't know, good man, uno caballero.' And he left me to serve less than caballaros further down the bar.

'You must be hungry.' It was not a question, it was a statement from Carmelita, and it was true. I had a good breakfast, a nap, shaved and showered and before the sun was thinking of rising I was settled on the third step, with my back against the wall and my left shoulder against the door of the American Consulate, in Tijuana, Baja California.

There were several big, luxury cars and limousines parked on the street above and below the entrance of the consulate. The uniformed chauffeurs cozy, undisturbed by the drizzle, were sound asleep in them. Some of them snored, some of them groaned occasionally, in some cars radios were playing.

This was my morning entertainment until one of the drivers woke up and got out of his limousine. He stretched, then relieved himself against the front tire, shook his equipment as he turned and noticed me with the biggest double take. He was buttoning his trousers as he asked, 'What are you doing there?'

'Having my usual morning siesta. What else?'

'Where did you park your car? The line forms down there. When did you get here?'

'I was born here. You asked too many questions – which one do you want me to answer?'

He woke up a couple of his peers. After a conference they approached me in a phalanx. When they stopped one asked, 'Whom are you standing in for?'

'For myself, who else?'

They had another conference, one of them got into his car and drove off.

The rain this time was on my side, it came down to investigate them and they withdrew into their dry cocoon. I was well protected in the doorway and dozed off.

The murmur of voices brought me back to reality. The street started to come alive. The driver was already back, the chauffeurs were devouring a boxful of Tacos, other goodies and lukewarm-looking cartons of coffee. A few 'civilians' showed up, trying to find parking spaces. A small crowd started to congregate on the sidewalk not too far from the consulate entrance, bunched up in twos and threes. I was the odd man out. They were watching me as if I was a freak on exhibition. I knew most of them, at least by sight.

Two of the limousines pulled out, the others jockeyed back and forth to spread, leaving not enough room to park between them. Aren't humans lovely? My favorites are the ones who watch you running to catch the elevator then frantically push the button several times quickly to be sure you are left behind. I am not nice. I always wished the guillotine doors of the elevator would crush their heads, but no. As the crack of the door narrows you see them with a content, evil smile, riding up or down. To hell, I hope.

The two limousines came back. Important-looking people with more-important-looking briefcases arrived in them. The other drivers jockeyed again to let them in their old places. One of the arrivals I knew well. He got out of the car and came to me directly.

'You look uncomfortable, come on, get in the car with us.'

'I am fine, just fine, thank you.'

'Suit yourself.' He headed back to his car, but after a couple of steps he stopped. 'How did you find out?'

'Since you didn't tell me I asked President Roosevelt and he tipped me off.'

The consulate entrance door opened. The man who opened it almost fell over me sprawled out on the doorstep. The worms scurried out of the woodwork. The man stopped everybody. 'Hold it, stop. Halt.' He spoke with a heavy, Mexican accent. With whatever accent he spoke he meant what he said. He instructed two Mexican policemen, not unlike the two bouncers of the 'Molino Rojo', not to let anybody, he repeated anybody, jump the queue. Then he told us applicants to stand in line. As I started to back down the stairs, he growled at me. 'You, applicant?'

'Yes-sir.'

'You think I do not speak good English?'

'You speak very good English – sir.'

'If I speak very good English why do not you understand? I said applicant stay. You applicant?'

'Yes-sir.'

'Applicant stay, line from here. Understand?' He yelled louder to the policemen, 'Line from here. Understand?'

Two imposing attorneys wiggled up the line a few steps. 'You applicant? Stay in line.'

'No. We are attorneys representing – '

'No applicant?'

The attorney now spoke louder, carefully enunciating every word. 'We are attorneys representing applicants who – '

'No applicant?'

The attorney made a grave mistake, especially for an attorney. He got annoyed. 'Can't you understand, we are attorneys who – '

'I understand good English, you understand good English, you are attorney – '

'Right, my business card,' and tried to hand over his card.

The man didn't even glance at it. 'No applicant. OK? No card, OK? No attorney in line, OK? Go.'

The rain painted polka dots on the impressive briefcases and the Sulka ties as the hastily summoned applicants and their high-powered attorneys were cooling their heels at the end of a long line.

Just as we were about to be let in a police car pulled up, lights flashing, sirens howling. One of the attorneys was led away by two policemen, the charge was trying to bribe an officer. My respect was growing for the US Department of Immigration and the Mexican police.

The consular offices were so spartan they were almost ugly. The personnel was impersonal. I was the first through the assembly line. Questions, answers, multiple choices, more questions. Some of them I found to be childish. Finally I was ushered through the big door of the consul's office. From the corner where it stood, the American flag dominated the large room. Seeing it, as always I had difficulty swallowing the lump in my throat, I was prepared to recite the 'allegiance'. I was so naïve I did not know I would have to wait for that big moment for a few years.

With his back to two big windows facing the courtyard sat the consul, behind a fair size desk, on the top of which was a name plate: Barton McLeary, Consul of the United States of America. The consul slowly swung around his chair and laughed. I was speechless, Bart had the advantage, he knew I was coming.

Luck! At the right time in the right place, even a whorehouse could be the right place if you are lucky.

9 The Stork's Egg

Miki was not a good driver, he was not a bad driver, he was just a driver, although lots of people on the road used to call him a roadblock. Driving me back from Tijuana with my dream in my pocket, when Noah's Ark would have been a more suitable transportation, he drove like a maniac. He was in a hurry to get home. 'We'll celebrate. And you'll never guess who will be there, Mitzi and George!'

My first, my only previous trip to Tijuana had been with George years ago and had ended in dismal disaster. I was wondering all the way back if Mitzi still intended to keep her promise to kill me. She was certainly capable of doing a silly thing like that.

Probably one of the most visible, the most identifiable exposed single objects in the world was and still is the torch held high in the hand of the Statue of Liberty. In the mid-thirties, early forties the breasts of Mitzi were just as exposed, just as visible. They were not as high but they didn't have to be held up. They stuck up there all by themselves. The torch was only a single piece protruding toward the sky. Mitzi had two protuberances. Her husband, George, was more proud of Mitzi's exhibits than she was and this was saying a lot. It puzzled me, since he had achievements he should have been more proud of. But men are very strange sometimes. Mitzi was the reddest natural red-headed Hungarian, with green eyes and a temper that went with it. She was not dumb. For her 'Time Marches On!' meant more than an RKO short, she knew the footprints of time could flatten everything in their path. She wanted something permanent to be proud of, something time could not destroy, like a title.

George was an aviator – he didn't like to be called a pilot – he was an aviator with his long white scarf blown by the prop-wash in the open cockpit of his biplane. He never stated he flew with the Lafayette Esquadrille, he only talked as if he had. George was not a liar, he was a writer, a successful writer with a vivid imagination.

It was not difficult for Mitzi to make George believe that he was the descendant of aristocracy, because his family name was Scottish. A title of Baronet, no less, would have been acceptable to both of them. But preliminary research showed George's Scottish title of Baronet was a bit cloudy. However, further research indicated that George's ancestors left Russia for Scotland in the early Middle Ages. When the official tracing of the complete genealogy became acceptable to the Office of Heraldry of the Czar, the family's ancient armorial insignia, the armorial ensign and the rightful title of Count was restored to George's family. The unexpected, pleasant surprise of being a verified Countess, not just a mere Baroness, cost Mitzi a few extra dollars, to be donated to the Heraldry Office of the Czar, which was located in Paris, where the White Russian emigrés camped out in the Ritz, George V, or less luxurious tenements. Most of them of course were Romanoffs and direct cousins of the Czar.

The intermediary who placed George back on his ancestral throne, was a Romanoff, naturally. I called this intermediary Prince, whose name I always forgot, 'Princey', and he always shuddered hearing it. I enjoyed that. Mitzi always kicked my shin if it was within her reach, I did not enjoy that. She was impressed by the Prince and bowed to him deeply to express her gratitude, which gave the Prince an excellent view of Mitzi's belly-button between her two exhibits. Tit for tat, and for that the Prince was grateful too, and he risked 'everything including lives' to smuggle out of Russia the ancient ensign and other family memorabilia for the Count and Countess from Saint Petersburg.

Selling papers to create new identities, thanks to Hitler, was a booming business. When it saved lives, as occasionally it did, it was a commendable business, but in George's and Mitzi's case it was a deplorable sham.

The newly found nobility changed everything. George's once comfortable early-American ranch house was transformed into a graveyard of fakes and the home of imported, trained moths and wood-worms to enhance the antiquity of the Count's family heirlooms. It was all heaven on the north-west corner of Tujunga and Ventura on the Count's and Countess' six-and-a-half-acre spread. He had two houses on the property, the very spacious main house and a small bungalow where I lived. George was a successful freelance magazine story writer. Luckily, being a Count did not interfere with George's desire to become a screenwriter. And that is where I came into the picture.

Géza Herczeg was one of the former very good friends of Mitzi. He introduced me to George, suggesting we should collaborate. The Count eagerly agreed, provided I did not take credit. I agreed just as eagerly, for a shamefully large sum, more than a roof over my head – a lovely bungalow all to myself for a while, until the rain came – plus any or all meals with the Count and Countess in the main house or in the bungalow, served by the butler.

Subsequently 'Tiehappy' moved in with me. Tiehappy was a hundred and seventy pounds Great Dane who was in love with ties, that is where his moniker came from. He preferred Sulka or Countess Mara ties, but was not very fussy. We preferred the old comfortable early-American furniture which was auctioned off by Newman on Wilshire Boulevard.

After that the Prince reappeared and for an additional donation to the Heraldry Office of the Czar he arranged to cleanse the home of the Count and Countess. He brought with him the blessings of the Patriarch plus a Greek Orthodox Bishop in full regalia with his full entourage, a large choir and several vestrymen burning incense in rattling golden pots hanging on chains.

This was very disturbing, but what broke Tiehappy's heart was Mitzi's kick. She had kicked him for the first time, for what? For something that made Tiehappy famous, for something that made him the life of many a party. I understood him, he was sensitive, he felt it and he decided to move in with me. He was a master of surprises. Usually before dessert he snuck up from behind, his head towering above the victim's head but nobody was aware of him until one of his paws landed on one of their shoulders with a heavy thud. Surprised they always turned toward the impact of Tiehappy's paw and in that blink of a moment Tiehappy grabbed their tie from the opposite side. One yank and the tie was gone. He shook it with a ferocious growl and dropped it into the fireplace, lit or dead, made no difference.

On this holy occasion Tiehappy snatched, instead of a tie, a dangling golden tassle from the Bishop's ornate vestment, because it was there. But he did not deposit it in the fireplace, he vengefully shredded it then dropped what was left on the floor and wee-weed on it.

God's ways are mysterious, but sooner or later always just. Clouds started to accumulate, first on the horizon and then above the house of the Count and the Countess – which was not called the spread any

more, it had become the estate. Whatever it was, it was next to something
that was laughingly called a 'river', the 'Los Angeles river'. A travesty of
a geological expression. Justice started with sudden lightning and a clap
of thunder almost simultaneously, then tentative raindrops decorated the
giant swimming pool with ever expanding rings. George and I grabbed
our papers off the table next to the pool and truth poked his sometimes
ugly head through the camouflage. 'Let's go to your place,' the Count
yelled over the distant rumble of thunder.

It puzzled me, he had a wonderful office in the big house, untouched
by the holy cleansing and the files were there. The bungalow was a few
hundred yards from the big house, on the highest spot of the estate. He
sat down on the porch, silent, listening to the rain drumming on the tile
roof. He wanted to have a drink, I brought him one. The clouds rolling
over the Hollywood hills from the south-west had no silver lining.

'No?'

'No, I don't feel like having a drink.'

He slushed his over the railing. 'Smart, I shouldn't have one either.'
His face was as cloudy as the sky above us. 'I had a nice spread here.'

'Estate.' I corrected him.

'Fuck the estate. I hate feeling sorry for myself and I hate being a
sucker.'

We sat listening to the increasing rhythm of the raindrops. It was peace
in the San Fernando Valley. Suddenly George laughed. 'OK, I've said it
out loud, I feel better and now I can have a drink.'

I brought him another drink, Tiehappy followed me out of the porch. I
thought the floorboards would crack as he crashed down on them to
settle next to me and my thighbone as he dropped his head on my leg.

'You are smarter than I am, Tie, old boy. May I have another?'

By the time I came back Tiehappy's head was in George's lap and, for
the first time since he had become a nobleman, George seemed to be
content. From an evil thought an evil smile surfaced as he crossed his
fingers. 'It happened once, three years ago, maybe it'll happen again.'

The most unjust, inhuman decision was to put the Los Angeles river in
jail. Why? Exuberance was no crime ever. Then why was its liberty taken
away with two ugly grey, graffiti-covered cement walls? Oh, there were a
few decent people with guilty consciences who painted some great, some
not so great frescos on the prison's grey walls, but that was little consolation, if any, for what was taken away. Before its imprisonment the river

bottom was the playground of the winds chasing dust devils. But when it rained up north – not in Los Angeles where the skies could have been smog-blue – suddenly, unexpectedly the water just happened, like a light turned on in a blacked-out room. Suddenly the light was just there.

That's what happened now. Between two blinks of the eye the lower edge of the estate was not an emerald green lawn any more, it was a foaming, swirling yellow destruction. Two more blinks, it reached the house, and two more, it was in the house. Mesmerized, I sat there not knowing what to do. George's smile widened before it became a full-hearted laughter. 'God, it's good, how much I was hoping for this.'

The flood had reached the window sills when Mitzi pulled into the driveway which was considerably higher than the house, but it was still a miracle that the car was running. 'Don't move,' said George to me, and we watched her overcoming the pressure of the water against the car door as she got out in the knee-deep water. She left the car door open, stamped her feet and screamed wordlessly.

George put two fingers in his mouth and let out a shrill whistle, then waved his arms, 'Come on . . . come on.'

Mitzi looked back at the car, ignored her shopping bags eddying through its open door and swirling off. The inside of her car became a sitz bath; she kicked the front wheel and screamed again. It was impossible to tell from the distance if her screams came from frustration, anger or if she had hurt her foot. Whatever it was it did not stop her from kicking at the water as she trudged uphill.

Before the spread became a spread or an estate with manicured lawns and prize-winning rose bushes, it was a walnut grove. The bungalow had been built over sixty years ago by smart people on the highest section of the land and it remained the only dry spot around. Mitzi, panting, reached us and started off, not exactly in the King's English, but very fluently, 'Shit-shit-shit-oooh shit!'

Coming from a Countess, I thought it was funny. Unfortunately I laughed, and she let me have it in Hungarian – and Countess Mitzi had a fabulous vocabulary of dirty cuss words in both languages. As I walked back into the bungalow I heard her tearing into poor Count George, 'You stupid son-of-a-bitch, you oaf, how in the fucking hell could you build a house in a ditch like . . .' and I closed the door behind me.

Mitzi stayed heartbroken for two reasons. One, the heirlooms were destroyed, two, when the Prince suggested he could replace them for a donation to the Heraldry Office of the Czar, George literally, bodily threw him out. Mitzi fainted. To put the house back in order with early American furniture, as the contractors guessed, would take a minimum of a month or 'so'. The Count and Countess moved in with me in the lowly, but dry bungalow. They were very quiet. They didn't speak to each other.

I asked George if he would mind shedding his nobility forever. 'I shed mine with the flood. Mitzi the bitch-o-mine is the problem.'

My time had arrived to come to their rescue. I was fond of ignoble Mitzi and George. I invited them to the 'Bublitchki', a Russian restaurant on Sunset Boulevard, and the trap worked: the Greek Orthodox Bishop who had cleansed their home was one of the busboys and his vestry men were his helpers in the kitchen. Mitzi fainted again and I believe the Bishop came close to fainting, too.

The weeks of sleepless nights I had spent at Miki's suggestion watching the back doors of the Russian restaurants in town finally paid off. It was worth it. George hugged me and said 'Thanks.' Mitzi didn't speak to me for quite a long while.

Weeks had gone by and the contractors not only couldn't begin to work, they could not find a pump available to pump the water out of the sunken living-room. The sewers smelled better than the dry upstairs. And when a dead cat floated out from under one of the collapsed heirlooms exactly when Mitzi was checking the damage with an insurance adjuster, the plan George was pushing for came to a head, thanks only to the dead cat – I am not suspicious of George and his magic powers.

The staff were to move back from the motel to my bungalow. Mitzi was to stay in Palm Springs with friends, he and I were going to Baja California to get back to work.

That was my first trip to Baja California. We settled in the Rosarito Beach Hotel, and spent an awful lot of time with the horses at the Agua Caliente track, wasted an awful lot of my time and emotion rooting for the bulls in the Tijuana Plaza, but strange as it may seem we did a hell of a lot of work on the side. The germ of two of George's big subsequent hits were sown then.

After a couple of months a disaster struck. The big house was put in order under Mitzi's supervision and we had to go back. George did not object too much to the new decor, except to the 'dusty-pink' bedroom, but unfortunately it was functioning. Functioning until one day when Mitzi came back from town and did what she had never done before.

She drove up directly to the bungalow and with screeching brakes came to a panic stop, jumped out of her car, leaving its door wide open, as she often did, stormed up the steps, tore the screen door open, and left it open of course, screaming, 'Get out, get out, geeet-oouut. Get-out-of-here before I kill you . . . get oouut!' In a hysterical frenzy she was running around the room grabbing out of closets and drawers clothes, shirts, shoes, everything she could reach, kicking them, throwing them out the front door. When she picked my typewriter up off the desk it dropped on her foot, and that did it. She went completely berserk, she started to kick me and everything else in her way.

The better part of valour is discretion, and with all the discretion I could muster I jumped off the front porch to freedom. As this saying does not exist in Hungarian, she followed me only to crumble to the ground at the bottom of the stairs.

Tiehappy was gamboling uphill in slow-motion to investigate the fracas. George formed a megaphone with his palms and called to me through one of the open windows of his office, 'I called her doctor already, he is on his way.' George was an astute and educated gentleman, he knew the saying about valour and wisely stayed away.

Tiehappy didn't help matters with his nosey inquiries; she kicked at him. I brought down a chair for her, no use, she kicked at me, at the chair, she kicked at anything and Mitzi had no panties on. That did not stop her, she kept on kicking, and cursing and accusing me, 'It's all your fault.' I didn't know what my fault was supposed to be but I accepted it and apologized, hoping that would quiet her down. It backfired, she became more hysterical, 'You led him astray, you ungrateful snake,' garnished with a new surge of filthy cuss words.

The doctor arrived with a nurse and sedated Mitzi. As they carried her into the big house she started to scream again, 'I fucked everybody and I never had it,' repeating it over and over, but as the sedatives slowly took effect she stopped bragging. They put her in bed in the 'dusty-pink' bedroom with the nurse in attendance.

George looked more like the drowned cat than the drowned cat did. He always wanted to be the conqueror, he liked to pick his own trophies, the Moulin Rouges for him were too easy hunting grounds. One of his Baja California victories was now costing him dearly.

George was very selective in everything. One of his selections was a lovely, young thing. 'She was a virgin,' he told me proudly. Little did he know she gave him a bonus with her virginity, a bacteria known as Neisseria Gonorrhoea. It sounded better this way than 'the clap' when a virgin presented it. To add to the problems, none of which I was aware of until that memorable day, George was allergic to penicillin and other antibiotics like tetracyline, ceftriaxone or spectinomycine were unheard of or unavailable and the treatment of George was lax and spotty, but the lab tests he was told were clear when we left Tijuana.

George tried to stop me from moving out of the bungalow but just the same, that very afternoon, I moved into the Knickerbocker Hotel on Hollywood Boulevard. When I checked in a message was waiting for me at the desk, 'I heard the news, see you for dinner at the Little Hungary. – Géza.'

Luck again, at the right time on the right spot. I was on the right spot, but poor George was not for a long and miserable time to come.

'Good,' was Géza's first word when I walked in the restaurant, then he went on, 'I wanted to borrow you from George anyway to kick around some ideas.'

I moved to Géza Herczeg's glued-to-the-hillside, stairs-entwined, three-stories-deep, Los Angeles-style architectural abortion on Los Tilos, off Outpost drive. The lowest floor was mine, closest to the swimming pool which was used only by me and lots of four-legged deers, a few discriminating two-legged dears and some courageous coyotes. No other mountaineers were willing to climb the hillside or the narrow, risky stairs. Climbing up and down didn't hinder me, we came up with something that brought the Oscar for Géza and for me my first Academy Award dinner at the Biltmore Bowl, in downtown L.A.

With Géza Herczeg I met the crème de la crème of the industry socially. Professionally I did not exist, but I didn't care for credit, I was well reimbursed.

Hollywood was living high on the hog, I drifted with it paying my share of the freight. The stakes in the gambling rooms of Herman Hover's Ciro's on the north side of Sunset Strip were staggering. On the south side, down the strip west from Ciro's was Billy Wilkerson's Trocadero where the Sunday amateur night try-outs were among the 'musts' to attend. On one night, among the amateurs was a young, skinny fellow with a lot of hair who brought down the house. His name was Sinatra.

Frank, I believe. What he lacked in voice he more than made up for in feeling.

On the same side of the strip, east of the Trocadero almost across from Ciro's, Felix Young reigned in the Mocambo with his big macaws behind glass in their cages sunk into the walls around the main room. They were brilliantly plumed in every color of the rainbow, plus white. They were very nice but they bugged me, I had no idea whether they could fly. I was born with gnawing curiosity. I also had a fetish to learn. Driven by these two curses, one night I decided to fill this gap in my knowledge. But the night's experiment left a still unanswered evolutionary question. Did the busboys descend from macaws or macaws from busboys? I was also a firm believer in liberty. I thought when I let the macaws loose they would fly around in their happy newly-found freedom and land and nest on the chandeliers and live there free, not in glass cages. No. I was wrong again.

It became evident the macaws were only capable of table-top-high short hops. Except one. The hefty wings of these big birds were not for flying, they were for clearing tables without training just like the busboys. However, there were big differences between them. The busboys were painfully slow and expected tips; the macaws were incredibly fast clearing off the tables and expected nothing. They were givers.

Generous givers. They dropped their larger than saucer-size memorabilia everywhere: on the floor, on table tops, on the heads and shoulders of anybody who didn't duck under the tables, which were indiscriminately swept clear of everything, glasses full or empty, porcelain dishes with only bread and butter or Baked Alaska.

It turned out to be a memorable evening. Only one of the birds acted like a bird. That bird flew and flew around beautifully, then landed on a chandelier, swung on it back and forth whilst screeching a happy song of freedom. Sparks, more sparks. Then total blackness. From above an ear-piercing screech, a jingling crash in the dark. And I was barred from the Mocambo for months.

As a revenge I spread the rumor that what Felix Young was serving for Thanksgiving was not turkey. He had saved me a lot of money by not letting me in, so I was grateful to the macaws.

I owe a great deal of thanks to big birds, of all kinds. They have had a strange influence on my life, starting with my childhood friend Sam, my grey crane who helped to eat the luncheon I was supposed to eat but detested. To the macaws for helping to save my money. And many,

many years later for my Academy Award nomination to yet another big bird, a stork.

I was married, on that occasion legally, to an extremely vulnerable young lady. We were walking out of a nightclub, Sherman Billingsley's Stork Club in New York, and stopped at a table to chat with friends. A shrill scream turned me around. A young man had grabbed my wife from behind and was pumping her breasts.

This jerk made two almost-fatal mistakes. His first mistake was he despicably assaulted a lady. That was a no-no any time, anywhere while I was around, plus, this lady whose breasts he was mangling happened to be my wife. His second mistake was he swung at me when I pushed him away from her.

Unfortunately, I could hit him only once. But more unfortunately it happened at Walter Winchell's table and in his Winchellian manner he described the incident in his column and on his radio show, quoting 'atomic punches' and all that crap. I was barred from the Stork Club for fighting on its premises or because of Walter's world-wide publicity. This was against the grain of the club rule: no fighting for any reason on the premises of the Stork Club. (It was all right to scuffle outside!)

During those overcharged years fights were a nightly occurrence, even in some of the plushest clubs. The action stars were the main targets – 'So you think you're so tough?' – and pow, the fights were on, even in the Stork Club. Not to scare away the celebrities, the well-oiled PR machine kept it out of the media by heavy publicizing: 'There has never been a fisticuff in the Stork Club.'

It was known that Winchell hated the club. He called it a phoney meat-market. But they swallowed this and kissed his ass – he was too important to rough up. But the swifty PR hounds got even with him, blew a high C charge on their trumpets and turned to their advantage the 'for the club not too favourable news break' by adding their well-known pitch 'so far'. With the PR drums rolling world-wide, I was barred from the Stork Club forever for fighting on its premises, never mentioning that Winchell, in his blurb, strongly approved of my reaction to the provocation. But Winchell always approved or disapproved of everything. There was no half-way with Walter.

Whenever I bumped into Winchell after this incident I had to give him a new one-dollar bill as a token of the considerable amount of money he saved me by publicizing the event and getting me barred from the Stork

Club. If I didn't have a new one-dollar bill on me, he was willing to accept as a courtesy, as he put it, any old one-thousand-dollar bill, or in lieu of that I had to buy drinks and dinners for him and sometimes his eight or nine friends, all thirsty and hungry. After a while I learned my lesson and always carried a new one-dollar bill on me. He said I was a cheapskate.

Nobody scooped Walter Winchell, so I am sure he knew I bribed an understanding undertaker and sent a brand new one-dollar bill with him on his last journey to help him cross the river Styx.

I was stupid enough to believe courage knows no fear. Like most people in their Walter Mitty world, I, too, wanted to be a hero. I had no yellow streak on my back, I believed I had no fear. Well, I learned an overdue lesson the hard way with the help of the Stork Club and Walter Winchell.

I was minding my own business sitting at the bar of the Smokehouse in Burbank across from Warners' studio, waiting for a friend to join me for dinner, when a hand grabbed my shoulder from behind, whirled me off the barstool and took a swing at me, 'So you think you're so tough, you atomic shit!' The man swung again. He was so drunk it would have been unfair to hit him. I shoved him and he fell over on his ass just as my friend walked in with a friend of his.

'Good-oh, you got it sooner than I thought you would. Winchell is widely read,' he laughed. 'I hope you don't mind, I asked Johnny to join us? He is a pleasure to have around.'

I did not know Johnny well, I knew his nickname was 'pick-up-the-check-Johnny-Meyer'. Nobody could pick up a check when Johnny was around. He was Hughes's man for all seasons. Hughes encouraged Johnny to pick up the checks, that was part of his job, like Paul Dugan's was to spread 'Guest of TWA' airline tickets around. It was good public relations at a bargain rate. Hughes was a bargain-hunter on the one hand, but he could be very generous.

On the south-east corner of Santa Monica Boulevard and Las Palmas was an 'A' – Associated – filling station and garage, owned by Hughes personally. The filling station was ramroded by Capo Alberto, who had a face in color and texture like a sun-dried apple on which several snow-tires had left their imprint. The rumor had it Alberto once worked for Ettore Bugatti, and was one of the racing mechanics of the legend himself, Tazio Nuvolari.[1]

1 The all-time great Italian racing driver who drove everything with four wheels and an engine and broke every record. Some of Nuvolari's records set in the mid-thirties are still standing.

Alberto was a virtuoso of engines of any kind. He did not speak in any one language. On the rare occasions when he spoke at all he mixed several languages in one single sentence, but he talked to engines for hours and hours, imitating their sounds perfectly. 'Brroohhbrroowh-grwhoooo-dats-vat-I-vna-hear-brrrooooh-growhooooo-ecco-ecco-eccolo, grrrowh ottimo-bravissimo,' came the symphony from under the hoods. I do not believe, except for his posterior, any part of his body saw sunlight more than ten minutes a week.

Through that corner filling station passed, if not the world's, then certainly Hollywood's most beautiful young ladies. To them the gas, the service, the tires, everything was free. The cars belonged to one of Hughes's companies. These Lincolns, Cadillacs, Mercurys, coupes, convertibles were each assigned to one and only one girl to drive with an added restriction, she was not supposed to drive it out of town.

I was working at General Service Studios on North Las Palmas, just south of 'the' filling station. Capo Alberto took care of my cars. Maybe because of my fractured Italian or because he realized we could lie to each other about cars and races we used to have an occasional cup of 'dis is not, not real cofe'.

'Next time I piss in yours, Alfredo.'

'Alberto, stronza!'

'Vana more cofe?' asked Lil, imitating Alberto.

We were in 'Lil's', the only café on the General Service Studio lot. It was impeccably clean. All three tables always had blinding-white tablecloths on them. Out of the twelve chairs it was safe to sit on ten. Lil's menu had a great selection: steak charred and rare, rare, medium or, as Lil described it, spoiled. But two things were sure, the salad was always fresh and the steak always came up charred and rare. Lil was very independent.

Alberto was as tortured as only an Italian could be. He said some of the 'bambolas' were insulting him for a long time, 'Merde allora, je sui not a stupido.' He surprised me. I thought people could not reach the Capo's feelings, for him they simply didn't exist. His life was engines, and since his beloved engines never lied to him, the truth was, the 'stronzas rubato Mr Sam'. Sam was one of Hughes' many 'code-names'. Translated, what Alberto meant was, 'The bitches robbed Mr Hughes.'

Some of the little lovelies used to drive in two or three times a day to fill up the empty tanks of 'their' cars with only twenty to thirty miles on their mileage counters. It crushed Capo Alberto's pride that anybody would even suppose he would allow an engine he took care of to guzzle that much fuel per mile. 'I am no stupido. They sell gasolino or give boyfriend. I was stupido long enough basta cosi. I tell Mr Sam OK. Merde alors!'

After Alberto told Mr Sam what his engines were telling him and how long he had been standing by like a stupido, one more restriction was added to the previous two. At the Capo's sole discretion the privilege of using any of the cars was revocable at less than a second's notice. Some of the silly little starlets who drove in 'their' Lincolns, Cadillacs to fill up had to walk home using their own foot power. Capo Alfredo filled up their car, checked the mileage, made them sign the slip with a smile showing off his surprisingly whiter-than-white teeth and asked them very politely to get out – he had something to do with the car, which was immediately driven away by a mechanic, then he waved goodbye to the awestruck beauties.

Bad news travels faster than good news, especially in Hollywood. The fishing season opened unexpectedly and, like a taxi stand in New York in front of a deluxe hotel in the rain, all types of drivers and cars were waiting in line, risking traffic violations, to offer their good samaritan services to the desperate.

I was present on one of these tragi-comic occasions and I wanted to offer a lift at source to the stranded beauty. The Capo grabbed my arm, 'No! Mr Sam not like it. Watch.' He held on to me tight. Dejected, the stupefied little beauty, whose name by the way was quite legible on billboards, walked off toward the honking line of cars. Making a quick decision, she picked a Mercedes. But Alberto still held on to me until a nondescript car pulled out from the rear, then he let me go. 'Detective follow every stronza. Mr Sam very angry.'

Money did not matter to Hughes but he had a phobia of being taken for a ride, of being 'cheated'. Mistrust, the seeds of schizophrenia, were beginning to take charge of a unique man. Hughes drove gun-metal-grey Chevrolets. These cars were delivered to him direct from the factory. The drivers were ordered to drive them through muck and every puddle on the way. Hughes's cars were never washed. But the very special engines were maintained to perfection. I believe Hughes loved engines more than his stable of starlets and kept them longer.

Hughes could not understand Johnny Meyer, who changed his shiny new Cadillacs at least twice a year, always to a different model and color. His answer to his boss's query 'Why?' was 'You can afford to drive those dirty junks, Sam, everybody knows you are important. You don't need a status symbol.'

Johnny Meyer was a middle-aged, middle-sized, innocuous baby-pink-cheeked statue of peace, with a benevolent smile. It was known he objected to smoking and, to my surprise, the minute he sat down the waiter brought him an extra large ashtray and an extra napkin without being asked for it. Johnny carefully placed the ashtray in the center of the napkin, twisted its four corners tight together to form a handle. Satisfied, he placed it on his left thigh, comfortably close to his left hand. He was left-handed.

'Oh shit,' I put down my second drink without even taking a sip.

Johnny didn't need any explanation, 'Where?'

I pointed them out. The drunken slob who had whacked me was back with a friend, a pretty big bruiser. They were approaching us.

Johnny excused himself and left the table carrying his napkin-bundled ashtray. I thought he was a wise man to get out of this mess.

'You better leave the table too because – '

'Better? Hell no! Nobody is going to spoil my drink,' said he, savoring his Gibson, as cool as the drink in his frosted glass.

'Look, you don't need any more of this kind of publicity, you had enough of – '

'Chum, that's what keeps me going.'

The big bruiser grinned from cauliflower ear to cauliflower ear, 'Ooohh-look who's we got here,' the drunken slob grabbed for me – and that was it. From nowhere Johnny Meyer was behind them, his napkin flashed twice and they weren't around anymore.

The waiters dragged off the floor two unconscious bodies and carried them out. The manager rushed over to apologize. Johnny sat down and politely asked for a clean napkin, the one with the ashtray in it was bloodstained.

That was Johnny Meyer. He sipped his Dewar's White Label on the rocks in silence. The general hubbub filled the room again. All I could say was, 'Wow!'

'Yeah, I said that lots of times. Now you know how it feels to be a target. Sometimes it scares me. It scares the shit out of me.'

Did I hear right? My friend, the swashbuckler of all swashbucklers on or off the screen, said he could be scared. Was he just kidding? Anyway, the stork laid an egg for me and it started me thinking.

In Dodge City, Tombstone, Arizona, or in Any-town of the spooky nowhere of the West could Billy the Kid, Bat Masterson, Wyatt Earp, any of the gunfighters, all 'targets', walk up to the bar, order a Sassparilla and admit they were scared without being stamped as yellow-bellied cowards? What had accelerated human understanding within less than two generations? The armor-clad shining knights of the Middle Ages rode their armor-clad steeds alone. The fighter pilots of the First World War rode their kites alone like the fighter jocks of the Second World War rode their Mustangs with 1,695 horsepower in their V-1650-7 Packard-Merlins alone. Did they meet fear? Would they have said so if they had?

Then the sitting ducks of the ack-ack – the bombers – took to the skies, with crews packed together, tightly. Could you blame 'Joe the tail-gunner' if he was afraid crouching in a foetal position in his plastic bubble between two guns. Sealed in. No parachute, not enough room for it, but an unobstructed view of the flak coming up. The 'Joe' who told you in the ready room before take-off he still felt the warmth of his wife's embrace, the kick of the baby within her – if Joe confessed he was scared, would you call him a yellow-bellied coward? Would you call 'Joe' a hero if he said 'Eh-shit-man, I ain't got no yellow streak on my back.' And up there next to nowhere, humans packed together in a shithouse in the sky next to the truth, learned to know themselves, and after that each other, and the real heroes were born who knew how to handle fear.

I have to thank Errol, tail-gunner 'Joe' and another Joe. They helped me to hatch the egg the stork laid in my lap. It hatched, strangely enough in the Stork Club.

'I thought this was a safe place, but it's not. Night before last I was sitting in this booth when a little shit of a schmuck came to the table, punched me in the face to show off to his date. I am afraid to go anywhere.'

'You . . . afraid?'

'Hell yes! Every time I stepped in the ring, except the first time with Schmelling, I knew I had him. I learned.'

Was Joe Louis a lesser man then than the Dalton Boys, Billy the Kid or any of the other gunfighters?

It took a long time to hatch the stork's egg, but it was worth it. *The Gunfighter* came out of it to pave the way to its glorious cousin, *High Noon*.

Bill Bowers, a great guy, a butt-to-tip-lit smoker – of whatever – a devout alcoholic at that time, he had to have a sip of – whatever, he wasn't fussy – every twenty minutes. We liked to work together and crossed many rough seas during many rough nights; he loved 'moonshine'. We fit.

To drink alcohol on studio premises was a capital N.O. To run out to the closest bar twice an hour was a short cut to the pink slip. This injustice hurt Bill so much that he developed a deep, nervous, rumbling cough. An ugly, pitifully whizzing cough. Being a generous but considerate gentleman, Bill refused to spread his germs around, and when his coughing fits came he covered his face from eyebrows down with the right lapel of his jacket to cough inside of it.

There was a quart-capacity douche-bag installed in his jacket's right inside pocket with a long plastic straw attached to it. And Bill was happily sloshed all day, but under all conditions a genius of a writer, and we came up with the true, the 'naked, no shining armor covered' story of a *gunfighter*, as it should be told. I wanted Gary Cooper to play it. It was not enough. It was torpedoed before it ever reached Cooper, as I found out when shooting *Springfield Rifle*.

Harry Cohn liked the story – 'with more action and some changes' – but accused me of being unpatriotic – heil McCarthy – by wanting to defile American heroes if I insisted on going on with it as it was. Wanting to present real human beings? I agree it may be ugly, but it is sure not a crime.

Bill lost heart or his douche-bag sprung a leak. I was alone fighting for *The Gunfighter* and I felt like Don Quixote fighting the Hollywood windmills, except their sails had razors for edges and could refine you to finely chopped mincemeat.

Don't let dreams turn into nightmares, ride'em cowboy. It bothered me, but I understood, Bill needed some quick ready cash, and so did I as always; however I suggested putting *The Gunfighter* on the shelf. I never went back to it, Bill did, but I disagreed with the resurrection process. I respected Zanuck, a lousy polo player but with audacious guts, who finally went for *The Gunfighter*, only to lose his famous audacity and guts. Hollywood filed off his rough edges, for me emasculating the image of

The Gunfighter. It was the only time it showed he fought the war from Paris. He was not the man I was working with before, nor was Bowers. It hurt me to see that Hollywood turned Bill's principles and talent into a soggy olive left overnight in the bottom of an empty Gibson glass, waiting to be flushed down with the morning clean-up.

But I'm lucky, because the fun memories of *Pitfall* and all the others we worked on stayed with me. Bill was working for Universal during the days and a few nights a week, and on the weekends we were turning out scripts in Palm Springs. Once I picked up a book, Jay Drattler's *Pitfall*, it had a nucleus of something I was interested in and wanted to do someday.

'If that's what you want to do with it why buy the book? . . . And why do that story in the first place? . . . It's immoral.' I heard the words over and over again. Nothing happened. Bill was with me but there were no takers, I couldn't move it. Then it came home years later out of the blue. There was no studio involved, it was an independent venture and a venture it was. And fun.

I had never met Dick Powell till the day he called inviting me and my wife for dinner. Our wives,[2] both of them being in the business, knew each other, so there was nothing bizarre about that, but everything else turned out to be rather odd and unusual, to say the least, making that picture. Right from the moment of our first meeting at The Beachcomber swimming in Navy Grogs[3], followed next day with a flight down to Palm Springs, to have a meeting with Dick's co-producer, Sam Bischoff, whom of course I knew. What I didn't know was that Dick had a plane and he was a pilot. Well, it turned out to be a very memorable flight; since then I have believed in miracles.

The menace of John Ford and Michael Curtiz on the road fused into one would have been a peaceful straight-driving blessing compared to Dick in the air. He was all over the sky. Sometimes I thought he was heading back; the approximately 55-minute flight took us over two hours, proving only one thing – it's not enough to own a fast-for-its-time, very good, single-engine 'V'-tail Beech Bonanza, it is who is at the controls that counts. The engine got tired of his flying too, I suppose, because it quit. Two coughs and one bang. That's all folks.

2 Powell was married to June Allison, de Toth to Veronica Lake.
3 A strong, very large tropical drink with various rums. Lethal.

It can be very disturbing up in the wild blue yonder, watching the stationary blade of the propeller of a single-engine aeroplane sticking up in front of you like a bloody exclamation mark pointing skywards, while you're diving earthwards, as the pilot (?) lets go of the controls, and pays no attention to the altitude of the plane, to the gauges. He picked up the mike and crooned: 'Mayday . . . mayday, this is Dick Powell. Mayday, my engine quit . . .'

Luckily, the plane was so badly trimmed – too nose-heavy, thank God – that, instead of stalling and snapping into a spin (an extremely dangerous, forbidden manoeuvre for that type of plane), as it would've done with a dead engine and no controls, it started to dive, while Dick Powell crooned, 'Mayday, mayday, my engine quit I'm . . .' he turned to me, 'how high are we?'

I told him, '10,000 feet. Tell'em your position first.'

But he only kept repeating, 'Mayday . . . mayday. This is Dick Powell . . . may-day-may-day-may-day . . .'

I checked the gauges and noticed the radio was still tuned in to the Burbank tower – where we had taken off from – so I let him croon 'mayday'. I knew these models had two fuel tanks; the gauge showed one was empty, but the second was full. This type of Bonanza had one single-control, swing-over yoke, so I took it from pilot side, swung it over and took the controls. Our diving speed increased, I turned on the full tank and after a forever-lasting – four or five – seconds and a few coughs the engine started to purr. One of the nicest sounds to anybody's ear who has ever had the luck to hear it.

Because it's not too smart to pull out of a past-the-red-line-speed dive of a plane too abruptly, I babied it gently toward Banning airport, which I knew was in the middle of the pass at 2,219 feet, and I levelled out, hedge-hopping at 2,800 feet over the highway, leaving almost 600 feet of safety between us and a possible disappearing act. I looked up, on my starboard the peak of San Isidro at 10,800 feet, on my port the peak of San Gorgonio scratched the feet of my real co-pilot up there. I said a quick prayer of thanks. And to my luck.

As though nothing had happened, Dick took over the controls. I took the mike and reported our position, heading and altitude to traffic control, adding that all was 'A-OK'. Dick was climbing and climbing, when 5,000 feet would have been a higher-than-safe altitude to reach Palm Spring airport. But he climbed and climbed till we reached the ceiling altitude of the plane and it started to mush, and we were getting blue under the fingernails from lack of oxygen.

We arrived above Palm Springs airport at 16,000 feet to land on the 495-foot altitude runway. We were almost high enough to turn back and land at Burbank airport without an engine, and because of the terrific thermals of the desert heat the plane kept ballooning. After more than an hour over the airport trying to get down, and almost out of gas, he landed. Landed? Well, sort of. After several mile-high bounces we were finally on the ground. The 114° heat never felt better.

He never said thanks, nor did he ever speak about this stunt. After we finished our meeting with Bishoff and resolved everything, he asked me if I would fly the plane back to town because he wanted to stay for a while. For that I said thanks because I had to be back, but not in a body bag.

My original deal was to write a screenplay with Bill Bowers. Dick wanted to co-produce *Pitfalls* with Bishoff as a first film, the foundation of a production empire. After our historic flight and landing in Palm Springs, and hours of story meetings, I thought what a well-meaning schmuck Dick was, what a pity he doesn't play the main character, Forbes, as well. Perfect casting.

Schmuck or no, Dick Powell was a kamikaze pilot, but he wasn't a dope, nor had he mental telepathy. He was a showman, an old circus horse with horse sense. A few weeks later, as we were going through the script, he asked me, offhand, if I would do him a favor and direct the picture too. 'A favor' and 'direct too' made me sure there was no telepathy involved, just good business. He expected me to direct the picture 'too', for the fee he gave me for writing the screenplay. He won and so did I. I directed *Pitfall* – and with joy.

For the part of Forbes's 'pitfall' there were very few around in Hollywood then who fitted the part as I saw it. Not a fashionable Hollywood bambola to cheapen the story, not a tit-swinger actress. I wanted a warm, sincere and proud human being. She had to have talent to *feel*, not *play* the part. For me there was only one who could do it, Elizabeth Scott.

'Can we sell the picture with Scott?' and a long list of 'saleable' and available tit-swingers was put in front of me. 'They would sell.'

That was a mistake. 'Why do we need anybody, we have Dick Powell,' I said.

'Right!' he agreed. 'You have me. Scott will do.' And Elizabeth Scott had the part.

His wife in the film was difficult to cast. A demanding part on the razor's edge of emotion. I didn't want a self-pitying, poor Miss Pitiful Pearl, a marshmallowy wilted flower, or a nagging bitch for the wife. I wanted somebody with inborn dignity and pride, with the strength of understanding, a real human being. Not only a good actress. It was a woman-dominated story, she had to be the strongest. It took some time to find her, but once the name came up there was no problem. Jane Wyatt. She had it all.

But then came trouble. Who was to play Mac, the private detective? Everybody had an idea who was Mac, the 'shoeshine' on the lot included: 'What's wrong with Humphrey Bogart,' he snapped his rag with venom to emphasize his point, 'Bogart! . . . Bogie! What's wrong with him?' Snap-snap. 'What's wrong?' Snap. He demanded.

I still don't know if he got the idea from Bishoff, or Bishoff got it from 'shoeshine', but not having a rag to snap, Bishoff pounded the table, 'God damn it, what the hell is wrong with Bogart? What's wrong?' he bellowed. 'What is wrong with Humphrey Bogart? Tell me what's wrong, what's wrong?'

A new field for him, Dick Powell was a seasoned pro in show biz, but was at a loss in the production labyrinth and in the 'whys' of casting. He only sighed. Different names were tossed in the hat. My answers to their 'what's wrongs?' were identical – short 'nopes'. In their one-track thinking they saw only from a Humphrey Bogart type down the line to an Alan Ladd figure. That was the mode, those pictures made good money.

The 'green menace' never blinded me. Having only one eye to lose, maybe I was doubly scrupulous. I didn't see Mac out of the money-making mold of the successful private eye types. I thought his menace shouldn't come from clipped, tough words, threatening poses, it should come from inside, because he is rotten. He should be an unknown menace; a large, silent, all-engulfing shadow of disaster. Mac represented doom to me, without opening his mouth. A lumbering, heavy silhouette of catastrophe.

'He doesn't know what he wants,' reported back the aghast agent and the casting director after I plowed through the dozens of photos they showed me.

'I don't believe that,' Bishoff stuck by me. 'I've worked with him before. Give 'im every fucking picture you got on file of all the geecks.'

The tired and fed-up casting director dropped his briefcase and from it a stack of photos slid onto the carpet. He started to shove them back with his foot, apologizing, 'Sorry, they're nothing,' and pushed the portfolio closer to me on the coffee table.

What would a detective or a movie director do without that magic bag of instincts? I've learned to trust it. I got down on my hands and knees and started to shuffle the photos around. And there it was. I got up with it. A photo of the unknown, in a strange way handsome, Raymond Burr.

'That's it, but don't tell him yet. I want to talk to him first.'

'You're joking.'

That was the beginning of Raymond Burr. It couldn't have happened to a nicer guy. It's a pity he became another one whom the 'green menace' stopped from reaching the peaks of his talent.

With all set, it took us two more Palm Springs' weekends with Bill to polish up the script; it was a snap, right down our alley. But being under contract to Universal, Bill couldn't take credit, and I didn't want it alone. That would have been unfair to Bill, who did at least as much as I did, so *Pitfall* was added to our many creditless efforts. Until *The Gunfighter* separated us. I missed him as a friend.

Many years later, a living ghost of the Old Bill, still puffing one cigarette while the next was still smoking, with his bony fingers nervously twirling a full glass of ice water and ordering another glass at Musso Franks: 'Shit,' he said, 'I must be getting senile, because I think I missed you all these years . . . I should never have stopped drinking. Now, had we stayed together, I bet you would've never let me. I know . . . Right? . . . Right!'

He left the table, no excuse, just got up and with wobbly knees shuffled out of the restaurant. The last I saw of Old Bill Bowers. Bye, Bill, I miss you.

The one who took credit for the screenplay of *Pitfall*, and who most probably never even read the script, landed a fabulous deal with Zanuck only to disappear in the Hollywood quagmire. That's Hollywood, hail credits. As Sam Goldwyn said, 'A verbal contract is as good as the paper it's written on.' A credit is as good as your knowledge that you have really done it. To hell with the rest, the paper.

Wake up. It does not work like that, especially not in the land of dreams and nightmares, Hollywood. The capital of the living dead, the has-beens buried alive in its painfully short memory. I was intrigued by its tough, crude hardness. It never deceived me. I knew it then, centuries ago, when I decided to go and come back better equipped to pick up its challenge. I still don't understand it, but if I did it would rob me of its magic.

The fall was mild, the top was down and I meandered north following the coastline until I found out that top down and seagulls are an indelibly bad mixture. The damned birds chased me further inland, only for me to be grateful to them for forcing me to exchange the morning fog for steel-blue sky and the colors of the forest that put the South Pacific rainbows to shame.

Zigzagging eastward across the Canadian border and the northern states would have made me, had it been possible, fall more in love with this country. This love affair of mine could have become deadly. The further east I got, the faster and more recklessly I drove, and I collected a string of speeding tickets. And when I answered one cop's routine question, 'What's your hurry, bud?' with the truth, 'I wanted to get away as fast as possible so I could come back home sooner,' I lost half a day. He took me to the loony bin. It took me that long to explain what I meant. But once they got it, I had to pay the ticket. However, they gave me an escort to the state line. One of the nicest rides I ever had. Mother of presidents, I love you Ohio.

The weather was lousy, I was alone on the deck and, as the skyline of New York melted in the fog, I swore, 'I shall return.' Sorry, General, I said it first.

10   A Slim Twist

The Goddess of Justice is blindfolded so she has an alibi for her performance throughout the ages. Being only half-blind was not enough to alibi
my judgements.

I buried Vienna when she was only half dead. During the second half
of the thirties Europe scratched and the old lady started to get rid of the
cobwebs from her hair, ears, sex organs, put on her make-up and pump
up her flow of blood. During the nights she almost looked alive. During
the days she still mourned her unreachable past. The termites of time
hollowed her heart.

The decade of the 1930s became more and more the decade of confusion in every sphere of life. Poor naïve Chamberlain wanted to protect
the world from a volcanic eruption with a tear, a smile and an umbrella.
Brilliant Churchill, through clouds of cigar smoke and fumes of brandy,
while working for Korda, saw the future clear in his crystal ball while
Korda was financing, with British money, *The Battle for the Matterhorn* for
Lúis Trenker. But Korda was not alone in the world of gullible optimists –
if that is the correct definition. Universal financed Trencker's *Der Rebel*,
an early and mild Nazi propaganda film for Dr Goebbels's 'artistic
library'.

In Hollywood, on the Warner Bros lot, in Géza Herczeg's office, on the
white wall behind his most disorderly desk, above his tattered favorite
chair, hung in a large ornate frame, was a numbered photogravure of
Mussolini. It was personally dedicated to '"Il Commendatore" Géza
Herczeg from "Il Duce"'. Below it, under a glass cover in an azure blue
velvet box, was the gold medal befitting the title, to be worn around the
neck on its colorful ribbon. Géza did just that on all occasions that
merited the honor.

In Rome, on the sidewalks, Herczeg would have been called, 'Ehy,
Commendatooh', with a good laugh. Here in Hollywood they started to

whisper 'Géza Herczeg a Jewish fascist', without a '?'. Nobody ever proved it, even though he went back to Rome almost before the breezes started to blow under Il Duce's head.

And in Hollywood the genius of Leni Riefenstahl was snubbed by everybody except Walt Disney and Miki Dóra. Both survived. Disney, because in Hollywood some backbones can bend to suit opportunities and individual purposes without breaking. Unfortunately. Dóra survived because he acted according to his belief.

Riefenstahl went to dine in the 'Little Hungary' and some of the emigrés in the restaurant demanded that Dóra refuse to serve her. He told the objectors, if the US government let her in this country he would serve her and reminded them they all came to escape racial discrimination, segregation and the curtailing of human liberties. 'If I discriminate, I am worse than they are because I know better. I shall serve her.' Actually this is not a verbatim quote, I am translating Dóra's fractured English.

Everybody had a good dinner. Leni Riefenstahl departed from Hollywood after a few days and life went on. If we lived strictly by the rule of 'an eye for an eye and a tooth for a tooth', sooner or later there would be no more eyes nor teeth left.

Wouldn't that be a blessing? So far we cannot be too proud of our achievements in the field of understanding brotherhood.

Emigrés arriving in Hollywood by the droves with respectable credits and talent were having difficulties landing assignments. Stories, treatments, screenplays written on speculation were being delivered to the studios by the truckload. Many of the emigrés, disappointed at not finding heaps of dollars on the street corners waiting to be picked up, went back to Europe. For reasons like, 'I couldn't swallow America and I don't want America to swallow me.' Out of their cocoons, facing the sometimes very rough American competition which lacked the polite European finesse – the smile while throats were being cut – frightened without admitting it, and not ignoring the fact that they were foreigners here, they took off. Too bad. The industry lost some great talent. Some got lost forever, some sprouted new roots in the familiar soil of Vienna, Rome, Budapest. A few even went back to the foxily manipulated Berlin of Dr Joseph Goebbels's organized confusion.

The leader of the disappointed brigade, living up to his trademark of 'pessimistic realism', was G. W. Pabst. His parting words were, 'I don't want to be the second Lubitsch here – when I don't even like the first one

– and become the servant of Hollywood finance. No!' So he left Hollywood to face, on the day of his arrival in Berlin, an assignment direct from Goebbels. The Berlin red carpet scared him off and he went on to Paris to work for 'Hollywood finance'.

Germany had two brilliant foxes, masters of confusion, delusion and deception. The Desert Fox, Field Marshal Rommel, of the African desert, and the PR fox of Berlin, Dr Goebbels. As early as 1930 he unfurled the flag of his dream, 'to put Germany into a state of spiritual isolation'. His ideal was 'a profound marriage of the spiritual nature of the heroic concept of life with the eternal laws of art'.

As time went on, more and more in control, Goebbels conducted the 'orchestras' and Hitler sang his arias: 'It's not the Jews, not-the-Jews . . .' On his agenda was only the systematic extermination of 'unhealthy Aryans' (Aryans with hereditary diseases). After all, Goebbels himself was at the 1933 première of *Ein Lied geht um die Welt* (*A Song Goes Round the World*). The star of the film, from a Jewish script, was Josef Schmidt, a cantor-voiced Jewish tenor, directed by a Jewish director, Richard Oswald. With Goebbels whispering from the wings, 'National Socialism under no circumstances should be a licence for artistic failure.' The film ran till early 1938. Only then was it banned.

In spite of his bad leg Goebbels was capable of some very fancy footwork. *Flüchtlinge* (*Refugees*) got the best film of the year award as late as 1939, directed by the Austrian Gustave Veicky, starring Hans Albers, with a foreigner, the Hungarian Kathe von Nagy. Albers's name was not mentioned, because he was married to a Swiss Jewess and they lived in Switzerland, but he did receive a plaque.

In *Wilhelm Tell* Emmy Sonnemann – aka Mrs Herman Goering – was playing opposite the Jewish Conrad Veidt. With Fritz Lang's *Die Niebelungen*, 'Even the most stalwart of the National Socialist movement were deeply moved,' said Goebbels. But on the other hand, Lang's *The Testament of Dr Mabuse* was banned. And Herr Hitler recited Dr Goebbels's new lyric, loud and clear: 'The only possible art is one which is rooted in the soil of National Socialism!'

Way before the Hitler-Stalin non-aggression pact was signed, Goebbels quoted something Lenin was credited with. 'Of all the arts, Film is for us the most important.' If he did it knowing Lenin had said it, he had an awful lot of guts to quote a communist, let alone Lenin, at that time. If he did it unknowingly, it shows both were thinking alike and were planning to employ the same PR methods to achieve their goals.

Having his attack on the film industry pretty well set, Goebbels turned to 'organize' other forms of art 'seen by sick minds'. The persecution of jazz musicians and 'disapproved' composers started to strangle the artists who were caught in Goebbels's net. 'Die Brücke' ('The Bridge') – a group formed by world-famous German Expressionists fighting for free expression and artistic freedom – was shattered. Ernst Ludwig Kirchner, the pillar and one of its founders, was dismissed from the Preussische Akademie der Künste (Prussian Academy of Arts) in Berlin and Kirchner was forbidden to exhibit. Despondent, he destroyed many of his paintings and committed suicide. The days of the German avant-garde movement, of 'degenerate art', were finished when the 'Entartete Kunst' exhibition opened. The works of great artists like Beckman, Chagall, Dix, Gross, Kandinsky and others were ridiculed at home. In Lucerne, Switzerland, in June 1939, clever Dr Goebbels organized an exhibition and turned 125 confiscated 'degenerate art' paintings and sculptures into hard currency for Nazi Germany.

'It is not your business to think, this faculty is reserved for the Führer!' was Goebbels's prologue. And a smooth 'gentleman' by the name of Karl Ritter wrote the epilogue: 'Good National Cinema is the middle-ground between entertainment and the Führer's views,' as he started on his next film, *Condor Legion*, to glorify the Luftwaffe's and Wehrmacht's intensified training, in the already bleeding and torn Spain.

One has to compliment the Germans; they did not sneak around corners to hide their intentions, it was all in the open for us to see.

The pendulum of propaganda started to swing bolder and bolder. Goebbels arranged an International Film Conference in Berlin, inviting forty nations and two thousand delegates. It was, of course, a platform for propaganda but it was also a very lavish, spectacular affair for Aryans and non-Aryans alike, without any sign of discrimination. At the last minute the British representatives cancelled. Dr Goebbels was slighted and he breathed fire. 'The British, with their blend of ruthlessness, mendacity, pious hypocrisy and sanctimonious holiness are the Jews among Aryans.'

And as the decade was coming toward its end, Herr Hitler bellowed in January 1939: 'If international Jewish finance, both in Europe and outside, should succeed in plunging nations into another world war, the result would not be victory for Jewry but the eradication of the Jewish race in Europe.'

Still, films complimenting the British were not banned till after the outbreak of the war. But the usual anti-communist films were replaced by anti-Jewish propaganda. The traditional, beloved, comic Jewish figures of the German, Austrian, Hungarian cabarets became villains. But to add to Goebbels's smoke-screened deception, as late as 1941 'disfavored' or Jewish writers were allowed to write under pseudonyms and were invited to some of the glossy Nazi functions.

Hurrah for Dr Goebbels, the dust in our eyes worked. We saw what he wanted us to see. And we made fun of the moustached Austrian paper-hanger who screamed, waving his Parkinson's guided arms, 'To die for something, that's the best thing there is. I wish I could die like that.'

His wish came true. Hitler died in the fire he lit himself. Unfortunately, and to our everlasting shame, we just stood by till it was too late and millions went with him in the inferno. We were burned too before the international fire brigade was able to quell the fire.

How long will it take to heal the wounds? Forever? When I finished typing this sentence I leaned back and looked up at the calendar. It was the first anniversary of the Gulf War.

My father, a true-blue Hungarian Huszár officer, warned me once, 'Son, you can collect anything you want, but don't ever collect enemies if you want to sleep well.' He took a big gulp of Hungarian barack pálinka, looked straight into my eyes, and said, 'Kill 'em!'

I looked at his old sword hanging on the wall, which he was so proud of, still razor-sharp, I looked at all his medals collecting dust, I knew he meant it.

He died in that fire Hitler lit. My brother died later in another fire, 1956, lit by Kamerade Stalin.

For most of the blessings of those still tightening screws we feel today we should be thankful to Monsieur Georges Eugène Benjamin Clemenceau. Clemenceau, the father of the fungus that fertilized the fear, revenge and hate he sowed in the treaties of Versailles St Germain and Trianon after WWI, after the war to end all wars. Forever. In his fear and blind hatred Clemenceau overlooked the fact that, by destroying the centuries-old balance of Europe, he was paving the way for Herr Schickelgruber. As a personal vendetta he robbed Germany, Austria,

Hungary of their most valuable asset, their pride. Humiliated, they were desperate to follow any path to regain their self-respect, to resurrect their national pride. The cross Clemenceau nailed them to became the basis of Hitler's cross, the swastika. That brilliant maniac promised a way to fulfil their dreams. It almost worked. Almost. At that time.

What about now? Thallophytic plants, like hatred, revenge, hunger and discrimination are hard, if not impossible to eradicate with simple chemical fungicides. Chemicals? Maybe mustard gas? Hydrogen bombs? But out of upheavals things can grow, like out of the big bang and chaos of the cosmos this globe – from space so beautiful, but within a decaying mud-ball – we proudly call Earth was born. Where are we heading? Another big bang?

Like storm-fed waves hitting the shores, the waves of aggrieved discontent, the political confusion, the chaotic financial disarray clearly influenced the style and approach of film-making in Europe. I was lucky to absorb, one-on-one, the do's and don'ts, the differences between the American, British, German, French and the Italian approach to picture-making at a crucial time in its development.

France went about making pictures in her own inimitable French way – as she always did everything in art, revolution, politics, love, life in general. Vive la France. Her politicians at large were busy defecating in their own and their opposition's nests and unlike Lenin and Hitler they neglected to utilize films for propaganda to further their political aims. Film-makers were left alone to blossom with virtually no censorship to restrict Imagination in the land of individualists. It is not unusual that in France, continuously drowning in political turmoil and boiling with innovative new-path-finding in film-making talent, nobody came up with any significant political film. Maybe to avoid stepping on toes to preserve this complete artistic freedom, the 'auteurs' smartly kept away from head-on political subjects, but, hidden in light-hearted French froth, their razors dissected characters mercilessly. The free-spirited artists broke away from preconceived ideology. Their quest for psychological and visual realism, as in *Quai des brumes*, created the film noir, which ultimately led to the realization that film is a new form of expression.

It was all contrary to the American Bible of film-making, where, unlifelike, the 'good' had to triumph and the 'bad' had to be punished. The culmination of a love affair was a closed-lips kiss. America, a 'forward-thrusting country' of sturdy pioneers, was not interested in exploring new ways to further a budding art form. Business was the slogan. She was licking the wounds of victory wrapped up in the dust bowl of the deep Depression, trying to forget the blood she had shed in vain to save the world. For their 5 cents they didn't want to see the bitter truth. And a style was born, 'Escapist Cinema'. There was always a large pot of gold at the end of an MGM Technicolor rainbow.

England, with stiff upper-lip, unperturbed and cool as a cucumber sandwich left between the window panes in January, sailed through the storm – on an even keel, as always. The British films weren't bad, but they weren't remarkably good either. Like cucumber sandwiches are never bad, but never really good either.

Conquered Germany's film industry flourished with Herr Goebbels holding the reins to a 'guided freedom', cleverly blinding us with stardust to cover the truth.

In Italy 'unguided freedom' was the rule, and with real Italian 'bravura abandonata' even those who couldn't swim plunged into the whirlpool of picture-making; the brass bands across the Alps playing the 'Horst Wessel' couldn't drown 'O Sole Mio'. Aloof and happy-go-lucky Italy went along making films. Film-makers stretched for new horizons, freely expressing their views according to their own slogan. They had their cake and ate it too, and succeeded in sowing the seeds of post-Second-World-War Neo-realism. And with it Rome became a significant epicenter of the world's film production, with its largest office, the Via Veneto. With commendable Italian audacity the path they cut was wide, stretching from *Bicycle Thief* through spaghetti-westerns to *Icicle Thief*, which only proves one can't trust the Italians. I know, first-hand, I have a son, a six-foot-four piccolo Romano. A budding film director. What else, the fool.

According to the Romans, specifically to Barone Luiso Sanjust, 'Il Barooh' in Rome, who made me fall in love with Italy, there were three Italies – Northern, Central and Southern – and three distinctly different Italians. The differences between them were obvious; 'Napolitani cantano – they sing; Romani mangano – they eat; Milanese lavorano – they work.' And since the Second World War, Americans have been accepted as honorary Italians: 'Americani pagano – they pay.'

He was not only right, I found out the Italian 'dogma' Barone Sanjust was talking about in Rome was binding world-wide, before I became an American, and years before the Second World War started. I found out

Basil was well aware of the 'dogma'. He consistently flattered me throughout the crossing, 'Oh you wonderful Americans, sir.'

I thought it was strange, I had the same cabin outbound, and Basil was my steward. But the ship was packed full that time, why should he remember me after all the passengers he had seen in the interim. Being taken for an American flattered me, so I did not correct Basil with a 'not yet'. And I paid for it later.

Basil was packing my trunk before disembarking in Southampton, he sprung his knowledge, 'Mind you, sir, I used to sail around the Cape, but this, this crossing was not very smooth, was it, sir? But you were the only passenger who stood up to it, but of course, oh you wonderful Americans are so tough. And, if you don't mind me saying so, tip so well.' What could I have done?

Basil must have been satisfied that I was a 'wonderful American', because for years, even after the war broke out and he rejoined the Royal Navy, he sent me postcards to my Hungarian address which was registered on my return ticket.

Physically, the *Aquitania*'s comfort and subdued opulence (which only the British can create) was undisturbed. But something was amiss. The same distinguished Captain was there too, pink-face and silver hair, gold braids, medals, and all. I sat across from him at the Captain's table, he was still the gracious host, but he was only the shell of the Captain I remembered. His inside was drained. His speech had changed. Had he been more 'British' he couldn't have talked at all. He swallowed his words half way and the half that came through came through his nose. A lost king in an empty kingdom.

One evening, sloshing his Delamain in his brandy snifter, he looked around the room and, after an unfinished tired gesture, he sighed, dropped his hand on the table, 'Soon, sooner than you think, all of this will be gone. Too bad.' He lifted his drink in a feeble salute, 'I shall be ferrying troops and this . . . we will never be the same. And we, the victors, will shed more blood than the vanquished. A pity.' He watched me as he had a sip of his brandy then put the snifter on the table.

'Are you sure that . . . the . . . only . . .' my voice trailed off under his steady gaze.

The Captain smiled, unexpectedly. 'British patience . . . it is too late now.'

'I don't think so.'

'It is obvious, otherwise you would not go back now.' He lifted his glass. 'Egéségére,' ('to your health,') he said in perfect Hungarian. It bowled me over. He had a sip of his drink, I needed two.

As clipped as only a British person could be, he asked, 'Why?'

'I have to finalize things, then I'll be going back, for good.'

'Oh, you'd better hurry. The extremes are spawning danger. The mixture of too much optimism and panic is a volatile one.' Without looking for it, the Captain reached out and there it was at his fingertips, held by a waiter standing in attention, an open box of cigars. Like a piano virtuoso's fingers gliding over the keys, the Captain's thick fingers slid over the row of cigars to stop over the one he wanted. Another waiter with a silver instrument circumcised the cigar the Captain picked. The first waiter held up a flame, both waiters' feet were glued to the deck, they were standing rock-steady in the wildly pitching and rolling ship.

All the way through this ritual the Captain never took his eyes off me for a second. The flames under the snifter-warmers swayed as the ship rolled. The snifters were exchanged with fresh ones and replenished. After a few puffs the Captain surveyed the empty room, 'Outbound, westbound, the ship is always over-booked. We are packed like sardines, and it smells like that too. The sardines are looking for the paradise that cannot exist.' He sniffed his Delamain, 'In bound . . .' he continued, then laughed into his snifter, 'look around, I feel like the captain of a resplendent floating funeral parlor.'

The salons, the bars, the dining-rooms were deserted. Most of the few passengers on board were sea-sick and cabin-bound. When the *Aquitania* crossed the 'valleys' between the Swiss-Alps-size waves, her airborne propellers revved to a high-pitched scream, and when she plowed back into the waves across the 'valleys', the sea buried her decks and her groans reverberated through the almost empty ship and she shuddered and she shook like a wet dog. And the band played on to the empty dance floor, nobly fighting a losing battle against the rattling dishes and the squeaks of the battered old gilded tub. One night one of the saxophonists neatly threw up in his instrument, but the band played on. Rules are rules.

Every evening, hell or high water, Basil carefully laid out my tuxedo, 'Nothing to it, sir, have a good evening. Could be worse, you know, we could catch an iceberg,' and he jiggled the ice in the pitcher while fixing me a dry Martini. British sense of humor? 'If you don't mind, sir,' he handed me my glass, 'old Martinis and old women are hard to take,' and he quickly filled a bucket-size glass to the brim with what was left in the pitcher. 'If you don't mind my saying so, sir, it is sinful to be wasteful in this terrible world.' And at the little bar in the corner, with his back to me, Basil with one big gulp and a sigh evaded the sin. Not a drop was wasted.

By the time the *Aquitania* dropped her anchor Basil had earned his halo, he didn't sin once. But the unexpected kindness of the Atlantic during the last forty-eight hours of the crossing ruined my chance to earn my halo. I sinned. I sinned several times. I did not instigate my immoral stumble but, what made it worse, I enjoyed losing my halo.

A few still-green-around-their-gills diehard passengers started to congregate around the bar, where I was actually not listening to a softly stuffed, pear-shaped Dutch man, with a walnut-size black and blue bump on his forehead. He was well-oiled, hyping himself how he would sue Cunard White Star for everything they owned for the bruises he received during the rough crossing because of inadequate protection for passengers' safety.

As he droned on with his plans I was making my own for my immediate future, until a gentle tap on my shoulder and a female voice – 'A very dry Bombay with a slim-twist,' – made me turn around to face a bundle of sable and in it a lady of about thirty, studded with jewels. She slid over to me one of the two identical drinks in front of her, 'It is yours. We share Basil, I know how you like it.'

'It seems she travels quite a lot,' the Captain told me, 'we have had her on board before.' However, when she shed the bundle of fur, the mileage didn't show, but everything else did and she was obviously proud of it. Rightly so.

I did not intend to write an encyclopedia of sins, there is some valor in discretion. I remember this fragment of my life, not because of the forty-eight hours I spent with the baroness, but because of my qualms about her title and her magnificent collection of jewels. Other assets she had I knew were real, no doubts about them ever entered in my mind, nor did I have time for such trivia while we were together.

I was all packed, ready to disembark, when the cabin door burst open and the baroness flew in, still in her negligé which was more revealing than nudity. She embraced me with a stranglehold. 'You got to save my life, loff-bug!' She had an accent I could not peg, but who cared? I untangled myself, she shoved in my hand a small package. 'You are

going to stay at the Dorchester, no? You must-got to help me. Please.'
She closed my fingers around the package, 'Please take it to the "Dorch",
a present for a friend of mine, I call her from Edingbourough, she picks it
up, Margaret will pick it up, don't you do nothing.' She laughed at her
double entendre, 'I be jealous, she-is-very-very . . . you know . . . Watch
it!' She drowned me in kisses. When we came up for air she went on,
'You saved my life. If I miss connection to Edingbourough, I die, and if I
stop at the "Dorch" I miss connection. Thank you-thank you,' kisses,
'thank you, thank you,' more kisses, 'see you in a week at the "Dorch".'
Another stranglehold embrace, a peck on my cheek and she was gone. I
didn't have a chance to say one word. I stood there smeared with lipstick
and with a small package in my hand.

The custom hall in Southampton wasn't uglier than custom halls are all
over the world. But one nice thing about this one was, it was almost
empty. When I arrived, the baroness was already there. How did she do
it? When she left me nuder than naked, I was packed, dressed and ready
to go.

The baroness stood out among the sparse crowd. She was aghast,
noisily aghast; she was the only passenger whose every piece of luggage
was open and every piece which had been once in the luggage was laid
out on the long counter with customs people swarming over the exhibition of her frills.

Her small box in my hand suddenly felt very heavy. I felt uncomfortable holding it. I put it down.

'Is that your luggage?' asked an inspector.

'Yes.' And I carefully stopped the pointing arc of my hand before it
came to the small box on the counter. In the background the baroness,
the center of attention, continued to complain about the barbarous treatment she was receiving.

My inspector openly, as openly as a British official with a stiff upper lip
could be, was annoyed with the scene the baroness was creating, and,
during his few perfunctory questions, he was more interested in the
commotion the baroness was creating than in my answers or what was in
my trunks he was clearing. And after a mechanical 'Have a pleasant stay in
England,' I was following the porter with a sigh of relief toward the exit.

'Your package, sir?' the inspector called after me. I froze. He was
pointing at the package the baroness had given me, now looking forlorn
on the long and otherwise empty counter. Before I could say anything he

went on, 'You forgot it,' and motioned to the porter to pick it up. I said a heartfelt 'thank you' but he never heard. He was on his way to watch the commotion with the baroness.

I never found out what was in the package. I never found out how 'very-very' Margaret was. After a couple of days a man called up from the hotel reception, saying he was to pick up a gift for Margaret. 'Margaret is the name,' he repeated it, as if it were a password.

Between patent leather hair and a pair of patent leather shoes, in a black, thick-pinstriped, double-breasted suit, a blindingly white shirt and sporting the widest, loudest, ugliest tie ever, was a pasty-white-faced man. Londoners would call him a 'spiv'.

'Margaret sent me,' and he reached for the package before I brought it up belt-high, took it and walked out of the lobby. But that was not the end of my affair with the baroness.

In Europe I found in the café houses that laissez-faire had taken over from the habitual over- or under-reaction to events, important events such as soccer results or political assassinations. After all, nothing new, really new was happening. Very much like today, only the names were different. Events were carried by their own momentum. Most of the 1930s went by with deaf ears, blind eyes and unvoiced thoughts.

Long before I left Europe, the monarchy in Spain was already gone and the Japanese sun was burning through Manchuria to Mukden. Hitler was the Chancellor of Germany, warming his hands by the embers of the Reichstag. Japan, then Germany resigned from the League of Nations. The US recognized the Soviet Union. The Third Reich was formed and signed a non-aggression pact with Poland.

Nobody of importance who could have done something about it seemed to care. Was the only reason I remembered that July in Vienna when Dollfuss was shot because I woke up the next dawn in a morgue?

The following month the headlines screamed that Hitler had become the 'Reichsführer' and before the sanitary stacks of newspapers had to be replaced in the privies, the fresh editions for the toilets let it be known that the Saar had returned to Germany and Hitler had denounced the Treaty of Versailles. But in a 'Goebbelsian' twist to confuse them all, Hitler signed a 'Naval Limitation Treaty' to reduce the naval arms race.

Mussolini had to play second fiddle. He only invaded Ethiopia, and the Ethiopians were only black people. And while the League of

Nations voted economic sanctions against Italy, King Victor Emmanuel became the Emperor of Ethiopia.

Then Hitler trumped Mussolini again; he announced that Germany had guaranteed Austria's sovereignty. He didn't specify for how long and nobody asked him the question, so don't blame Hitler alone for annexing Austria two years later. It is easy to blame Hitler. My question is, who was responsible for leaving the door open for the burglar so long? It seemed nobody cared. Why not try again? he thought, and it worked. He broke the Locarno Pact and re-occupied the Rhineland. Quietly. The noise was coming from the Spanish Civil War.

The noise was too far across the Atlantic from the US. France was enjoying her after-lunch nap, Great Britain was savouring her cool cucumber sandwiches with her afternoon tea. Hitler was looking for nourishment and gobbled up Czechoslovakia. For dessert he had Austria and he took Poland for a midnight snack. But it's good to remember it was not cholesterol that killed him. Roughly we know what happened. And it all happened in less than a decade. How, and why it was allowed to happen will take historians a long time to figure out.

Europe was in well-organized confusion. Outside of Germany there was no coherent, or even incoherent planning. Only Hitler and Co. knew the path they wanted to follow. The wizards of the café houses either pooh-poohed or read the signs correctly. It didn't matter. Nothing was done.

That was not quite true.

Covertly and above board international money, including Jewish, maybe spurred by blind hope, wishing to turn the clock back, or triggered by sharp eyes for business opportunities, continued to finance Nazi and fascist ventures from heavy industry to films. Whatever reason prompted capital's action, it added to the vacillation of the sheep, and on the bottom line the yield of human blood outweighed the financial gains. The endangered species, not only Jews, who still could have found safe havens elsewhere, hung on, confused by the false signals.

The film industry was booming in England. The Korda magic had worked. It was not the point how good or how bad those films were. The point was that a dead – no! worse than dead – a non-existent industry had come to life, it was turning out product. Product accepted by the world market, including Germany.

Germany, UFA – Universum Film Aktiengesellschaft – in UFAstadt-Babelsberg on the Berlin-Potsdam elevated line, through pine forests, twenty miles from Berlin, not too far from the 1936 Olympic Stadium, next to posh Grünewald, was the Babel of mixed-up Europe in the thirties. An efficient, giant factory of not only films but deadly hopes. French, German and some English films were rolling off its assembly lines, nurtured by Aryans, 'unhealthy' Aryans, Jews and craftsmen of various nationalities. Goebbels's evil genius lulled the hopefuls into false security.

A strange breed of Jews in Germany were more German, more proud to be Germans than Kaiser Wilhelm II's Prussian officers. And they were just as arrogant. They belittled the wise ones who saw the indelible writing – the Nazi graffiti – on the walls and departed.

Unknowing, unthinking, filled with admirable patriotism, another group of 'unhealthy' Aryans and Jews stayed on the seesaw, but sent their children out of the country, 'only to learn languages'. They served Hitler, who wanted the world to believe 'alles in ordnung' – everything was fine. It was for him. It enticed foreign investment, created additional jobs, and the factories went on making aeroplanes and shovels needed to dig the future mass graves.

Having had the chance to drive around Europe in various countries on assignments for Alex Korda, I was exposed to first-hand stories, all 'authenticated', all contradicting each other. The conflicting 'expert opinions' transformed Europe to a rumormonger's paradise. I had no bead on the situation.

It took Zoli Korda to set me on track. The only way he knew how. Straight and simple. 'You can't solve it, forget it. We'll get these couple of pictures out of the way for Alex, then go back to Hungary, direct a few pictures . . .'

'But –'

'You will, and after that I'll see you in India . . . or in Hollywood.' Zoli dismissed my 'but' with a simple shrug, for him my problem was solved. Zoli gave problems that could not be solved only to himself.

We had the pictures 'out of the way' and Alex grumbled, 'You are not going to arrive in Budapest by train. It is ridiculous. Zoli told me you should direct. Do you want to direct? Arrive in Budapest by aeroplane from Rome.' He held up his cigar, 'On your way –' he pushed the intercom, 'Mrs Fisher, bring in Mr de Toth's itinerary and his tickets,' he pointed his cigar at me, ' – on your way, I want you to take care of a few things for me.'

My itinerary was certainly no short-cut from London to Budapest. I was not looking forward to it. I was spoiled: crossing borders by car was the same old routine, but train crossings had become arduous. Inevitable and unpleasant delays had become the norm as states clamped down to prevent the flow of life savings from state to state. Convertibles such as platinum, silver, gold, even wedding rings, gold watches, any kind of jewelry or objets d'art, rare stamps – which were the easiest to smuggle across borders – and the least valuable of the 'convertible-valuables' – cash – were verboten to be taken in or out of the countries of Europe without special permission.

Permissions were close to impossible to obtain. The penalties for breaking the law were very stiff. The couriers took great chances, but had great rewards. The control officials on the borders often became the 'finders' of what they had legally confiscated.

In the second- and third-class train compartments the passengers were sitting in each other's lap. In the corridors they were treading on each other's toes on their way to the toilets. Travel in first-class was bearable. Food in the dining-cars was sometimes edible; it all depended, Alex warned me, how well you tipped.

Two-three stations before reaching the borders apprehensive passengers with their noses pressed against the windows fogged up the view of the uniformed police, border guards and customs officials boarding the train.

Then the noose of uneasiness tightened. The chitchat died down. The train's safety controllers, usually wrinkled and smudge-faced, were checking the wheels with long-handled hammers, tapping them to listen for 'cracks'. The sharp, high-pitched, reverberating 'clings', of 'healthy' wheels were blasted by the noise of the 'official bulls in the china shop'. The stench of air hitting them when they ripped the wagon doors open was not enough compensation for all the miseries they caused.

My only fellow passenger in the first-class compartment for four was a symphony in grey and green loden. Above his head, on the fishnet luggage rack, his green jäger hat, with a foot-long, beaver-tail 'shaving brush' stuck to it, was so full of souvenir pins I was sure it was bullet-proof. His only interest so far on the trip had been smoking, rubbing and admiring his ornately carved first-size meerschaum pipe. Years of abuse had turned the originally white 'seafoam' material into the color of connoisseur's choice ocher with a touch of gold in it. His greying, wax-tipped handlebar moustache was a fair competition to the horns of any longhorn from Texas or Hortobágy. He knew he was beautiful.

'I hope they hang them!' It surprised me when he spoke. More because of what he said than that he spoke at all after the hours we had been sitting across from each other in silence. I followed his scrutinizing look. On the platform, two men, hands manacled behind their backs, shoulders hunched, heads bowed so low their faces were parallel to the ground, identical twins by terror, moving statues of fear, epitomes of distress, were being herded off the train.

'Hang 'em all.'

'Why?'

'They are Jews.'

'How can you tell from here? And what if they are?'

'They are not taking just anybody off the train. They have good judgement.' Challenging, he looked straight at me, 'Are you a Jew?'

The door to the corridor slid open, two men in uniform and one in civilian clothes stood there. No greetings, no please. 'Papers, passports.'

Old 'longhorn-moustache' handed over his documents while I was getting my passport out so I could not identify with what papers or passport he was travelling. All I heard was the clicking of heels and a 'Gute Reise.' When I looked up, he was already putting away his papers and indolently asked me again, 'Are you Jewish?'

I ignored the question. Not the three officials. I did not have to hand over my passport, one of them took it out of my hand and they withdrew to the corridor. While they scrutinized my passport and had an animated conference, 'longhorn-moustache' was watching me with a victorious smirk. I believe I surprised him when I took his meerschaum pipe out of his hand and stomped it to dust. To clarify my sentiment I told him, 'Fuck yourself.' He sat there wordless, with the tips of his moustache trembling, watery-blue eyes bulging with tears. 'It's not because you called me a Jew, it is because if I were one you could have gotten me in deep trouble, you shit.' To add more weight to my sentiment I broke the stem of his deceased pipe in two. As it snapped, the door from the corridor slid open and the three men came back.

Stuttering in falsetto, and with thick purple finger pointing first at the debris, then at me, he complained, 'Look . . . hee . . . heee.' He stopped sobbing.

The three officials were looking at the mess on the floor, I was looking at my passport in the hand of one of the men in uniform. For a while the only sound came from the long-handled hammers tapping the wheels. I broke the silence, taking the bull by the horns. 'You are lucky I didn't smash your head like your fucking pipe.'

Two hands held my shoulders. Not roughly, but strongly enough to let me know they could mean business. 'Please, calm down,' said one. 'I would be upset too if anybody referred to me as a Jew,' said the second in uniform.

'Look at the mess, you shouldn't have done that,' lamented the man in civilian clothes. 'You will have to pay for cleaning it up, you know that.'

I reached in my pocket and pulled out a modest stack of single dollar bills, which I had legitimately. They all, including 'longhorn', were watching the money, hypnotized. I quickly figured; they were three of them – nine, no, not enough. God bless Alex Korda, his schooling helped, fifteen will do better.

'If I get off the train I may miss my connection. Please, would you be so kind to help me and take care of it for me?' And as I spoke I counted out fifteen nice green dollar bills, slowly. I took it for granted they agreed, reached for my passport and exchanged it for the money. 'Longhorn' was gaping with occasional squeaks.

'Maybe it would be wiser, sir, if you could, if you would move to another compartment. There are places.' The civilian didn't have to suggest it twice, I thanked them and was out on the corridor with my baggage.

Behind me 'longhorn' was complaining. I heard them explaining to him I had the right to the foreign currency since I had declared it when I brought it into the country.

Exasperated, 'longhorn' insisted, 'But he could be Jewish, the "de" in front of his name means nothing. There are Jewish barons, look at the Rothschilds.'

One of the officials summed up their verdict for him: 'He came back recently from America. No Jew would have come back to Europe now.'

I have to grant it to 'longhorn', he didn't give up easily, he went on grumbling, 'Passports could be forged.'

A train employee came down the corridor, I handed him a dollar bill.

Without uttering a word he took the dollar first, then my luggage; I followed him as he bulldozed his way through the garlic-smelling sardines on the corridors of the second- and third-class cars.

Finally, I could get a fresh breath of air. One of the windows of the first-class corridor was halfway open. 'Hope you don't mind? The lady in the next compartment asked for it, she likes fresh air.' He came to a halt in front of an empty compartment with a reserved sign on it. It was locked.

He put the luggage down, raised his left hand as if he were giving me a blessing, pulled out a piece of red-checkered rag, once a table cloth, now a handkerchief, blew his pock-marked, bulbous nose, trumpeting like a herd of elephants on the Serengeti in rainy season. Satisfied, he ceremoniously folded the retired table cloth and put it away, then pulled out from a bulging pocket a large key-ring with millions of identical keys on it. Without looking he picked one, inserted it in the lock, and it worked. The train started to move, he didn't wait for my opinion, he dumped the luggage and ran to get off.

Alone in the compartment I stretched out and dozed off. The screeching of the braking wheels on the rails blended with the screams of the baroness in the customs hall in Southampton in my nightmare. I felt the train pick up speed, the mechanical screech of the brakes died off, but the human screams continued, gaining in volume and vulgarity. The baroness from the *Aquitania* and the Southampton customs hall was cursing and shrieking like a demon at the half-open window of the corridor, flailing her hands.

I thought I was still dreaming, but no, there she was, bedecked with garish jewelry, otherwise as elegant as she always had been on those rare occasions on board when she was dressed. She was surrounded by the usual, now obviously dumbfounded passport control and customs officials.

'You want this one too?' she screeched, as she tore one of her earrings out of her ear and chucked it out of the open window. 'I told you bastards they were fake.' With blood dripping down on her shoulder from her ear, she repeated with another high-pitched, piercing scream, 'Fakes, aaall aaare f-aaa-k-e-s!' and threw out of the window one of her large bracelets. 'Why don't you cut my arm off with it, stupid shits. If they were real, wouldn't I hide them, you stupid shits?' She shoved her hands with at least eight rings on her fingers in the face of one of the aghast uniformed officials, indicating the rings, 'Take one!' He hesitated, she insisted, 'Take one, take two, take all, throw them out, keep 'em, go ahead.'

Tentatively, the civilian reached out from behind the challenged man and slipped one of the rings off a finger. He scrutinized it for a long time, the train rattled on at high speed, swaying the carriages.

She prodded him. 'Throw it out, keep it, do something.'

Finally he did, he threw it out the window. The other man in uniform, encouraged by his partner, now reached out bravely, yanked off one of her bracelets and threw it out promptly. He thought it was fun. Then the shy one in uniform followed suit, grabbed a brooch and flung it out.

It became a game, they started to enjoy it. She kept on encouraging them, 'See stupid fools, they are false, faaakes!' Then unexpectedly the baroness tore her dress open. Between her exposed breasts, hanging on a gold chain, was a gold cross. The flustered officials drew back, bewildered. She picked up the cross and kissed it tenderly. 'This, this is real, you bastards, but for this you have to kill me.' She burst into hysterical tears, 'My mother gave it to me before she died.'

She stopped crying but looked up at them with silent tears rolling down her cheeks. A pitiful Madonna from hell's ugly, vulgar fury. The only sound came from the wheels chattering against the joints of the rails.

She kissed the cross again, whispered, 'I am coming from her funeral . . . She died a week ago,' and collapsed.

Even I believed her.

'It was extremely wise of you not to interfere,' said with a worried brow 'Rechtsanwalt' Dr von Arx, Korda's legal and financial adviser in Zürich. 'You could have been held as an accomplice, you know. Negatives are hard to prove.' And the 'matter' for him was closed. He was a taciturn, antiseptic, an honorable Swiss. I respected and liked him very much.

But the 'matter' for me was not closed. After von Arx left, I sat in my room in the Hotel Baur Au Lac, mulling over and over what I could have done and didn't. I found no solution or absolution. The phone rang.

'A cold Bombay Martini with a slim twist is waiting for you in the bar.' The caller, a man with a heavy Swiss–German accent, hung up.

Who was that? Oh, one of my friends had received my message that I was in town. It's good to have friends. Perfect timing, I thought in the elevator on the way to the bar.

The place wasn't crowded, but I couldn't spot anybody I knew. On the bar, away from the few customers, in front of an unoccupied barstool, was a lonely Martini glass, full, with a slim twist on its lip.

I stopped a few stools away from it, with my back to the bar, and surveyed the room again. There wasn't a soul around I knew or who knew me, it seemed. I moved further away from the lonely martini and ordered one for myself.

I tasted the drink when the bartender delivered it and complimented him on how perfect it was, which was true, but I was fishing for information. I indicated the untended drink.

'What a shame to let it sit there. Who ordered it?'

'I don't know, sir.'

'What do you mean, you don't know?'

'I was only asked on the house-phone to call you, sir, of course you understand I cannot give out information.'

I understood that, of course. What else was to be expected in a tower of Swiss discretion in the Hotel Baur Au Lac, on Talstrasse since 1844. And the bartender had been there ever since. As a matter of fact, he still is.

I was in no mood to play, I asked for my bill. As I was about to sign the tab I was hugged from behind.

'You are my guest tonight,' said the baroness when I turned. She was as nonchalant as if we had last seen each other at Chez Max for dinner the night before. She held on to me tight, bit my earlobe, gave me a peck on my cheek, and let me go.

Let me go! If I ever needed a support I needed it then. I was agog.

She sat on a barstool opposite my empty glass and tapped it. 'Two similar, please.' She motioned to me to sit on the stool next to her. Still dazed, I did. She picked up my right hand, held it to her cheek, then kissed it and whispered, 'Thanks, you saved my life. You were great.'

The soap-bubble of the initial jolt burst, but I was still off balance. 'Thanks? Great? I saved your life? What the hell are you talking about? What happened? What were you doing on that train? Stupid, bedecked like an over-decorated Christmas tree, stupid-stupid! And what are you doing here? How did you get here?'

'One question at a time, which one do you want me to answer?'

The martinis arrived, she lifted her glass, 'Salute,' and almost drained it before I tasted mine. I noticed a small band-aid on her right earlobe. She wore no jewelry. She finished the last few drops of her drink and ordered another round. Suddenly, I felt sorry for her. She looked vulnerable, she was not the same person whom I had met on board the *Aquitania*, seen in the customs hall in Southampton or on the train. I needed another round of drinks like a hole in my head, but the drinks arrived. She took her glass almost before it was on the top of the bar, her lips touched the rim of it, but she put it down without tasting it.

'I am glad you're here and I am doubly glad you didn't come to me on the train. When I got a glimpse of you through the window of your compartment, I almost died . . . I felt I had stepped in an elevator which wasn't there . . . I was falling, falling down the shaft forever. If you had interfered, we wouldn't be here now. I wouldn't be, that is for sure.'

She leaned over to plant two kisses on my neck, below my ear. She didn't notice that she knocked over her martini. By the time she straightened up, the mess was cleared away. A fresh drink stood on the counter, carefully placed further from her elbow. She lowered her voice. 'I think it is high time we should be properly introduced to each other . . .'

I thought for a minute she had thrown her marbles out the window too. 'Look, this charade must stop. I – '

'Yes, you. All I know about you for sure is that you are not Jewish. And what do you know, know about me? You may have some guesses, right or wrong, but . . .' Her voice trailed off in a smile. 'Life is funny.'

'That is a profound statement.'

She went on as if she were talking to herself more than to me. 'You don't know, you can't imagine how good I felt suddenly, and I don't know why, when I spotted you in the lobby sitting over there as I was checking into the hotel.'

I said nothing, she was stamping out Olympic rings with the wet bottom of her glass on the top of the bar. The cocktail hour's cacophony of several languages ricocheted off the walls. She came to a decision, moved closer and whispered anew.

'My name is Kathe Holzberg, I am not a baroness, I am a German Jew who lives with five pseudonyms and five matching passports. Now you know one of my aliases, and after Southampton and the train you probably put two and two together. Yes, I am a professional "schieber".'[1]

Not only the bar, the room, the world started to spin the wrong way. Not because of the martinis. I always thought I had a fair vocabulary, but all I could think was, 'Oh-shit!'

1 A schieber is a professional smuggler of cash and other valuables, like precious stones, jewels, stamps and other forbidden articles. Schiebers never touch narcotics.

1 *Café New York, exterior.* The palace of creative bedlam. The home of artists and fakers, literary geniuses and illiterates, apostles of peace and the future makers of the atomic and hydrogen bombs. *In short a full-blown nut-house.*

2 *Café New York.* One of the smaller throne rooms of one of the kings where the waiters in white tie and tails glided through the SRO throng for twenty-four hours a day as if they were skating on ice.

3 *Alex Korda.* The king of chameleons. A bon viveur. A genuine deal maker. A lover of beautiful women and motion pictures.

4   *Antonia Farkas.* a.k.a. Maria Korda, a.k.a. Maria de Korda, a.k.a. Maria Corda, a.k.a. Maria de Corda, a thoroughbred looney, Alex's first wife and nemesis, literally till he was lowered into his grave.

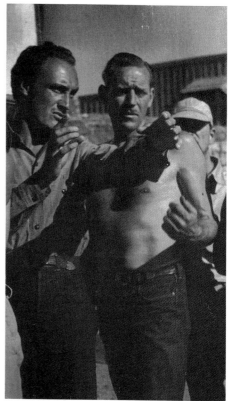

5   (Left) *None Shall Escape* (1943). A fighter for equality, de Toth wanted to put four blacks, Latinos and Asiatics on the jury of a war crimes trial by the as yet unestablished United Nations. It was an unheard-of request and it almost cost him his job. Finally he and the studio came to a compromise and de Toth seated Jesse Graves, a dignified black American, on the jury of that fictional United Nations. Not numerically but morally, it was a victory.

6   *Ramrod*. Discussing a scene with Russell Harlan, one of my favorite 'cameramen' for tougher westerns. During those years there was only one director on a picture but the 'cameramen' contributed just as much as today's 'directors of photography'.

7 *Veronica Lake.* A typical victim of a stage-mother's dream turned into nightmare.
From a miserable childhood packed with broken promises, shoved into the pitfall-littered
labyrinths of Hollywood, where the bouquets of roses can have more thorns than flowers.

8   *Springfield Rifle.* High up in the sierras, high in spirit. With his stomach still empty but full of hopes, Fess Parker (who could've come closest to the prince of them all, Gary Cooper, without imitating him), in front of the camera for the first time. Coop is gone west, but his memory will live. Fess Parker is buried under Davy Crockett's coontail hat, and the rubble of his millions. It's a pity.

9   (Opposite, top) *House of Wax.* Charley Bushinsky, a promising young actor who is now lost and buried by the millions of Charles Bronson, on the set of *House of Wax* behind his wax image in the electric chair. In the foreground is Phyllis Kirk. Next to the freight-wagon-size monster, the Natural Vision 3D camera, is Robert Burks, one of the three cinematographers on the show. And another buried man, buried under the weighty name of Warner, Jack M. Warner is peeking from behind the camera.

10   (Opposite, below) *House of Wax.* This photo is a monument to THE Warner, J. L. Warner. Only HE had the guts, foresight, sense of humour and gambling spirit to bet on a one-eyed director, one of the four in Hollywood, to shoot his first 3D movie. J. L., where are you? You're missed.

11   *Pitfall*. The worry and concern on Dick Powell's face is not good acting, it's a genuine concern. 'I can't hit 'im,' he protested. 'Fake it.' 'What if I miss and I hit him?' 'It'll be that much better.' 'Right,' piped up Raymond Burr, a great guy and good sport, 'show it to him.' After our fifth demonstration Burr piped up again. 'Do it, Dick, for Christ's sake, he'll kill me.' The scene worked.

12   *Play Dirty*. There are lessons in this photograph. Acting can be dangerous. So is too much talk. This punch connected. The recipient made three mistakes. After too many *copas de Jerez* (sherry) in a cantina, he disclosed to a crowd and the first aid woman on the show (who is standing by in the photo) that he was celebrating his early retirement. He'll lean into the punch and collect insurance. Being a gentleman or being greedy he lived up to his word. He did lean into the punch. Now he is retired minus two front teeth and insurance. No biz like show-biz.

13 *Riding Shotgun.* A great golfer, a cool gentleman, Randolph Scott, is strutting down
Main Street with the *Wall Street Journal* tucked in his belt beside his trusty six-shooter.
Don't monkey with 'im on or off the set. He has no tears to shed for you.

14 The quirks of life in show-biz. It was Maria Korda who went to the studio to annoy
Alex, and in the commissary she, not Alex, discovered the one who became what she
herself wanted to be but could never have been, a *Lady Korda*. Estelle Thompson, a.k.a.
Queenie Thompson, a.k.a. Merle O'Brien, a.k.a. Merle Oberon, was a lady in capital
letters even without the title.

17 *The Day of the Outlaw,* had many similarities. Nobody wanted to make them. Both had hurdles to overcome: the night shooting of *Crime Wave*; the cold and snow of *The Day Of The Outlaw*. But the two principals made them fun to make. Robert Ryan and Sterling Hayden came out of the same mould. Too bad that mould isn't used more often.

15 (Opposite, top) *Indian Fighter.* What Scott lacked Douglas had a double dose of. The icy stream didn't cool his acting with Elsa Martinelli, in her first picture, discovered by the casting director of the picture, Mrs Kirk Douglas, Anne. That's show-biz.

16 (Opposite) *Crime Wave.* How far can the often deaf always blind Goddess of Justice obliterate all human emotions in an officer of the law without robbing him of all feeling for compassion and still leaving him/her a good representative of law and order? That is the theme of *Crime Wave*. There was only one actor around not to play, but 'be' the part. Sterling Hayden, a strong and straight man of firm convictions with a heart in his panzer – one of the most overlooked talents in Hollywood. With the famous and imitated toothpick in his mouth, Phyllis Kirk over his barn-door-size shoulder and Gene Nelson, the dancer in his first dramatic film next to him. This film and –

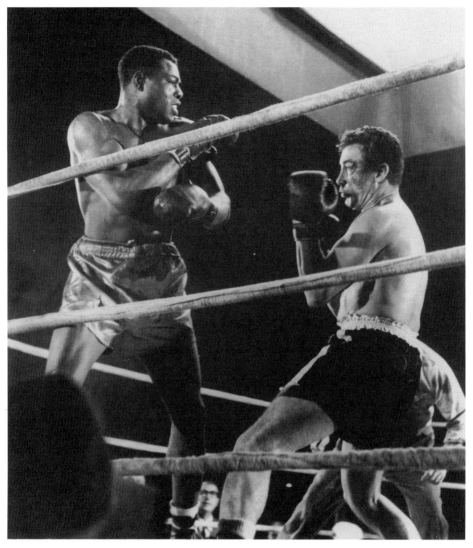

18   *Monkey on My Back.* Like voices in the wind, blown away unheard, are the voices of those still-alive unfortunates whose talent was buried by money. Or the horses that shit on the bright future of Cameron Mitchell. Or narcotics as in the 'true rehabilitation' story of Barney Ross. Three days prior to the release of the film the 'reformed dope addict' was picked up overdosed. That's show-biz again.

19   (Opposite, top) *Man on a String*. An authentic story from the horse's mouth of a man lost in the labyrinth of dirty politics. A true tour de force of the many-faceted Ernest Borgnine. A true pro portraying an amateur spy.

20   (Opposite) *The Billion Dollar Brain*. Lunch one hour. A lone camera on its dolly in white emptiness.

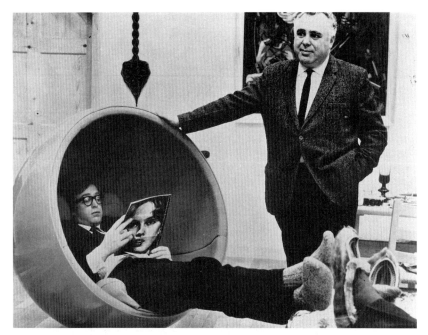

21 *Saltzman & Caine.* Lunch one hour for them too. Strange as it sounds, the below zero weather was kinder to the camera than Ken Russell, the director of the film, was to Harry Saltzman and Michael Caine. The camera didn't break down, Saltzman did. Caine, not a hero but a wise survivor, hid in the quiet of the Finnish womb-chair.

22 *Play Dirty.* But there was no rest for Caine on this film which he dislikes intensely – *Play Dirty*, where he had to play dirty and climb the Himalayan sand dunes in the heat of the desert where only the wind-whipped sand wiped off the sweat. But more credit to the pro he is, he did it. But not with a smile, mind you.

23 *I Wanted Wings*. No, she didn't. She wanted a farm, children, horses and cattle, in that order. She never wanted the wings, wings that stuck on her, that took her to heights she was unprepared for, that she never dreamed of. She was afraid and lonely and lived alone with her fear. Too proud to call for human help. She nailed herself to the crooked cross.

24 *Hooked*. The bronze is in her memory, a sign on the crossroads, a reminder.

I must have been thinking out loud, too loud. She got it, and with the tips of her fingers stroked the back of my hand. 'I understand. I am sorry about Southampton.'

'You are sorry?'

'But I was certain you were a sure bet to get it through.'

The stark realization hit me of what her 'certainty' could have done to my future if the obviously illegal 'it' I was transporting, courtesy of whatever her name was, had been discovered.

Her eyes clouded up and, before I could say one word she repeated, 'I am sorry. Please, believe me, I am really sorry.'

'That's water under the bridge now, but it beats me how you could have been so asinine to leave "it" with a stranger, whatever "it" was? It must have been something of value. I could have walked off with "it".'

'No, you couldn't have. You were followed, and watched to see if anybody else was following you. Did you open the package?'

'No. Of course not.' I got up and asked for the tab again. She hooked her arm around my elbow, gently trying to guide me toward the exit. I hung back to settle up.

'It's all taken care of, sir,' said the bartender, and with dignity rebuked my attempt to leave a tip, 'gratuities included, sir.'

Kathe said, 'Thank you,' to the bartender, who said, 'Thank you, madame,' to her, then she faced me. 'I made a reservation for two at Chez Max on Seestrasse – and I took the liberty of laying on a car. Shall we go?'

Curiosity killed the cat, I warned myself, but curious I was, and I didn't need any further persuasion.

The dinner, pre-ordered, was luxurious, my epicurean dreams were being fulfilled, but my curiosity was starved. Not a word about Southampton or the train.

'Kathe! When did you get back?' a man descended upon us and burbled on with a heavy Romanian accent: 'Why didn't you call? I was concerned. Is everything all right? God, it's good to see you back. Don't do that again, call me the minute you –'

'– I only got back today, I was delayed and –'

She was pounced on with an 'Everything is all right, I hope,' but it was not a question. It sounded more like 'It had better be all right.'

Kathe dismissed him with royal aplomb, 'Andre, meet Oscar Causescu,' and she introduced me to a man, too-too well-dressed in all hues of grey, with an ash-grey, lardy face and steel-grey, fright-wig-like hair. And grey eyes behind grey-rimmed glasses.

He was slick and oily. When we shook hands I felt that, if I firmed my grip, his limp fingers would slide out of my palm. Looking straight at me he adjusted a chair to sit close to her. 'I would like to talk to Kathe.'

To say the least, it was an insolent proposition to get me to leave the table. He put me in limbo. Kick him? hit him? or walk away? I didn't know their relationship and did not want to get involved in a family explosion.

After an awkward pause Kathe broke the tension, 'Go ahead, Andre is a friend.'

I picked up her tone. 'Don't mind me, Oscar, I am a good listener and not a gossip.'

Oscar knew he was on the wrong track. 'No-no, it is – it's nothing special or urgent,' he reached for and patted Kathe's hand resting on the table, 'we–' he emphasized 'we', '– in the office were concerned about her.' His benevolent smile at Kathe exposed his grey teeth. 'She works for us occasionally, a great linguist, a translator sine qua non. So you – '

Oscar stopped when a waiter came, anticipating his order. He looked up at the waiter, hesitated, then expectantly looked at us. Kathe pulled away her hand from under Oscar's with its high-gloss fingernails. We looked at them in blank silence. He got the message.

'Nothing, thank you, I am expecting somebody, I am at the bar.' The waiter left. With a deep grunt Oscar got to his feet, handed over three of his cards, sighing to me a grave secret. 'I disdain the world we live in. Well, we are all glad you're back, Kathe, and safe.' He moved away, then came to a slow halt as he turned back to Kathe.

'You're staying – '

'The usual place. I'll call you, 'night.'

I looked at Oscar's three cards, in three languages, in too-too good taste, but not grey, and Oscar Causescu – Rechtsanwalt/ Avocat/ Avvocato – had a good address. We finished the dinner as if it had never been interrupted.

'I am tired,' Kathe said as she crawled into bed, but the sun was trying to peek through the slits of the heavy drapes and we were still talking. With her head on my shoulder, her light fingers were painting invisible designs on my face, chest, in my hair. Her voice was soft and monotone.

'I hate them, I hate them all. Not only because they are Nazis, but because they didn't shoot him. They kicked him, clubbed him, stomped him to death.'

The ice in the bucket next to the bed had melted, the bubbles had escaped from the bottle long ago. She reached over to the nightstand, groped for her glass and poured a few drops in it, wet her lips and kissed me.

'My father was trying to protect what he loved in life most, his books. It was silly of him, I know.'

She dropped her head. Silent. She stared at the drink and her tears drowned in the flat champagne in the glass in her hand. 'They should have shot him, not kicked him to death, the bastards . . . Bastards! Burned his books.'

She kicked the sheet back, got out of bed, picked up the phone and ordered a bottle of champagne with a few strange tit-bits, like Spanish caviar, the best.

'I am getting even with them, hitting them where it hurts. I am helping Jews, Aryans, I smuggle for anybody who wants to hurt them.'

'Don't you get hurt chasing your revenge. I was never so lost in my life like I was on that train. God! I don't get it, how, I mean those jewels out the window!'

'I am proud of that trick. It was my idea but I can't copyright it and I can't use it too often, only when something big, some heavy stuff comes around.'

She lifted her hair, there was a fine scar on her left earlobe from the hole for an earring down. On her right earlobe the little band-aid covered the new scar.

'The earring is the pièce de résistance, the blood helps. The rest is easy, but I have to remember which earring is the fake. We grind the hoop of it razor sharp. Nothing to it. But on the train those bastards lucked in on two good pieces. You gain some, you lose some, can't win 'em all.'

There was a knock on the door. Kathe slipped on the hotel's bathrobe, 'Stay there, I'll get it.' She took the order from the waiter and declined his help to set it up.

After she arranged everything on the nightstand next to me, she let the bathrobe slide off her. 'It's a shitty life, I wanted to quit it so often, but then I see my father on the cobblestones, trampled flat like a dirty rag doll, with the ashes of his books around him in front of his burned-out book store, and I am back to fuck 'em.' She shrugged, had a sip of her fresh drink. After the second sip her tension eased, 'And I am making good money,' she said as she sat on the edge of my bed and leaned over and kissed me.

She straightened up with a laugh. 'You know, it's funny. Oscar knows less about me than you do. He is one of the "filters" of the game, he is a big shit on the circuits. The trips come down through him, but he only knows my real name. We couriers can't afford to give out our aliases. To make a pact they can rat on us and we are eliminated. Finished.'

Her smile vanished. She took a sip of her drink and sank in mile-deep thoughts. 'It happens all the time. I didn't like what happened in Southampton or on the train, they were too hard on me. Maybe I am marked. If you ever see me by chance again somewhere, anywhere en route, please, ignore me. God, you were smart on the train. Are you a courier?'

'No.'

'You acted according to the rules. I thought . . . Do you want to be one?'

'No. I told you what my plans were. I have to go to Prague from here – then down to Rome – then up to Budapest. And after I make some pictures of my own there, back to America. To stay. Nothing will change that. Nothing will.'

She lifted her glass but changed her mind and poured the remainder of her drink in the ice-bucket. She cuddled up in bed, hung on to me tight and started to cry. 'Oh, God, how glad I am I met you.'

So was I. And the moment she fell asleep I got dressed, tiptoed out of the room.

We made no plans to meet but on the chance that we should, I arranged to stay over for a few days. The only fixed date I had which I couldn't have changed was with Dr von Arx, and that was proceeding according to schedule. On Swiss schedule to the split second.

During our luncheon, en passant, I asked von Arx if he knew anything about an attorney by the name of Oscar Causescu. With Swiss precision all three Swiss attorneys stopped their forks in mid-air, exactly halfway between their plates and their mouths, in perfect synch. Worry-ditches cracked the marble-smooth brow of von Arx. Again in synch, all three attorneys shook their heads and after a tercet of 'Hmmms' proceeded with the lunch in silence for a while. With the arrival of coffee we returned to the business of the day.

Before von Arx's boney posterior hit the comfortable chair behind his imposing desk in his office, he started to fire questions. Questions like a prosecutor would ask from the accused in court. Unrelenting. Where had I met her, how had I met her, how long did I know her, was I in love with the 'lady'? Did I meet her before or after I met Causescu?

No, he had nothing concrete, no 'strictly illegal' activity to accuse Mr Causescu of. 'His garish taste and attitude is not a criminal offense and it really should not offend us who are more secure,' he said demurely. 'Oh, we may be accused of being square, but, believe me, we are not,' he went on. 'I admit, though, the hard edges of our convictions may cut deep.'

He reminded me of my multiple responsibilities: that is, first to myself and then to Alex Korda, who certainly 'would look down disdainfully' on my association with anybody of Causescu's type or his affiliates. He got more perturbed when he 'fully comprehended' that my 'association' with Causescu was through Kathe. 'You see the way he is operating, his ethics, are unacceptable for us. Mind you, as far as I am aware, what he is doing here in Switzerland is not quite illegal, but it is everywhere in the world around us. Swiss discretion, you know.'

He got up slowly, burdened with thoughts and stood in front of the most imposing row of gold-embossed, leatherbound editions, studying them with his back to me. He reached for one of the thickest volumes on the highly polished mahogany bookshelf; hell, there went my after-noon with Kathe. He pulled out one of the books and the whole row of books swung with it. They were the cover of a treasure hoard of crystal decanters in a small red-leather-lined cache behind them.

'Mrs von Arx is definitely right. I should stay away from desserts,' he sighed. 'But I love them,' he added as he carefully lifted out one of the decanters, encased in a silver cage.

He carried it to a coffee table, surrounded by an array of easy-chairs. Seen through the corner windows the inner-city traffic seemed more degrading of civilized humanity than through your own car window. He gestured me to join him as he let his brittle bones land gently on the down-filled cushions on one of the chairs in the corner. While I walked over he fished out of his cigar-pocket a small silver key on a chain and unlocked the safety door of the silver cage guarding the crystal decanter from unauthorized intruders.

'The best for heartburn, Unicum, from Hunga– oh I am sorry, of course you know, you're Hungarian.'

He filled two dainty liqueur glasses and handed me one, then closed his eyes and sipped the horrible stuff. Without feeling any guilt I quickly slushed mine under my chair; if it was good for heartburn it could not harm the carpet, I thought. Then I closed my eyes like he had and did not open them until I heard von Arx saying: 'Heavenly.'

If this was his heaven I wanted to be somewhere else, like in bed with Kathe, at this moment. But the gates of heaven were locked for me for a while. Dr von Arx leaned forward and put on his glasses. I felt he was putting me under a microscope again.

'Please, no offense to the lady, I am sure she is one, but I – we would prefer it if your relation would be a short one.' I wanted to interrupt him, but he held up his hand. 'Please, I understand, oh I do, but you have to understand you cannot afford this liaison. She is known in some circles here, let us say, as one of Mr Causescu's best assets; she may well be marked by the authorities. Mind you, I don't want to infer she is involved with anything illegal here . . . but we – you – cannot afford to expose yourself by being associated with her.'

Without asking he refilled my glass, nothing I could do except hope he would close his eyes again when he doctored his heartburn. I had a slow burn which he didn't help by not closing his eyes this time around. He was well-meaning, but strangely it added to my anxiety to get the hell out of there. He droned on.

'Mark my words, you will be approached, if you haven't been yet. Causescu's business is growing, but getting more and more complicated and risky. There is a shortage of dependable couriers. It would be very déclassé to call them smugglers. So they call them couriers and pay them well. Some of them are ingenious, but they are expendable. In the end, if something goes foul, they are the ones who pay. Dearly. The Causescus are taking no chances.'

Dr von Arx must have had a terrible heartburn because he poured himself another dose of his medicine, which I found out was supplied by Alex. After a leisurely sip from the slop, von Arx leaned back with drink in hand appraising me like I was an object on exhibit.

'With your Korda association as a cover you would be an ideal smuggler and they would pay you handsomely, but I have to warn you, if you accept any offer from Causescu we would have to discontinue our association, I mean between you and me, and I would have to inform Mr Korda immediately. We cannot afford to be, we don't want to be, associated with any of Mr Causescu's associates.'

'You don't have to worry about that, Dr von Arx. If I would explain to you my connection with Causescu's associate in more detail than I have done, it would be pornographic and certainly not gentlemanly . . .'

His unexpected outburst of laughter took me by surprise. My biggest surprise was that his laughter was sincere; it came from the bottom of his heartburned heart. Was it possible there was a human being hidden in the center of this bone collection?

His arthritic symphony blended with the slight traffic noise filtering through the double-paned windows as he got to his feet to escort me to the door. 'Please don't take this as an implication, but about as many business transactions are torpedoed daily in bed as on the stock market. Many of them inadvertently, of course. Please put your papers in the hotel safe.'

At the door he put his hand on my shoulder, 'Between you and me, I envy you,' he said. 'Actually,' he continued, 'I met the lady in question once at a party. She was very lovely and very intelligent. How could she associate with somebody like Causescu?'

'Money and convictions or convictions and money. Or money alone. I'll find out, it interests me too.'

'That is what worries me. Watch it. As I told you, we would prefer if your relation remained strictly personal and were a short one.' He reached out a skeletal hand but I did not feel the bones, I sensed a warm friendship and a grave concern. 'I understand you, I think,' and he shook me by the shoulders, 'Have fun, but be careful!'

'Hell, I don't know how to be careful and have fun. If she had venereal disease, it's too late now to be careful. So I am going to have fun. Short term, I promise.'

His smile vanished. 'No flippant jokes now. Please. You understood exactly what I meant when I said be careful.' He picked up a briefcase from a little table next to the door and handed it over with a set of keys and a warning. 'Everything is in there. If some of the information leaked it would hurt Mr Korda's business affairs, my reputation and worst of all it would hurt you.'

Swiss knives were famous the world over.

Zürich was a miniaturized, antiseptic New York. I didn't like streetcars, but in Switzerland even those were somehow less offensive to me.

The people, with their gyros set and neutered, were on their way to wherever, inoffensively. It was a fresh, late afternoon. It was always a pleasant experience to walk in Switzerland, so I decided to walk back to the hotel.

Much as I admired Rodin's masterpiece it was not a good example for me. I remained a walker-thinker and Dr von Arx gave me a lot to think about, but the closer I got to the hotel the faster I walked.

There were no messages at the desk. I put the briefcase in the hotel safe. The small bouquet of flowers I had bought on the way smelled nicer in the elevator than on the street. Sachlich (mátter-of-fact) Zürich had never looked beautiful before. The forty-eight hours I stole from Korda promised to be better and better. Until – I opened the door of my room.

To say that it was in a mess would have been an understatement, even in Great Britain, with the stiffest upper-lip. One could have said everything was upside-down if one could have determined what was up and what was down. Everything in the room was slashed open, from the lining of my luggage to the ripped-off heels of my shoes, to the bellies of the armchairs with their guts pulled out, hanging loose.

I called von Arx before I reported it to the hotel. He praised me for that, and he was there, it seemed before I hung up.

Dr von Arx took over. He instructed the hotel manager not to file any report – to protect the privacy of its guest and the 'renommée – the fame, prestige – of the hotel. He called in private investigators and handed over the case, to the great relief of the hotel's top management.

My room looked like the old Grand Central Station in New York during rush-hour. Herr von Arx was above it all, elegantly in charge. He sat in a corner watching the convergence of the investigators checking for clues.

'Oh-no-oooohh-nooo!' moaned Kathe as she stopped in the doorway. 'The bastards!' and with outstretched arms she came in the room to embrace me. 'I am sorry, the least I could say, and I really am if this happened to you because of me. I wonder? I – '

'So do I!' intervened von Arx from his corner, as he got up to join us.

'Who are you?' Kathe asked him perplexed, then she turned to me. 'Who is he?'

I introduced them to each other, told her von Arx and I were associated. 'Oh,' said Kathe. 'Please follow me.'

We did. With a grand theatrical gesture Kathe swung open the door of her room. 'Please step in and enjoy the show.' Her room must have been hit by the same tornado that had hit mine. 'I didn't report it yet, I wanted to talk to you about it first.'

'You made a very astute decision, Miss Holzberg,' complimented von Arx. 'I shall handle it from here.'

'Do you think you should, Dr von Arx?' asked Kathe with obvious misgiving.

'Shouldn't I? Actually I can't. It never happened. Did it?' and von Arx picked up the phone.

With 'profound apologies' and flowers befitting a Godfather's funeral we were transferred to a two-bedroom deluxe suite, as guests of the management for the rest of our stay in Zürich.

As we were bemoaning our predicament with caviar and champagne for appetizers – as guests of the management – in the dining-room, von Arx proposed I should stay for a few days longer than originally scheduled.

'Fine,' I jumped up. 'I'll arrange it right away.'

'Why?'

Better get it over with quickly, I thought. 'I had already pushed back my departure forty-eight hours.'

'Before this happened?'

'Yes.'

'Hm, clairvoyance, was it?' he inquired, smiling.

'What do you suggest?' I asked him.

'Make it a week,' recommended von Arx. I didn't argue. I was grateful to the burglars for the week and I was anxious to leave the two of them together, to give them time to size up each other and form their opinions.

By the time the dinner ended I thought Kathe could have twisted old brittle-bones around her little finger. She was dignified and painfully straightforward. I faced a new side of her. Very hard. She blamed herself for the mess.

'Immediately upon my arrival I was supposed to deliver the transfer as usual. I didn't do it. My fault, I knew the game. I was wrong. Then, to add to my mistake I was spotted by chance, here in the hotel,' Kathe put her hand on my forearm, 'with him, before even reporting in on the telephone. From then on I knew I was covered, it made no sense to call in any more.'

It was interesting, she did not mention Causescu, who had spotted us, by name. She shrugged and smiled. Dr von Arx was engrossed, 'And then?' he asked.

'Then this morning I delivered the transfer I was trusted with, about five and a half million dollars worth of jewelry, minus two rings, worth about two hundred and fifty thousand.'

'How come?' asked von Arx, but I took over. I never mentioned Southampton, but filled him in on what had happened on the train. He was impressed and horrified. Horrified enough to order a round of drinks, making sure he would be personally charged with it, not the 'courtesy of the hotel'.

Kathe took over. 'Couriers sometimes go astray. Your associate was an unknown number to them, he could have been an accomplice in moving the rings. I should have known they would be looking for the goods before dumping our bodies next to the tracks or selling our skins for sieves. I am too valuable for that. Had the rings been found, it would have been another story. Actually there wouldn't be a story at all; we wouldn't be here.'

We were silent, she swirled the drink around in her glass. Before tasting it, she bowed down as she said, 'I am sorry for the messy trouble I caused you,' and kissed my hand resting on the table.

'It's a suicidal game, why are you doing it, Kathe?' asked von Arx quietly.

'I had my reasons and now I have a plan. Three more transfers, that will be all. I am going to get married.'

That was a surprise announcement, but it had no effect on our relationship and it was not referred to by either of us until the night we parted.

Our week turned out to be only four wonderful days. In the middle of the night Kathe got a call, she packed up, had a long shower, got dressed without a word, kissed me at the door and with happy anticipation reminded me of her wedding plans. This one and two more to go. And she was gone.

Without her Zürich lost its glaze, returned to its former old self – business. Clean and efficient and dull as hell. (I don't know, I may revise this statement, hell may not be so dull after all, considering its inhabitants.)

'We are just going to stick to our schedule,' said von Arx, babying his heartburn with Unicum. 'I understand you. Oh, I do, she was a remarkable lady, thank your good luck and don't be restless. You cannot afford to be.' And I had to sit out the rest of the week in Zürich.

After the dullest train trip, I checked into the hotel, I don't remember its name. It was on Vaclavski Namesti, where a fellow on an unruly horse reigns over the lovely square. This was my first trip to Prague.

In Vienna the old oxen docilely pull under their yokes, hiding their resentment of the world in general; in Prague the same beasts use their tails – and not only to swat flies off their rumps. At that time in history it was useless but pretty courageous. And not too long after my trip the tails and the rumps were all chopped off in one fell swoop.

The two large armoires in my hotel room in Prague, would have passed as antiques or traditionals in Switzerland; here they were just plain old clumsy pieces of furniture. I couldn't even open the door of one of them. The bathroom door was as large and massive as the entrance door to the room. When finally I succeeded in yanking it open, in the large bathroom, in a large bathtub, kept off the tile floor by gaping lion's heads, was Kathe, taking a leisurely bath, bubbles and all.

She didn't need the bath towels to dry up, and we didn't speak to each other for a long time and when finally we did, her first words were, 'I love you.' And I believed her, maybe because I wanted to.

With the right key the door of the second armoir opened easily; it was stuffed with flowers and her clothes. She sat on the edge of the tub while I was taking a bath, filling me in with the 'boring details' of the uneventful 'transfer'. It was a 'test run for me' she said, 'it was tempting bait for a courier who wanted to go astray, but not enough for my trousseau; and I knew I had two dumb tails on me. I could've cut 'em off, but it wouldn't have been worth it.' She waved off my suggestion to quit. 'And what are you suggesting I should do? Go to Jewish heaven, the Bronx, if I can get in, and sell brassières in Macy's basement. No. I've changed my outlook on life. Till now I lived for hate and revenge. If every Jew had hurt the bastards as much as I have done, they would've gone "kaput" long ago. I told you and von Arx I have made my plans: two more heists and I will quit and get married. That's it.'

But it wasn't it. She slid in the tub with me, half-dressed, and we forgot about her marriage plans.

My plans had changed and Kathe decided to come with me to Berlin from Prague but suggested we travel on separate trains. In case she was 'caught in the net', I would 'drown with her'.

I got worried. 'Are you carrying something?'

'No! I am not pregnant and you know it, dummy,' and she laughed. When she realized how serious I was she turned serious. 'No, I would never do it travelling with you, or anybody else for that matter.'

Then came one of the biggest surprises of my life. The train was nearing the German border, I was listening to the approaching 'boot-steps' and the scraping of the opening and closing doors of the neighbouring compartments. Kathe didn't speak a word of English, but was submerged in a *Harpers Bazaar*, opposite me, next to the window.

The two other passengers in the compartment closest to the door handed over their passports, one Czech, one German. I gave them my Hungarian passport. They were impressed with my American visa and remarked on it. Kathe was still slowly turning the pages of the glossy magazine and they made a remark on that too.

Kathe turned to me apprehensively: 'Didn't you give them my passport.'

My heart stopped, I stuttered, she grunted an 'uuh', as she rummaged in her backpack-sized purse. Everybody in the compartment was watching her, waiting. Finally, without hurrying, she came up with a Hungarian passport, handed it to them first then half stood up, leaned over to kiss my forehead and apologized, 'I am sorry, darling.'

By the time she leaned back in her seat they handed over her passport with a 'Danke sehr, Frau de Tóth.' She smiled at the departing men in shining boots and impeccable uniforms. Before they pulled the compartment door shut she beamed at me, handing over her Hungarian passport, 'Here, darling, you keep it, you know I don't travel without you.'

Kathe! I couldn't wring her neck in public and by the time we were alone I didn't want to wring her neck. Even when she said, 'That passport was worth every penny of the fifty dollars for the look on your face.'

Two days later in Berlin, 'Frau de Töth' had a phonecall in the middle of the night in the Adlon Hotel. She packed up, took a long shower, got dressed without a word. At the door before she left she kissed me. 'I see you in Paris next week in the George V. Right?'

'Right. Take care.'

'Right. I promise I am not using the Hungarian passport for work. That was reserved for fun. A tout à l'heure!' she said in her fractured French and was off.

Off, never to return.

After an extra few days in Paris and no news from 'Frau de Tóth', I went back to Zürich. Dr von Arx was surprised to hear from me, but wasn't surprised at all when I told him I wanted to marry Kathe. He didn't even utter his customary 'Hmm'.

Causescu was gloomy when he came to see me in the hotel. 'Your call surprised me.' He continued after a long silence, 'What can I do for you?'

We both felt there was no love lost between us. I came to the point. 'I would like to contact Kathe.'

'Why are you asking me?'

'Because you are the only one in Zürich I know who knows her. I am sorry to bother you.'

'Why do you want to contact her?'

'It is a private matter.'

A waiter came, he spat a 'Nothing for me,' at him. 'A cup of coffee for me, please.'

Causescu made an act out of consulting his paper-thin gold wrist watch. 'You will excuse me, I have an appointment. I came here because I thought you might have something, some news for me. Obviously you haven't. I can't help you.' He rose from his chair.

'I want to marry Kathe.'

Had his legs been shot out from under him, he couldn't have dropped back into his chair more quickly. His ash-grey complexion turned magenta, blue veins popped up under the thin skin of his temples, pulsing.

The waiter delivered my coffee. 'An espresso for me,' Causescu squeaked, then, speechless, he watched me drinking my coffee. His eyelids were fluttering.

His espresso arrived. I asked the waiter to repeat the orders and in addition bring two brandies. Causescu didn't object, I knew I had him.

'Please, give me her phone number or address.'

He finished his espresso and stared at me over the rim of the small, empty cup. No answer. The waiter came back with the new order. Causescu tasted the brandy before drinking his espresso. 'Strange,' he said. From his coat pocket he pulled out an envelope and dropped it on the table in front of him. 'Strange' he repeated, then finished his brandy. 'I thought you two were married.'

Now he had shot my legs out from under me and he knew it. He ventured, with a twitch of his thin purple lips, what I guessed was a smile.

'Why did you say that?'

Causescu shoved the envelope across the table to me. 'Open it!'

I did. In it was the counterfeit Hungarian passport issued to one Kathe de Tóth. It was bloodstained.

11   The Great Dane from America

Mussolini had three loves. The first, most sincere, all-engrossing love of his life was, naturally, himself. Aviation and voluptuous actresses were vying for second and third positions. Very much like Howard Hughes. With the passing years his pendulum swung to aviation. Not because of his age, but because General Italo Balbo's flight around the world made him realize the potential of airpower and air-transport.

In July 1933, General Balbo took off in a formation of 25 Italian-made Savoia-Marchetti flying boats to fly around the world. Which he did with bravura Italiana, save two mishaps, one in Amsterdam and one on the home-leg in Lisbon. During the remainder of the flight they plowed through, in formation, violent rainstorms and dense fog to face the greatest hazard his squadron had to endure during their historic flight, according to General Balbo – the five-day celebration in New York, which they survived – and with the United States Distinguished Flying Cross on his hairy chest, Balbo led the 23 remaining flying-boats in tight formation over Rome and landed safely on home waters. Mussolini kissed Balbo's cheeks twice, in spite of his beard, made him Air Marshal and decided to build a world-wide Italian Airline network.

On the assembly line of life, heroes and broken records are quickly forgotten. Who are the two 'immortalized' in stone at London's Heathrow airport, ignored by the millions who pass through? Jack Alcock and American-born Teddy Brown, the two who first crossed the Atlantic between St John's, Newfoundland and Clifden, Ireland, in 1919. Handing over Lord Northcliffe's £13,000 prize to them for being first to cross the Atlantic, Winston Churchill quipped, 'I really do not know what we should admire the most, their audacity or their good fortune.' In the same year Alcock was killed during an air show in France. Brown never flew again.

The 'Flying Fools' who shrank the world are mostly forgotten. Who remembers the 85 killed, 162 seriously injured barnstorming pioneers during only one year, 1923? And the martyrs of the air, among them Nungesser and Coli in their L'Oiseau Blanc. And who remembers those few who succeeded? Bert Hinkler, who flew solo in 1928 from England to Australia in an Avro Avian, small enough to fit in a one-car garage.

The crackpot genius, a millionaire in his spare time, Howard Hughes, in his 'Flying Laboratories', set new standards for aviation pioneering. He proved money and knowledge mixed with luck and courage were unbeatable. In his new Lockheed Vega 12 (he bought three before selecting the one he ultimately flew), with a crew of four, Hughes better than halved Lindberg's 1927 Trans-Atlantic hop to Paris.

Of course Lindbergh flew alone, without radio, sextant or fuel gauge, in a single-engine Ryan, built in sixty days, with a cockpit 37 inches wide, 32 inches long and 51 inches high.

Wiley Post was better equipped than Lindbergh. He had Australian Harold Gatty as navigator with his latest instruments in 'Winnie May', a Lockheed Vega, but still a far cry from Hughes's navigational aids.

Also in a Lockheed, a Lockheed 14, Hughes and his crew flew around the world, again in record time, halving Wiley Post's five-year-old record. The fact that Hughes never deviated more than a mile or so from his charted course was more important to him than the world speed record he set with 352 mph. His goal was to prove the feasibility of a world-wide air transport system to bring humanity closer to each other – or to hell.

His records were no accidents, nor the power of money alone. Hughes was a man of sometimes annoying lint-picking precision. I got a taste of it at Burbank airport, in front of United Airlines Hangar No. 1, where I hangared the fulfilment of my newest dream: my just-off-the-assembly-line North American Navion. It was one of the first private planes built after the War, designed by Dutch Kindelberger of North American Aviation, another aeronautical genius, who, in May 1940, at British request, designed the 'P51' overnight! Within five months from drawing board to air, Vance Breese took off in the NA-73 X, the P51's prototype. Again at the request of the British Purchasing Commission, the plane was renamed from 'Apache' to 'Mustang', and the plane became the single greatest factor of Allied supremacy in the air over the superb German Luftwaffe.

Nothing ever looked as beautiful in the air as the dream of all fighter pilots, the '51'. Nothing was a greater joy to fly than the Mustang –

provided you had a strong enough right leg to conquer the torque on take-off and a very strong heart to keep on pumping when at 19,000 feet the supercharger cut in automatically with a wretched thud and disintegration – and did the little beauty shiver and shudder! After that you weren't home free, yet. Before facing a rather 'sporty' landing your heart had to still overcome, at about 15,000 feet, another shock. The supercharger cut out with a lesser thud and shudder. So, you 'greased' it on the runway. Runway? Ground? All you saw ahead of you was a long engine-cowling. Then you had to 'S' the monster where the tower told you to tie down. Still, ask anybody who survived all that what they want to go up in to have some fun, they would all say the 'Spam Can', the little beauty. The Mustang was built to fly.

The Navion had a silhouette remotely resembling the Mustang, since Dutch Kindelberger drew it on a paper napkin during dinner. It was understandable, after all he had designed the Mustang.

I was sitting in the cockpit of the Navion familiarizing myself with the instruments and my concentration was rudely cut.

'How did you get it here, by truck? Dutch never concocted anything yet that flew.'

It was Howard Hughes. He was interested in anything that flew, from kites to the Spruce Goose. And interested in Ma Brady's cornbeef sandwich with Ma Brady's kosher dill pickles, and above all, Ma Brady's pecan pies. I didn't know where Ma Brady was, but my mechanic 'gooseneck' Jack, did, and on his Moto Guzzi he usually got Ma Brady's poison to us before Hughes could re-tie the laces of his dirty-white sneakers.

We had it real good right after the War. We could pick up almost new surplus aeroplanes for a fraction of a tenth of what it had cost the government. Of course, if anything went wrong with them, repair was out of the question; even the government couldn't have afforded it. So we junked the airframe, sold the radio equipment to HAMS, recouped most of the investment, flew back to Kingsman, Arizona, picked up another plane, like a Mustang, for about $4,000, which had cost the government/taxpayers about one million.

Hughes used to wander around the airport, on his way in and out of Lockheed on the north-east end of the field, and often stopped by to watch me tinker with my various types of newly acquired aeroplanes. And laughed.

After we disposed of Ma Brady's culinary masterpieces, sitting in the cockpit he asked me, 'Do you think, really think this thing would fly?'

'I flew it over yesterday from North American.'

'If you say so. Prove it to me.'

He had never flown with me before. He called me a 'junk-yard pilot', unsafe. Coming from him it was ironic since most of the time he flew experimental equipment.

I naturally moved from the left seat to give him the command, but he insisted on sitting on the right. It bothered me, he knew it and enjoyed it. Hughes had a hidden sense of humor but quite an up-front presence; and as the tower was giving me taxi instructions for take off, I became more and more aware of that presence, his life achievements in general, and specifically in aviation.

As I was cleared to take off, he said, 'Don't you forget there are old pilots and there are bold pilots, but there aren't any old bold pilots.'

After sharing this infinitesimally small part of his wisdom with me, he remained silent for a long while in flight, listened, watched. It was very annoying. He finally spoke and asked about different power settings and the behaviour of the Navion under various conditions. My answers did not satisfy him, nor did my alibi: 'This is only my second hour in this plane.'

'It shows,' he retorted joyfully. 'May I take it?' He never touched the controls until I said, 'Please.'

During the two hours he flew and talked and I learned how little I did know. He probably saved my life. I heard his voice flying through a snowstorm when everything was grounded, en route to Denver to attend the opening of a picture, and one of my lovely wives set the radio in the plane on fire so she could extinguish it with her mink coat. She hated furs more than she hated the 'on course beeps' of the radio, and, she said with an angelic smile, it would have been good publicity for her. Little did she know, without Hughes's many tips on what not to do 'when the shit hit the fan', her write-ups would have been in the obituary columns. She probably remembered that Daedalus and Icarus flew and had some good publicity over thousands of years. But I landed safely in Salt Lake City, without radio, in the blinding snowstorm, and her fame was shorter-lived than the two Greeks. But I have to give her credit, she tried.

Air travel was no longer thought of as suicidal, but it was still considered an adventure when I took off from Rome for Budapest in late

1938. The once-a-week arrival of the big Italian Savoia Marchetti, with its three engines looking very much like the American Tri-motor Ford with corrugated fuselage, was a notable event. The large crowd in Budapest, as around airports generally, consisted of the doomsters, who crossed their fingers expecting the planes to crash, a bunch of Walter Mittys, who thought they flew them, and the few neutrals waiting for the daredevils to board or stagger off the planes, hitting the ground with rubber-legs, spring-green faces and with strangely soiled lapels, shirt-fronts and ties. A sorry lot the pioneers of the early air transport system.

Except for another stork, nothing could have looked more like a stork than a man in the small group waiting for me with Dr Basch and Eiben. He was squeezing an overstuffed briefcase under his left armpit, his right side was glued to a short, overstuffed woman, who in turn was glued to two red-headed, freckle-faced, small, overstuffed, dumpling-like girls in perpetual motion.

The cool autumn breeze helped to spread the aroma of Eiben coffee on the tarmac. Eiben grunted, 'Flying is stupid, unnatural and it's for idiots. Welcome back. Let's go.' He turned and walked away. Eiben didn't feel home anywhere except on a set.

Basch gave me a rib-cracking bear-hug, 'Perfect timing,' he said, 'coming by plane was a great idea, very impressive arrival,' and patted me on my back a couple of times, whispering on our way 'Dr Steinmetz, there, would be instrumental in financing a production. His daughters are air-enthusiasts. Perfect.'

I met Dr Steinmetz and family hanging back by the exit. I kissed Mrs Steinmetz's fat hand, shook hands with the girls and had a hard time getting loose from their fat little clinging grips. Eiben didn't wait for us, walked straight through the gate and was gone. 'He is shooting,' explained Basch, 'you know him.'

'How was it?' asked the Steinmetz quartet before saying how do you do. They did not wait for my answer. They popped one question after the other, mostly in unison. Questions about flying, about the wild Indians on the prairies, scalping and buffaloes and the exact height of the sky-scrapers in New York.

If storks flew like Steinmetz drove, they could not deliver babies, but with luck, after a hair-raising slow drive, mostly on the wrong side of the streets, in the big, wide, Czech-built, teardrop Tatra, with bench seats for three in front and three in the back, very much like the V12 teardrop

Lincoln Zephyr of the mid-1930s, we had survived. He bumped over the curb and came to a jarring halt, halfway up the sidewalk, in front of Gundel – the best restaurant in Budapest – and then had the gall to ask me, 'Isn't flying too dangerous?'

'Nooooo,' sang the little girls in an off-key duet.

One of Alex Korda's most annoying habits was being right so often, and he was right again to suggest I should arrive by plane in Budapest. Without it, I believe I would have never landed my first directorial assignment within four hours after the Savoia-Marchetti's wheels touched the Hungarian ground. It was ridiculous.

'I wanted a director with style, guts and class . . .'

'And courage,' interjected Mrs Steinmetz.

'Would you take us flying, Daddy, please?' The girls even had fat voices.

'SShhh, quiet,' warned Dr Steinmetz and continued. 'The minute you stepped off that aeroplane I knew I found the man for my picture . . .' He droned on and I switched off.

He made me the Great Dane from America. At least he spared me from being the Dachshund of Sunset Boulevard. If I had stepped off a Rome–Budapest sleeping car, would I have been a lesser man? The offer was offensive, sadly debasing. And, unfortunately, how true.

It was a difficult decision for me not to walk out, then I remembered Alex Korda and I didn't. Was it my Lady Luck again, being in the right place at the right time? Could it be this time in the right place at the right time with the wrong people?

Steinmetz pulled out three books from his bulging briefcase, ordered three Tokays for us, asked his family to take a taxi and go home. 'We'll get down to business now.' Had he driven as fast as he conducted his business he would have been a world champion Grand Prix driver. 'Would you object to working with Jews?' he whacked me with.

'What a question. Why should I? I would object to working only with no-talent idiots.' I got to my feet, excused myself, 'I will take a taxi.' I ignored the three books on the table, his offer to drive me to the hotel, and was off.

In spite of Basch's prophetic promise during luncheon – 'You could sleep fifteen, twenty minutes longer in the Royal. You'll be shooting and driving across the bridge at dawn in the winter when the freezing fog above the river is a mess. That's why I booked you in the Royal instead of the Gellért Hotel,' – I couldn't go to sleep now for a long time, a rarity, and as I just about dozed off not a knock but hard banging jerked me back to ugly reality. I didn't know where I was.

'Let the bird fly and open the door before I kick it down,' growled Eiben. To kick the door down was not an empty threat. I opened it at the wrong moment and he almost kicked my knee-cap off and came flying in the room. Basch was following him, carrying the three books.

'What the hell are you doing in bed?' complained Eiben, 'it's seven-thirty. I just finished trying to make shit look like gold. I'm hungry, let's order up some slop.' He opened two little liqueur-cabinets in the living room, one for wine, one for hard liquor, both were empty. He started on Basch, 'What the hell is the matter with you, Lóránt? You didn't order up anything; just because you don't drink everybody else should rust?'

Eiben picked up the phone to ask for menus and a wine list. Without answering him, Basch sat down, carefully placed the three books on the coffee table and had barely laid his palms on them, when there was a knock on the door. He jumped to his feet, opened it with expectation and with the smile of a Cheshire cat stepped aside to let in a bell boy carrying two wicker hampers, filled with different wines and hard liquor.

Examining the contents of the hamper, Eiben grumbled, 'I can't make up my mind if you're thoughtful, Lóránt, or cheap.' He turned to me, 'He saved you at least fifty per cent on the room-service liquor bill ordering this.'

The dinner was garnished with my stories of the States. The waiter rolled out the table, put the second bottle of Vichy water in front of Basch and the first brandies in front of Eiben and me. Eiben opened up, 'Now, Hapshikám, I don't want you to screw me up. Got it?' Pointing at the three books he went on, 'All three of them are equally shitty. Got it? And one of them you are going to make, got it? I don't care, Lóránt here doesn't care which one, got it, but one of the three you are going to make, goddamn it! Got it? . . . Don't interrupt!' he warned me.

'Pishtukám,' Basch tried to calm him.

'Don't try to calm me, Lóránt!' He knocked back the brandy, which I had never seen him do; he loved to savor it. 'OK,' he turned back to me. 'Now, listen to me you cattle-chasing Hungarian demi-cowboy, you can't let me down. Steinmetz will go ahead with one of them and I gave my word to do it. If you don't do it, I may end up with somebody –' Abruptly he stopped, only to continue with more fire, and yelled at Basch and me, it didn't matter to him we had not opened our mouths, 'What the hell do you two mean "somebody"? You old Shatterhand, you are doing it! Got it?'

Out of steam for the moment, Eiben got up to pour himself another drink, Basch took over. 'You impressed Dr Steinmetz very much and –'

'Yes, a lot of bull. Because I flew in, instead of hitchhiking, thank Dr Steinmetz for me for the compliment and shove it.'

'Gooood,' yelled Eiben from the liquor cabinet, 'just cut your fucking throat with a hacksaw.'

'I wish, Pishtukám, you wouldn't use those words all the time.'

'This is not all the time,' shouted Eiben, 'this is the fucking best time, OK? Sir Lóránt. And up you too Sir cowboy.' Satisfied with himself, he joined us again and sat down with a sigh. 'We are in production, Hapshi, like it or not. And listen to me, you better like it, OK?'

'Now, both of you listen for a minute, after that you have my blessing to kill each other.' And as usual Basch ended up having the upper hand. 'He was impressed by you – and don't interrupt – because you walked out on him when he brought up the Jewish question. He is half Jewish and very sensitive about it. He is pessimistic about the future, overly so, I think. He despises motion pictures, but he wants to make them, because he thinks it is a way to build up foreign equities legally and get his family out of here. He thought your knowledge, awareness of the English and the US markets, slight as it may be, will more than compensate for your inexperience in directing.' Concerned that he may have roughed up my ego, he corrected himself, 'the lack of first-hand experience. I agreed with him. Eiben didn't, he said you could've done it without going further than the next public toilet. There are the three books, read them, the sooner the better, and make up your mind –'

'Bull shiiiit!' Eiben jumped up. 'I made up his mind, he is going to direct *Toprini Nász*. That's it. Got it? Or I'll kill 'm, simple.' And he walked out, slammed the door, then re-opened it. 'You're lucky. I got to be on set at six-thirty. Damn it.' Then he slammed the door hard.

After several first-hot-then-cold showers, by the following noon I had finished reading all three books. They were not bad but *Toprini Nász* offered the best possibility for a feature. It annoyed me that the old fox, Eiben, was right; but it annoyed me more when I called Basch to tell him I had read all three books, he took it for granted.

'Of course you did. Get dressed, when you're ready call me and we shall meet Dr Steinmetz to talk over all the details, dates, etcetera, etcetera. Sorry, I am in the middle of a meeting, but I wanted to talk to you, 'bye.'

Just like that. My dream was fulfilled and I wasn't jumping for joy. I was let down. A hot-air balloonist, I thought, would have felt like that if, after feeding all the heat, he realized it was not necessary, he could have shut the flames off and the balloon still would soar, filled with a miracle.

The whole affair of making my first feature film was absolutely, positively anti-climactic. I was so ready, when it came it became almost a boring routine. I felt, and still feel, I was robbed of something, especially after listening to some of my peers' exciting adventures and heroic deeds to 'get in the saddle'. It was nothing. I shot it in eight days; before finishing I received an offer to write and direct my second film.

Within two months of 'go', *Toprini Nász* (*Wedding in Toprin*) was running in the theaters. By then I was preparing my third feature which I had written and was to direct. It was so fast I had no time to enjoy it.

I had nobody to argue with. Every time I looked at Eiben, I felt like a prize fighter in the ring throwing punch after punch and winning as the trainer – Eiben – at ringside jumped up and down with joy, laughing. Luckily he never said, 'See? I told you so.'

If I was not in the cutting-room, the nights were mine and I used them. No. Misused them. Writing scripts at a small round marble table in the Café Japan, at 'my table' in the back. If not, I was enjoying getting into trouble, with great success.

I came to my senses with shock. Dr Steinmetz died, for me unexpectedly. Cancer. I wanted him so much to enjoy what he had done for me and he couldn't.

It was in the middle of the night on the day of Dr Steinmetz's funeral. There was a tentative knock on my door, then another and another more demanding. I slipped on a robe and opened the door a crack. It was Mrs Steinmetz, still in her funeral black.

'Oh,' she said and slipped through the crack and collapsed in the nearest chair. 'Oh!' she gurgled again, 'I need something, badly. A drink, maybe? Do you have one? If not, don't bother.'

She knew damned well I had drinks in my suite, she and her husband had had a few dinners in here with me. 'What'll it be?'

'Oh, strong, something strong, I need it so badly.'

I gave her a double brandy, which she immediately sunk, then lifted the snifter for another one. I complied with her silent request. When I came back to hand her the new drink, she scooted forward in her chair and put an arm around my waist, leaned her forehead against my stomach. 'Oh, what a day it has been.' She took the drink but continued to hold on to me.

'Did you know that he was half Jewish?'

'Yes, I did.'

'Oh, but he was such a considerate man.'

'What do you mean by "but"? You're trying to tell me, Mrs Steinmetz, half Jewish people are not considerate?

'Yes.' As she put the glass down on the floor, her hand slid from my waist to my buttocks. When she straightened up she grabbed my buttocks with both hands and started to sob. 'Yes,' she repeated, 'in this new order they don't know where they belong.' Holding on to me tighter and tighter with kneading fingers, and trying to wipe off the tears, she rubbed both of her cheeks against my stomach, the robe slid open and she lamented to my naked stomach. 'They are scared. They all are. Did you know he was afraid? He was. He was afraid for us.' She stopped rubbing her cheeks against my naked stomach and tried to stick her nose into my bellybutton. It didn't fit, her nose was too fat. I froze with mixed emotions, disgust, pity, nausea. She babbled on. 'Did you know he was Catholic, got baptized? You know what he said to me? He said, had he known this new world was coming he would never have had children. That's what he said. Oh God,' she cried out and started to kiss my stomach. 'Oh, God,' she carried on, 'I am born Catholic but he wanted to kill us all once. But he was a considerate man and he died instead, we are now –'

I lifted her up and she started to move toward the bedroom. Then I grabbed the frock covering her fat ass and a handful of hair on the back of her head and shoved her out of the room, and slammed the door behind her. And vomited.

A stepping stone in my path, it taught me a lesson – look beneath the surface. And I dug.

'You really want to know? I can't tell you. Those who are writing the proposed laws don't know. This ambiguity gnawed on poor Steinmetz. It doesn't bother me and I am Jewish,' said Basch.

I didn't know. He was more German than any German I ever met. He even had 'Mensurenschnitten'[1] on his right temple, the indelible mementos of his university years in Heidelberg. He represented several large German corporations in international legal tangles.

'Surprised?'

'I never gave it a thought one way or the other.'

'Good. Why do you want to know now?'

'Something happened last night and I started wondering how serious this Jewish question is here in Hungary.'

'From 1 January 1939, Jews will be divided into three categories; first, the Jews, period. Second, Jews who should not be taken for Jews. Third, those who are Jews but who should be exempted from restrictions applicable to other Jews. The first category is clear; a Jew is a Jew, OK? Now, if one of the parents, two or three of the grandparents, before and on 4 May 1939, are Jewish and Judaism is their religion, they are Jews. If their offspring were born after 4 May 1939, they are to be treated as Jews. However, they are not to be taken for Jews if the children and parents were baptized before 1 January 1939 and they have stayed Christians. The Jews baptized before 1 August 1919, who remained Christians, are to be looked upon as equals. Those whose ancestors lived in Hungary since 1 January 1848 have to be considered unrestricted citizens. Exempt from all restrictions are the recipients of certain battlefield decorations, disabled veterans, widows whose husbands died on the battlefield and Olympic champions.'

This appalling 'law' was never strictly enforced in Hungary but that did not absolve its disgraceful existence. The cruel Spanish Inquisition, the barbarous bloodbaths of the Pogrom and other ugly chapters of human history were gone. Why did anti-semitism persist through milleniums, from the Pharaohs to Hitler and up to now in some circles? Was it deprivation of religious freedom, resentment of Jews as a foreign tribe within another country? Is Judaism a religion or the stigma of that particular race? Did the hatred grow from envy, jealousy?

---

1 Mensuren is a German student duel in which the object is not to cause serious harm. Combatants always bandage vital parts of the body prior to the duel which is conducted with razor sharp rapiers and fought by students representing different 'corps' within a university. Because the *Mensure* is comparable to an athletic feat it has remained a feature of German university life, albeit closely regulated. The main target to attack was the face. The diehards inserted a hair into the fresh cuts, 'Schnitten', to assure a well-visible scar.

Why did we think we could find a solution during luncheon to a millenium-old puzzle? Around us in the restaurant they were setting up for dinner. The State of Israel was an unspeakable dream then.

In August 1939, Victor Bánky was shooting a film, *Áll a Bál* (*The Ball Is On*), in Warsaw, Poland. One midnight I received a call from Eiben, who was on the picture.

'Hapshikám, come on up to this hell-hole, I don't know what the fucking hell is going on around here but they want me to shoot stuff that has nothing to do with this shitty picture. Something is off. They are sending my negative I don't know where but to my laborato – '

We were cut off. I couldn't get him back, nor could anybody from the company in Budapest get in touch with the production unit up there from then on.

Bánky, the director, was a strange duck. He was the brother of the great Hollywood silent star, Vilma Bánky, which he told you before he let your hand go after introducing himself. He was the cutter on two films where I was first assistant, but he was inclined to make everybody believe he was born as a director and had never done anything else but direct important features. In short, he was a pain in the, yes, there. But I doubted anybody could have been so great a pain as to prompt Eiben's call. Eiben never asked me for anything. Maybe the 'soul' of his coffee ran out – and that spelled disaster. I took off, well fortified for him, of course.

At the station in Warsaw a well-dressed, German-speaking, 'very military-looking' man whom I had never seen before came to me straight through the crowd, greeted me by name. Why and how did he spot me? His answer to my thought puzzled me even more.

'I am from the company.'

We had not been able to get in touch with anybody in Warsaw to tell them I was arriving, and on which train.

He was curtly polite in a typical German way. He took and carried my bag to the front of the station where we sat in a black Mercedes. He drove well, and en route to wherever we were going, he pointed out sights of interest. Rounding an impressive, grey, Baroque building, the car pulled up at its back entrance. Without any signal or anybody being in sight, the small gate opened and he drove through a tunnel-like passage to a large cobblestone-paved yard, littered with several cars and motor cycles.

'Please, leave your baggage, it will be taken care of.' And he led the way into the building. Long corridors with light grey-green walls,

studded with darker grey-green doors, no nameplates, only numbers. It
was spooky. There were no uniforms around, but it had the air of a military
or police establishment. He opened one of the doors for me and ushered
me in.

Large square room. The blinding-white walls were empty above rows of
filing cabinets. From behind the two desks in the room two men stood up
to attention to greet my escort. He ignored them, motioned me to follow
him. Through the two large windows a nice view of the square below hit
me first. The harshness of the white walls was softened by an array of
aquarelles of, I guessed, the Polish countryside. Mostly railway stations.
Obviously somebody was queer for railway stations painted in water-
colour. There was nothing on the shiny top of the large, functional desk.
From a well used, leather upholstered armchair, a thin man with a
pot-belly came around to meet us.

'Wolfgang Pröhle.' As my escort excused himself Pröhle said, 'Helmut
will be taking care of you while you are here,' and ushered me to a corner
seating arrangement around a coffee table. As we were seated he popped
open an elegant, slim, silver cigarette case and offered me a cigarette.

'Don't smoke, thanks.'

'Coffee will be here any minute.'

While he lit his cigarette he watched me. I watched him without a prop.
Something was fishy. The whole atmosphere was of a military or police
establishment. It flashed through my mind maybe Eiben had committed or
was accused of something. Pröhle spoke. 'Mr Eiben spoke very highly of
you.'

'Nice to hear it. Are they shooting far? I would like to . . .'

'Do you think he is a good cameraman?' he interrupted me.

'Eiben is not good – '

Pröhle leaned back, nodding, as if this was what he wanted to hear.

I continued, 'He is a *very* good cameraman, one of the best.' This quite
obviously did not please him.

'Hm. Strange . . .' he mumbled to himself.

The door opened after an inquisitive knock, but Helmut did not wait for
a 'Come in.' He walked to Pröhle and handed him a slip of paper. He
glanced at it, 'Excuse me,' walked to his desk, and took out from one of the
drawers a file, slid the note he received from Helmut into it and came back
with his right hand reaching, 'May I have your passport? We need it to get
some clearances for you.'

I didn't like it, but there was little or nothing I could have done. The door opened, now without a knock. A bursting-everywhere-from-health lady came in, in a shiny black blouse to enhance her gifts from God, carrying a large tray laden with tit-bits, two tea cups, a pot of tea, two small glasses, a bottle of schnapps. She put her load in front of us and withdrew with her polka-dot skirt swinging.

As she opened the door a harassed-looking man with haystack hair oozed through it with a large camera and a flashlight around his giraffe neck. He charged at me and, before anybody could take a second breath, he blinded me with two flashes. One shot straight on, one in profile and before the lady could close the door behind her, the photographer was out of the room.

'If you don't mind,' said Pröhle belatedly, 'we need it for the ID papers.'

Helmut withdrew with the file, Pröhle, now visibly more relaxed, poured two teas and two glasses of schnapps. 'Grüss Gott,' he toasted me unabashed.

The tasty tit-bits, I had to confess, hit the spot, but 'Now what?' I asked as we were nibbling. And he, without any prompting, explained that 'we' are only remotely associated with the production, but by previous arrangements . . .

'Arrangements with whom?' I asked, which he disdained to answer, as he disdained to answer 'How did Helmut recognize me at the station and how did you know I was coming at all and on which train?'

'Oh, there are ways, you know . . .'

'No, I don't . . .'

Helmut came in, after a knock, and handed a typewritten page to Pröhle, who, after a cursory glance, told Helmut, 'Bring it in,' and refilled my schnapps glass and tit-bit plate. Helmut went and came back bringing a large 'Minifone' – a way-ahead-of-its-time, large German wire recorder – put it in front of me and gave me a set of earphones.

'I know you were recently in America. Would you, please, translate for me. Roughly, only the gist of it.'

I did. It was a routine, almost daily BBC broadcast warning Hitler not to make any rash moves. The date was 30 August.

During Pröhle's hogwash I was beginning to guess where I was, but had not even the slightest inkling how I got there and why was I where I happened to be. Luck? The wrong place at the right time?

Finally Helmut came in again bringing with him my 'papers' but not my passport.

'Where is my passport?' I asked. Helmut looked for an answer to Pröhle.

'Your safety is our responsibility, and inexplicably some of the misguided would be willing to kill for a passport other than Polish. We are holding it for you. It is a precautionary measure.'

He got to his feet, 'Your passport is held here for safekeeping, it will be handed back to you at the station when you wish to depart. The car is ready now to take you to see Mr Eiben, if you still so wish. If you have changed your mind we shall take you to the station – ' he consulted his watch '– to catch the next train to Budapest.'

He moved toward the door. I was in one of the biggest holes I have ever been in, having no idea how to crawl out of it or which way. I have to admit, for a moment, disgustingly, I thought of demanding my passport and heading for that next train.

In the courtyard Helmut opened the trunk of the same or an identical Mercedes, I believe to assure me that my baggage was safely tucked away inside. It was there, next to cans and cans of film and camera bags. I thought nothing of it then. We had a driver now, Helmut sat in the back with me. He knew the town and its history well and instructed the driver to go out of his way so he could show me points of interest. I would have been interested at any other time, not then. I wanted to get to Eiben.

Knowing it would have disrupted the progress of shooting, I didn't show up till Bánky called it a day. When he spotted me, like a Bantam Cock before a fight he ruffled his feathers and welcomed me with a 'What are you doing here?' Before I could answer he shot a second and third question in an equally friendly manner, 'Who sent you here and why?'

That was the sum of all our dialogue for the rest of my stay in Poland and for the rest of his life.

'Hey-hey! Hapshikám,' hollered Eiben from a mile away, 'you got it?'

'I got it, Hapshi!'

'Get it then, Hapshikám, and come on over with it. On the double.'

The stack of Hungarian newspapers I brought for Eiben were gone from my locked baggage, but the baggage was relocked, the two bottles of 'soul' for Eiben were intact and everything inside was neatly in order. Stepping across the threshold of Eiben's room I started to complain, 'Somebody took – ' Eiben put up his fingers to cover his mouth and shook his head, a silent no. That rattled me more than I already was. This wasn't like Eiben, he always spoke out loud, often too loud, and always clear, whatever was on his mind, regardless of whom it flattered or whom it hurt, including himself.

He had one of those stinking nautical alcohol stoves in his room. 'No son of a bitch could make coffee in this shitty joint,' he pontificated, unnecessarily loud, then he checked the coffee pot on the contraption, and continued, again too loud, 'can you imagine, some shit-filled son of a bitch had the gall to steal the 'soul' of my coffee? Good God, am I glad you came! Just in time to save my soul from that contamination they call coffee here.' He shut off the blue flames under the pot and generously mixed his newly arrived 'soul' with the steaming-hot coffee, only then did the aroma of the Eiben coffee win the battle with the nauseating fumes of the alcohol stove.

We talked about generalities, how the picture was going, how the score for my last picture was shaping up, where should we go to eat, and whatever. Eiben, 'soulful', got to his feet, 'Let's go for a walk.'

This was one of the biggest shocks of my trip, and I had plenty, because on the set, on location, Eiben was tireless, but he never took half a step for the sake of walking.

'I am a fucking spy, Hapshikám. I am, they made me a fucking spy.'

That was for openers. Eiben never dilly-dallied. My sympathies for the father-confessors grew, for the burdens of others they were required to carry. I felt uncomfortable. Guessing, knowing, somehow I was or would be involved.

'Why are you telling this to me? What can I – what do you want me to do?'

'OK, go ahead and ask why the fuck did I ask you to come up here. Ask, you have the right to ask. OK? . . . OK, so you don't. I tell you, I needed somebody to talk to, somebody I trust. OK?'

He stopped to spit in the pond next to the path. We watched in silence the rings reaching for the shore on the mirror-smooth surface of the water. We started off, he stopped again to spit once more, but we were too far from the water and his spit disappeared tracelessly in the night. And with it his gloom. He started to laugh. We sat down on the large trunk of a once-proud tree, now lying on the ground, dead and defiled by stray dogs, heartless ants and now by us; trying to dove-tail our guesses to make a cohesive story out of them.

'You know, Hapshi, I don't want to direct, but I have to know what's what in the story and why, to be able to add that extra something to the image.' He got up, spat, then sat down, feet dangling, his heels kicking the tree trunk. I had never seen him so agitated. 'I had to photograph buildings, crowds with long lenses, focusing on jokers they pointed out to me. "What the hell for?" I asked; "Fuck the script, change it, I don't care, but where in hell will this shit fit in the story? I want to know." Shit-head director said, "Just shoot it." Travelling shots, most of the time on roads leading to railway junctions, streets to railway stations.'

'Hold it. Railway stations!' That hit home. In every watercolor on Pröhle's wall there was a railway station in the picture. It all became clear: railway stations, railway junctions, all probable military targets. How much easier it would be for a stranger to find them through visual references, memorized from pictures, projected films, rather than through maps. Such simple, brilliant planning if – No! Europe – the whole world? – so badly wanted to believe: 'No war in our time,' ignoring the German noose tightening against the arteries. In April, Hitler disclaimed his non-aggression pact with Poland; in May, Germany formed a military alliance with Italy; and in August signed a ten-year non-aggression pact with Russia.

'Shit, Hapshi, they made me a fucking spy. That's what I thought. I wasn't sure. That's why I called you to talk to you about it, but they cut us off, made me sure I was right. I couldn't warn you not to come any more. Sorry, Hapshikám, I dragged you into this . . .'

'Forget it.'

'Bullshit, but you're here, I am sorry and I am glad; so let's have some fun. You know what I did? I fucked them already. I shot everything, every fucking frame so out of focus they wouldn't be able to tell their grandmother's face from her ass.'

Now I understood, but I did not tell him Pröhle's doubts about his talent as a cameraman. I only suggested he should shoot some of the stuff in focus.

Eiben enjoyed his revenge, got to his feet, kicked the tree trunk again, this time with venom. 'Like what?' he asked. 'No way, Hapshi. But I sure would like to see their faces during rushes,' he laughed. He enjoyed his 'counterspy' activities. 'Until now I was the international, one-man, Hungarian FBI. Got it? But now you're in it too.' He was having fun. 'When they found out you were coming they asked me if you could use a camera; if not, I would have to make sure you could. I don't know why, but they are in a hurry to shoot some stock shots.'

The dawn of 31 August 1939 was breaking above our heads.[2] It was to be an unusual day for Eiben, he actually had to shoot scenes for the film. He hated it. For me the day brought nothing but surprises. I tried to open the door to my room and, before I turned the key, the door opened a crack. I was sure I had locked it. I swung it open wider and stepped back, like a Raymond Chandler detective. In the murk of the early dawn a figure rose from the only armchair in the dingy room. I backed away further. Scared, unlike Chandler's detectives.

'Don't do this again, please. Checking on you, I knocked on the door and there was no answer. I was concerned and told the manager to open it. Don't forget, you are my responsibility. Where were you?' fretted Helmut.

'I was out walking.'

Like a hunting falcon he swooped down on me. 'Walking? All night? With whom? Where?'

'Do I have to have permission to go to the toilet? By the way, this one doesn't flush.'

'I assure you it will be taken care of. Since you are here, we thought it would be a good idea if Eiben would concentrate his talent' – he said facetiously – 'on the production, while you take the load off his shoulders by shooting stock shots for a film we are interested in.'

He got up, stretched and walked out of the room. Passing me in the doorway, he 'suggested' without looking back, 'I will see you for breakfast in the dining-room within the hour.'

I was hungry, but to show my independence I was a half hour late. It was silly, I missed Eiben. The company was on its way to the set when I marched in. Worse yet, I missed annoying stuffed-shirt Bánky with my presence. Helmut was surrounded by the driver of the Mercedes and three other men. They had finished their breakfast and were enjoying the chicory-adulterated, mud-grey slop, blasphemously called coffee, in thick, once-white mugs. Both Helmut and the driver spoke fluent Polish to the three other men. To my surprise there was no remark made about my being late when I arrived. I took my time ordering and eating a big, unhealthy, delicious breakfast. I wasn't hurried. Ignoring me, they conversed in Polish.

2 At dawn on 1 September, German troops invaded Poland, triggering World War II.

By the time I had finished, aside from us, the dining-room was empty. I slowly got up from the table, signaling, if not my eagerness, at least my readiness to face the day.

'Please,' said Helmut, indicating the chair I had vacated. I sat down again. He spoke Polish to the men at the table. The driver and one of the Poles left and he turned to me. 'How much do you know about cameras?'

'Not much.'

'Eiben said this morning you were good. I believe him. It will be very exciting, very interesting for you. Maybe a once-in-a-lifetime chance.'

He ignored my question, 'What is it?' and the 'maybe' once-in-a-lifetime chance became an almost once-in-a-lifetime. Period. A long period!

The driver and the Pole came back carrying camera equipment and cans of film. A garlic-smelling, otherwise handsome woman appeared to replenish our 'coffees'. This new dose was piping hot at least, and the scalding muck camouflaged the foul taste of the fresh slop and the taste of the two subsequent meals.

As Helmut laid out the camera equipment on the table, it was evident he knew what he was doing. The two Arriflex[3] cameras had everything that could be needed under any conditions. Enough batteries for eight, nine hours of continuous shooting, a good selection of lenses and filters, carrying harness and rain-protection gear.

To be onerous, I inquired, 'No lights?'

Helmut actually started to laugh, the others joined in. 'Where you are going to shoot the last thing you would want around would be light.'

'What's the big joke?'

Helmut quietened down the group. 'What I meant was you are not going to shoot at night.'

He turned out to be wrong, I shot at night; the burning barns, the churches, the human torches running around the villages . . . There was too much light – I had to be careful not to over-expose. The tracers through the nights were horrifyingly beautiful. I was so tired I couldn't even throw up, not even when the 'raiders' at night were counting ears. Human ears. But only left ears counted. Whoever had the most ears won the pot. The 'entries' were high for the pot, about as much as an American nickel. But there were restrictions. Only grown-ups' ears counted, they were gentle

3 The German company of Arnold & Richter introduced the Arriflex, the first hand-held 35mm motion picture camera, in 1936.

folk. I am still wondering how St Stephen, the patron saint of Hungary, felt about it up there, because a group of Hungarian renegades, proudly wearing their insignia, the Arrow Cross, were involved in the 'game'.

The 1st of September 1939 set the world on fire. On the 3rd, England and France declared war on Germany; on the 5th, the US proclaimed her neutrality. That is what Russia was waiting for, and on 17th September, invaded Poland. By the 28th of the month Poland disappeared, gobbled up by Germany and Russia.

Call me a coward, but I didn't hang around that long. The German onslaught was a superlative of swift precision. I was sure they knew where they were going. 'Aquarelles'? 'Stock shots' supplied by unsuspecting cameramen over the course of months?

I was alone with one of the Poles, who didn't speak anything but Polish. Helmut was killed. Killed by the Germans. If you were in civilian clothes, the Germans shot at you; if in uniform, the Poles. We were targets for both sides. That way was quick and easy. Finding you with a camera was the worst death. Each side, with their own special method of torture, interrogated you inch by inch, second by second, to an everlastingly slow death.

I had other plans, so I quit. The first and only time in my life to date I had quit something. When I broke my neck, the first time, in Switzerland, skiing, I was told 'Don't try it. You'll never walk again.' I didn't quit. By the following season I was on the slopes again, and stupidly showing off as before. I suppose my walk from Poland to Hungary was a good training.

The Pole was sticking to me. I disliked him, he was a traitor to his country. But in many ways he was instrumental to our survival. I buried him when he bought it. Unnecessarily. Greed. I never knew his name. We borrowed compasses, maps, knives from dead German soldiers. Feasted on the flesh of not yet rotting farm animals. Water was a problem sometimes.

I was often asked about that escapade in my life and I have refused to talk about it until now. But I have had enough of it. It was easier to live through it than tell it now. One day, maybe, God willing, I will put the rest on paper to serve people who listen for one reason only, to learn what not to do.

12   Growing Up

The normally well-balanced madness of Budapest went out of control while I was away. The laughter, genuine or forced, was louder in the packed nightclubs and cafés. Everybody played the violin while the world started to burn around us.

I finally succeeded in fighting my way through the mob and settled at 'the table' in the packed Café Japan. 'You look like hell!' was the most complimentary greeting that was awaiting me.

'Where have you been? With whom were you shacking up?' I was jumped by two aghast writers with whom I was supposed to be working on the script of my fourth film. 'Shit!' screamed Tony Takács, an old friend from Berlin, producing his first film. 'You almost killed me before I could see the first day's rushes.'

'You would have died in vain. You were not going to see rushes. Remember?'

'Oh, yeah. I have bad news for you. We lost Eiben in Poland.'

He almost killed me, but luckily he spoke fast, 'Finally, through the German embassy, I got through to him – '

'You talked to him?'

'Yeah, sure he – '

'Was he all right?'

'Yeah, sure. But we can't have him because they're way behind. He was sorry and was asking about you, then we were cut off, that was it. We couldn't get him back. The man at the embassy said we were lucky to get through in the first place.'

Eiben was a foxy cookie. He 'got it' right away; if Takács didn't ask about me then he didn't know where I was and Eiben let it lie. I poured oil on their guessing game – with whom was I shacked up – I led them on. For me the chapter of Poland was closed until chapter eleven of this book.

Basch was a tower of strength. He believed the 'Hitler mania', as he called the movement, was 'the epitome of self-combustion', it would exterminate itself. He had lined up six productions for the next year for me.

'No more, Lóránt. I'll be shooting *Six Weeks Happiness* when I finish the script, which will be any minute. I am committed to *Semmelweis*, not only by the contract but by sentiment; in memoriam of Stephen, Lillian and Dr Erdös, in a way of Vienna too. Then I want to think, I have a lot to think about.'

'You're changing. Does it hurt?'

'Hurt what?'

'To be growing up.'

I thought, I hoped I was, but I never suspected it was showing. Basch, the wise old owl, sensed something. It annoyed me, I wasn't ready to play 'face-up' poker, I didn't yet recognize the cards Poland had dealt me . . .

'Don't insult me with this "growing up" stuff, I don't like grown-ups.'

I lived high on the hog. I was ridiculously overpaid. For what? I never worked a day in my life. I loved so much what I was doing – and still do – I would have given – it's not much now – whatever I own, for what I was overpaid to do.

The tragedy was I made so much money with so little time to spend it. It was bewildering for someone barely over twenty, but I tried. I had the best seats, the best – yes, it's all good, but I had the best of what you are thinking of. Disgusting as it was, I had a new toy, a Mercedes 540SK convertible, to wreck after I wrecked my Steyr 220 convertible. I was being spoiled rotten, and I did not comprehend why. I didn't go out of my way to do anything special, I was doing what I loved to do. It was easy. I wasn't even satisfied with what I had done – one of the few good habits I had that stayed with me. I didn't understand the reason for the fuss, although I took the fullest advantage of it. Why not? What else did one need? Kept and unkept promises, I had them all.

Envy, jealousy, thank God, more often destroy the beholders than those they are envying or are jealous of. Ultimately, the envy and jealousy of one of my peers helped me more than I could ever thank him for.

I was shooting later than usual on the night in question. Selfishly, it didn't bother me, I was sure they would hold my table for me at the Gundel's. I guessed right. But I didn't guess the commotion that would cause.

As I walked in the restaurant I heard an irate voice complaining, 'Don't tell me you are full. Look, look, loook, there is an empty table, see it? Right there, what's wrong with that?'

'I'm sorry sir, but – '

'No buts' . . . and the incensed voice of Márton Keleti, a not untalented but usually unemployed assistant director whose greatest achievement was keeping himself out of work. Like a mad dog, hungry, thirsty, chained to a gatepost he was barking indiscriminately at everybody on sight. He had an audience now, ranted and raved and was having a field day.

'Look at it. That table is reserved for two, we are four. It is bad business, you're losing money.'

I stayed in the background in the doorway to enjoy my importance, the scene. The Fö-úr noticed me.

'Good evening, sir. Your table is ready. This way please. I will tell the chef, sir, you have arrived.'

On my way in Keleti stepped in front of me. Not nose to nose, but pretty close.

'You think you are so fucking important?'

'I know it. And keep sex out of it. Yes.'

Keleti was boiling. 'And you think you're so goddamned talented?'

'I don't think, I *know* I'm very talented.'

'You're just damned lucky.'

'I know it. I'm very, *very* lucky.'

But Keleti wanted to have the last word, which he did, and I am eternally grateful to him for it. He wielded the straw that broke the camel's back. He woke me up with a well-deserved kick in the pants.

'I tell you something, big shot. If you were Jewish you wouldn't be working. Heil Hitler,' and gave me the Nazi salute and marched out.

He gave me the most fruitful sleepless nights but robbed me of the joy of going on the set, making the picture. He planted a gnawing doubt which grew and grew. Was he right?[1] I did not want to be successful by taking advantage of the inhumane injustice inflicted on innocent people. I didn't want to ride on top because I was not Jewish. 'What if Keleti is right?' was

---

1 Between January and November Andre de Toth directed and also wrote or co-wrote five feature films. His first film, *Toprini Nász* (*Wedding In Toprin*), received the 'Most Artistic Film Award' from the Hungarian Ministry Of Culture. His second film, *Öt Negyven* (*Five Forty*), was chosen as the Hungarian entry in the Venice Film Festival. His third film, *Két Lány Az Utcán* (*Two Girls On The Street*), also sole screenplay, was awarded the UFA Silver Cup for the 'Most Avant-Garde Film'. For his fourth film, *Hat Hét Boldogság* (*Six Weeks' Happiness*), he received the 'Best Director Award'. In the United States he received an Academy Award Nomination as co-author of *The Gunfighter*, and a Lifetime Achievement Award from the International Stereoscopic Cinema Association.

the first question I asked myself every morning and last thing every night. I had to find out!

I rushed *Semmelweis*, my fifth picture, and for me it showed. I buzzed through post-production, delivered the picture way ahead of schedule. And all way through the rush I felt I was letting down Stephen, Lilian and Dr Erdös. But I kept on pushing, I had to. I wanted to get out.

As you couldn't run away from your shadow no matter how fast you rode, I couldn't run away from Keleti's question. I couldn't enjoy the best seats, the special treatment, the deluxe dinners, my pride the car. What if it was true? If it was, I was worse than the ear-cutting bastards, I was robbing the living of more than the special treatment, deluxe dinners and wealth. I was robbing them of their pride, their dreams.

During dinner I was offered two more films, one of which was originally a project of a Jewish peer of mine. It was like being doused in a shower of vitriol. It hit me hard in the middle of the meal. I got up from the table. Went home. Packed. Drove to the East Railway Station, parked my Mercedes, locked it carefully, then dropped the keys down the drain and boarded the first train out of Budapest going west, and, with every hour behind me, I felt cleaner. I was on my way to find the answer. Thanks, Márton Keleti.

Rome was every bit the same madhouse as Budapest or Vienna, except instead of brown shirts, the shirts were black and the uniforms weren't as well starched and pressed, and the boots weren't as shiny. Naples I had always loved, but with *S.S. Rex* towering in the harbor she looked better than ever. But when I found out she was overbooked and scheduled to sail the following day, *S.S. Rex* didn't look so good. Shipping agents refused to talk to me about getting on board. 'Not even steerage,' they said.

Alex Korda's voice came to me in the cool silence of the Excelsior Hotel's lobby. 'The concierge usually has the solution, there is always a table, a seat, a ticket, a solution. The concierge!'

The conversation with the majestic factotum started with ten US dollars changing hands. After twenty more dollars I was assured he 'probably could get' third-class passage with three other passengers in a way-below-deck cabin, next to the engine-room. Korda must have overheard because he spoke to me again and an additional fifty changed ownership. Within one hour I was 'almost' guaranteed a north side 'B' deck cabin to share with one 'nice gentleman', said the concierge. Korda nudged me again, I followed his advice and started to roll slowly a hundred dollar bill into a tube, muttering, '"A" deck, south side, alone. Per piacere' ('please'), I added for good measure.

'Vediamo' ('We shall see') he said and gently pulled the rolled up century note through my fingers. 'Scusi,' he whispered as he left his lustrous mahogany and brass post. He waved to one of God's lesser creations to take over the post, not his place. I watched him through the window, he took a taxi and disappeared.

After three hours I was sure he had disappeared and my hundred and eighty dollars with him. At least I was entertained watching the onslaught of travelers with outhouse-size trunks, full of glossy 'look where I was' stickers.

'I am sorry I kept you waiting so long.' I didn't see the concierge come in; he continued sotto voce, 'We may have a little problem.'

'Little problem, only little problem?'

'I had to take the liberty of making a decision for you, but it is not irreparable.'

'Yes?'

He took his time. He pulled out of his briefcase an envelope, out of that envelope another envelope. 'I undertook an obligation for you, but the final decision will be yours, of course.'

From the third envelope he came up with what looked like a steamship ticket. Had he said 'voilà' as he handed it over he would have completed the image of a magician.

It was a first-class, south side, 'A' deck, single-cabin ticket, issued in my name. I almost hugged him, 'What's the problem?'

'My obligation is for another hundred dollars. It is not your obligation, it is my obligation. Please don't worry. I will be able to dispose of the ticket.' And he reached out for it.

He withdrew his hand with another hundred dollar bill. And I was the happiest passenger to board the *S.S. Rex* the next day, on what turned out to be her last crossing of the Atlantic. She was sunk next time around.

13 Rabbits Running

Hitler's cruel and powerful arm reached out and whipped up the South Atlantic to punish the 'Flüchtlinge' (fugitives, escapees). The tops of the smoking waves looked like the peaks of the Swiss Alps. Sea-mist crawled through the keyholes. Some of the portholes on the north side of the ship as high as the 'B' deck were battered in; and that was about ten, eleven stories high. Ankles were twisted, collar bones broken. The bruises were treated internally at the bars. On the dance floors the obliging storm made even the Christmas trees do a spectacular 'Big Apple'.[1] What I am trying to say is it was a hell-of-a-party for those who were not 'bunk-bound'. The weather, aside from playing tricks, was a good host, though it added four days to the scheduled five days crossing. The longest in 'Rex's' illustrious history.

Nobody noticed or cared that the food was lousy, the service – service? – non-existent. And though only half of the passengers could manage to stagger around, there were still enough people left to run interference for you and save you from colliding with railings and sharp corners as S.S. Rex thought she was a loco-bronco during the Calgary Stampede. And it was easier to ride those loco-broncos than negotiate the stairs on 'Rex'. I have tried both, courtesy of my range boss, Eddie Cline.

New York swayed into sight, and, as maggots scatter from under an overturned rotting tree trunk, the 'bunk-brigade' came up squinting, to have the first sniff of freedom. The Statue of Liberty. Tears and handkerchiefs.

I heard Keleti's voice. I felt again like I did then – as the underdog climbing into the ring to fight the champion. So far I had earned no applause, only boos. If, if, if Keleti was right. But there were no ifs in the ring, it was yeah or nay.

1 The dance-craze of the time, choreographed by chiropractors.

The ring, the shore of the USA, was floating closer, I was bucking the threat of another yeah or nay.

Blood smells the same everywhere. Specially your own blood, and specially if your nose is like a lump of stepped-on raw hamburger. I had lost my mouthpiece several times during previous rounds. My lips didn't hurt, they simply weren't there any more. The world looked like a narrow ribbon through slits that once were eyes. I heard only two sounds, one was a distant train whistle as I was trying to breathe, the other was applause. Loud. That ringing, steamrolling applause. It was not for me, but it was mixed with a few boos. That was not for me either. Yes? No! I didn't care. I wanted to stay alive.

The train-whistle stopped for eternity, the solar plexus cramped under the blows. There was no sound left in the world until the train-whistle restarted, deafening. So did the applause and the boos. My knees were buckling, the world was rocking, so was my head. Then I hit. I hit up from the depth of unconsciousness. From the floor. The uppercut connected so hard, a hot poker pierced my shoulder and it extinguished all sound. A distant sharp crack. The back of his neck hit the rope as he fell back. Dead.

I never stepped in the ring again. But for a long, long while it haunted me. Poland, the wholesale death, the death of innocents eased the noose of the lonely ghost. And as the Copper Lady from France greeted me, I forgot the boos and the applause. I picked up Keleti's gauntlet.

Below me the tiny tug boats were gently nudging the helpless behemoth toward her berth. The 'bunk-bound' human maggots were beginning to regain the complexion of the living, muted hoots of ships near and afar, frozen droplets hanging in the air. New York in winter.

'Here is your confirmation,' said the chief purser on board the *S.S. Rex* as he handed me a piece of paper at the railing. 'I am glad it worked. With all the "coniglionis" ("rabbits") running from Europe – I do not know why but they are – it was difficult,' he continued officiously. 'Believe me, it is important, if you have no relatives, have reservation. Relatives with good address is good, no relatives good hotel will impress immigration officers. I know, I see it all the time.'

He had told me two days out he had a brother-in-law who was the concierge at the St Moritz Hotel on Central Park South in New York City. You guessed it, that is where I checked in. The 'Korda method'. Ugly, but it worked as usual.

A short walk from the hotel, 729 Seventh Avenue, among the many film companies under the same roof was Danubia Pictures, a distribution company specializing in the US distribution of Hungarian pictures and tours for Hungarian celebrities in the country. Danubia had three equal partners, but only two of the three partners were on speaking terms with each other. I had met all three during my previous visits. Dezsö and Béla were bachelors, fussy, prissy stoics. Elemér, the 'not-spoken-to' partner, was by no means a silent partner, he was verbose, sloppy and married to Tzuntzi. That added to the problem.

She indulged in a crime a Hungarian wife can not be forgiven for, certainly not by characters like Dezsö and Béla, both gourmets, specializing in Hungarian cooking. Tzuntzi loved to cook, but she was a disaster in the kitchen. Had she only wanted to poison Dezsö and Béla to gain control of Danubia Pictures, they would have understood. She insisted on having them for dinner every time her husband was on the road with Danubia's films. Which was often, because the Hungarian – and only the Hungarian – films had a mysterious habit of disappearing if traveling alone. Taking the prints by hand was a must. It was also a must for Dezsö and Béla to face Tzuntzi's dinners. This was the only line of communication the two old codgers had to their business, since they didn't talk to Elemér.

Dezsö and Béla swam to the US from Hungary before the Mayflower dropped anchor, but their combined vocabulary in English would not fill half a page of the smallest dictionary. The few expressions they knew in English were hidden by their thick accents; they were understood only by Hungarians, but why speak English to Hungarians? they questioned.

Elemér did all the traveling around the country, to the delight of Tzuntzi, who thought she was better off without him. In more ways than one. In fact, she was running the business single-handed, quite successfully. She was half Hungarian and half Rumanian, but she spread the rumor she was French. Tzuntzi spoke the language just enough to get away with it, but her approach to life was definitely French and there she got away with more than poor Elemér bargained for. She was not bad-looking at all in a well-worn way.

The Danubia offices looked like a used office furniture store at the turn of the century. Elemér's office was dotted with painfully out-of-place Art Nouveau lamps, as a result of Tzuntzi's presence in the office. When I, unannounced, walked into the office, Frau Nussbaum, the secretary, who spoke only German well, seeing me coming through the door, got excited and screamed at the top of her lungs, 'Noooooooo! Ach lieber Gott nein! Wie ist das möglich?' ('Oh, my God, no! How is it possible?')

Her three bosses ran out to investigate the reason for her screams and to face me. In the excitement a miracle happened. The three equal partners actually talked to each other without noticing it and, Elemér's office being closest to the entrance, we settled in there.

I was suffocated by the questions and answers they gave to their own questions. It was like being in the middle of a tornado of words.

'Why don't you speak Hungarian, you jerk, so we can understand it?' Dezsö stopped the Babel for a second.

His equal partner, Elemér, puffed himself up like a turkey before gobbling, but protested in Hungarian, 'I speak any way I choose in my office. In my, my, my office, cabbage-head.' He looked at me victoriously, 'There! So welcome, but why did you come back?'

'Why didn't you let us know?' asked Dezsö. 'Where are you staying?' asked Béla.

But again they didn't wait for an answer. Overlapping, overriding each other in a verbal vortex they were trying to convince me I had made a big mistake.

'Over there you were king . . . You should have taken advantage of it . . . Here you are one of the millions of refugees . . . but don't forget you didn't have to come here . . . you are a refugee without a reason . . . you really shouldn't have come.'

It was a hell of a reception committee. Luckily the door burst open and Tzuntzi blew in on a cloud of Chanel Number Five, dressed to kill. She kissed everybody in the room with varied fervor, except Elemér. Instead of a kiss, he was reprimanded. 'Frau Nussbaum had to tell me the news, you couldn't have called me, of course.' She planted another long kiss on my forehead, 'Welcome to the Big Apple,' then with a dramatic sway of a hula-dancer she undulated to face the others, 'this is an occasion to celebrate. We all have dinner tonight, all of us.' With her threatening finger tipped with long scarlet claws, she ticked off each of the three equal partners, 'Understood, messieurs?' Not a grunt of dissent or agreement from the equal partners; she smiled sweetly and went on, 'I have already made the reservation.' This seemed to relieve, somewhat, Dezsö's and Béla's reticence; Elemér succumbed. Tzuntzi was in her full glory.

The food in the small, naturally Hungarian restaurant was good, Tzuntzi was a gracious hostess. They all even seemed to enjoy each other, but less so as time went on. Not halfway through the dinner they were back at each other's throats again, now on my behalf. They ignored my presence while discussing me, à la Bolváry and Eiben in Vienna or Molnár and Basch in the Café Japan. That was my fate, it seemed. But on these occasions it hurt. It was painful to be dissected alive. In Budapest Keleti was wielding the scalpel like a meat axe; here the Danubia trio bludgeoned me with a sledgehammer and both sides made me feel like shit: inferring I was taking advantage of a situation I despised.

On the other hand, Tzuntzi was telling me Kate Cameron in the *New York Daily News* gave my first film three and a half stars in her column; it was the highest ever awarded to a Hungarian film. 'We shall go on a tour with the film.' She really lit up, she grabbed hold of my hand, her crimson claws dug into my skin, 'We are going to make a lot of money on the tour.' The thought of money must have excited her, her claws dug deeper, she wet her lips, 'And we are going to have fun, fun like you never had before.'

She kept her promise. But her keeping some part of her promise was resented by Elemér, and my association with Danubia Pictures, not with Dezsö and Beéla, was cut short. That was a welcome relief, but my aim was Hollywood, not the Hungarian cinema circuit of the East Coast, in winter, with Elemér driving an old clunker, no heater, and Tzuntzi in the back, griping she was freezing-freeeezing cold. After a day she got on Elemèr's nerves and he asked me to sit in the back to keep her quiet and keep her warm. Tzuntzi must have been very, very cold, because from then on, every night of the following week, she came to my room to be kept warm. I guess that got on poor Elemèr's nerves too.

I took the train from Cleveland. Tzuntzi and Elemèr continued the tour, making nothing else but money. In New York Dezsö and Béla were waiting for me with a laurel wreath and ear-splitting smiles. Took me to Horn and Hardart, their favorite non-Hungarian eatery, to console me with, 'Don't feel too badly, you are the fifth we know of.'

Ivan Tors[2] was a writer friend from way back in Hungary. He had been

2 Ivan Tors (1916–1983) was a Hungarian-born playwright, who became an American film producer of long-running television series such as *Flipper*, *Daktari* and *Sea Hunt*, as well as of a number of features with animal stars, such as *Clarence The Cross-Eyed Lion* (1965) and *Namu The Killer Whale* (1966), mostly shot in Florida.

planning to go to Hollywood since he left Budapest six or seven months ago, but he was afraid to face it. To add to the delay, he fell in love with an Irish lass named Eileen, from Hoboken, New Jersey. At the same time he fell in love with a 'brand, brand-brand new' gunmetal-grey Plymouth coupe, through her brother, a car salesman. A frugal man, Ivan assured me it was a 'steal'. I assured him it was the worst piece of 'brand, brand-brand new' junk. Ivan was a bad salesman, I didn't like the car, but I bought it. Bought it for one reason only, my faith in Ivan's talent; I wanted to blackmail him into driving to California with me.

I meant he should ride with me, not drive. He was the most aggravating driver, he either crawled or his size 13½ foot tramped the accelerator through the floorboard, neither at the right time, in the right place or under the right circumstances. But even I would have let him drive had it been the price to pay to get Ivan to Hollywood; I was certain once he was there he would connect. I didn't like to listen to the radio while driving, but Eileen had a pleasant voice and sang 'When Irish Eyes Are Smiling' often and well. I was looking forward to the drive, I told the two equal partners.

'Oh, he won't be back for two weeks or so.'

'He left only yesterday, you're supposed to be on the tour for three more weeks,' Béla added to the good news.

'Have a French apple pie,' offered Dezsö to ease my disappointment.

They had Hungarian friends in Hoboken, they could have helped to intercept them, had I known Eileen's surname. Dead end.

I saw all the plays, the Rangers in the Garden, the ice-floe on the river, I was filled up with Napoleons and other famous poisons of Rumplemayer, walked the endless miles of the museum corridors, enjoyed the Rockettes. The next best thing for me to do was get the hell out of New York. How? With no car and all my luggage I had one choice, the train.

'No compartment, I am very sorry, sir,' cried the concierge at the hotel, feeling sorry for himself because of losing the sure gratuity. Dezsö's and Béla's Hungarian Mafia achieved the impossible with ease; within twenty-four hours I was on my first cross-country on the train, in a comfortable little cell called a compartment.

It seemed the White Russian Mafia was better connected than the Hungarian Mob. In a plush travel bureau in Beverly Hills, taking care of 20th Century-Fox, was a Russian gentleman who was aware of the movement of the gods of the lot. This same gentleman was also aware of the movements of a Russian friend of his, Gregory Ratoff, Griesha to his friends and creditors – who adored him equally.

To follow the movements of Griesha was no big deal, he had to restrict his movements because to re-heel his shoes was too great an expenditure for him. He was a neat man, he had talent, a great sense of humour, good ideas, he had everything. Almost everything. Griesha had no money and no connections to the 'right people'.

'We'll fix that,' said his friend from the travel bureau. But he almost gave Griesha a heart attack one day when he handed him a ticket on the Super Chief to Chicago, with connection to the 20th Century Limited to New York. The royal route.

'Zanuck[3] will be in the next compartment, to New York and back. You're on your own.' He added, as a good Russian friend would, 'You'll pay me back from your first pay check from Twentieth. Double. OK?'

And Griesha was on the train. Got onto it in Pasadena, that was 'the way to do it'. Only nutnicks boarded the train in Los Angeles, Union Station. He played small parts, his face was not unknown. On the race tracks, to his detriment, his face was well known.

Zanuck was a gentleman, he was in the picture business, he was a lover of horses too, so it was not a miracle that, when Griesha, with his 'familiar face', from the screen and the tracks, nodded a 'hello' to Zanuck, he returned it to the 'familiar face' when, as a miraculous coincidence, they boarded the train simultaneously.

Miracles can go too far. By Chicago Zanuck was an unhappy traveler. Griesha was $5000 ahead playing Gin Rummy, a dollar a point, he couldn't do wrong. The trip was leading to disaster, not a job.

The train pulled into New York with a happy Zanuck, but a much happier Griesha on board. He owed Zanuck $32,000.

Griesha was a good actor, he was downcast when he asked Zanuck, 'When are you going back? I need a revanche.'

Zanuck checked his ticket, Griesha pulled out his, with a checkbook. They studied both tickets.

'What a surprise, same dates,' said Griesha, taken aback, and he

3 Darryl F. Zanuck (1902–1979), the only swashbuckling studio executive in Hollywood. At eight he played an Indian boy in a silent Western. At 15 he lied about his age and saw action in WWI in France. From being a writer of Rin Tin Tin stories after the war at Warner Bros he had a meteoric rise from the dogs to the polo ponies. A gambler. An inventive writer, producer, a demigod of 20th Century-Fox.

pocketed his ticket and his check book. 'We'll settle in Los Angeles then.'

Zanuck was first to board the train in New York on their return trip. He greeted Griesha like a long lost brother when he boarded the train with a minute to spare.

As the train was pulling in the station in Pasadena, Zanuck was $75,000 wealthier. He patted Griesha on the back, 'Well, let's settle it then.'

This time Griesha didn't have to act to be sincere. 'I don't even know how to write down $75,000, I haven't got a pot to pee in.'

Zanuck sank back in his seat, for the first time in his life speechless. The train pulled out of the station in Pasadena. They sat in silence, staring at each other until Griesha had an idea he had never thought of before.

'You got to give me a job so I can pay you back – with interest,' Griesha added.

'You just thought of it.'

'No. I planned it,' said Griesha simply.

Zanuck stared at Griesha – as he told me, for an eternity – then burst out laughing.

When the Super Chief pulled into Union Station in Los Angeles, railroad history was made: Zanuck had not gotten off in Pasadena. By the time they left the train in Los Angeles, Zanuck's car from Pasadena was in front of Union Station.

'Get in. I'll drop you off,' Zanuck told Griesha.

In front of Griesha's apartment Zanuck told him, 'Seven tomorrow morning in wardrobe.'

That was Darryl F. Zanuck. Their friendship lasted and Griesha clicked in Hollywood. I am sure they are playing Gin Rummy now, in heaven or in hell.

However, 20th Century-Fox changed its travel agency. That's Hollywood. No inside information, please.

14   Comedies of Error

Leon O. Lance was one of the dozens of Hollywood agents who lived on inside information. Without it they would starve to death, taking with them hordes of the hopefuls. They gathered information from little people. They represented little people. They were little people. They were the signposts in the kingdom of little people with big dreams and empty stomachs. They were on the job twenty-four hours a day, sniffing, digging like ground hogs collecting fodder for the winter. Hollywood winters could be very long.

Leon O. Lance was in the upper echelon of these future-builders. He had an office on the top floor of a building on the south side of Sunset Strip, a few doors down from the Trocadero. He had a bronze nameplate on his office door: 'Leon O. Lance – Personal Management'. He was very proud of this bronze sign. Stability. It was a good address, although his office was so small he had difficulty fitting in his enormous briefcase, loaded with photos of girls, boys, men and women, dogs, horses and birds. Leon O. Lance had two live telephones; Leon O. Lance was glued to the telephone. With his menagerie it was a must.

He could deliver at a moment's notice anything from a virgin to a giraffe. One phone call. That was it. There were no second calls in that bracket.

I still have no idea how I fitted between a virgin and a giraffe, but Leon O. Lance delivered me to Woody Van Dyke[1] at MGM the week after my return. Through inside information, from Elinor Prentis, who fitted in between a virgin and a giraffe with Woody Van Dyke, Leon learned that Woody, like everybody else, was looking for a 'different story'. Leon decided I had one; while I was sunbathing, he listened fully dressed,

---

1 W. S. 'Woody' Van Dyke (1889–1943) came to prominence as a director in the 1920s; he became one of MGM's most reliable directors, with films such as *San Francisco* (1936), *Bitter Sweet* (1940) and *I Married An Angel* (1942).

sitting in the shade of one of the chimneys on the tarred flat roof of 1842 North Cherokee, an apartment house north of Hollywood Boulevard, on the hill below Franklin.

I moved in because I met a lovely little lady on the train out from New York, and that was where she lived. It was an old building then – it was demolished recently, a pity. It had big rooms with never-functioning air-conditioning boxes that were fixed through the bottom halves of the windows to obstruct the good views of the Hollywood rooftops to the south. I would never have picked the place, and I would have been wrong again. I would have missed, short as they were, some of the most fun-filled days of my time in Hollywood.

The building was peopled with the top-line second-stringers of the town. Gypsies, hoofers, small-bit players, musicians, stunt men. They all had a common bond. No dreams. They knew where they were. Exactly where they wanted to be, a happy, 'every day is a holiday' bunch. More than half of them were under the 'personal management' of one Leon O. Lance. There were also a few employed, and unemployed, unhappy writers with and without ideas or typewriters. All full of dreams.

'Congratulations,' said a fellow on the stairs, with genuine tears in his eyes, who followed me down from the roof to my apartment on the third floor.

'Thanks. For what?'

'I overheard your story, I heard what Leon said. You have a job. And My God, with Woody Van Dyke, tops.'

'Well, thanks, it's only an interview and –'

He interrupted me, ' – man, you're going to meet Woody, maybe even Hedy Lamarr[2] woo-woooo – ' he put his hands up to his breasts, ' – he is shooting with her. I'm a writer too. If you need any help . . .' he let the suggestion drift, pulled out a card from his pocket: 'R. Chandler', under it simply 'writer'.

'Raymond?'[3] I asked facetiously.

2 Hedy Lamarr (born 1913) was an Austrian-born actress who came to fame in 1933 as a result of a nude sequence in the Czech feature *Ecstasy*; she was an exotic leading lady in such Hollywood productions as *Algiers* (1938), *White Cargo* (1942) and *Samson And Delilah* (1949).
3 Raymond Chandler (1888–1959) was one of the best known American authors of tough detective fiction, including *The Big Sleep* and *Farewell, My Lovely*, both of which featured his private investigator hero Philip Marlowe.

'Rayfield Chandler,' he answered without being slighted. 'Everybody calls me Ray, though.' He followed me into my apartment without being asked. 'You have a coke, I presume?' Without waiting for a word from me, he followed his presumption, opened the refrigerator, 'Do you want one?' and took out two cokes. 'Glasses?' he asked uselessly. He went to the kitchen and came back with two glasses, poured, handed me one glass filled to the brim. He took over, checked my typewriter, 'Not bad.' He sat behind it, zipped in a sheet of paper and started to type with the speed of a machine-gun firing. 'Smooth, I don't have one now, I write on a pad,' he said and went for another coke. 'I don't drink hard stuff before sunset. I used to, that's a bad kick.'

'Rayfield – '

' – Ray!'

'Ray, I am glad to have – '

'Yeah. You want to get on and polish your treatment. Remember? I am a writer too. I know. Know it real well. But this goddamned town, I haven't been able to get a job now for five months, almost half a year!'

Ray had his third coke. He was a clean-looking guy, conservatively dressed. Leon didn't approve of that style. You got to 'cut through', was Leon's motto. He did, sporting black and white or brown and white shoes, with his tall, bent, skinny body hidden between the enormous shoulder-pads of his painfully loud plaid sport-jackets. The fashion plate's head was topped by pomade-soaked and dyed black hair; he had a moustache with waxed tips pointing menacingly forward like the horns of an angry Aragonian bull ready to charge the matador. Leon O. Lance cut through all right. Ray didn't. He was a living apology. I felt sorry for him when he stopped at the door, with his hand on the doorknob, and shamefully confessed, 'I am selling cars now.'

'It's great. Nothing wrong with that. I love cars.'

He perked up a bit, 'You do?' and let go of the doorknob to pull out a card from his pocket. Handing it to me he said, 'I've had no sale for the last three weeks. Terrible. I will have to move out of here next Monday.'

The card read: 'Rayfield Chandler. Sales representative, A. E. Nugent, Chevrolet'. I have forgotten the address, somewhere on La Brea. As I was reading the card he asked tentatively, 'By any chance, do you have a car?' And obviously crossed his fingers.

I was not superstitious but, I don't know, sometimes those crossed fingers can evoke miracles and I became the owner that afternoon of a maroon Chevrolet Convertible, with red leather seats. It was not the car or the color I would have picked, but Rayfield was working for Chevrolet and that was the only car the dealer had in stock. I owned two cars, neither was my choice. A year and a half later an accordion-pleated, gunmetal-grey box, derivation of a Plymouth coupe, pulled up in front of the General Service Studio, where I was working. Ivan, big, sweet and clumsy as always, got out of it, ignoring the protesting door's ear-splitting screeches and grunts, and said simply, 'Thanks for letting me use your car.'

I had to beg him to keep it. 'Oh, yeah! Thanks for remembering today was my birthday.' He did keep it for another six or seven never-serviced years. His next car was a Rolls Royce, but by then he had got too successful to have fun or to learn how to drive a car and got no joy out of having a street named after him in Florida. By then he was gone.

'I never understood you, how could you have been so absent-minded as to forget that car in New York,' he told me shortly before he left us. 'If I hadn't been there, that wonderful automobile would still be rotting away in storage.'

For Ivan that gunmetal-grey Plymouth coupe was 'Rosebud'. For me that maroon Chevy rag-top was anything but 'Rosebud'. Its top was always down, rain or shine. I didn't mind getting wet. I knew the top leaked, but never from the same spot twice. Leaving it down I eliminated the surprise – where was I going to get wet from. That 'from where' bugged me. The only good thing about the car was, it was slow. It never rattled faster than a hundred, hundred and ten – downhill. With the brakes it had it was a blessing. In all truth, the car became a blessing during gas-rationing and it rattled after three years like it rattled the day it was delivered.

And that was the day. I was rattling over the pot-holes on Motor Avenue, which could have been more aptly named Oxcart Boulevard, on my way to MGM to meet the legend in his own time, Woody Van Dyke. He was a multifaceted legend. On the top of the list of his legendary features was he shot a film, any film, in eighteen days, put it together in eighteen days, rewrote scenes, wrote new added scenes in eighteen days, reshot the epic in eighteen days, then delivered it in eighteen days, complete.

Today, if you're famous and rich, especially in the field of entertainment, after you bathe or shower from 24-carat gold fixtures, you sprinkle yourself with Armani's new scent, 'Sweat', a $5000-an-ounce creation. After that, to be sure everybody out of smelling distance will also know you are famous, rich and important, you have to be clad in Armani-, Brioni-, Battistoni- or Nieman-Marcus-created imitation-homeless attire for $2750–6000. In the less expensive 'Golden Days', if the trousers were pressed to match a razor's edge, shoes shined to blind, shirts clean and ironed, ties tied, and you had on a jacket, you were 'on the beam'. One could be judged or misjudged inside a less expensive wardrobe. Nothing has changed, really, only the 'uniforms' are different and everything has got a little more expensive.

I was wearing the appropriate 'uniform', neat, tidy and clean, not the least prepared to change a flat tire. And that is what I was doing on blessed Motor Avenue, at 10 a.m. Changing a flat tire. It was already stifling hot. I was sweating profusely. Armani could have made a fortune collecting my droplets. The speeding cars whizzed by doing at least 25 to 30 miles per hour, whipping up the dust, augmenting my thirst and not helping my appearance. I was cursing in five languages. Maybe that was the reason I was punished.

My appointment was for eleven. There was not a chance of going home to change and make the date. On the dot of eleven I pulled up at the studio gate with screeching brakes, not screeching tires.

It would have made no sense to inquire about a bathroom when the man at the gate said, on hearing my name, 'Mister Van Dyke's secretary just phoned asking if you had arrived.' He told his number two, in the booth, 'Jimmy, you better go with him and show him the stage, you know Mister Van Dyke doesn't like to be kept waiting.'

Jimmy didn't like the assignment but he had no choice. Number one gave my morale a boost.

'Shit, this seat is burning my ass!' complained Jimmy. 'Why don't you have the fucking top on? You look like you're drowning in sweat.'

Another boost. I needed it. Badly. It made me more conscious of the sweat dribbling down my spine. My sweat-stained shirt stuck to my chest. A bell rang.

The car was still crawling, Jimmy hollered, 'Stop, right there,' and yanked the door open before the car stopped. 'I told you, pull up there.' I pulled up with a jerk, he got out, I got out, picked up my story. A second bell sounded, 'They're ready to shoot, better get in 'cause he locks up sometimes for an hour.'

'Thanks,' but Jimmy didn't hear or care. He was walking away, cursing his fate at having to go back to the gate on foot in this heat.

I got inside the stage just as a man was about to pull down a heavy crossbar on the stage door. 'Watch it, man!' he said, maybe too loud, because a man sitting in a director's chair next to the camera 'hisssssed' at him. Ray was right. Hedy Lamarr was there and Spencer Tracy was there. I guessed the 'hissssing' man was Van Dyke. I had never been star-struck, I liked people but some of the stars weren't. I was interested in one of those upside-down bottles filled with nice, ice-cold water. I spotted one, not too far, behind the set. The sight of it already made me feel better, I edged toward it. Van Dyke now 'hissssed' sharper, looked at me and shook his head. With a nod and a feeble smile I froze. Standing still made me feel the restriction of the wet shirt sticking to me, its least saturated piece, the collar, remained the whitest, contrasting with the sweat-stained front of the shirt. If I pulled the lapels of the jacket too close together to hide the sweaty front, the sleeves exposed the mementos of changing the flat tire, the grease-stained cuffs.

In England they would have said I was on a 'losing wicket', but I was in the States; standing there all screwed up, all I could say was, 'Oh, shit.'

Now the 'hissss' came with the strength of a steam whistle. I must have been thinking out loud, too loud. They started to shoot. Hedy Lamarr was beautiful in life, like on the screen, but couldn't act. Poor Spencer Tracy, one of the greatest among the greats, was trying his best, which was doing less. Contract players had to live with disadvantages.

The scene was over. I made a mad dash for the water, the bottle was empty. My mouth was stuck closed. They started another scene right away. I was sneaking around in the back of the set looking for another source of water.

'Stand still!' yelled a new voice.

'Who the fuck is moving around?' continued Van Dyke.

I froze once more and stayed frozen. I felt the sweat and the dust was caking a mask on my face.

'Two more scenes.' Van Dyke was fast, quick, one after the other.

Finally, they were opening the doors. I took a mad dash for the nearest, to hell with them.

'Where are you? Come here.' It was unmistakably Van Dyke. I turned back to join him. 'Bring him a chair,' he asked the propman who was handing him a tall glass of water, crystal clear. The ice cubes clinked in the glass as he took it.

Somebody shoved a chair under my butt, I gave up the losing battle to hide my sartorial disaster. I watched him draining his glass.

'One more, Mr Van Dyke?' asked the propman. Van Dyke nodded, turned to me, 'Well?'

'May I have one too, please?'

Tracy was walking off the set, stopped and looked at me.

'Get 'm one,' Van Dyke told the propman. 'Move.' The propman did. All other movement on the set stopped, Tracy sat down on the closest chair.

I tried to clear my throat. It didn't help much, and it didn't help either that Van Dyke was scrutinizing me. I handed him my treatment and he, without looking, dropped the pages on his lap.

'Go ahead, tell me your story,' he asked me.

Determined, I rasped, 'I had a . . . hm-hrm . . .' and that was it, all I could come up with were unintelligible 'hurrumps'.

A snicker from the background broke the silence. 'Shut up!' snarled Van Dyke. 'OK, tell me the story in five sentences, tell me what happens,' he said. I started to clear my throat once more, he got impatient. 'What is the matter with your throat?'

Hoarse and rasping, I started to tell the story. I knew I had to, there wouldn't be a second chance here. When I looked up after the sixth sentence I knew I had him. He was still listening. And when I saw the propman, my saviour, he was holding out the water for me on a tray. The cold glass in my hand – sweat, dust, flat tire and hell, I made it.

'Excuse me. Thank you,' and I took the first, so-much-wanted, big gulp. It was frozen heaven – I was saved, I felt I was home free.

The second swallow became choking burning hell. I wanted to spit it out, some of it came through my nose. Through tear-blurred vision I saw Van Dyke get up, from his lap my pages scattered on the floor, heard his voice through the haze, 'OK. Next set-up.' Something was funny, I heard laughter. I saw feet walking over my pages.

I have despised gin ever since.

'Everybody knows Van Dyke drinks gin like camels drink water before crossing the Sahara. You won't survive in Hollywood.' And Leon O. Lance didn't want me to benefit from his inside information any more. I embarrassed him. Leon O. Lance turned out to be not only a personal manager, but to my disgust a prophet too. It seemed I would not survive in Hollywood.

Hollywood was overcrowded, the dog-eat-dog competition was saturated with resentment; not only toward newcomers who were not forced to escape but toward any new arrival, regardless of their race or religion or gender. Most of the 'Flüchtlinge' ('fugitives') loved their native countries, and were more patriotic than those who robbed them of their wealth, human dignity and freedom. They couldn't understand why anybody would come to 'gullible, uncivilized' America of their own volition. But they accepted what the US had to offer, with complaints of course. No punishment under any circumstance. For some of us 'fortunates', who were not 'forced' to flee Europe, it was not the right time to join the queue of the uprooted, bitter émigrés. I was welcomed in Hollywood, correction, unwelcomed with a reception about as heartwarming as I got from the Danubia trio in New York. In Hollywood it hurt more.

I never understood how people who suffered so much from prejudice and were victimized through racial discrimination could trample on others with the same loathsome force. Fear had strange bedfellows. If bulletproof vests had been in mode and available, I would have run out and got one for myself. No, not one, two.

In my disgust I had forgotten that looks and whispers could do the job too. Actually, they are more dangerous and painful than bullets. Bullets either kill you, then it's over quickly, or the wound heals, and then it's finished. I had known that from experience. But sniping with dirty rumor hurts you more than a bullet, and it never heals.

I have been accused of a lot of things in my life before and since, but that time I was incriminated with something heavy: I was a Nazi spy. That could have killed me worse than dead. I could have been made a living dead in Hollywood.

'I don't know what to say, they're killing you,' said Miki Dora. 'You got to do something. Why don't you give yourself up?'

He had a strange sense of humor. I knew that, but those who overheard it didn't. My grave was dug deep already, he just laid me in it. It took a long time to crawl out of it.

Neville Chamberlain's umbrella finally leaked. Between the first week in April and the first week of May, Germany invaded Denmark, Norway, Belgium, the Netherlands and Luxembourg. Chamberlain resigned as prime minister of Great Britain. The vacillation ended, Winston Churchill took over in early May.

The 4 of June 1940, Dunkirk, the boldest and luckiest strategic withdrawal in the history of warfare. Over 200,000 British and more than

100,000 French troops crossed the Channel in rowboats leaving every-thing, dead and material, behind. By mid-June the Germans were in Paris and France surrendered.

Hungary and Romania joined the Axis. The restaurant 'Little Hungary' was steaming with true and fabricated horror stories. I stayed away from the place, not wanting to ruin Dora's good name and his good business with my tainted presence. All he needed was some joker renaming the restaurant 'Spy's Nest'.

The United States remained more than 'uncommitted' in the conflict; the waves of anti-British sentiment were lapping the shores of the 'Hill' in Washington. Churchill wanted to turn the tide and with Churchillian candor suggested to Alex that he come up with a propaganda film to that effect – except that it should not be an 'obvious propaganda film'.

'Is that all? Easy,' said Alex in his unflappable manner. I was not there, but I am sure this was the way it happened. They had lit a fresh cigar, had a sip of Delamain, and Alex asked, 'What did you have in mind for the story?'

Naturally Churchill had something in mind, and knowing him as well as Korda did, he knew it. The two general geniuses made Napoleon more Hitler-like than he actually was and *That Hamilton Woman* was born as a propaganda film – produced and directed by Alex Korda, with Vivien Leigh fronting as Emma Hart, aka Lady Hamilton, and Laurence Olivier as Admiral Nelson pulling the propaganda wool over the audience's eyes. Successfully. The coup de grâce, the essence of the film, Nelson's memor-able speech, '. . . you cannot make peace with dictators; you may have to destroy them . . .', was written by Churchill himself. It created a furor *among* isolationist politicians in Washington.

Thanks to Churchill, Alex Korda was called before some fire-eating Senate Committee. Without it I probably never could have cleared myself of the stigma of being a Nazi spy. It swung my pendulum the other way, since Alex was allegedly working for British Intelligence and, as I was associated with him, the rumor now had it that I was working for MI5 or MI6 – or why not for MI7, 8, or 9, just pick a number. Through Alex Korda anything could happen. And it did.

Parts of the 'Golden Years of Hollywood' were dark and confusing. They could have been called the 'Years of the Witch Hunts'. The world was on a see-saw and so was the Town.

Walter Wanger, a well-known socialite and film producer of mostly 'tit-and-sand' epics, announced he would make three films a year in Italy, with the 'marvelous', 'plain', 'sympathetic' Mussolini, who 'knows everything'.

Italy declared war against Great Britain and France and invaded Greece. Miki Dora changed the name of his eatery from 'Little Hungary' to 'Little Gypsy'. Otherwise, nobody else paid any attention to the news.

Wanger was called 'only a fool'. It took him many years to prove it, but finally he did by missing one of Jennings Lang's[4] balls with three shots at point blank range. His alleged excuse was, 'Lang's balls were too miniscule.'

Victor McLaglen[5] had over-sized balls one could not miss, as he rode his steed of 'good intentions' heading his 'California Light Horse Regiment'. He was stamped as 'fascist'. But the word 'fascist' was ignored by Metro-Goldwyn-Mayer's prominently Jewish bosses. The world-wide giants 'gratefully' accepted the gold trophy Wallace Beery received from Mussolini's 'National Fascist Association of Motion Picture and Theatrical Industries' for *Viva Villa*. I wondered whether they were learning from Dr Goebbels's 'mix and confuse the real issue' or was Herr Goebbels imitating them? It worked, both MGM and Goebbels were doing good international business and I kept on wondering who would ultimately benefit from this charade the most? We, 'The People', certainly did not.

Like rabid politicians during mud-slinging election years Hollywoodites went berserk. For a while the stamp of 'fascist' was a death warrant and 'communist' was the badge of honor. Then came McCarthy. The graffiti changed, but not its writers. The deaths were identical. 'Americanism is an unfailing love of country; loyalty to its institutions and ideals; eagerness to defend it against all enemies; undivided allegiance to the flag; and a desire to secure the blessing of liberty for ourselves and posterity. Therefore, Americanism is the foundation upon which we are building the Hollywood Hussars. We are solemnly pledged to uphold and protect the sacred principles and ideals of our country.'

Based on these words Gary Cooper was stamped as fascist. A fascist because he pledged allegiance to the flag? I had the privilege of knowing

4 Jennings Lang (1915) was a Hollywood agent from the 1930s to the 1950s and later a producer. In 1951, he was shot in a parking lot by producer Walter Wanger, who claimed Lang was having an affair with Wanger's wife, actress Joan Bennett.
5 Victor McLaglen (1886–1959) was a popular character actor on the screen from 1920 to 1958; in 1935, he won an Academy Award for his performance in *The Informer*.

him. One-to-one. He was a man deeply in love with his country, with liberty and equality and justice – equal justice – for all. He was deeply hurt by the smear. But the tempest was only in the Hollywood teapots. Grassroots America drinks little tea and the storm kept brewing under the lid.

Germany grabbed Yugoslavia, part of Greece and, ignoring the not-quite-two-year-old Russo-German 'non-aggression' pact, German troops invaded Russia.

In General Service Studios, on North Las Palmas, we had our own battles to fight. A battle initiated by Alex. A conflict he inherited the day he acquired the remake rights of *Thief of Bagdad* from Douglas Fairbanks, and with it a 'halfway commitment' of 'the professor', Dr Ludwig Berger, to direct it. I had never met 'professor' Berger, but from what he shot of the film he should have been shot for it and the assailant acquitted.

Korda wasn't a man who loved to suffer and he didn't suffer long. Based on hearsay, but 'from reliable sources', Alex tackled the bull by the horns from the rear on the third day of shooting. He stood on the set close behind 'professor' Berger, and before his director could finish his instruction, Korda countermanded him.

'To the right . . . lower and – ' asked Berger.

'To the left and higher,' demanded Korda from over his shoulder.

A farce like this couldn't last long. It didn't. The contract of 'the professor' was settled, but it was not the end of the directorial pandemonium; the mosaic of directors, six or eight of us, some credited and some uncredited, finally finished *Thief of Bagdad* in Hollywood. To set the record straight, *Thief of Bagdad* was duck soup compared to Alex's *Elephant Boy* misadventure.

Actually this potpourri of 'Kordaism' wasn't as big a mess as it could have been. Up front was the venerable Michael Powell. To 'add to' and 'clean up' were the forever-ready Zoli and Vincent with their brotherly love and talent to save Alex. It was their habit. They had good training.

But the third cataclysmic venture Alex got into surpassed the difficulties of *Elephant Boy* and *Thief of Bagdad* combined. However, every drop of blood, which actually flowed on the set, and all the sweat we were swimming in was worth it. *The Jungle Book* turned out to be the biggest financial and artistic success of the three, with six Academy Award nominations. Sadly it became a farewell to the magic of London Films, and the last time the three Korda brothers worked together.

Alex Korda had taste, brilliant ideas and occasionally money. Starting *Elephant Boy* he lacked the last, but he never lacked snobbery and, being impressed with Robert Flaherty,[6] he scrounged up enough to finance Flaherty's dream of making 'something' about elephants. But the 'something' was totally different for Korda than it was for Flaherty. Quite different. Korda was thinking of Rudyard Kipling's *Toomai of the Elephants*, Flaherty was just thinking of 'something' and while he was doing it he disappeared into the Indian jungles with his crew for over a year. No contact.

Sam Spiegel had to face a not dissimilar situation during *Lawrence of Arabia* when David Lean fell in love with the Jordanian desert and melted in with God's furnace on earth. Except that stubborn David fought Sam for a better screenplay, while Flaherty simply 'forgot' to take Korda's script with him to India.

When Korda discovered it – after close to a year – for the first time in his life (if you discount women) he got anxious. The budget trebled and more than 400,000 feet of 'something' was piled up on the cutting-room floor and nobody knew what to do with it.

There was a fascinating similarity between the producers, Korda and Spiegel, and the two directors, Lean and Flaherty. All four were heading in the same direction, quality. Korda once owned and wanted to make *The Bridge on the River Kwai* and *Lawrence Of Arabia*.

Both producers were entrepreneurial gamblers and unconscious spenders on their own needs. But no matter how much Spiegel spent on himself, or changed his name from Sam Spiegel to S. P. Eagle, he remained Sam Spiegel, hoping to become Alex Korda, royal and impeccable even in rags from Savile Row. Both bobbed up and down in their ocean liners in one of the Riviera's fashionable yacht basins. Spiegel on board of his *Malhane*, looking like a Bronx tourist renting it for a day to impress somebody, Korda on his *Elsewhere* left you no doubt he really owned it. Both were capable of charming the skin off a snake, gracious, lavish hosts as long as you served their purpose. They had easy tears and firm hands on production budgets. Sam promised you anything to get you where he

6 Robert Flaherty (1884–1951) is generally regarded as the Father of the Documentary Film in recognition of his achievements with *Nanook Of The North* (1922), *Moana* (1927), *Man of Aran* (1934) and *Louisiana Story* (1948); despite a number of opportunities, he never proved capable of working within the 'Hollywood system'.

wanted you, but you couldn't trust Sam farther than you could throw his yacht. You could trust Korda, he never promised anything.

Both directors, Lean and Flaherty, were dreamers. But Lean controlled his dreams, he made them up, and made them happen; like when he told his cameraman, a cameraman par excellence, Freddie Young, 'I want a mirage here.' As simple as that, and it happened because Lean willed it. Because of his cutting-room background Lean shot almost as frugally as John Ford, who overdid it sometimes by putting his shovel-sized hand in front of the lens four or five frames too soon. Both Lean and Ford were very tough people, Flaherty was not. He and Lean shared poetry and sadness. Ford shared Michelangelo's chisel to cut the marble and the bullshit. Flaherty was waiting for his dream to happen, he photographed what 'might have been'. He was not a director in the strict sense of the word, he was a selector.

Flaherty was not alone by all means; many successful 'directors' saw 'it' after 'it' had happened, or only in the cutting-room. And many times they needed an editor who could pick it up from the proverbial cutting-room floor.

On *Elephant Boy* there was on the cutting-room floor, unfortunately not in Flaherty's mind, more than 400,000 feet of 'something'.

In charge of a rescue squad despatched to India, not to rescue Flaherty but Alex, as usual, were Zoli and Vincent. Zoli knew how to reach point 'B' from point 'A' only in a straight line, he never recognized any obstacles. Flaherty walked around anthills for miles so as not to disturb the ants, followed by his unhappy crew lugging the heavy gear. Zoli was General Patton in film-making. In theory, Flaherty was a beautiful man too, deep and sensitive. He fell in with an Indian sect to preserve life, but forgot he was killing his crew, not to mention Alex.

One day, watching ants removing elephant dung from their path in the stables of the Maharajah of Mysore, Flaherty discovered Sabu, a stableboy.

Some of the footage Flaherty shot was magnificent, but neither he nor anybody else could come up with the 'something' he was thinking about until Zoli cooked up a story with Kipling's simplicity in mind. Vincent's ingenuity created India on Denham Studio's backlot and, cursing in mixed French and Hungarian, he was also building what Zoli called 'bloody rubber feets' of elephants, hundreds of them, for Zoli to shoot the famous *Dance of the Elephants*. In England, of course.

William Hornbeck[7], from whom I learned the difference between editing and cutting, fused the best of Flaherty's shots with Zoli's film, and
the *Evening Standard* in 1937 wrote of *Elephant Boy* with the authority of
knowledgeable critics: 'Pictorially magnificent, the skilful work of an
individual mind. Sabu is a discovery.' Individual mind? Which one? Heil
critics, and Ave Venice Film Festival Jury which bestowed the best
directorial award on the film. On whom?

Awards are strange phenomena. Had it been an award for mayhem,
The Jungle Book would have won it, hands down. Had there been an
award for a comedy of errors behind, around or next to the camera, *Jungle
Book* would again have been the winner hands down. For miraculous luck
that nobody was killed or seriously injured, *The Jungle Book* would have
collected the combined awards disbursed throughout that and the subsequent year.

Working with the three Kordas together was the surest and easiest way
to commit suicide. All you had to do was insult one of the Korda brothers
or take sides when they were ventilating their differences of opinion,
which were often, violent, vulgar and always loud. If it wouldn't have
been too messy, Alex was always ready – not to die – but certainly to kill for
his two brothers. But if you were not initiated in their family 'discussions',
you would swear they were about to kill each other.

To insult all three of them at the same time was safe. Alex and Zoli
carried on vendettas against each other. Vincent was above it all; a
philosopher with two regrets, but when he realized he had left a part of his
heart and art in France, he got over the first and floated through life. The
second, that he wasn't a better father, he carried with him when he left us.
Vincent was not difficult to live with – he wasn't around – and his
Alex-prescribed marriage made philandering more fun. I wasn't a good
father either; I understood him, we were free spirits, we were friends.

Zoli was not difficult to live with, he was around and downright
impossible. Joan, his wife, beautiful and talented, gave up a career for him
and the children, and deserved a halo.

For more than eight months of shooting *The Jungle Book*, every weekday

7 William Hornbeck (1901–1983) was voted in a 1977 poll to be the best film editor
Hollywood had produced. He began his career in the 'teens, working with Mack
Sennett. In the 1930s and 1940s he was supervising editor for Alexander Korda in
England and the US. From 1960 until his retirement in 1976, he was head of the editing
department at Universal.

at six in the morning on Appian Way on the top of Lookout Mountain I rang the bell to pick up Zoli. He hated most things most of the time, but he hated to drive all the time. According to Joan it was too early for the help to be up, so she opened the front door, crisp, starched, impeccable. The early morning dew parted in front of her British accent, her smile cured my occasional hangover. Like from a lost ship at night boomed Zoli's foghorn voice, 'I'll be down in a minute, two-eggs-sunny-side-up,' and a door was slammed upstairs.

Zoli wasted no time with unnecessary frills and formalities like 'good morning' or 'how are you'. He dropped two fistfuls of vitamin pills on the table. 'Another bloody day,' he announced to no one in particular, 'I am downstairs' and the whole neighbourhood knew it, not only Joan in the kitchen.

Zoli pulled out his prized possession, a 'Bugyli bicska'[8], and stared at the eggs Joan put in front of him for a long while in hostile silence. When somebody stares at cold stuffed cabbage in a restaurant it is bad enough, but it isn't as disturbing as when somebody stares at fried eggs, cold fried eggs, sunny side up. Without taking his eyes off the eggs, with a whip of his wrist he flipped open his blade, picked up the large uncut Sheepherder bread from the middle of the table, held it against his chest, and with the point of the knife scratched the sign of the cross on the round bottom of the bread and sliced two large pieces, crossing his eyes several times.[9] Joan stood behind him holding a cup of tea on a saucer watching the daily ritual. She was a perfect statue of patience. Zoli attacked a slab of Hungarian bacon and chopped off a thick chunk. Using his uni-utensil bicska as knife and fork, he held bacon and bread in his left hand alternately slicing and consuming a piece of each.

'Zoli, your eggs are getting cold,' pleaded Joan.

'I can't eat the bloody things.'

'What is wrong, Zoli?'

---

8 The 'Bugyli bicska' is an ancient Hungarian instrument. Its razor-sharp blade is six to eight inches long and was used as a 'persuader' by the highwaymen of the Hungarian Sherwood Forest, the Bakony. Aside from 'persuasion' it was used for shaving, skinning and butchering the prey and also served as the knife and the fork during meals at the table. It folds into a wooden handle without a spring to keep it open or closed. It is a special art to use the knife and retain all ten fingers. A very basic and versatile utensil.

9 A more superstitious than religious peasant heritage.

'They are cross-eyed. I can't eat bloody cross-eyed eggs.'

Joan picked up Zoli's plate. I thought she would crown him with the cross-eyed eggs, but she started to laugh. The yolks *were* cross-eyed.

The second helping of the sunny-side-up eggs turned out wall-eyed and Zoli refused to eat wall-eyed eggs too. It was getting late; we left the eggs with their eye problems behind, taking only Zoli's problem with us, and off we were for Sherwood Lake around Thousand Oaks, our location.

The sadists of freeway planning had not created the bottleneck alley of the century – Route 101 – yet. One could move if needed. The top was down on my Chevy rolling down Laurel Canyon, and before we reached Ventura Boulevard Zoli opened up.

He had a dilemma, a big problem that bothered him. I learned long ago through bitter experience, don't ask questions and you won't be saddled with the same problems. On this occasion I didn't even have to listen, I was well aware of the problems. The problems were that Alex didn't have the slightest inkling of the serious problems we had on the picture, when he was the major cause of them.

I wasn't listening to Zoli mumbling more to his pipe than to me. He was trying to light it; in an open car it was always a mess. I loved to drive mountain roads, it sharpened your skill.

'You're not listening again.'

'No. I am not. But fretting and complaining will not solve the problems.'

'Alex is a bloody idiot.'

Now, in that instance Zoli was right, but if I had agreed verbally, Zoli would have gotten out of the car and I would have been out of a job I loved.

'No, Zoli, and you know it. We have no solution, we don't know what to do, when we know we'll make a decision and go for it.'

'I found the solution and I am going for it.'

'Good.'

'I am going to commit suicide.'

'Just like that?'

'No. That is my problem. I don't know how.'

The news, not me, drove the car off the narrow hard surface of the road. We were engulfed in a cloud of yellow dust.

'Watch it.' And he concentrated again on his pipe, and I on my driving, pushing the rattle-trap as fast as it could go. It had never been over a hundred, now we were sashaying over a hundred and ten, downhill. I felt like the maniacs driving across the canyons from Beverly Hills to the Valley or vice-versa. Crawling uphill through the curves, but full speed downhill, negotiating the same curves when the momentum, the inertia was against safety.

I was worse than those I made fun of, because I knew it, the idiots didn't, but I wanted to get Zoli to our first aid to give him sedatives. Call Alex. Zoli was capable of doing the most unexpected things at any time. He was worse than a hero, he had the courage of a fool. He sat morose, staring at the floormat. Muttering.

'My only problem is I don't know whom I shall kill first, Joan or David. It would be irresponsible to kill myself only and leave them here, unprotected.'

With screeching tires I took the curves in four wheel drifts.[10] My leg had cramp from pushing the gas pedal so hard against the floorboard. Another silly thing to do, since you have no reserve speed left for safety. The only mementos of sanity left in the car were the safety belts – unusual then, hangovers of my racing days. They were God's blessings. Zoli never could undo them, otherwise I would have been forced to stop and put the top up, which could have been a traumatic experience. I watched Zoli toiling with the buckle. To my relief he left it alone when he started to speak again.

'I made up my mind, I will take David first . . . no, Joan, no, maybe I will just kill myself, that would be better, no, my family is – ' He suddenly wedged his back against the seat and screamed, 'You are going over a hundred, are you crazy? Do you want to kill me or something?' Reaching over with his left hand, he turned off the ignition key which locked the steering wheel. Out of control we spun and stopped with the front of the car hanging over the lip of the roadside ditch.

'Goddamn-it! Why did you do that, Zoli?'

He answered serenely, 'I didn't want to die.'

Sanity won, only to be engulfed with the insanity of making *The Jungle Book* in Southern California's Sherwood Forest and Lake – in the rainy season – and on the lot of General Service Studios, 1040 North Las Palmas, next to Howard Hughes's Associated Gas Station on the corner of Santa Monica Boulevard. That's show biz.

10 A late 1920s innovation of the all-time great Italian race driver, Nuvolari; a must for safe high-speed cornering, a technique when the front wheels are pointing away from the actual path of the car, drifting.

15 Faking It

Alex Korda was a film-maker; 'If you can fake it, fake it,' was his credo. Oh, he wanted quality all right, but only if the price was right. He learned to quote in his Sam Goldwyn-tainted[1] King's English the Old Hollywood Testament: 'A tree is a tree, a rock is a rock, shoot it in Griffith Park.' 'Who could tell?' Korda added, 'make it look rich, give it class.' And Vincent's without-any-fuss magic made Alex believe it was easy.

The trouble was that tigers, black panthers, king cobras and pythons didn't speak Korda's King's English or appreciate his cigars. As a matter of fact one of my best friends in life, Captain Jiggs, hated Korda's cigars so much he used to grab them out of his mouth and piss on them. At ten dollars a squirt. Captain Jiggs was an orangutang from Borneo, younger than Sabu and smarter.

I was responsible to Zoli and had to work with individuals who were less impressed with Alex than I was; nor did they care about the rising insurance premiums due to Alex's drive to save on the insurance costs backfiring.

Alex, sight unseen, bought from a bankrupt circus an impersonator of Bagheera, the magnificent shiny-black panther of *The Jungle Book*. This initiator of the insurance problem looked like a mangey alley cat with half of her teeth missing and what was left was worn down to yellow-green-black stubs. Runny nose, no whiskers. In all fairness, she was docile. Not by nature, but because she couldn't stand up on her poor arthritic legs. Seeing for the first time his Black Prince of the Jungle Alex ordered an immediate and complete rejuvenation. Anesthetizing their object of art,

1 Samuel Goldwyn (1882–1974) was the great Polish-born producer of some of the biggest hits of the 1930s and 1940s. Like the Kordas he never mastered the English language, butchering it with quotes such as: 'A verbal contract isn't worth the paper it's written on.'

the make-up department used everything from hair-dye to black shoe polish on spots of her fur-less hide, trying to restore the splendor her ancestors once sported in the jungle. Alex was thorough; 'No good,' he objected. 'The fangs. The fangs. Get a dentist.' Alex was happy, the dentist was happy, Bagheera's impersonator was miserable. She had fangs all right, like a creature from the Pleistocene epoch, but whimpered day and night. I suspected the dentist did a shoddy job, no root-canal work.

When Alex proudly introduced the 'thing' to Zoli he just stared, unblinking; a sure sign of trouble. 'What's that bloody thing supposed to be?' demanded Zoli.

Somebody from make-up whispered, 'Bagheera.'

And that did it. But not what I was looking forward to with dread. Zoli burst out laughing. 'To begin with, Bagheera was male.'

'No problem, Zolikám,' Alex assured him, 'we'll fix that too,' and opened the door of the cage as he motioned to George Bagnall[2] and a couple of gentlemen from the insurance company to follow him into the cage. 'You see, George, there is no, absolutely no reason for that extra coverage I am objecting to. I assure you the tiger will be just as docile.'

The poor beast only whimpered. No food could pass the white picket fence of human cruelty in her mouth. With parched tongue she licked her lips and a few of her prop-whispers fell off. Zoli and I walked away. Far away. And Alex made his deal with the insurance company.

The following morning the panther was found dead. I wondered, did she commit suicide because of shame and pain? Show business is deadly. Alex, with a black arm-band of mourning hidden inside his soul, gave orders to a taxidermist to 'make her a male,' and inquired, 'When is the tiger going to be ready?' The taxidermists in record time, and for record remuneration, did a better job on the panther than the make-up department. The stuffed 'Bagheera', Alex's pride, now with balls and moveable extremities, with his/her menacing fangs well in evidence, was perched in a tree of the large jungle set encircled with a double-link, high, Ford fence, on the General Service Studio lot.

Alex was a showman. To emphasize the danger for the visitors and press, he ordered the double-link fence to be reinforced with another double-link fence, and, to my horror, put a ceiling over the whole set.

2 At this time George Bagnall (1897–1978) was Vice-President of Security First National Bank, in charge of film production finances.

This robbed me of the possibility of showing sky, openness, freedom when eventually I was to be shooting on the set. Of course, the doors opened the wrong way. Alex liked to be right, especially in public. I ordered the ceiling torn off and the door rehung – which saved his life at a later date. In spite of that, he never forgave me.

To add to my persona non grata status with Alex, without his approval or knowledge I got two black panthers for Bagheera and two magnificent Bengal tigers for Shere Khan – from India, not circus or zoo leftovers. Zoli backed me all the way. He was like a kid playing hookey. Through his mysterious connections he came up with a Hungarian tiger-tamer. Luis Roth was about fifty, fifty-five years old and had a mane like a lion. That mane was fifty per cent of his body weight. He had a set of false teeth and whatever he was saying was full of whistling ssss's. Next to Luis, an Egyptian mummy would have looked like Mr Universe. He arrived with a very small suitcase, a whip which produced an ear-splitting crack and a rickety old chair: his 'magic chair'. And magic it was. Thank God.

I watched with amazement how much easier it was to work with these wild beasts fresh out of the jungle. To get a performance out of them was easier than getting one out of some conceited actors.

The day had arrived, both for Alex and for us. The day of reckoning. Unknown to us, the taxidermist delivered Alex his tiger. Unknown to Alex, we had decided the time had come to bring in Bagheera No. 1 to acclimatize himself to the 'jungle on the lot'. The roofless cage was panther-safe, secure. The door shut the right way, the foliage was 'panther-friendly'. We put a padlock and a big sign on the door: 'Keep out! Wild Animals! Danger!' It was early dawn, before the lot woke up. The black prince of the jungle was sound asleep when he arrived from the jungle of California's Sherwood Forest. We had difficulty in dislodging him from his cage, but once out he was awake. He checked every link of the fence, charged at the door, finally settled down to urinate all over the jungle.

'It's his now, he is marking it,' and Luis showed his false choppers to the rising sun, a happy man. He pointed, 'He'll settle there.' We waited and waited. Bagheera urinated and urinated. Finally he settled on the spot Luis said he would. 'Let's have some breakfast.'

Satisfied, he placed his magic chair next to the door, pocketed his key to the padlock of the jungle and came up with a card he stuck on the sign on the door: 'To be opened only by Luis Roth, Lion-Tamer.'

The breakfast tasted wonderful until yells of 'help' yanked the bites out of our mouths. All hell broke loose. The trouble started with the prop department. They gave us the lock all right, but not all the keys to it. Herman, an assistant propman, was expecting Alex's tiger from the taxidermist. Luckily Alex's tiger was to arrive in two parts; his 'tiger' was an oversized Great Dane fitted by the taxidermist with a tiger-skin. The fangs glued to his ample lips were to be the courtesy of make-up. Wardrobe refused to be any part of this operation, quoting Union Rules.

We had no idea about these subversive activities. They did come to light though, narrowly averting a tragedy.

It was discovered during fittings and rehearsals that the poor miserable dog in the tiger-skin smelled worse than Bagheera's extempore-stuffed impersonator, so they decided to house Alex's tiger in a 'king of the jungle' doghouse, befitting his status, in the jungle on the lot.

And what a jungle it turned out to be.

Thinking the sign was simply a sales pitch for reality, Herman ignored it, went in the cage to figure out where to put the doghouse.

The door of the jungle cage was half open when I arrived. The frightened, hysterical mob was senselessly clamoring for God and guns and help. Luis wasn't in sight anywhere. In the 'jungle', up on his perch, Bagheera was holding Herman's apparently lifeless dangling body by his right arm. My first instinct was to close the door of the cage.

'Don't touch it!' roared Luis, coming up on the double with a side of pork ribs. 'You wan 'im killed?' he snarled at the group. 'Keep quiet, don't move around! You –' he ordered me, '– pick up my chair, if he goes for you, shove all four legs of it at 'im and growl. Let's go!'

He went in first, then he swung me with the chair in front of him. 'Keep on goin', steady an' slow.'

For me Herman disappeared, I was mesmerized by Bagheera's tail. It was swinging rhythmically like a metronome, left to right, right to left, and he curled the tip of his tail in the opposite direction of each swing.

'Slow down, then stop,' said Luis in a tone as if he were saying, 'have a nice day.'

I followed orders that weren't delivered like orders. 'Stop now,' he suggested. I stopped. He handed me a big chunk of filet mignon as he passed me. 'When I'll give 'im the ribs, you shove it against his mouth from the other side. Don't you rush it. Let 'im take it in his sweet own time.' As an afterthought he added, 'Don't let the chair's legs touch Bagheera.'

'Touch' – touch the black panther – brought me back from a nightmare to reality, which was worse.

'Do it now,' sounded like 'pass me the salt.' No please though.

I did it.

Bagheera preferred the beef to the pork-ribs and snapped the meat from me and let go of Herman's arm. Before Herman slipped to the ground, Luis grabbed him under the armpits and dragged him at snail's pace, backing away. I wanted to run.

'Don't you turn your back. Lower the chair's legs. We have all day, slow.'

I had all eternity and I would never forget its end, the first cup of hot coffee outside the cage. Nor would Herman ever forget, he stuttered, 'the revenging ghost' of stuffed Bagheera diving at him as he passed out.

'Lucky he fainted,' remarked Luis. 'Had he struggled, the real Bagheera would have killed him.'

Bagheera No. 1 was retired from the jungle and the film. We shot the picture with No. 2. Without Zoli and Eddie Small[3] I would have been forced to retire in the jungle of the unemployed.

News traveled faster on the radio without waiting for TV newsvans being despatched to the scene, but the ugly side of the news was equally exaggerated. By the time the early 'check-ins' drove through the studio gate, they were informed about the 'wild beast's deadly rampage' on the lot. The make-up department paid the closest attention to the news. They were certain Alex would nix all wild animals, if not from the picture, for sure from the lot. They doubled their attention to Alex's tiger.

We moved. Bagheera No. 1 was on his way to Sherwood Forest, Shere Khan No. 1, 'Rajah', was on his way to the studio. We had to prove and prove fast we could work even on the lot with wild animals. We were not quite ready, but our only chance of survival was to take a chance. Little did we know about our consolation: the make-up and wardrobe departments had their problems too. The fake Shere Khan ate his rubber fangs

3 Edward Small (1891–1977) began his career as an agent, but soon became a producer in the 1920s, specializing in costume dramas and farces. As evidence of the scope of Small's productions, his films include, beside several classics of Alexander Dumas, *I Cover the Waterfront* (1933), *Getting Gertie's Garter* (1945), Andre de Toth's *Monkey On My Back* (1957) and *The Christine Jorgensen Story* (1970).

as fast as they were glued on. When they forced the tigerskin suit on the Great Dane he laid on his back, four legs skyward, wriggled and howled. It was impossible to coax him to stand up; he behaved very un-tiger-like. Putting tiger-striped body make-up on the dog caused further complications. The tiger-dog grabbed the make-up applicator sponges, ate them and promptly threw up.

(1) According to the rules of the American Kennel Club, the minimum requirements for being acknowledged as a male Great Dane were, among others: height 31½ inches at the withers and weight about 135 pounds. This wretched tiger-striped Dane was at least 170 pounds with make-up on, and would have been 33 or 34 inches high at his withers had he been held still long enough to be measured. For a Great Dane he was big and tall and handsome, but only Alex was sure it was enough to impersonate a tiger.

(2) According to the rules of the jungle, a male Bengal tiger is supposed to be 10 to 12 foot long, with a 3 to 4 foot tail, between 34 to 38 inches tall at the withers and weigh between 400 and 640 pounds.

(3) According to the rules of Hollywood, height and weight didn't matter, a producer was judged by his bank account. Eddie Small, from his 'elevator shoes' to the top of his head, was a 59½-inch giant of the film industry. He was a dapper gentleman, a millionaire who was helped to amass his fortune by a couple of noble men, like 'Count George Bruce', the writer, who introduced him to Alexander Dumas's Count of Monte Cristo and others of Dumas's brain-children.

It was not difficult, it was impossible to find a common denominator for (1), (2) and (3) within the confined space of this shrinking world.

The dissolution started when Eddie Small, using a periscope to see over the hood of his big Lincoln, pulled up at the gate of General Service Studio. 'Is that panther still on the lot?' he asked the guard.

'The police wanted to shoot him, but he was whisked off rightaway, Mr Small,' the guard volunteered solicitiously. 'But, imagine, they replaced the panther with a big brute of a tiger. I would say crazy, sir.'

Small halted at the gate where normally he didn't even slow down to say 'Good morning.' As he was mulling over the possibility of personal danger, the guard tapped his side-arm to assure him, 'Every chamber is full, with split-head dumdums. I ain't gonna take no chances, sir, don' worry, sir.'

With a firm decision and squealing tires, Small headed toward his VIP parking spot, one of the few in the shade. He pulled up with a whistle-like squeak of the brakes but still hit the cement safety block harder than usual. In his hurry to get to the shelter of his office he didn't notice the impending danger.

Dogs, even if they were supposed to impersonate tigers, like shade – especially in heavy make-up. The arrival of Eddie Small interrupted the Great Dane's merrily undulating, inverted hula grinds on the tarmac as he tried to get rid of the tiger make-up on his back.

Eddie made two mistakes. One unknowingly: he got out of his car. Two, seeing the 'ersatz tiger' coming to greet him, he started to run. His screams for help were mostly stifled by the friendly 'tiger's' tongue as he was lying on top of him, licking his face profusely and transferring his tiger make-up off his stomach to Eddie's white shirt and light linen suit with great success.

The backing of Zoli and Vincent, the Eddie incident and Captain Jiggs on my arm, embracing me tightly, took some of the edge off the wrath of Alex. 'Admit you're all wrong. I know what I am doing. If I fooled Eddie Small, if he believed – up close, real close – that a tiger was attacking him, with short cuts, quick flash cuts, through the foliage the audience will – '

At my prompting Captain Jiggs interrupted. If I rubbed his big toe he could not only imitate, but produce strange variations on the sound of the expulsion of human intestinal gases. Captain Jiggs furled his large, floppy lips and let his symphony go, with variations.

'Take that ugly monkey out of here, it is disgusting,' squirmed Alex.

He got so infuriated he forgot to fire me, which I was sure was the reason for the meeting. I loved Captain Jiggs, he got me out of a few hot spots.

As I was walking out of the office Alex called after me, 'How is the tiger working now? I hope he wasn't too upset.'

'The tiger isn't upset, we're doing fine.'

That was the truth. I only forgot to mention the tiger was Rajah from Bengal, 11 feet long with a 3½-foot tail, weighing 550 pounds and 36 inches at the withers. The 36-inch withers was the closest similarity to the Great Dane. Not telling Alex was one of the biggest mistakes of my life, and I have made a lot of them; some of them I am even proud of, but this one still haunts me occasionally.

The Jungle Book was shot in Technicolor, the latest color process of the era. Apart from its great advantages, which are still valid, the system had two built-in disasters. One was easier to handle, the size and the weight of the camera. The other was tough to live with, 'color consultant' Natalie Kalmus, the wife of Herbert T. Kalmus, a lovely little milktoast, the owner of Technicolor. The production had to pay for Mrs Kalmus's services (?) and give her credit on the screen and advertising. Allegedly, she was color-blind; obviously she had no taste. She was an unavoidable pain in the derrière, if you wanted Technicolor.

Through the courtesy of Vincent's talent the jungle in the cage on the lot of General Service Studio looked more like the jungle I have seen in India. Rajah felt comfortable and so did I after the first few hours with Luis next to me with a whip in one hand and the magic chair in the other. Two of us in one cage with 11 feet and 550 pounds of uncurbed deadly beauty. Rajah was awesome, majestic and magnificent. I loved him almost as much from a distance as I did Captain Jiggs from close. Luis pronounced me safe, he said the wild beasts sense one's feelings; I kept my fingers crossed for Luis to be right.

The wife of the camera operator didn't believe in Luis and begged her husband to stay out of the cage so he surely would see their first child, due in four months. He rigged up a remote-controlled Selsin motor and with the focus-puller they could handle all technical requirements through the chain-link fence. I was operating; he received the danger money, but I was overpaid having the fun.

The camera was rolling with a fresh load. Rajah, 'seeking the scent' of Mowgli/Sabu, followed Luis's movements as I wished, moving his head right and left, slowly and fast, showing both sides of his great profile. He was more co-operative than Claudette Colbert.[4]

'I can't understand why Zoli –' he raised his voice '– and you argue with me all the time? Look at him, he looks great.'

'Don't move a muscle,' whispered Luis. Alex was in the cage with us, waving his cigar at the tiger, giving him instructions, praising him, 'Good dog . . . good doggie.'

Rajah, hypnotized, followed every move Alex made.

'Where is the bloody operator?' he demanded. 'Roll it – you,' he pointed his cigar at me.

'We're rolling.'

4 The popular Hollywood actress Claudette Colbert (born 1905) was famous for not letting her right profile be photographed.

'Good.' Korda charged at the tiger, 'Get 'im boy.'

Luis lifted his magic chair but didn't move. The tiger whipped his tail faster and faster, slunk closer to the ground behind the foliage. Luis spoke Hungarian.

'I think this is about enough, Mr Korda. You did beautifully with him.'

Not the voice, the language stopped Korda. Surprised he turned from Rajah to Luis. 'Are you Hungarian?'

'Yes, Mr Korda.'

'You are training the dog?'

'Yes, Mr Korda.'

'Good, keep up the good work,' Alex said magnanimously. He left never knowing how close he came to being not a DOA, but a DOLTC (Dead On Leaving The Cage).

Alex was halfway through the cage door when black-striped, red lightning streaked through the air. Rajah, with all his 550-pound might, hit the door. The outward-closing door crashed shut with a big bulge in the links. Rajah towered on his hindlegs 14 feet above Alex, who was lying on the other side of the cage, out cold, sprawled in the dirt, with his cigar splattered on his face like a rambling rose.

Silence.

The sudden pandemonium. Jabbering people swarming to help Alex. Nobody cared what would happen to us in the cage.

'Goddamn-you-all, shut up and stand still!' Luis's command cut through the racket. The sudden realization of our situation woke up the mob's morbid curiosity. Unfortunately the tiger's too. Luis whispered, 'Don't move, don't look at Rajah, just stand still.'

Rajah stood still too. His claws were hooked on the chain-links of the fence 14, 15 feet, 100 feet high. He turned his magnificent head toward us. The silence brought Alex back to the living. Slowly he sat up, his moaning stopped as he looked up at the tiger above him and, in a dead faint, he fell back to the dirt.

With as much noise as snowflakes hitting the chimneys, the tiger's paws connected with the ground. Rajah became interested in us. He didn't walk toward us, it was more like he 'appeared' to be closer and closer in spooky silence. I remembered Luis's warning, 'Don't look at Rajah,' but I had to. I was drawn to him like a pin to a magnet. It seemed to me Rajah was listening. The only noise I heard was the 'whirrr' of the camera.

Luis spoke up, the first time he had spoken Hungarian to me. 'Turn off the fucking camera and freeze.'

I did both. It wasn't difficult to 'freeze'. Rajah didn't stop, he just wasn't getting closer any more, the fear had evaporated and a strange thought sprouted: If I had to face a firing squad I would decline the blindfold. I would want to face the muzzles. I was facing one now. I had been in danger facing death before, but never felt such total calmness. Rajah nudged Luis's 'magic chair', licked the grease off the metal legs of the tripod.

The breeze waltzed away with the sweet smell of the tiger's urine, Rajah resettled in his lair. Korda looked funny, undignified on his hands and knees, with his fringed cigar still in his mouth. Some 'do-gooders' who would have loved to kick him, helped him to his feet. Alex looked at me, not as calm as the tiger minutes before, but he snarled, in Hungarian: 'You are a son of a bitch.' And those were Alexander Korda's last words to me – at least I thought so for some years afterwards.

Some idiots outside started to applaud, I couldn't figure out if they were applauding us inside the cage or Korda outside. I had a long time to figure – Rajah got excited, charged the door again and put another dent in it, and it took the tiger more than an hour to settle down.

From the very beginning Alex and I had a – to put it mildly – strange relationship. He needed, no, he could use me and he was generous, but he was never good to me. I despised his Hungarian and other bloodsuckers around him as much as Zoli, Vincent and basically Alex himself did. But he needed a court and court jesters. And I realized how ghosts must have felt; I became a ghost in his court. Alex Korda didn't ignore me, he did not snub me. He couldn't have done either, for him I ceased to exist, I just wasn't there. It became a ridiculous three-ring circus. Vincent, the sage, made no waves, only squinted and gently shook his head, so as not to disturb the perennial cigarette ashes glued to his lower left lip. Zoli, who had a slight sadistic streak, enjoyed the situation and took advantage of it. Captain Jiggs and I profited the most by our newly found freedom since Alex was the only one who curbed our antics.

After his tiger incident, Alex became an expert in wild animals. Zoli just couldn't stomach his trying to interfere even with the smallest details involving the beasts and ruining everything. He didn't interfere directly with Zoli as much of course as he did with me by countermanding my orders, but Zoli's and my set-up was totally dependent; they were, so to speak, fused with each other. The damage and confusion sired by Alex hurt Zoli's results – and the snakes too.

Snakes since Eve have always been unpredictable, unreliable and very difficult to cope with. We on *The Jungle Book* had two snakes to contend with: the magnificent king cobra, guarding the treasure, and wise old Kaa, the giant python.

Alex's first jab hit me through the cobra. He, she or it was 14 feet long and was owned by a – strange as it sounds – Mrs King, who made the cover of *Life* a few years later by being killed by her pet, the king cobra of *The Jungle Book*.

Alex cut out of my budget the car allowance to pick up the two 'kings' – Mrs King and the king cobra – in the morning and take them back home at the end of the day. He ignored the fact that neither of the 'kings' could drive. Alex wanted to oust the live king cobra, he wanted to be the only king on the lot.

We parried this by buying a used oboe case in a hock-shop. We drilled lots of holes in it and Mrs King every morning folded and packed – if I remember correctly – the longest cobra then in captivity, inside it, got on the bus and reported in, always on time, to General Service Studio. The preparation for the homeward-bound trips in the evening became tedious to say the least – to use a British understatement. The snake had to be warmed up; when cold, Mrs King couldn't fold the cobra into the case. I learned a very useful fact, king cobras don't bend when they are cold, warm them up first.

Alex Korda knew this and surely knew there was no additional insurance coverage for king cobras to travel on the bus in a used oboe case. He knew everything except how much the overtime would cost for a sneak warm-up – not in budget. It added up to as much as it would cost to buy a bus. The oboe case cost only 75 cents, tax included.

Kaa, the python was more demanding, it cracked his budget. Kaa was elusive. We tried to find one to fit Kipling's words. We searched in the Brazilian jungles – after the Flaherty débâcle Alex, at first, didn't want to hear the word India, thus we had to start with Brazil.

Alex was proud of 'his' tiger scene, he had run it over and over. He wanted everything real. Circus rejects and Great Danes couldn't substitute for pythons any more for him. Alex wanted a real python, a 30-footer at least. It turned out to be easier to handle the 11-feet, 550-pound tiger, Rajah, than an equal length python. But Alex insisted on a

30-footer. Since we couldn't do a thing with an 18-footer, the best we could come up with was what Vincent and Larry Buttler, special effects supreme, were giving birth to; what we called among ourselves a '3F', a 'Fake Forty-Footer'. (The '4Fs' were the rejects, the unfits for military service in the US forces.) With all the children God blessed(?) me with, I never paced the corridors as much as I did waiting for the birth of that big 3F. And it turned out to be a big, limp, rubber sausage.

To have the fewest possible witnesses to our failure we were launching it at night. 'What is that bloody thing?' asked Alex one midnight in Sherwood Forest. We all stood silent, knee-deep in the water, looking up at him standing on the shore above us. Somebody had tipped him off. 'Vincikém, the length is almost right, maybe five, maybe ten foot longer, but alive,' and he walked off only to stop with an afterthought and advised us over his shoulder. 'That puddle looks like a children's wading pool. I want it ten feet deep and wider. The water will look more like water, dangerous, real.' And the night swallowed him till next meeting.

Zoli was prepared. Captain Jiggs and I knew a serious meeting was coming up because Zoli grew his fingernails extra long and paid special attention to the flowerpots in the corridor leading to Alex's office. Captain Jiggs imitated Zoli's every move and added to it hooping noises and slapping his resounding rump.

The day had arrived. Zoli scraped up dirt from the flower pots with his fingernails on the way to Alex's office, Captain Jiggs followed Zoli's example with great glee and ruckus. Meetings which used to last for hours now were quickly over. Alex just couldn't stomach Zoli's fingernail cleaning contest with Captain Jiggs. When Zoli wanted to finish a meeting quickly he took out that razor sharp 'Bugyli bicská' and started to clean his fingernails with its point. It was an unrehearsed signal for Captain Jiggs to take a flying leap onto the top of Alex's desk, grab his sterling silver letter opener, scurry back to my lap and imitate Zoli, picking at his fingernails with Alex's letter opener. No meeting ever lasted longer than it took Zoli to clean three, maximum four of his fingernails. Once the 'Bugyli bicska' came out of Zoli's pocket the meeting was practically over. Alex couldn't take it. I was not there for Alex, so how could he ask me as he did before, 'Stop the bloody monkey.' And nobody else did. Alex must have expected us because he made the mistake of hiding the letter opener. Captain Jiggs took umbrage, shook the desk, then banged on the top of it with his two clenched fists, and won his case.

Kaa, the Alex-approved python, I told Zoli, 'looked like a German sausage left over from the Munich Oktoberfest'.

'We were bloody rough on Alex. Let's shoot it, let him see it, then we'll make the changes,' said Zoli. I must have made a face because he continued, 'I'll shoot it.'

The follow-up was short, as I learned. I was shooting with the black panther, Bagheera No. 2, in town. Zoli, who could not swim, was shooting Kaa in Sherwood Forest on a camera barge above the 'ten-feet-deep real water'. Alex was visiting him.

Zoli had wonderful qualities. Patience was not among them. It was one of those days when nothing was working. Zoli was jumping up and down on the barge, which finally overturned. Alex got hysterical, which he was capable of under lesser strain than seeing his brother drown in the 'ten-feet-deep real water' he had created. He screamed, 'Save him, saaave him, he can't swim!' Nobody moved, as often happens in similar disasters. Alex was jumping up and down, but he was on the shore, pleading, 'Do something, do something, he can't swim,' as he watched the unyielding surface of the dirty water under which his brother was drowning.

Zoli finally ran out of air and stood up in the four-feet-deep water. He knew, of course, that we had dug only a four-feet deep 'children's wading pool'.

For a while Alex was off our backs, but without Zoli's 'Bugyli bicska', *The Jungle Book* would be still shooting.

Working with the Kordas, specially on *The Jungle Book*, was a great experience. To my surprise, Alex emerged once again in my life. Vincent, without cigarette ashes glued to his left lower lip, and I, just the two of us, celebrated his last birthday in the Terrazza in London. We got loaded, not only with memories. Unfortunately, except for a short stint with Zoli on the QT on Columbia's *Sahara*, it was my last professional association with the Kordas as such. I owe them a lot.

'It'll be as easy for you to make the desert around Barstow look like the Sahara as it is for babies to shit in their diapers,' shuddered Zoli as he quoted Harry Cohn to me. Zoli hated dirty words, he used only 'bloody'. But only once every two minutes.

Zoli had a great talent and the reputation of making places look totally different from what they really were. 'You made *The Drum* for your brother in South Wales look like India,' Mr Cohn encouraged him, 'and you did it without Bogart, with Bogart on the screen you're home free, even I will believe it's the Sahara. No trouble.'

There was trouble. It started and persisted with Bogart who didn't believe the desert around Barstow was like the Sahara, he didn't believe in the story and didn't believe Zoli was the right director for the picture. Bogey loved Zoli's *Four Feathers*, but classified him a British Imperialist. Those days were Bogey's 'b.B.' (before Bacall) days, everything was exaggerated. By midday Bogey and Mayo – the reigning Mrs Bogart – got the crew drunk in the 100° plus heat only from the evaporating fumes of their morning shower, which was gin, and the follow-up eye-openers, extra dry martinis, which were perpetually available all day from a large glass pitcher, which Mayo occasionally used as a weapon. Bogey and Mayo were an odd couple.

So were Bogey and Zoli, but at least they had a common denominator and that is what kept the picture going and Zoli on it. Both loved to play chess. Both were good players. Both were stubborn and both of them were bad losers. Bogey forgot his compunction about *Sahara* and Zoli and tortured himself between set-ups with reading books on chess. He could hardly wait for the end of the day so that, with his new, fortified knowledge, he could restart his daily battle with Zoli. But not once during the film did he come close to even a draw. In the end both were losers. It was neither Bogart's nor Zoli's best picture.

But *Sahara* introduced me to the caste system of Hollywood, specifically Harry Cohn's kingdom: Columbia Pictures, in Gower Gulch, and on Hollywood Way in Burbank, The Ranch.

16 Traffic

In the Heaven of discrimination and segregation – in Hitler's Third Reich or during the darkest hours in the 'South,' in caste-riddled India – segregation spelled equality compared to the unwritten law of the studios, in the 'Land of the Free'. There were no walls to separate the pariahs of the film industry from each other. Even the joy of beating their heads against the walls was taken away from them. Glue and molasses guarded the borders. They were typecast and kept alive stuffed in segregated boxes. No bridges. If they crawled out of their patches, quicksand was their bonus. A dreadful and final disappearing act.

'Do it, you're not stuck yet, take chances,' was the throw-away line of Bert Allenberg as he was giving me advice between telephone calls to and from other hopefuls. I felt like a lost but street-wise dog must feel in traffic. And the traffic was heavy, I saw the fatalities. Allenberg nudged me to jump off the curb into the traffic of Columbia Pictures, the Hellhole of Dreamland.

'Irving Briskin saw two of your Hungarian films –'

'– How? I didn't know –'

'I got them for him from New York. He liked them and he liked your *Jungle Book* stuff too. I assured him, if you handled the tigers you could handle a "Lone Wolf".[1] The script stinks, but you're going to do it. Do the best you can.'

At Columbia next to, not below 'God Cohn' was sanity, dignity and

---

1 *The Lone Wolf* was a jewel thief turned detective character created by Louis Joseph Vance. He was portrayed by Bert Lytel, Melvyn Douglas and various others, but his best known essayist is Warren William, who enjoyed a career which included performing on Broadway. In films he played everything from Julius Caesar in C. B. De Mille's *Cleopatra*, to Pearl White's leading man, to Perry Mason, Philo Vance and the Lone Wolf in eight Columbia features, beginning with *The Lone Wolf Spy Hunt* (1939) and ending with *Passport to Suez* (1943), Andre de Toth's first feature in the U.S.

elegance personified, B. B. Kahane, a vice-president, when the title meant more than a raise in salary. After him came the various units, like the Sam Briskin Unit for top 'A' pictures.

The slimy tracks of the slugs crossing the sidewalk lead to Sidney Buchman and other frantic climbers. After 55 billion light years of walking, if you weren't hit by cars while crossing the Boulevard, you reached the Briskin Unit.

The names of Sam and Irving tagged to Briskin wasn't a coincidence, it was nepotism. But both were good in their own patch. 'What do you think of the script?' asked big and burly Irving, a second-hand Selznick but a real executive producer, not only an addition to the credits.

'It stinks.' I told him my honest opinion. I didn't really want to do the picture, but I didn't want to turn it down, I wanted him to nix me.

'Good,' he agreed. 'What could you do with it?'

'I could do my best, but I don't know if that would be good enough to save the shit.'

'Good,' he said the second time, 'do your best.' He picked up the phone and called Allenberg, 'He'll start tomorrow. Yeah, OK.' He got up from his desk, threw a script at me, 'It's a rewrite, not much better. You'll start to shoot Monday,' opened the door and walked out. 'Come on, meet your producer.'

That was Thursday.

In the Briskin Unit everything was second-hand. My first American producer too, an ex-vaudevillian, Wally MacDonald, a second-hand Brynie Foy.[2] Both of them were lovely men. They left you so alone as a director that you sometimes felt lonely. Wally would never push you, but if you fell into the sea of molasses surrounding Wally's little island, he had no muscle to pull you out.

No Monday ever came faster and I started the picture. I had a – generous for that unit – seven-day schedule. By the end of the third day I was three days behind. Wally shed sincere tears, 'I'm always crying at funerals, even if I hate them,' he confessed. 'Don't you commit suicide by going over schedule,' he warned me. 'We are making lots of these

2 Brian Foy (1896–1977) was the son of vaudevillian Eddie Foy. At the age of four he was the star performer of the family troup, the once-famous Seven Little Foys. He became a legendary producer of classy 'B' pictures, and was known as 'The Keeper of the B's', but he also directed the first all-talking feature, *Lights of New York*, in 1928, and produced a number of major Hollywood features, most notably *House of Wax*.

pictures here and you could keep on making them.'

He bowed his head as he said 'Mr Cohn' and delivered the message; I was to see Mr Cohn after wrapping for the day. 'I hope I'll see you tomorrow,' sighed Wally as we parted.

'What's the problem? There are people working for Cohn for years and never saw him. So go and see him. He is a son of a bitch, but straight. Tell him whatever you want him to know, if you can get a word in edgeways. I am not writing dialogue for you. Call me after, I'll be at home.' Allenberg hung up. The evening traffic buzzed along Sunset, I had difficulty kicking open the door of the tight, urine-smelling wooden phone booth. I didn't merit a phone in my 'office'.

The damned useless classic education haunted me again: 'Ave Caesar, morituri te salutant,' I hyped myself as I entered through the Gower Street entrance to the slaughter house.

At a large desk in a small room a well-fed middle-aged-lady with a thick finger and dirty fingernail pointed at an empty chair next to the far wall in bad need of a new coat of paint. I don't remember if the room had windows or not, but I remember it had a discreet scent of kosher dill pickle and pastrami. Fingers had left their dark, greasy, pastrami imprints on the edges of the three visible once pearl-grey upholstered wooden chairs lined up against the wall. The other three chairs were filled with muscle. In those days they weren't called bodyguards. Endearingly, they were called 'Gorillas'. A mystery still unsolved: they were on duty usually in odd numbers, one or three, not two or four; in their uniform of blue serge suits, white shirts with narrow ties, to emphasize their barrel chests, cauliflower-ears of various sizes and twisted noses of various degrees. They were unmistakable.

Like someone emerging from a sauna, a disheveled bundle of twitching nerves stumbled through the door desperately squeezing under his armpit a stack of multicolored loose sheets of paper about to flutter to the floor. With the increasing speed of an escapee with safe haven in sight he was dashing toward the exit.

'You can go in now,' said the fat lady to me, but before I got to my feet two of the Gorillas, like lightning, were inside the room on each side of the door, the third held it open for me. Rumor had it, it was much easier to get out of Harry Cohn's office than get in. The propulsion out-bound was right behind me at the door.

I had never seen Harry Cohn before, this was my first time in his office.

I couldn't describe it, when Cohn was around he filled the space. He wasn't sitting behind a desk, he sat at the head of a mile-long board-room table with piles of papers in front of him. Next to him sat an elegant, distinguished looking elderly gentleman, B. B. Kahane. A statesman.

What first struck me about Cohn were his eyes. You knew when he looked at you how the asphalt must have felt when a sledge-hammer drilled it. He had a strong open face, wore no jacket, the cuffs of his shirt-sleeves were open and the large, garish cufflinks clanged on the table when he banged on it for emphasis. He was a wound-up bundle of nervous energy, in contrast to Kahane, who was so relaxed, so limp it was a wonder he didn't slide off his chair.

Cohn wasted no time. Before I was half-way between him and the door behind me he clang-banged on the table, 'Do you know what is the schedule on the picture?' And he whacked the table again for no apparent reason. Before I could answer him.

I quickly slipped in, 'Yes, sir,' before another clang-bang.

'Mr Cohn,' he spat at me.

'Yes, sir,' – I accentuated sir – 'Mr Cohn.'

A long silence followed and the sledge-hammer eyes worked on me. After he thought the desired effect had been achieved Cohn picked up a paper at random from the table and studied it. Carefully. Suddenly, with an exaggerated clang-bang, he slapped the paper back on the table, pointing at it as if it were my schedule, 'You have a seven days' schedule and you are three days behind in the first three days. What do you say?'

'Nothing, sirrr,' I added, 'Mr Cohn.'

Kahane leaned back; Cohn leaned forward, stared at me, a two-fisted clang-bang punished the poor table.

'A fuckin' nothin' he says,' he whispered to Kahane, then roared at me. 'No excuse, no alibi, just a fuckin' nothin', that's all?' He turned to Kahane again, whispering, 'Did you hear 'im, nothin' he says.'

I took advantage of the momentary quiet, 'Mr Cohn, I still could finish on schedule if – '

The ceiling cracked, the dingle-dangles on the crystal chandeliers sounded like timpanums as Cohn bellowed, 'If. Eeeeef? What do you mean if?'

He was on his feet with two hands on the edge of the table, leaning forward, not unlike Mussolini on his balcony on Piazza Venezia, chin out with a snarl.

'If we change my contract.'

He sunk back into his chair. The Gorillas got to their feet at the door. Kahane didn't move. After two attempts Cohn spoke to him. 'Did you hear that?' He whacked the table again and screamed, 'Did you hear that? He wants to change his contract.' He threw himself back in his chair and laughed, loud, almost hysterically.

Kahane was quietly amused, 'Why don't we listen to him, Harry?' Cohn leaned forward, Kahane asked me, 'What do you want to change in your contract?'

'My contract says I am to perform to the best of my ability. Right, sir?' I asked Kahane.

'It is a standard phrase in everybody's contract,' answered Kahane with narrowing eyes.

'I know, sir.'

'What do you object to?'

'Nothing. I am living up to it. Take it out of the contract and I will finish the picture within the original schedule in seven days. I am giving you gentlemen my word.'

Kahane shrugged with a smile. Cohn stared at me again in silence, then exploded. 'Get the hell out of here.'

I turned, the Gorillas were coming to help me out. Cohn yelled at them. 'You too. He knows his way out.'

I walked out unassisted. The contract wasn't changed. I finished the picture seven days behind the seven days schedule. I did my best, but even film directors can't make gold out of crap.

'Mr Cohn is the boss,' said Wally, with a shrug next day. 'I want to make better pictures too, but I am not responsible for quality, I am responsible for the budget.'

'When I wanted to replace you, Mr Cohn wanted to see the rushes. You were lucky, he was in a good mood. He liked them. But don't get too big for your britches,' Briskin warned me, 'you may never work again. Certainly not for me. I can't establish a precedent.'

'Don't you ever change,' suggested Sheldon Leonard,[3] one of the

---

3 Sheldon Leonard (born 1907) was a character actor in the 1940s and 1950s, specializing in gangster roles, who became a very successful television producer and director with *The Andy Griffith Show*, *The Dick Van Dyke Show* and *I Spy*, often working with his one-time partner comedian Danny Thomas.

actors (in fact, the only actor among the dead wood on the show). 'Keep that camera moving. I like it,' he added.

I didn't know how privileged I was to be allowed in the cutting-room till the end. When we finished, Harry Cohn asked me, grumbling, 'Was the seven, seven fuckin' days behind schedule worth it?'

'No, Mr Cohn. It was not worth making it.'

Cohn walked away. Wally was offended, 'You just discredited my picture,' then added with glee, 'but cut your throat.'

By the time I walked back to the Briskin Unit, a stranger was sitting behind the desk in the nine-by-nine windowless cubbyhole I had proudly called my office an hour before. The few pieces of my belongings were shoved into an old cardboard box in the corner. I was notified my parking space was assigned to somebody else and I should move my car off the lot. My entry permit to the studio had been revoked. The few people I knew on the lot were giving me a wide berth so as not to be exposed to the contagious, deadly disease – communicable on sight – I was carrying.

I did the only thing I could have done, I left the dump. Left it head high, grateful for the chance, proud and happy because I did my best under the circumstances.

'Do you have something in mind you would like to do now?' asked Allenberg on the phone.

'Yeah, shit in the beef-stew in the commissary at Columbia.'

'Watch it, you may eat it yourself. Harry Cohn has something in mind for you. I'll send it over.'

Two weeks later I had, in the main building on Gower on the directors' corridor, a 'large' – about sixteen-by-sixteen – office with two windows, a phone I could dial out direct, a secretary from the pool when needed and a respectable parking space among some name directors – I had arrived.

The very first minute of the very first day as I walked in my office the phone was ringing.

Without the modern-day electronic surveillance equipment, Harry Cohn in Columbia Studio knew where everybody was every minute of the day and what they were doing. 'Take castor oil if you're constipated. If you are mentally constipated don't sit on the fucking toilet on my time an hour every day,' Harry Cohn told a trembling writer and fired him for mental constipation. The poor fellow couldn't get a job. No-money-no-food-no-necessity-to-go-to-the-toilet, the normal vicious circle of life, but for him it was worse. The only place he could think was waiting for things to happen on the toilet, as ultimately they did, but his good thoughts came always after. Now that Harry Cohn had spotted only half of his shortcomings, no way could he prove 'King Cohn' wrong. It sounds like a pure Shakespearean tragedy in Hollywood, doesn't it?

'Mister Cohn wants you –' click. Whoever she was hung up. Why waste time? She knew there was one answer only. I was on my way.

'Are you a Nazi?' Cohn asked me before the door closed behind me.

A nice reception. Seven, eight people around the big table, fourteen, sixteen eyes, different colors, were giving me the once-over. Some blinking, others with a blank stare. Crossfire. Was I the slave on the bottom of the Colosseum's floor in Rome? 'Panem et Circenses.' They had the 'bread' from Harry Cohn, I supplied the 'circus'.

'No, Mr Cohn – why did you ask me that?'

'I was told.'

'By whom? Who was the fuck who –'

Cohn held up a hand, ' – I don't like four letter words.'

'I would like to meet the gentleman who told you I was a Nazi so I can kick the shit out of him, sir, Mr Cohn. If I were a Nazi I would have stayed over there making good pictures, not shit for the Briskin Unit.'

Harry Cohn could smile with his eyes, I discovered. The people around the table looked like a tableau of stiffs from a morgue or stars in an MGM glossy picture – clean, neat and antiseptic, the Lion in the trademark being the only one alive. From around the table eyes like slow-moving beams of a lighthouse scanned the space between Cohn and me.

'How did you like the story?'

'The script stinks, the –'

'I didn't ask you about the script, I asked did you like the story.'

'Yes, sir. I would love to make that story, not the screenplay.'

'Didn't you hear me, I asked you about the story, not the script. The writers of the original are in your office now. Be back here at three.'

Cohn went back to the meeting as if it had not been interrupted. No 'goodbyes' or 'see you laters'. I evaporated.

Alfred Neuman and Joseph Thau, the authors of the original story, were sitting on the edge of the just-not-long-enough-to-stretch-out-on couch. They got to their feet as I walked in, the springs in the couch sounded like a chord from an out-of-tune guitar. The springs in the comfortable-looking armchair in the corner were not musically inclined, they were special surgical instruments for castration. I sat on the corner of the desk. Neuman and Thau wore the identical masks of refugees, ingratiating smiles and discreet tear drops in the corner of their eyes. A silent unwritten plea.

Their masks cracked as we talked, but they treaded easy. Like peeling an onion, it finally came out they were unhappy with the screenplay. They saw, felt what they were writing about, but the screenplay lacked the understanding of the human beings Neuman and Thau had lived with and were writing about. It was something I had wanted to do since 1 September 1939.

It was 1943. The world was on a blood and fire diet. It was two and a half years before the Nürnberg Trials. In *None Shall Escape* we invented a name for the asthmatic, breathless, thoughtless and impotent League of Nations: 'United Nations'.[4] A moniker of utopia. Those of us who were singed by the fire and hallowed by the blood were craving for justice. Not revenge. Revenge will never spawn justice, it is a vicious circle. Justice or revenge – a point where I differed with one of the screenwriters. But, living off Hollywood Boulevard, how could he feel it? But Harry Cohn did. *None Shall Escape* was made for justice.

Well-camouflaged – so he thought – behind the bulwarks of bogus crudity, Harry Cohn owned a heart which he was ashamed of. He possessed human understanding which he occasionally misused. But on those rare occasions when I could peek behind his bastions there was a sensitive human being. Hiding. He would sooner die than admit he had understood me, or anybody. He was a continuous 'tester'. He wanted to be sure that you were sure, you really believed in what you were clamoring about. He wrote no blank checks. His mistrust was planted in the deep trenches of yesteryears' hurts and disappointments. I respected him. I liked him. He loved pictures, he lived for motion pictures.

Aside from our legal entanglement, where I was wrong and made a hell of a mistake, we had only one head-to-head battle, like two spring bucks in mating season.

'Do you want to ruin me?' screamed Jack in New York, so loudly he

4 The League of Nations was created by the Treaty of Versailles (1919), and dissolved in April 1946 by its 21st assembly. *None Shall Escape* was shot in January 1943. Its subject was the trial of a war-criminal. The United International War Crimes Tribunal opened in Nürnberg two years and six months later on 20 November 1945.

could be heard in Los Angeles without the phone. 'You're nuts? I couldn't sell the fucking picture in the South with four niggers on an international jury of the United Nations' Court. You are out of your fucking mind!' And he hung up.

In the sudden silence, with his sledge-hammer look Harry Cohn riveted me to the wall as he repeated the questions I had heard through the phone. Verbatim. Twice. When he spoke quietly he was dangerous, now he whispered. I said nothing. After a very pregnant silence he descended from his throne, turned his back to the room, and me, to watch the mutely gliding traffic on Gower Street. His room was totally soundproofed. He didn't want any noise to interfere with his dictums.

There were no first names when we had our 'discussions'. I called him 'Mr Cohn', he called me all kinds of names, none too flattering. After a while I tried to divert his attention from the Gower Street traffic.

'Mr Cohn – '

' – Are you still here?'

'Obviously – '

' – Smart ass. No!'

'You are famous for your guts, Mr Cohn – '

' – Stop the bullshit.' He said without turning around. A good sign.

' – Not having blacks on an international jury would be like walking down Hitler's alley. Dirty Jews, jungle bunny blacks, negroes, faggots, discrimination is discrimination, racial prejudice is racial prejudice.'

He never glanced at me when he climbed back up to his throne. 'Get me Jack.[5] I know it's three hours' difference, they ought to know where he went to lunch. Get him, and tell Sam Bischoff[6] I want to see him.'

He slammed down the receiver and that was the only sound in the room till Sam Bischoff arrived. He didn't tell me to leave – a good sign.

5 Jack Cohn (1889–1956) was the lesser-known brother of Harry Cohn, who entered the film industry in 1908 with Carl Laemmle. Co-founder with brother Harry and Joe Brandt of C.B.C., which became Columbia Pictures. Jack Cohn handled the adminstrative and distribution end of the company from New York. Jack hated the coast, Harry hated New York. A perfect partnership. Brotherly understanding.
6 Samuel Bischoff (1890–1975) was a prominent hands-on producer, primarily at Warner Bros and Columbia, from the mid–1920s to the mid–1960s. Among the stars who worked for him were Errol Flynn in *Charge of the Light Brigade* (1936), James Cagney and Humphrey Bogart in *The Roaring Twenties* (1939) and Jane Russell and Robert Mitchum in *Macao* (1952).

He didn't tell me to sit down – not a good sign. I might as well sit down, I thought. Before Sam had a chance to close the door Cohn jumped on him. My mental abacus started clicking: Cohn had referred to me to Sam as 'your director', not a bad sign.

'Your director lost his marbles. He wants to put some blacks on the jury. What do you think, Sam?'

Sam was an old Hollywood fox. 'Let me think, Harry.' Now the three of us sat in silence while Sam was thinking. 'How many?' asked Sam from nobody in particular.

'Four. Four blacks on the jury of the United Nations.'

My abacus stuck, there was no reaction from Sam. He dropped his chin and was engulfed again in a 'thinking silence'. 'Four?' he muttered after a while.

'Four! It's going to ruin me. The South – '

Cohn picked up the phone, he was loud enough to be heard in New York, demanding, 'Where in the – ' he stopped. Obviously the operator anticipated his question. Cohn listened, slamming down the phone he exploded, 'That fucking brother of mine, he didn't tell 'em where he went to lunch. I hope he chokes.'

Sam, calm as always – if no ladies were around – asked me, 'You want four, huh?'

'Yes, at least.'

'At least,' screamed Cohn on the top of his lungs.

'I have an idea, Harry.' Sam snapped his fingers as if the idea just occurred to him. 'Let's have two. They won't stick out so much.'

The phone rang. 'Where in the hell have you been?' Cohn asked his brother, but didn't wait for an answer. 'Two-fucking-hour luncheons, no wonder the business is in a slump. Did you see those sheets? Listen, Jack, this crazy director of Sam's wants six blacks to sit in the jury . . . What jury?' Cohn shook his head in disgust, raised his voice, which was loud enough before, 'The jury of the United Nations in *None Shall Escape* . . . Don't interrupt. Don't tell me about the South . . . Yeah . . . Yeah! . . . I know the South. I agree!' Cohn turned to Sam and me, 'No blacks, understand?'

My abacus cracked, my heart sank, that was the end of my first big Hollywood dream.

'Sorry, Sam. I am off the picture.' He patted my forearm, 'Take it easy. Let's think.'

Cohn ignored us, he was busy on the phone bestowing more and more endearments on brother Jack.

'You're a fucking salesman, aren't you?' he kept on barking. 'Get off your ass, don't have no two-hour luncheons, you're too late. I already told them they can have one, only one black man.'

I didn't think of it at that moment in Harry Cohn's office, but I was wondering ever since if he was aware that the presence of 'only one black man', a lonely black person, made my statement stronger.

Paul Lukas was a gentleman and a friend who had helped me to fulfil my dream to become an American. Lukas signed the affidavit I needed to get my quota number. He was an international star, a big hit on Broadway in *Watch on the Rhine*, an Academy Award winner. Harry Cohn and Bishoff wanted him for the picture.

I didn't.

Harry Cohn knew of my association with Lukas – Harry Cohn knew everything. 'You are an ungrateful bastard, aren't you.' It wasn't a question.

'He liked the script,' interjected Bischoff.

'That's another reason I don't want him and I told him so.'

'You made a big mistake.' Bischoff shook his head.

'What did he say?' came Cohn's whiplash.

'He agreed with me, Mr Cohn.'

'Oh, shit,' sighed Bischoff.

'Get out of here,' yelled Harry Cohn. Before I shut the door he warned me, 'Don't you talk to actors except on the set, if you ever want to work here again!'

The phone was ringing as I walked into my office, 'God' himself was on it. 'Where in the hell have you been, taking a walk?'

'No, a leak.'

'Get up here!' Clang. I could even see Cohn slamming down the receiver.

I opened Cohn's office door only a crack, in case some missiles were coming my way – it was rumored to happen. The attack was only verbal.

'You ruined our deal with Lukas.'

My mental abacus rattled, one for me, they had talked to Lukas, I scored. Not the pompous ass casting jerk.

Cohn finished him quietly, 'Out'; he didn't even earn a shout. The slime slid out the door. 'Lukas is out, no blacks,' Harry Cohn informed me in a surprisingly civil tone.

Bischoff could cry on command. Real or manufactured tears were welling up now in his sad eyes as he looked at me, waiting for the tears to roll down his well-nourished cheeks. He must have forgotten I watched him negotiate in Palm Springs when he was trying to convince a lovely little buttercup how misunderstood he was at home. 'Tears are more effective when they are rolling down. That's the right way.' He scored.

The tears had arrived, to help them to roll down he shook his head. The tears had dropped on the lapels of his cashmere jacket, on his Countess Mara tie, it was very effective. He spoke barely audibly. 'We may have to cancel the picture. Too bad,' – a deep sigh – 'Why did you do it?'

'Shit,' Harry Cohn belched the word. 'Why did you fuck it up? What do you have in mind? If anything. Lukas is a good actor.'

'That is exactly what I don't want.'

'Listen to him, Sam, he doesn't want a good actor.'

'*None Shall Escape* shouldn't be acted, it should be felt, thought, lived. An ugly slice of life. Real, the truth as it was. As it is now. I lived through it. The faces shouldn't be déjà vu.'

'He is speaking French now. Aren't you impressed, Sam?' He snarled at me: 'What's on your mind?'

'I would like Alexander Knox[7] to play the part.'

Empty stares, long silence. Intercom buzz, 'Get me a file on Alexander Knox.' Cohn cut off the 'sir' after the 'yes' on the speaker. Bischoff's tears dried up. Cohn's sledge-hammer look took over. 'Where did you meet this Knox?'

'I never met him.'

Exchanges of knowing looks between the brass. Sam spoke, quietly, politely. They were a good team.

'In what picture did you see him?'

---

7 Alexander Knox (born 1907) was a serious actor, both on stage and screen. His most important film appearance was the title role in the 1944 Darryl Zanuck, 20th Century-Fox production of *Wilson*, for which he received an Academy Award nomination, but it failed to bring the stardom he deserved. The Award went to popular crooner Bing Crosby (*Going My Way*).

'I forgot the title, it was in one of lustrous Litvak's[8] phony crap. Only Knox was real. And I saw him on Broadway in Chekhov's *Three Sisters*.'

Cohn got up and went into his adjoining private projection room. Sam followed him, well-trained. Heeling, without a visible leash. And, at that time, he was one of the three or four highest paid producers in town. He turned back before disappearing in the darkness of the projection room, 'We'll let you know.'

Two weeks passed. It depended on whom I was talking to; they told me, 'They are drying you out on the line,' or, 'They have put you on ice, you're in the freezer.' For me it felt as if I had been put in a decompression chamber but somebody had reversed the procedure – they were giving me the bends. This was the legalized method of robbing someone of one of their most valuable possessions, self-respect. A slow but sure method to kill those who had innards.

I had my office, the lights were on and my phone was connected, I retained my parking space: these were the only signs that I was still among the living. I am sure the 'in' expression 'just hang in there' was sired and/or given birth to by somebody who was hanging in there. Hanging like I was on an unseen rope held by the powers that be. Hanging, and being swayed by the wind of hope.

'You're not very smart, are you?'

'No, Mr Cohn. Otherwise I wouldn't have come in every damn day for three weeks, hoping. Wanting to hear at least a no.'

'Sit down,' he pointed at one of the four armchairs encircling a coffee table below his throne. The chair he indicated was facing the big French windows. He plopped down, stretched out opposite me, already having the upper hand. Gower runs north and south, I was facing the setting sun filtering through the lovely Brussels lace curtains. The dancing shadow patterns of the delicate lace made it more awkward than facing the direct sunlight.

Sam Bischoff came in from the projection room, a secretary brought in on a tray three cups and a pot of coffee. It was all arranged. This was my first 'social contact' with Harry Cohn.

8 Anatole Litvak (1902–1974) was a Russian-born film director who worked in Germany, Britain and France as well as his native land before being brought to the United States in 1937 as a result of the international success of his film of the previous year, *Mayerling*. His best work in America was with melodramas such as *Sorry Wrong Number* (1948) and the *Snake Pit* (1949).

'Did you tell him, Harry?'

Cohn didn't answer Bischoff. Watching me, he poured himself a cup of coffee, then tasted it, made a face and pushed a buzzer hidden beneath the top of the coffee table. He barely had time to withdraw his finger from the buzzer when the door opened and before the secretary was able to say a word he rode her, hard. 'Is this hot? Taste it.'

Mumbling a 'Sorry, Mr Cohn, very sorry,' she backed out and returned with another tray with a new pot and only one cup on it. It was on the table in front of Cohn before Bischoff finished pouring himself a cup from the pot Cohn was complaining about. Then he poured me a cup too. He didn't touch his. I tasted mine. It was scalding hot. Harry Cohn knew not only showmanship, he knew gamesmanship.

'Your actor friend is a snake in the grass. Now that's between us, after I told him you suggested him for the part the son-of-a-bitch wanted Milestone[9] to direct the picture, not you.'

'Milestone is a very good director and – '

'Bullshit, I told him you're under contract to me and you're directing the fucking picture. Make the son-of-a-bitch sweat blood, work his balls off.'

I never counted my 'first picture' in the US a 'picture'. It was, as Allenberg called it, 'a key to the door of Hollywood'. Walking through that door so far there had been nothing but hurdles of various heights in my path, but it was fun to get over them. Except one.

I must have risen in Harry Cohn's estimation or he needed a new sacrificial lamb for his luncheon ritual: I was extended the dubious privilege of eating luncheon in 'his dining-room at will'. To be invited to use the 'executive', 'private', 'Mr Cohn's' or other special dining-rooms on the various lots in town was an expensive privilege. The food in some – to be complimentary – was atrocious. The food in 'Lil's' humble hole in the wall with her steak, steak or steak menu on the General Service lot was an epicurean inner sanctum compared with Mr Cohn's halfway-house to a mortuary. But Harry Cohn had in his dining-room an electric hot seat controlled by him from the head of the table.

I was prepared for it by Sam Bischoff. He was concerned I would bolt or turn the table legs up.

In Zanuck's elegant dove-grey dining-room at 20th Century-Fox the

---

9 Lewis Milestone (1893–1980). To an outsider he would have been an obvious choice to direct *None Shall Escape*, because of his work on *All Quiet On The Western Front* (1913).

food was excellent, the dry martinis superb, the cigar smoke could be cut only with sharp steak knives. The comfortable chairs around five round tables were cradles to enjoy the after-meal cognacs.

Matching the personalities, Jack Warner's dining-room had one long but wide table with twenty large, sturdy armchairs around it. Behind the 'boss' an almost 'wall-to-wall', richly inlaid antique screen – now in the Santa Barbara museum – covered the service entrance. The meals had an atmosphere of a large family gathering around the turn of the century. Aside from a soup-to-nuts set menu you could order just about anything ahead of time. It had smaller martinis but a better wine cellar than Zanuck's.

I enjoyed the possibility of having drinks at mealtime but it bothered me – occasionally – that less lucky mortals were fired if they drank or had in possession even a can of beer on the studio premises. 'Insurance problems', I was told. Or prohibition hangover?

Harry Cohn's cramped dining-room, with one skinny table in the centre and Mr Cohn at the head of it, was a heartburn-projecting, ulcer-promising drab room at the back of the lot, upstairs at the head of a weather-beaten wooden staircase, next to his barbershop. I was antici-pating, with not much joy, dining the first time with the firsts among the firsts in the studio. Cohn only had to push a button to deliver his surprise, usually with soup, stew or other 'spillable' nourishment. It was more fun that way. The victim's cleaning bill was not included in the lunch bill.

Clinking sounds of dropping spoons against saucers under the soup bowls settled on the room like baking flour through a sieve. Bischoff coughed to camouflage a smile, I spoke up, lying through my teeth.

'Thanks, Harry, for extending me the privilege of using this dining-room. The soup is excellent, my favorite, by the way!' And I kept on ladling, with slurps that would have driven my mother over the hill – or she would have driven me into the doghouse.

It turned out to be one of my most enjoyable luncheons. All through the meal Cohn was pushing the button with swelling annoyance and less and less concern who would notice it. I did. And I felt the current connect my teeth with the spoon, producing miniature lightnings with its prongs in my mouth. I was glad for the frugal meal. One more course and Harry Cohn would have won. Unfortunately, I did not witness the Grand Finale of my obstinacy.

According to Sam Bischoff, Harry Cohn came close to spontaneous combustion. He wanted to fire on the spot the head waiter and the electrician responsible for the fiasco. They had insisted the rig worked. 'It didn't.' 'It does.' 'It didn't.' 'It does.' To save his job and to prove to Cohn he was wrong (which was a foolish and dangerous thing to do), the electrician urged the head waiter to sit in the chair to show it was working. The head waiter refused. The electrician, instead of sacrificing his job, sacrificed his ass, sat in the chair . . . jumped off the chair with a howl before Cohn lifted his finger off the button.

Cohn was livid, felt cheated and fired the electrician on the spot. To justify his action he sat in the chair himself screaming, 'Push it, push the fucking button. You're scared because you have let me down and lied to me. Push it!' Nobody volunteered. Cohn was jumping up and down in the chair. When he threatened to fire the head waiter too the poor slob succumbed, pushed the button and Harry Cohn went through the ceiling screaming and cursing.

The electrician was fired, the head waiter was fired. I started to shoot the following week *None Shall Escape* with Alexander Knox in the lead.

Harry Cohn was as frugal in production as he was in his dining-room, but he was destined to serve some of the finest films of that period when his well-hidden taste came out of hiding, which in his dining-room was forever concealed.

Columbia made 50 to 55 features a year. To save on film, laboratory cost and time there was a rule not to exceed five takes per scene. Should a sixth take be necessary, the first assistant was to remind the director of this rule.

I took my first assistant with me from the Briskin unit: a beautiful drunk, an Irishman, Bill O'Connor. He had a purple face, watery-blue eyes and a set of choppers the Hong Kong ivory-carvers would have loved to get their chisels on. For Bill it was a big step up to work on *None Shall Escape* – 'on the other side'. He went out and bought himself a new wardrobe. His new shoes were shining, so was his unruly red hair he now tried – unsuccessfully – to plaster down against his bowling ball-like head. He was a good man. He was a pro. He had one problem. When Bill had one or two too many and got excited, he had a sneezing fit. And when Bill had a sneezing fit, he ejected his choppers with the velocity of cannonballs. Subsequently, the whole crew on hands and knees would look for Bill's false teeth, usually to be found in the most unlikely places.

It was Friday, one of those do-or-die days. Bill dutifully notified me I was on my fifth take and asked if there was anything he could do to help, all according to the Book of Cohn.

'Don't do this to me,' begged Bill. 'They'll send me back to the dumps. The tenth one is coming up, I'll have to call production office.'

'Do it, that's your job, Bill.'

Bill mumbled, 'It won't be for long,' as he went to the phone.

Jack Fear, reserved and professorial with sparkling rimless glasses, floated in with a 'What's wrong?'

'That's easy to answer, Jack, everything.'

'Can I help?'

'If I thought you could, I would've called you long ago.'

'You know the rules.'

'I sure do and I am living up to them, doing my best.'

Fear shook his head, his glasses quivered and the reflections of the lights from above sprinkled them with added sparks. 'This is no joke, Mr director, I have to report this to Mr Griffith and Mr Cohn.'

On his way out he stopped occasionally to gather information from the crew; I expedited his exit, 'You're holding me up, Jack.'

I smelled toothpaste, Bill was at my shoulder. I knew he had had a couple of swallows of courage. 'You are killing me and yourself, but my wife is pregnant and you're not,' he moaned.

Gordon Griffith was the studio production manager. He had been a baby Tarzan in silent films with Elmo Lincoln, or something. He was six-four, the width of his shoulders was six-four. He had no hips and no feet. He had flippers, as large and as flat as a rubber welcome mat in front of a church in Vermont in January. By the time he marched in I was shooting my forty-second take. It was so unheard of there were no provisions in the Book of Cohn on handling a situation like that. I was lucky it was the weekend. Nobody could be found with authority to fire me. Gordon Griffith didn't have that big a clout.

'I could ask a silly question, how are things?' Griffith smiled as he put his arm around my shoulder. 'Let's go over there and I'll have some other questions.'

Gordon lived four doors down from me on top of Miller Drive, above the Strip. He was a straight shooter and a gentleman.

'Stop this nonsense. Cohn likes you, Bischoff likes you, they like your stuff – so far. They are talking about the next projects for you. You're on the threshold of a good career, don't shut the door. Break the scene up. I know what you're trying to –' He held up his hand, as big as a snow shovel in Vermont in February, 'Let me finish,' he said. 'OK. Don't break up the scene, move the camera a foot to the left or right, I don't care, then give it a new scene number. If the scene still doesn't work after five takes – OK, six – move the damned thing again. Don't print this scene. OK?'

'No, thanks, but no. It's a principle.'

'Don't stretch your luck. Jack tried to reach Cohn and Bishoff in the Springs, he couldn't. If he'd reached them, you would be off the picture by now, you know that. Please, as a friend, all I can say is, be sensible. It's four-ten now, how far behind schedule are you today?'

I didn't answer that question. 'Thanks, Gordon, I appreciate what you were trying to do. I can't cheat myself, I have to do it my way.' We shook hands and parted as friends.

It was five-twenty. Bill smelled like a burst-open toothpaste factory. I said the much awaited words, 'Print the eighty-fifth and eighty-seventh takes.'

By five-fifty-five, Monday's sequence was roughed in, positions marked on the floor with chalk. That put us ahead of schedule. 'That's all for today, see you Monday,' Bill hollered. I was proud of him; I told him, 'No sneeze in the tight squeeze.'

At five-fifty-nine, leaving the stage Bill whispered, 'It was nice to work with you,' and he, like the others, slunk out of the doors, avoiding looking at each other and me, like a funeral where the mourners weren't sure if the corpse had moved in the coffin.

I was the last to leave. I usually do that. I love the magic of thought as it fills the empty set, a fata morgana, a mirage in a tinderbox.

Across from Gower Gulch on the north side of Sunset was the Birmingham. It was a great place. The service was lousy and very slow, luckily for the out-of-jobbers, nowhere-to-goers. They could sit there forever waiting for their small orders to come without worrying about being ogled out. The food was lousy too – thank God the portions were small – but the drinks were large and the stools around the big bar were comfortable.

As a Friday night ritual, like birds in the rain on a powerline, we used to commiserate, lined up at the bar. The few of the habitués who were there that evening excused themselves with transparent alibis and left shortly after my arrival. Hollywood friendship.

'I told him,' said Gordon as he sat next to me.

'What did he say?' I shot the question.

'He didn't blow up, he said nothing, the worse sign.'

No calls Saturday. No pink slip by messenger. Being fired was the fastest spreading disease. I found out it was contagious through the telephone. Nobody answered or returned my calls. No messenger, no calls till Sunday evening.

'You must have been sitting on the phone, you answered it so quick,' said Gordon. 'What's so urgent? Four messages.' I told him the story. 'Strange,' he said. 'There was no message from Cohn. I don't like it.'

After one of the few sleepless nights of my life, Monday arrived. And I arrived earlier than usual at the auto gate of Columbia. I didn't know who was more surprised, the guard seeing me there or I when he said with astonishment, 'Well, no orders to the contrary, you can drive in. You're early. Aren't you?'

I was the first on the stage, turned the lights on, a few mice scurried to safety, afraid to face the day. So was I.

The stage floor was spotlessly clean, no tell-tale signs of Friday's rehearsal, the chalk marks were gone. I understood, 'they' didn't want to embarrass the director who would take over from me. Very thoughtful. Sitting alone on the murky stage brought no magic images this time. Horror was hidden behind the decor, phantoms were creeping high up on the bridges among the dead lights.

'I wonder who will take over?' asked a faceless voice. A 'sssh' from the dark. I felt warning fingers pointing at me. Tentative 'Good mornings'.

'Another lousy day,' blastered Bill. 'Oh!' he gulped his words. 'Good morning,' and continued with the same breath, 'who was the son-of-a-bitch who wiped off the marks?' but did not wait for an answer.

With ill-hidden surprises and uncamouflaged 'ohs' the new day began. We re-rehearsed the sequence, started to shoot and by ten o'clock the 'ohs' and the 'whispers' rotted away in the fungus of the minds.

There was another rule in the book of Cohn, nobody but God could ring through to the stage during shooting. About eleven, in the middle of a take, the phone rang. A sudden tidal wave from a deep freezer paralyzed the set. We all knew it must be Cohn or God, in that order of probability.

Bill came running, 'Mr Cohn wants you in his office.'

'Good, tell him I'll be there when I am through with this shot.'

Not pink, but purple pink, Bill stuttered, 'I can't do that.'

'Why?'

'I can't talk to Mr Cohn and I can't tell him that.'

'Leave a message.' At snail's pace he dragged himself to the phone, we rehearsed the scene.

Disaster struck. Bill came back from the phone on the double, desperate, trying to deliver Mr Cohn's message between sneezes. 'I did –' sneeze, 'I actually –' sneeze, sneeze, sneeze. He stopped to take a deep breath. I was worried he would have a heart attack. Strands of his red hair had rebelled against the glue and were popping up like box-springs from a discarded mattress every time he sneezed. 'I actually,' more sneezes, 'I did talk to Mr Cohn –' he stopped, staring at nothing with glassy-eyed incredulity, gasping for air, 'to Mr Cohn.'

'Fine, what did he say?'

Between a flurry of sneezes, he squeezed out words – a minor miracle – 'I won't tell you, but,' I felt so sorry for him I had no time left to feel sorry for myself. Finally he sneezed out the words, 'He wants you now.' With that his choppers flew out, and Bill O'Connor turned into a red-headed Medusa on his hands and knees, looking frantically for his choppers, pleading and sneezing, 'Go, please go.'

Defiance or fear of facing my doom, I dilly-dallied and finished the scene, rehearsed the next one and learned how cattle must feel on their way to the slaughterhouse. Cohn's office door was open, flanked by the three Gorillas, watching me. The fat lady at her desk didn't waste her eye muscles looking up as she said, 'In the projection-room.'

I had been in Harry Cohn's office before, but I had never been more impressed by it. The bright sunshine through the Brussels lace on the windows on the right, the comfortable seating arrangements in front of them, inviting. In contrast, on the left, the long, sombre conference table surrounded by eighteen, twenty chairs. Beyond it, flush with the wall, was the door. My door to hell. The door to Harry Cohn's private projection-room. Opposite, in the far right corner of the large room on a quarter-circle three-feet-high pedestal, was the throne behind a massive desk. In front of it were four very comfortable armchairs but lower than the desk, just enough lower to force you to look up at 'King Cohn' on his throne. Behind the throne, in a triangular glass cabinet, golden Oscars sparkled under hidden blue lights. It was awesome. I had seen them before, but that day it seemed there were hundreds of them.

The room was longer than it ever was before, but I reached the door more quickly than I wished. I didn't have to open it, one of the Gorillas did it for me and shut it behind me.

Hostile ghosts in the dark projection-room. Coming in from the blinding glitter of the office I couldn't see anything, but I knew they were there. NASA's command post controlling a space flight would be a piker's toy compared to Harry Cohn's set-up in the center of the projection-room; it was like the flying bridge of a battle cruiser high above the mortals below him. Telephones, switches, blinking lights, buttons – he could control not only people, but machines too. He was in charge of the projectors, the sound. Harry Cohn was in charge.

I had been in the projection-room before. I didn't have to see them, I knew he was sitting up there, alone of course. I knew below, way below him sat his staff, and his flunkies. I knew the floor of the projection-room floor slanted toward the screen and was dotted with tricky stairs. I was caught off balance anyway: the minute I walked in he turned off the lights. I hung onto the doorknob.

The slate came on the screen with the pertinent information – the title of the picture, the director's name, the date, scene number and take number, 85. The second identical slate came on, except this of course had the number of my second printed take, number 87.

The long black silence was slashed suddenly by the harsh 'cleaner's lights', but only on my side of the projection-room. Muted sound of a buzzer. The door opened behind me. The shadows of the Gorillas standing in the doorway were a mile long on the projection-room floor. Cohn's voice from the darkness, disturbingly polite. 'OK. Which one do you like, Herr director?'

'Neither, Mr Cohn.' I might as well go out in glory. I added for emphasis, 'Both shit, sir, they stink.'

I felt the breath of the Gorillas on my neck, and that was the only sound in the dark room for a while.

Maybe in contrast to the long silence, maybe because of his frustrated anger, I never heard Harry Cohn's voice louder, he boomed out of the darkness. 'Get the fucking hell out'a here. You wasted enough of my money, back on the stage, ffffuck-off!'

'He knows the way,' Cohn barked at the Gorillas.

Had I said I liked the 85th or the 87th take, I would have been flying on Harry Cohn-ignited Gorilla power.

Out of the 87 takes only five were completed scenes. Cohn instructed the laboratory to substitute the slates of the 85th and 87th takes with two of the three scenes completed but not printed.

That was Hollywood. It was tough, I loved it. There were no guessing games in shooting pictures. Cohn was right to have his propulsion ready for me if after 87 takes I accepted the 40th, 31st or 57th take.

I respected Harry Cohn for his professional understanding and his love of making pictures. Cohn could be rude and crude – he often was – but never phony. I should never have left him and Allenberg and embarked on my happy 'yo-yo-years' in a make-believe world.

But from that day on nobody asked me 'Was this take necessary?' As a matter of fact, after I left Columbia and Selznick, nobody asked me anything. The truth was when anybody asked me 'How are you?' and meant it, it turned out to be a red-letter day.

This sounds maudlin and very melancholic, but those days weren't at all what they should have been; I didn't know better then. They clarified themselves after the fog of youth and conceit was devoured by time, the time that tarnished the playboy-years. Now, reflecting, without self-pity, those years were fun, I would do them again. Sometimes it is more fun making mistakes than being right and dull.

17 Dangerous Waters

He had the MGM 'Lion' by its tail in more ways than one. He had an office on Sunset Boulevard just before it was split in the middle by the bridle-path. Except between October and Christmas, when the seven acres of red poinsettias bloomed across the large bay-window in the corner of his office, his office was more Godfatherish than all the three Godfathers fused into one. As brilliantly as Brando played Corleone – as he played everything else – had Coppola known Frank Orsatti, he would have picked him for the part because he was the Godfather. There was never any void around him, he filled up everything. He was power. He used it. He knew how to use it, and as all powerbrokers he knew how to misuse it. And did. He was very selective, allegedly he meddled only with 'pro-s', like pro-hibition, pro-stitution, pro-duction – all on the highest level, of course, according to the rumor.

Coming from a good Catholic family Frank had several brothers. If he had sisters they were locked in the closet of virginal pro-priety, out of sight. Only two of his brothers were visible. Ernie was a dehydrated image of Frank, perfect casting for a 'getaway-man'. He was Frank's assistant, carrying Frank's heavy briefcases full of ? and driving the limousine. In the office Ernie was the only one authorized to answer the direct line tele-phone on Frank's desk in his absence.

The most visible Orsatti was Victor, the youngest of the family. Hand-some, flamboyant, not flashy but a big-spender. A full-time playboy, a full-time agent, a full-time pilot. Anything he did, he did full-time. I met him in the airport coffee shop in Burbank. He was an auxiliary pro-duction check-pilot at Lockheed. He took off, flew once around the field, landed, signed the paper testifying it flew and the various Allied costumers happily went to war with the equipment. If the weather was exceptionally nice and there was an exceptionally nice, fresh little buttercup to impress, he buzzed the beaches, after duly informing her of the occasion, the time and the place. And they all were always duly impressed by the test-pilot's performances in the air and subsequently on the ground, while they lasted.

'You mean you have no agent?'

'No.'

'Yes, you do. I am representing you from now on.'

I didn't take him seriously, there were a couple of stewardesses to impress within earshot. The Orsatti agency had the key to the back door of MGM, but somehow I had the feeling the lion of the trademark was the most alive, the least submerged in the Metro-Goldwyn-Mayer gloss.

'We are working with other studios too, you know,' said Victor loud enough for the stewardesses to hear him. And within fifteen minutes he was working with the stewardesses, representing Victor Orsatti, Lockheed test-pilot, with connections to the studios.

The following day, asking Tower for taxi instructions, I was advised before taking off to collect urgent and important documents from Airport Security. 'Will do,' and collected a script of *Dark Waters*, with a note – 'Fast enough?' – signed 'Vic'. 'P.S. Merle Oberon is committed to play Leslie. Immediate start.'

It was a new lesson for me, I learned that to underestimate could be more embarrassing than to over-estimate. But it was even more embarrassing to read it. The script was atrocious, an insult even to mud-heads.

That week was to be a week of surprises. The next day, out of nowhere, Alex Korda called, inviting me to luncheon. He never did that before when he should have.

I met an older Korda, one-on-one. He was edgeless, so to speak. I was on a teeter-totter. Was I facing a chameleonic Korda performance or was I talking to a real, warm, sensitive human being? The latter would be the first time throughout the years. I was hoping it would be so, I was hoping very much. But almost half a century later I still don't know.

Alex came to the point, he sometimes did, but never before that quickly: 'Merle made a mistake, I would like to help her. We are divorced, but I want to help her' – am I talking to *the* Alex Korda? – 'She made a commitment she can't get out of. The script is bloody awful – '

'– It's worse than that.'

He was surprised, scrutinized me over the rim of his glasses. He was the old Korda from Denham.

The maitre d' came, Alex studied the menu, discussed it in great detail, we ordered luncheon, then he asked, 'How do you know?'

'I was asked to direct it.'

He was fast on the trigger. 'Did you talk to Merle about it? What did you tell her?'

'No. I turned it down, I couldn't do anything with it. Can't she get out of it?'

'She doesn't want to. She wants her-her . . .' – Korda stuttered? – 'her love to photograph her – '

'– Lucien Ballard?'

This was below the belt, but I didn't mean it. He ate in silence for a while, then continued without looking up. 'You know she has this skin problem on her cheeks, she thinks, or he told her he could . . .' He faced me square, it was difficult for him but he said it, loud, 'He is not going to photograph the picture.'

'How do you know?'

'I know it.' And we ate in silence again.

The lunch was over. Korda was going through his cigar ritual when he started to speak again, quietly. Very quietly. 'Actually I didn't discover Merle. Maria did during one of her periodic and most unwelcome visits to Denham. She refused to accept our divorce was legal, final. It was over years ago.' A faraway look, his cigar stopped midway to take a puff, no tremble, 'Maria of all people. She called my attention to her in the commissary. She did. But I made Merle Oberon. She is my creation.' He took a deep breath as if he wanted to say something more, to continue, but abruptly he fell silent. For a moment I couldn't tell if the two shimmering glints were tears in his eyes or reflections in his glasses. When he continued I was sure they were tears. 'I still love Merle, I wanted to ask you to do the picture, to help her.'

I believed he loved Merle, almost as much as he loved himself. Alex Korda was human after all. The loneliest man I have ever met.

'Vic? . . . Yeah, I changed my mind. If *Dark Waters* is still open, I'll take it.'

When I got back from the phone Korda was gone. A self-conscious maitre d' ran to the table. 'Oh, Mr Korda was very sorry, he regretted very much, asked me to excuse him, suddenly he felt very ill, he had to leave . . .'

Fabrications. Alex Korda's dictionary did not contain any of those words, he didn't know them. I was sure he never said a word. I understood him. He was running away from me, running away from himself.

For a fleeting second he stood naked in front of me, in front of himself. The realization of it must have hit him hard, he didn't even pick up the check, a 'first-in-history' event.

I owed the Kordas more than a lunch.

The water was full of eddies, dead bodies, undercurrents, crocodiles and seven (!) drowning 'producers' with script pages splashing around in the sewage of *Dark Waters*: the four Nasser brothers owned General Service Studios, with ambitions to become Warner Bros; Benedict Bogeaus, handsome in a Romanian way, married to a Dodge heiress; Arthur Landau, an ex-agent crumbling under tons of photographs and scripts; and Joan Harrison, a lovely lady and a gifted screenwriter. All of them, first time in the starting gate, producers on a muddy track. Separately they were housebroken, together they became a seven-headed dragon in panic. They more sensed than knew the disaster they were facing. That the studio was available for a certain period only, that was the number-one concern of these second-hand Warner Bros – not the script? 'Merle said you'll fix it, let's get on with it,' they recited. Bogeaus had a one-track mind and that track led to the toilet of disaster. 'I'll fix it,' he threatened. Landau was shedding sawdust tears worrying about losing actors who were not right for the parts anyway. Joan, the only pro in this unholy co-op, was out-voted but hung in there, standing firm against a bunch of male chauvinists.

I admired Joan Harrison, beside her talent she had guts. I supposed that was what the six resented. 'We have a woman "producer". I hope it will not offend you,' said Bogeaus during our first dinner in his pseudo-baronial hall in Beverly Hills, California, à la *Henry VIII* Vincent Korda dining-room set in Denham, England.

'What's wrong with women producers?' asked his heiress wife with a formidable frown.

'Nothing, dear, as long as they are producing children.' He couldn't reach her hand, the seats around the table were too far apart. He walked over to kiss her pudgy, ring-bedecked fingers. All ten of them; separating the syllables with his kisses. 'Like-you-will-my-dar-ling.'

'Eeh-heeh-heee,' she giggled.

The dinner was too good to throw up.

It was clear what I was to face, and Joan made it easier. The script needed a rewrite, we both knew it; John Huston needed money, everybody knew it. The horses were running. Joan had her hands full countermanding six asinine orders in order to keep the production's lifeline open. I was shooting. According to Jules Buck (a gentleman in black silk suits, Sulka ties, and perennial cigars protruding from every one of his body openings, who was a confidant of John Huston) John was free, betrayed by the horses and happy to go ahead. Selfish as it was, Joan and I were happy too; the other six were not, but gentle blackmail, or call it diplomacy, worked.

'OK. Out of the hundred and twenty pages how many do you want rewritten?'

'Oh, eighty or so,' piped up Jules Buck unexpectedly.

The old air-conditioning unit hanging on the window always rattled; now the heartbeats of the six gave louder warning their service life was about coming to an end.

'Eighty?' they tremoloed. 'And what will be our guarantee if he hits a long shot he will not walk out on us? You can't trust anybody.'

Pompous as a courting turkey cock, Landau piped up, 'I took care of that, I have a safety valve for that, but eighty pages?'

I was not aware Jules Buck and Landau had 'tentatively' agreed that John was to be paid per page, half of the estimated pages to be paid up front. Finally they agreed on a sixty page minimum guarantee, but to be paid per page as delivered. Provided I approved the pages.

John was John, big, expansive. The talent that oozed out of him and flushed down the toilet was more than many were praying for and never were blessed with. What a joy it was to have fun with him and Joan. It wasn't work. We discussed at night my requirements for the next day, Jules delivered the pages in the morning, I initialed them, he collected the cash which John left on the track by mid-afternoon. After that he came on the set with Joan.

'I think, kid, we'll need an awful lot of pages for tomorrow.' He leaned close and told me a secret everybody could hear from my ear to Amarillo, Texas, 'Sure a tip, a long shot. What do you think, kid?' Joan was shivering. She had given birth to this Machiavellian arrangement and was to be the recipient of its blunt end if –

I was disconnected. I didn't ask any of the six not to come on the set while I was shooting. I was too well brought up to be so rude. Curiosity, not politeness killed the cat, I was well aware of that, but I took a chance whenever any of them came to hover. My father and General Szirmay would have said, 'Kick'em out.' Mother would have been very proud of my good manners. I asked props to bring up a few chairs. I made them sit down, 'Are these chairs comfortable enough? No, oh no. Props, please bring something better for the chiefs, thanks.' Then my known curiosity took over and I asked question after question, from their dogs' bowel movement to the fluctuation of the stock market, about their and their neighbours' health. When they wanted to leave I retained them, 'Please, stay, it's great to have you here.' The propman was well trained and shoved the chair against the back of their knees, their legs buckled, they sat. When they ostentatiously checked their diamond sprinkled watches to call my attention to the time I usually made them feel easy with 'Don't worry, you're not holding me up,' and as an afterthought I added, 'Oh, overtime won't start till . . .' and that always did it. Couldn't have hog-tied them to stay for another second.

Jules was late, unusual. I was already winging the first set-up. 'Do I – no, actually John has a surprise for you.' He fanned a big stack of pages in front of me, then carefully selected a few pages, 'These are the scenes in this set, as you discussed. Check them over.' I glanced at the pages he handed to me; no surprises, the scenes were good. I had no time to check the rest of the pages, I initialled the top sheet, Jules was off, and I continued shooting.

I like a quiet set, and it was quiet, maybe more than usual, but I was too involved to notice that I was being watched by cast and crew alike. As I was looking through the camera the operator whispered, 'Look behind you.' I did. Lined up against the stage wall, as if they were waiting for the firing squad to relinquish them from the joys of living, were the six, all six of them. Before slinking into the shadows between a fireplace on wheels and a cupboard Joan, as a signal, drew her fingers across her throat. The propman and his helpers were lined up like sprinters on the starting line of a hundred-meter dash, waiting for the gun, ready to move with the chairs. Jim, the senior and most sensible of the Nasser Bros, politely declined the lurking comfort, 'No chairs, please.'

As we walked into my trailer, all started to speak at once, pointing at the pages each had in their hand.

'Hold it, please. It must be something serious, otherwise you wouldn't hold up shooting. Let's get Joan,' I asked them, then, without asking for the reason for the honor of their presence, I went into the bathroom and left them in their stew, whatever that was.

I knew Joan had arrived because the crosstalk flared up in force. I joined them and I was defeated, unable to convince them to talk one at a time. Like a burst dam they were flooding me with jumbled sentences, most of them starting with 'Why?' I believed Joan suffered more than the six did. In a way she was responsible for Jules. He was her friend. But, in fact, the sure tip on the long shot was responsible solely for the momentary tragedy.

'Why did you change the name of the characters? The new scenes are good, but where do they fit? Do we have to build all those new sets? How many days will this add to the schedule? . . . We'll be ruined,' lamented Jimmy. 'Please, don't run away with our trust.' Finally silence. They were all spent.

I was perplexed. From the desk I picked up my copy of John's whole new batch which I had not read before. I read them all now, carefully, all twenty-eight pages, and couldn't stop laughing. John was a genius!

'Please, don't laugh, it's a tragedy, we're wasting all this time, terrible,' whimpered the youngest of the Nasser Bros. 'Terrible, we paid him for all twenty-eight useless pages, he blew my safety valve,' mourned Landau.

'Not all of it is useless, part of it was already shot today,' Bogeaus put his two cents in the pot of discontent.

I left them in the trailer. Joan caught up with me, 'What now?'

'John needed the money so he padded the script with twenty-one pages from *The Maltese Falcon*. No problem, I have enough to shoot for two more days, by then John will deliver.'

And that he did, of course, but the long-shot was still running, with the twenty-one pages worth of 'advance' from *Dark Waters* on the nose.

The waters were dangerous, the deadly white streak of a torpedo flashed through beneath the waves. The white streak became a blurred image of newspapers whizzing through the press. The news. Headlines. Another ship torpedoed. Few survivors picked up after fourteen days in the stormy seas. White. Out of the whiteness of a hospital pillow one of the survivors, Leslie Calvin/Merle Oberon sits up into an extreme close-shot. Her face is haggard, it reflects every hour of the fourteen days of the watery hell in a lifeboat. A scene not to be 'played', to be 'felt'. Lived through again as it was spoken.

'Have you ever been at a funeral where the minister forgot the service?' were Merle's first lines. I wrote them, I still remember. She was superb, her skin problem was working for her, she wasn't acting, she was the survivor who lived through the fourteen days in a lifeboat, with bodies being dumped overboard around her. Her eyes were frozen, glassy, set deep in her face, a weather-beaten, white, marble statue. Without moving a muscle tears rolled down her parched cheeks.

That was the first take on the first day of shooting *Dark Waters*. She was applauded, but without it she knew she was good. She pulled me down to sit next to her on the bed. She hugged me and she trembled, saying, 'Thanks.' I didn't know why, but it made me feel good, we were off to a good start.

I went back to the camera to check, but before I reached it she called me: 'Please, can I have it once more?'

My reply was prompt, 'Sure. Once more.' I was impressed by her desire to do better. It was fine with me, but after the eleventh 'Please, may I have it once more?' I felt she was draining me down the toilet. I was an unknown director, working with a strange crew, I looked like a puppet director, their respect was ebbing away.

After the twenty-second take I noticed that my seven producers, yes, the six and Joan, were lurking behind the set exchanging meaningful glances. Then I noticed him – handsome, confident and elegant – Lucien Ballard, a great cameraman and Merle's heart-throb, who was her choice to shoot *Dark Waters*.

I wanted Merle to look straight into the camera, which was one of the picture-making no-nos at that time. I wanted her to ask the question to the audience, 'Have you ever . . .?', involve the viewer one-to-one, so to speak. But she turned her head, changed her look up, down, left, right, various degrees every take. After the thirty-fifth take, to end this charade I applauded, but I was alone. That didn't work. 'Once more, please.'

I had never felt so small, so useless in my life. After I broke my neck the third time, with four screws in my skull, and weights on my ankles stretched out like a buffalo skin in the sun to dry, I felt more in command. It would have been easy to say, no! I quit. Patience. I had the solution.

After the fortieth take Merle smiled, she thanked me, she was happy, the fainting seven producers were very happy. I decided to make Merle even happier. I opened the camera, pulled out the exposed negative of the last, the fortieth take, wrapped it around her neck, 'You were happy with this, I want you to have it,' and kissed her cheek. She never again asked, 'Once more, please.'

It took me some time to catch on, long after everybody else did on the set. It all happened behind my back, all I noticed was that she never looked at me after a take, but I gave her the benefit of the doubt, she was embarrassed to ask again, 'Once more.' I should have been sharper. Johnny Mescal, the cameraman who started the picture, asked me quite obviously after the twentieth take, 'Should I change the lighting?' It slipped by me, I said, 'No, why?' That, after the thirtieth take, Mescal stomped on his hat, I took for the manifestation of alcohol mixed with his famous temperament. That he hated Lucien, a similar class, sensitive, fine cameraman, added to Mescal's explosion.

Lucien was in love with Merle, he wanted her to look the best under the circumstances; I was in love with making pictures, I was after reality, to show the transformation, the mental and physical development of the character after her terrible ordeal. I wanted her to look as horrible as possible. After every take Merle looked at Lucien at the back, he directed her from there. If he shook his head, no, she asked for another take and followed his head movements, he was trying to make her catch a more flattering light.

It was fun making pictures. I never heard anybody complain that it was boring. I was sure it was not boring for my seven producers. I was never bored in my life, there was always a chance to get into trouble and now there was Victor to help me. He did.

'Not because I represent her, I give you my word, no. Wait till you meet her. She is going to be the biggest star ever, wait till you meet her.' With an assuring gesture he informed me, 'She is just divorced.'

I was ready to play, I didn't want to save my money for my old age when I wouldn't know what to do with it. Or worse yet, how!

'When?' Mistake number one. Many more to come.

'Tonight, at eight, La Rue.'[1]

We met. She was petite, very pretty and vulnerable. Tough because she was scared and had been hurt too often. Smoked like a chimney, drank like a fish. She had a sense of humor but there was something sad about her. She filled the room with a silent cry for help, and nobody heard it. I sat with a star who was born to die.

A week after we got married Victor turned on the cold shower while I was in a tuxedo. 'She owes us ten thousand dollars, you're her husband, are you responsible?' We were at Romanoff's,[2] a restaurant I liked and

1 La Rue. Subdued, expensive, elegant, it was one of the 'in' places of the period on the Sunset Strip at Sunset Plaza Drive.
2 Mike Romanoff (1893–1971) was the self-proclaimed half-brother to Czar Nicholas, and ran a very plush and popular Beverly Hills restaurant from 1940–62. In reality he was born Harry Greguson in Brooklyn, New York, where he started his career before becoming a prince in Hollywood as a pants-presser in the garment district of New York. That is America, where dreams can come true.

didn't want to be barred from. Victor's straight nose and china-white teeth for the time being stayed intact. 'Frank thinks so, but don't worry, I have a way, we are friends, right? Not only it won't cost you any cash, you will make a thousand on it. OK?

The bizzare, the macabre thwarted my revulsion. I decided to play it their way. 'Whom do I have to kill for the thousand?'

He liked that, he laughed, 'We could handle that,' and ordered two more martinis. 'The dinner is on me.'

'I hope so, because I am going to eat a lot so when I get home I can throw up.'

He didn't quite get it, but he thought, 'It's funny. Now, there is an agent who wants to take over your contract with us for ten thousand dollars. Ten grand, strange coincidence, good omen. We're friends, right. So it won't cost you any cash. You have to agree, of course, and that's where the thousand comes in. If you agree you wipe out her debt. To prove we're friends we'll accept nine from the ten and tear off a grand for you. Cash if you want cash. OK?'

'Who is the agent?, I want to know.'

'Sam Jaffe.[3]

'A deal. I want the check, now.'

He got up from the table without a word. I finished my drink and asked for the check. He intercepted the waiter on his way back to the table, grabbed the check off the tray, 'I told you, dinner is on me.' He sat down, 'What's your sudden hurry? Your check will be here within thirty minutes.'

It was.

I had never met Sam Jaffe. When I did, I gave him the check.

'What is this?'

'It is a check for a thousand dollars from the Orsatti office, for cash.'

'I can see that.'

I told him what happened. 'Do you have a favorite charity?'

His was the same. Roosevelt's March of Dimes was the vogue, that is where it went.

I had barely closed the front door behind me when she descended the

---

3 Sam Jaffe (1901–85) was involved in production before becoming a partner in Schulberg-Feldman-Jaffe talent agency in 1934. The following year, he formed his own agency, Sam Jaffe Inc., which he ran until returning to production in 1959. He was an art connoisseur and collector.

stairs. Was it coincidence or was she lying in wait? She was stunning, as always. An unreadable blond sphinx.

'I'll fix you a drink.' She was good at that. Too good. She came to the point as usual; an admirable trait she employed only when it was harmful, to herself mostly. 'Do you have a thousand dollars, cash? Now.'

I added this query to her long list of surprises, I did not ask what for; experience taught me she would dish out some more. She fired her next question.

'Do you want to adopt her?'

In spite of the fact I was aware of her bag-full of inexhaustible surprises she scored. Bull's eye. She knew how much I adored – and still do – her little girl from a previous marriage and how badly I wanted to adopt her, but the mixture of a thousand now and adoption puzzled me. I didn't have to ask a question.

'Her father is in town, I saw him this afternoon. Finally he will sign the adoption papers. Thank God, he needs money and for a thousand, now. Cash.'

'It's late. A check for cash is the best I could do right now. Why now? Tomorrow morning when the banks – '

'I don't want him to change his mind.' She pulled out a stack of papers, 'Sign above the "X's".' She was in a hurry. She handed me a pen, shoved one paper after another in front of me. 'I'll try a check for cash, a thousand.'

I signed it. She was radiant, she smiled, 'You got her easier than giving birth to her. See you later,' and she was gone.

I understood her elation, I was just as happy and went into the nursery to play with my COD baby.

It took me some time to find out where the money went. Then it was strange how within an hour two one-thousand dollar checks brought me what I wanted. More later.

I believe beside luck the single most important factor of success in pictures hinges on having a good, creative and dedicated agent on your side. Of course, the lightning of success can strike without an agent. That is not luck, that could be an accident.

Many had tried but no book could describe, do justice to what the 'Garden of Allah' really was. To begin with, it seemed inappropriate to call it the 'Garden of Allah' when it was a place where alcohol flowed as freely as waters over Niagara Falls. The truth is: 'The desert is the only Garden of Allah from which the Lord of the Faithful removed all superfluous human and animal life so that there might be one place where he can walk in peace.' On the corner of Sunset and Crescent Heights? Please! Even Hollywood couldn't be that sacriligious. The place was built and owned by the highest paid star of the silent era – $13,000 a week – Alla Nazimova, and the painter who put up the sign thought her name was spelled with an 'h'. Nobody noticed it, and this spelling error didn't stop Natasha Rambova from marrying Rudolph Valentino there. I boycott McDonald's because they defiled the Garden of Allah's once sacred grounds. It was the nest of glorious sins, the birthplace of fledgling geniuses, the shelter for the living dead of the world cinema, the burial grounds for those who burned the candle at both ends. An unholy commune.

'Where in the hell have you been?' asked John Ford as I entered the watering hole of the 'Garden of Allah'. Now, by 'watering hole' I don't mean the pool, which was large and usually dirty, and in spite of the fact he was serving in the US Navy, he hated water in any form. 'You're making us late.'

'Us late, where? To my recollection – '

'Let's go.' And he drove. Drove? If what he was doing could have been called driving. Ford was the 'boss', the captain of the ship; one of the most positive, decisive men on the set and in life in general except in an automobile; there, he was not in charge. He didn't drive the car, the car was the boss. But his car couldn't read and was color-blind, so stop signs, red, yellow and green lights meant nothing to Ford's car, it sailed through all that kind of nonsense. John Ford's car was a speed maniac.

Without losing our steady speed we turned right off Melrose onto Bronson and immediately left through a studio gate where the guards were scrambling for their lives. I closed my one eye, not wanting to lose it from the flying debris as we were about to arrive on a stage right through its wall which was in front of us. No! Defying the centrifugal forces, a 90° turn to the right and we were heading straight again, stopping as gently as hitting a cement bulwark, in a red-marked 'fire zone' an inch from the entrance to a low Spanish bungalow, in Enterprise Studios.[4]

---

4 Enterprise Productions Inc. was founded by David Loew and Charles Einfeld, to make high quality motion pictures with a different approach, and produced more than a dozen films, the first and second being Andre de Toth's *Ramrod* and the *Other Love* (both released in 1947). The Company suffered a disastrous loss as a result of its big budget production of *Arch of Triumph* (1948), starring Charles Boyer and Ingrid Bergman; it ceased operations in 1948 and its assets were acquired by the Bank of America in 1951.

Ford turned the ignition key the wrong way, and before the starter's shriek for help died he was out of his kamikaze vehicle. 'Come on, what are you waiting for?' were his first words since we left the 'Garden of Allah'. A friend is a friend, I had followed him from the 'Garden of Allah' without question, why not now. Nothing could be worse than the ride. As he strode through three offices I was wondering, who copied whom? Wayne did Ford, or vice-versa? What Ford lacked in mass he made up for with speed. They both moved impressively.

It was a large bright office, pastel colors. The beige leatherbound books on the shelves were pertinent, not bought by the yard for decoration. Two identical desks with silver accessories. Flowers in Baccarat vases, fresh fruit in baskets on coffee tables. Good lamps. Subdued, quiet elegance. Hibernating bears in their lairs would have been awakened by Ford's arrival. 'Hi, Charlie – David.' As skinny as he was, Ford filled the room. He was in command. Two gentlemen rose from behind their desks. Charlie Einfeld and David Loew.

'Glad you could make it, Jack,' said Einfeld.

'We appreciate it,' added Loew.

Ford nodded his head toward me, I was hanging back by the door, 'He kept me waiting.' I received curious glances and restrained, polite smiles. Ford introduced me and added 'Tommy Mitchell[5] saddled me with him.' The door opened behind me, a butler in a dark suit wearing white gloves guided in a mahogany trolley; on it a tray of petit-fours and a Herendi porcelain coffee service for four! Since they certainly did not expect me, most efficient and elegant. Memories of my first visit to Korda in Denham.

Einfeld and Loew were heading toward the comfortable armchairs in a corner, I followed them politely, Ford didn't move. 'Jack – ?' gestured Einfeld invitingly, but Jack was heading back toward the door. Confused, I tentatively moved toward him. 'You stay,' as he held onto the doorknob. 'Charlie, David, he is going to direct *Ramrod*, I can't get rid of my commitment. Talk to him, give him a script, I lost mine. He'll be all right,' and the door closed behind John Ford, the man known for surprises. The three of us stood there, dumbfounded.

The shock of my being there slowly wore off. To my lesser surprise the

5 Thomas Mitchell (1892–1962) was a memorable character actor on screen from the 1920s to the 1960s. He was Scarlett O'Hara's father in *Gone With The Wind* and won an Academy Award for his role as a drunken doctor in John Ford's *Stagecoach*.

coffee in the Herendi porcelain service turned out to be tea; after a cup of it Einfeld excused himself and left the room, Loew gave me a script of *Ramrod*. I thanked him for it, ready to leave, he asked me to stay on. An ever so gentle inquisition, what do I know about the west? Who was my favorite western author? Strike one. An extremely well-read man, Loew had never heard of Karl May. He dug deeper, who was my favorite western star? Did I ride? Where did I learn to ride? And a thousand more questions before Einfeld came back.

An afternoon of surprises, Loew recited my history from Hollywood, Florida to riding the range for Eddie Cline, to Thomas Mitchell working with me on *Dark Waters*, which they had luckily both liked.

'But that is not, not a western!' said with finality a disgruntled Pop Sherman, the uncrowned king of the Alabama Flats, above Lone Pine and below Mount Whitney in the High Sierras. He was the producer on *Ramrod*, a lovely man, who was born old. I liked him. I didn't think he disliked me, he just didn't know into which of the small square boxes in his brain he could fit me. It bugged him, I bugged him.

He knew the west, the only west where villians – always in black, at least in black hats – charged from the left and never won the final battle; the good guys in white hats rode to victory from the right. His modest-budget westerns with venerable 'Bill Boyd – Hopalong Cassidy' on a white horse, of course, always fresh from the dry cleaners, shiny and unreal, were utopian entertainment, making money. So, he was right. In Pop's world the women of the west fell into two major categories: first, the lovely-dull schoolmarms and dishwater-dull housewives; second, the frowned-upon easy girls. Only in Ford's classic, break-through western, *Stagecoach*, were the 'whore ladies' (as Michael Curtiz called them), like Claire Trevor, allowed to have golden hearts. Heroes couldn't waver, they never made love, were not allowed to take off their spurs, day or night, even when stalking their foes. It was not stupid to keep them on, jingling on the rocks and giving away their presence, it was sporting. Pop didn't take off his spurs either while stalking me. I respected him for that. He was a gentleman in a never-land of Quixotic grandeur. The passing time was his windmill. His films were far above their class, but their high gloss couldn't hide the never-land of fable – real life in Pop's mind – where the characters lived.

I was looking at life, reality, through a microscope. We were a basic mismatch. It hurt him and I felt for him more deeply than he ever imagined. I wanted to get off the picture. Ford put an end to that with a lengthy argument. 'No, you can't let me down, fuck 'em all, do it!' That was it, that was all he said. That was his argument.

He won, I stayed. Pop and I agreed to disagree on the two main characters, we saw two different stories. I was looking for a human being, not a powerful locomotive speeding through the night without lights and without giving a thought that the tracks ahead may be broken. Someone who was vulnerable. 'A vulnerable western hero! No, never!' moaned Pop, and shuddered as he accepted for the female part a wicked, conniving lady, stronger than a man, with velvet balls.[6] Pop still had the pre-*Stagecoach* mentality living in utopia, but he was a true-blue professional. With tears in his eyes he pitched in to help. Shalom, Pop!

It was five-fifteen, I didn't have to look at my watch, I knew it. My office door opened, as it did every day, and the butler, white gloves and all, rolled in the trolley stocked from vodka to caviar, from foie gras to champagne, from prosciutto and melon to salami, liverwurst and cheeses, gin, Jack Daniel's and various other poisons welcomed up and down the corridor. The afternoon trolley was more enticing than the ten-thirty morning arrival. Enterprise Studios, Einfeld and David Loew knew how to spoil us.

One afternoon the butler handed me an extra encouragement. A screen-play based on an Eric Maria Remarque short story, 'The Other Love', and a note, '. . . Please, read it overnight . . .' I did. I found out Einfeld and Loew had to confirm a Barbara Stanwyck commitment the following day. Would I do the picture with her in the lead? What a question. Would I? But in the rush they had forgotten to mention, or they weren't told by the producer – whom I didn't know – that he had already committed an actor for a major part and a lady for a lesser role. The Ladislas Fodor script gave no big problem, but the lady and the gentleman did.

Barbara Stanwyck, the pro of all pros, was bulging with talent, but not with breasts. Nature tried to make up for the producer's find's lack of talent with two enormous bulges. They were so grotesque I had photo-graphed her from as far, far away as possible without getting her off the set. Even then never in profile. The producer was upset with me, bouncing between the floor and the ceiling, and I was sure he would wear out the ceiling before the carpet. When his trembling fingers found his mouth he

6 The two parts were played by Joel McCrea and Veronica Lake.

took such quick, deep drags from his ever-present cigarette that I was sure it was a question of time before he sucked in his burning cigarette and his fist with it. I had my fingers crossed it would happen.

'Why, why-why are you doing this to her? You are a pro, you are . . .' and he whined on and on in falsetto; his protegée complained I was sabotaging her talent, and destroying her future.

I assured him, 'I was destroying nothing if she thought her only talent, nature's only gift, was what looked like the two cantaloupe-size wads of kapok where her breasts did not exist.'

'How do you know?' he snapped. Professional curiosity. It couldn't have been jealousy. 'Come on down next time we have a scene with her.' Satisfied, he dropped anchor and sat down while we were discussing less important matters, like being behind schedule.

He was no dope, he had taste, talent and tons of neuroses which wiped it all out. And in the end it helped to wipe out Enterprise Studios, the entire beautiful Einfeld-Loew empire.

He was uncomfortable on the set. He stood next to me, watching the scene. For the first time she was close to the camera and in profile which surprised everybody, except her. She whispered a meaningful 'Thanks,' to the producer, loud enough to be heard.

After the take and a 'Hm, I see,' the producer wanted to leave.

'Please, stay for a minute – wardrobe.' She was right there, she knew I had tried it before.

'Pull it out, please.'

She pulled out a six-inch drapery pin I had stuck into her sex appeal. The pin never touched her talent. It was my turn to say my thanks, as I handed the pin over to the producer. Barbara hugged me with her thanks and added, 'It bugged me too, the bitch.' But she had never let anybody know that it bothered her.

That was Barbara Stanwyck. Only David Niven was heartbroken, 'My, I am so gullible,' he sighed.

We all were, thinking Enterprise would last forever. It was too civilized, too good to be true.

18   Monkeys, Tyrants and Slave-drivers

A gravely-ill Roosevelt in Yalta, against Churchill's advice, accepted Stalin's plan, and sowed the seeds of the Cold War. He lived just long enough to see the Marines raise the flag on Iwo Jima's Mt Suribachi. Within a month of Roosevelt's death Italian partisans captured and executed Mussolini; Hitler committed suicide in his bunker under the Reich Chancellery in Berlin; the following week Germany surrendered.

Colonel Daryl F. Zanuck was fighting the war from his HQ in Paris, the Hotel Plaza Athéné. In Hollywood the 20th Century-Fox studio was a more dangerous battleground. When Zanuck went to war, Bill Goetz substituted for him and led the studio from victory to victory on the box-office front and on the slippery field of awards. Having a reliable crystal ball or being an astute politician, he resigned from Fox before the end of the war.[1]

After his departure the battle for Zanuck's throne was on. Bill Perlberg[2] was riding high on the crest of the Hollywood wave and with General Patton's speed, audacity and cavalry tactics simply occupied Zanuck's office to the dismay of Fred Kohlmer,[3] another aspirant, a senior producer on the lot but no hero, who did the next best thing, moved into Perlberg's old office. They smoked a peace pipe and other equally healthy substances thinking they would live happily ever after.

Then unexpected tragedy struck. Truman pushed the button, the war

1 Bill Goetz (1903–63), a son-in-law of MGM's boss Louis B. Mayer, joined Fox in 1930. During WWII he substituted for Zanuck but he never occupied his offices.
2 William Perlberg (1899–1969). An erstwhile agent, then Harry Cohn's personal assistant. Producer from 1936 with Academy Awards and many commercial successes to his credit. His films of great variety included: *Golden Boy*, *Charley's Aunt*, *Coney Island*, *The Song of Bernadette*, *Miracle on 34th Street*, *Forever Amber*, *Wabash Avenue*, etc.
3 Fred Kohlmer (1905–69) was a former agent, Samuel Goldwyn's executive assistant before becoming a producer in the late 1930s. His films vary from 'Bs' to small 'As'.

was over; Zanuck's mop-up operation in Paris was coming to an end. But Zanuck lingered on in France and the news, mixed with eucalyptus oil and sweat, filtered through the pores in the sauna baths of Finlandia on Sunset Strip; Zanuck might not come back at all. That was just fine with Perlberg, in Zanuck's office, remodeled to suit his taste. Fred Kohlmer sat in Perlberg's old office, redone to suit his own kinky taste.

The mushroom of the atom bomb was only a flash of a match compared to the news one Thursday: Zanuck would be back the following Monday. Only the moths chewing on Zanuck's rugs and the termites devouring his polo mallets in a backlot storage were more unhappy than Perlberg. Fred Kohlmer, smug, in Perlberg's office was as happy as the crafts were, working on golden hours overtime all through the weekend to carefully restore Colonel Zanuck's office to its original state without a tell-tale sign that it had ever been touched. Naïveté! But all was ready by Monday.

Zanuck didn't show up, that kept everybody on edge. The frizzled nerves on the lot were more visible than fringes on the top of a surrey on a bumpy road. Under these ideal conditions, on that Monday, I started my assignment on a strange lot on the script of *Slattery's Hurricane*, hired by Bill Perlberg. It felt like I wasn't in the right place at the right time! Luck? Bad timing?

Perlberg, upset by Zanuck's return and the thought of being stuck in a lousy office, had a chip on his shoulder. He was not in the most receptive mood for anything. I knew before I opened my mouth his answer would be no. I had to fight him for everything except for the check at lunch in the commissary. The toughest battle was to get Bill Bowers on the screenplay. His talent was always acknowledged, but the fame of his douche-bag had superseded his other attributes. I swore Bill had seen the light, he was so dry he was eligible for canonization by the AA; then Bill swore the malicious old rumors were unfounded, people could change; then Perlberg asked Bill to give me, his friend, in front of him, his word of honor he wouldn't touch a glass until the screenplay was delivered. Bill complied, and finally he was on the picture, and he was keeping his word.

To Perlberg's great concern Bill's word not only didn't cure his cough, but made it worse. The seizures lasted longer and when they became more violent he stuck his head deeper under the side of his jacket and covered his head with his lapel. But the attacks couldn't have hurt him because after the fourth or fifth spell he surfaced with an angelic smile on his lived-in face. Perlberg was hugging him every day more and more often, feeling for the douche-bag in Bill's breast pocket. Nothing. But Perlberg said one day with thoughtful suspicion, 'The son-of-a-bitch is getting loaded, but how? We are with him all the time during the day. He looks sober in the morning. I don't know . . .'

I told Bill about Perlberg's suspicion and asked him point blank, 'Are you drinking?'

'Would I do that to you?' He made me ashamed for the question. 'How can you ask me that? How could you think I would break my word? My word to you, my friend. I never touched a glass since I promised you I wouldn't.'

He made me feel terrible. With clear conscience I guaranteed Perlberg: Bill was keeping his word. He was a gentleman, and a friend.

Carelessness causes many disasters, it strikes quick, leaving grief and devastation in its wake. Bill's misfortune caught us without warning. A minute before we all were happy, ready to start the morning story conference, when it hit. At ease and with unrestrained abandon Bill threw himself back into his chair across from us. Then it happened. Because of the sudden pressure Bill's derrière exerted on his 'busmen's friend' through a thin IV tube attached to it vodka squirted as high as the ceiling and rained upon us instead of violets. No wonder Perlberg could not find the douche-bag in an inside pocket of Bill's jacket. Bill's life-line of inspiration was attached from his 'busmen's friend', strapped to his crotch between his legs, then hidden behind his wide braces high enough for him to reach it.

Wordless, Bill got to his feet, collected his papers from the table, left the room, the studio and his self-respect for being caught, as clever as he was. They all are clever deceivers if they are ashamed of their different monkeys on their backs. What makes it easier for them is that we want to believe them, desperately.

Bill was out. He was a simpleton compared to someone else I had to carry through the picture. Her two monkeys were hiding in squeezed empty toothpaste tubes in her bathroom, needles behind picture frames on the walls. Those monkeys caused more devastation than the real hurricane did in *Slattery's Hurricane*, but they changed the title for me of the Barney Ross story from *God Was In My Corner* to *Monkey On My Back*.[4]

4 Barney Ross was a legend in his own time in the ring, holder of several world championships, some categories simultaneously. Enlisted in WWII. A combat-decorated Marine sergeant wounded on Guadalcanal. Allegedly the monkey climbed on his back because of field-administered morphine to ease his pain.

Slattery's Hurricane started with a bumpy ride. I felt wetter from a few drops of vodka in Perlberg's office that day than flying into the eye of the hurricane from Opalacka naval base in Florida in old leaking PB4Ys. That was easier to take, I expected that. Actually after a while even that became fun, betting on which one of the four engines the rain would short out.

Zanuck arrived, then came the repeat of the 'Selznick treatment' – my first meeting with him. By then it was old news in Hollywood that for a large number of those unfortunates hired during Zanuck's war years the only hope was to cross the rough years of joblessness in a leaking dinghy with a pink slip for sail. And the seas were turbulent, the air was jammed with frantic SOS signals.

Zanuck and Selznick were very similar in many ways. Both in love with making pictures. Both were inclined to over-season their chef d'oeuvre. Selznick used a bulldozer to reach his goal, Zanuck a razor. Zanuck developed from Rin-Tin-Tins and German Shepherds to horses – playing polo, badly – but he had courage and tried. Selznick wanted to be looked upon as a unique exhibit in the window. Zanuck wanted to be part of, belong to the élite, not a curiosity, a famous freak on display. I wouldn't have trusted either of them with my life and now I was in Zanuck's hands for the next six or seven months anyway.

The phone rang: 'Sorry, Mr de Toth, Mr Zanuck is tied up, but he wants to see you tomorrow. The same time, two-thirty.' The same message for the fourth consecutive day, came at the same time, at two-fifteen. But tomorrow was Saturday.

'Don't come in tomorrow, I won't be coming in either.' I took Perlberg's advice, I didn't go in, I was looking for a life-jacket during the weekend. On Monday my hand was resting on the phone all morning. No call. Two-twenty, no call. Two-twenty-five, it rang. 'I'll see you downstairs,' said Perlberg.

Zanuck's two-sectioned office was a bizarre mixture of subdued elegance spiked with out-of-place, show-off safari mementos, trophies, pieces more befitting a stable, garish junk, good paintings; it was an absurd combination, still one felt good in it.

Selznick dressed like a bum, Korda like a British banker, Zanuck like an international playboy – not a gigolo, one with money. He was an elegant show-off, without intending to be one. He was a fox and he was the hunter, rough without showing the edges. The more I knew him the more I respected him; I liked him. The first thing I learned through my first-hand experience with Zanuck was how those fakirs I saw in India felt walking over broken glass, nails, fire and cow dung. He made me go through all that.

Before this, the first story meeting with Zanuck, we had ironed out all our story differences and production wrinkles. 'Watch it,' Perlberg warned me, 'he is funny, he wants to be sure we believe in what we want to do. If he objects to some of the points we have agreed upon, just speak up.'

The first blow came before we sat down. With too obvious innocence he asked Perlberg, 'Why did you switch offices with Fred? I thought your office was much better, more prestigious.'

He waited for no answer from Perlberg, asked me, 'How did you like working for Selznick?'

'I enjoyed working with him, short as it was.'

He was sharp, he got it. 'You like to work with people?'

'Sure, as a director I have to work with them.'

'I see,' he said.

Perlberg was morose, puffing on his cigarettes – the plural here meant he always had several lit. After a few deep puffs he left them abandoned, smouldering in ashtrays all over, but he rarely picked them up again. Perlberg had a fetish for lighting cigarettes. Zanuck was a neat smoker. His torpedo-size cigar was between his buck-teeth perpetually, except when playing polo – he tried that once but it backfired on him. Being a connoisseur of alcohol beverages and a true gourmet, he relinquished his symbol of manhood during mealtimes. There was a rumor he couldn't make love without having his cigar in his mouth.

With my inexperience, political non-savvy and eagerness to impress I started off according to Perlberg's instruction, 'Just speak up.' I did. I was championing a point which actually was Perlberg's idea and we had agreed to fight for it if Zanuck objected; it was a must for us. To my great pride and satisfaction Zanuck was agreeing with me down the line, a first-round victory, until Perlberg said a loud and clear 'No, absolutely not!' with emphasis.

I was defeated; I suffered in silence as their battle royale of hurt egos raged on in the smoke-saturated office for weeks – two, three hours a day. If Zanuck said 'yeah' to anything, Perlberg's 'nay' was immediate, and vice-versa. I had no desire to get involved in this futile venom-venting. And that cost me a lot.

I had never smoked in my life, and never since. In self-defense I took up pipe-smoking, being the most involved mode of self-destruction. I never dreamed how expensive it would be. A small fortune. For pipes? There was *the* London Shoppe on the north-west corner of Beverly Drive and Brighton Way – the deluxe nightmare bazaars of today's Rodeo Drive didn't exist then. My office called the Shoppe and they kept it open till I was through for the day in the studio.

'I would like to have six pipes, the best you have.' A choir of salesmen responded, 'Yes, sir, certainly,' as if that was the minimum order of pipes one should buy. They weren't impressed at all. I wanted to impress them and added, 'Make it a dozen, please.' The salesmen waiting on me stopped their motions in mid-air, stared at me, then the one's 'Certainly,' overrode the other's 'Are you sure, sir?'

Beside the twelve pipes, I acquired a three-pronged, gold pipe-cleaner-scraper-tobacco-tapper instrument, several different pouches for various occasions, gold snap-on protection covers so the pipes would function 'perfectly' during high winds and be kept dry during rainstorms, six pounds of Christian Pepper Crumble-plug – a finger-thick two-square-inch compressed tobacco block – 'for beginners the best and the easiest to handle', I was assured.

The salesmen carried the boxes to my car and they were still shaking their heads as I drove off. By then I was shaking it too, being $2,168 poorer. But wiser. I learned something about straight-grain, cross-grain, briar, silver and gold connection bands for the pipe stems; rum and honey were the best to 'break in' the lethal weapons. I was told about an ingenious 'smoking machine' that would turn the harsh white of my new Meerschaum pipe into the warm, mellow amber color, identical to the color of the centuries-old carved masterpieces in museums, and only in six to eight months instead of centuries. 'Guaranteed.' It was reassuring I didn't have to wait that long and I left my future museum piece with the Shoppe. Never picked it up.

They had no 'smoking machine' for sale and I had eleven pipes to 'break in' with honey, or the mixture of rum and honey, or pure rum. The rum-created pleasant memories of Eiben coffee weren't much help. I was half loaded and sick by the dawn's early light.

I staggered into the office next day, green and nauseated, laid out the pipes on the table. Nobody noticed them. Nor did they notice for six weeks that I couldn't keep the damned pipes lit, I was puffing on wood

smoke of the always-fizzling-out kitchen matches. The red-hot smouldering debris of tobacco and sparks from the pipes, the broken-off
magma-like-match-heads burned through everything I owned: my jack-
ets, ties, shirts, they smouldered right through to my bare skin. I was
itching and continually scratching. I didn't even bother any more to slap
dead those nasty little sparks landing on me. I smelled and felt like an
escaped bargain from a fire sale.

But, all in all, it was a successful operation. I didn't want to get
involved in this farce, and I didn't feel any more like a dummy, a bump
on a log just sitting there. So on those occasions when my opinion was
asked for I didn't answer, I didn't even look up. I had things to do, I was
busy refilling, lighting, cleaning one of my eleven pipes lined up in front
of me. During the last meeting, annoyed, Zanuck growled at me, 'The
trouble with you, de Toth, is you smoke too much!' It was an inauspicious way to launch the picture in Perlberg's leaky dinghy.

Most people involved in *Slattery's Hurricane*, on or off screen, were
living in their own private little hurricanes. The picture, the whole set-up
promised to be anything but dull.

Richard Widmark, a complex character in his own life, interested me.
Never a hero, Widmark was not a bad man, he was an edge man. You
never knew on which side he was going to jump off. He projected that
famous image of pushing old ladies down the stairs, even in private life.
'Shed that image,' said Zanuck to me simply.

Linda Darnell wanted to shed the turmoil in her private life, being in
love with one of 20th Century-Fox top directors who was happily married. A dead-end street.

For Veronica Lake it was again a part to shed her established image,
which she hated. She loved the part, the challenge, but was riddled with
doubts of being able to do it. She was jumpy. When we got married I
didn't know a monkey was on her back. A big one, a hungry one, but
hidden from me for a long time. Marriages could bring lots of surprises. I
could say in my defense I was naïve, trusting. No. I was just plain stupid
to begin with. That 'Thousand dollars now!' should have opened my eye.
No, and when finally I discovered the monkey I saw it as the dragon and
myself as St George the saviour. That was no stupidity, that was conceit.
I ended up like the poor slob in Greek mythology who had to roll a
big-big rock up the mountain over the ridge and, as he just about did it,
right on the tip-top of the ridge, the stone always rolled back down the

hill and he had to start all over again. She and her monkeys were in the dinghy, staring at me.

A condensation of the Hollywood tragedy. Actually she, the real She didn't exist any more. 'That one was sold,' she told me, at fifteen, as a down-payment for her mother's dreams, not for Her own dream. In the bed they put her to dream the dreams turned into a nightmare and She gave birth to her alter-ego. Appalled, the alter-egos ran away from each other. One hurt, timid and scared, hid. The other loud, bitter, boisterous got lost in the 'fucking Hollywood jungle'. In her resentment for 'tinsel town, the shit capital of dreams', where she drowned herself in blind hatred. One was hidden and so quiet; the other up front, so boisterous no one could hear their pitiful cries for help. I heard, I tried. The extravagant monkeys in the end beat me. Another beautiful soul got lost.

During the eight years while we were more or less together between us we made twenty-five feature pictures, she fourteen, I eleven. She abhorred making every single one of them, scorned most of her co-workers. She was longing to be with her alter-ego in the Sierras, in Oregon, on a ranch anywhere, with horses, dogs and children, in this order. She took out her revenge for her busted dreams on Hollywood. Why? 'Fucking Hollywood, shitty tinsel town' was nice to her. Her mother's umbilical cord of dreams tied her to Hollywood. Then the monkeys took her over.

We had to declare bankruptcy, I shuddered, she enjoyed that. 'Just finished shooting; I am at Lucy's, we'll have dinner and celebrate. I am waiting for you.'

'We' became an additional dozen or so moochers. The monkeys had a ball. She was happily pontificating, stopped for a second, 'Darling, would you sign the check?'

I, for the first but unfortunately not the last time in my life, hated to be a gentleman. But would you have left a drowning person in the water when you thought you could swim? Even a stranger, not one for whom you felt great compassion.

Unfortunately that portrait fits many of her contemporaries. But not many – if any – were more insecure, shy and vulnerable. She was not real in a never-land where she had been transplanted by her mother. The early forties were the stage-mother's dream years. The adoration of lonely, grateful GIs guaranteed success. The applause for their children tore up the cobwebs that covered their warped old dreams. Satisfied, on the peak of their vicarious thrills, they pushed relentlessly harder. The laudable patriotic fever of the children helped to burn down their own barricades of doubts and qualms. They all became stars as they deserved to be; they gave their all for their country, throwing themselves on the funeral pyre of their future and the smoke of the fire covered their own dreams. The unlucky who awoke found only their burned-out skeletons facing no tomorrow. 'Rosie the Riveter' gave her all too, invisible and unknown but solid on the ground; and when it was over she knew where she was. They were passengers in hot-air balloons once high and visible in the nebulae (where they didn't belong in the first place), and when it was over and the fires had gone out, either crashed to the deep hell of self-pity or floated in the eternal limbo of cruel non-existence.

I was conceited. I thought I could help and almost drowned myself. Luckily, the monkeys took her away, she left with the ethereal smile of a Kamikaze, she knew she was committing suicide. I was left with no bitter memories, my Doberman and a bunch of wonderful children who deserved to have a better way of life. I did the best with them – I thought I knew how. I spoiled them. They were full of surprises and ideas. One day they wanted a bird; they said most of their playmates had birds which they kept in gilded golden cages. 'In gilded golden cages, no way,' I told them, but I promised them a bird that wouldn't fit in one of those stupid things. 'It is dishonest to do that to a bird born to fly in freedom,' I told them. 'A cage is a cage, I hate them, if they are gilded golden, I hate them more.' So I went looking for birds. God it was a stinking, messy job. These creatures, born to be free and fly, sure paid back their jailers with shit.

'Yes, sir, they're . . . well . . . the truth is birds are dirty. Have a big one, sir, they don't mess more than small ones and usually their leavings are firmer, easier to clean,' said one of the dealers. 'This bird is a magnificent specimen and an Einstein of parrots.'

'Then why doesn't he speak?'

'Well, he has a little trouble. He is a little shy; he was mistreated but once he is settled in he will speak. Money-back guarantee and a bonus.'

Next day I started on *Springfield Rifle* for Warners and the happy troops received the Professor in a cage big enough for the children to move in with him. On its stand it looked like a tree-house. He unloaded on me, an obvious novice bird-owner, stacks of dishes and sacks of food – 'the caviar of parrots', I was told. 'But watch it, no champagne,' said the dealer. 'Birds can become alcoholic,' joked the dealer.

Except for the terrible mess the Professor created, nobody could tell without seeing him that there was a living parrot or any bird in the house. Three days of anxious, anticipation-filled days went by, everybody tip-toeing around so as not to upset the Professor.

On the fourth day AP – After Professor – I brought home the writer to discuss, in peace during dinner, some problems with the script and the producer. It was his first time in my home.

'Fuck yoouuu, g't oooouut,' greeted us – the rough voice of a woman accompanied by Harry James's trumpet at its best, loud, ripping up the ceiling. 'F'ck oooff . . . g't ooouut baaaaasta'd, hahahahaha . . .' and a flow of four-letter word combinations.

And the Professor flew and the petshop owner flew protesting, 'You must have played Harry James . . . I forgot to tell you, the bird went berserk hearing Harry James,' and he forgot to tell me the Professor was an alcoholic who 'suffered from withdrawal tantrums' and also forgot to tell me the Professor came in on a tramp steamer the week before I bought it.

The dealer didn't want to take away the big cage, the dishes and the food, saying 'that wasn't in our agreement'; he didn't know 'what to do with all that', which bugged me, but with tears in his eyes he refunded the money. As he tried to shove the big bird into a small cage to take the cursing Professor away, the bird bit his hand and hung onto it, flopping his big wings. It became a contest between them who knew more dirty words. The last I saw of the Professor was the first time I saw something looking clumsy in flight. He was hedgehopping down my quarter-mile driveway with the bleeding dealer chasing him.

Had the North American AT-6[5] I rented been armed, I'd have raced to the airport, taken off, hunted down and shot to pieces both the dealer and the Professor. In lieu, I took off next dawn and started to shoot pictures of mountain ranges from Durango, Mexico to British Columbia for *Springfield Rifle* locations.

I laid out twelve thick albums full of photos on the desk of Jack Warner. 'On any of these dozen locations I could shoot *Springfield Rifle*. You two

5 An advanced trainer, the last step before being checked out in fighters. Navy designation SNJ.

pick. Go ahead.' As the producer in his eagerness kept leaning over for a better view of the pictures, two heads kept on colliding. It wasn't a wise move, inadvertent as it was, it was not a wise move to constantly bump Jack Warner's head.

The big crash came when both simultaneously came to a decision and poked the same album at the same time, 'That's it.'

I didn't even get up from my chair, 'It's fine with me, I told you.'

They didn't sound like the Andrews Sisters, but they were pretty much in synch, 'Where is it?'

The albums were identical with the same number of photos in each; I had to walk over to identify the location.

It is not very nice to say and most annoying to hear 'I told you so,' but I would be a hypocrite if I dared to say I was not gloating inside. But I didn't say it.

'Where?' Warner repeated the question. 'Where?' echoed the producer.

'Above Lone Pine.'

The quick contraction of nerves in his stomach burped up a 'No!' and the producer sank and almost missed his chair behind him. J.L. smiled, I shrugged, we all remembered: 'No way will I agree this picture to be shot in Lone Pine, this is a big "A" picture, a Gary Cooper picture, Warner's biggest western of the year. No,' foamed the producer, 'this is not a Hopalong Cassidy. Find another location.' He raised his hands heavenward, addressing Jack L. Warner, substituting for God, 'Please, Jack –' Aghast, he stopped talking and dropped his hands.

I enjoyed the air-Odyssey, the circle closed, and I was shooting *Springfield Rifle* above Lone Pine. I was there, the horses were there, all three hundred head of them, but nobody knew where Cooper was. The sun was sinking, so was my heart.

Had Coop been more relaxed he would have been a puddle. He and Churchill must have had similar genes, but Coop's worked without alcoholic help; he could doze off standing still and he was always still.

The horses were moving around restlessly, then broke; a stampede, it was a horrifyingly beautiful, humbling sight in the low golden light of sunset: the power of speed and freedom, the flying-hooves-manes-tails-flashing-colors-shadows in a blur like a flood engulfed, rolled over everything, equipment and men and Coop, sleeping soundly next to a boulder.

The herd was headed off and rounded back to the holding place. It was over. No injuries, minimal damage but 'Where is Coop?' was the cry. Stretching up from behind the lee side of a boulder with a yawn, slapping the dust off himself with his hat, Coop came lumbering, 'Must have been a terrific shot, Tex,' he told me after spitting some mud to clear his mouth. We just stood. 'Wasn't it?' and spat some more mud.

'Where the hell have you been?'

'Had my nap. Why?'

'Where is the balloon? Your balloon?'

'Ouh,' Coop looked down on the sagging, pathetic deflated balloon tied to his belt-buckle, but he kept his promise, he was co-operative, considerate and he saved us a lot of trouble and time when he stretched out 'for just a lil-shut-eye' in the sagebrush, because we could find him under the dancing balloons in the up-drafts.

'From now on two balloons.'

'Hell, Tex, two? They'll take off an' Ah'll fly.'

Balloons or not, it was a pleasure to work with Coop, a friend, rain, shine or snow. And it was snowing and it was foggy up at the Portals on the slopes of Mount Whitney, above nine thousand feet and the weather was not much better in the valley.

It was a perfect day to sleep in, thought the crew. A good crew, but no mountaineers. Old 'Twopants', I called my first, the most senior on the Warner roster. He always had two pants on – during summer 'to keep the heat out', in winter 'to keep the heat in', he said. Now in three pants braving the weather, he grumbled, 'Boss, even you can't shoot in this weather.'

'No way!' said Eddie DuPar firmly, the dean of the cameramen on the Warner lot who was present when the brothers were born. He was a hard-headed stubborn mule. I called him 'Marblehead'. He was proud of it; wanting to live up to his moniker, he refused to shoot. 'I don't think it will work.'

I was stubborn too, and I didn't think, I *knew* it would, 'I'm going ahead with or without you.'

'It's too early to call the Studio, Jack will kill me if I wake him up at home, so OK. Till I hear from them I'll shoot under UP (under protest) on the slate.'

'Fine with me, but I'll put on the slate POU.'

'UP is customary, but what the hell does POU stand for?'

'Piss-On-U.'

'You can't do that. Jack Warner will fire you. I hope he will anyway.'

'Will it work, Tex?' asked Cooper.

'It will.'

''kay. Don't worry. I'd go with you.'

I noticed he kept his fingers crossed. So did I. 'Roll it.' And we started to shoot.

The morning messenger brought up a note from the producer, 'Stop shooting.' Coop read it over my shoulder, 'What now, Tex?'

'We stop now?' asked 'Twopants'. 'Better,' said 'Marblehead'.

I kept on shooting all Friday. With luck again, the weather held, we worked on Saturday and on overtime on Sunday.

On Sunday night Coop and I got loaded, something I never did during shooting; not a drop was the rule. I had seen too many casualties. On our way back to the motel the stars were out. Big and piercing and bright through the clean frozen air. It was almost as beautiful as my first night in the Sierras on my first cattle drive.

'Nice.'

'Nice.'

I stopped. 'I am going to ask you a favor.'

Coop stopped. 'No need.' He called a spade a spade, 'If Jack hands you your walking papers you don't have to look over your shoulder. Ah'll be walkin' behind you.'

'I'm asking you the opposite. Stay on. No matter what happens I can't lose. I learned.'

There was no horse-turd around so he kicked the next best – Coop kicked at a pile of snow and almost fell on his behind on the icy pavement.

'Watch it, you can't catch up with me on crutches.'

'Ah am not joking, Tex.'

He was always quiet, but he spoke quieter than usual. He didn't move. He was there, you knew he always would be there. The silent power, the symbol of honesty.

That was one of the qualms of the producer of *Springfield Rifle*: 'Nobody – no! – no-bo-dy would believe Gary Cooper was a spy!' He suffered.

He didn't see my point. If anybody believed or suspected the character Coop was supposed to play was a spy, there wouldn't be any play to be told. We crossed swords, rewrites, rewrites, writers and more writers.

Months and months went by, I was climbing walls, ready to quit in the lull of the 'dolce far niente' (sweet doing nothing). Luck again.

Behind one of the 'walls' was Brynie Foy, a circus horse in full glory, prancing and waltzing to music he alone could hear. He led me to the finish line of my dream track: a remake of an old, two-color Michael Curtiz film *The Mystery Of The Wax Museum*. With Brynie carrying the flag and Coop behind me *House Of Wax* was born. With a Caesarian section, as Jack L. Warner picked up his steak knife and pointed at me during one – I'll never forget – luncheon in his executive dining-room.

My place was mid-way down, on the left side of the table from J.L.'s point of view. Coop usually sat next to me, away from the head of the table. He was hiding and smiling as the usual J.L. flak was zinging across the table. Brynie's throne was the last place on the right side of the table, next to Tenny Wright, at the opposite end from J.L. Tenny, with his perennial fresh carnation in his blue suit's lapel, and always smelling like pigeon shit. An avid carrier pigeon breeder, an over-fed bear, a beautiful man. A pro of pros. The studio's production manager. On his right, if he ate at all, was Charlie Greenlaw, his number one. Lean and sharp, an icicle with a heart. He and Tenny, tough and fair, were the last words on schedules and budgets.

'You!' came the voice from the head of the table. 'You' could have been anybody around the table; conversations stopped, like compass needles pointing north, all eyes focused on J.L. The steak knife was pointing at me. No doubt. Some returned to their intakes, some watched like vultures on the roof of a slaughterhouse. 'Listen, you,' J.L. shook the knife at me before slapping it down on the table, 'if you think you can get away with blackmail you have a few surprises coming.' He picked up his knife again pointing, 'That goes for you too, Brynie.' He didn't raise his voice, it worried me. It came from deep inside, it didn't sound like a surface storm.

Brynie smiled and nodded in agreement; he agreed to anything anytime, then did it in his own merry way. Tenny Wright next to him raised his hands in surrender, he and J.L. were a great team. Charlie Greenlaw studied the level of the soup in his plate, the only one who wasn't looking toward the head of the table. The only three around the table – in the studio – who had carte blanche. Well, almost.

'And you, Coop, better stay out of this.'

'Yep,' said Coop, kicking me in the shin under the table and starting to eat. Warner started to roar.

'I don't want to hear a word out'a you,' as he with steady hand pointed the knife at me, 'a million and fifty days, that's all, a mil-li-on and fifty days!'

'Boss, I, I – ' I was taken by surprise. I was expecting much less. 'Boss . . . thank you, but I think – '

Warner hit the ceiling, he spoke direct to Coop and Brynie, 'Did you two hear me? I stand for no blackmail. OK, I want it big, I want it good or he is off the picture, off the lot. I don't want to hear one word out of any of you.' He placed the knife on the table, gently, as if he had suddenly realized he was waving it around. J.L. spoke quietly to me. 'You were bugging me with this crap long enough, not a word out'a you either, sixty days and a mill-and-a-quarter. That's all. Final.'

The Caesarian section with his steak knife was successful and thanks to Tenny Wright and Charlie Greenlaw's departments, within ninety days from J.L.'s OK, almost to the hour, *The House Of Wax* was running on the screens at a freight cost of twenty-eight shooting days and $628,000. A far cry from sixty shooting days and a million-and-a-quarter. Warner never said thanks. Why should he? It was my job. I wanted to do it, I said thanks to the Boss.

The same J.L. – a man of surprises – who on Monday, the Monday after that stormy weekend shoot in the snow, in the Sierras, sent a special messenger to eleven thousand feet up on the side of Mount Whitney with an envelope.

'Don' forget, Tex, Ah am with you,' drawled Coop. Marblehead smiled, he imagined me hanging from a pine branch as Christmas decoration. 'I am sorry, Boss,' mumbled Twopants. The wind stopped whistling through the scrub-pines as I opened the unusually thick envelope of my walking papers.

'Watch it, Tex,' Coop warned me, 'may be the whole damned legal department's in there.'

I froze. Then laughed. 'Efficiency plus! They sent me the wrong envelope.' It was filled with a big, thick stack of one-hundred-dollar bills.

As I was stuffing some loose bills back into the envelope a note slipped out, Coop caught it before it fluttered to the ground. He read it. He didn't laugh, he howled, 'Now you can bet your life, Tex, I'll be walking with you,' and handed me the handwritten note. 'I won this on chemin de fer during the weekend. I gambled for smaller stakes than you did. You gambled with your tomorrow. You won. That's your bonus. Stay stubborn, stuff looks good. – J.L.'

It was $10,300, cash.

Jack Warner; one of the moguls of a bygone golden era of tyrants and slave-drivers. But somehow, they weren't ashamed to be human. I miss their warmth and their love of picture-making. God bless them wherever they may be.

I'd have gladly given back all the $10,300, plus what I had, if that would have been the price for letting me experience all the mistakes and have all the fun I had in making *Springfield Rifle*. Among all the firsts, that picture gave birth to a new star. On a cattle call[6] a lanky, shy kid caught my eye who let everybody step in front of him and he politely stepped further and further back. Before he was almost pushed out of the back door I picked him, 'You, tall-one, have you been in pictures before?'

He clicked his heels, straightened up, adding another two inches or so to his over six-feet height, 'No, sir. I'm sorry, sir,' and started to walk out the door.

I liked him and I was afraid I'd lose him. 'Hey, come back. No recall, get over there, give 'em your name and tell 'em to send you to wardrobe. Tell 'em I said you are a Southern soldier.'

'Yessir.' He clicked his heels again, 'Excuse me,' unheard words on a cattle call, 'excuse me,' he kept on repeating as he was running the gauntlet of jealousy.

Without imitating him, he was Cooper. Both were born under the same star. Coop was fascinated. So was I.

'Let's help 'im. Nobody helped me. Put the kid under contract, you and I, Tex.' The papers were drawn, we kept on shooting and watched him and gave him a small part. He was getting better every day.

The lawyers kept nudging us, 'Did he sign? If he is half as good as you two think, get him under contract, it could be a good investment.' And I think that did it for both of us. We went to the lunch-tent with pen and contract in hand. We stood by the entrance, watched the kid. Doing nothing, he radiated in abundance what the others around him only dreamed about. The sure sign of a born star.

---

6 A degrading mob-call for the hungry dreamers to be picked for an extra job, any job or at least to be called for a 'call-back' so they can extend their hopes for a better tomorrow. For those who have the power to pick, it is a disheartening affair too.

'I don't think so.'

'Nor do I. We would hurt the kid more than help.'

'Yep,' and we tore up the contract.

It was the end of our 'mogulship' and the birth of Fess Parker; the beginning of Daniel Boone and a future land baron of Santa Barbara. I wouldn't believe it had I not seen it, the shy Cooper image blown up be a fat cigar-smoking millionaire. The kid never forgot a line of dialogue then, now he didn't remember the words 'Excuse me,' shut up in the cold, closed clamshell of a poker-player. That's life on the track of 'the green menace'.

I missed the kid and wondered if he did too.

19 Watching Camels

World War II was over, according to the rumor spread by those who never read the bloody pages of history. The Second (?) War achieved as much as the other wars before it, nothing – beyond sowing the seeds of new hatred and the fungus of discontent. Old countries split apart, new countries sprung to life on the map and in dreams that became night-mares. Former allies turned on each other with venom. Old enemies formed mutual defense alliances. Like wild fires during the hot summers of California, bloody conflicts jumped across real and imaginary borders.

The patriotic zeal of the war years used up the adrenalin of Hollywood, unconfessed doubts tightened the production strings. The gut bravado was washed down the drain by the diarrhea of doubts and fear of the uncertainty of what would happen to the lucrative foreign market.

The 'Hollywood Colonels' and the 'Fort Roach Commandos' were jockeying for position with those who came back from where things really happened, ignoring what to do about the newly evolving breed of couch potatoes; as television grew and got more and more colorful the color slowly faded from old Hollywood, eclipsed by a new brand of less ebullient personalities, more befitting the couches of the living-rooms and the cans of beer than the champagne and caviar bubble of old Hollywood. New dynasties of entertainers were born on the eight-to-ten-inch boxes. In black and white!

'Let's make the films larger. Project 'em on bigger screens!' 'Let's make 'em in color!' were the battle cries. Few thought making 'em *better* could be a solution to save the picture business from the impending disaster. The Warner brothers were sometimes short of capital, but never short of guts and pioneering spirit. J. L. Warner jumped in swinging. 'Let's make 'em bigger, make 'em better, make 'em in color! – And cheaper!' After another flash of thought he whacked the table so hard it almost split. The Greek philosopher Archimedes yelled 'Eureka' when he discovered every body submerged in water loses as much weight as the water it displaces. There is no record of J. L. Warner yelling 'Eureka', but he was just as happy as old Archie when he discovered the real weight of gold sunk under the dirty pools of TV. He wasted no time and set up Bill Orr, a good tennis player, a handsome playboy, erstwhile thespian, an amusing raconteur, one of the warriors from Fort Roach, to head a Warner Bros TV production unit, and struck gold.

Bill Orr was a probing, restless 'Zanuckian' talent, without Zanuck's lead in his pants to stay with his 'Old Faithful' -like, forever popping-up ideas. While the lead in Zanuck's britches hampered him only in playing polo, the lack of it was a blessing for Bill, kept him ahead of the fast moving pace of television production. It was a joy (no pun intended, his wife's name was Joy, J.L.'s daughter), a real joy to work with him and watch the sparks flying.

His number one was a genius fire-chief who never dampened Bill's sparks, he fanned the fire without letting it consume Warner Bros studio. He was Hugh Benson. Together they came up with a half-a-dozen or so top quality long-running TV series unequalled to date.

To 'make 'em better' wasn't too difficult for J.L. either when a great array of not only stars but talented stars, writers and other creators like Hal Wallis, Michael Curtiz and Co. were warming up in the bullpen waiting for his signal.

Now, 'make 'em in color' and 'cheaper!' was a different kettle of fish. So was having a larger format to shoot and project the future masterpieces, hopefully, if not to exterminate at least amputate TV's legs before the two industries' marathon run for gold. The Technicolor process was – still is – the highest quality color process. It exposed three black and white negatives simultaneously, which tripled the negative and the high laboratory costs, while lugging the heavy, cumbersome Technicolor cameras around the sets considerably lengthened shooting schedules. The few films shot in the available 'True Color' (a one-strip system) were less than inadequate, with their washed-out unreal colors and peopled with lookalike fugitives from a funeral parlor made up by apprentice embalmers. It was similar to today's early 'colorized' black and white abortions on TV.

Michael Curtiz, disappointed by the sad results of his 'Two Color' *Mystery Of The Wax Museum*, refused to experiment with J.L.'s and

Eastman Kodak's new venture into a new single-strip color process. Thank God and my Lady Luck.

I was sitting on the fence, restless, and repeating my old slogans like 'Doing nothing is death,' and 'Do something even if it is wrong, mistakes are the best teachers,' didn't help. I could not even make a mistake, nothing came around in the barren zilchland except unpaid bills. If you sat on a picket fence too long, the sharp tips interfered with your judgement – through the wrong end of the brain.

'You like horses, let's gamble, I have a – '

'– Punish your other clients. Don't pick on me.'

'I wouldn't do that to you, now would I? I am talking about a western for you, but it involves a gamble,' said Ned Marin, my agent, nudging me off the fence as he took the first sip of the very dry martini I fixed him. Stirred gently with a glass rod in a pitcher, both fresh out of the freezer, not a bruised martini from a metal shaker. 'Good – very good,' he repeated between the second and the larger third sip.

He was a sharp businessman with a great horse sense for human talent and absolutely no sense for horses. On the racetrack he was a disaster. Ned lived for and died because of horses and gambling debts.

'Michael Curtiz turned the picture down,' he informed me, 'and I don't think anybody wanted it on the lot, but J.L. doesn't particularly want another crazy Hungarian. We'll see him tomorrow at eleven-thirty.' He smiled sheepishly, 'We may see him earlier, tonight, he is having dinner at Chasen's.' He picked up the phone, made the reservation, shoved his empty glass in front of me, 'I dare you to make it as good as this was.'

Inside information is the mother of the majority of the 'deals' in Hollywood. It always had been. We 'accidentally' bumped into J.L. at Chasen's. One of his deluxe lackeys in attendance with him arranged for the script to be delivered to my home by the time I got back from dinner.

The picture was to be the first feature in the world to be shot in the new single-strip as Warner Color, aka Eastman Color, a process most films are shot in today. I liked the challenge of firsts, I loved westerns, I loved horses. I liked J.L.'s tactful approach of a meat axe, I didn't like the script, I needed the money, the pastures started to look much greener on the other side of the fence I was straddling.

There were horses around all right but the green grass Ned Marin promised, from close turned out to be ocher-colored dust squeezed between rust- and beige-colored boulders on the west end of the San

Fernando Valley. There were so many westerns shot there through the years that the rocks called the horses by their first names. The people riding them were so insignificant they had no names.

However, there was a bonus in it, the film was a Warner Bros 'epic', but with a western star whose complexion matched the rocks, with Sassparilla frizzing through his aging veins. I called him 'Granite Jaw'. Even the horseshit was sterile around him, a perfect gentleman on or off the set who never read a script, which showed he was wise too. But he was a reader all right, an avid reader of his bible, the *Wall Street Journal*, and wherever he was, on horseback or in bed, he was engulfed in the antiseptic cloud of a dry-cleaning establishment. A blue-book millionaire via his wife and in his own right, with a hobby which he thought was acting.

He produced his own films with a partner, a bright, lovely little man whose picture-making wizardry was miniaturized in his desert turtle-like small head adorned with a turtle beak and heavy-lidded, lazy eyes, on top of his butter-ball body. He moved more slowly than turtles move in the Mojave desert in mid-August but as purposefully as the turtles did. But in contrast, he spat out words as fast as an Uzi spits out lead, while generously emitting through every pore of his body the anesthetizing fumes of Jack Daniel's. He made an alcoholic of my dog who kept licking the booze-beads off the back of his hand and his bald pate, residue from his last night's consumption. No Sassparilla for my Doberman.

I met 'Granite Jaw' with his boots and spurs on, resting atop a worn leather couch in his partner's office, ready to ride the bull market. When he heard the news about the single-strip color, he dropped the *Wall Street Journal* on his chest, looked almost alive, and asked me, 'Do you think it will work?'

'I don't think I – '

'– Oh,' he cut me off and went back to his bible.

'– I know it will,' I continued. 'It worked with the tests I shot, no reason why it shouldn't work with features. I'll just have to be careful with my set-ups, because the negative is "blue-sensitive". No problem.'

'Oh,' and he sat up accompanied by a symphony of his arthritic bones and the pinging of tired springs in the ancient couch. It was an effort. For a moment he sat on the edge of the tormented couch.

The great mystery of motion pictures is the power with which they can register and project thoughts on film. The danger of this power is that it magnifies the lack of it too. As he sat there to gain strength after the exertion of getting up he didn't stare at me, he looked, and I was delighted. His look would have been a 'print'. He was evaluating me, he actually did have a thought above his 'Granite Jaw'.

Hope started to sprout; this may all work out. Then another pleasant surprise, he moved swiftly and well to a phone on the desk, dialed and hung up after one ring but kept his hand on the receiver, an obvious signal which was answered almost immediately, the phone rang. 'Right,' he said into the receiver, '. . . yes, twenty thousand Eastman Kodak,' and hung up.

That was it, and with his flame extinguished, silver spurs jingling, he moseyed back at snail's pace to the couch to disappear in the clouds of high finance.

All in all it was fun trying to differentiate a Pliocene actor from the Genezic era's Quarternary boulders who retained the Pleistocene ice in the place where some degenerate humans had mistakenly put their hearts. The war was over and most of these had been forgotten. The twinkle of over-stuffed starlets on the contract lists was turned off by the retrenching studios as the doors of the once glorious stage-door canteens they had served so well were closing. Tinsel town was overrun with its refugees. Despair, loss of identity gnawed off the tinsel, the town became a meat-market for international playboys, jerks or future presidents alike. Howard Hughes was certainly not alone in playing the bourse of flesh, but most certainly he was the most generous player.

I got lucky again and Lady Luck led me out of the horse-dust and hooked me on to a few projects that were worthwhile wasting time on – only to come up against illiterate, pontificating censors judging scripts. Their power was awesome. I caught one of them, a Knight of Malta, without his sword, cape, shako and medals, in flagrante delicto, naked-assed in bed. I didn't blame him for that, he was a good man. It happened after a Sunday noon mass he always attended at the Good Shepherd, on Santa Monica Boulevard, in Beverly Hills, with his wife, a chattering, fat bore and five chattering, ugly fat kids.

But his cup over-runneth when the hypocritical old goat blocked a script I wanted to make because its theme was adultery and divorce. The film brought up the question how long should an otherwise good husband and father be penalized for adultery because adultery did not exist in America where divorce was also unheard of – in films. 'To end a film with a divorce,' he pontificated sanctimoniously, 'please, don't be ridiculous!'

Purple is a lovely color under some circumstances but no purple hue ever looked better than that flooding this hypocrite's face when I was arguing for the script to be passed in the boardroom of the American equal of Dr Goebbels's office of censorship. 'The script addresses a real-life problem, it has to be honestly told to understand one of the tragedies of daily life – divorce – the pitfalls of which, unfortunately, I am fully aware of. Were I only after 'exploitative sensationalism' as I am accused of, I would have written about a blackmailer who caught a very respectable man in a high and vulnerable position committing adultery after a Sunday mass and not about a lowly, dull insurance investigator who committed adultery once. One of the millions of decent, chained-to-their-jobs citizens of either sex.'

Boardroom bingo. The script was passed with a few negligible suggestions. Most of them were ignored.

To succeed in the picture business, I was finding out, you need on your side not only Lady Luck but some gentle blackmail too. It could be a dirty business sometimes.

Unfortunately, luck couldn't bring to light the ugly truth showing the end of the rainbow at the end of derailed dreams: the snake-pits of Lexington, Kentucky, the first and only withdrawal ward at that time in the States. I didn't have enough clout to put real life on the screen. 'We wouldn't release it . . . It will scare, shock people,' I was told.

'Thanks for the compliment, that was exactly what I wanted to achieve with *Monkey On My Back.* Scare them off committing slow suicide with dope.' I battled on only to find deaf ears and shaking heads. The golden age of picture-making. How happy I would have been to exchange some of that gold for a little freedom of expression of today. To stomp my foot and quit would not have been the solution, would not have served the thought I wanted to put through in the first place. I did what I thought I would get away with, but even that was held back from release until an operetta version of drug addiction had been released.

The monkeys were stronger. God was not in Barney Ross's corner any more,[1] the monkey was on his back. Two weeks before the planned première he was picked up stoned out of his mind in New York.

1 *God Was In My Corner* was the title of Barney Ross's autobiography which the film *Monkey On My Back* was based on.

'You see, you were wrong,' I was told gleefully, over and over again.

Was I wrong for not giving up hope for those who needed it so desperately? Even McCarthy couldn't make me give up hope, waging his war in the name of American justice, swinging a scimitar, slashing at anything openly or covertly tinted red – including watermelons. The laurel wreath of victory often slips down to cover the eyes of victors and they stumble in the belly-high debris left from their ticker-tape madness.

Ink was always available to sign abortive peace treaties, but not being sure of how long the treaties would last, the US dropped its hydro-genized expectation appropriately on a Bikini Atoll. The British had a better sense of humor and dropped their hope for the rebirth of sanity on Christmas Island. The third H power, Godless USSR, sent a dog up to lift his leg and defile the pristine space, then hit the moon with a rocket.

All good news to cheer up forces fighting on the ground from the Congo to Korea, but at least the vanquished always had hope to look forward to a better tomorrow.

The stench of the canals in Venice disseminated the bloodstained memories of the war, but the fat pigeons, symbols of peace, still fought for airspace above St Mark's to unload their opinion on the heads of the tourists. They wheeled above them, jockeying for position in the white-cloud-littered, blue-blue sky like the fat-assed cherubs on a Rubens kitsch.

In Rome, the 'Wedding Cake' (a sparkling white, overbearing monu-ment to King Victor Emmanuel III and to the Italians' sense of humor) had assured Kodak's booming business, while 'the beach' (the Via Ven-eto) assured immortality to the 'oldest profession'.

Italy was buzzing with life and discontent as always. By 1960, Italy churned out 195 films a year, 24 more than the US, not including the foreign productions shot there like Willy Wyler's megahit *Ben Hur* (famous for its chariot race) and *Cleopatra* (famous for her cleavage and comedy of errors).

Rouben Mamoulian, the first director on *Cleopatra*, started it in London, to simulate sunny Egypt. In October! Every member of the half-naked cast turned an identical color, blue. Even in black and white he couldn't have gotten away with it, because the goose-bumps of the slave girls were larger than their breasts and, according to the sales department, those were bigger box office assets than Richard Burton's talent. The magnificent sets in England were destroyed: blueprints which had been sent to London from Hollywood went on to Rome, and the production was transferred to sunny Italy. Without Mamoulian but with careful consideration of the difference between the US-British and the Continental metric linear system. Simple.

In happy Italy the luck finally changed, everything worked to perfection, and great strides were made to catch up with the time lost on the, until then, damned production. The production encountered only a small hitch. It was impossible to assemble on the stages of Cinecitta the off-the-lot prefabricated sections of the sets. They were too big, they didn't fit onto the stages. They wouldn't have fitted into the Basilica of St Peter's. Somewhere a minor detail was ignored: communication. The skilled Italian craftsmen, not being aware that the courteous British had translated the figures of the blueprints from the US-British to the Continental metric system, took it for granted blueprints originating in the USA were in inches. *Once you're lucky, you're lucky.* Back to square one.

Post-war Italy's Neorealism, the era of *Bicycle Thieves* and *Open City*, of directors working without scripts, an epoch of true film-making, became corrupted by the glossy images of Super Spectacles, stories of Roman Emperors, mixtures of the Bible and mythology. With the enormous world-wide success of *Hercules* with Steve Reeves, a legion of steroid pumped-up American strong men invaded Italy and roamed the jungle led by a new breed, the so called 'fly-by-night' producers who sneaked onto and pirated other productions' sets at night and – if they weren't caught and chased off in a few nights – actually finished their epics. Tartars met the Vikings, chasing girls, and if it was nudey enough, they were successful. Blood covered the incredibility.

The old Maestro, Alessandro Blasetti, finally put on the screen his long-planned *Europe By Night*, a tasteful super-vaudeville extravaganza which became a super hit, legitimized nudity to a point and opened the floodgates to – for want of a better word – art, such as *Paris By Night*, *America By Night*, *World By Night*, *Nude Sexy*, *Sexy By Night*, and of course *Nude World*, and so on.

The reaction came with films like the crudely true *Mondo Cane* by Gualtiero Jacopetti, a world-wide hit, the start of the 'inquest' period, followed of course by *Mondo Cane No. 2*, and a new, worthwhile, not sensation-hunting but honest effort to bring back reality and art to films. Of course, it was flushed down by the usual quick-money-chasing hyenas. And, of course, from the hills around Rome, to save the day, as so often before, charged the American cowboy. A posse led by Sergio Leone, with one of the two real cowboys in the history of the western. I am sorry I didn't make the ideal western with the two of them, Clint Eastwood and Gary Cooper together.[2]

Once again, a new epoch of the old west (which had been discarded at home) brought life and fresh air to the movies – and fresh money. For the time being? Cowboys swarmed around them thar hills of Spain, and then Yugoslavia, without a Sergio Leone or Eastwood, and succeeded in leaving nothing again but horseshit in the lap of the audience. Maybe Eastwood's *Pale Rider* and *Unforgiven* will make them forgive and forget. Tempora mutantur et nos mutamur in illis (time is changing and we are changing with it).

Rome became the film capital of the world and Italy the international tax dodgers' heaven, where tax evasion always had been considered an honorable sport. In the delicate art of tax dodging Italy was second to none, aiding and encouraging it with an archaic system. The honest tax payers were ridiculed, Americans included. In Italy 'gli furbi' (the foxy ones), 'the Artful Dodgers', the Grand Masters of evasion, were national heroes, their chess game with the government was followed as closely as any sporting event: 'Il piu sportivo vince' ('the most sporty one wins').

The living-room of the Americans in Rome, the Via Veneto, was a twenty-four-hour beehive filled with the blinding flashes of the paparazzi's lethal weapons of blackmail. Cleopatra, aka Liz Taylor, added her two mounds to the seven hills of Rome, freely disclosed to the public by her decolleté down to the cobblestoned piazzas. But eleven members of our congressional committee – ten Democrats and one Republican – on a European fact-finding tour had to leave Rome dissatisfied with seeing only the seven original hills of the Eternal City. Liz kept them waiting at Cinecitta for a whole day without letting them have a glimpse of the attractions she had added to the panorama of Rome. Was it unpatriotic of Taylor to prevent the US tax payers, who financed the trip, from getting all the facts? When blamed, she was fearlessly protected by her husband of the hour, a sparrow with the voice of a nightingale.

Spouses can be strange birds. One pro-tem-lady of my life was a peacock (and as we know, peacocks can't fly) and had twice as many and

---

2 Fred Zinneman came the closest to the ideal western by remaking *The Gunfighter* as it should have been done first time around: *Twelve O'Clock High*.

more colorful plumes, all of them ruffled all the time. She arrived unexpectedly, with six large trunks – 'Just for a couple of weeks' – too many even for a year-long around-the-world, deluxe cruise. She came by air, of course.

The Excelsior where I stayed was not fitting enough for her for that 'just for a couple of weeks' stay. By the third day after her entrance I had to bum a ride back from work – she had commandeered my driver and the car. I survived that not really unexpected surprise. But – maybe I was being unreasonable to be pissed off. After twelve hours of location shooting I was anxious to have a shower, then sit out on the sidewalk next door at Doney, where they were trained to have a Jack Daniel's on the rocks ready. After that, dinner around the corner in front of Il Piccolo Mondo and, after that, relax some more across from the hotel on Via Veneto, at the Café de Paris with friends. A perfect way to end a busy day. To top it off, on the way back to the Excelsior, have a chat with my friend Dominic, the traffic cop on the corner, who always held up the traffic for me. Then fold up to get ready for a seven on the set start of another day.

'Sorry, signor de Toth, but you don't live here anymore, peccato, the signora moved,' and the conceierge handed me a note.

After a shower in my old suite, I had to put back on my dirty clothes. I read her note with my Jack Daniel's at Doney, I re-read it after dinner in the Café de Paris. By then it was funny. 'It says,' said one of my Roman friends as he tapped the note, 'you love surprises, so she did it to please you. Say thanks, a very good address.'

It was. On Monte Parioli, in the Mussolinian Bel Air of Rome, on Via Gramsci on the top floor of a quite decent apartment building, with an elegant elevator that seldom worked, a wide, majestic, marble staircase with a frilly wrought-iron railing. In the, as she put it, 'jet-sety' apartment miles of echoing marble corridors connected five marble-floored bed-rooms, six enormous bathrooms, with marble walls, tubs, sinks, and gold faucets and no hot water. Twelve other rooms of various sizes, seventeen rooms in all! Each had marble floors in every blessed color of marble to be found on earth, with pink dominating. White marble floor in the soccer-field-size kitchen and even in the storage-room. Today I still can't look at a marble cake. She had signed a one-year lease. 'Just for a couple of weeks'?

The following week – 'Just because you like surprises' – some of the children arrived with more trunks and a new nanny, fresh out of the pages of *Vogue*, wearing, and wearing very well, some of my lady wife's designer clothes. A very unlikely person for her to hire.

'Just to save some money. I will not be obliged to buy her new clothes. After all, our governess (governess?) has to fit into the milieu we'll be living in.'

'Congratulations, very economical, so now you can go out and buy for yourself twice as – '

'– Right,' she cut me off with pride.

'And what milieu are you talking about?'

'You know, the jet-set and all that.'

'I am working seven days a week, twelve, fourteen hours a day, I am starting another picture, I am not jetting anywhere.'

'Fine, good, that's why I thought it was such a good idea, I'll be representing you. I thought of everything, that's why I didn't bring any clothes with me – '

'– What's in those fucking trunks – '

'– Oh, they are half empty, I don't have to buy luggage, I thought of everything. I planned. I have judgement.'

She certainly had judgement, it was proven on the third week; our 'governess' was picked up for prostitution. The local hookers reported her and she was on her way, at tax payers' expense, to Brooklyn. We ended up with a nice, fat Italian mama, who could cook too, and how.

The 'just for a couple of weeks' was going on its sixth surprise-full month. The biggest sustained surprise was that she was putting on weight and didn't buy any new clothes; she was wearing clothes returned to her after the 'governess's' departure, with let-out seams by our Italian mama, the queen of the other help.

The status quo worried me. I didn't surprise her, she knew I'd be leaving for Yugoslavia within a few weeks, 'Why don't you and the children go back home, I'll be away for at least three months. We talked about it, we've drifted so far apart. You're right, I am, I was the worse – '

'– You're right, but I have changed my mind – '

'– When did you change your mind? Why? Just now, just this minute?'

'It doesn't matter. I want to be closer to you.'

'I won't, I can't be here, I'll be shooting in the boondocks on location, not even in Belgrade, no phone I'll – '

'– I know, but it's still closer than Pacific Palisades, California.' Then came the surprise and all the marble collapsed on the top of me: 'You will be a father again.'

Ten months after her arrival in Italy she presented me with a piccolo Romano. For this I am very grateful to her. But because it was she, it couldn't be a simple note telling me that I had become a father again. And of course I was in the boondocks. The message reached me through the US embassy in Belgrade: 'If you want to see your son alive, return to Rome immediately,' signed by the obstetrician. Now that was a hell of a way to find out that I had a son.

In a white flannel blanket a skeleton squirmed, weightless and silent. Purple temples pulsing in a paper-thin skull, ugly and pitiful. Sighs from two dejected doctors, a sobbing nurse, a wordless, staring wife. I heard the screeching brakes of a streetcar, saw red and yellow and green. Yes, and blue and a ball 'this big'. A Viennese waltz.

'Goddamn it, it's not going to happen again. You're as good as dead if he dies! Got it?'

Two squirming doctors: one stuttered in English, the other spoke Italian. 'It's an amoebic infection, it's – '

'– Don't say it. Move, don't just stand around waiting for your own funeral. Move, work, work for a miracle!'

The miracle worked through Major General Costello, the American embassy, the antibiotics, two thimbles full of my blood for tranfusion, the superhuman effort of the Italian doctors, and prayer and faith. I was proud again to be an American. How lucky we are, how little we appreciate it. The 'piccolo Italiano' is six-foot-four now, but would he have been, were he not an American?

I never felt closer to my wife, she had gone through hell. Alone. And still she was to be alone; I had to go back to Yugoslavia to finish *I Mongoli* (*The Mongols*). After the trauma, her parting words as I was leaving I shall not forget.

'I am disappointed in you – '

'– To say I am sorry isn't enough, I understand – '

'– No, you don't.' She waved me off. 'You never asked me why I didn't buy any new clothes. But don't you worry, I am going to catch up now,' and she was trying to catch up with her dreams of grandeur when I came to the hospital to say adieu, au revoir – and it turned out to be a goodbye for me.

'The people I came over to meet are not here, they are in Switzerland – '

'– What people you're talking about?'

'The jet-set!' She was annoyed that I didn't know, 'Rome is only a short lunch-stop on their way from the Côte d'Azur to Davos, Arosa, St Moritz, Gstaad, Cortina d'Ampezzo – '

'– Cortina is in Italy – '

'– Ohhh, it's up there in the Alps – '

'– The Dolomites.'

She shrugged, angry, frustrated – I had spoiled her dreams for the moment – looked at her watch, the first present from her son, 'Don't miss your flight, Miss Ekberg will be angry. I am sure she missed you.'[3]

For me, being in the film business always meant being on the extremes, being spoiled and given a lot, but robbed of a great deal of things others take for granted, like watching your monsters grow up. And what I had to do then in exchange for all the booty was: go off to watch camels.

The closest I came to camels before *Lawrence of Arabia* was the camel on the packages of Camel cigarettes; since I don't smoke, even that wasn't very often. I had never eaten sheep's eyes, raw slippery balls tough to hold even in your fingers, ugh! to say nothing about swallowing one as it looked at you, as God gave them to the sheep. For the sake of art one could be compelled to do strange things sometimes, but our negotiators for the production were businessmen, good businessmen, except when negotiating for camels. Gabriel Pascal, filming G. B. Shaw's *Caesar and Cleopatra* wanted only 100 ordinary camels. David Lean, exacting and peculiar as he was, wanted 147 – not 140 nor 150 – plus ten-or-so silver racing-camels, the pride of every sheikdom of the sand world. The sheikh drove a hard bargain. Finally, after lots of haggling, the deal was set, and the money was to be handed over the following morning.

The morning came as usual but there was not a single camel or a soul in sight. Black tents, camels, Arabs all gone, disappeared during the silence of the night. It happened three times. Was it blackmail? Despair reigned over this puzzle. The camels were needed, the production was running out of time.

All three débâcles were identical. After the price was agreed every sheikh gave us a dinner to celebrate the deal. The food was good and identical, roast lamb, but the pièce de résistance was the lamb's eyes, one of which every sheik swallowed with great relish, then ceremoniously

3 Anita Ekberg, a sex symbol of the era, was co-starring with Jack Palance in *I Mongoli*.

offered the other to our man in charge of the bargaining, who politely refused to indulge in the joy of swallowing it. It was an unforgivable insult to refuse this great honor. The sheikhs marched out with their entourage. We were left with a detached eye looking at us. We were too slow to wake up, but a sheep's eye sliding down one's throat is – ugh.

Nobody could have done more for art and David Lean than swallow one. I always had hope, and a brilliant idea hit me: swallowing it may replace my blind left eye. No. No miracles. The thought of it makes me feel a lump stuck in my throat now. Ugh! Dr Heimlich, please help.

Camels are a troublesome bunch anyway, but imagine a seasick camel. Two out of the 147 got homesick and expired en route from North Africa to Almeria, Spain. The seven silver racing-camels, magnificent beasts, arrived dirty and mean. The camel drivers matched them, but rode like the wind, hopefully downwind from you.

Finally the day had arrived to reap the reward of the camel finders' expedition. That morning – dawn, at three-thirty – the smell of camels woke me up in my hotel room. Camels in my room? Maybe I shouldn't have had the second glass of the juice of Rioja, the 'Imperial'. I slowly opened my eye. Five camel drivers stood above me, silent.

'What the hell are you doing here? Get out!'

They stood staring at me, nudging each other. I yelled, 'Out,' pointing at the door, which was a ridiculous gesture, they came in through it, they knew where the door was. I realized it. Stopped pointing, I repeated, 'Out.'

All five of them spoke up at once in four different languages, Arabic, French, Spanish and English at the same time, wildly gesticulating and pointing in every direction of the compass. Repeating 'Shut up!' five times finally worked; they calmed down somewhat, then unloaded their burden. 'The camels are gone.'

Emphasizing every syllable, 'The – camels – are – gone? – Where?' was the worst thing I could have done, the floodgates of their unintelligible theories opened. 'All of them?'

'All, all gone. All-all-all. Gone-gone-gone. No camels.'

How could 145 ordinary and 7 silver racing-camels be just 'gone-gone-gone'. They kept parroting it again in four languages.

Disappeared? Where? In Almeria, then a hamlet with a main street ten paces long with potholes as large as a small swimming pool in Marbella, and blessed with three 'hotels' (where the bedbugs rocked you to sleep), four cantinas, a church, all surrounded by innumerable, forever-changing sand dunes.

I couldn't smell any hashish on the drivers' breath, they smelled only of camel dung and urine. I went with them. The corrals were empty, the camels were gone, disappeared. Disappeared the day they would have become film stars. A horrible thought sunk me: back on the sheep's eye diet!

'Now what?'

I didn't have to turn to find out who spoke. The sometimes offensive whiff of a cigarillo was now a welcome shield against the proximity of the camel drivers. The littlest 'giant' stood next to me. She could go on tip-toes under a camel's belly without her wavy, silver mane touching it, 'eva monley' – she spelled her name in lower case – our production manager. She was a handsome lady with pretty lips and good teeth chomping on a cigarillo, even in the showers, but she was never a 'lower case'. 'eva monley' always filled, no, dominated the space wherever she was, from Wadi Rumm, across the millenniums-old caravan trecks through the Nefud, the black basalt desert of Jebel Tubeiq in the furnace of Jordan, where the Arabs were indoctrinated to believe then that anybody wearing a pair of trousers was the enemy, a Jew, and thus a free target in the early sixties. Without a blink she faced the threat of the Jordan sniper's bullets. In Morocco she found the roofs of two hundred toilet cabinets which had been blown off by sandstorms. In comparison the sand dunes of Almeria would fit on a dessert plate.

'We'll have the stinking camels back by tomorrow!' 'eva' assured me and I had no doubt.

The Guardia Civil is one of the toughest military units whose tricorne black patent-leather headgear was designed to be a constant reminder of the tradition of the outfit: if they had to face the muzzles of a firing squad it had to be with open eyes, without blinking. But the Commandant blinked when 'eva' charged into his office brandishing her cigarillo like an insulted eighteenth-century Spanish grandee flaunting his rapier and demanding satisfaction, and she held the Commandant responsible for the camels.

But the camels had heeded no authority and had disappeared. After weeks and weeks tracking down horror stories about strange ghosts looming up in the morning mist all over the countryside, scaring the faithful, finally the Guardia Civil rounded up 133 out of the 145 ordinary camels and five out of the seven special silver racing-camels. The descendants of the successful fugitives are still propagating and enjoying their freedom.

'All accounted for,' 'eva' reported to David Lean. 'Two silvers are indisposed but replacements are on their way.' David was as happy as he could ever be and never knew, nor did I or anybody else, that the quality and grandeur of *Lawrence of Arabia* was lessened by a dozen stinking beasts. Nobody counted the camels and who would dare to doubt 'eva', the miracle worker, who set up a tent city in sand-land, and ran it without a hitch for over a year, keeping several hundred spoiled costumers happy in hell.

Years later, working with me on *The Billion Dollar Brain* in the deep-freeze above the Arctic Circle on the outskirts of Finland, when a herd of reindeer performed a disappearing act on the picture like the camels did in Spain, 'eva' confessed that she 'didn't tell the whole truth' about the camels, but she assured me that reindeer couldn't hide.

20 Guardian Angels

Coincidence again put me on the top of the world on the tundra. My nickname, Bandi, and snow forced the coincidence. Except for being white, the snow on the Rothorn above Lenzerheide was quite different from the snow of the tundra, where earth and heaven melts into one horizonless, white, dull eternity – truth with no end or beginning. In the Swiss Alps, in Grison, the unreachable peaks crudely slashed the horizon, stabbing the blue sky, and the blinding sun was life, excitement. Excitement that almost killed me.

That was the first time I broke my neck. And if it had to happen it couldn't have happened on a nicer day. It was my fault, not the Alps, not the snow's nor the sun's. I was showing off. I should have bought it then, but somebody doesn't want me up there, saying, 'You, stay down there!' Or likes me very, very much. Thanks anyway.

It had been snowing all night. The silence was soft. The harmony of sleigh bells just hung in the air as the few hefty horses shook snowflakes off their manes in front of the couple of hotels in the gateway of this tucked-away paradise for skiers, undiscovered by the international jet-set, to the dismay of my jet-set-chaser lady wife, and to my delight. The peaks around Lenzerheide reminded me of the twisted tips of whipped cream surrounding the top of the first Moron's Delight I had in the thirties at Brown's on Holywood Boulevard. That almost killed me too.

After the first run with the ski school, a group of us decided to split. 'I understand, but watch it,' warned Roland Bläzi, the head of the school, an Olympic skier for Switzerland, a champ and a friend. Above the tree-line the sky was bluer, the snow seemed whiter, the powder deeper, fluffier; we had a magnificent first run.

To feel the power of the ear-bursting, freedom-flying aerobatics in an old open-cockpit Stearman biplane, or to be engulfed by the enormity of the silent loneliness of the sky in a sailplane, or to feel one's insignificance diving in the ocean above the rim of a wall of bottomless depths are the thrills of living – next to skiing in virgin powder.

Gaining confidence, the second run was even more exciting. On the third we started to out-do each other, three of us boys and the girl. In a cocktail lounge we wouldn't have given her a second glance, but she was as good a skier as any of us. No, I was better and I knew it. Stupid male chauvinism, spiked with the never-admitted twinge of inferiority. 'Drop the shackles, let's goooo,' I yelled. 'We have time for another run.'

That run was the best thing that happened to me. I broke my neck. The first time. I was way below and ahead of the group, squirting the drifts with every turn, not touching the little gulches between the humps – not bulldozed-out, man-made moguls, God made them more exciting, no rhythm built in them, unpredictable. I knew I was travelling too fast. I would have never done it on the racetrack, overdrive the potential of the machine, maybe I was a better driver than skier.

'Eeedeeeooot,' I yelled, and the scream made me feel better, cool.

There was a rock in the next drift.

No, I wasn't flying through the air in spectacular slow-motion; I burrowed in the deep snow, the world was a swirling blur of azure-blue and white, an extended crrr-rack of slow-breaking, dry twigs. That's all. That was it.

Not exactly, the rock gouged and partly shredded off the running surface on both of my skis. The safety binding was bent, it didn't release as it should have. I was trying to straighten it out. I still couldn't understand why, it would have been impossible to use the ski anyway.

'Gott sei dank, gar nichts passpiert' ('Thank God nothing happened') said the girl, the first to catch up. 'Vous êtes OK?' ('Are you OK?') asked one of the fellows. 'Vous avec beaucoup de chance' ('You are very lucky') noted the last to catch up, panting. They were all very happy I was considerate enough not to spoil the rest of their afternoon by needing help, and headed for the piste without me. That was the end of our international friendship. Not the usual behavior on the slopes.

Nothing hurt, my limbs felt heavy and stretchy, and I was having a hell of a time trying to put on the skis with the twisted bindings. I was certainly not thinking clearly, I lay on my back (!) hoping I would be able to handle it that way. I sank in the deep, soft snow. It was comfortable, felt good. And that was almost it, but I was lucky again.

I woke up in Swiss heaven. I knew it immediately because I heard two sturdy guardian angels speak 'avec acksan Feterall'[1] as they were touching me ever so gently, 'Dough ganz werrück dah Kerl' ('The kid is totally crazy,'). The other agreed, 'Yoh, blööde.'

I moved, trying to get up to see if there were better-looking angels around with long blond hair. 'Bleib ruhig' ('Stay quiet') and firm hands held my shoulders. They had a conference I didn't understand a word of. They came to a decision and with the magic of the angels or the power of two Bernese Oberländers, lifted me up expertly by my armpits. One checked the skis; 'Och,' he grunted, 'sheiss mit reis' ('shit with rice').

To please my angels, trying to imitate Switzerdütch, I spoke up, 'Ich-ab' die Diät nie-g'hört' ('I have never heard of that diet').

'Hör mal, er spricht doch Deutsch' ('Listen he speaks German') said the one holding my 215 pounds up as if it was feather.

'Ein Amerikaner.' It wasn't a question. The one trying to fit on my skis looked up at me and from there on they spoke grammatically perfect English, using a mixture of Stratford on Avon and New York on the Hudson English words with the fresh scent of the pines of the Bernese Oberland. Finally we communicated, they understood what had happened and, as a duet, sang their strong disapproving 'yoh' in Switzerdütch.

The mountain was beginning to live up to the name 'Rothorn' ('red horn'). The slowly setting sun was beginning to tint the peaks. I have never seen it so magnificent. Blessed innocence. Innocent or dumb, they didn't like it, they were smart and wanted to get the hell off it. The snow was too deep, it would have been impossible to descend without skis or snow shoes. They moved away and had a serious confab, not a word of which I could grasp. Unfortunately, some awareness started to seep through the haze of the tumble. Alone, I had about as much chance of getting down as the biblical camel had of getting through the eye of the needle. With my past, I had about as much chance getting into heaven too.

They broke their head-to-head session and came up with a plan. They stomped a small platform so we weren't sinking knee-to-waist-deep in the snow every time we moved. They carefully scrutinized what once

1 A dialect and particularly heavy accent of the capital of Switzerland, Bern, and its Canton. Mixed with 'Switzerdütch', mostly spoken in the rough, almost inaccessible, beautiful Bernese Oberland, virgin ski country.

were skis, now obviously useless. Each tried to put them on. No way. Their boots were fresh out of a museum for hundred-year-old ski equipment and my 'latest safety bindings' fit the custom-made two-week-old 'Molitor' boots. Their wooden skis had loose-heel bindings and nipples on their tips to hook on the 'Seehundfellen' ('seal skins') for climbing. I tried to put my 'skis' back on. 'Nie-nie' the 'mountain-men' objected as they took them away from me, 'if you didn't break your neck with your last mistake, don't do it now.' After a reassuring gesture with their two snow-shovel-size hands, they were off.

'Where are you going?' I called after them. They waved back again and went off toward the trees, taking with them my 'equipment' and my bootlaces. I never felt lonelier in my life, before or since. I watched the dark shadow of the far horizon creeping up the red horns. They were ugly.

I had no pain, but, just tired of standing up, I lay down for a second only; when I opened my eyes they were dragging me onto one of the most comfortable platforms of transportation I have ever traveled on: my two bent ski-poles, the wrecked skis, and pine boughs fastened together with their 'Seehundfelen' and my bootlaces. They lifted me onto it. 'Bleib still, sei ruhig' ('Don't move, be quiet') and a journey to heaven began. The peaks of Rothorn never looked more majestic, stretching up into a purple-pink velvet sky. Suddenly, a pale moon played hide-and-seek between the skyscraping trees sliding by above us. I was lifted again by my shoulders, we were next to the halfway hut. Soft music, the gentle smell of 'glüevie' (hot wine and cinnamon). 'You need some medicine, that will fix you now, but see a doctor tomorrow.' I thought the three doses of 'medicine' I was not able to pay for would fix me forever. My whole body felt like a funny-bone, it tingled with the smallest jar, even putting down on the table a full glass of 'glüe-vie'.

On the sleigh ride down to the hotel from the hut the 'mountain men' vehemently discussed, in their excitement mostly in Switzerdütch, the 'code', the 'laws of the mountains'. They were appalled and couldn't get over the fact that I was left alone up there. They didn't understand my saying how lucky I was. Our group would have stayed up there forever. 'They were not as good skiers as I was,' I said, more in a way of bragging than in their exoneration.

'Nobody could be worse,' they whipped me in duet. 'Unmöglich!' ('Impossible!') the taller one added salt to my wounds; 'Es war unsinnig'

('It was foolish') rubbed in the shorter one. Shorter? He was only about six-two, built like a brick shithouse. Those two didn't mince words, I got the coup de grâce. 'Sie sind no skier' ('You're not a skier'). 'Es war stumpfsinnig' ('It was more than stupid') and both shook their bare heads. The evening breeze couldn't move one strand of their barbed wire-thick, rust-coloured hair, held in place after a fashion by pairs of grandmother's loving-hands-knit, dazzling ear muffs. They could have been brothers. The last ones to compliment my skiing ability. Their advice that, to be a skier, a good skier, you have to think, not just do, stayed with me. It came almost too late.

They refused to come into the hotel and have dinner with me – they had a 'rendezvous' which was 'unmöglich' ('impossible') to cancel – they declined my offer to take the sleigh to wherever, but, 'Auf wiedersehen,' they waved back, as they walked down the hill from the 'Kurhaus'. That was the last time I saw them. I didn't know their names, where they came from. They appeared, saved my life and were gone. I never thanked them one-to-one even for the 'glüe-vie'.

I didn't feel like skiing for the rest of the winter. Easy slopes, bunny-pistes, halfway huts, sunny terraces, anesthetizing 'glüe-vie', phony windbags, empty conversation, everything I have always despised; stiff mornings, wasted days on the fast track to a dead end. Cold turkey, a U-turn.

I loved to play golf and was proud to be a very long hitter, I was often followed beyond the first tee. Not because I was such a good golfer, but I occasionally hooked so viciously my golf balls became boomerangs. I was famous in my home clubs, Lausanne, in Aqua Santa and Olgiata in Rome, Wentworth near London. I knew it was foolish to be proud of this notoriety, but I was. Slowly I was robbed of it by becoming a slicer like the rest of the duffers. It worried me, not for the right reason, but because it took me the regulation three on a five-par hole – not two – to get close to or on the green. The long four-pars were beginning to ruin my score. I had some good silver to show for my luck. Thank God, one of my lovely lady wives in one fell swoop relieved me of all my trophies. It was one of the very few favors the darling lady did for me.

I was beginning to feel tired. Tired? Even the word wasn't in my dictionary before. Those trophies were rubbing it in that I was getting older. Older? Around the turn of my half-century. No way! I rebelled and took on a rough assignment with a German company, which I had nixed before, to write, produce and direct a western, in Spain.

This turned out to be, among the others, probably the best mistake I ever made. Looking for locations above Granada, only barely above nine thousand feet, I could hardly move. Back to my old stomping ground, Almeria, at sea level, I couldn't move. Nothing hurt, nothing worked. Some of the nothings were embarrassing. The first serious symptom that started to worry me. But I couldn't worry too long.

The company didn't like what I wrote, it was too rough for them, so they conveniently ran out of money. I even had to bail the recce crew out of Spain. They never paid me a penny. Actually they owed me 10 per cent less than the contract called for because I made that deal without an agent of course.

I went back to Switzerland to find out we were living in Le Mont sur Lausanne, in the Canton Vaud, in a three-storey-plus mansard farm-house, built in 1785, on 164 acres. The rolling fields were studded with cherry, apple, prune, plum, all kinds of pear trees. Snow-capped Alps on the skyline, Lake Geneva on the horizon. No cows with bells, the only cow, with bell, belonged to Mme Ecoffeé, whose family built and owned the spread. Gertrude was the sole supplier of Madame's daily milk, butter, whipped cream, sour cream and cheese requirements.

Madame Ecoffeé lived on the premises on the ground floor behind a mountain of cord-wood in a – I don't know what to call it. It was a very large room, with a loft, stacked full of hay. One very large faience stove at one end, a very large cast-iron stove at the opposite end. In dead center was a very large iron stove on eagle claws clutching a ball legs, next to an enormous bath tub – again on eagle claws clutching a ball. In the farthest corner from the entrance was a tennis-court-size bed with pillows piled high on a straw-stuffed mattress. In the closest corner to the entrance was a long dining table surrounded by a dozen large wooden armchairs, below shelves loaded with beer steins, mugs, glasses, bottles of all kinds, full and empty, a couple of different guns and large pistols. From the rafters above the table hung like necklaces various sausages, cheeses in sacks, bunches of grapes. Every piece of furniture, the commodes, cup-boards, everything was hand-carved, naked wood. Everything was bright, spotless, clean and smelled of hay, woods and Yardley's to match the chintz and lace clouds. And Madame Ecoffeé, straight as a pine tree, all 6 feet 2 inches of her at 90.

One side of this heaven of hers was attached to the main building, the other to a large barn, Gertrude's bedroom, which she shared with ancient but shining-new-looking farm equipment and hay, hay and hay piled in the half-loft under the cathedral ceiling.

At first I didn't know why we had moved from the small but big-enough Swiss modern monstrosity we had been leasing from Mr and Mme Theodore Tealdeaux. He was the nosiest vermin in the world. He was terrified of the two Kuvaszok we had imported from Hungary. They kept him snooping around the house under the pretext: 'S'il y a jamais quelque-chose à régler, faîtes-nous savoir vous Américains, vous êtes si gâtés. Nous ferons tout le possible pour que vous vous sentiez chez vous ici dans notre petite Suisse' ('If there is anything to be taken care of, just let us know, you Americans are sooo sooo spoiled. We want you to feel at home in our small Switzerland'). He bowed and smiled ingratiatingly, very unlike the Swiss pride. I suppose the uncivilized, proud pagan blood of the Hun-Magyar-Tartár heritage of thousands of years on the steppe boiled up in Keve, the male Kuvasz. He finally put a stop to Tealdeaux's intrusions. He ultimately accepted the monthly rent by mail instead of picking it up personally. 'Ça me gêne de vous imposer la visite à la poste chaque mois, mais . . .' ('I hate to put you to the inconvenience of going to the post office every month, but . . .') and he pitifully shrugged.

The troops didn't fit around the table in the dining-room, we were having cheese fondue in the kitchen; my lady wife, four of the children, their nurse, and 'Tündér' ('Good Fairy'), the female Kuvasz resting her chin on my instep under the large dining-table. In the living-room, pardon me, salon, Bing Crosby crooned 'White Christmas' on the Blau-punkt console. It was the night before we all were off to Lenzerheide. Tranquility.

The heavenly peace on earth was only interrupted with an occasional 'Watch what you're doing,' or an 'Oooh, look what you have done,' as Nissat, the five-foot-short and five-foot-wide nurse in charge of the children tried to peer over the rim of the large crockery pot above the flames to fish out the piece of bread one of the children had dropped in the gluey yellow goop of cheese.

Richter scale 8, the table moved as Tündér jumped up growling and charged at the door. There are great differences between growls and growls. This wasn't a 'don't bother me' growl, her growl meant business. Her growl at the door was answered from outside with an 'Au secours!' ('Help!') and another miserable 'Au secours'; Keve's answer from the outside rattled the windows.

The Kuvaszok were serious, no monkeying around with those dogs; they left their cousins, the still-existing breeds of the Tibetan mastiffs, the Mongolian sheepdogs and the Tartár sheepdogs behind with the Huns and the Magyars during the Great Migration, arriving in the Danube basin during the end of the 9th, beginning of the 10th century AD. Loyal and fearless, they were irreplaceable defenders of the livestock from the wolf packs then roaming the plains. Their courage is still unparalleled by any canine, save the giant Komondor. King Mathias of Hungary (1458–90) had his bodyguards replaced by Kuvaszok. Since nobility evolved from the most successful shepherds, it was the natural progression for both the human and canine species to move together from the grass and mud hovels to the stone dwellings and castles. The Kuvasz became the dog of the nobility, not unlike the magnificent German Weimaraner up to 1946 or so. The name Kuvasz means the defender of nobility.

So Monsieur Tealdeaux shouldn't have been so distraught, after all he wasn't pinned to the ground in the snow under the aluminium ladder by an ordinary dog. It appeared he was peeking through the kitchen window on the top of the ladder, not a noble deed, and the noble Keve took umbrage.

'Out!' I commanded Keve. He was a well-trained Schutzhund III; not very happily, he got off Monsieur Tealdeaux's concave chest, Nissat dragged the ladder off him as she asked, 'Vous nous espionnez encore, monsieur Tealdeaux' ('Spying again, Mister Tealdeaux?').

I calmed Keve, who was snarling and pawing the snow; 'A friend, a good friend, a nice friend,' pointing at Tealdeaux, squirming in the snow. I must have overdone it because, with a sudden lunge, he licked the face of the whimpering Monsieur Tealdeaux who promptly fainted. And from there on our contact with Madame and Monsieur Tealdeaux was restricted to the telephone and the excellent Swiss mail service. They were relieved, I believe they were relieved, when my lady wife asked them to cancel our lease. Sometimes she made good mistakes, and she moved into the farmhouse, where the door to the second floor had never been opened.

Nothing to be ashamed of – being humiliated by a dog like Keve, with his 110 pounds of muscle and one-inch fangs on top of you – but by a paper-clip? I couldn't pick them up from the top of my desk. That I started to slice not only my woods but my irons was disastrous enough, but being ridiculed by a paper-clip? No way would I be defeated by a silly old paper-clip, I tried to master them for months. My fingers felt like sausages, their tips went numb. Was it the revenge of the cursed paper-clips? Watch out for them, they have their own mafia, they screwed up the showers for me too – my only joy left after a lousy golf game, a hot then a cold shower. But it seemed the paper-clips mafia was running the Swiss plumbers union, the water was never cold enough and never hot, only lukewarm or scalding turning the skin to blistering crimson.

I read the books, I had lessons from the top pros, 'Don't strangle that club, no white knuckles as you swing.' As sometimes I did overdo things I really must have over-corrected. One afternoon on the first tee my driver flew out of my hands. Everybody thought it was a funny joke. I asked my caddy to pick the driver up, that was it for that afternoon, I thought. That afternoon turned out to be damned long. It is still on.

I drove to my garage on the way home, my steering wheel was sticking, it was a hell of an effort to turn. They found no trouble. Mercedes services were usually very good world-wide, but in Switzerland they had to be extra thoughtful – at that time there were too many spoiled tax-fugitives with heavy-number accounts. Monsieur Probst asked me with thousands of apologies if I had had something to drink, it happened to everybody sometimes, they would be happy to drive me home. I made it home, hoping for a better tomorrow.

The inconsiderate morning sun burst through my windows. Unreal puffy white clouds with pink edges stuck on a corny-blue sky. It seemed an ideal morning to play golf, I decided to play 36 holes, just for the hell of it. Whatever bugged me I wouldn't give in. Let a golf club fly out of my hands. That was stupid. The mafia of the paper-clips could not be that powerful, I got out of bed.

I encountered one minor and unexpected detail, I had no legs under me to hold me up.

'Good!' said my understanding lady wife as she stood over me, gloating, 'there is justice, now you're going to pay for your conceit. You thought you were an iron man, I am telling you, your rust is showing.'

It certainly did and little could I do to hide it. There was only one telephone in the old farmhouse, it was in the kitchen. I was trapped. I couldn't have opened the door she considerately shut, so I did the next best I could have done, dragged down a pillow from my bed and lay back on the hardwood floor. Nothing hurt. Outside the damned birds were singing, the children laughing as they were stacked in the car on their way to school. I had time to think. I should have – forever hindsight – listened to my Bernese Oberländers in Lenzerheide, maybe I should have seen a doctor.

The door opened, Keve and Tündér charged through, and after licking my face lay down next to me. The lady of the house marched in dressed to kill in her most out-of-place and expensive dressing gown. 'Want a coffee or tea or something?' and she answered before I could open my mouth, 'Nope, better have nothing, let's wait. I called the ambulance after the children left. I didn't want to upset them.' She could be considerate.

The ambulance arrived and the circus started. Keve sat on me, Tündér straddled my head between her forelegs. They didn't bark, didn't charge, just sat on me and growled at the entering ambulance attendants, exposing their frightening fangs. Could I have gotten up and commanded 'Ssitt' there would have been no trouble at all; they ignored it, sensing I was helpless.

'Those goddamned dogs of yours,' shrieked the lady of the house, most incongruously with her high-fashion elegance.

'Don't move,' I asked the attendants. I didn't have to ask them twice, they froze smartly. 'Step in front of them,' I asked her. 'Now, all of you, back out, slowly . . . Fine . . . now close the door, slowly, very slowly,' she complied till the last foot or so of the opening, then slammed it fast. Keve didn't move, Tündér flew at the door snarling. She meant business.

'Now what?' she yelled in a louder voice than necessary.

'Ask them to leave and come back in ten minutes,' which she did, happy to show off her passable French. The front door opened and closed, the ambulance's door opened and closed, its engine started, Keve didn't move, Tündér charged to the window and stayed there looking out, barking savagely. My bedroom door swung open, she stood on the threshold like mother-god of the Furies.

'You have embarrassed me!' That was all she said.

Dressed in white, the nurses slid by the open door, silent like a Swiss ski-patrol in the Alps. The bed was white, the coverlet was white, the snow was white outside the large window, the smock of Dr Claude Schneider, associate professor of neurology of the University of Lausanne was white, the milk-glass against the white wall was whiter, the X-rays snapped against it looked blacker than they actually were.

'Quelle horreur' ('What horror') he stated simply, turning away from them. 'As you Americans say it so aptly, you are in a hell of a mess.' No truer word could have been spoken. My arms and hands were about calling quits. 'Why did you wait for so long?' was a silly question from a brilliant man.

'What are my chances?'

'Straight?'

'Straight!'

'Not too good. You'll be paralyzed only from waist down, at best.'

'At worse?'

'Totally.'

'Thanks, that was straight enough, I appreciated it. But you're wrong, I'll be, I want to be back in the saddle.'

He was puzzled by my attitude and the expression, 'In what saddle?'

'Never mind, I am asking for one thing only, don't put another vege- table in the garden of the living dead.'

'Pardon?'

'Never mind, I'll be walking within a month.'

'C'est ça, beaucoup meilleur [that's much better]. I believe you.' He came close, reached out his hand, smiled, 'Shake.' I tried. 'Harder.' I tried, he shook his head, not enough, harder . . . harder. Whenever I saw him he demanded, 'Harder!' And from that feeble handshake formed a strong, lasting friendship.

Life is strange, what is lasting? He left and I am still here to the surprise or disappointment of some. If the dead could comprehend, I knew then exactly how they would feel as 'They came to pay their last respects.' Even the three 'bankrupt' German geniuses who had abandoned me came with a haywagon full of roses to ease their guilty consciences or pacify my ghost not to come back and haunt them. Nobody wanted to touch me. I felt like a sausage covered with a coat of green rot hanging in limbo. I never could find out what really motivated my lovely lady wife – to really help me or impress her 'jet-set' friends – but she went as far as to call Professor Diamant of the Amsterdam University to come and see me, which he did. He saw me for 30 minutes then flew back to Holland, saying before he departed, if he were as badly off as I was, he would ask Professor Zander if he would be willing to take the chance to operate. But Diamant himself would not touch me with a Dutch barge-pole. All for a small fee of $5,000. Cash.

Only Claude Schneider and Professor Zander realized my determination to walk, to use my hands again and Zander decided to operate on me. Nine and a half hours on the operating table, then on my stomach for seven days and nights with careful hands turning my head every thirty minutes from one side to the other. Every thirty minutes I had to watch my left then my right hand, dead, next to my face. Both hands – dead! Praying, 'Move,' didn't help. Cursing them to move didn't help. Willing them to move, nothing. Wishing them to move, nothing. Nothing! They were useless pieces of dead meat.

After watching, watching, staring at two dead hands for hours and hours and days and days of eternity, finally they turned me over on my back like I was a side of beef. With blurred vision I saw a circle of anxious faces above me, Zander barked, 'Move your toes . . . move them.'

'Please,' asked Claude Schneider from the background.

I tried, I tried and tried, I have never tried anything so hard since or before. I felt nothing, nothing was moving.

'Try harder,' barked Zander louder and whacked my legs with full force. I could see it. I had no feeling.

'Again,' he commanded.

Zander was a full colonel, not medical but a regular colonel in the Swiss army – where the eagles weren't perching as quick and easy on the shoulders as they did in some other armies around the world. He was well over six-feet-two inches, a Heidelberg graduate, with several Mensura schnitts to prove it beyond the diploma in his office.

Zander, as tough as a marine drill-sergeant, hit me again with brute force. 'I believed you, so now move it!'

I felt nothing.

'Don't worry about your arms and hands, they'll be all right.'

In Switzerland, like in many European countries, courtesy was almost as important as your knowledge. Associate Professor Schneider opened the door for Professor Zander, the dean of the university, and the door closed behind them. I don't worry about your arms and hands, they'll be all right, fine.

'What about my legs?' I called after them.

No reply came back. They either didn't hear or didn't know, and they left me behind with my unqualified doubts. I closed my eye, squeezed the lids tight, so tight they hurt, and I was glad, at least I felt something.

'Goddamnit, I am going to move, I'm going to walk, write, direct pictures, hunt deer and fish for trout again in the High Sierras – '

' – Bien sur' ('For sure') said the nurse, and she put a warm compress on my eyes and a cold one on my forehead. It surprised me, I had forgotten when I spoke out loud I had a nurse in attendance twenty-four hours a day. I was glad she covered my eye. When, after a week on my stomach, they turned me on my back, it was a relief at first, but staring at the white ceiling for days turned it into an endless ski-slope without horizon and I was really moving through the knee-deep virgin powder faster and faster, leaving vapour trails of snow behind me until I hit a boulder. But this rock wasn't covered with snow like the boulder I hit on the Rothorn run, this one stood there naked and as I was racing toward it, it grew and blocked my path. I hit it. The rock shattered and I started the run anew, over and over again. No feeling. A floating puppet on a string. 'Keep your shoulders parallel with the slope, bend your knees more, your legs are the springs, your power is coming from your hips. Uphill, ski slightly forward as you start your turn. Don't drag your poles. Don't let the tips dig in,' yelled Roland Bläzi at the top of his voice. The edges dug in deep, the cock's-comb of snow reached the sky, covered everything. This time I was determined to avoid the rock. I put in everything I had. I screamed.

'Congratulations' said the voice, gentle hands wiped the sweat off my brow. 'You made it! . . . That's fine. Relax now.' Schneider and the nurse stood above me. 'That was enough, don't try it any more. You have moved your toes. Tomorrow we start the physiotherapy.'

Ten months after I broke my neck and after six weeks of twenty-eight hours per week physiotherapy I walked out of the hospital, no crutches, no sticks. No neck-brace.

I wanted to surprise them at home. And it turned out to be quite a surprise.

'I never saw a Kuvasz before, I'd like to see them,' asked the cab driver. I was talking about them all the way up. My taxi pulled up in front of the farm.

'Keve, Tündér!'

Nothing. The front door cracked ajar, I called again. Quiet. No Keve or Tündér came to greet me. The door swung open. 'Here they'll come,' I whistled. 'Keve, Tündér!'

'I had to get rid of those wild beasts. They were unmanageable, what

are you doing here?' were the first words of welcome home from the lady
of the house when she emerged, dragging two suitcases. 'Is that the taxi
you came in?' she asked as I was paying the driver.

'Why? I – '

' – We ordered one, I thought this was it, at first I didn't see you behind
the cab.' Annoyed, she checked her watch, 'It should've been here long
ago. Damn, it spoiled my surprises for you.'

'Oh, and what else?'

The surprises started to drown me, one of her daughters from a former
marriage appeared lugging two additional suitcases. 'What are you doing
here?' she asked the same question her mother did. Maybe I had more
reason to ask her questions, since the last I knew of her she was in jail in
Arizona for alleged shoplifting, but I didn't ask her. She ignored me
anyway, brooding, turned to her mother, 'He ain't gonna spoil our
vacation, or is he?' and continued as if I were not present, 'this is my
twenty-first birthday present, he could drop dead and I wouldn't care,
we'll be goin' right, right Mom? You promised.'

I didn't drop dead, I didn't stop them, I only stopped my taxi from
leaving when their one cab arrived to pick up the bubbling, happy tribe
emerging with skis, ski-boots, parkas, favorite toys and good-luck charms:
five children, Nissat the 'governess' and her.

'How on earth you thought you could fit all of you in one taxi with the – '

' – Stop directing, we managed pretty well without you. So – ' she never
finished the sentence, which was one of her better habits, and off they
went to ski, not in Lenzerheide, but in 'jet-set-land', St Moritz.

I watched the taxis sashay down the hill on the icy road. The children
screamed with joy, 'We'll see you tomorrow . . . We love you, daddy . . .
We'll see you up there . . . Hurry up . . . Bye-bye,' and the cabs disappeared behind the snow banks around the bend. The end was fast,
funny and painless.

'I have nice hot chocolate with whipcream, some walnut and apple torte.
Come on,' and Madame Ecoffeé hooked a strong arm around my
shoulders, picked up my small valise. 'Let's go, it's cold out here,' she felt
my shoulder as she guided me with care on the icy driveway. 'God, you're
skinny. I'll fix you some good dinner – '

' – Thanks, but I better – '

' – No buts,' and she firmly propelled me away from the still ajar front
door. I couldn't match her strength.

'I'll lock it later, after I set you up in my place.'

'But I – '

' – No, you're not. They didn't expect you and your wife gave three weeks Christmas vacation to the help. She is very considerate, you know.'

I did.

21 Nicknames

Andor, András, Endre, all had the same nickname, 'Bandi'. Why I don't know. It's Hungarian logic so my nickname, 'Bandi', was not unique or unusual. So it was not unusual that George Marton, a well-established literary agent cum writer working out of Hollywood and Paris, had a younger brother named 'Bandi', a well-respected second unit director in Hollywood.

Jenö Csepreghy, aka Johnny Shepridge, was an unsettled gentleman with several films as an extra in Hollywood and two or three films as director in Hungary to his credit. A ladies' man supreme and international playboy extraordinaire, thus it was not unsual for somebody like Johnny finally to land an heiress, Fea Hunter, an international-Argentinian junior Elsa Maxwell, a millionairess in her spare time. Neither was it unusual that they settled in London and Marbella; however, what was somewhat unusual was that Fea carried her Yorkshire Terrier in and out of England through the quarantine in the sleeve of her mink coat or in her purse.[1]

Johnny was always thinking big, often too big for his britches, so it didn't surprise me at all when, in 1958, he came to me. 'I took an option on a gold mine,' he beamed.

'What are you going to do with it?'

'You are my partner, a Corniche for me, and I always wanted you out of that silly, isolation-booth, gull-wing 300SL Mercedes of yours, a Lamborghini for you –.'

' – Make mine red, OK?'

'This is no joke. Did you hear of Ian Fleming?'

'No.'

'Did you hear of 007?'

---

1 It couldn't be done today, there were no security checks then.

'No.'

'Aoh,' he grunted and extolled at length the potential of the Ian Fleming properties. 'I took a six-month option on them,' and handed me a book. 'We'll start with this one.'

I read it, the title was *Dr No*. It was good. But for five months trying to get it off the ground I heard nothing but 'no's', we couldn't even get a positive 'maybe' to encourage me to go on. This wasn't unusual either, but I became saturated with 'no's', and finally I said 'no' to Johnny.

'OK,' he shrugged, 'I'll find somebody to pick up my extension of the option for another six months.'

He found 'somebody' by the name of Harry Saltzman, a bright-eyed Canadian who started to pound the rough road to the calvary of 'no's' with as much success as I had had. With a week remaining out of the six months of his option, without a chance of renewing it, despondent, Johnny suggested as the last straw to take the project to the Godfather of all American film-makers working in London, Cubby Broccoli, known, respected and loved, with considerable success in his wake on both sides of the water.

Cubby was a picture-maker with an uncanny instinct, a gift that could not be earned or learned, and a Calabrian heart as big as his old grey battleship, a classic Rolls Silver Shadow with a license plate: CUB 1, the envy of the Cuban embassy in London and lots of others. It wasn't unusual that Cubby read *Dr No* overnight, got on the plane the next morning to New York and, after landing it, took all of another hour and a half – lunch included – to put together the package with United Artists' Arthur Krim. And so the seeds were sown for the James Bond series, the most successful independent venture in the history of motion pictures, by the oddest odd couple: Cubby Broccoli and Harry Saltzman.

From there on everything became a very strange chain of unusual coincidences; 'ifs' and luck again took over the tiller of my tomorrow and, in the ensuing confusion, the very usual name 'Bandi' became the common denominator for the most unusual, royal mix-up.

George Marton sold Harry Saltzman a vague story idea, *Deadly Patrol*, and with it the venerable French maître René Clement to direct. Being a snob, and wanting to prove to himself and to the world he was a better picture-maker than Cubby, Harry grabbed the opportunity to work with the highly regarded around the world, specially in highbrow circles – René Clement, soft, vulnerable and gentle.

That *Deadly Patrol* had no story to tell, no point of view, didn't bother either Saltzman or Clement, each being sure he was the one who would find a story they wanted to tell. Both were right. Each came up with one. There were two *Deadly Patrol* stories as different, as far apart in concept as three persons could have been – Madame Clement put her two cents in the pot too.

It was no wonder that after the first 'How do you do?' Harry Saltzman and René Clement, exasperating each other, had nothing but trouble with each other and rather than developing the story, in their own civilized, impotently-silent hatred, developed nervous tics instead. There were no steam-releasing, hysterical shouting matches like the constant and volcanic blow-ups between Saltzman and Ken Russell on *The Billion Dollar Brain*, a picture I ended up producing for Saltzman while he was preparing *The Deadly Patrol*, which almost killed him.

Actually, I got involved involuntarily with both shows because my nickname created confusion. Harry had heard of, but never met 'Bandi' Marton, the famous 'Who did what?' second unit director of Willy Wyler's *Ben Hur*. Had he heard of Andre de Toth, there was no earthly reason he should have known that once upon a time 'Bandi' was Andre de Toth's nickname, reserved for close friends.

For Johnny Shepridge there were 'only two mountains' in Switzerland that weren't silly: 'One had Gstaad on it, the other St Moritz.' Wanting to help me and get me off that 'silly mountain of mine', which he hated – it was 'too-too quiet' for him – he told Harry that 'Bandi' had made a remarkable recovery after he broke his neck skiing, he was ready to go back to work. Harry, badly in need of George Marton to smooth out the daily 'misunderstandings' between him and Clement, jumped at the opportunity to please George by hiring his brother to do second unit on *Billion Dollar Brain*.

Before Johnny could finish his sentence, Harry, impatient and anxious to help, cut him off, 'I want you to talk to "Bandi". Find out what he is up to. Call him now.'

I wasn't home. There were no message machines, thank God. Out of nowhere, in the evening, Johnny called again.

'What's up? What are you doing? Not much I suppose.'

'No. Not much. I finished a screenplay of a Jules Verne book for –'

' – Which one?'

'Can't tell you, Johnny. They are having some legal entanglement with it, they've asked me to keep mum.'

'Another never-never land.'

'Could well be.'

'How well do you know Harry?'

'Harry who?'

'Harry Saltzman of the Saltzman-Broccoli-Bond empire.'

'Never met him.'

'He seemed to know you and wants to talk to you about an assignment.'

'Why?'

'Don't be funny, leave the goats on that stupid hill, talk to him, he'll send you a ticket and set you up here. It'll be good to see you anyway. When do you want to come? Can't lose.'

'Don't know, let me think – '

' – Yeah or nay, he wants to know now, I have to tell him.'

'I'll let you know, I – '

' – Yeah or nay?'

' – I'll call you.'

I had known Cubby Broccoli, Saltzman's partner for years. Why didn't he call, I thought; I thought and thought. In this business people are so quickly forgotten. People who shouldn't be. I had been out of it for two years leaving no mementos behind; I was not satisfied with anything I had done till then and what I had done during the two years on my back was patch up script jobs, nameless and better forgotten. But I was aching and eager to get back in the saddle, so I stopped thinking and started packing. I was on the next flight to London.

'Good,' said Johnny when I called him, 'I hoped you had come to your senses, when do you want to come?'

'I am in the Dorchester.'

'Fine, tell me when so Harry can set you up. But you know the quarantine regulations, you can't bring your damned polar bear with you.' Johnny had the sometimes very aggravating, sometimes blissful habit of not listening.

'Johnny, I am calling you from the Dorchester, and I came without Macko [my 192-pound Komondor].'

After a long silence, during which I heard him through the phone taking a slurping sip of his always scalding hot coffee, another aggravating habit he had, he sighed, 'You're nuts. Why?'

'Why am I nuts? I don't know why, but I like it that way. I am kind of used to it.'

'He-wanted-to-send-you-a-ticket. Are you suddenly that rich or are you crazier than I thought you were?'

'Pick your own answer. I didn't want to get obligated before I knew what I was –'

I heard another, louder, slurp through the phone as I was talking, then he interrupted me. 'You woke me up –'

' – Be glad there wasn't any earlier flight out of Geneva.'

'Order me up ham 'n' two eggs, basted easy, rye toast, Scottish marmalade, you know how I like my coffee. I'll be over in ten minutes.'

His opening words when he walked in were, 'Let's order another pot, I'm sure this is not hot enough.'

The third pot was OK, he was finally satisfied. I wasn't. He had no idea what Saltzman wanted me for. 'He kept on talking about a chariot race like the one in *Ben Hur*, except in the snow.'

'He should've called Yakima Canutt.'

'He wanted you –'

' – He wants me for a second unit –'

' – So what? I want you back in circulation. We'll get Macko in here –'

' – Yeah, yeah , he won't fit and you can't afford a mink coat with big enough sleeves –'

' – Talk to him, it can't hurt, you're here. I'll make him reimburse you whatever happens.'

'I don't want to be reimbursed, I –'

He held up a hand, checked his watch, 'Let's go, he doesn't like to wait . . . Yeah, I told him you were here. He was impressed. Let's go. I'll walk you over.'

We didn't speak until we stopped, 'This is as far as I go, you're on your own,' and he walked off.

Saltzman's office was a hop, skip and a short jump from the hotel; it occupied half of three floors of a lovely old building on Audley Square. The carefully observed other half of the building was Cubby Broccoli's kingdom. Everything in the building was deluxe, more than what I was expecting, not garish.

Saltzman's office was on the first (US second) floor; it was large and long, oblong with his almost wall-to-wall desk at one end of it. It was a big desk, the biggest I have seen, and the most cluttered I have seen.

Without any doubt it was an office. There was no backgammon board and table in sight like in Cubby's office on the same floor, which was spacious and square with two identical museum-piece 'partner's' desks, a memento from the early London, Cubby and Irving Allen days, now with one of his chairs empty, an invitation Harry never accepted nor refused, just didn't fill. Too bad. Both men sat alone.

Partners shouldn't compete with each other. Alone by his own choice, Harry sat in Buddha-like fashion, and endowed alike, in a big high-back, red leather swivel-rocker chair, wiggling his toes in red stockings half-way hidden under him. He was rocking in the dangerously tilting chair, stuffing himself with bonbons from a large box in front of him on the desk. When I walked in he threw himself forward. I was sure he would topple over, I rushed forward to catch him. No. He rocked himself backward, so far backwards that the back of his chair and his body was parallel to the ornate ceiling, then he rocked so far forward his chin almost hit the top of the desk and with speed and surprising dexterity grabbed two bonbons, threw them into his mouth on his way back to face the ceiling again. 'Are you hungry?' he asked.

I was, but, seeing he was gorging himself, I lied, 'No.'

'Good,' he said and with the same breath he instructed one of the secretaries officiously holding a note book, 'Reserve a table for four at the Gay Hussar. Tell Victor it's for me, on the Tory side.'

The Gay Hussar was a fabulous, real Hungarian restaurant. The place was little wider and longer than a railroad carriage, and was always crowded with politicos. The right side was reserved for Tories, the left for Labour. Then prime minister Wilson sat opposite us. I was impressed, it was not a media hangout.

As we were seated, he finally introduced me to the two people, which he had neglected to do in his office, only as 'Bandi': 'He'll be with us.' That was all. We talked about everything except why I was there. He rattled on about how great a chariot race-like sequence on sleds in the snow, deep snow, very deep snow would be in *Billion Dollar Brain*; this meant little or nothing to me at that time, I hadn't read the book and as the ugly credit bickering about who had shot the chariot race in *Ben Hur* had always appalled me, I disconnected from the conversation. I was at the table only in body. The question nauseated me, I didn't care who did it. Who did it? Was it Bandi Marton? (the top second unit director of the time) or was it Yakima Canutt (the king of the stuntmen for decades)?

Willy Wyler, who directed the film, said Yakima did it; Bandi Marton said he did it; Yakima shrugged his massive shoulders, twitched his big ears, scratched his nose, said nothing and smiled in silence as the undignified, repulsive credit hussle went on – even years later in London at the Gay Hussar.

'Gay' meant what the word originally was used for. I liked Victor, the owner, for retaining his old trademark when the word acquired another connotation, and for his excellent food. I didn't want Harry and Co. to spoil my meal with the old Hollywood muck. 'Let's talk about something else.' And in my annoyance I didn't pick up one of the flunkies saying, 'Modesty, modesty.'

I thought it was quite elegant not to talk business during our first luncheon, but when we got back from lunch the first thing Harry did was kick off his shoes, climb back into his rocker, grab a handful of bonbons and throw them toward his mouth. Various shapes of chocolate were flying through the air like buckshot, reinforcing a belief in miracles – not one piece of chocolate missed his mouth. I slipped forward on my seat, ready to jump to perform a Heimlich maneuver as he swung himself backward. He didn't choke.

Silence. In slow-motion Harry sat up straight as a die and switched off, staring at nothing. An effigy of void. Nobody moved. It was nothing like Churchill's famous doze-offs, with which I was familiar. Churchill was alive even then. Saltzman, with his large, dark, usually sparkling eyes wide open, stared sightlessly. A wax figure, he, the man wasn't there any more. It was eery, and it went on. I cleared my throat, stood up, his two men threw disapproving glances at me and returned to their own reverie on each side of Saltzman's throne. I was ready to leave the office, London. This macabre wax museum.

Like when a coin drops in a machine to animate the puppets, Harry stood up, looked straight at me, he was alive again. 'We'll have a talk a little later, look at your office now,' he said on his way to his private bathroom and shut the door behind him.

I found a nice office with two telephones on the desk, and a battle-axe secretary who explained that the second telephone was for Mr Saltzman to get to me without going through the switchboard; he didn't like to wait, so I shouldn't use it except, of course, if I wanted to talk to Mr Saltzman direct. Little did I know then how important that second phone was. Throughout the years while I was working with Harry

Saltzman that phone never rang once.

It seemed I was going to be important in the outfit. I was impressed, let's wait and see, I thought, sitting behind my desk in a comfortable chair with a cup of good coffee and Len Deighton's *Billion Dollar Brain* in front of me. I took toll of the situation. The mistaken identity became more and more evident and I was beginning to enjoy the charade. I wasn't hurting anybody, I was not going to take 'Bandi' Marton's job, I was paying for my own freight. Why not have some fun?

I started to read, I didn't notice it had become dark outside. A soft knock on the door, my battle-axe came in, put a slip of paper in front of me, 'Excuse me, sir, for disturbing you but if you have nothing special for me to do tonight I shall be leaving now, good night Mr Marton.'

I laughed out so loud, she must have thought I had gone off my rocker, and with her British scuffle was backing toward the door, on the double. I didn't blame her.

'Did Mr Saltzman – '

' – Oh yes, sir,' she cut me off eager to get the hell out, 'Mr Saltzman called, but when I told him you were reading, he didn't want me to disturb you, sir, his message is in front of you, sir, good night, sir.' And she was out.

'You knew it, you son-of-a-bitch, didn't you?' I told Johnny in the Dorchester bar later.

'Of course.'

'Then why?'

'You're back in circulation. For Christ's sake you know the business, they buried you already, wake up. Nobody got hurt, don't tell Harry – '

' – But – '

' – Wait, let him find out on his own. Being one of those lucky humans who has never been wrong, he will never admit he has made a faux pas. Let it ride and everything will be perfect.' Johnny turned out to be right.

But until Saltzman found out who I really was we had some very weird meetings. On the other hand, even when one knew what he was talking about, it was sometimes difficult to understand or follow him, bright as he was. To help him to make pictures was easy, he loved the idea of making pictures and he had flashes of genius, but his brilliant ideas usually didn't fit the characters or the situation of the moment in the story. But before you could object, he came up with at least five more new ingenious ideas that had equally no place in that particular story. Luckily, he got bored quickly and left the story, the picture and you alone. He had to have a dozen 'thought-balls' in the air to juggle.

Poor methodical René suffered and continuously argued about petty, meaningless details Harry never even thought of and didn't want to be badgered with. Had Clement shrugged off Harry's verbal diarrhea, he could have used the few brilliant thoughts that were always hidden in Harry's diatribes. But no. He too was in love with himself, his own ideas and was convinced they were always better than Harry's, or anybody else's. Clement wanted credit more than anything else, but wanted to earn it. He was a very proud man. The big difference between Clement and Harry was that, in the end, Harry didn't care whose the idea was, he knew it was his anyway.

It would have been impossible to find three more different men in the same business in the world. Here they were under the same roof: Clement, Saltzman, Broccoli. There was no similarity between Clement and the other two. The only similarity between Saltzman and Broccoli was that they both loved to make pictures, and that was it. Cubby just wanted to make films, make them well and sanely. Harry wanted to make them to have power and money for the fulfilment of his dreams. His dreams were beautiful, commendable and mostly impractical. He had an artistic soul. He was complex, intricate, complicated and sensitive; he was a living invitation to be hurt, he was a masochist. For him no straight line ever existed between 'A' and 'B', even if taking it would have led him to the jackpot. If there weren't any, he caused complications. Cubby knew only one straight path and he followed it even if it bruised him. He was no pushover by any means, he was known to move mountains out of his way, but his blood from the south of Italy made him avoid all exertion if possible. However, he still often got there first. His love of making pictures was for the sheer joy of making them, and a joy it was to make pictures with Cubby. He had another hobby he loved aside from making pictures: gambling. He was a good loser and an even better winner, one would never know whether he was winning or losing.

I could not compare Cubby to any of the Selznicks, Kordas, Zanucks, Harry Cohns or Jack Warners, the giants of the past with whom I had worked. He was Cubby Broccoli, unique in his talent. He was closest maybe to Jack Warner in his approach to solving problems and the concept of film-making in general. He was as tough as Jack Warner if need be, but in general he was softer and probably enjoyed life more. Nobody ever had and nobody will ever have a nickname that fit better: 'Cubby'.

Harry Saltzman had all the talent and all the faults of yesteryears' giants; unfortunately, it all mingled, and what a turbulent mess it was. He was closest to the semi-giant Sam Spiegel, also vying for the title 'the biggest snob'. Both came from a past they were not extremely proud of, both Harry and Sam occasionally subdued their excellent taste with a garish display of their good fortune, to submerge their insecurity, and choked themselves with brilliant non-sequitur ideas. Foolish spenders to impress. When it came to production costs Sam became a downright miser. Harry remained a big spender. Neither had any patience or tolerance. They were charmers without Korda's class. Spiegel wanted big, 'entertaining' films, Harry wanted award-winning art films and blockbusters at the same time. Had they been partners they would have killed each other. Harry would have done the job himself in an anger tantrum, Sam would have hired a professional to do it. One had to feel compassion for Harry Saltzman. Hidden, well hidden inside him was a generous, beautiful, tortured man. Sam improved with his success, unfortunately Harry didn't.

Harry Saltzman looked down on the Bond pictures. They were beneath him. Basically, he looked down on the motion-picture industry as a whole and on those in general who made them, but he accepted the millions the pictures scattered in his path. He wanted to be a successful West End and Broadway producer. That was class.

And class was what he was looking for, like Woodlands, Bucks, his country cottage with its half-acre-size living-room, through which his oldest son drove his mini-midget electric car from one side of the estate to the other to avoid going around an acre and a half of other buildings, not counting the indoor swimming pool, where butlers from the 'shore' – with white gloves naturally – served the drinks inserted in small life preservers. They skimmed the drinks expertly to your floating chaise while you had a story conference. I always wondered how the butlers could find us in the temperature-controlled London fog depositing large droplets of condensation on the cold glass ceiling. Those Sybarites who criticized it, enjoyed it usually as much as the rest of us. I wallowed in it, it eased the discomfort and helped to mend my broken neck. The pool was home for Harry, a bore for Jackie – Mrs Salzman – who couldn't swim and hated water, except Evian in a Baccarat glass or scented in an extra large tub. By the way, all this was set in two hundred magnificent wooded acres with two trout streams running through, in which the life expectancy of the trout was forever, the life expectancy of the fishing lures was three castings, maximum. After that, like crazy Christmas ornaments, they were hanging on the surrounding trees.

The swans in England are Crown property, the Queen owns them. It was unfair as far as Jackie Saltzman was concerned. If the Queen had swans, she wanted swans too. At least six of them, 'Cherieee, mon cherieee, at leeeast,' Jackie bubbled. 'You can't have two lakes without swans.' The lakes were big enough to have a couple of small boats on them. 'One of the lakes for boats, cherieee, one for swans, six, cherieeee!' Jackie pronounced the verdict with conviction and two big, noisy, wet kisses on Harry's well-cushioned cheeks. His dark eyes lit up. They truly loved each other and both hated the Broccolis. I never found out why, nor did I want to.

To own one swan was an impossibility, because they were the Crown's but Harry came up with three. It was one of those magic English summer days, the sky was so blue that it was a lie, no such blue existed. The picnic set-up was more poetic than any image the French impressionist 'déjeuner painters' have put on canvas. The breeze was just right, gently swaying the corners of the overhanging Brussels lace tablecloths. Saltzman's oldest son, taking the picnic set-up as a gymkhana course, whizzed his kamikaze vehicle between them. Two big Chesapeake Bay retrievers divided their attention between happily crunching the ice from the solid silver champagne-cooler buckets and chasing the little maniac on his chariot of destruction. So it was all set up for an idyllic Sunday picnic in the British countryside to celebrate the miracle, the arrival of the three swans in Jackie and Harry Saltzman's little country hideaway.

Competing with the swirling puffy white clouds in the blue sky above, Jackie, in a tulle, Schiaparelli-pink cloud, swirled around below, seemingly without her feet ever touching the emerald green grass, a most gracious hostess wanting to be sure the guests were gorging themselves with the most expensive of the best. The Saltzmans were overdoing being good hosts, but they overdid everything.

Among other connoisseurships, Harry was a connoisseur of caviar, and from that sprung two disasters, the first on that otherwise perfectly normal Sunday afternoon, the second in the Hotel Marski in Helsinki, Finland in the middle of a long frozen winter evening. Jackie and the swans had nothing to do with that.

Jackie Saltzman, like all nouveaux riches, liked to flaunt her good fortune; after all, the swans belonging to the Crown must have been used to 'the good life', she wanted to prove to them they were not slumming, she would be worthy of the title she was hoping for one of these years, so she had decided with the help of her good friend Dom Perignon to involve her aloof new royal wards in the celebration in their honor. With ping-pong ball-size globs of caviar on a bed of slim slivers of various bread, laid out elegantly on a silver platter, like an ominous pink cloud of tornado, carrying her offering, followed by the approving applause of the appreciative, three-sheets-to-the-wind guests, Jackie descended on the swans bobbing up and down in the water, 'They are reeegal, reeegal, cheriee, thanks.'

The swans were a peaceful, elegant and graceful sight; they were much less elegant or graceful when they took off from water, or land for that matter, but the low sun transformed the spray whipped up by their heavy wings into a mirage of rainbows. It was a magnificent sight. Jackie was exalted, so were the swans, sounding like a brass band with cracked horns as they skimmed barely above the water heading for their new sovereign. She reached the shore of what now was designated 'swan lake' and tragedy struck.

The reason was never clear: whether the swans got scared by the dizzying cloud of swirling pink tulle with a large, menacing metal object charging toward them, or whether they disliked Harry's brand of caviar or Jackie's way of serving it, or Jackie herself, their substitute sovereign, for whatever reason – the bottom line was that the three swans attacked her and the bottom line hurt the most. Two of the swans created an impromptu striptease, tearing to shreds the pink dream of Jackie and her couturier, while the third held on to one cheek of Jackie's by then almost naked derrière in his/her (?) vice-like beak and all three with their wings were beating her flesh pinker than her former dress. The gardners came with rakes and shovels to fend off the birds; Harry, swinging a chair, took on one of the swans, a courageous, noble deed indeed, the dogs and guests got into the mêlée, overwhelmed the swans and the birds withdrew into the lake and the swan-fighters into the pool to soothe their black and blue limbs in the warm water. Jackie was screaming, 'Merde,

merde-meeerde! Give the fucking birds back to the Queen, cherieee I don't want them,' and unusual as it was, even she got in the pool in the little coverage the swans had left on her.

It was easier said than done. Nobody wanted the swans. Jackie came up with not a very practical solution to get rid of them, 'If the lakes were covered with chicken-wire, cherieee,' she was sure, 'the fucking ugly birds would leave.' The plan fizzled out, of course. Harry forbade the grounds keeper to shoot the swans and Jackie, a superb cook, to cook them for a thanksgiving turkey dinner for people they didn't like. As far as I know, the swans are still happily bobbing up and down on the 'Swan lake of Woodlands'. Unfortunately, Harry and Jackie are not there any more; but nobody could enjoy it any more than they did, swans and swan bites.

With me Harry was generous; thanks to Johnny Shepridge and Bandi Marton, he helped me more than he realized. Unfortunately, he never helped himself. I call my years I worked with him the years of frustration. I was grateful and I wanted to help him, save him from his worst enemy – himself. He was a ruthless, vicious enemy. To protect him from himself was like fighting windmills with razorblade sails.

I had to wait for my turn to become one of the Don Quixotes, others had the priority and it took me over a week for my turn to see him. Reading the book twice didn't help. 'Action, action, action will be the key to the success of Deighton's *Billion Dollar Brain*,' he harangued, not character, ignoring the very essence of the piece as I read it. Yes, it had action but what prompted the action was the core of the story, that was what interested me, it was something that should have been told, I wanted to tell long ago. Curiosity is a good glue, so I stuck, biding my time, wanting to find out Harry's angle, his solution which eluded me. And I was looking forward to the final curtain of this charade. It didn't end the way I anticipated. It was an utter anticlimax. It slaughtered me.

Finally the day of reckoning came. My 'battle-axe' called, 'Mr Saltzman wants' – not 'would like' – 'to see you tomorrow morning at ten, Mr Marton.'

By then if anybody had called me Mr de Toth, I wouldn't have answered.

'Please tell his office, fine. Thanks,' and burst out laughing at the thought of the day of rechristening.

I had barely put down the receiver, when the phone rang again; my battle-axe must have heard my outburst; 'Is everything all right, Mr Marton?' she inquired worriedly.

I was Harry's first appointment of the day; one thing was sure, I would be getting in. Had it been the third or fourth it wouldn't have been so sure. I walked into Harry's office as he slammed down one of his phones, 'Merde, merde-merde alors,' two bonbons, 'Merde!' two more bonbons straight down his throat. 'The "UA bunch" is here with the new international production chief, whom I don't know, and I have no script, no director.' He reached for more bonbons but stopped himself halfway, 'Merde alors. Let's go.' While extricating his two crossed feet, in red socks, from under his overhanging Buddhan stomach, he murmured, 'The idiots, why didn't they call a week ago?'

'They did,' whispered one of his secretaries.

'Why didn't you tell me?' he screamed.

'I did, sir.'

'You didn't,' he screamed louder. 'You did not,' he repeated and picked up a red leatherbound date book, opened it where it had a marker, stared at it in silence. Evidently, she was right, 'Get out-a here, get oouut.' He was loud without hysteria.

Wisely she left. Harry wiggled off his big rocker, 'Come on,' he said to no one in particular, stepping into his ever-under-him pair of moccasins, by Bally, of course. 'Come on, Bandi,' he called back to me, over his shoulder, at the door. No director, no writer, what in hell does he want from me? Substitute for Bandi Marton?

It was not very befitting the elegant environment, but all I could think was, 'Oh shit,' and I expressed it out loud.

'What did you say,' asked Harry peeking back around the doorjamb, and without waiting for an answer he moved on, impatiently yelling back, 'Come on!'

Why not? We rode in silence in 'Eon 1', Harry's brand new Rolls Royce, so big one had to use a pair of binoculars to see the chauffeur, and to talk to him was a long-distance telephone call.

Harry received the red carpet treatment; like greased lightning through butter, without being announced, we were ushered into the fair-sized, subduedly elegant, British boardroom of UA's main office in London.

'Bandi!' the 'UA bunch' chimed in like a choir before we got halfway through the room. I had made several pictures for UA and had known them all decades longer than Harry had, except the new international chief.

'Oh, you know Bandi, he will be working for me on *Billion Dollar Brain*, right,' Harry nodded to me. 'Chariot race nothing, right? You will see some action sequences never done before, in the snow. We will out-do the chariot race, this will be in the deep snow. Right?' he prodded me to say something.

What could I have said? Nothing, so I remained silent, just smiled and watched Harry when I was introduced to UA's new international production head, as Bandi 'de Toth'.

I watched Harry like a hawk and he bowled me over with the self-control I never guessed he had. Whatever he thought remained hidden, not a blink. I still don't know if Johnny took him for a ride, or he took us. It was a nice ride, but I was happy the arrival of the 'UA bunch' cleared up the 'Bandi mix-up' and Harry's enthusiasm for the 'sensational chariot-like race in the deep, deep snow' subsided. I was lucky, because within a few more weeks I wouldn't have known which 'Bandi' I was. It felt like shedding a millstone from around my neck and regaining my own identity, miserable as it may have been.

Johnny had blown one of the many gaskets he usually blew when I told him I didn't want to direct *Billion Dollar Brain*. 'Now you're digging your own grave, go ahead dig it, dig it deep. I am not going to drag you out of it any more. Lay in it. I could have gotten you a doctor's opinion, two, any insurance company would have accepted. Gladly.'

I believed him, Johnny was capable of producing all kinds of illegal miracles. It never occurred to him I was the one who would have had to live with it.

He was so livid, his impeccable manner in public slipped and he slurped his coffee at the dignified 'Les Ambassadeurs' so loudly people at the next table stared at him. 'Now you really have finished yourself, herr director.'

Luckily, he was wrong this time. Johnny hadn't finished his tirade when a phone was placed at our table. He took it for granted it was for him, and picked up the receiver.

'Shepridge . . . yes, he is here,' and handed over the phone, 'for you.'

When I walked into my office a totally confused battle-axe greeted me. 'Mr de Toth . . .? Mr Saltzman wants you in his office right-a-way.'

I was dumbfounded, 'How did you find me?'

'Mr Saltzman told me to phone the decent restaurants in Mayfair and Soho. Mr Saltzman wanted you right-a-way, Mr Mar – ' swallow, ' – de Toth.' She checked her church-steeple-size wrist watch, 'You better go, sir. I told Mr Saltzman I had found you.' She looked worried.

That was Harry's way, the only way of dealing with the situation now.

Harry was on his usual perch, he didn't look very happy, he was chewing his bonbons, slowly, they didn't fly down the garbage-disposal. He was thoughtful. 'Why did you turn down directing *Billion Dollar Brain*?' Naturally, without waiting for my answer, he continued with the same breath, 'If you didn't like it, why didn't you tell me? Why?'

'I like it, very much, it has great potential. The characters interest me. I didn't quite understand why a chariot race was so important.'

The penny dropped, he didn't pick it up. Or did he? 'Why?' he snapped.

'Well, one of the reasons was, I am not Bandi Marton.'

That stopped him, dead. He threw a large handful of bonbons down the garbage-disposal, he was back on the tracks. I rolled on and explained I would not hire myself at present as a director with my freshly mangled neck. It would be a downright misuse of trust. He never thought of that.

Harry had the most beautiful dark eyes when they weren't dead. Now they lived. He stared at me, no bonbons. He eased up. 'I have decided you will work on the script with me and produce. UA likes you, it will be all right with them.' He never asked me, would I? I still believe the truth was the 'UA bunch' wanted me to head off Harry's extravaganzas.

Little did I know then that the continuous eruption of the Russell-Saltzman volcanoes[2] would ignite intellectual fireworks, create ulcers, cover with ashes mediocre dreams and give birth to a junior genius who, instead of climbing the Himalayan peaks of motion picture-making where he was heading, sunk into the valley of self-adoration. And drove poor Harry up the wall, screaming bananas.

For me it was never painful, always an exhilarating cataclysm I selfishly enjoyed.

Usually alone, I have to confess.

2 Russell is Ken Russell, director of *Billion Dollar Brain*; see next chapter.

22 Billion Dollar Battles

'Join the services and see the world.' If you are in the motion picture industry and want to see the world join the makers of the Bond films; the slogan fits better. When Broccoli and Saltzman split, Harry, not wanting to be outdone, started to look for stories taking place in faraway places, but not 'Bondian' fantasies. *Billion Dollar Brain* fit the bill.

'Before starting on the screenplay let's find the locations according to the book.' It was a good idea, he wanted the picture to look like a documentary. We found the locations and Harry signed Melvyn Bragg, urbane and elegant, suave and restrained, an Establishmentarian-looking, suave figure, who loved cucumber sandwiches in the Dorchester lobby. From the other end of the scale he picked John McGrath, a playwright, a no-nonsense, down-to-earth talent, a beautiful man with convictions, stubborn as an artillery mule and pulling as strong as one to the left, a dyed-in-the-wool anti-Establishment stalwart. Both good writers, neither with any picture experience. A lethal combination, even without Harry's sparks, which he always let go off when the three of us were beginning to see eye to eye. The three of us, as far as I knew, because with Harry one was never sure how many other writers were working on the same script – writers he picked up the night before in a restaurant or club.

Happy with the turmoil he created, Harry left us for Paris to annoy poor René Clement. His picture was to start after *Billion Dollar Brain* was delivered. He had been on the picture about two years, but neither of them was clear what the picture should be about. Sadly, both of them were sure only that the other's ideas were wrong – the poison of so many producer-director relationships and a guarantee for everybody to get hurt at the end. The big, unsolved, many-times-ugly question: who was to decide what the tone, the core of the picture was to be.

My only concern was *Billion Dollar Brain*. It was way overdue to have a director on it; we knew it, and Harry knew it, but he only moaned, 'Who – who – who should direct the picture?' But before a name could be suggested, as if he could read your mind, he whined, 'No, no, no, not him.'

One of the unfathomable, heartbreaking quirks of the picture business is how one gets – in any capacity – a job on which the whole future depends, regretfully, often through mistakes. John had an idea about a director and had shown me some exceptional BBC films on composers (Elgar, Bartók, Delius) by a man I had never heard of – Ken Russell. By then I had learned never to suggest anything directly to Harry. 'Why don't we look at some of the films of that director you talked about the other day, somebody like Ken, Ben, Len Richards or Russell?'

He pushed the intercom button, 'Get me all the films of –' he turned to me, '– what's his name?'

'Ken Russell,' I said without hesitation. It was safe, by then he paid no attention to me, he was concentrating on which bonbon to pick.

He yelled into the intercom, 'Did you hear?' It was not a question; translated to Harry's language it meant you had better have heard it. 'I want to see his films tomorrow at ten.'

'Only his films, sir, or TV – '

'– Features!' Harry screamed, and almost pushed the intercom button through the desktop to cut her off.

'Oh shit, stop him,' whispered John next to me. 'He made only one film and it stinks.'

'Then why did you suggest him? Can't undo it now, let it ride.'

French Dressing was bad, so bad Harry didn't fall asleep. John squirmed, Melvyn snickered. When the screening was over he stood up, imperial in his valediction, 'Russell is so talented he could hide the few gems that were in the picture.'

'Who, who, who?' moaned Harry as he was walking out of the projection-room, hanging onto his Cuban cigar as if it were his divining rod to find directors. John stayed behind, I understood how he felt, sat next to him. He muttered, 'I didn't realize till now how bad, really how bad it was . . . but . . .' and he drifted off as usual when he was thinking. He had the bad habit of thinking too much and that ultimately hurt him in the business. He was declared 'dangerous'. Sometimes that moniker could not be lost or forgiven.

'Don't worry. I was glad Harry asked for the film otherwise the roof would have caved in.'

John, a true Scot, frugal even with movements, scratched his head, then squeezed out of himself a surprising 'I am sorry.'

Next morning at one o'clock my phone rang and John McGrath broke his record the second time when he said, 'I am sorry, I was thinking. I would like you to meet Ken Russell. I have already arranged it with him. OK? Lunch. It's important to me. I'll pick you up at eleven, OK? Thanks. Go back to sleep,' and hung up.

I was in the Dorchester lobby at eleven. I wanted to meet this director who could come up, after those fine TV portraits, with a mish-mash jumble like *French Dressing*. The quiet of the Dorchester lobby was shattered by the approaching sound of crackling gunfire; I knew it was John announcing his own arrival, on the dot. I walked through the revolving door as he pulled up in his 'car', mostly resembling a Volkswagen, with the Rolls Royce angel on its hood – pardon me, bonnet – which didn't resemble any other car's bonnet.

The doorman, although shuddering at the sporadic gunshots emitted by John's chariot, politely opened the passenger's door, which was a different color from the color of the driver's door, which again was a different color from any other part of the car. It was not a mismatch, it was John's statement; most pieces of his miracle of locomotion were made in different countries – a symbol of 'international unity' – and assembled in his back yard. I looked back and saw the doorman change his white gloves as we blended into the London fog with our own created smoke and sporadic gunfire.

John didn't use his car like everybody else – as a lethal weapon. He was a slow, agonizingly polite driver, with a 'we all have equal rights' sticker on his bumper. He waited for everybody who wanted to cross an intersection to get up, get dressed, get in their car, and drive through it before he moved. Like an old, tired bird flapping its wings to take off, the fenders of the car were making the same valiant effort, helping the springless jalopy across the potholes where otherwise it would have sunk forever.

A crunch, a sigh from the engine and we came to a most welcome halt in front of one of those then-in-vogue 'Cafe Houses' in Chelsea. Austere, antiseptic and spotless to the point of being uncomfortable. It was filled with people who I was sure took a mudbath after their shower to fit in with the rest of the crowd, sitting nose-to-nose across dinnerplate-size tables on the edge of their postage stamp-size chairs, intense and conspiratorial. That is where I met Ken Russell, fresh from his mudbath, in a crackling-white shirt. You felt immediately he was ready to fight.

'You are wrong,' screamed out of him before you had a chance to open your mouth.

I liked him at all cost, and he could cost an awful lot, to nerves and pocketbooks alike, if wrongly handled. I still like him.

An hour and five cappuccinos later I believed Russell would do justice to what the book was all about. For me not 'who-who-whooo' any more but 'how how how' to proceed was the big question. From avant-garde David Chasman and UA I expected no problems, my hurdle was Saltzman, who, like an Indian dancing around the campfire, was chanting 'who-who-whoo' in tighter and tighter circles, without receiving any suggestions.

Lightning struck and broke through the circle. 'I saw secret – something like trailers or something of Warner's, I think – future programs on classic composers. They were extraordinary.'

Harry had taste in music and was a snob, a competitor and above all loved and lived for intrigue. As I hoped, he took the catchword bait 'secret' and 'classic composers'. 'I want to see them, how can I get them? Would something like that fit my program?' His final downfall occurred because anything would have fitted his 'program' since he didn't have one.

'I don't know, you would have to see them to judge that. I have no idea and – '

'– 'How can I?'

'I'll try.'

With two phonecalls within thirty minutes we had the films from the BBC in our cutting-room. We cut off the titles, the films started with the action. Saltzman pushed the button. The projection-room became dark, I crossed my fingers. The first anonymous film ran. The dim lights came on, no comment from Saltzman, not a word. He avoided looking at me, pushed the button, dark again. The second film had the same reception. Harry's attitude didn't change when the third was finished, the only change was the room remained dark.

A voice in the dark from the projection booth: 'Shall I start your material, Mr Saltzman?'

'Go ahead.'

Then it came, down like a ton of bricks on my head, with their BBC credit on, all the three films of Ken Russell ran one after the other without interruption.

Before the lights came on Harry Saltzman walked out. I was alone in the dim, blurred murk and never felt smaller than in that projection-room with my only companion in the dark the cold cigar smoke of Harry Saltzman.

'Now what?' I asked, but I had no answer. I was very much alone in that mournful projection-room.

Ignoring the rain which had started, I meandered back to my office. I walked in and stayed longer in that reproachful dark than I realized; my battle-axe was gone, only to lunch I hoped. There was a note on my desk, 'My lunch hour starts at noon, I waited till 12.03, be back 1.03. Mr Saltzman wanted you in his office at 11.47.' I didn't use the 'private phone', but went through the switchboard, and before I said my name, the operator cut me off, 'Please, let us know in the future where you will be, sir, we couldn't locate you. Mr Saltzman wishes to see you in his office.'

'Now what?' – but that question (for which I had no answer) was answered by another question, 'Are you free for lunch?' Harry asked as I was halfway through his door. He had never asked before, he took for granted I was free when he was.

We didn't speak in the car, which was usual. During luncheon it was unoffendingly easy not to speak to each other, because his international hangers-on were outdoing each other, spewing out gossip which Harry ate up with more appetite than he ate his luncheon. The first time Harry spoke to me direct was after lunch in front of the restaurant, after I had said to no one in particular, 'I am going to walk back to the office.'

'But it's raining,' he said.

'It will be good for him,' chimed in the trio of rats, as they happily scampered after their piece of bread in the Rolls Royce. The hearse drove away, I walked back.

'My goodness, oh my goodness you had no brolly [an umbrella for the lesser civilized world],' lamented my battle-axe, bundled up like a cocoon in heavy Harris tweeds, shawls and scarves, more stuff than any of us had on at the North Pole. 'That is the way to catch your death of pneumonia.' She handed me a list of messages, adding to it, 'Mr Saltzman called three times.'

The hour of reckoning had arrived, I thought on my way to his office.

No. We talked about his problems with René Clement, the cameramen for that picture (scheduled to go eight months hence) and the weather in the Middle East, North Africa and Spain that time of the year. Not a word about *Billion Dollar Brain*. The closest I ever came to fainting was when halfway out the door, after a perfunctory 'See you tomorrow,' 'I made a deal with Ken Russell. He'll be here at eleven.' That was Harry Saltzman, not the easiest man to work with.

But in my room a mysterious bottle of Jack Daniel's greeted me. No card, nobody seemed or wanted to know where it had come from. Harry was incapable of saying thanks and he would sooner die than say you were right.

Was I?

There was no way around the next hurdle. No tricks. Saltzman was very shy around women. He was polite, courteous, he liked them all right, 'as long as they stayed where they belonged, after all they were only a small part of man, a rib'. For Saltzman to swallow that a five-feet-two lady with an unruly silver-grey mane, a perennial cigarillo in her mouth, could, would or should be able to run a show physically, logistically as difficult and demanding as *Billion Dollar Brain* was to be, would be impossible. Sam Spiegel's plug for her was actually no help. He wanted to prove to Broccoli, to himself and to the world (in that order), that he could be successful on his own, without anybody's 'interference'. But Harry was a pro, and the fact sunk in that that little dynamo had been the production manager for *Lawrence of Arabia*, responsible for two or three second units running simultaneously, lodging and fodder for a horde of 4–500 people, food and water for camels and horses, and setting up camps on three continents in sands where the camels refused to go. 'Film folk' were generally spoiled. Even in Kansas they rolled out the red carpet to the privy up on the hill for them. But where men weren't used to taking orders from women it was a different set-up. Still, all functioned flawlessly. Little cigar-chomping eva monley carried it without a hitch and without a red carpet.

It was different in Finland, we were royally received. The Finns worked according to strict rules, but Thor, the god of the skies, for the first time in memory ignored the rules, and during the winter of our discontent there wasn't a snowflake in Helsinki in February! For humans the rules remained rules. The Helsinki sanitary squad descended according to schedule on the town every night at nine to get rid of the snow before the onslaught of the morning traffic. This created a free circus for the Finns. They stopped in their tracks to applaud the strange convoy of the 'bizarre film folk', and with stiffly frozen fingers tapped their heads, making kooky signs at the drivers of the snow-laden trucks rumbling by during the day to distribute their cargo on the clean, bone-dry streets, rooftops and window sills of Helsinki, only to be cleared away during the night. The blind grind of bureaucracy was winning.

Ken was enjoying the situation as much as the Finns did; he worked faster than ever before running out of cover sets – much to Harry's annoyance. Something had to be done to soften the hard rules of the Helsinki snow-clearing schedule which was about to destroy our schedule. It was becoming a desperate situation.

eva invited a few chieftains, hoping to convince them to break the rules and stop the wheels. Notoriety and curiosity have great power; the acceptance was 100 per cent for a 'flag dinner' to commemorate the first UK–US–Finnish co-production, 'Harry Saltzman's *Billion Dollar Brain*'. Harry Saltzman was easier to pronounce for the Finns than Len Deighton – so decided Harry's PR-machine. Len Deighton's name was dropped from the elegantly engraved invitation, and who in the hell was Ken Russell? they asked Harry and themselves, but they forgot to ask Ken Russell. Had I known the explosion Ken was to create to make his existence known, I wouldn't have laughed so loud at this oversight.

Harry came up to Helsinki to host the celebration and hated every minute of it more than he hated Ken. But Saltzman was always a gracious host, especially when the occasion served his purpose. Fresh vegetables, fruit, champagne and wine were brought in from Italy and France, the scotch, the gin and the steaks and English roast beef arrived from Scotland, of course. Everything else was from Finland, except the caviar. Harry paid a great deal of attention to the menu, and rightly so, he wanted to treat our hosts to a memorable meal. He succeeded beyond expectations.

The pre-eruption rumble of the volcanoes started, I think, when dinner was announced and the dining-room doors opened. Ken was the first to charge through and promptly seated himself on Harry's right at the head of the table. Whether he saw or whether he defied the place-card was unclear, but Harry's voice, as he pointed at the place-card in front of Ken, was clear: 'Move, Ken, that's not your place.'

Ken looked over his shoulder at Harry, who was standing above him like an angry god ordering Adam out of paradise, with pudgy finger pointing toward the other end of the long table. Ken turned, and destroyed the artwork of the white-as-virgin-snow and starched-stiff napkin in front of him. With undue care he spread it on his knees. He had absolutely no intention of moving.

A tableau. Silence.

The maitre d' whispered something to Harry, who nodded. In turn the maitre d' nodded to a sturdy squad of waiters, in their white tie and tails looking like the curious penguins of Antarctica as they shuffled off their station toward Ken. Their intention was obviously not as benign as those greeting the explorers of the South Pole. Ken had a lot of faults, but courage was not among them. He got up. The penguins marched away. Harry himself held out the chair for the tall, elegant Finn standing on his right, the minister of culture, in charge of film production, who stone-faced, unperturbed, sat down in the still warm chair vacated by Ken.

The din of the scraping chair legs being pushed under the backsides of the honored guests, the swelling hubbub rinsing away the momentary embarrassment was cut through by Ken's voice, loud. 'Where is the caviar, Harry? There is no caviar!'

A sudden silence again, another tableau.

Beaming in the new spotlight of attention, like a civil war general surveying the battlefield from a hilltop, Ken stood above the table set up against a wall for the cold appetizers. 'No caviar,' he repeated shaking his head gravely, 'you promised me, Harry.'

Harry trembled, his face turned turkeyneck-purple. The maitre d' whispered to him again and Harry started to smile as he listened, his color changing to his normal ashen-grey as he nodded in agreement. A staccato order in Finnish, and out of their line-up two 'penguins' moved with surprising swiftness.

'Mr Rooselow,' the maitre d' turned to Ken, 'please be seated.' He indicated to him his seat almost in the next room. One of the 'penguins' held out his chair for him, the other with a flourish popped open the tortured-by-art napkin and placed it in Ken's lap. 'Your seat, Mr Roosclel,' the maitre d' said with satisfaction. The Finns could be snobbish.

Ken sat down, it was more apparent under his silver-grey mop that, in turn, his palor had changed to purple. The dam of the embarrassed silence broke again and conversation flooded the room only to stop again when the maitre d', with an imperious gesture, pointed Ken out to the two returning 'penguins'. Like the revolving light in an old lighthouse, heads turned to follow the path of the two large silver trays carried by the 'penguins'. On one tray in a silver urn sunk in crushed ice was a glass dish with a kilo tin of Beluga caviar, open, untouched. The second tray was loaded with small slices of paper-thin bread, and several glass dishes for the various condiments to disguise the taste of the caviar for those who really didn't like caviar but thought it was chic to consume it with savior faire. The caviar-bearing 'penguins', like pallbearers for the funeral procession of the unborn sturgeons, came to a halt at Ken's side. He looked around. The other guests were being served different appetizers, nobody else had caviar.

Ken was an extremely sensitive man, in some aspects of life; in others he had thicker skin than a rhino. He was not going to be defeated by Harry's one-upmanship. Defiantly he served himself a large but not exaggerated portion of caviar, condiments and bread slivers.

Harry was an extremely sensitive man, in some aspects of life; in others he had thicker skin than a rhino. He too was not going to be defeated. 'Are you satisfied, Ken?' he asked his director stuck on the far end of the table.

Like a grand seigneur, Ken answered, 'Excellent, Harry, excellent, thank you – '

'– Would you mind, Ken, if I tasted it?'

'But of course not, Harry, please do taste it.'

This was beginning to be too thick. Sooner or later, I knew shit was going to hit the fan and we'd have indelible freckles and we, we the company, would be stuck with the cleaning bill. And was I right! Never did I see or hear of anybody tasting caviar as if it were wine, but Harry did; he could not swirl it in the spoon to smell the bouquet, but he closed his eyes and smelled it anyway. Then he spat the caviar out on the little spoon and dropped it on the plate in front of him. The horrified 'penguins' whisked away the mess.

'This is terrible, Ken, I thought you knew caviar.'

All conversation stopped and suddenly it was colder inside than outside in the icy wind; eva whispered, 'Oh shit'. Harry was whispering to the maitre d' who apologized then, followed by his two 'caviar penguins', left the guests immersed in deep study of their own plates, not eating, only scrutinizing the superior food. Ken kept his eyes transfixed on Harry.

Dirty line call as it was, but love-fifteen for Harry Saltzman.

Led by the maitre d', the procession of 'penguins' returned with a second tin of opened but untouched caviar; it was brought directly to Harry. He tasted the caviar and went through again what was now known as Harry's caviar ritual. 'No,' he said, 'not for Mr Russell, he is one of the greatest connoisseurs of caviar. No-no, not for him.' We sat in silence with surreptitious looks at each other, but for Harry there wasn't anybody around; he had only Ken in his sight, he wanted to teach him a lesson. He tasted the third and fourth tin of caviar and sent them back, 'Unfit for the fine palate of –' he emphasized '"– caviar connoisseur" Mr Russell.'

I admired the maitre d's dignified composure, but when Harry asked for the fifth kilo of caviar, his stiff and snappy Prussian bow and his quick turn around with a clipped 'very well, Mr Saltzman,' bared a slight annoyance. He was human after all.

Harry called after him, ' I want you to open the next tin here at the table.'

The maitre d' stopped, turned, clicked his heels, 'Very well, sir,' and departed.

It was fifteen-all in this dirty little power game, but Harry overstepped the line when he served.

Nobody was moving in the room only Ken, he was chewing a large piece of bread. The fifth tin of caviar arrived which the maitre d' ceremoniously opened; Harry tasted it in deeper silence than the silence at 282 feet below sea level in Death Valley at noon in August.

'This is good,' he finally proclaimed to the by-then-couldn't-care-less maitre d'; then, smacking his lips to savour the after taste, he smiled at Ken. 'This is caviar, Ken.'

'Thanks, Harry,' Ken nodded.

The relieved guests picked up their interrupted lives, the murmur of conversation was reborn. The caviar reached Ken and he asked the 'penguin' to serve him. He tasted the caviar, like Harry did, with all eyes on him.

'Well, Harry, this is good. Good for this . . .' and he picked up his large soup spoon, dug deep in the tin and spread the Beluga caviar, soup-spoonful after soupspoonful, on his shoes and shined them with his once-white table napkin. It was a glorious mess.

A tableau to end all tableaux.

This was only the beginning. But somehow, with more luck than sanity, the picture came to an end without Harry and Ken killing each other, and I surprised myself feeling sorry that it was over. It was fun, it was a challenge to end all challenges to keep it on the tracks.

Meanwhile, in Pinewood Harry battled with five different projects and René Clement. He not only fought him in London, he went over to Paris every week not to listen to him.

'I don't know what to do with him,' was his first sentence before I could defrost in London.

'Listen to him.'

'I can't.'

'Then don't, just let him do what he wants. He is good, he is – '

'– not for this. After two years he has no – '

'– He sees it differently than you – '

'– Eh, maybe he is getting too old, he is afraid of it. I don't believe he would survive Israel.'

'Israel! Why Israel?'

'Because I want to shoot the picture there.'

'Why?'

'I want to help Israel, and as you know, it would please Arthur.'[1]

'No, I didn't. But would that be right for – '

'– We'll shoot it in Israel.'

Harry was always full of surprises, this was the first time I had heard about Israel as a location possibility, and there was still no story. Clement was apprehensive and disinclined to scout locations in Israel. Harry had a delivery date for the picture without the slightest, no, with a dozen conflicting ideas of what the picture was to be about, but he wanted to help Israel as much as Mrs Krim – the power behind the throne – did.

The bottom line: I was sent off to Israel to look for locations. For what? That's show biz.

1 One of the gods of UA was Arthur Krim. His wife, Mathilde, was a leading Zionist.

23   True-Blue Pros

It was a unique experience; Israel during the 5, 6, 7, 8, 9 and 10 of June 1967; I occasionally thought I would remain there till the end of eternity. This assignment almost cost me my happy life, not then during the Six Days War in Israel, but six years later in the wake of the Yom Kippur War in Egypt, 6–23 October 1973.

Strange, it was again on an assignment involving UA in Egypt. It happened again because of mistaken identities. I was not expected to stage a sleigh ride à la *Ben Hur* chariot race in the snow that time. It was in Aswan, where I was taken on what was supposed to be my last ride with the barrel of a 45 automatic against the back of my head, between C1 and C2, the sure spot, execution style. Those characters were not joking, they must have seen too many American-made mob pictures. Weird, in the heat of an Egyptian night the steel of that gun barrel felt ice cold.

I wouldn't have minded anything cold against me on the way from the Aswan airport to the hotel Aswan, dragging our suitcases on the road in the pungent heat for miles in ankle-deep dust and blinded by our own created dust cloud. Our commercial Egyptian airliner was denied landing permission because the runways were being kept open for the Aeroflot bringing in a Russian agricultural delegation. After giving me a strange once-over the harassed-looking officials at the airport had a hush-hush conversation among themselves, but after conferring with our 'reception committee' waved me through. But it didn't help; for us it was too late. That the members of the 'committee' ran like scared jack-rabbits didn't help. The pleading of our limo drivers didn't help either. Nothing could have helped, save a scatter-bomb to eliminate the surging Fedora hats and heavy blue serge suits of the uniformed Russian agricultural delegation. They commandeered every car, including our three limousines.

So the trek began for Ann, from production, Ron, one of Cubby's battery of attorneys, one interpreter travelling with us and six, yes six members of the 'reception committee'. Two for each of us, the interpreter didn't count. He was Egyptian.

In front of the hotel 'our' three drivers, sheepish and apologetic, explained that the Russians hadn't released any of the cars, that was the reason they hadn't come back to pick us up. Which seemed to be true. In each car, Fedora-less, but in their heavy blue serge uniform, a KGB man was crawling under the dashboard of the 'appropriated' cars, looking for bugs, I hazard to guess. They were impressively thorough.

Inside the hotel the reception clerks were sheepish and apologetic, explaining the Russian delegation had taken over our reserved rooms. I asked Ann to give me my confirmation slip. She reached in her briefcase and seemingly without looking, out of stacks and stacks of papers she came up with one sheet, the confirmation of my reservation. You can't blame me, I married her.

'I want to see the manager,' I didn't ask, I demanded. I received only strange looks from the people behind the counter.

Instead of any of them answering me, the apparent head of our 'reception committee' spoke up with a frozen smile, 'Why? Please, he is too busy.'

'Too busy? Damn it, so am I. I want our reserved rooms, pronto. Let's get it over with.'

'Hm,' he grunted, then exchanged a few words in Russian with the hotel personnel.

'Everybody's room has been confirmed and we are going to stay in our confirmed rooms. Savvy?'

In the back of the counter a door opened and a dignified Oxford don emerged. He thrust out his hand, 'I am the manager of the hotel.' I forgot his name. We shook hands, 'Welcome, Mr de Toth. I understand how you must feel, I shall see personally that you and your party immediately will be having the rooms that were confirmed.'

One: I became sure the manager's office was wired to the lobby or the front desk, otherwise how could he have appeared on cue?

Two: the other thing that made the situation look fishy was that the clerks behind the counter became obviously puzzled and confused hearing their manager's promise.

Three: Houdini couldn't have done a more impressive trick: the manager clapped his hands and out of the thin, hot air a waiter appeared with a large tray loaded with mysterious-looking, various-colored liquids in identical glasses, with real, jingling ice cubes in them!

With a grandiose gesture dropping his chin to his chest, the manager pointed to a comfortable-looking corner, 'Please, be seated there or anywhere you like, the hotel is yours.' Backing away he added, 'I shall now personally check your rooms.'

One thing became certain, there was absolutely no color distinction in Egypt – regardless of its color all drinks tasted alike, as we knew already, like Coke, Pepsi or Dr Pepper. And they were all equally dangerous. Your lips could stick to the rim of your glass and could only be removed surgically with the knowledge that lips were cheaper than glasses.

'Your confirmed rooms are ready,' announced the beaming manager. He emphasized 'confirmed' and apologized profusely 'for the inconvenience'.

Time leaves indelible marks on everything. The numbers on the doors of our rooms couldn't cover the marks time had left, the outlines of the original numbers on the doors identical to the numbers of our confirmation slips. That they were out of sequence with the other room numbers of the corridor was only a minor detail the KGB wouldn't overlook.

After a long shower where you couldn't tell the hot water from the cold, I walked down to the bar to clear the dust out from my inside too. The manager was there at a corner table with a group. He smiled at me with circled forefinger and thumb together giving me the OK sign, the others at the table, one of them in the heavy blue serge uniform, glared. It bugged me he thought I was stupid enough to swallow his trick.

I barely had time to sit on the stool on the corner of the L-shaped bar, the best vantage point of the room, when the manager was next to me, 'Anything Mr de Toth orders is on the house.'

'That's very nice of you, thanks.' I'll catch them, I thought. 'A Jack Daniel's on the rocks, on lots of rocks.'

'I am sorry, sir, but we haven't – '

' – Yes, we do,' the manager overrode him.

'Of course, sir,' came the bartender after a long and significant pause.

'That is very nice of you, I take it as a special privilege to have a Jack Daniel's. You are a very astute hotelier.' The manager beamed and looked around to see who had heard the compliment. I got up, 'I would like to show you something.'

Puzzled, he followed me, and as we proceeded he slowed down. As I started to mount the stairs toward the third floor he stopped. 'Where are we going, may I ask you? Your room is on the second floor, Mr de Toth.'

'I want to show you something. Something that taught me a lot, and I am sure a man of your caliber wants to learn.'

'Sure . . . sure,' he stuttered, becoming more and more apprehensive. When I turned the corner of the corridor he stopped again, I ignored him and walked directly to the door of the room I was supposed to have. When I lifted my hand to point out the number he pleaded, 'Please, don't disturb the guests. Don't knock on the door.'

'I won't,' and only touched the traces of the old numbers clearly visible on the door. 'You are too good a man for anybody to play such a dirty little trick on you, an insult to your intelligence.' He stayed frozen in front of the door gaping at it. I spoke as I was walking away, 'And now I will have that drink, thank you.'

By the time I got back to the bar there were two more Russians at the corner table. At a table in the opposite corner of the room six young men, uniformly dressed in identical beige pullovers, sturdy and taciturn, sat staring at the different colored liquids in their glasses. A large Jack Daniel's on lots of rocks was on the bar. The offer to pay for my second drink was seriously refused; it was an unheard-of gesture to refuse cash in that part of the world.

The manager came back with a sweat-bathed rotund little Russian and without a glance toward me sat down at his corner table; the Russian checked me out before he sat down. A few tourists and locals were wandering in and out of the bar, it was quiet and peaceful, the Jack Daniel's never tasted better. There was no sign of Ann or Ron.

Unexpectedly, the drowsy place came to life. The manager left his party, and, on his way out, wished me 'a pleasant evening'. The first Russian in a hurry I had seen blew in, came to a screeching halt in the doorway, scanned the room then joined 'the six in pullovers'. Without my ordering, the bartender brought me another Jack on rocks and dashed away before I had time to protest. After a short but animated conversation, the 'speedy Russian' joined his comrades in the other corner. The 'pullover brigade' came to the bar and sat right next to me, three on the long and three on the short end of the 'L' of the bar. Like dust devils on a deserted country road springing to life quickly and fizzling out more quickly, it all became peaceful and quiet again.

'Why are you making fun of us?' asked the one on my right. I looked around, he couldn't have been talking to me. Wanting to be polite and not block their line of communication I reached for my drinks to move away. 'Stay where you are!' commanded the one on my right. The one closest on my left placed his hand on my forearm, holding it down against the bartop. At the same time, two of the farthest from me at the counter came up from behind.

'Don't move.'

'Stay quiet.'

Two pointing fingers (?) gun barrels (?) were shoved against my two kidneys. More fear than curiousity made me turn to find out whether they were fingers, pencils or guns. I barely moved, both jabbed me hard; I didn't have to see, I knew they were gun barrels.

'Now what? . . . why? You are making a mistake.'

'You made one.'

'What do you mean? I – '

'– Don't talk, just follow orders.' One of the gun barrels was shoved against me harder, 'I'd hate to make a mess here, but don't tempt me.'

Ann came in lugging her heavy, forever-present briefcase, 'the office.' She stopped at the door, trying to get her bearings.

'Your friend. Tell her to sit down, you'll be back.' I hesitated. The jabs of the barrels hurt. 'Tell her.'

I did and, surrounded by the six, I was whisked through a back door I was not aware of. The two with the guns felt like they were glued to me. As we reached the door on the end of the narrow service corridor, it was opened from the outside. At the same moment a blindfold was dropped over my head from behind and tied with unnecessary force, a pair of trained hands frisked me, other hands slapped handcuffs on my wrists behind me. They were swift, efficient, silent. They were too good just for lifting a little currency. They were class pros, I had no doubts about that, I had doubts about the celebration of my next birthday.

A car with a terrible-sounding engine pulled up. The mind is a weird phenomenon, mine is anyway. The blindfold especially hurt my bad eye, and because of its pressure on my good eye I saw red, blue-green, yellow circles and flashes blending with John McGrath's miracle of locomotion in front of the Dorchester. The image changed into shooting stars as strong hands pushed my stomach in and forced my head down, but I still bumped it as they shoved me in the back seat of an obviously small car. I was sandwiched in between two well-built shoulders. They didn't give. The one on my left smelled of hashish, the one on my right of Yardley's aftershave. I had no idea how many were in front, but I was sure that John McGrath and whoever drove the car went to different driving schools. Nobody spoke, only the poor car complained, especially after it had left the main road. Dust was coming through the open windows, the potholes became larger and louder, the tired springs underneath us sang louder and jabbed our behinds harder.

Be happy with small mercies, the car finally came to a stop and I was sure it couldn't be happier than I was, but if this was the end I wanted it instantly, not another ride to shake my screws loose till insanity. The dust, mixed with sweat rivulets trickling down my back and dripping off the tip of my nose, smelled like camel dung; I was itching all over, and every time I stupidly tried to scratch, the handcuffs cut deeper into my wrists.

Those in front got out and walked away, my two bookends didn't budge, we sat squashed, silent. Unintelligible voices in the distance. I thought they were looking for a suitable grave site for me. I was hoping they'd bury me deep. I never had the ambition to be dinner for jackals. Returning footsteps, the doors were yanked open. Relief, fresh air. I bumped my head hard as they pulled me out of the car, nobody cared. By then I didn't either. My knees had gone to sleep during the cramped ride, I could hardly stand up, a gun barrel hit the back of my head, I heard the question on my way to the sand, 'Are you Dayan?'

The hero of the never-forgotten Six Days War was Israeli General Moyshe Dayan. We both had a black patch; he had a very short supply of hair, I cropped short what hair I had. Our silhouettes were vastly, or 'waistly' different, but through the distance in time and the glasses of hatred, his pear-shape was forgotten.

With brilliant planning and bold courage the Israeli forces under his command trampled the Arabs' pride. The Arabs were virtually caught with their pants down; I saw rows of dead bodies on latrines, countless armoured vehicles with their radiators drained dry in the June heat of the desert by the thirsty, ill-supplied Arab soldiers. Sitting ducks. In spite of their tanks, armoured cars with seized engines were blasted, opened up, their armour looked like petals of a wilted old rose, exposing the corpses of the still-strapped-in, mostly headless heroes inviting the vultures to pollinate the world and spread peace. Mementos, not unlike those the Germans left in their wake during Hitler's also brilliantly planned Blitz-kriegs in Europe. I saw them too. Wars are equally ugly, no matter on which side you fight them. Are they justifiable?

A few events from the six-year span between the Six Day War and the Yom Kippur War – did it all have to happen for me to have two guns in my back, expecting someone to find my grave site in the Egyptian desert? I had no idea how long I was out. The last thing I remembered before folding was the question, 'Are you Dayan?' The first I remember when I was picked off the ground was the same question, 'Are you Dayan? Answer.'

I couldn't wipe the the spit off my face, it trickled down with my sweat.

'Are you?'

'Are you?'

The second spit smelled more putrid.

'Answer!' I was grateful for the kick, no spit.

'You are or not – '

'You're dead!'

'Masquerading as Dayan – '

'Who sent you?'

'You made us a laughing-stock in front of our allies and friends,' barked a new voice.

A hard kick in my ass made the blood throb in my bad eye-socket, another kick made it worse. I took it for granted they were talking about the Russian delegation, I saw them with one of them in the bar before they picked me up.

'I didn't know they were here and I am not – '

'Fucking liar . . .' and I was slapped across my face, another relief after the spit. Look for the best in everything, so as not to lose hope and survive.

'Why don't you take a look what's under my black patch? You will – ?' I was slapped across my face again, it was a new touch, a new taste, blood and camel-dung. A dessert for my last supper? They kept on slapping me. My knees buckled, they grabbed me by the shoulders and held me up before I hit the ground again. It was easier for them to slap me when I was upright. 'If it matters I am . . .'

I stopped; the sweat, the dust, the blood clogged my throat. They shook me. 'What are you doing here, Jew bastard?'

'If you stop and listen . . . listen, my money is in my back pocket – '

'Don't insult us more, you shit,' and they kept slapping me harder and harder. I wanted to speak but the words stuck in me somewhere, my face was numb. I heard the slide being pulled back on an automatic, the kicks and the slaps didn't hurt any more.

A quirk of the mind, eerie images erupted: my father in his den engulfed by his trophies, swords, guns, medals; his cousin, General Szirmay in his imposing office in the Hungarian Military Academy I was supposed to attend. The thought pierced me, I might as well go out like a man, go like my father and General Szirmay would expect me to go.

'Shitheads. Stop, you stupid bastards, whatever you want it's not the way to go about it. Listen, listen to me, idiots!'

A couple of commands in Arabic, they stopped the abuse and let go of my shoulders. Limp as a wet dish-rag I met the ground. After a flurry of Arabic, I was lifted straight up and held by my shoulders.

'Good, speak!'

'Whom are you working for?'

'We'll make it easier for you!'

I witnessed it in Poland: nerves cracked when the stress limits were passed, producing the strangest reactions. I started to laugh. Suddenly everything was very clear. Every word was swallowing embers, but I could talk.

'United Artists, an American motion-picture company sent me to look for locations for the next James Bond film and check the feasibility of making the film here. Understand? That would bring lots of dollars here. Don't fuck it up, assholes.'

They took my wallet from my pocket. Out of the loud and long discussion that followed in Arabic I understood two words – Moyshe Dayan – repeated and repeated over and over with venom. Every time I heard it I tried to interrupt the gibberish. I thought it was a futile attempt until rough hands tore off my black patch from under the blindfold. A strong beam of a flashlight hit my face, the left side of the blindfold was slid down a bit, the eyelids of my bad eye were forced open. A variety of halitosis-, hashish- and coffee-smelling breaths robbed me of the desert air as the six took turns to examine my bad eye, expressing their opinion loud and fast. The name Dayan was mentioned again and again in their diagnosis.

That won't work, it hit me, Dayan had an injured eye too. I kicked out hard, found no target, 'You idiots, idiots, I am not even Jewish.'

My fly was zipped open, I was bared. That is all I remembered.

When I opened my eye, ice cubes wrapped in a napkin were on my forehead and next to my face, I was cleaned up on the top of the bed in my room with the manager hovering above me.

'What happened . . . You shouldn't walk in the desert alone, especially at night. It could be very dangerous.' He carefully changed the icepacks. 'What happened?' he asked again. 'You're very lucky some decent people found you.'

It took me some time to reorient myself.

'What happened?' asked the manager anew, extremely interested in my answer. 'It's very important for me to know. Were you held up?'

'I don't know.'

'You had money with you –'

' – I did.'

'I know.' That surprised me, he noticed it. 'I took the liberty and checked your wallet. You are a motion-picture director, that's nice. How much money you had on you?' and from the nightstand handed over, with my wallet, my passport with my Rolex. 'Strange,' he sighed and watched me. It was a surprise for me too.

'Yes, it is.'

'Count your money.'

I did, 'It's all here.'

'Strange,' he repeated.

'It certainly is.' My question, 'What do you make of it?' surprised him. He thought before answering.

'All I can say you were very lucky. Be grateful.'

'I am very grateful indeed. I wish I knew whom to thank.'

'Your good luck. The nice people who brought you in must have scared them off.' He was sizing me up before he spoke, 'Would you recognize the assailants?'

'Would the "nice people" recognize them?'

This question upset his equilibrium, he opened his mouth twice before he spoke. 'Well no . . . but it is more important, would you?'

I tried to put the pieces together, my head was clearing and old experiences came in handy. I hesitated with my tentative, 'Well, I . . . I . . .' and I changed my attack on the puzzle. 'Did you report it to the police?'

That took him aback, I felt he was squirming inside before squeezing out his answer, 'No, I didn't, I –'

' – Why?' I threw at him quickly and he was quick coming back.

'Mr de Toth, I asked you, would you recognize your assailants?'

'Well . . .'

'Yes or no?' he asked very intensely.

His game had been given away. I had better be careful. I shook my head and took my time to answer him, thinking hard, mumbling my answer, 'I am thinking, thinking hard. It was such a traumatic experience . . .'

He was watching me in silence, radiating tension, I felt it. I put on no Academy-quality performance but, without being immodest, I thought I was pretty good. It worked anyway, thank God, and the 'nice people'. My answer was full of conviction.

'No!' I put it on thicker, apologizing, 'I am sorry, but it all happened so quickly.'

He was openly relieved, more for his own sake than mine at not getting involved in any possible mess. He became solicitous, but still hesitantly asked if I wanted him to call the police.

'No definitely not!'

His first sincere word, 'Good,' slipped out, but he rectified it immediately. 'Anything like this creates bad publicity and with the tourists . . . you know how they are . . . I have to be careful . . . and since you were lucky I thought, but if you want me to I – '

I was quick and firm, 'No. Don't.'

'Well whatever you wish, but you know, without positive identification, but if you want to – '

'No!'

He was anxious to get the whole thing over with, he was jumping from subject to subject, 'So you are a director, how exciting. Your friends were very worried. They are still waiting for you in the dining-room. I kept the kitchen open for you. Are you hungry?'

I put the breaks on him. 'I would like to thank the people – or was it only one?'

'Oh, no, well, there were more,' he stuttered.

'I would like to thank them personally.'

'No, no,' he answered too quickly, then regained his composure. 'They are very shy, but if you think of some little present for them I will be happy to transmit it with your gratitude.'

'How many?'

That stopped him cold for a minute. I heard the wheels rattling in his head, then he came up with 'four'.

'Well, what do you think, eighty, a hundred dollars would be right? I want to do what you think would be right.'

'Well . . .' after a quick calculation he came up with: 'A hundred twenty would be fine.' Based on my offer, the correct figure for 'the six'. I had him in my trap, solid.

Maybe I was conceited thinking buying my life back for 300 dollars was a bargain. I handed over three one-hundred dollar bills. He was surprised and I still would like to thank 'the six'.

Ann said, 'Never do that again, I was worried sick.' I couldn't tell her I hoped I didn't have to. She poured a drink out of a fresh bottle of Jack Daniel's on the table. 'The compliments of the manager, he was worried too. He was very considerate.'

In the farthest corner from us in the otherwise empty dining-room sat, without sweaters, 'the six' with two other men. We ignored each other. I was sure, had I been caught by zealous amateurs, I would be the remains of a well-digested jackal dinner in the desert, covered with camel dung. I had respect for them, they were pros and it is possible to deal with true-blue pros, the trouble is always with zealous amateurs. That was confirmed again during our next trip to Egypt when a true pro, Ann, saved my life and that was a tougher situation because she faced zealous amateurs.

In no other business could one have more fun than in the 'Eden of Charades', the motion-picture business.

24 Playing Dirty

Looking back at the sleepless nights of fretting about how and from where to import snow in mid-winter to Helsinki without being more ridiculed than we already were, how to live down the shameful echoes of the 'battle of the caviar', how to survive in the cross-fire between Harry Saltzman and Ken Russell, all the stifling aggravation in a place where you couldn't take a deep breath to clear your mind without freezing your lungs and your brain with it, how to be sure that the sinking boat of *Billion Dollar Brain* reached safe port and did not go under the ice of the Gulf of Finland in the Baltic Sea – when I got back to England it all seemed picayunish. It proved again nothing could be so bad that something worse couldn't top it and there is always something good in every disaster. I learned to look for the good, forget the bad. I had a lot of practise before and since looking for that little promising good and I always found it. And that 'little good' always grew big. Try it. It works.

London had never looked better, but I wished I was back on the Baltic with an idiosyncratic director, a suicidal, maniac star who was ready and willing to kill her male star, who was in the midst of trading the smell of the fishmarket for Chanel No. 5, and the real stardom he certainly deserved. I wished I was back there, not because I missed the reindeer steaks and cloud berries from the tundra, but because the battle between Clement and Saltzman had deteriorated into an ugly war.

Clement hated London, and as usual the world outside France. He was a Frenchman, refined and civilized, and civilization kept him from blowing up. Clement kept it inside and suffered. Harry didn't suffer, he blew; Ken also blew all the time and Harry understood that, and as the abyss grew deeper between him and Clement, Harry's tolerance of Ken's antics grew in proportion. He wanted to 'replace', or if he was very mad at Ken 'throw him off' the picture, but as time went by I didn't have to defend Ken. That he finished *Billion Dollar Brain* was largely due to

Clement's, not Ken's transformation – he remained as obnoxious and as talented as he ever was.

When I walked into Harry's office, Clement was sitting on his left with his back to the large windows looking out on South Audley Street. After one of the most hair-raising drives of my life the only acknowledgement of my arrival I received was Harry's silently pointing finger to the seat on the left side of his desk, the interrogation hot-seat, facing the blinding windows, seeing only silhouettes. They ignored my presence. Harry was still trying the impossible, to convince Clement his approach to the story was wrong, his visual concept was off. He was more insulting than the tone he had used to bludgeon Clement to submission before I left to freeze in Finland months ago.

'If you don't want to shoot it in Israel, "vous êtes un génie, René" ("you're a genius"), shoot it in Spain,' a place neither of them had seen; and after all the time I had been away in deep freeze, still neither had a clear idea of what the story was about. They were sure about one thing: whatever the other proposed was wrong.

Harry was putting away a five-pound box of bonbons within forty-five minutes, which made it impossible for him to scream. 'Tell 'im – ' one bonbon, Harry urged me, ' – go ahead, tell 'im – ' four bonbons quickly in one gulp. And while the chocolate was sliding down, I was wracking my brain what on earth would Harry want me to tell Clement now. I had heard their unpleasant arguments umpteen times before: nobody asked me for my opinion, and I was grateful. Harry just wanted to exhibit to me and, many times, to others around too his power over a world-renowned director like René Clement. It took me a long time to find out why he didn't walk. When I found out, he and I disagreed; the only time we did.

Why was Harry asking me now? I hadn't thawed out yet. At the airport, his driver had yanked me from Customs, 'Mr Saltzman wants to see you, sir, right away.' I was dreading seeing Harry right then. He politely held the door of Harry's hearse open for me, 'The papers are on the seat, sir, as usual.'

I never knew the driver's name, I dreaded his driving, he was a faceless, nameless blend with the shiny woodwork of the Rolls, he was the perfect funeral driver for a hearse, dignified, smooth and agonizingly slow. No! Not that day. He was like a hopped-up maniac driving a getaway car as I was helplessly slammed against one side of the car then the other, my ass polishing the slippery leather seat, getting to town in record time only to find myself on slippery ground as I walked into the office.

'Tell 'im – ' one bonbon, I hadn't even sat down, ' – go ahead, tell 'im – ' Harry urged me, two bonbons, a sip of Evian, ' – tell him. You were there with David – ' four bonbons in one gulp could have been deadly for anybody, ' – David Lean – ' Clement wanted to say something, I got worried, Harry overrode him, harsh, loud. 'No! no-no, nooo, never, I am not trying to equate you with anybody, no-no-no, René. You are the only. You are René Clement.'

That seemingly pacified Clement, Harry grabbed the last two bonbons – they kept him from talking while he put the top on the empty box. I knew the sign and it bugged me. He was ready for a serious attack. He looked at Clement with fire in his eyes, opened his mouth . . . and the phone rang. I thought he would have a stroke when he jerked the receiver off its cradle, and held it in his clenched fist with hatred; out of his opening and closing mouth only agonized breathing came out.

'Mr Saltzman . . . hello . . . hello . . . Mr Saltzman, Mr Saltzman, are you there?' chattered the receiver.

'Where in hell do you think I am?' roared the lion, 'I told you, don't put any calls through! Who was it?' all in one breath, holding the receiver so tight that the lobe of his ear turned purple. Harry's curiosity and secrecy was insatiable; he knew if the call was put through it must have been important and didn't want us to hear it by chance. He released the pressure on his ear; then, as if he were throwing a punch, he snapped his elbow and shoved the receiver toward Clement's face. Had Harry Saltzman connected, René Clement would've lost both of his bridges. With disgust Harry slid off his throne. Without shoes, and in his red socks, he shuffled to his bathroom, closed the door only to open it in a second, 'See you tomorrow at ten,' and shut the door again.

Clement hung up the phone, 'I am sorry,' and picked up his papers. He asked me on our way downstairs how my trip – trip? – to Finland had been. He knew, we all knew, that his wife was the general. René Clement was not a strong man, she was one. Had she not been put through, without hesitation she would have marched in and that would have been a sure pink slip for everybody downstairs. Madame Clement was in the lobby.

Harry put Clement 'out to dry', as he phrased it, and I was left alone to wind up the production with eva in comparative peace, laying low, staying away from Harry's pies in the sky – none of which was ever eaten – which in turn increased his appetite for more punishment; he was a glutton for punishment.

Billion Dollar Brain was about to be delivered and as with every project a piece of my heart was going with it. I was ready to change course and set sail for less turbulent waters back home, then came a call from Harry, like hundreds before, 'Have dinner with me.'

'Sorry, but I am – '

' – No, you're not. I want you there, I had a good meeting with René this afternoon, all set, we'll celebrate.'

This call was not like many other 'unrefusable invitations' I was hoping to duck, this was an 'Of course Harry,' call. I was glad they had finally seen the light. It promised to be an event not to be missed.

Harry, thoroughbred schizophrenic, was capable and happy to stomp on your guts with joy at 5.30 p.m. in his office, only to be your most gracious host at 7.30 p.m. for dinner.

If Harry Saltzman had known stories as well as he knew wines, all of his projects would have turned out to be as delightful as 'the help' to digest our magnificent meal. He was his sparkling brilliant self, he even mesmerized Madame Clement with the help of 'the help'. By the time the second brandy and the port for Madame had arrived and Harry's cigar was halfway to its inglorious, soggy end, they 'definitely' agreed, if Clement would agree to consider shooting the picture in Spain, Harry would consider dropping his idea of Israel.[1]

The next day during luncheon, to really cement their pact, I convinced Harry in public that, of course, he had 'won the first round'; he savored the accolade and royally asked me to take Clement to Spain. That took the wind out of my sails, but I felt sorry for Clement, I wanted him to make the picture, and above all I owed a great deal to Harry, who – Bandi Marton or Bandi de Toth, chariot race or not, with a broken neck, taking a risk – held on to me. Thanks.

'You won the first round,' I told Clement, born and bred in the birthplace of political connivance.

'Did you tell the same thing to Harry too?' he asked me.

'I did.'

---

1 At that time there was no completion bond or cast insurance available for Israel, thus no finance could be obtained for the picture.

'Eh, bon, pourquoi?'

'Because I believe that's true, the first step in the right direction to sort out this unproductive discord.'

'Could we shoot it in Spain?'

'Yes, we could.'

'Bon, you were there with *Lawrence*, bon.'

Bon means fine, OK, good, for anybody except Clement; for him it meant 'maybe?' – a positive 'maybe?'.

'Is he going to Spain or not? What did he finally say?' Harry asked me, in one anxious breath.

'He said "Bon."'

'Merde! We are back to square one.' He knew Clement better than I did. 'Why doesn't he quit if he doesn't want to do the picture? Well, take him anyway.' After three bonbons and an afterthought, he added, 'Maybe he'll change his mind,' four bonbons, 'I hope.'

What Harry was hoping for I didn't even guess.

The air-conditioning worked on board the Iberia flight between London and Madrid, but nothing could have been strong enough to obliterate the nauseating pungency of the mixed odor of garlic emanating from Madame and the heavy, sweet, supposedly sensuous scent of Schiaparelli. The garlic was winning hands down every time Madame Clement turned around in the seat in front of me and aimed at me one of her endless questions about Almeria. I didn't listen, and with every question I became more and more anesthetized. I wanted to evade the answers; as I understood it, the town had changed since the days of *Lawrence*.

For some it became contaminated. No more crumbling walls with pleading signs, 'Mas agua, mas arbores, mas industrias, Franco' ('More water, more trees, more industries, Franco'). The slender mamacitas of the cantinas and bodegas had become spread-out mamas of restaurants and nightclubs. No more showers of bedbugs were coming down in the mornings from the mattresses as they were hung out for airing in the higher windows of the two 'hotels'. No more stray dogs, donkey-shit and potholes on the main drag. The main street was paved with marble, dotted with department stores offering everything from Madrid or Paris. Two deluxe hotels of international standard. No more mule trains, but direct flights from Madrid to Almeria. Brigitte Bargot's white Rolls and other matching modes of transportation with fitting traffic jams. I was bowled over, Almeria was caught up by the doom of civilization, but the cigalas were still walking to your table before being grilled on charcoal in front of you. I was glad to see civilization wasn't totally victorious.

'Bon,' said Clement, 'C'est parfait,' said Madame, adding her own garlic to the cuisine. They were content, 'so far', they said together cautiously. That I had no idea what Clement was looking for was bad enough, but that he didn't know it either was a bit disconcerting. To say he was not very talkative would be an understatement, and as time went by he talked to me less and less. To make up for his days of silence with me, he never shut his mouth during the evenings, sitting in the corner of some restaurant shunning even their noisy compatriots. 'Un deux' ('a twosome'), the engrossed Monsieur and Madame Clement were rattling in French, like a drum roll interrupted occasionally by the harsh, castanet-sounding voice of Madame. They would have been ideal models for a Norman Rockwell painting: 'The Perfect Couple'.

In a way I understood Clement's bewilderment and growing mistrust of me. Almeria was not the place I described. A sleepy shamble of adobe hovels in the middle of an arid nowhere, endless sand dunes on the horizon, camels. I didn't blame him, I too was bewildered at first. Cops directing traffic between Sean Connery on horseback and another company's stagecoach and a third company's herd of cattle between the 'endless dunes'. Well, the only thing that remained of my description were the descendants of *Lawrence of Arabia*'s 'escapees'. No more 'mas aqua' signs, overhead sprinklers were watering the flowers and fresh vegetables for the film companies' tourists' tables. The demand for 'mas arbores' wasn't quite fulfilled yet, but everybody welcomed the destructive fulfilment of 'mas industrias' and ignored the fingers pointing skyward at the impending doom of this mudball: the smokestacks of industries were belching smoke toward the once blue, now industrial-grey sky. Who cared, money was pouring in, the small businesses were blooming making artificial flowers and 'antiques' in backyards, tourists wanting to be taken for a ride and the 'millionaires' easy with the 'dinares', film crews eager to spend their – according to the union – nice daily living allowances. I felt guilty which I shouldn't have – I had nothing to do with it, except maybe in a minor way I enhanced the start of the madness, so to speak. Time and progress did the rest.

I misled him, Clement told me. But on the other hand a David Lean, a Zoltán Korda, a John Ford and others with pre-vision of a scene had the gift of seeing what they could get out of the geography, never noticing what was useless for them. They wouldn't have been so distraught.

After a miserable week I still didn't know what Clement was looking for. I showed him every place I could think of around Almeria, some still untrampled, unblemished by the leftover plastic cups of film companies and tourists, some nooks I had selfishly kept to myself for possible future use. It was useless. Clement didn't talk to me, he refused to talk to Harry and the fact that Harry wasn't disturbed by it at all added one more puzzle to this strange, not too pleasant, assignment.

Without Harry being directly responsible for the finances of this project, I would have been fishing for trout in the High Sierras long before we boarded the plane in Almeria to return to London. But my motto, 'there is some blessing in every disaster,' was proven right again, except I didn't have to look for the blessing, this time it was negative. I didn't have to smell it – Monsieur and Madame Clement sat as far from me as space permitted on the plane back to London, I didn't miss the garlic at all.

In London separate transportation was arranged for the Clements, so I didn't even mind Harry's driver whisking me away from Customs, but this time he drove – no, he didn't drive, he crawled in his normal funeral style – to take me not to the office, worse, farther, to my surprise to Harry's 'shack' in the country, Woodlands, for the weekend, where Harry and his usual weekend retinue were already waiting, bobbing up and down in their floating armchairs in the 90-plus degree water of Harry's private ocean.

I never welcomed more a glass of Dom Perignon than the one that was floated to me as I joined the idle rich. But before I touched my glass Harry spoiled my first joy in a week: 'Is he going to quit?'

'I don't know, Harry, I haven't got the faintest idea. He hardly spoke to me at all.'

'Good – '

' – Thanks for the compliment, and what is that supposed to mean?'

Harry laughed. He had a good laugh when his laugh was sincere. 'We'll talk about it Monday in the office, welcome back.'

I wasn't a bad swimmer, but 'welcome back' almost drowned me. Something must be wrong somewhere. That was off the main line Harry traveled. And that was only Thursday.

During the Friday afternoon bobbing-up-and-down session the phone was floated to Harry. After he listened poker-faced, he covered the phone with his wet palm and turned directly to me, 'George Marton, from Paris. He wants to come out tomorrow,' then listened and listened more without saying one word, very unlike Harry Saltzman. Finally he spoke. 'You know, George, I don't do business here during the week-ends' – which was an outright lie – 'but I'll see you, you know that, sorry I won't be able to put you up, we have the place full . . . yes from the pool . . . like sardines we are. We'll see you tomorrow then . . . no-no, George, I'll have a car pick you up and take you back to the airport.'

Harry Saltzman could wilt when he was defeated. He wilted when he hung up the phone.

George Marton arrived in the morning with a pound of caviar, a box of cigars and a big smile. They were closeted for two hours or more; Harry emerged more wilted and after big hugs, 'au revoirs' and 'bientôts' George Marton departed.

In spite of the pale, happy-pink table linen, the sparkling silver, the snow-white wrought-iron furniture above the brick-red tile floor of the terrace, surrounded by emerald-green grass with tiny water-beads twinkling among their proud blades like miniature rainbows under a happy British-blue sky, a dark cloud like the sword of Damocles was hanging over the table. Harry was morose and when he was, it was no fun to be around him. He didn't taste George's caviar, poked at the food before him, he never said a word of what went on during his two-hour meeting with Marton.

'Sorrry, sirrr,' the ex-Yugoslav butler woke me up, 'Mr Saltzman was wonderrring verrr you verrre. He is in the pool,' and he withdrew.

I had escaped the gloom that must have been reigning in the billiard-room during the routine after-lunch games, stretched out after arid Almeria on the plush grass with the two Chesepeake Bay retrievers next to me and a book someone tried to palm off on Harry, and quickly fell asleep, the book ending up on my face to keep off the flies. The book was so bad even the dogs didn't chew on it while I slept. But the lovely, peaceful afternoon was over, thoughtlessly interrupted.

Have you ever been at a funeral where the minister has forgotten the service? Well, the atmosphere at poolside was like that when I got there. The mourners were bobbing up and down in eerie silence. I waved off the drink, slid into my floating armchair. Harry never said a word to me and I continued where I left off on the grass. Actually, it was very pleasant, I took toll of the whole situation which I hadn't done before.

I did the Almeria abortion as a favor to Harry. Officially, I had nothing to do with the project nor had I any desire to fall from the freezing pan of the Baltic Sea into the molasses of a tug-of-war between Harry Saltzman and René Clement. I didn't want to let Harry down, he was more than fair with me and I was aware the time wasn't right to tell him I'd be off fishing in the High Sierras; I knew I had to wait till it would be appropriate without being unappreciative. The melodic slap-slap of the waves against the sides was very soothing. I cleared my conscience and fell asleep in no time at all.

'That son of a bitch won't quit,' woke me up with a start. The first words I heard from Harry since the Marton meeting. Luckily, I didn't have to ask 'Who?' Harry was extremely Francophile, but blurted out with venom, 'That French bastard.' The bomb that hit the water surprised everybody, me the most.

Denis Selinger, a lovely gentleman, always quiet and polite, an agent handling among others Michael Caine, spoke up softly, 'But you gave me the impression, Harry, you wanted to work with him very much. The prestige you said – '

The drops of condensation that collected on the glass roof of the pool house came down like a tropical shower as Harry howled, 'Are you telling me or asking me, Denis, I made a mistake?'

Harry asked the wrong question from the wrong man. The milquetoast veneer busted, Denis had more guts than a loaded Irish pub-champ. 'If you feel the way you have sounded, yes, Harry. A big one.'

The ping-pinging of the droplets hitting the surface of the pool was the only sound for a long while, then Harry grumbled, 'Talk to you later, Denis,' and we bobbed in stupefied silence until noisy Miss Sunshine, Jackie, ripped it apart with laughter and chatter; with her around nobody could put in a word edgewise.

As quickly as she descended, she was gone with an order served on a laugh, 'Cocktails and Jack Daniel's for the peasant' – she meant me – 'in the den in forty-five minutes.'

Nothing could evacuate a place faster, everybody was gone. I looked back, there was Harry, alone in the big pool, eyes closed, bobbing. Somehow I couldn't leave him with his loneliness, I slipped back in the pool and started to do some laps. To stomp out the soft spot I conned myself it would do me good, I needed more exercise.

Harry, usually the last to leave a festive Saturday dinner table, was the first to break. There was no usual brandy and cigar ceremony. 'Bandi,' he said on his way out, 'in my study.' The first words he said since we sat down to eat.

By the time I joined him and sat down in a very comfortable, dark-red leather armchair across from him, two snifters, warmers with dancing blue flames, a bottle of dark Delamain were already on the little side-table next to him. He took his time. I heard clearly the soft cracks of the big cigars as he tested them, smelled them, licked them with affection and finally lit one with long-stemmed wooden matches. Everything was quiet, smelled good. It was peace. Harry locked the gloom out. Then the roof fell in.

'I want you to take charge of this fucked-up mess. You told me once you were nursing an idea, something similar, remember? . . . Remember?'

It felt like I had run off the end of the diving board like Donald Duck and was running on thin air and getting nowhere with a bottomless pit under me.

'But René Clement – '

' – Fuck René Clement and – '

' – Can't, I won't do – '

' – Don't interrupt all the time. I told Clement – '

' – But – '

' – You stop interrupting. Clement knows I want you to take charge of a new script.' Strike one.

'What did he say?'

Harry didn't answer me, he picked up the phone, dialed. The phone was ringing and ringing and Harry was cursing and cursing the phone. Finally, he hung up but dialed again immediately and there was an answer after the first ring.

'René? Andre won't do it unless you ask him personally,' and without any further ado he shoved the phone over to me. 'Talk, talk to him.' Strike two.

It was one of the most difficult surprises I have had to face.

'With whom can you get a script out fast – ' Harry asked me when I hung up.

' – And good?'

'Egh!' he grunted annoyed, 'no time for bad puns. Anybody you can think of.' Strike three. Harry was pitching hard and very fast balls. I needed time to recover.

'I have to think.'

'Then go and think,' he was sharp. I didn't like it at all.

'Think during the Sabbath, please, Harry.'

He got up abruptly, he could be surprisingly agile, especially when he got irritated, and I succeeded. He always wanted his own way in his own time. With cigar in hand he stood there looking at me in silence for two hours, I thought. I had never noticed before he had long eyelashes. Abruptly he turned, he was irked but he left me in the room with a 'See you in the morning.'

I sat for a while before going to the smallest of the guest cottages, the farthest from the main building.

The two retrievers were waiting in front of it; nobody else would let them inside any building but me. They dropped next to my bed, stretched out, closed their eyes and pronto were off to their happy meadows to chase rabbits. They didn't care how I was going to flop over them on the bed to face a long, sleepless night.

The sky was brightly promising another nice day before I closed my eye, it felt like it was only for a minute. The two damned dogs wanted to go out, I let them out to greet the morning with wagging tails and happy yelps. I couldn't go back to sleep.

Harry's hours were always unpredictable; it was not unusual for him to be the first at the breakfast table reading the morning papers. He ignored my 'Good morning, Harry.' For him I wasn't in the room, on the planet. It didn't bother me that Harry had moods, he did the same to his wife whom he adored. I was halfway through my breakfast when, without looking up, he said, 'I hope you didn't sleep.'

I knew right then it was childish, but the truth is often embarrassing, it just slipped out, 'I didn't, thanks to you.'

'Good. With whom do you want to work, or do you want to do it alone?'

He didn't like John McGrath, he was uncouth and too radical for his taste. 'John McGrath,' I said without a moment's hesitation. I was sure that'd let me off the hook.

Wrong again, he answered also without hesitation, 'Fine.' Ball four I threw and he walked. I knew then he was serious.

I pitched again hoping to strike him out.

'Melvyn Bragg,' who thought Harry was uncouth, Harry knew that and didn't appreciate it. Ball one.

He said, 'Sure, you want both or one or the other?' Ball two and three too were gone with one wind-up. 'Anybody else you want whom I don't like is fine with me. This is your headache.'

That was Harry Saltzman, no dope was he. I lost the ball game.

To turn it down would have been a mistake, not only because of my obligation to Harry but more because of Lotte Colin. As it turned out, I never could have forgiven myself for letting her dreams down. The stone above her grave reads Lotte Colin. That's who she wanted to be. Her original name was a melodious Romanian Jewish name. Her old name, for her, was euphonic with the tunes of the marching bands of the pogroms, the Nazi persecution. For her it was the memento of misery. She wanted to be Lotte Colin, a writer, a screen-writer, a screen-writer in English. Dreams have no anchors – the fact that she could hardly read or write, not even in her own native tongue, Romanian, didn't stop her dreaming. She took English lessons, she worked on it, she could afford the best teachers, she was the mother-in-law of 'dee Harry', she was Jackie's mother.

We all are most impatient with those who are closest and dearest to us. Jackie and 'dee Harry' loved her deeply, but neither was famous for their patience. They sincerely appreciated and praised her for her cooking, bought her the most expensive dresses, which she hated, but they had no time to listen to her stories. In Harry's defense he didn't listen to the stories of writers to whom he was paying $5,000 a week.

After every weekend I spent in Woodlands I had to send to the cleaner every piece I had with me and after every three or four occasions I had to buy new luggage. She snuck into them badly packed, aromatic Romanian specialities she had prepared for me. I didn't want to insult her by locking the bags, I left them open and always, duly surprised, thanked her profusely for the goodies the next time I saw her. She hugged me, she was a 'born mother' and, as mothers do, she liked to read stories and she proudly read them to me for hours from a single sheet of paper with six or seven badly scrawled English words on it.

Dreams are beautiful. Could you awaken somebody like she was with the ugly, cruel truth? I couldn't. She sat quiet as a church mouse at a discreet distance from us in a corner when John McGrath, Melvyn Bragg and I were working during weekends in Woodlands on what became *Play Dirty*. She loved it.

Her daughter hated it. Harry felt about it like he felt about all stories he bought; nobody could tell – not even himself – how he felt, that was his usual attitude. Before he bought them they were the greatest. I believe deep down he got frightened of the inherent headaches and responsibilities that went with making them into a picture.

It was moonlight and roses until the slow fire of animosity between Harry and John turned into a continuous inferno and John for the 'benefit of the project' – and I believe because of his own pride, conviction and integrity – 'with regret' walked. Barely was he across the threshold when Harry sat in his chair. He didn't throw Lotte Colin out, he asked her to 'cook us something special for lunch', and she ran with a happy smile to oblige 'dee Harry', and he flooded us with ideas, many good ones, for other projects he was always working on.

'This is about what I wanted Clement to do,' he burped the words after the murderously heavy but fabulous luncheon Lotte Colin fixed for us. From there on he was not very generous with his presence at our story meetings, we had to chase him with the new pages and, of course, he never committed himself.

Melvyn Bragg, not belonging to the 'en famille bobbing circle', made it easier for me to hit Harry in the pool when he was relaxed – as relaxed as 'dee Harry' could ever be – and had his guard down.

'Do you read, Harry, those pages we send you?'

'Sure, certainly, they are fine.' Local knowledge helped, I knew when he answered too quickly he wanted to get off the subject. 'Fine' he added.

'How did Clement like the script?' I drilled on. Not a grunt for an answer. I got concerned, 'You are sending him the pages, Harry, aren't you?' Not a word. 'Are you, Harry?'

Harry Saltzman will go down in history as the great evader. 'It could be shot in Spain, is that correct?' was his immediate reply.

'Correct. Harry, I asked you, are you sending the pages to Clement? I haven't heard a word from him.'

He started to complain the thermostat was set too low. He picked up the ever present phone by his fingertips and ordered a higher setting.

'Harry –'

'– Call him. I am thinking.'

His 'Call him,' pacified me for the time being, after all he was right the first time he made me call Clement. He closed his eyes and in a little while he started to snore genuinely and gently. I snoozed off too.

'Are you trying to boil me? For Christ's sake turn-the-damn-thing-down,' – splash, he slammed down the receiver but missed its cradle – 'are you awake?' All in one breath, he woke me up.

'Thanks, Harry. I –'

'– I want you to go down to Spain one of these days and set the locations.'

'Did you check with Clement?'

'I don't have to check with anybody.'

'But –'

'Call him.' I got out of the pool, 'What's your hurry?' he called after me as I left the tropics to face the frost of a normal English spring day on my way to 'my' cottage.

Have you ever had a phone conversation with someone who was talking to you, but wasn't there at all. I was talking to Clement, I recognized the voice, understood the words, but he couldn't have been there.

'Bon, pick them,' he said. 'They will be fine, "bien sûr" ("surely"), just pick them.'

'The script, I would like to –'

'– Bon, I will call-you-an-ve-tak-about-it. Thank you for calling. Au revoir,' and hung up.

I went to Spain, picked the locations, sent photos of them to Clement; not a word from him. We finished the first draft. Lotte Colin thought it was the greatest, Jackie, her daughter, was convinced it was horrible.

'Merde, who wants to watch the truth, mon chereeee?' Jackie asked Harry who, true to himself, remained non-committal.

Michael Caine didn't like the script at all and doubted Clement would like it. He was bitten by 'Clementitis', as Harry must have been when he signed him. As a matter of fact, Caine still doesn't like the picture. A climber, he wanted a credit, a picture – good, bad or indifferent – with *the* René Clement. The part Nigel Davenport played was originally turned down by Richard Harris; United Artists said good riddance, approved the script, the budget and scheduled a release date.

Saddled with a staggeringly high overheard, there was no other choice for Harry than abandon the project and write off a small fortune or start the picture. Sets were built in Almeria, still not a word from René

Clement. Trying to reason out his strange behavior was like beating my head against the wall.

Not as one of the writers, but because of the responsibility of this whole mess dumped on my shoulders, I asked Harry's legal eagles to messenger me in Spain all contracts; it is a sine qua non for a producer to have them on hand and I was discharging the duties and functions of one again for Harry. My fractured French was good enough to get service in restaurants, but far from being good enough to decipher the complicated French contract of René Clement. After wrestling a night and a day with the help of French–English dictionaries, trying to make sense of the René Clement puzzle, it still remained unsolved. I refused to believe he stayed with the picture only to receive the last instalment of his salary on the last day of shooting. I wanted to be convinced, no matter how big it was, he wouldn't sell his integrity. The puzzle became more confusing as the days dragged by.

Clement, the meek, reserved gentleman and his garlic-storage drill sergeant Madame arrived a week before shooting. I felt justified in having trusted his integrity. Perfunctorily, he drove with me to the sets and to the locations, dodging on the way cowboys and Indians chasing each other; we were held up in our progress by a stagecoach being held up, wagon trains toiling their way through the rocky terrain trailed by rag-tag starving pilgrims; there was life everywhere except in René Clement. He became more disconsolate with every turn of the wheel. I felt I was driving around with a fugitive from Madame Tussaud's, a wax figure of the famous director René Clement. He never said a word about the script, I didn't ask him. He didn't speak. He rubbed his chin. Harry came down unexpectedly.

He loved garlic, but I still felt sorry for him. For the remainder of the week every night during dinner he, Monsieur and Madame Clement had their foreheads glued together over the dinner table and she was doing most of the agitated talking. Even across the largest restaurant Harry looked deflated. He joined Clement's club and hardly spoke to anybody. The information he needed, eva was supplying ably.

Joking, witty and bright Michael Caine – always competing with the David Niven image – had become taciturn. A rumor started with the Spanish crew members on the second day of shooting that Clement was quitting. Their news came through their compatriots, from the bilingual waiters of the various restaurants, the only living creatures except the

restaurants' flies being within earshot of the nightly huddlers, Harry and
the Clements, during their tense dinner confabs. I have never experienced being with a crew so splintered apart, especially in a foreign land.
eva did her best to hold the lethargic company together.

On the third day Harry commandeered a car to take him to the airport
and he himself went to pick up George Marton. A royal welcome.

'Bandi, how are you?' Marton grabbed me, kissed me on both cheeks –
not a Hungarian custom – and, hanging on to my elbow, dragged me to
the farthest corner, literally cornering me, sticking his nose so close to
mine he almost got cross-eyed looking into my one good eye, whispering, 'Between you and me, only you and me, on my word, do you
want to direct this picture?'

Had he spat in my face, it wouldn't have rocked me more. It took time
to throw up a 'Hell, no,' and he mistook the pause.

'My word of honor, just between you and me, I, only I have to know it.
Do you?'

'Did you forget what no means in English? N-O, got it? What I really
want is to get out of this whole fucking mess. Do you read me, George
Marton? Now fuck off.'

He didn't, he stuck, hanging onto my elbow. 'Is it that bad?'

'Ask your client, I've got to go now.' I shook his hand off my elbow and
left him in the corner where he urinated on himself as far as I was
concerned. That was the last time I ever talked to him.

The following morning the sun of the Costa del Sol shone on different
Clements and a very different Harry Saltzman. For the first time since
their arrival in Almeria, Madame and Monsieur Clement came down to
the dining-room for breakfast, late but smiling, saying good morning to
everybody. George Marton waltzed in with his ears in danger of falling
into his mouth, his smile was so wide. Harry was so depressed, so
deflated he looked like he had shrunk to the size of a dried-out prune
during the night; radiating misery he sat alone in a corner with yesterday's French papers which George Marton brought him.

'Now what?' asked eva.

'I wish I knew. Harry should be walking on air.'

Well, Harry Saltzman didn't walk on air, it would have taken too long
to walk on air to London; instead, he took the next flight without a
goodbye. George Marton stayed on for another day.

A different Clement had walked onto the set thirty minutes ahead of us. He was moving props around himself. The René Clement we were waiting for arrived, observant and meticulous about details. Before the actors were on the set, he was changing lines in the script, all for the better. Everything moved and faster. Sour Caine turned so happy he almost out-quipped David Niven. The dirt underfoot started to smile. I was the happiest. I didn't care who had performed the miracle, whether George Marton's hypnotically shrewd thinking had turned Clement into sainthood or Harry had twisted Clement's arm – it worked, we were beginning to function like professionals. My lost respect for Clement emerged from the garbage shinier than I had dropped it in.

Although he remained convinced and expounded it freely, it would have been ill-timed, ill-advised to shoot a picture about Israeli commandos in Israel now or shoot any picture in Israel ever. However, this version 'may have a chance', he said. Hail George Marton or whoever.

The Clements remained solitary. We never dined together which, being on location, was unusual behavior. But their routine became the source of an underground news service. When they dined in restaurants where waiters spoke French the spotty gossip that filtered through the waiters' eavesdropping, unreliable as it was, was still very disturbing.

The Clements hated Spain, Almeria, the food, the mediocre crew, the script, everything, but Madame wouldn't let him quit and lose the big lump sum due him the last day of shooting. I was becoming shock-proof by then, but this jarred. If this solved the puzzle, I wished it wasn't true. Who likes to be disappointed, to be so gullible? I threw my respect this time not in the garbage but dropped it in the portable chemical toilet on the set to be sure it would dissolve.

Being way behind schedule, with Harry screaming on the phone, 'You are killing me' – I was killing him? – 'I trusted you, how could you do this to me?' he kept asking me several times a day.

What could I have said, 'According to the waiters . . .' – Please!

'Clement will quit tomorrow,' came through the tom-toms in the morning. How would it have sounded in London on the phone before Harry had his bonbons – 'According to the waiters . . .'. – and it would have been unfair all around.

Actually Clement didn't quit, only raised hell wanting to revamp the set, change the wardrobe, find new locations, maybe in North Africa; in short, shoot another film. A panic call from the set and I was off to the location. The moment I walked on the set Clement left, went back to his hotel. I found a bunch of mixed-up zombies milling around aimlessly. 'Go home, the drinks are on the company tonight. See you in the morning,' and like a scared covey of sparrows the crew disappeared.

I called Clement and Madame told me he couldn't come to the phone, he was sick, very sick, and she hung up. I sent a doctor immediately. They wouldn't let him in. I called the insurance company in London. Harry was the next call.

'Clement got sick this afternoon – '

' – Did you call the insurance company?'

'I did.'

That was it, he hung up.

The Costa del Sol wasn't sunny that day, and at the end of our rainbow what was in the pot was certainly not pure gold but pure something else, and when the whirlwind of the Almeria desert hit it we all got freckles.

Some times making pictures was more fun than at other times but it was certainly never dull.

I gave the next day off and paid a hefty liquor bill. If it was spent to drink to Clement's health it was ill-spent. Clement got out of Almeria. He quit.

Harry called later in the day; when he got me on the phone he started to yell so loud I would have heard him without the phone, 'What are you doing in the office, do you know what time it is? You are robbing me. If you don't know it, you're already behind schedule. Why-why are you robbing me?' I had had about enough and was ready to walk when I heard, as I was hanging up on him: 'Get on the goddamned set and shoot,' and Harry hung up.

It was a strange way to get a directorial assignment, to say the least. But most film folk are strange, some are even nuts. I would have been a hypocrite to deny I wasn't happy. I had wanted to do a story like *Play Dirty* since I wallowed in the blood of futility in Poland. But as I always say, there is some good in every disaster; I also learned in Poland how to crawl under barbed-wire with fishhooks dangling on it, and if you were caught and the tin-cans rattled, you had no chance even to start your last prayer. And that all came in very handy making a low-budget epic. One never knows. To reach a dream sometimes one has to walk barefoot on thorns, but I never stepped on toes.

I hate to see a legend in the toilet. I rekindled my respect for Clement; after all, he finally won over money, Madame and Marton, but the fire was never as bright as it had been before. He became one of the 'lost talent brigade'; it is numberless.

Michael Caine was probably more disappointed than I, and I understood him and his resentment of the film. He felt uncomfortable, insecure in the film without Clement, which made his portrayal in *Play Dirty* so remarkable, considered by many one of his best, since both he and the character he portrayed were out of the safety of their rocking chair. The character was not an '007', facing ready-made mechanical solutions, nor even a Harry Palmer of *The Ipcress File* or *Billion Dollar Brain*. Thank God, he was young and not too experienced yet. My respect for his professionalism only grew as we drilled on under not the clearest Almeria sky. The unexpected rain performed a miracle. Magic. It turned the desert almost overnight into a – for the natives the most beautiful – flower garden. Nothing could be done for a week and it took us another week to destroy the beauty. Caine was a trouper, maybe because it gave him time to chase Brigitte Bardot until she threw a loaf of bread at him in a restaurant, then the sun came out.

I liked Almeria. I went back there often, I enjoyed the fun of dodging traffic cops, in the sand, making you believe they didn't exist. I defy you to point out where it gives away that *Play Dirty* wasn't shot where it really happened, on the cruel, naked desert. And even a professional liar wouldn't swear that the camels weren't descendants of *Lawrence of Arabia*'s fugitives, which of course they were. Otherwise, there would be no camels in the film, we couldn't have afforded them.

Challenges like this make life worth living and making motion pictures such a joy and fun, creating reality when it doesn't exist. After all we are working with make-believe. It is so easy to distort, falsify the truth. But making truth, something out of nothing, is what life is all about – for me. I always loved making pictures. I suppose by now you have guessed it.

Cases of cerveza (beer) in the heat and hard work faded the bitter memories of Clement. The crew became a unit. Harry was understanding and non-existent, it was a delight to work with Caine and the rest.

Harry had more trouble in London than we did in the flower-covered desert, he couldn't dislodge Lotte Colin from the projection room. She camped there and in the cutting-room in spite of her agonizing headaches and spent, according to her, the happiest hours of her till then not too blissful life.

Jackie was diagnosed as having breast cancer, she was scared of surgery and refused it. Harry agreed, 'Nobody is going to mutilate my wife.' The latest X-ray equipment was delivered one to the town house in London and one to the country cottage, Woodlands, Buckinghamshire. No chemotherapy, 'My wife is not going to lose her hair.'

'Thank you chereee, you're wonderful.'

If anybody had the right to hate, Jackie did, and she used it, she openly hated the picture. She tried to talk Harry into scuttling it, or at least re-cut the end; she mysteriously succeeded – only at the last minute before the release prints started to roll off the printer – in cutting out of Michel Legrand's score a children's euphorious, jubilant choir from under the morbid scene where Caine orders at gun-point his rebellious patrol to bury the bodies of their ambushed enemy. 'Mon dieux, c'est un sac- rilège,' Jackie cried, and her tears did the trick.

There was only one happy person in this sad congregation, Lotte Colin. I made up for her a loop of the title and the first scene of *Play Dirty*. She wore out the loop, she ran it whenever the projection-room was free, every day, all day for her Romanian cronies, it cured her headache she said.

The credit on *Play Dirty* reads: Screenplay by Lotte Colin and Melvyn Bragg, not Andre de Toth and Melvyn Bragg.

Lotte Colin died of brain cancer after running the main title of *Play Dirty* for her friends for one month. Her last words were, 'See, I told you. I made it.'

25 Changing Courses

There is an ancient Hungarian proverb: Man plans, God executes the way He sees fit. He had hidden the plan He had for me. It had been a big surprise landing at Enterprise: this time He had a matching big surprise for me. He landed me, through *Play Dirty* with NGC – National General Corporation – a multi-billion-dollar conglomerate. It was the beginning of the extinction of the dinosaur, multi-headed corporations were starting to gobble up yesterday's moguls.

But strangely enough, this giant was run as elegantly and as thoughtfully as Enterprise. The approach to film-making of Irvin Levin and Gene Klein, the two bosses of the corporation, was very similar to Charles Einfeld and David Loew. They both loved making films – of course, without the vast experience of the other two – but nobody noticed the handwriting on the wall: if Enterprise didn't succeed, they had no more chance than a snowball in hell of surviving. And the business at that time was closer to hell than any other place.

Both bosses of NGC were ardent pacifists and they were impressed by *Play Dirty*'s statement. Harry was anxious to get rid of me after I refused to have any part in some of his suicidal production plans and, hoping to open a connection to NGC's coffers to replenish his shrinking capacity to make mistakes, he gave his blessing – in those days with a very rare smile – and I was off to Los Angeles, after ten long years. When I got home, I realized how really long those years had been. An unripened new era in the picture business and the good old smog greeted me. I was more disappointed with the new business than the old smog. I felt like a ghost covered with slimy green moss, crawling out of an ancient forgotten grave carrying a deadly contagious disease. I was shunned.

I had the choice of producing or directing *El Condor*, a period swashbuckler. The script had already been written, under the 'super-vision' of a lovely elderly gent, whose only sport was going to automobile showrooms in the evenings and kicking the tires of the exhibits – he thought that was the sign of an interested buyer. But he never bought one in his long adult life – since he crawled out of his crib he had driven company cars. He was a controller of big corporations with as much story sense as Harry Saltzman. But Harry bought cars, always more than needed. After the hectic *Play Dirty* I wanted to live leisurely for a while and had decided to produce *El Condor* only. With Ann on board and my daughter Diana back from Paris to be the second-unit script girl – not script person, she was proud to be a girl. Smooth easy sailing, the Sierras looked very close.

We prepared a budget, added up the detailed figures. I fainted – more than twice as much as it would have cost in Almeria. To be sure, a script went off to eva monley. Her Spanish budget came back within a week. Damn it! One of those few occasions I was right. To the tune of a grateful NGC we were off to – guess – yes, Almeria, and Spain swallowed the Sierras.

I was beginning to get used to being prostituted. I wasn't proud of it, nor ashamed of it. I took it for granted and kept screwing up my future, spending the money unwisely enjoying the phony life only money can buy.

Words are powerful, spoken or written they can make you change courses. The magic words came through Western Union: 'Finally succeeded obtaining rights to *The Fighting Temeraire* Stop Please phone earliest Stop Regards Frank Poole.' Frank Poole was the head of Rank Distribution based in London. *The Fighting Temeraire* was a best-selling book about the psychological hurdles the crews of atomic submarines had to surmount on their long patrols. The book was full of suspense and a number of complex characters in nerve-wracking situations.

'We'll be going back to England next week,' and Ann started to pack.

We settled back into our old offices in Pinewood to face two exciting years in an atmosphere of strong men and electronic marvels. A submarine. Sardines packed in a steel hull. Bruised elbows, banged heads on the low ceilings, food of spartan morsels to be washed down with a thimbleful of tepid water. Climbing narrow, steep iron stairs mostly on hands and knees. How about an elevator? One only? Hell no! Five. It needed more talent to have bruised elbows and banged heads in the *Sherwood Forest*, where tomorrow's atomic salvation was stored standing up, ready to go from a thirty-some-feet-high, eighty-feet-or-so-long, little, cramped cubbyhole; of course you could bruise your elbow and bang your head in the bathtub in your home with less talent. But the healing would take longer without the roast beef – better than that served in what used to be Old Simpson's on Piccadilly – served from 'spoiled' to blood rare, as you wished, with all the trimmings.

The electronic gear, in one descriptive word, was awesome. In the deathly silence, the wake of the torpedoes as they left the sub reminded me of the lace trains of wedding gowns for the Angels of Destruction or whipped cream on beautifully sinful desserts.

Alice in Wonderland was an old bored bitch compared to how I felt. But I realized where I was, only after I was shoved with the help of a shoehorn into an 'A Class' sardine can and the bruised elbows, bumped heads became a dozen-times-an-hour reality as your heartbeat picked up the rhythm of the metallic throb of the large diesel engines – a different sensation of noisy claustrophobia after the stealthy silence of atomic subs.

I got lucky again: I was privileged to hear the last heartthrobs of the only survivor of her class from World War II. I was on board when she said goodbye to the deep in her old hunting ground, the English Channel, and became one of the very few who ever surfaced in a submarine in the River Thames. At her final mooring from the Embankment she looked so ancient, so small, so pitifully vulnerable in spite of the cannon mounted on her deck. A relic, a noisy threat of yesteryear's oceans, a museum piece on exhibit, robbed of her menace by time, the 'silent salvation' of a questionable tomorrow. Who knows the answers?

Sesame opened for Ann and me to spend memorable months with a group of the nicest, most straight-talking gentlemen of the Submarine Service of the British Royal Navy. Proud of their mission, a bit confused what that would be, but so was the whole world. Their hospitality matched their tireless assistance. They enjoyed working with us as much as we enjoyed their company and, even-steven, we picked up lifelong friends. Some were in a hurry to leave us, but their memory remains. You are not forgotten, Captain Colin Grant and Co. Wherever you are, do you have Glenfiddich?

The door of Sesame opened wider, and within the limits of the 'no-no's' of security breaches we had carte blanche. They liked our script; Ann said, with her sometimes annoying British understatement, it was 'not too bad'. She and her opinion were always important to me, but on this occasion Frank Poole's carried more weight. He and his lovely lady took us to dinner and he was not known as one of the last of the big spenders.

He didn't wait; as we were sitting down at the table he said very simply, 'It's terrific, we are launching *The Fighting Temeraire* tonight,' and that dinner tasted better than any other for a long time.

The torpedoes were called 'the silent menace'. This one hit bull's eye and silently sunk Frank Poole in the choppy waters of the hideous infighting of corporate politics. *The Fighting Temeraire* was despatched without a trace nor a wreath floating above her, to join in the corporate muck of other scuttled properties rotting in the depths, and Frank Poole, a gentleman, disappeared with it after our dinner celebrating 'the launching of *The Fighting Temeraire*'. Hearing the news, Mervyn, a friend of Poole who instigated the project, shrugged, only slightly. I didn't believe he didn't care, that was Mervyn. A strange man, a cipher. Not someone whom you could forget; no, someone whom you would honestly swear you had never met while you still felt the warmth of his handshake. He spoke five languages like all five were his mother tongue. You would remember his words, but not where the words came from. Mervyn wasn't his real name, I never found out what it was. I forgot where, how long ago and under what circumstances we met. Maybe Poland? I was always concerned about him, the lightest wind would have blown him away like the winter storm an autumn leaf. He was a weightless man with mousy hair, the no-color dead eyes of someone whose path you didn't want to cross; the only features of his you would have never forgotten. A cold, professional killer? With a dozen identical blue suits, shirts, ties, shoes; everything he owned was identical, a uniform?

He was one of those whose undecorated heroism was buried with their non-existence. According to whispers, he was with the Free French Underground through World War II. The only tell-tale signs were some of his French habits, he certainly lifted his chin as he shrugged with panache. I liked him and trusted him. His passkey opened the door of Sesame for Ann and me. He was instrumental in arranging our top-security clearance, he worked for the 'Defense Ministry, as what? I never asked him and I didn't think many people knew.

But his cover cracked, just a hairline crack but it did. His office in the building of the Ministry was hardly larger than a prison cell. It was spotlessly clean, its barren walls painted so white it hurt the eyes. One grey steel desk, of indeterminate age, with chrome edges and a greenish plastic top, four brown, straight-back, uncomfortable wooden chairs in front of it, one identical behind it, the only furniture. An old telephone. That was all. Nothing else. I understood why we had two – two-and-a-half-hour luncheons. I had never seen 'nothing' emphasized more.

Except the old black phone, that was something, power. Mervyn picked it up, 'Buck House, please.'

'Yessssir.' A click, 'Mervyn here, Major . . .' – I forgot his name – 'please.' Two or three clicks.

I didn't hear the answer, it was a male voice, then, 'Mervyn here . . . Thank you, Major, very well, thank you, and yourself? . . . Oh, I hate to hear it. Those nasty colds are a bother. I am calling to tell you I found the persons to . . . Yes, two . . . Yes, I think so, they are a team. If His Royal Highness approves of the plan, I shall take care of the necessary clearance, of course . . . Very well, Major, thank you. I hope you get rid of that nasty cold soon. Goodbye, Major.' Mervyn hung up, 'I think I'll have "something" for you, this will be "soigné" ("clean, polished, elegant") Now we are going to have lunch.'

He was referring to our bad experience with a fugitive from Hollywood, following the sinking of *The Fighting Temeraire*. We were gullible and taken for a ride by the king of the nefarious warts of the picture industry; he was so low he couldn't have reached a frog's ass if he stood on tiptoes on the top rung of a firemen's ladder. 'I am so absent-minded,' he said as an excuse with a wheezing sigh and a forever-frozen, slimy smile. He had forgotten not only to pay us, but also to buy the rights to the book on which the script was based, *Slayground*.

I have to admit he had good taste: the book was good, he liked our script, he lived in an ancient baronial castle, played a good game of croquet on the venerated grounds of British history on which the castle stood. But there was something missing from his magnificent dwelling, the page with honor on it was not in his gold-embossed, Morocco-leatherbound dictionary.

I was sure whatever Mervyn had in his mind would be 'soigné'. I am, modestly speaking, a genius and I was wrong again. Not only was the assignment 'soigné', it was something even a cock-eyed optimist like I am wouldn't dare dream of.

From bobbing up and down in Harry Saltzman's pool between drinks, through the silent, motionless depths of the oceans in a Trident class atomic submarine and ascending to end up 'bobbing up and down' between the smoking, sky-touching waves in the watery hell of the North Sea in gale force ten, in a shoe size 11 wooden tub, not in an atomic submarine – no – but on a Halcyon class, 152 foot length, 28.7 foot beam, 7.7 foot draft, 1115-ton wooden tub, with 39 crew: a minesweeper on her way to become a minehunter was the 'something'. Another of Mervyn's miracles. That Ann and I survived all that was not the end of the miracle. No. That old wooden tub, HMS *Bronington*, was under the first command of His Royal Highness, Charles, Prince of Wales.

Before meeting him, I had to go through the same routine familiarization with the etiquette of do's and dont's like everybody who was to be presented to attending royalty on some gala occasion. There were more 'don'ts' than 'do's'. The main 'no-no's were: do not speak first, do not reach out to shake hands first, and do not ask questions. That was easy enough to learn. It was tough not to chew my fingernails while waiting for my security clearance. It was smooth and easy for Ann. Her grandfather, Lieutenant-Colonel Edward Waring, served the Crown with the Army in India. An uncle, Colonel Eric Waring with the Sappers, served with the Royal Engineers. Another uncle was with the Royal Air Force, Air-Commodore Colin Grierson. Yet another uncle, Horace Waring, also an Air-Commodore, with the Royal Air Force. Please, add one more uncle for good measure, the 'bad boy' of the illustrious military family, again an Air-Commandore, Francis Waring with a Distinguished Flying Cross, who embarked on a 'flying machine' with the Fleet Air Arm, way before the Second World War and the birth of the RAF. He became famous for spending more time in the waters of the Channel than in the air: at first the malfunctioning engines of the precarious kites, later enemy fire forced him to take unwanted baths. During one of his long-distance swimming exercises, Frank got bored with being dunked so often, he went on to invent a self-inflatable life raft.

Ann was definitely coming from an air- and navy-oriented family. Finally I was cleared and we were off in an old Austin Princess, missed by the German buzzbombs: three of us, Chief of Staff of Naval Operations, Mervyn, and myself, with two smaller and older cars from the Ministry of Defence following us, destination HMS *Vernon*. If *Vernon* was a ship, Gibraltar should be called HMS *Gibraltar* too.

When we pulled up in front of a sprawling, neat one-storey building, I was glad we were on solid ground. So much brass piled out of the two cars that followed us, it would have sunk any ship.

The 'planning-room' was large, lit by 200 cruel neon tubes, one above each of the chair-desks, with one of the 200 in the back flickering. Rolled and unrolled charts on the walls, a large blackboard behind a big, slightly elevated table neatly stacked with pointers and various colored crayons.

A figure way in the back of the yawning room, in white shirt with rolled-up sleeves, loosened tie, almost hidden by an impressive pile of books with a thick, white mug next to them, was a perfect picture of loneliness. From the door it was impossible to see what was in the mug on the far end of the long room, but I was certain it was a half a cup of stale coffee. I could detect that sad smell from a mile and see the rings, the tell-tale signs of the size of the sips taken, on the side of the mug, the wedding rings of absent-minded concentration. It took a few seconds for the detached figure to realize his isolation had come to an end.

There were no swarms of secret agents buzzing in the long austere corridors in our path, maybe because of that ugly, penetrating damp cold. There was no knock on the door before we entered. After all, the Chief of Naval Operations doesn't have to knock on any door of a base to ask for permission to enter.

When the young man in the back of the largest freezer this side of Antarctica realized who the intruders were, he snapped to attention like any naval officer would have done. And the way he did, I was sure it wasn't just to show off the brand new gold stripes of a full commander on the sleeve of his tunic draped on the back of his chairdesk. My first impression of him: here was a tough hombre. The polo ponies don't respect rank or royalty, they do respect an ass that is glued to the saddle and sure hands on the reins.

I watched this lone, lonely man from the planning-room dumped from fifty feet into a sixty-foot-deep steel tank full of water, strapped in the pilot seat of a helicopter fuselage, not a mock-up, only the blades and rotor assembly were removed as they were for everybody – the water tank wasn't wide enough. I saw one, only one exception made: two more divers with ABA (Additional Breathing Apparatus) were lounging on the bottom of the tank in addition to the usual four.

The routine countdown reached '. . . and two . . . and one, and . . . theeere she goes . . .' Splash! The chopper hit the water full-force from fifty feet, the steel tank tower shook, the silhouette of a human figure scrambling in a dark mass behind a curtain of pearls of air bubbles floated by the peephole through which I was watching – the only one who was tense, for others at the various observation stations it was all routine, the only thing important to them was the question of how many seconds he took. The bets were on. The count on the blowers started, ten, fifteen . . . the outside limit being sixty seconds to get out of the cockpit and surface to pass the test. The figure of the crashed pilot slithered out of the cockpit between the twenty and twenty-five second count with the loose straps of the safety harness floating behind him.

'He'll make it under fifty.'

'No way,' Mervyn responded to the voice, 'he has the NAK (Nerves And Knowledge). He'll surface at fifty-six.'

Mervyn was wrong. Displaying his NAK, the pilot was breathing out continuously to avoid the danger of the dreaded bends, air-bubbles were streaming from his nostrils all the way up. He was checking his wrist watch and stopped from time to time to decompress; he didn't reach for the ABA strapped to him. He was cool, and surfaced in fifty-eight seconds. The coffee in the white mug handed to him was steaming hot, spiced with the seawater dripping off his nose. He shuffled in his soaked flight gear to the elevator, glued with spit and chewing gum to the side of the giant tank, and, with two dry pilots squeezed into the birdcage with him, descended in the squeaky contraption, which was dripping water like it would have done any other time with any other dunked commander in the cage and not His Royal Highness Charles, Prince of Wales, the successor to the British Throne.

The more I saw him, the more I liked him. The more I knew him, the more I respected and admired him – and I don't travel with too much admiration hidden in my traveling bag. I am quicker to admire what people have done than the people themselves. Most of my life I lived among the 'target people', the people who were carrying the millstones of their position or success around their necks. The fortunate victims in any profession who have lifelong open season declared on them. Leave them, shit-diggers, please, they have enough trouble left alone with themselves and their heavy burden of fame. I have lived with some, I have watched some 'fortunate miserables' fly, flutter and crash, I have known others who carried their crosses with lofty grandeur but none with more dignity than the one with the largest, heaviest millstone around his neck, Prince Charles.

Living around someone on and off for over eight months in the confined space of a 152-foot long, 28.7-foot beam wooden tub with blue sky above or engulfed in the hell-whipped waves of the North Sea, one would have a chance to know what makes a man tick.

The man in the white shirt in the planning-room got to his feet and walked toward the line formed under the blackboard, and with every step he took he got closer for me to know him. I was asked to stand next to Mervyn who was the last in the line-up. His Royal Highness stopped at the top of the line in front of the Chief of Naval Operations then slowly and – the first and last time I witnessed this – ceremoniously made his way down the line. He took his time, chatting, joking, he knew everybody.

Finally when he almost reached me I asked, 'I hope Your Highness won't ask me one question.'

He stopped, his friendly smile vanished, two kicks simultaneously, one from left one from right. Mervyn's almost shattered my shinbone. If dagger-looks could kill, I would have been standing there like a sieve in a knee-deep pool of blood.

He spoke after a minute of scrutiny, I felt I was dropped into a deep-freeze. 'And what would that question be, may I ask?'

'I hope you will not ask me how come that a Hungarian-born, one-eyed American cowboy from Texas was given this privilege. Your Royal Highness, I wouldn't be able to answer to save my life.'

In the Arctic the silence is exaggerated, so was the silence in the planning-room. Nobody inhaled from fear of freezing their lungs.

He moved forward at first tentatively, evaluating, then he thrust out his hand, 'Welcome on board,' and shook my hand with a firm polo-mallet-calloused grip. His smile resurfaced and I felt I was home, with aching shins.

He had a wry sense of humor, an insatiable curiosity and a steel-trap mind behind a poker face when he was prying for information; when he got through, you felt like a thirsty sponge had sapped you dry. I never left a glass of excellent white wine in front of me untouched except when he was putting me through the wringer. He was extremely well-read and genuinely interested in everything beyond his golden cage. He was a film buff. He wanted to know 'everything' about 'the Hollywood people', how real they were without their make-up. He was real. A fair driver and polo player, a good pilot. He loved horses, wanted to know about the cowboys, how much their lives had changed since the 'historical' yesteryears; he hoped their traditions would never get lost. He was human. He was a strange mixture of a wide-eyed, innocent child and a brilliant professor. Aching to live a life without the golden leash. He liked girls, nothing wrong with that.

'How does it look to you?' was his first question as he joined me at the railing on the lee-side on my first day on board of HMS *Bronington*.

'It's lovely . . . it's beautiful . . . it's really calm.'

'I meant the horizon, the waves, the ship, the world, around you?'

Like many men who have a one-track mind when they are concentrating on something they take it for granted you know what they are talking about, he was one of those. Once on a track he was on, hook, line and sinker. In an expectant silence he was waiting for an answer, I had nothing else to say and he realized he had crossed wires.

'I meant with one eye how does the world look to you?' He closed his right eye, looked around and realized I have the black patch on my left eye; he laughed, opened his right and closed his left eye and let go a waterfall of questions about what I could or couldn't do and surprised me with: 'I thought the story that a director with one eye had made the best 3D movie was only Hollywood publicity. I am curious to find out how you managed it.'

Discussing it, he surprised me with his knowledge of optics, but his curiosity and eagerness to experiment almost got me in deep trouble.

HMS *Bronington* was scheduled for a state visit to a small neighbouring country. Our shooting was suspended for a week and my motley crew and I were off the ship for a week. Before leaving, I sent him six black patches with a note: 'If things look bad, with this on they will look only half as bad. If things look good, look twice. If there are nice ladies around keep looking.' HMS *Bronington* arrived at her destination on schedule, of course, a reception committee in their Sunday best was waiting at the quay, of course, and His Royal Highness, Charles, Prince of Wales, of course, marched down the gangplank followed by his officers – all of them wearing a black patch over their left eyes.

Some circles didn't find it as funny as we did. But just the same, he put on the black patch as he waved goodbye when we were transferred at sea in gale force eight to a small tug, next to which HMS *Bronington* above us looked like a 60,000-ton aircraft-carrier.

I still heard his laughter after I lined up on deck with Ann and the rest of our crew to salute him, and an irreverent wave swept over the tug and washed overboard twenty-seven pieces of our equipment.

He had a great sense of humor. I appreciated it, but I would have appreciated it more if it had happened when we were boarding HMS *Bronington*. The issued equipment and the permanently seasick crew left a lot to be desired. But I learned soon enough one can't have everything, and Ann and I proved for sure we are immune to seasickness.

We watched HMS *Bronington* disappear on the far horizon heading north on a new, urgent mission, leaving me sopping wet, warm memories and a numbered bottle of champagne – unopened to this day – which I won in a bet with Prince Charles.

26   A Cup of Cubby Coffee

The Flying Scotsman from Edinburgh, shaking and rattling on the rails toward London, felt ridiculously stable after the roller-coaster of the North Sea. I wasn't all that stable after the celebration of our return to HMS *Pinewood*. If 'Vernon' was called HMS *Vernon*, why not HMS *Pinewood*? Both were standing on solid British soil, and the panelling in Pinewood Studios' library, bar and dining-room was not just a copy or duplicate, it was the real, original panels from HMS *Mauretania* – first class. There was a maritime connection there and 'HMAR *Pinewood*' ('His Majesty Arthur Rank's Pinewood') wouldn't sound too appetizing, it wouldn't have done justice to the food and drinks that almost matched what was served by the Royal Navy, especially on board the submerged atomic saviours.

'Bunty! when did you get back?'

I didn't have to turn to find out who asked the question, only Cubby Broccoli called me Bunty.

Nothing was more welcoming after missing the cold North Sea than this over-stuffed, 365-days-a-year, genuine Santa Claus warm friendship. He was always ready to help everybody, and at that time he certainly helped to rock the remnants of *Mauretania*'s bar. After being spoiled by our royal assignment – in more ways than one – Ann and I felt we needed a change of scenery and decided to go back home to California. The ancient Hungarian oracle: 'Man plans, God executes,' worked again; on this occasion Cubby, with the help of two Jack Daniel's, substituted for God. By the time Cubby and I – the last two guests – left the ex-*Mauretania* dining-room, we were committed to playing hooky for several years.

Being with, working with Cubby, was like playing hooky with your bestest friends. Not since grade school had I had so much fun. Some days, the fun started at six, six-thirty in the morning, with a knock and a question through the door of my room at the Dorchester, 'Now?' Cubby knew the answer would be a 'Yeap,' it always had been. He didn't like surprises, he liked to know the future in advance. And what always followed was no surprise either, kippered herring and scrambled eggs, easy over, with 'Cubby coffee' in a cup in the 'Dorch Grill'. Serving alcoholic beverages in a cup was a leftover from the good old prohibition days; 'Cubby coffee' was a modification of the custom to Cubby's specification, it contained Jack Daniel's all right, but with a few drops of boiling hot coffee added to it 'to enhance the aroma'.

The 'aroma' was the problem. Cubby had a lovely house – no, not only a house, a home on Green Street where the 'smell', not the 'aroma', of kippered herring and 'Cubby coffee' was not tolerated. For those uninitiated it was absurd that A. R. Broccoli, a hard-working, self-made millionaire, one of the most successful producers of, among others, the Bond films wasn't allowed to have kippered herring in his house because 'a single breakfast would stink up the whole house for months'. Cubby not only never denied this rumor, he poured oil on the fire of the gossip and enjoyed it. In fact, it was true that Mrs Broccoli's super-sensitive stomach churned and rebelled not only at the smell but even at the mention of kippered herring, some people and cold bacon drippings. Although she didn't drink Jack Daniel's, she understood it was an antiseptic.

Cubby was thoughtful of everybody and most considerate of his wife, but, being a 'Calabrese', for him playing hooky was fun, a secret venture of naïve school kids. Secret. We were reeking kippered herring and 'Cubby Coffee' all day after our covert breakfasts showed how naïve we were, and it showed how astute 'Lady Broccoli' was. A good sport not wanting to spoil our secret fun, she did not let us know how far ahead of us she was.

I admired the Broccolis. I felt always deeply sorry for the Saltzmans. The whirling, fluffy pink cloud, the perennial laughter didn't hide a deep sadness in Jackie Saltzman. Dana Broccoli, elegantly frill-less, smooth, was a shiny black marble statue of contentment. When I met her in Hollywood years before she married Cubby, she was a budding writer with a promising future, a single parent bringing up a son, Michael. In the forties it took guts. She always was a strong lady. Her strength paid off, now Michael is following in his mother's footsteps – writing, and taking some of the load off Cubby's shoulders by producing the Bonds. A solid family. It was the biggest miracle the Saltzman-Broccoli partnership lasted as long as it did.

Cubby, always in the front-line whatever he was doing, dug the trenches. He came close to digging my grave in Egypt.

TransAmerica needed 007's dexterity to open a few doors for them. I had learned from Alex Korda that being high in the film business could be utilized for various other business purposes as well. Before the sweatshirt realism took over from the astral, mysterious status of film people, curiosity opened many doors. In the feeding frenzy of the shark-infested bloody waters of big business one of the biggest, TransAmerica, gobbled up United Artists only to discover there was a fly in the ointment, indigestible by and incompatible with the Arabs' stomachs. Arthur Krim, one of the pillars, and part owner of UA, and his wife Mathilde, were flag-waving Zionists, and this caused serious financial constipation for TransAmerica.

The Arabs had long forgotten Mussolini's tough Bersagliere (sharpshooters) in North Africa; nobody could be mad too long at the Italians. The Germans were gone. Everything started to swing in the Arabs' direction. In 1953, Egypt was proclaimed a republic under Colonel Gamal Abdul Nasser's premiership. In 1954, Great Britain agreed to relinquish the occupation of the Suez Canal. The hope of damming up the Nile was coming closer to reality.

It was different with Israel, a thorn in the Arabs' side since 1948, and with the Six Days War Israel opened up deep, old wounds. This placed TransAmerica in a precarious position and the company was looking for a way to reinstate the normal functioning of their business with the Arab world.

Delavalle, I believe, was the name of one of the pipeline supply companies also owned by TransAmerica, doing around $240 million-plus business a year before the Egypt-led boycott cut off its lifeline. The God of TransAmerica was cognisant of the Korda short cuts. An adroit strategist, he was aware that A. R. 'Cubby' Broccoli would be the best carrot to dangle in front of the civilized Egyptian noses. An American of Italian descent, based in London, a most successful picture-maker, among others, of the 'billion-dollar-bracket'(?) Bonds. (The question mark refers to the publicity blurb of the sum 'billion dollar', not to the world-wide success of the Bonds or Cubby Broccoli being a picture-maker par exellence.) This carrot was served garnished to the Egyptians (who matched the British in their snobbery) with a Hungarian-born American who was professionally accepted by the highest circles in Great Britain and who they hoped would have a chance to find ears to listen to the lucrative possibility of Cubby shooting a Bond film in Egypt, which would bring great benefits to the hard-currency-starved economy.

In their anxiety to break through the boycott through this back-door they, and we, also, overlooked the possible complications my black patch could cause. Only on the spot did we realize it, a couple of times almost too late. But the Dayan 'lookalike-ship' caused problems only on the streets. We were well-received as high as deputy-prime-ministerial level without a black patch hitch. There only Ann suffered, her body was always severed from her right hand on every photo of those handshaking ceremonies – even though in respect of Moslem laws she had no short skirts, but wore her 'uniform,' grey flannel trousers with her blue blazer, and had gone to school at Farnborough Hill Convent School, in England, with the deputy foreign minister's daughter.

Otherwise, we were heading for an understanding, so much so that the God of TransAmerica sent his envoy to evaluate the situation on the spot and report. He was five-feet-nine tall, no hips, with five-foot-nine shoulders, an ex-marine major with a lovely, very much alive and very much pregnant wife. Delightful, not at all TransAmerica-like, harassed people. He had shorter haircut than me and, thank God, no patch.

One of the best restaurants in Cairo, among the many good ones, was on a fancy barge anchored on the Nile – the 'Omar Khayyam' or 'Sheherazade' or something like that – where, with a small ad hoc welcoming committee we were celebrating the arrival in Cairo of Trans-America's dove with an olive branch. I have forgotten only the name of the place, not the good food and wine they served and the fact that it came close to being the place of my last supper.

As we piled down the gangplank out of the shadows (Cairo had many), three young men not aptly dressed for the plush restaurant were heading toward us. Fast. They didn't give me much time to think before a razor-sharp knife cut through my linen jacket, its point digging into my skin on my right side. The blunt muzzle of an automatic was stuck against my left side. The third man grabbed my shirt and jacket collar from the rear and very professionally pushed me forward, at the same time he pulled me up by the seat of my pants to unbalance me. The unwelcome committee propelled me toward the rim of the quay, the river. Those on the shore who weren't swallowed by the shadows stood still like statues. Suddenly it was quiet. My funeral procession was only a few steps from the river, I heard the Nile gurgle against the stones of the old retaining wall. Then: 'Stop, you fools . . . Stop, I said!'

The surprising command slowed their forward momentum and helped me to regain some of my footing.

'Ann, get back!'

'You're silly too.' A muffled sound of a slap on a hand. 'Drop that knife, you idiot, you could hurt somebody with it' – Ann spoke up louder – 'and that senseless, stupid gun, put it away, right now!'

The pressure on my sides, the firm hold on the seat of my pants eased and Ann grabbed me by the shoulder like a mother would drag a naughty child caught with its hand in the cookie jar. She jerked me away from the dumbstruck trio.

'Now, you three go home, and don't get into any more trouble. Understand?' And she kept talking to them as she dragged me toward our car waiting at the gangplank. 'You, start that car.' The wax figure of the driver came alive, the engine started at the second try as we reached it. 'Let's go!' She yanked the car door open and I suffered the most serious injury of the venture – I banged my head as she stuffed me into the car.

Thinking back, I don't believe those three spoke one blessed word of English. The unexpected surprise of being intercepted, and by a woman, and a woman in man's trousers, dumbfounded them just long enough. Had Ann hesitated, had the car refused to start . . .? The last glimpse I had of them they were in a spirited discussion, gesticulating with gusto. We melted into the traffic, they were long out of sight but I still kept looking in the direction I last saw them.

Had they been successful, I thought, a body fished out of the Nile was not worth the newsprint, when before and after so many important things were happening all over the world: The US table tennis team playing in China; next to the same river in which I was supposed to start my new career as fishbait, Nasser dying of a heart-attack to vacate the chair for Anwar Sadat; the *New York Times* publishing the 'Pentagon Papers' on the Vietnam Wars; Monet, a better name than de Toth, and the $1,411,200 price for his 'Terrace at Saint Address' that started the sky-rocketing prices for real art were much better 'filler stories'.

This is not sour grapes, not getting my name in print and saving Cubby a large sum on a bronze coffin and other ancillary funeral expenses; he knew I always traveled first-class like him. Nope! it's too late in this book to start lying now, I thanked God and still thank Ann for being what she is. In short, I was goddamn glad.

Luck and coincidence worked again. The door was cracked open for TransAmerica. Some of the great locations Egypt had to offer were in a subsequent Bond film. It was moonlight and roses for all. But there are seasons for moonlight and for roses, and roses have thorns and those thorns started pricking me.

The Broccolis' friendship was warm and overwhelming, but real friendship is giving not only receiving. I wanted to give more – what? The right advice to Michael. I was born to be a bull in the china shop so I gave it and in the wrong way: he had to change his ways because I would be moving on, I had to. Cubby was adored, but Michael was not very well liked; he had the talent and all other gifts to take some load off Cubby, he was ready to get his feet wet but it would have been more helpful if he were liked. The large weekly checks burned my pocket, and that I blew them as fast as they came in certainly didn't give me any relief. My affection and friendship they would always have, no money could buy that.

Being with Cubby made me think more and more of home. Unrelated in a way, but strangely it was an indivisible part of making my decision, it made me more homesick. What is homesickness? Silly things like remembering. I wondered if Cubby did. We never talked about the shiny aluminium trailer surrounded by pine trees in buckets, the breath of far-away forests mixed with the scent of pitch oozing from the freshly cut trees that sacrificed their lives to give commercial joy to others for a week; that small trailer parked in the early thirties on an empty lot somewhere close to where Wilshire and Santa Monica Boulevards cross in Beverly Hills. How could one forget, especially if you were hungry, the mouth-watering smell of spaghetti sauce that bubbled over a charcoal fire all day in Cubby's trailer, the sales center of the pre-Christmas enterprise in partnership with Cousin Pasquale 'Pat' Di Cicco, a man about town in any town he had landed, and loved – mostly by women.

The trailer, the empty lot long gone with the red poinsettia fields off Sunset. Pat is gone. But the memories stayed. It was a warm feeling to be around Cubby, to share the 'Cubby coffee', but I was going back. The Sierras were sending their messages – express. I was sure sooner or later Cubby would return home too. Maybe he could spot where the empty lot was, I couldn't.

Returning after more than twenty years was a stranger feeling than arriving the very first time in Los Angeles. As I drove around the images blended. It hit me and it hurt, seeing the once sprawling old town dissected, familiar landmarks swallowed, worse yet, others only choked, the orange groves devoured by the hungry progress of civilization. Mammoth billboards erased the dazzling colors of the rampant bougainvillea on the rooftops. The once-beautiful jacarandas became 'the dirty trees', because they constantly shed their dirty little leaves on the asphalt that had robbed the jacarandas of the green grass beneath them that once hid their leaves and was in turn fed by them.

The peaceful 'lanes' and 'drives' retained their names, but became four-lane boulevards and the smoggy-grey color of the sky siphoned off the delicate hues of their flowers. And who cared? Nobody looked up any more when an aeroplane flew by and the few birds that survived men's mechanical superiority of the skies flew in silence, except, of course the crows, but they disappeared too with the walnut groves. But one thing not only remained unchanged from the past but grew with a flourish – those monuments of human discourtesy, the traffic jams.

Like a contagious disease discourtesy, the phalanx of inferiority complexes, took over as proof of power. Unanswered letters, phone calls not returned became the stigma of positions respected before. Hollywood, aka the picture business, became a fertile land for gods, lesser gods, demi-gods and viceroys. Viceroy means vice-presidents of all class from executive senior down to the low-class simple vice only. At a first glance the decentralization of power seemed like havoc. No It was like it had always been, except with a greater selection of people to call a son-of-a-bitch. The Baby Moguls aren't new either. They started with David O. Selznick: 'The son in law always rises.' 'Oh, you were lucky, you were here during "the Golden Age"'! The golden age of what? The surprise is that those we called 'sonsabitches' became 'The Golden Age Gods' of picture-making. And what was so 'golden' about it? We were all nuts, loved to make pictures. The only thing 'golden' about it was the gold – $$$ – necessary to make them, but that is inherent in this hybrid art? industry? form of anthropology? emasculated self-expression? business? or strange disease? We just loved to make them, the 'sonsabitches' loved to make them as much as we, the ants, loved to make them. If our love and dedication made it 'golden', if the feeling survived, every minute, every drop of tears or sweat was more than worthwhile. As long as this sickness, the love of making films, survives nothing will ever change and thirty, forty years from now, if you are able to grope your way through the smog to return, you will be greeted with: 'Oh, you were lucky, you were here during "the Golden Age"!' Except, there will be more 'sonsabitches' and more gods to remember. And, because of the high stakes, the 'sonsabitches' will out-number the gods on both sides of the cameras.

In the early nineteen-hundreds in the glorious years of the Austro-Hungarian Empire the son of the richest nobleman in Hungary disappeared. The Emperor Franz Josef himself ordered, 'Find him,' to ease the grief of one of His Majesty's favorite courtiers. Still, no luck for years. One day, the father of the prodigal went to a circus and, lo and behold, there was his lost son shovelling horseshit. The father, heartbroken, ran to his son. 'You're noble, you're rich, how could you do this?'

The son replied: 'I love show business.'

If you are unhappy don't blame the 'sonsabitches', have the guts to blame yourself.

That's show biz!

No end, always a beginning.